A Dream of Tall Ships

How New Yorkers Came Together to
Save the City's Sailing-ship Waterfront

by Peter and Norma Stanford

Introduced by John Stobart

(signatures: Peter Stanford / Norma Stanford)

SEA HISTORY PRESS
NATIONAL MARITIME HISTORICAL SOCIETY
PEEKSKILL, NEW YORK

We are grateful for the support of
FURTHERMORE: A PROGRAM OF THE J. M. KAPLAN FUND.

Furthermore:
a program of the J.M. Kaplan Fund

ISBN 978-0-930248-17-8

Printed in the United States

NATIONAL MARITIME HISTORICAL SOCIETY
5 John Walsh Boulevard, Peekskill, New York 10566

PATRONS

Publication of this book was made possible
by the generous contributions of the National Maritime
Historical Society supporters listed below.

Starboard Watch

ALICE DADOURIAN, *IN MEMORY OF*
ADMIRAL JOHN. M. WILL, USN
FURTHERMORE: *A PROGRAM*
OF THE J. M. KAPLAN FUND
WILLIAM G. WINTERER

Port Watch

REYNOLDS DU PONT, JR.
JAKOB ISBRANDTSEN
RALPH AND DOROTHY PACKER

Anchor Watch

VIRGINIA D. MARTUS
RONALD L. OSWALD
HOWARD SLOTNICK
CAPT. CESARE SORIO
GEORGE F. TOLLEFSEN, JR. AND FAMILY
IN MEMORY OF GEORGE R. TOLLEFSEN, SR.
CAROL E. VINALL
JEAN WORT

Launchmen

VINCENT & GALE BELLAFIORE
IN MEMORY OF GEORGE R. TOLLEFSEN, SR.
CADDELL DRY DOCK & REPAIR COMPANY
RADM JOSEPH F. CALLO, USNR (RET.) & CAPT SALLY
MCELWREATH, USNR (RET.)

Boatman

THOMAS J. GOCHBERG

DEDICATION

To the people of South Street who sailed for far horizons, and to those who keep their story alive today to enrich our tomorrows.

CONTENTS

Introduction   vii

Preface   xi

Acknowledgments   xiv

Prologue   xvii

Chapter 1: We Set Out on the Journey, *1965-66*   1

Chapter 2: *Athena* in Conroy's Creek, *Winter 1965–66*   12

Chapter 3: To Gloucester—and Beyond! *Summer 1966*   21

Chapter 4: Launching Friends of South Street, *Autumn 1966*   36

Chapter 5: Tackling the Establishment, *Winter 1966–67*   52

Chapter 6: Flags in the Wind, *Jan.–Feb. 1967*   66

Chapter 7: We Find the Right Chairman, *Feb.–March 1967*   79

Chapter 8: Headquarters In Fulton Street, *March 1967*   94

Chapter 9: The Seaport in the Market, *April–May 1967*   107

Chapter 10: *Athena* Opens the Museum, *May 1967*   119

Chapter 11: Kortum Finds a Ship for New York, *May–June 1967*   131

Chapter 12: Racing the Bulldozer, *June–Aug. 1967*   145

Chapter 13: Aboard *Athena*, *Summer 1967*   160

Chapter 14: The Schooner Race for the Mayor's Cup, *Autumn 1967*   172

Chapter 15: The Privilege of Continuing, *Nov.–Dec. 1967*   185

Chapter 16: Gains by Sea and Land, *Jan.–March 1968*   197

Chapter 17: A Southward Foray, *May 1968*   211

Chapter 18: Square Riggers '68, *Summer 1968*   230

Chapter 19: South Street's First Ships, *Aug.–Oct. 1968*   246

Chapter 20: Seaport Restoration Conference, *Nov. 1968*   268

Chapter 21: South Street Besieged, *Nov.–Dec. 1968*   280

Chapter 22: The Dreamers Get Moving, *Winter 1968–69*   295

Chapter 23: A Home for a Distant Ship, *Winter–Spring 1969*   315

Chapter 24: Launching a Seaport Campaign, *Spring 1969*   327

Chapter 25: The Seaport Plan, *Summer 1969*   341

Chapter 26: *Wavertree* Revisited, *Autumn 1969*   356

Chapter 27: Leaning Forward, *Autumn 1969*   369

Chapter 28: Sea Day Ushers in a Fair Tide, *Spring 1970*   379

Chapter 29: Our Ship Comes In, *Spring–Summer 1970*   395

Chapter 30: Beautiful Necessities of Life, *Aug. 1970*   410

Chapter 31: Celebrating City Waterfronts, *Autumn 1970*   422

Chapter 32: The Seaport Established, *Year-end 1970*   434

Chapter 33: Gathering Strength and Purpose, *1971–1972*   448

Chapter 34: A Place for People and for History, *Early 1973*   466

Chapter 35: Something Special for New York, *1973*   481

Chapter 36: The Changing of the Guard, *Jan.–April 1974*   498

Illustrations   513

Timeline   533

Appendices   543

Index   551

INTRODUCTION
The Sea Dreamers

I'd like to give a fair picture of my first encounter with my longtime friend Peter Stanford and his wife and co-conspirator Norma. But that seems an almost impossible task, since that meeting changed the course of my life as an artist—literally changing the world around me so that it's difficult to remember the world as I knew it before we met.

I do remember the excitement I felt as I headed south on the IRT subway, some time after the first exhibition of my paintings at the palatial Kennedy Galleries in midtown. There Margaret Wunderlich, matriarch of the New York gallery world, had told me to go and see Peter's new museum, where she rightly felt I would find ultimate inspiration for my ongoing quest to rediscover America's wharfside scene in the days of sail. This new museum bore the resounding name South Street Seaport Museum, and in my head were visions of a grand stairway leading to marble halls lined with portraits of old sea captains gazing down on meticulous small models of their ships, frequented by distinguished visitors likely to buy paintings that brought the viewer face to face with the great ports in the days of sail.

Finding Peter's office was like an enactment from *Pilgrim's Progress*. Opening a door from the street I recall being faced with a ramshackle staircase in severe disrepair that seemed to go up for three storeys until the top was accomplished. Climbing two at a time as is usually my wont—to compensate for endless hours at the easel with the only exercise being to wield a one-ounce paint brush—it was a test, but a treat was in store. I had not met Peter before, and when I did it was one of those rare occasions when I knew in an instant that he would be a friend for life.

In no time he was showing me copies of old daguerrotypes of ships berthed at South Street in the 1880s, the zenith of merchant sail, when the horse-drawn era, to which it was inextricably attached, was nearing its inevitable demise. This was exactly the world I was seeking, the wharfside scene having so rarely attracted the attention of artists of the time. Was this a treat or a miracle? Here was the answer to my quest and a plan for my life being handed to me on a plate: to bring back to life the scenes of the great ports in the days of sail.

Peter's office was plastered with signs bearing mottos like Nelson's "The Order of Sailing shall Be the Order of Battle," and Albert Schweitzer's adjuration, "It is better to create than protest," followed by the cellist Pablo Casals's memorable response: "Why Not Do Both?" Peter told me about the terrific battle he and Norma were leading to uphold landmark designation of an historic row of buildings across the way, which were threatened with imminent demolition by a proud developer who had said: "I am not accustomed to losing." Peter said: "We're out to give him that experience."

Puzzled, I remember asking: "But where's the museum?"

With a grin Peter responded: "As Christopher Wren once said, 'Look around you!' You're sitting in it, this is a museum that is a whole neighborhood. We're salting the museum experience into the cobbled streets and buildings that made up the city's "Street of Ships"—and the first two ships are nodding at you outside the window."

I looked, and there were the masts, moving to the harbor swell.

When I left our meeting, Norma took me down to visit the museum's rotund red lightship *Ambrose* and the shapely fishing schooner *Caviare*. Norma, one of the crew who'd brought the schooner in under sail a couple of months earlier, told me that passersby were welcomed aboard at set hours to raise and stow sail, followed by a talk with a fisheries veteran over a cup of coffee fresh off the Shipmate stove. I asked a question I'd hesitated to ask Peter: "Does the museum actually own these ships and buildings?"

Laughing, Norma said: "The ships, yes. The buildings—not yet! We're fending off the bulldozers, while our chairman Jakob Isbrandtsen is working to get the City to finalize an air-rights sale which will make it possible for him to donate the buildings he's been buying up. It's a simple arrangement Peter and I worked out, but dealing with official-dom seems to take forever. As for these ships, we own them, but they're here as squatters until we get title to the land."

I remember thinking that this blithe young woman did not seem at all troubled dealing with concepts and developments that frankly would have driven me up the wall. At her invitation I went on to visit the ex-tensive library which the group had pulled together out of thin air. And in future visits to this grand source of maritime lore and learning I got to know the museum staff and the skilled volunteers they'd gathered around them.

Norma and Peter told me that they relied on the expertise and ac-tive research pursued by leaders in the field like Karl Kortum, who was later to be so helpful to me in my quest to accurately record in a major painting the phenomenal harbor scene of San Francisco's Gold Rush harbor years. Karl was founder of the great maritime museum in San Francisco, whose word, I learned, was close to law in South Street. And then there were Howard Chapelle, maritime curator of the Smithson-ian Institution; Harvard's Oceanic Historian Robert G. Albion; and a local network of scholars and veteran seamen and shipmasters who just walked in the doors because of the growing reputation of the place. Among them I was delighted to get to know George Campbell, a Brit like me, who had designed the restoration in England of the world's last surviving clipper ship, *Cutty Sark,* and the distinguished Australian art-ist Os Brett, whom I still consult regularly.

All this was years ago, you see, when people whose names are now legend walked in the door to deliver first-class talks to staff and volun-teers and exchange views at the local pub. I was swept away by all this, carried to a different world. I'd always sought out scholars and seamen to understand the world whose ships I was painting, but here that vanished world I sought to record on canvas surrounded me, and I soaked in its message. I was becoming part of a seafaring community in touch with its past and present.

I was excited to learn that they were working to bring in the classic square rigger *Wavertree*, which had survived as a sand barge in Argentina after being dismasted off Cape Horn in the early 1900s. When Peter asked me to paint her picture, I felt a dizzying rush: I would play a part in saving the ship! I immersed myself in photographs and stories about the ship and then made a sketch of how I imagined her. The sketch showed the big iron ship setting sail with her great foresail lifting in the fresh northwest breeze as she left her berth in the Kill van Kull after her visit to New York in 1895. When Peter saw the sketch, he invited Os Brett, Bob Herbert, the maritime scholar and sailorman, and the Cape Horn veteran Archie Horka to meet us after work at the Square Rigger Bar. The ensuing talk was priceless and I was soon changing the sketch to satisfy these veterans, as they relived their experiences. Archie even called out the orders that were needed to get the set of the sails right, clewing up the topgallants and easing the foresheet. It was my job to make these changes on paper as one of the crew summoned for this occasion.

This launched my career painting the life of the American seaports. In this quest I was welcomed everywhere as part of that maritime world of South Street that Peter and Norma summoned into being. The story of how they did this is told in the book before you.

Years later in San Francisco, Karl Kortum casually remarked to me: "Peter sees things that are not yet there." It's been an immense privilege to me to be one of the crew involved in making those things happen and to open for more people the deeply inspiring and endlessly rewarding heritage of American seafaring.

JOHN STOBART

PREFACE
A Personal Account

City streets have a thousand stories to tell. These stories, infinitely varied and each unique, turn by turn inspiring, discouraging, radiating hope like a beacon or heartbreakingly sad, together make up much of New Yorkers' experience of their city. The story offered here is one of people coming together forty-odd years ago to save a whole neighborhood of old brick buildings and cobbled streets that testified to the changing experience of a rundown district on South Street, facing New York's East River. The district was threatened with imminent demolition, which lent urgency to this idea if anything was to come of it. The people involved were explorers of city streets and searchers-out of different neighborhoods, driven by a thirst to know their city better and feel more part of its life. They were drawn by the robust, devil-may-care life of the Fulton Fish Market in that rundown neighborhood just south of the Brooklyn Bridge or by the sea-worn wooden fishing boats which still brought their catch ashore here or by the simple desire to walk through a neighborhood redolent of a vanished age.

For Norma and me South Street had an almost mythological past as a street once widely known as New York's Street of Ships—a street which led right around the world, sending tall ships to sail out on the power of the ocean winds to the world's four corners.

And for all of us there was the mute appeal of the district's aged brick buildings leaning against each other as if sharing secrets, gazing back from windows that had been dazzled by uncounted sunrises striking in from Brooklyn Heights across the river, to begin who knew what kind of day in the seaport community. It is from that perspective of fresh discovery that Norma and I set out here to tell the story of the South Street venture. I act as narrator because, while the bulldozers were snuffling and grunting around the precinct, it became my lot to serve as the spokesman for the New Yorkers who went to work to build in South Street a new kind of center for people and for history.

The people who came together to make this possible came for their own reasons, bringing their own concerns, with their own stories to tell. Their stories are woven into the fabric of this tale, because without them, there would be no tale. What they brought us was the establishment of an historic district extending over seven blocks of downtown New York, gathering along the way the largest and most active membership of any maritime historical organization anywhere in the world.

It has been a joy to Norma and me to revisit these people, studying papers that carry their words and photographs that catch them working, cracking jokes, telling stories and, now and then, beaming in high glee at some current success in our shared endeavor. We've searched out those we could reach to hear their tales, while searching our own journals, letters and memories of events. This effort was supplemented by a handful of papers I gathered in leaving South Street. Fortunately the late Richard Rath also gave me two file drawers of his meticulously kept records of founding the South Street Seaport Museum, including his exchanges with his fellow trustees.

"What took you so long?" Joe Cantalupo, garbage man of the Fulton Fish Market, said when he appeared in the doorway of the fish stall at 16 Fulton Street where we'd just set to work to launch our venture. His question was reassuring to us, confronting as we did a future with huge questions hanging over us, as we scrubbed out the filth of ages on a cold March day. Joe, at least, expected us and expected something of us. We never answered his question, but this book perhaps does that, telling things as they happened—or as the Spanish serve broiled squid, *en su tinta*, in its own ink.

Come join me then on a wet and windy Sunday afternoon in January 1965, when Norma and I, with my children and a friend, made a remarkable discovery among the fishing craft that had taken shelter from the gale in the Fish Market wharves on South Street. This led us, all unaware, to set out on the road to South Street.

Peter Stanford

ACKNOWLEDGMENTS

"Now write that down for me!" Karl Kortum said, when I told him about the air-rights transfer we in Friends of South Street had proposed to Eric Ridder early in 1967. The air rights transfer was the only way we could possibly acquire the historic buildings of South Street Seaport, as Karl immediately understood. And at Karl's insistence we asked and secured Eric's confirmation of our report on this vital proposal, as it now appears in Chapter 6 of this account. Moved by Karl's strong interest in getting this story out as it actually happened rather than as reported by City officials, Norma and I began to think of telling the whole South Street story as we had seen it unfold.

So Karl effectively planted in our minds the idea of telling the story of the Seaport Museum from the viewpoint of the citizens who made it happen, rather than the City officials who enacted the needed measures. And Karl's aide Anita Ventura, on her own initiative, packed up and sent to us the Kortum end of that correspondence, after our own museum files had somehow been mislaid. So she played a role as archaeologist in recovering lost layers of evidence of a fallen city—as, at least, it seemed to us.

Two people chiefly responsible for the actual founding of the museum, Jakob Isbrandtsen and Joan Davidson, went on to become the leading patrons responsible for the funding of *A Dream of Tall Ships* over the years of its gestation. Our work on this was constantly interrupted by the demands of our continued careers after we left South Street. Never was Dr. Johnson's harsh view of the patron more completely belied than by the helpful responses to our questions and unstinting support provided by these stout-hearted friends.

Other supporters of the Seaport Museum also contributed to the research and writing of *A Dream*, of whom the late Walter Handelman was a leader. Others, too many to be named here, contributed in many and varied ways.

We also got close-in support in the later stages of the writing, and this from a uniquely qualified group; a peer review panel appointed by our publishers, the National Maritime Historical Society's Sea History Press. Led by New York State Historian Emeritus Dr. Joseph F. Meany, Jr., the group gave this work a thorough airing, shaking out, and settling down—based largely on their own involvement in the story of South Street we were telling!

And there could be nothing more refreshing than their individual perspective on events. As concerned New Yorkers, they each had their own take on the South Street story. The panel, then, was made up as follows:

CHAIR: Joseph F. Meany, Jr., PhD, New York State Historian Emeritus, author of many articles in *Sea History* and other journals, whose interest in the heritage stretches across oceans;

Norman J. Brouwer, author of *The International Register of Historic Ships*, historian of the Seaport Museum 1972–2005, advisor at Mystic Seaport, South Street and other museums;

Robert Ferraro, a founder and later chair of Friends of South Street, formerly of ABC-TV and volunteer in ship research and public programs in South Street;

Lee Gruzen, secretary of the Ship Lore & Model Club (established 1927) and organizer of the important 2005 charrette on South Street, "SeaportSpeaks;"

Ronald L. Oswald, chair, National Maritime Historical Society, active in other maritime historical organizations, dedicated sailor, devoted to the worldwide reach of the seafaring story;

Terry Walton, coordinator of Friends of South Street, editor of *South Street Reporter* and later *Seaport Magazine*, author of the book *Harbor Voices*, and other works.

Besides new insights into our story, this distinguished group offered comments on content and style which would make a rewarding and entertaining publication in itself! How these people, each engaged with other concerns, made time to reflect on the story and help clarify its message is a wonder to both Norma and me.

And finally, the constant support, interest and patience of the trustees and staff of the National Maritime Historical Society, led by Ronald Oswald as chair, Jean Wort as trustee book liason to the board, and Burchenal Green as president, Shelley Reid as senior editor, and Steven Lovass-Nagy as production editor have been a great encouragement to Norma and me in our long voyage to bring this story into the light of day.

PETER AND NORMA STANFORD

Prologue

The Road to South Street, *1965*

Rutgers Club Farewell—Fish Market Visit—Lady of Good Voyage—
Sailing a Schooner to New York—"The Grownups' *Hour"—
Dream of a Revived Seaport—the City Beyond* Athena's *Bowsprit*

The northeaster had been blowing in its full winter fury. It blanketed the city with snow, followed by a driving rain that flooded the slushy streets of New York. On the Lower East Side the gutters became icy rivulets, gurgling their way toward the grey rain-speckled waters of the East River. By Sunday afternoon the howling winds had died down, but we knew the gale must have stirred up heavy seas outside the harbor. So we decided to walk down to the Fish Market piers on South Street to see what fishing boats had taken shelter there.

On this particular afternoon Norma, our friend Jim Kirk and I with my children Thomas and Carol in tow, were due to make a stop at the Rutgers Reform Democratic Club to pay our respects to the club's new leaders. Two years earlier Norma had been the secretary and Jim treasurer of my campaign against the established district leader, P. Vincent "Duke" Viggiano. This effort in an old-line Tammany stronghold had won a few County Committee seats in a campaign waged by volunteers who had scrubbed out tenement hallways and set up job clinics for the unemployed. Eleanor Roosevelt, President Franklin Roosevelt's widow, had come to the Lower East Side to support our work. Her talk was followed by applause that went on forever. But as she left, an irate citizen grabbed her arm to ask: "How can you drag your husband's name in the mud by interfering in our politics down here?" Mrs. Roosevelt responded simply: "Why, it's down here that politics matter." This perfectly expressed what we felt: politics did matter "down here."

But the new leaders, sensing an old-fashioned patronage victory within their grasp, had lapsed into the patterns we had come to change. "It's the same old same old," said Jim, as Norma, nodding, rose to lead the children out the door, while we all gave farewell waves. So we clattered down the iron stairs into Rutgers Street and made our way down slippery sidewalks and across rushing gutters, past Al Smith public housing to enter into an older world south of the Brooklyn Bridge. This crowded region of winding streets and ancient buildings was deserted this Sunday afternoon, as was all of lower Manhattan was on weekends.

As we neared the Fish Market, we came across a solitary ancient gnome warming his fingers at a fire of broken-up fish crates at the southeast corner of Beekman and Front Streets. The smoke of many fires had blackened the brick of the nondescript one-story garage that had been put up some time ago to replace the old market building that I remembered from childhood visits to the fishing fleet with my father in the 1930s. Further on, at the foot of Fulton Street, we came upon the customary watchman on the Fish Market pier, who nodded to us from his shed as we passed by.

As we had expected, the fishing fleet was present in force on this Sunday afternoon, a jostling flotilla of old wooden vessels, driven in by the foul weather. An easterly blow can be terrible along the sandy coast south of New York, driving great surfing seas before it in the shallow water that extends miles out to sea.

We walked out on Pier 17, nodding to the watchman as we passed his shack. My father used to talk his way aboard the boats when we would walk across the bridge from our house in Brooklyn Heights to visit the fleet. Sometimes we would end up in the narrow fo'c'sle of a fishing schooner that had been converted to a motor dragger, exchanging stories over a cup of dense coffee, which the fishermen enriched with sweet condensed milk.

None of the fishermen were on hand this afternoon. But here, anyway, were the boats, a generation after those visits in the 1930s. Then there were still converted sailing schooners in the fleet, operating under diesel engines with cut-down rigs. But these had long been weeded out, replaced by boxy hulls built for the heavy engine and powered gear of the motorized fisherman. I explained to our troop that the graceful, elliptical-sterned schooners I remembered from my childhood had been entirely replaced in the passage of years.

But then something caught my eye and I broke off my elegy in mid-sentence: "No!" I said. "There's a schooner! Just over there—look at those masts!"

Across the way at Pier 18, amid the stumpy upright masts of the motor draggers, was a pair of slender raked masts, and there were empty topmast bands on the foremast—unmistakable evidence that the vessel had been built to carry topsails. We were looking at a real schooner—one built to travel fast under sail.

We could see the tapered flanks of the Gloucesterman nodding to the river swell under those slanting masts, and her name, *Lady of Good Voyage,* was incised in white capitals at her bow. This magical name was lettered again around the curve of the stern, along with her home port Gloucester, the renowned fishing port on Cape Ann north of Boston. She was one of the fleet built to go out in all weathers to the Grand Banks off Newfoundland and fight their way home against the prevailing westerly winds.

We stood gazing at this noble thoroughbred as the light died and a chill wind got up, sighing through the masts and rigging of the tied-up fleet.

"Time to go," said Norma, moving on ahead with the kids in tow. The three figures were an enlivening sight trotting down the pier, as Jim and I followed more slowly. We caught up with them as we walked past the slope-roofed buildings of Schermerhorn Row, whose soft pink brick seemed to glow through the grime of ages, as though charged with the life that had swirled around it for so long. Talking of what we'd seen, we made our way down South Street till we came to the bright windows of a bar on Old Slip kept open on weekends for the sailors in the Seamen's Church Institute building next door. Stepping in the door, visibly chilled, we were greeted by the bartender with the exclamation: "Those poor kids!" His name, we soon learned, was Joe, and he immediately set about making hot chocolate for Tommy and Carol. When Norma and I got our Beefeater martinis and Jim his Dewar's on the rocks, we drank a toast: "Fair winds to the *Lady of Good Voyage!*" There was still a Gloucester schooner in the world.

Why did schooners matter? An unanswerable question. We were plainly enraptured by these vessels of antique, ineffably graceful rig. We had recently acquired a vessel of this traditional rig ourselves; a forty-year-old, 43-foot schooner built in 1925, a smaller version of the great Gloucester fishing schooners, and she was waiting for us in a yard in Maine. We'd had a long search for a proper schooner of traditional style, and when we found her lying in winter quarters in Camden in late 1964, we'd recognized her breed instantly. She belonged to Robert Amory, who had sailed her happily for years with a convivial crew of friends under the name *Heart's Desire.* We re-named her *Athena* for the Greek goddess of wisdom, who served as inspiration to the Athenians in the age of Pericles. In a time of unrest in city streets and college campuses, we admired the classic moderation of the Greek civilization, which shone for us like a beacon across the twenty-four centuries between Pericles' time and our own.

John Alden of Boston had designed our schooner with a fine bow leading into a full body topped off with a saucy sheer and sustained by powerful after sections to help her stand up to her canvas in a breeze. She had been built and finished fisherman style, with plain galvanized fittings, with railings and cabin house painted rather than varnished, fitted with a rugged iron fisherman's wheel and an old-fashioned fisherman's anchor.

Still, the *Lady of Good Voyage* continued to haunt our thoughts as we walked the South Street waterfront on weekend afternoons, rejoicing in a generalized affection for old bricks and lanes with unexpected turnings, the memories of the tall ships that had sailed from under the windows of these very buildings for the four corners of the world, and of the songs, stories and vanished lives of South Street, the Street of Ships—and of course the comings and goings of the fishing fleet, with the *Lady of Good Voyage* occasionally turning up among them.

Our city walks ended with the coming of spring, as other concerns took over our lives. First and foremost was to bring *Athena* home from her distant port in Maine.

"Heads up, Boats!" I called to Norma—Boats, short for boatswain, being her nickname—from my perch at the top of *Athena*'s foremast. Three and a half stories high above the schooner's decks, I was in heaven. I had finished pulling the new jib halyard through its masthead block, and when Norma stood aside, I tossed down the rope coil I had gathered. She then hauled the line taut and secured it to a belaying pin on the fife rail around the foremast, secure in its assigned place in the web of the schooner's running rigging. This was just another in the multifarious tasks to be done before the schooner, which we had last seen as a hulk under a snowy tarpaulin, was ready to set sail. We were in Camden, Maine, the schooner's longtime home, outfitting her for the voyage to her new home in City Island, at the western end of Long Island Sound. We had dreamed of this day—but what dream could match the reality of reeving off halyards for the sails we'd soon be setting?

Aboard for the passage were David Johnston, a young, very deliberate Scottish trainee at Ogilvy & Mather, the advertising agency where I had worked until just recently. David had a considerable taste for adventure, having worked his passage to New York from Australia after service in the army. With him was Dan Northup, an older person I'd met through the reform movement, a bon vivant and artist who regularly inscribed *"Achtung – Spitsfeuren!"* on his calling cards. Norma and I finished reeving off new running rigging while Dan, David and his fiancée, Jane Coulson, brought aboard the provisions, charts, books and papers we'd brought with us in David's car, which Jane then drove back to New York. We all set to work dragging the sails out of the cabin where they had spent the winter tied up in huge, ungainly bundles. By day's end the schooner's rig was complete; jib, staysail, foresail and main bent on to the booms, gaffs and stays, with halyards ready to hoist.

There was not a breath of air, so as shadows crept across the narrow harbor, we started up *Athena*'s wheezy engine and headed out to sea, motoring into the chilly April night, the stars brilliant above us mirrored in the water we tramped through.

As *Athena* stuck her nose into the glassy swell outside the harbor, she began to take in water through the dried-out planking of her topsides. It took until midnight to get her old-fashioned pump to work (we discovered it needed a very heavy priming). By that time cold seawater was slopping about the cabin floorboards, which may have contributed to an attack of seasickness that drove Dan Northup to take to his bunk.

In the succeeding days we had wind a-plenty and found that the old schooner stood up well to her considerable spread of canvas, stepping out in lively fashion when it breezed up. We had various adventures along the way. Dan Northup, unable to shed his wracking siege of sea sickness as we bucked head seas, left us at Newburyport to take the train home. Later, stopping in at Gloucester in a freezing gale, we sought sustenance ashore at a waterfront bar. Wrapped in dripping oilskins with watch caps jammed down over our foreheads, we welcomed the warmth and quietude of the barroom, until the bartender barked at us: "No women allowed!"

David and I gallantly accompanied Norma back to the schooner, mystified as to how the bartender had detected her under the layers of wool and bulky foul-weather gear that encased her with only eyes and nose visible. We soon had a fire roaring in the Shipmate stove that dominated *Athena*'s main cabin, and we had our mug-up in peace, while the wind hummed through the rigging overhead.

The next day we arose to find the world under a dusting of snow and we sailed the vessel on south through the Cape Cod Canal, to the Elizabeth Islands, tinted with faint green in the advancing spring, and so westward toward New York. Coming into the sheltered waters of Long Island Sound we were caught up enough on our schedule to stop off at Milford, Connecticut, where my father, Al, came aboard for a visit. He had owned a Nova Scotia-built schooner in the 1930s and admired the breed. We enjoyed dinner with Al and his wife, Berenice, who gave us a pot of hearty stew she had thoughtfully prepared for us for the remainder of our journey.

And on the chill bright Sunday morning of 25 April 1965 we made an early start for New York. The light breeze soon died out and we resigned ourselves to using the engine to cover the remaining miles to City Island—until, some miles short of the goal, the wheezing engine gave a final stertorous cough and died. When a breeze struck in at last, it grew rapidly in strength and *Athena,* sailing close-hauled with taut sheets, picked up her pace, leaning over to the wind until the sea came sloshing through the lee scuppers to race around the white-columned bulwarks before gurgling overside. As darkness drew on, an icy rain began to fly into our faces.

Ordinarily we might have pulled into one of the friendly harbors that dent each shore of the Sound, but we knew we had to be back at work the next morning, Norma at the National Committee for an Effective Congress, David at Ogilvy & Mather, and I to report to Hicks & Greist to write ads for Beefeater Gin, a job I'd taken just a week before this cruise.

"Isn't this wonderful!" I said to Norma, as we stood up forward to spot lighthouses and lighted buoys as they came up through the dusk, with the lights of Manhattan glowing in the distance. We had just finished lighting our own running lights, kerosene lamps mounted in the foremast rigging, and everything seemed to me in proper order, with our stout vessel racing through wind and rain to get us home on time after our adventurous cruise. Norma thought "wonderful" a bit overstated, but said she might accept "exciting." I told her she looked great with wet hair plastered across her face.

On this rainy, blowy night, it looked a bit tricky coming into the City Island anchorage. But we shortened down to foresail and staysail and headed into the sheltered water behind the island, where we lowered the two sails and coasted into the Minneford's pier with no trouble (it fortunately had a lighted sign on it), landing so gently that we wouldn't have cracked an egg coming alongside. Norma and David, standing by fore and aft, simply handed our mooring lines to Harry Naverson, the dockmaster who had spotted us in the offing.

"Where did you get that schooner?" was his gruff greeting. "Don't see many of them around these days." We introduced ourselves and felt an immediate bond with the old salt. And then, with the rain coming down in buckets, we scurried below, pulled the hatch after us, lit the cabin lamp and the stove, and sat down to Berenice's splendid stew, finishing up as Jane arrived in David's car to drive us back to Manhattan.

We resumed our accustomed daily routines, with the well-rounded shape of a handsome Gloucester schooner luring us back to City Island, a long subway ride and short bus trip from Manhattan, every weekend and quite often week nights as well. *Athena* was a demanding mistress and, not having been as well kept as she might have been in recent years, there was endless work to do, alow and aloft. At Minneford's yard Harry Naverson, a veteran of square rig, took joy in looking after the old schooner, sharing bits of maritime lore and counsel. Young friends from Ogilvy, rounded up by David, turned out to help clean out and to lend a hand with caulking, painting and odd bits of carpentry. We celebrated *Athena*'s 40th birthday with champagne in the forecastle, right in the bows of the vessel amid hanging coils of rope and sailbags. Thomas, age six, offered the toast to *Athena*, celebrating her new name, while Norma and I cheered.

Then in late May we broke off work to get in a weekend sail down the Sound. Tommy for the first time found himself aboard a big boat with plenty of line-handling, deck swabbing and other needed tasks to be carried out. His previous sailing had been done in a 25-foot sloop with little room for walking about the decks, but aboard *Athena* there were enclosing bulwarks and one could even go out on the bowsprit and look back at the whole schooner, with her multiple sails driving her forward. And he discovered that one could get one's legs washed down when the skipper headed into the wake of a passing motorboat.

Back where the elders gathered around the wheel, talk was largely of the advertising business. David and Jane had joined Norma, Thomas and me on this trip. David was doing well at Ogilvy & Mather, where business was booming. And we chatted about my move from Ogilvy to the small firm of Hicks & Greist to write the ads for Beefeater Gin. I had secured the job on the strength of a long phone call David Ogilvy had made to H & G about my work. This extraordinary gesture from one of the titans of the industry made me wonder if I could live up to this kind of billing. The client, Kobrand Corp., distributors of Beefeater Gin, had never run an ad of over eleven words. But, feeling there was more to say about this gin, I wrote an ad of 1,100 words, which would require almost a full page in the *New York Times* and two in the *New Yorker*.

Headlined "The *Grownups'* Hour," the ad set forth "A time and a way ... to cut off the cares of the day and enjoy a great martini." Replete with counsel not to ask one's wife to "preside over the swift chilly marriage of gin and vermouth," this expansive disquisition had been approved without change by my new clients. This I think had something to do with my having insisted on doing research by spending a week behind the bar at Costello's on Third Avenue, a cherished hangout of *New Yorker* writers and newsmen as well as people who appreciate a no-frills Irish pub, followed by another week at Whyte's Restaurant, on Fulton Street just off Broadway, before writing the ad. Habitués had tended to spot me as a ringer, but the Costellos in their good-natured way took pride in increasingly fantastic explanations for my bumbling ways behind the bar. And in Whyte's many of the staff remembered a Rutgers Club dinner held there in my honor, which gave them a ready-made story to tell. But I did learn that martini drinkers liked to talk about their martinis. This conclusion made the judicious David raise a quizzical eyebrow: If they were already fans of the martini, why would they read a long lecture about it? But Jane enthusiastically applauded, perhaps from superior understanding of the male psyche.

When we reached a quiet cove in Huntington, Long Island, we enjoyed our grownups' hour at anchor, until a squall that had been building in the west swept down upon us and we scurried below to talk about sheep farming in the Scottish highlands, past adventures in Lower East Side

politics, and even of sailing *Athena* into the Fulton Market one day, to
bring the sight of gaff sails and a fidded topmast back to the slip that
had once been a nest of schooners carrying this antique rig.

Going up on deck to check on the kerosene riding light hung on the
forestay I looked at the schooner's bowsprit pointed toward the haze of
light that represented New York. What would become of our doings
there, and what would become of Jane's and David's Highland dream-
ings? What about our dream of sailing ships coming back to the heart
of the city in South Street? I could not help thinking that we live in two
worlds: the one of dreams that do not go away, but grow in one's mind;
the other of the everyday realities that get people to work every morning,
knitting their complex and changing lives into patterns too elaborate and
variegated for any one mind to encompass—the kind of effort that kept
the subways running through the rabbit warrens of the city, whose lights
glowed against the sky beyond *Athena*'s forestay. Could one bring an
actual fishing schooner back to teach the slower rhythms of life in this
preoccupied, hurrying, noisy environment? I thought that these musings
and visions of things half-remembered or still unknown could hardly affect
the world of physical cause and effect, the screech of subway wheels, the
scurrying of street traffic and the tramp of myriad feet. But who knew
what actually lay before us in New York? It was a peaceful night, and I
was asleep minutes after I went below.

Weekends throughout the summer of 1965 found us working aboard
Athena with our volunteer crew of schooner-struck friends. They seemed
somehow to find joy in such operations as hoisting our worn-out engine
out of the vessel, using the main gaff with its sturdy peak halyard as a
derrick, then clearing the dirt of ages out of the engine room, which received a thorough scrubdown and a gleaming coat of fresh white paint.
My "*Grownups'* Hour" ad hit the papers in August with a considerable
splash, as letters both heartfelt and jocular poured in, asking for reprints.
This meant a redoubled workload for me in my new job. So I found

myself in the anomalous position of hammering away at a typewriter on the new dining table we'd built for the main cabin, while people around me wielded real hammers, scrapers and paintbrushes to improve the surroundings. Fortunately these things were meat and drink to Norma, who had grown up as her father's leading assistant in keeping up the old wooden buildings of the Franceschis' country home in Westchester.

But other developments were in the making to change the even tenor of our ways, as our first summer in the old schooner ended.

CHAPTER 1

We Set Out on the Journey, *1965-66*

On the San Francisco Waterfront—Historic Ships—
Balclutha—*Remembering Plato's Academy—*
Stackpole Signs On—Anita Lights a Candle

A fine evening in October 1965 found Norma and me together in San Francisco, and after an early dinner we set out for the waterfront and Fisherman's Wharf. Our hosts, the local distributors for Beefeater Gin, had entertained us royally at a Nob Hill hotel, but they tactfully released us early to find our own way to the harbor. So, hand in hand we hopped on the Hyde Street cable car and, breasting an intervening hill, we saw before us the waters of San Francisco Bay gleaming in the lights of the shore establishments. This, evidently, was no deserted waterfront. Passing the cheery windows of the Buena Vista Cafe, we disembarked and made out against the night sky the aspiring shapes of masts—masts evidently belonging to a sailing vessel!

We were surprised and delighted to be where we were. The trip had taken shape amid a welter of canceled appointments and a hurried wedding ceremony at New York's Municipal Building, with Ed Parmelee as witness and best man. We three had to suppress giggles as the clerk with a serious speech impediment stumbled incomprehensibly through the reading, and Norma has since suggested that we were not properly married, since our names were never pronounced in recognizable form. Nonetheless, our marriage was a fact. And, to my delight, my clients at Kobrand Corp. said they'd be glad to have Norma join me on their annual West Coast trip for the Beefeater Dinner in Los Angeles and to a subsequent trip up the coast to review the advertising campaign with several Beefeater distributors.

As we traveled up the coast, Norma and I discovered that those authoritarian bosses, Rudy Kopf the chairman and John Bush the president of Kobrand, had passed the word that this tour was our wedding trip. We found the sober businessmen—who kept me busy telling the story of the "*Grownups' Hour*" ad to their salesmen during the day—were conspiring to let us have time on our own in the evenings, excusing us early from the obligatory dinners. So we raced together down to the Hyde Street Pier where we had seen tall masts against the sky.

As we arrived at the pier, a big three-masted schooner took shape in the darkness before us. Our hosts had told us that there were some old ships on the waterfront, and here, evidently, was one of those ships. Along with another tourist, a young sailor is his dress blues, we boarded the schooner and found she was the *C. A. Thayer*, built in 1895 by Hans Bendixsen for the lumber trade. Bendixsen was a well-known builder of these beamy, shoal-draft schooners with their short, stout masts and no topmasts—a breed quite different from the last of the tall, deep-draft East Coast trading schooners I had seen as a boy in Long Island Sound. Below decks amid a grand array of old photographs we saw one of Bendixsen himself, a fine mustachioed gent, proud of his gabled Victorian house, his majestic wife and well-scrubbed children. And we learned a lot more about the people who'd sailed in this shapely 156-foot vessel, both in the lumber trade and later in the North Pacific fisheries. We followed the vessel's story in family photos, letters, newspaper clippings and logbook pages. Some tutelary genius had found out how to let the actual experiences of real people speak for themselves—and the people became real to us, as we entered into their world. I would not have been too surprised if someone had tapped me on the shoulder, to turn around and face old Bendixsen himself, asking what we thought of his ship. Back on deck, I took hold of the main peak halyard and leaned on it, just to see the blocks along the gaff stir and lift—and to imagine what it must be like to make sail on this vessel, whose every aspect dwarfed the working gear we were accustomed to in our *Athena*.

Norma joined me on deck to point out another vessel just ahead of us along the Hyde Street Pier. It was magic to us that the pier was still open at 8PM, but it must close at some hour after all. So we hurried down the gangway, prompting the quiet watchman at the rail to say: "Easy does it, people, she's not sinking, you know!" Farther down the pier we mounted the gangplank of a great wooden steamer bearing the Indian name *Wapama*, after California's Wapama Falls. (It was customary for vessels in the McCormick fleet to have the names of waterfalls.) This white-painted, multi-tiered vessel had a marvelously primitive, antediluvian look to her. Having learned about steam schooners from Peter Kyne's great novel of the schooner trade, *Cappy Ricks, or the Subjugation of Matthew Peasley*, I knew *Wapama* for what she was—one of the crude, wheezing dinosaurs that used the brute force of the triple-expansion engine to lug huge cargoes of lumber down the coast, crowding graceful schooners like the *C. A. Thayer* out of the trade.

We soon fell under the raffish charm of the quarters in the big house in the stern. In the mate's cabin a navy blue cap and jacket hung from a hook above a pair of sea boots, while a copy of the *Police Gazette* had been thrown down on his bunk—as if he'd just been called on deck. The newspaper was of the era the vessel had been launched in, 1915—and it was printed on pink paper. I had sung the song about "the girl I'll not forget, in the pink *Police Gazette*" but had never expected to see a copy of the paper. Entering the main saloon by the curved stairway, we plunked a coin into a vintage "music machine." This sprang to life with a honky-tonk tune, which resonated with the newspaper engravings of the era hung up all around us. Finally we had to leave. We went back to our hotel entranced by the life we'd felt in those solid wooden ships.

The next day, a Sunday, was the last of our tour, and we were on our own. We made haste to get back to the Hyde Street pier and found that the magic in the old ships still held by daylight. We'd heard that there was also another big ship, a square rigger, on the waterfront, and looking about we caught the glint of morning light on the unmistakable masts and crossed yards of a square-rigged sailing ship to the eastward. Making our way past the small fishing boats of Fisherman's Wharf we pursued our way down the waterfront until we stood face to face with the actual ship—a grand trumpet blast of a ship!

A white, far-gazing figurehead stood over our heads on the arched bow of a great grey hull with painted gunports topped with the sweeping line of black bulwarks. Aloft, the shining spars that had first caught our notice stood supported by the maze of rigging required to drive the big hull across the waters. This was the full-rigged ship *Balclutha*, built in 1886 in Scotland. Seemingly reborn from one of Jack Spurling's paintings of the steel sailing ships of the closing era of deepwater sail, she was one of the British ships that took California grain round Cape Horn to feed the growing cities of Europe and her native British Isles. The newly formed San Francisco Maritime Museum stepped forward in 1951 to save the vessel and to tell the story of her life, the cargoes she carried, and the men who sailed in her.

One of those men was the marine artist Gordon Grant, who had made a passage north in the ship with the Alaska Packers in the 1920s. His vivid sketches were placed about the ship to show men in action, as seen by one who'd been there. Another who became part of her story was one Norman Pearce, who, after sailing in British coastal trades, had decided at age twenty-one that he wanted to go deepwater. Joining *Balclutha* in the spring of 1887, he was in the fo'c'sle as she was towed out of the Welsh port of Penarth on the Bristol Channel by one of the ubiquitous paddle-wheel tugs that pulled sailing ships out to sea against the prevailing westerlies. Since the ship had been towed down from her builder's yard in Scotland without being rigged for sea, the carpenter had not yet fashioned wooden plugs to stopper the hawsepipes—the big heavy-lipped holes through which the anchor chain fed into the fo'c'sle, where the men lived. Pulled relentlessly by the threshing tug, the ship stuck her bow into the Irish Sea. Cold salt water jetted through the hawsepipes into the seamen's quarters, flooding everything, soaking straw mattresses and carrying away the men's sea chests and personal belongings like loose garbage. The men tried to stem the icy flood by stuffing seabags, shirts, pants and towels into the hawsepipes, but the sea repeatedly burst in, rampaging through their dwelling place. This example of the sea's implacable strength, Pearce wrote, frightened him more than the screaming winds and mountainous seas he later encountered off Cape Horn.

Pearce had written all this down in 1954 at age eighty-eight, in a letter to the museum, whose people had the wit and energy to track down his story. Norma and I had a stunning sense of the reality of that distant occasion, as we read his account standing beside the hawsepipe the sea had rushed through, while sunlight dancing off the waves below filled the quiet fo'cs'sle with wavery light.

Catching the cable car back to Nob Hill, we picked up the car we'd rented, a big metallic gold Chrysler convertible, more than a bit showy for us but the only car available, which we drove gleefully across the Golden Gate Bridge and onward to the wine country of Napa Valley. There we sought out the back roads, eventually finding a valley stream where we stopped to cool our wine and enjoy the picnic lunch the hotel had packed for us. We built a rough dam to make a small pond, and a light breeze ruffled its face, making it a miniature sea. The sea is one—and this water was bound for the same sea that glittered up at us earlier in the day through the hawsepipe of the *Balclutha*.

The sea is all connected, like time, with past and future flowing through the present moment. We talked of Plato's Academy, where people walked under the trees exploring such ideas. What if there were such a center in New York, not under the trees, but under ships' masts that stir to the tides that bind the world together?

We carried these musings back to New York, and Norma and I often talked about the ships of San Francisco. Six weeks later, when Al and Berenice came to dinner with us in our apartment on East 11th Street, we told them of our adventures in San Francisco and described how the *Balclutha*'s figurehead gazed over the crowded streets of the city, while her questing bowsprit hovered over the heads of the people who came to wonder at her boldly shaped hull and heaven-challenging rig. The ship's story, we said, was told aboard the vessel in such vivid detail that one came away feeling one had met the ship's people and had come to know the far horizons of seafaring under sail.

Dad was a trustee of Mystic Seaport, so I asked if he thought we might get in touch with Mystic's former curator, Edouard Stackpole, about finding a great square rigger for New York. Ed, I knew, had recently retired from Mystic Seaport to pursue his scholarly studies with the historical societies in his native Nantucket. He and Al had first met as young men writing stories of the sea in the 1930s, and I dimly remembered a visit to Nantucket aboard Dad's schooner, *Tom Cod*, in 1932, when I was five years old, when Ed and Mrs. Stackpole came out for a day's sail. Now, in 1965, the two men were still in touch, pursuing their quite different lives. I said I would write Mr. Stackpole if Dad thought that was the thing to do.

"Hell no," said Al, who loved to quote Winston Churchill's dictum—which the Prime Minister had made into stickers for his memos: "ACTION THIS DAY." Berenice gave me a look meaning: "Here we go again!" as Al continued: "Let's call him up. Where's the phone?"

The telephone was produced and I can see my father now, leaning back with a big grin, to yarn with his old friend.

"Yes, I know it sounds a little wild, but what's the use of being young if you don't do wild things now and then." We could hear only one side of the conversation, but it was not too hard to guess the other half. "Well, the kids say this idea has really worked in San Francisco—better than anything they've seen in Mystic."

I winced at that, since he was speaking to the curator who had presided over the displays at Mystic. I need not have worried. Al added, with a bigger grin than ever: "Well, you'd better talk to Peter yourself—I'll put him on." He handed me the phone.

"Peter, I think this is a wonderful idea," said Ed Stackpole. "To get some real historic ships into the old South Street waterfront would be a great thing for New York. How can I help?" Not knowing exactly what to say, I asked if he would serve on an advisory committee for the project, which as yet had no name. He instantly said yes, and we agreed to stay in touch.

———◆———

Al Stanford brought more than a casual interest to our East River seaport idea. As a young man breaking into advertising in New York, he had written novels featuring young men finding their destinies in seafaring under sail, and the world of South Street had seized his imagination. In one novel, *A City Out of the Sea*, he even had a young lawyer put out with a pickup crew in an old schooner used as a bar in South Street! In 1934 he went on to write what became a classic photographic narrative of the North Atlantic fisheries called *Men, Fish & Boats*, a work that held me fascinated as a child.

Dad had served briefly in the US Navy in World War I, and in World War II he volunteered at age 42. Using Washington connections, he got to embattled England to serve as deputy commander of the artificial harbors, code-named Mulberry, which the Allies built on the Normandy beaches to support their invasion of France in 1944. He later wrote a story of this, *Force Mulberry*, which featured an introduction by the Navy's official historian, Samuel Eliot Morison, a peacetime sailing friend.

Al's sailing friendships kept cropping up. When Al enlisted in the Navy, his sailing pal Freddy Paine, who had quit his own bookshop business to join the Navy, found us emergency lodging, since Al had to give up the family's palatial Gramercy Park apartment, which he couldn't afford on a Navy salary. So we bedded down in Freddy's famed midtown shop, ALFRED W. PAINE, BOOKS RELATING TO SALT WATER. Here I reveled in the serried ranks of authors ancient and modern, turning from *Jane's Fighting Ships* to *The Odyssey*, with Masefield's *Salt Water Ballads* for an encore. And I never heard anyone complain about reduced living standards.

After the war, he and my mother, Dorothy, were divorced. Fed up with advertising, Dad fulfilled his lifetime ambition of running a small-town newspaper, buying *The Milford Citizen*, a weekly paper in the Connecticut town where he and Berenice moved in the early 1950s. Before the war, Dad had served as commodore of the Cruising Club of America, and sailing remained a great thing in his life. He believed seafaring under sail fostered solid values and exposed false pretenses, which he felt he'd seen enough of in his varied career. A book he wrote just before the war, *The Pleasures of Sailing*, celebrated his deep satisfaction with life afloat, which he and Berenice continued to enjoy in the small cutter they kept in Milford Harbor, in front of the house they'd built in that quiet corner of the world.

Despite our strikingly similar interests, and Al's interventionist style in life, he made it a rule not to intervene in his children's projects. He would willingly give advice if asked—but then you were on your own. This made his advice welcome in the East River dreams that were clearly beginning to take shape as some sort of project in Norma's and my life. And I was glad to see his positive reaction to Norma's go-ahead approach to things, which indeed had quite a bit in common with his own.

Another family member who soon became involved in our seaport dreaming was Norma's father, M. Peter Franceschi. Mr. F, as everyone called him, was looked up to by a large extended family, and his story was one of remarkable achievement. Having immigrated to New York at the age of six with his parents from a small village in the remote mountains of Tuscany, he went to work straight out of high school, nailing up shipping boxes in a factory while studying art at night at the Art Students League. He soon got a job in the bull pen of an ad agency, and from then on there was simply no stopping him. In 1935 at age thirty, he was married, had two children, lived in the city and bought a country home in Westchester. By the early 1950s he'd risen to vice president and general manager of Foote, Cone & Belding, serving as the right-hand man of Emerson Foote, one of the great ad men of the postwar era. When Foote quit the ad business over the industry's continued advertising of cigarettes, Mr. F found the ad game tougher going, especially for a person of his polite but quite definite views, but he was managing to continue his career against odds as he advanced into his sixties at this stage of the story. Norma became Mr. F's right-hand aide in family affairs; they worked well together and enjoyed each other's company. As the business of the seaport scheme began to take over our lives he cheerfully played a supportive role in our work.

But Mr. F had locked horns with Norma in one famous disagreement which was to have a notable impact on the seaport idea. This was her plan to spend her junior year of college at Marymount in Rome. Mr. F, persistently American in his views, clearly thought this a retrograde step in education, a viewpoint he maintained even as he signed the necessary papers—up until departure day, that is, when a marvelous photo was taken of him beaming from ear to ear as he waved goodbye to Norma —departing for Italy aboard the *Cristoforo Colombo*!

"Perhaps spending a year away from the city you love is a good thing," Norma later wrote. And having also managed to spend a traditional Christmas with my cousins in England during her year abroad, she added:

> *I returned from Italy and England with a freshened view about cities. I had a new respect for the concept of neighborhoods, for resident landlords, for individuality, and for "smallness." I had impatience with ugliness, a mistrust of "bigness," and contempt for the prevalent notion that the city is here to be exploited. That attitude, whether harbored by a bank president or a bus driver, is, I suggest to you, the biggest threat to this or any city's well-being.*

These views became familiar to all who came to know Norma's work in South Street. In fact, they represent a fair picture of the governing spirit of the place as it was coming into being.

On 20 January, a few weeks after Al's visit, Norma, sharing Al's bent for "Action this day," wrote a letter to San Francisco. It was addressed simply to :

Director

San Francisco Maritime Museum

Foot of Polk Street

San Francisco, California

"Dear sir," it opened, coming right to the point: "New York's Fulton Fish Market, the last enjoyable bit of New York waterfront, will soon be closed down. It has already been suggested that the waterfront be filled in and luxury apartment buildings be built on the site." It went on to mention that, on a visit to the fish docks the previous winter, Norma had noticed an old schooner cut down and refitted for use as a power fishing boat, and that the neighboring streets had buildings from the mid-1800s, which were "certainly doomed with the Market." She continued:

> Some friends and I were wondering about the difficulties involved in the establishment of an historical marine park. Before the proposal could responsibly be put before the Department of Parks we would need an idea of the problems involved. We thought you might be able to help us.

It was Norma who decided we needed advice from the head of the museum whose ships had so stirred our imaginations. We'd agreed that she should take the lead in this, since she had a gift for cutting to the heart of any problem. For my part, I was wary of launching any effort that might involve the day-and-night work it had taken to run the Rutgers Club in view of my demanding job in advertising.

In a little over a week we had a response to Norma's request for help—and what a response it was! It came from Anita Ventura, registrar of the museum, and in it she explained that Karl Kortum, director of the museum, was out of town on a long trip. But she knew he would be interested in our project and apparently felt we had come to the right place for guidance. She told us: "Mr. Kortum's first act in the creation of a maritime park area here was to interest major publishers." With this support, he had persuaded the State of California to take over the Hyde Street pier as a public park, and to maintain the ships there, which were run under the supervision of the Maritime Museum headed by Kortum. And, very helpfully, Ms. Ventura enclosed a swatch of clippings to show how Kortum got the museum's story across in papers and magazines, as the great vision of an inner-city floating museum had come into being. Commenting on our own situation as Norma had presented it, she added that she knew that the Fulton Fish Market was a tourist attraction, and we noticed she mentioned Sweet's restaurant (which Norma had not mentioned) as well as Sloppy Louie's, showing an acquaintance with our part of the world.

Ms. Ventura's last paragraph explained that more than a passing acquaintanceship was involved—and made us love the lady:

> *I would only add that I hope very much that a group is formed and succeeds in preserving that area of New York. I formerly lived for four years at Broad and Water Streets and know just about every inch of the ground and buildings of Manhattan below Wall Street. It is my favorite part of the city, and as I write to you I can see, smell and feel it. I miss it very much and know that there are many like me who would do whatever they could to preserve it.*

As things turned out, a year would pass before we got back in touch with Anita. But we did not forget her letter. It lit a candle in that part of our lives where the old South Street neighborhood made its mute appeal to be saved, a gleam among the shadowy shapes of the half-forgotten past and unrealized future.

CHAPTER 2

Athena in Conroy's Creek, *Winter 1965–66*

The Sound in October—Winter Lay Up—
Rocco's Chippewa Tavern—Conroy's Marina—
Rocco Stands Up for Free Speech—A Champagne Departure Party

After San Francisco we had taken a week off to sail around Long Island Sound in *Athena*—memorable days of bright skies and screaming October winds, salt spray in the face and the schooner's decks constantly awash in cold salt water. *Athena* was in her element, careering along with a cascading bow wave as she charged through the sea, steady on the helm and easily handled by the two of us. We were grateful for the warmth of the coal stove in the evenings, when we anchored in out-of-the-way coves and nearly deserted harbors. Only a few vessels were still about, and with only seagulls and occasional porpoises for company the Sound was a wild, vividly beautiful place to be.

This was the last sail of the season, and we needed to find a place to lay up the schooner. Most yachts were hauled out of water for the winter, but we knew *Athena*'s heavy wooden hull would be better off in the water in some quiet corner away from moving ice. Minneford's in City Island would be too exposed for us, but their dockmaster, Harry Naverson, took a special interest in *Athena*, whose old-fashioned rig and gear took him back to his seafaring youth, sailing in square riggers from Buenos Aires to Marseilles in summer vacations before World War I. He heartily agreed with our plan to keep *Athena* in the water over the winter, and he said we should take a look at Conroy's Marina in Westchester Creek, where a mixed bag of party fishing boats and small cruisers took refuge in sheltered slips over the winter.

So one Saturday morning we sallied forth from our East 11th Street apartment and boarded the Lexington Avenue subway for a long trip up through Manhattan and then under the Harlem River to the Bronx, where the train burst out into the open air on an elevated track like a dusty animal coming out of its burrow. The dun-colored subway cars swayed and rollicked past low-rise brick houses that characterized the outer boroughs of the city. We got out at Westchester Square and came hurrying down the clanging iron steps that led to the street.

Saturday morning—a time to be up and doing! The street was full of life; women shopping with children in tow, as the men of the households took it easy after a week at work, while teenagers pursued whatever their weekend adventures would be. Halfway down the stairs Norma pointed out a sign, "Rocco's Chippewa Tavern," just ahead of us.

"What a cockamamie cultural stew!" she said. But the sign was readily explicable, I explained. In the late 1800s the Tammany Hall clubs of the Democratic Party had taken Indian names. Practically all these clubs had their headquarters over bars, usually Irish, but sometimes Italian after the great immigration of the 1890s and early 1900s. Then, in the reform-minded 1930s, a law was enacted: No bars connected with political clubs! Usually the club just moved around the corner, keeping up its convivial relation with the bar. Norma looked skeptical at this, so I bet her a glass of beer that there was a Chippewa Democratic Club nearby. We went in and ordered our beers. The bartender, a sullen-looking bruiser of a man with reddish-blond hair, whom we would come to know as Schultz, slid a couple of glasses across the scarred mahogany bar. When I asked if there was a local Democratic club, he said:

"Yeah, the Chippewa club, just around the corner, other side of the block," he said. "Not open this early. Usually open up around eleven o'clock."

Norma cheerfully paid for the beers and, having got directions to Conroy's Marina, we pursued our way down a side street where the respectable brick buildings around Westchester Square soon gave way to low-rise industrial buildings and junkyards guarded by vociferous dogs. After a while the pavement gave way to a gravelly road and we came to a compound of square, white, one- and two-story buildings huddled together like tents of the French Foreign Legion along the Stygian waters of Westchester Creek.

Here we met Adrian Conroy, a retired tugboat skipper who seemed much at home in this out-of-the-way corner of the ocean world. He informed us that he had put up stranger vessels than ours—including a Chinese junk and a big Nova Scotia schooner which I remembered having seen years ago from the Hutchinson River Parkway on the other side of the creek. The Scotiaman, I was sorry to learn, had put in for repairs that were never completed and she had finally been towed away to a scrapyard.

Despite this ill-omened precedent, it was clear that this was a snug home for our own schooner. So I wrote a check on the spot to rent a slip. And Conroy's, with its convenient source of refreshment at Rocco's Chippewa Tavern, became a center of exuberant life for us that winter of 1965–66, as we worked with David, Jane, and a few other helpful friends to rebuild our schooner's accommodations. The restoration of the *Athena* became a project with a life of its own. In the evenings we would tramp up the street to Rocco's, where we found that Schultz had a fine hand with the pasta dishes he cooked up, and a marvelous way with the children, who were with us on many weekends. His sullen look reflected God knows what disappointments he'd encountered in life, and he would sometimes vanish on expeditions from which he returned looking the worse for wear—but when he saw the kids he beamed and he loved to get them talking.

The three youngsters—Tony now being old enough to join our outings with Tom and Carol—got to know the ins and outs of the buildings ashore, and became familiar with the tippy floating walkways which served as piers for the dormant hulls of party fishing boats and other local craft. *Athena* became a snug cottage on the frosty nights as ice began to form around her hull. The winter cover, made up of tarpaulins erected over the afterdeck and the cabin house between the masts, made the decks a kind of indoor playground for the children.

And then, those nights at Rocco's! It was thirsty work in the bowels of the ship, as the crew were wont to point out, so at quitting time of a Saturday evening we would tramp up the road to claim the central table in the back room. Usually there would be a couple or two at a side table. On occasion we were joined by Joe Rocco himself, a tall, shy, soft-spoken man. He usually dined with his wife, Madeleine, who had kind eyes for the kids beneath her formidable beehive hairdo. I worried a little about our boisterous ways in this decent neighborhood bar, ways that occasionally extended to singing a song or two. But the Roccos seemed more amused than shocked by our carryings-on.

One day Rocco pulled up a chair at our table. "I understand you got a boat down to Conroy's," he said. We said yes, that was what we were doing in the neighborhood.

"Schultzie tells me you got a hundred-foot mast in that boat, is that right?" he asked.

"No, not a hundred feet, more like fifty," said Norma.

"Well, actually fifty-five," I added. I was proud of that soaring topmast, the spar from which you hang the fisherman staysail, turning a schooner from an earth-bound plodder into a winged Pegasus.

"Well, okay, that's some boat," said Rocco. "I guess you'd call it a yacht, right?"

"No, no, not a yacht!" several voices protested. "Hell ship is more like it," someone added. And we explained that *Athena* was basically a working vessel built on fishing schooner lines and that we were doing some needed work on her before we took her sailing far and wide.

Joe said he'd have to get down our way to visit the schooner. Oh yes, we all said, great idea. Please come. Why not stop by tomorrow afternoon? Maybe Mrs. Rocco would come. But to our lasting regret, they never did.

One evening at dinner we had been holding a lively discussion of the resumption of bombing North Vietnam after the Christmas bombing halt. I recounted how on Christmas Eve, on my way to buy a Christmas tree, I had stopped to make a pay-phone call to the *Herald Tribune* to urge an end to the bombing. I reached Raymond Price, who had published an op-ed piece of mine on city government the year before, and he invited me to come up to see him with my concerns.

Meeting in Price's oak-paneled office I told him that our policy had led to designating whole stretches of the country as "free fire" zones, where anything moving could be killed. This, I added, met Clausewitz's definition of a war against a people, where strategy ends and extermination begins. Clausewitz concluded; you simply had to go on killing until you'd killed off the people of the country you were trying to subdue.

"And what did Mr. Price say?" asked David, who maintained a judicious neutrality in these discussions.

"He talked about the Asian states falling like a row of dominoes if we didn't fight in Vietnam. And I said this was old-fashioned European *realpolitik*, which regards war as a game played with soulless pieces—a policy far removed from any strategy of freedom. Then he walked over to a big world map on the wall, turned to me and said: 'We're too deeply committed to pull out.' Now, any real fighter knows there comes a time to take your losses and abandon a failed strategy. So I just thanked Mr. Price for his time and wished him all the best of the season."

All this was thirsty going, and while the rest ordered supper, I took the empty beer pitcher off the table and walked through the green curtain that separated the dining room from the bar, to get the pitcher refilled. There I saw an intense young man halfway down the bar glaring at Rocco, who was polishing a glass.

"Hey, Rocco, you know what you got back there? A bunch of freaking Commies, that's what you got!"

Clearly, the man felt action was called for.

Rocco put down his towel. He laid his big hands on the bar, leaned forward on his arms and looked steadily at this irate patron. Conversation died down the length of the bar.

"So maybe they're Commies," Rocco said at last. "If so, they're *our* Commies, see?"

Rocco turned around and walked to my end of the bar, where he saw me and proceeded to refill our pitcher. Conversation again resumed along the bar. Another night at Rocco's, where a remarkable man held sway.

———◆———

Along with carpentry, politics, and the goings-on in the advertising world in which we worked, a few things happened during the winter to move us forward on the South Street trail. One was an accidental meeting I had in February with the assistant editor at the magazine then named *Popular Boating*. This was Richard Rath, whom I had met in San Juan, Puerto Rico, when he was captain of an inter-island cargo boat working out of that fabled city of the sea. We now renewed our acquaintance to meet occasionally for drinks. I told him about our idea for an East River Seaport (as we then called it) and he told me of his dream of getting a Gloucester schooner sailing from the Fulton Market to catch fish at sea with a crew of disadvantaged city kids. Learning this traditional trade with its harsh but valuable disciplines could really change their outlooks and their lives, he felt. I was moved by this vision coming from a person with a tough-guy attitude and Runyonesque way of answering his phone with the growled monosyllable: "Rath." Norma was as interested as I was to learn of another person thinking of bringing a working schooner back to the Fish Market, though the scheme seemed as far-fetched as our vision of a restored seaport in South Street.

Another step was a letter Norma wrote to the English journal *The Mariner's Mirror*, a letter that reflected the impact of our visit to *Balclutha* in San Francisco and Anita Ventura's letter written on behalf of her boss, Karl Kortum, who believed in the power of the square-rigged ship to attract and inspire people. Norma's letter, sent in January and published in the August 1966 issue, read as follows:

> *A group of residents of New York City are interested in forming a maritime museum centering on the past of the East River Waterfront. For this purpose they wish to locate old sailing-ship hulls, with an eventual view to acquisition and reconditioning for display.*
>
> *They are particularly interested in acquiring a deepwater square rigger. It would be greatly appreciated if*

any reader having information about the hull of such
a survivor of the age of sail would communicate with
Mrs. Norma Stanford
210 East 11th Street
New York, N.Y. 10003

And however fantastic this vision of a restored seaport in the heart of the city might seem, Norma and I began to form an idea of how the historic buildings might be saved. A few years earlier, in meetings at LENA—the Lower Eastside Neighborhoods Association—I had been outraged by a plan which called for tearing down a row of mid-1800s brownstones inhabited by long-established Irish families, which lent architectural variety and ethnic diversity in a depressed minority neighborhood. I was informed that the city zoning laws called for open space to be created opposite the new school to be erected across the street—and that any attempt to get a variance to save the buildings and keep these established families in the neighborhood would delay construction of the needed school by at least ten years. So the plan went through, the families left, and the narrow "park" set up where their homes had stood became a frowsy wasteland with drug users' needles scattered among the mangy tufts of grass.

And at that very time, in the early 1960s, Jacqueline Kennedy had saved the historic buildings on Lafayette Square in Washington, DC, with an innovative plan that allowed developers to build the high-rise buildings they wanted behind the historic frontage, with the taller building height making up for the ground area they'd lost to preservation.

Historic preservation in big cities was then in its infancy—but here, at a stroke, a popular First Lady had broadened its scope from saving individual buildings to saving historic streetscapes. Why couldn't we do something on these lines in New York? Just by shifting the allowed building volumes around, we could rationally aspire to save our old buildings and their historic streets.

Norma worked at developing the principle into a usable planning tool. It was a matter of dealing with building volume flexibly and accepting cobbled streets and historic buildings as having urban value—perhaps a more humane value, indeed, than angular sculptures stuck into the barren plazas mandated by the current zoning practice.

Spring came to Conroy's Creek—as local boatmen regularly called it— and to the schooner that was now the center of our world. The ice faded away and equinoctial gales stirred the muddy waters into steep crested wavelets which slapped *Athena*'s broad haunches. As the weather turned milder, our crew began to work on decks and rigging, while striving to complete the detailed work below. This interior work took much longer than any of us had expected, since right angles were few and most sur- faces were curved. But we all persisted and the accommodations below were transformed. The layout centered on the large main cabin table illumined by an ornate brass lamp of 1911 from a pilot cutter my father had once owned. These accommodations were to serve as the meeting- place of our adventures and discussions aboard *Athena*, the sea chariot that would carry us leagues down the long road that led to South Street.

And the day of departure finally arrived, well into June. We celebrated the occasion with a late morning champagne reception honoring Mr. Conroy, along with Dutchy, skipper of the party fishing boat on the other side of our float, with whom we'd formed a grand alliance after a rocky start-up involv- ing some strong language he used with a female member of our crew about whose docking lines went where on the limited number of cleats on the float. Once that matter had been settled, he became the soul of generosity, giving us old but usable flares the Coast Guard had condemned for use on his passenger-carrying vessel, and above all lending us his engineer Micky, who did wonders to get our ancient rebuilt engine back in operating shape.

The log entry for our departure read:

Saturday, June 18, 1966

1150 Motored downstream from Conroy's gas dock after morning working on wrecked dinghy Conroy gave us in ex- change for ABS dinghy [my father's dinghy, too small for our crew], Jane's heroic vacuuming below, and chaps messing

about with carpentry, cabin sanding, fitting bowsprit, and fi-
nally a 15-minute champagne reception in Mr. Conroy's honor.

So we steamed off in the best of spirits, our gang working about the decks to coil down docking lines and lace the sails to the booms, gaffs and masthoops. As we approached the Bruckner Boulevard drawbridge, we expected a dour reception from the hurrying motorists forced to endure a delay on our behalf. Apparently the sight of an old-time schooner outward bound with a Tudor rose burgee flying from our lofty topmast pleased the onlookers on both sides of the highway, for there were smiles and cheerful waves as we passed through. All this was much in keeping with our frame of mind, as *Athena* at last made good her departure from winter quarters, to escape to the broad and sparkling waters of Long Island Sound.

CHAPTER 3

To Gloucester—and Beyond! *Summer 1966*

A New Base for Athena—*State Museum Announced—*
Schooners in Gloucester—Lady of Good Voyage—
Nantucket Wisdom—Athena *Romps Home—We Change Jobs*

With *Athena* freed from the narrow confines of Westchester Creek, we spent our weekends roaming the length and breadth of Long Island Sound, making our base in Milford, halfway down the Sound, at my father's invitation. We berthed the schooner at Al's pier with his sloop *Vision IV* on the other side. From this happy coign of vantage, either end of the Sound was within a day's sail, from the rocky outcroppings of the Norwalk Islands to the enchanted reaches of the Connecticut River.

There was naturally much raillery between the two boats. *Vision IV*, named for the staunch, straight-stemmed English pilot cutter Al had once owned, was a fast-traveling, slippery boat. Designed by Olin Stephens, who had consulted with Al among others to get full headroom and open, roomy accommodations in a 33-foot hull, she was fully ten feet shorter than *Athena*—but proved almost impossible for the bigger boat to catch in the prevailing light airs of the Sound in summer. We longed for blowy weather, which never came on an occasion when we were out together. But even in a blow Al's boat would have been tough to beat. The twenty-three years between *Athena*'s launch and the debut of *Vision IV* had seen more change in yacht design than in the preceding hundred years. Olin was a pioneer in developing those changes, and Al a race-winning skipper.

We wanted to let the schooner lengthen her stride in a venture eastward, and settled on a plan to take her to Gloucester to track down the *Lady of Good Voyage* in her home port. We would look for other schooner hulls as well while picking up more background on the fisheries. For somehow the dream of a restored East River seaport refused to go away, but seemed to grow with a life of its own.

In the spring Norma had left the National Committee for an Effective Congress to work at Arts Councils of America. Her co-worker and friend, Maal Kiil, had told her husband Leevi, an aspiring architect, of our vision of the restored seaport. Maal had suggested that Leevi could build a model of the project, so we'd have something to show people, and Leevi had agreed to take this on. Maal had also discussed the seaport idea with Bob Ferraro, a former Peace Corps worker she'd met in the teacher training classes they were both attending. Bob spent his weekends photographing old buildings in Lower Manhattan and was interested in saving some of these relics of an elder New York. And there was Dick Rath, with whom I stayed in intermittent touch, a practical sailor and writer with his own vision of outfitting a Gloucester schooner for sail training. And there was our pen pal Anita Ventura, she of the lovely name and warm heart, who had caught the magic of South Street from 3,000 miles away. The seaport idea drawing in people from far and wide.

Meanwhile, other things kept breaking in, as they have a way of doing. Things had begun going awry in my work for Beefeater gin. "The *Grownups'* Hour" had made a considerable splash when it hit the streets in mid-1965. Martini aficionados requested reprints of the ad, and it was extensively discussed in several articles in the trade press. It even got a pat on the back in the *American Journal of Psychiatry*. And this *succès d'estime* had been confirmed as sales figures rolled in showing that Beefeater had resumed its commanding lead among premium gins, which competitors had begun to challenge.

Early that year, however, a new manager had been hired by the Beefeater importers, Kobrand Corp., to reorganize the firm's growing business. Beefeater's success, of course, owed everything to Kobrand chairman Rudy Kopf, whose visionary leadership made things hum in the Georgian-style office building they'd built on East 40th Street. My work for Kobrand, which included premium wines as well as Beefeater gin, followed Rudy Kopf's convictions about each brand he took under his wing. The authenticity people found in my ads stemmed from that fact. Creativity worth its salt is not a matter of fiddling with words, after all, but of ideas forged in the fires of conviction.

But the new manager was not impressed by the success we'd been achieving. He continually called for a "fresh, new look," quoting the latest fads reported in the trade press, which he read assiduously. I could tolerate and learn from Rudy's sometimes scorching criticisms of my work, but any solid exchange of ideas simply sank in the new manager's frothy suds of borrowed notions. I finally asked Harry Hicks, president of the ad agency, to carry my ads to the client—where he got them through with better success than I. This meant, however, that I did not talk with Rudy to get any useful criticism of my work. Not what you'd call a healthy situation.

But it was also one that worry wouldn't help. And so, having reviewed this unpleasing state of affairs with Norma, I decided to forget business politics and enjoy our life afloat for the summer now opening upon us. I also pursued some new advertising possibilities with our great friend Ed Parmelee, who had worked with me at Ogilvy and also had preceded me on the Kobrand account. He had his own boat, a schooner a little younger than *Athena*, which fully engaged his time afloat, so he wasn't often with us aboard *Athena*. But we got together in town and, at Ed's insistence, looked into starting our own agency, with Ed for market research, me as writer, joined with the grand touch Norma's father could bring as business manager. Ed was particularly enthusiastic about this and Mr. F. was broadly tolerant of our shenanigans—while I was coming to think it wouldn't hurt to have another iron or two in the fire.

On this somewhat unquiet but enjoyable scene there burst an extraordinary new development. This bolt from the blue came in an excited phone call from Maal Kiil's friend, the Peace Corps veteran Bob Ferraro. He told us the *New York Times* had a story reporting that on 2 August 1966 Governor Nelson Rockefeller had signed into law a bill establishing a New York State museum, to be known as the South Street Maritime Museum, in the buildings of Schermerhorn Row. This row of slope-roofed buildings, a monumental testament to the city's seaport origins, was central to the seaport district we envisaged. We had been inspired by the confident assertion of its repeated doorways and windows punctuating a rosy brick facade still surmounted by stately brick chimneys. Beyond its defiant old-world roofline loomed the high-rise towers of Wall Street and skeletons of glass-fronted office buildings going up amid the racket of riveters and grunt of bulldozers clearing away the remains of the historic city.

The law establishing the new state museum was sponsored by State Senator Whitney North Seymour, Jr., who had recently served as president of the Municipal Art Society of New York, a civic organization formed in the civic reform era of the 1890s. A call to the City Planning Commission confirmed that Seymour was the person to see about the new museum, so I wrote him a letter on the seaport project as it was taking shape in our minds. And at the end of the hot summer day of 10 August Norma and I foregathered to meet with Bob Ferraro for the first time in person and then trooped together into Seymour's office at 120 Broadway. The senator, a vigorous man with a very open manner, bade us a smiling welcome and expressed interest in our idea of bringing historic ships into the South Street waterfront, which I'd made much of in my letter. This idea, he added, was part of the thinking behind the waterfront museum, and he was interested to hear of our visit to the ships in San Francisco, for the San Francisco waterfront renaissance was a much talked-of phenomenon in planning circles. He was also glad to know that we had interested a former curator of Mystic Seaport in our seaport idea.

Seymour then set out for us what the museum act provided: It empowered the state to acquire Schermerhorn Row, but without providing any money. The governing board had still to be appointed, and it would be up to that board to pull together funding to acquire the site, restore the buildings and set up the museum—perhaps $5 million or more. Before any money could be raised, architectural and feasibility studies were needed and it was important, he emphasized, to avoid premature funding appeals which could put off major potential donors. Such fumbles could doom the project as amateurish and disorganized, he warned, and I said that we understood that. We went on to agree upon five areas in which we could play a role in the development of the museum. I noted these down as follows:

1. Developing public discussion and publicity

2. Building a display for exhibition at the Chamber of Commerce

3. Searching out historic ships

4. Accumulating a file of suggestions and ideas

5. Searching out prospective money donors for Seymour's list

In high spirits after this businesslike meeting, Norma, Bob Ferraro and I made our way from the senator's office down Fulton Street and so to Schermerhorn Row, where we were due to meet Leevi and Maal Kiil to report on developments. After a sidewalk meeting in the style of the many waterfront meetings held in this precinct in sailing-ship days, we all proceeded upstairs to Sweet's Restaurant for a celebratory dinner overlooking the waterfront, fancifully imagining the historic ships that would soon lie outside the restaurant windows.

I was struck by how closely our thinking moved together. We were all concerned with saving the storied streetscape we'd walked through, and we longed to bring fresh life and interest to a revived seaport neighborhood. A single museum building could hardly contain the voyaging spirit that had made South Street the "Street of Ships," a heritage still living in the fishing smacks that called in there. And as for the ships we dreamt of bringing in, they should be welcomed by streets that had echoed to sailors' songs and draymen's curses, with varied stops along the way—again, an experience that could hardly be contained in a single building. My notes on our meeting put this strongly: "The demands of *people* in a successful museum simply won't be met in less space."

So we agreed there must be "an initial push" to save the buildings stretching for three blocks along South Street from John Street to Peck Slip, reaching inland to save the facing buildings on Front Street. This effort could not wait long, considering the headlong pace of development in Lower Manhattan, and the first need was to make people aware of the district and its value. Leevi Kiil's model of these buildings would declare

their unique character and stimulate people's interest. Plans in the newspapers suggested that the new towers proposed for the waterfront were
erected in empty space, as though the ground were blank paper—but we
would show it furnished with century-old buildings crowded with past
life and awaiting rediscovery today.

We decided against organizing as a committee for action until we'd
talked with more people and gathered more support. But I felt we'd made
a beginning. And as the long summer evening faded and shadows crept
over the river running outside the windows of Sweet's, one knew it was
out there running quietly in the dark, freighted with future possibilities, as it had been when the city at large came down to the waterfront
to keep in touch with the wider world through ships moored in South
Street.

Norma and I left our new friends in good heart, looking forward to
our forthcoming trip to hunt down the *Lady of Good Voyage* and learn
more of the heritage of the wind-driven ships that had done so much
to make New York the city it was. And we would be embarking on this
quest under sail, in a schooner of our own.

Late on a Friday night two weeks later we found *Athena* lying before us
at a mooring in the Connecticut River, where our friend Jock Bartlett
had left her after a two-week charter. The river was wreathed in swirls
of mist, illumined by a moon that made the dark corners full of mystery.
The schooner loomed huge in the night as we came alongside, her spars
gleaming dully in the cold moonlight, her halyards whispering in private
communion with the night wind sweeping down from the hills to the
north. Norma, Tommy and I climbed aboard quietly from our dinghy
with the cat, Scratch, who traveled with us, to fall into our bunks, looking forward to our setting forth next day. As a youngster I had sailed in
small craft from these waters upriver into the hills and downstream into
the broad waters of Long Island Sound on voyages of discovery and adventure, but I never felt more surely that these things lay before us than
I did as I turned in that night, surrounded by the stout timbers of the sea

chariot which had carried us so far—not so far, perhaps, in actual miles, but certainly in our lives together.

After a pleasant passage via Block Island, the Elizabeth Islands and on through the Cape Cod Canal, we made a quiet crossing of Cape Cod Bay and brought *Athena* to anchor inside the Gloucester breakwater just after midnight Monday night. On Tuesday, 30 August, we weighed anchor after a leisurely breakfast and made sail to a very light breeze to enter Gloucester Harbor in proper fashion—a scion of the Gloucester schooners come home under full sail: main, foresail, staysail, jib, capped by main topsail and fisherman staysail.

Coming up to a large red waterfront building bearing the legend "Tarr & Wonson's Paint Manufactory, established 1863," we saw people waving from the windows. Norma and I had recently slapped two coats of Tarr & Wonson's copper paint onto *Athena*'s bottom—an economical, sure protection against the shipworm which eats away wooden bottom planking, so we knew who they were. But now we were astonished to find that they seemed to know who we were! For as we neared Tarr & Wonson to enter the inner harbor, more people crowded the windows, waving caps and handkerchiefs, and as we drew alongside the building, the factory whistle blew three resounding blasts, and there were cheers and a mighty waving of caps and handkerchiefs. I quickly bent an American ensign to the flag halyard at the end of the main gaff and ran up the flag so that Tommy, age seven, could dip it in response to these salutes. So we arrived in Gloucester, in a welcome that we agreed made up for the scurvy treatment we'd received at a local bar when we had put in there a year earlier.

The people had clearly recognized *Athena* as one of their own, perhaps from memories of the last schooners out of Gloucester under full sail in the fisherman's races of the 1930s, or from family snapshots stuck in bedroom mirrors or in flyspecked photos on the walls of local bars where the legendary past lives on. Once inside the harbor, we found the man in charge at the boatyard full of information. He told us the last of the pure sailing schooners, built before the era of engined craft, had been featured as the *We're Here* in the epic film *Captains Coura-geous* of 1937. That lofty, clipper-bowed schooner, restored for the film to go to sea under an acre of canvas, had been sailed with her decks half underwater, carrying away her main topmast in a tangle of gear as a result of that hard driving as part of the film—a price too often paid when the schooners were pushed to be first to market from the fishing grounds. Talk of saving this vessel as a museum had gone nowhere, and she'd ended her days hauled ashore and buried in waterfront landfill. Sailed hard by working fishermen, she gave the film its awesome authenticity, including the close-knit nature of the crews, where the skipper ate with the men at a V-shaped table in the forward section of the bows, and every man had a voice, though the skipper's word was always final.

Clearly taken with *Athena*, and perhaps intrigued by her unusual crew of two grownups and a child—our knowledgeable friend went on to name five schooners currently in port that carried sail, though built to accommodate engines too. The oldest of these was the *Evelina Goulart*, a largely unaltered 83-foot hull built in 1927, followed by *American Eagle*, the *Edith L. Boudreau*, *Columbia* and the youngest, *Lady of Good Voyage*, built in 1942. Because of the shortage of fuel in wartime America she had been rigged with bowsprit and topmasts to go fast under sail. Somehow she, the youngest of the group, had retained best the lines of a classic Gloucesterman.

After we'd re-provisioned our ship and taken a walk with Tommy through the historic streets of Gloucester, the great home of schooners, we climbed into the dinghy and rowed over for a close look at the five schooner hulls our boatman had pointed out. We saved the *Lady of Good Voyage* for the last. Her dark green hull was warm to the touch in the late afternoon sun, as I traced out occasional graving marks on the planking forward—marks which, when connected in a line, established what must have been the old waterline, interrupted by the replacement planks that had been installed in the past two decades. Since her sailing days, the vessel had been heavily weighted aft to lift her bow two or three feet higher in the water. Just above this mark on the battered and oft-repainted stem, we made out the indented shape of what must have been the cutwater iron, for the fitting that secured the stay that had held down the long-gone bowsprit. We noted these marks and measurements on a bit of paper, and later when we returned to *Athena*, we figured out that the bowsprit must have been between 15 and 20 feet long, appropriate for a 90-foot vessel.

The *Lady of Good Voyage* embodied to us the toughness of these hard-working Gloucester schooners, which survived in changing forms to avoid the nemesis of technological change while bearing the scars of their primordial struggle with the sea. We were delighted to see her still active in the fleet, her unique shape revealing her lineage as a true Gloucester-man. Pursuing our mission, we were up early the next morning to make sail to the southward, heading back for the Cape Cod Canal, on the way to meet Edouard Stackpole in Nantucket.

After a leisurely three-day passage in light airs and fog, we picked up a fine westerly breeze on Friday afternoon and *Athena* settled down to her work, beating out a lacy wake across the sun-daubed sea to finish the run in grand style, the waves of her passage sweeping across the sands of Brant's Point, at the entrance to Nantucket Harbor, like a silken train. Amid the muffled thunder of canvas shaking in the wind, the squeal of halyards running out through their blocks and the creak of swaying gaffs, the sails came down, guided by the lazyjacks to nest on their booms as the sail handlers Norma and Tommy hurried about their tasks and I stood at the helm to steer the vessel to an anchorage off the Nantucket Yacht Club. There we met Ed Stackpole and his son Rennie, who came aboard *Athena* for a mug-up.

I had written Ed a few letters asking guidance on the East River sea-port project, and he had urged that we begin hunting down the ships we wanted to bring into the seaport. I told Ed how his friend Al had vigor-ously agreed with him, saying: "Give them something to get their teeth into. If people disagree with your choices, you've given them something think about. That'll get 'em involved." Ed grinned at this: "That certainly sounds like Al!" And he had of course been delighted to learn of the state museum act, and to hear how we'd staked out a role for our work in our meeting with Senator Seymour. Before we parted we agreed to meet next day with an old schooner hand, one Charlie Sayle, a good friend of Ed's and equally interested in seeing a sea museum in New York.

On the next day, Saturday, our friend Ed Parmelee, his friend Claude Martinot, and his son Trevor, along with Richard Henstock of the *Athena* restoration crew, joined us for the sail home over the three-day Labor Day weekend. While our guests did the marketing and explored the old whaling town, Norma, Tom and I went with Ed Stackpole to meet Charlie Sayle and his wife, Mickey, in their modest shingled house on Union Street. Charlie turned out to be a quiet-spoken, avuncular-looking man with bright blue eyes sparkling above a white beard, and, at our request, Ed soon had him telling us about his seafaring life, supported now and then with lively comments by Mickey. Although he was born in the Midwest, a longing for the sea had brought Charlie to the East Coast, where he sailed first in the Gloucester fisheries and then in the last of the coasting trade in sail, ending up aboard the 73-foot schooner *Alice S. Wentworth* under the redoubtable Zebulon Tilton. Scion of an old seafaring family in Martha's Vineyard, Tilton kept the aging schooner sailing in a variety of trades. The handsome schooner was known to me; I'd met her in Maine waters in 1948 sailing in my 25-foot sloop *Whisper* and had made a sketch in my log of the *Wentworth* cruising among the islands of Casco Bay in her final career, carrying passengers for hire. Charlie, pleased to know I knew his ship, was glad to tell me her story.

Built in South Norwalk, Connecticut, in 1863, the *Wentworth* was a beamy shoal-draft vessel designed to take small cargoes to odd corners of the coast where she made her way up small creeks and coves, lying on the beach to pick up or unload cargo where there were no docking facilities. She started her career carrying brick from Hudson River plants to supply the building boom in New York and its suburbs after the Civil

War, later turning to cheap cargoes as varied as oysters (cheap in those days), sand, coal and cordwood, in which she could compete with the steamers that were taking over coastal trades. When around 1940 these varied trades gave out, with trucks on highways carrying the cargoes schooners had carried, the *Wentworth* was put up at public auction to pay her bills. Captain Ralph Packer of Martha's Vineyard, who had retired as skipper of Texaco tankers to run Texaco distribution and a marina ashore, stepped forward to buy the old schooner, backed by a syndicate including the movie stars James Cagney and Katherine Cornell. Zebulon Tilton was then reinstated as skipper, carrying cargo when he could get it, supplemented by outings with tourists.

Charlie had kept sailing with Captain Zeb and remembered carrying cargoes of brick so heavy that water flowed easily over the *Wentworth*'s deck, only her hatch coamings keeping her afloat. He spoke also of fast passages under sail, with the lee rail buried and bow wave thundering, and of parties in the main cabin aft. As Charlie recalled in a letter he later wrote me:

> *Many a party was held in her spacious cabin, and I have been present when twenty-one people were in her cabin, the accordion player on the locker in the fore port corner, a quahog chowder simmering on the stove, and two couples dancing in the middle of the cabin floor.*

As we left to rejoin our friends aboard *Athena*, I began to realize that we had discovered more than another schooner to add to our list, valuable as she was; we had met a lively, real-life veteran of the schooner trades. We had encountered the living continuities of a vanished way of life. This was borne out when Ed and Charlie came aboard *Athena* for a farewell cup of coffee before we set sail. Charlie was much taken with *Athena*, recognizing her workboat style. He tweaked halyards to follow their leads, and spoke with approval of the lazyjacks which bundled the mainsail as it came down, a great help when sailing with two grownups and a boy. But of course, he had sailed with Zeb—just two men in a vessel almost twice as long and perhaps four times as heavy. When I rowed

Ed and Charlie ashore, Charlie turned in his seat to look back at *Athena* and, noting her lofty topmast, asked if we used it to set a topsail. Yes, I said, and even better, a fisherman staysail.

Charlie said: "Aye, that's the schooner's glory."

After stopping overnight at Tarpaulin Cove in the Elizabeths, a longtime refuge for schooners in the coasting trade, we began the next day swimming from the pristine beaches stretched in a gleaming arc around our anchorage, and then, returning to the schooner, donned foul weather gear, weighed anchor and put to sea in a blowy, rainy southeaster. As *Athena* gathered way, she found herself in her element, racing along with a boiling wake and lee rail dipping into the rollicking seas that chased after us. Tommy and I, out on the bowsprit, reveled in watching *Athena*'s bow slice through the water under the press of canvas overhead—until the schooner ramped up to bring a breaking sea crashing over the afterdeck, where our guests were gathered in the shelter of the bulwarks. These proved no shelter at all as broken water came surging aboard, with everybody hanging on for dear life. I decided to shorten sail to rein in the schooner's wild careering. So we hove to, amid a great thundering of unleashed canvas as we half-lowered the straining mainsail and tied in reefpoints to reduce its size, while the vessel bucked and cavorted under our feet, impatient to get away.

Athena ran more easily now, and was noticeably steadier on the helm with the mainsail reduced by a third and the jib lowered and lashed down on the bowsprit. Norma, not really an aficionado of rough going on the water, surprised me by saying she was sorry to end our wild ride. But even under short canvas *Athena* charged ahead, her columned bulwarks dipping into the water racing by to leeward, as she reveled in the wet, riotous ride the wind gods had sent us. We raised Block Island through the rainsqualls ahead and dropped anchor there in time for Tommy and Trevor Parmelee to take a turn in the dinghy through the Great Salt Pond, while the grownups sat talking over the day's run and a great stew simmered on the stove. On the way home the next day, the last of our vacation, Norma and I found ourselves talking over the discoveries we'd made on our passage east, which we agreed were considerable.

Back at work Monday morning, I was called in to meet the new creative director Harry Hicks had taken in as partner in Hicks & Greist. Harry had told me over our morning coffee a few weeks before our vacation that he had to bring in a partner to provide working capital and attract new business—both badly needed for the struggling agency, which had recently lost its only major account besides Beefeater gin. And Beefeater was showing signs of restlessness.

So I was prepared for change when I stepped into the new director's office, but hardly for his welcome: "Ah, so we meet at last the genius of 'The Adults' Hour!'" This mangled version of my "*Grownups'* Hour" ad told me all I needed to know about my future at Hicks & Greist.

But before leaving the agency, I submitted the sketch of a new ad I had dreamed up. I asked Harry Hicks to get it done up in finished form to show Rudy Kopf, after he had rejected the jazzy ads the new team had prepared—as I felt sure he would.

My ad, all white on white, except for the green olive in the welcoming face of the martini as you looked down on it, was headed: "First name for the martini: Beefeater." A few more words told how the Beefeater Martini became the one people asked for by name. Much depended on the photograph, and here Harry did us both proud. Its smiling face made me, too, smile when a month or so later, it greeted me in the pages of the *New Yorker*. It went on running there, and elsewhere, for years to come.

By the time the ad began its long run in print, I had secured a new job at Compton Advertising, a job paying more than I had been earning. This was helpful, for maintaining *Athena* and other life commitments were putting more burden on our finances than Norma and I had expected. And I was glad I'd shed the turmoil of the Beefeater account for the orderly procedures of the Stock Exchange account as handled by Compton, one of New York's leading ad agencies. Norma, meanwhile, was finding her work at the Arts Councils of America peaceful and rewarding, where the calm and order of a Rockefeller philanthropy was a relief from the hurly-burly of unending political campaigns at the National Committee for an Effective Congress.

Under these less intense working conditions, Norma and I lunched together whenever we could, walking along Fifth Avenue between her office at Rockefeller Center and my office at Compton Advertising near the Plaza Hotel. I enjoyed the half-mile stroll up this eminently civilized international boulevard, where one met people from all over. Coming back from one of our luncheons on a bright autumnal day, the kind whose heightened air seems born for interesting encounters in New York, I ran into Joan Davidson. Joan was a classmate of mine in high school, whom I hadn't seen in years. Having heard that she had moved to the Pacific Northwest, I was delighted to see her in New York, and we stopped off at the Palm Court in the Plaza to catch up on things over a cup of tea. There I learned she was apartment-hunting in the city, where she and her young family planned to return next spring. Keenly interested in politics, as she had been in school, she was interested to hear about goings-on in the City Club and the excitement of the reform congressman John Lindsay's triumphant election as mayor a year ago.

"So what's next?" she asked.

"Well, if you must know," I began—and blithely proceeded to tell her of Norma's and my interest in a project to recover historic ships to tie up in South Street.

She'd known about Senator Seymour's bill for a maritime museum in Schermerhorn Row through the Municipal Art Society, but the seaport idea was new to her, and she readily agreed that real ships in South Street might add a whole new element to the downtown cultural experience. I then told how we'd made a trip under sail to Gloucester and Nantucket that summer to learn more of the realities of the sailing era from surviving sailormen, a world quite new to Joan. I had been talking for quite a while when we both suddenly became aware of the time on the curlicued clock at the entry to the Court. As we exchanged addresses and said our good-byes, Joan said she was quite taken by the seaport scheme of replanting this vanished experience in the heart of the city.

When we met again the following year, she told me she remembered that I had been a lot more interested in old ships and seamen than in affairs at Compton Advertising. I also didn't forget the meeting; it wasn't every day one met someone so alive to city affairs and so ready to respond to a new idea.

CHAPTER 4

Launching Friends of South Street, *Autumn 1966*

*Norma Draws a Line—$1 Membership—Rath Signs On—
The Great Ship Hunt—Three Schooners—Kaiulani—
Schaefer's America—the Boating Circle—Lundgren*

"Peter, where do you really think we are with this South Street business?"

It was Norma on the phone, calling me at Compton Advertising in the middle of the morning. We had come down by train from Yorktown Heights, where we were now living. On the ride in, we had talked about South Street, searching for a center of effort to move the project forward, but we hadn't been able to come up with anything. There was a longish silence on the line.

"Well," I said at last. "The seaport model is coming along, the sketches Lee Kiil has done look great—and that should attract some attention to the project. As for progress on the ground, you know we've hit a blank wall in Albany. Apparently, no one even has a file on the state museum." I reminded Norma that I had talked by phone with Ralph Miller, director of the Museum of the City of New York, to ask his guidance. The City Museum had taken over the Marine Museum of New York, incorporated in the 1920s with Governor Franklin D. Roosevelt as one of its distinguished board—a venture nipped in the bud by the Depression of the 1930s. Miller had even added some exhibits to the collection, but he did not feel this would serve as a springboard for the State Maritime Museum. And he doubted our trying to stir up public discussion of the project would move things forward. What was needed was a plan the State could act on, and his final word on this—kindly meant, I reminded Norma—was: "Museum planning is a job for museum professionals, after all."

This tore it for Norma.

"Listen," she said, "I've had it with this endless talk. The bulldozers are moving while we talk and talk. We need to save a whole neighborhood, and now we find we can't even get action on a museum in one block in that neighborhood—a museum that has been established in State law. I say we act now to get the project moving. Either we do that or I'm dropping out. I won't attend another meeting that leads nowhere."

"Boats," I said, "I can't tell you what to do to make the South Street thing happen and it's beginning to look as if no one else can. In the meantime, I have a new job to tend to, dammit, so let's finish for now and talk about it tonight."

I was not altogether happy with Norma's attitude. We'd decided early that fall to move from the city to join Mr. and Mrs. F in their house in Westchester. It had been hard to give up our East 11th Street apartment, but Mr. F had talked of selling the country place, and by joining forces we could share household expenses and see to it that the old house, which had served as a family gathering place for thirty-odd years, would stay in the family. This would relieve our own finances, hard-pressed to meet the cost of the apartment on top of our schooner's multifarious needs—which followed the rule of thumb for old wooden boats in regularly exceeding any estimated costs.

So we'd spent the last few weekends lugging furniture, books and papers down three flights of stairs, to deliver them 45 miles north in a rented van, an hegira made possible by the devoted labors of two of Norma's cousins and Bob Ferraro, and I'd found it impossible even to think much about South Street with these seismic changes going on.

When we sat down together that evening in Yorktown Heights we were surrounded by boxes of unpacked books on the second floor, where we'd agreed our library would be. This lent an air of a temporary encampment to our meeting and might also have suggested our continuing wide-ranging interests and the demands of the new career I was just breaking into. Somehow things did not work out quite that way, however. Norma, as expected, was adamant about her position on the South Street venture. It was act now, or she wanted no further part in it. I said there was one thing we could do, but it broke our rule that we would not go overboard on this project.

Norma asked: "Well, what's the one thing we could do that would get South Street off dead center?"

She must have known the answer as well as I did. But I spelled it out: We could form a citizen committee to raise funds, enlist a membership, rally public opinion and take the steps needed to bring the seaport into being around the slow-moving maritime museum. This would undoubtedly mean long days and nights devoted to the project, very likely to the exclusion of practically everything else.

Norma nodded her agreement at each item in this short list, and as I spoke these things the course ahead became clear. *Of course we'd do it!*

We began to plot out a course of action.

Leevi Kiil had the seaport model nearing completion in his home in Queens. We would get it on exhibition so people would begin to talk about it. We'd get a public discourse going on the project. And we knew we had to do something to support the maritime museum now enacted into law. Well, then—why not set up a Friends of the South Street Maritime Museum to campaign for the museum in Schermerhorn Row? This would focus all our efforts while we pushed beyond the museum toward the wider seaport plan. We'd get out a newsletter to build up a community of shared purpose. We'd then campaign systematically to get planning authorities, civic organizations, the press and ultimately funding and development forces enlisted in the plan. We found ourselves riding a surging flood of ideas on what to do.

The first thing to do was to ask Senator Seymour, as sponsor of the museum bill, for his approval to go ahead with the committee. So we made a date and solemnly trooped into his office on 15 November—Norma, Bob Ferraro, my aunt Alice Taylor (who was a fervent admirer as well as a local constituent of Senator Seymour), and finally Leevi and I bearing his elegant model with its trim pasteboard renditions of the buildings on the site. Seymour welcomed us warmly, and was clearly taken with Leevi's model. Here was something to catch the public eye! Even the most blasé New Yorker would stop to look at these curious old buildings from another age. Some might well be surprised to find this section of an elder city still standing within a long bowshot of the moguls of Wall Street. Seymour, or Mike, as he had told us to call him, quizzed Leevi about the model. He was absorbed by the miniature versions of buildings of the neighborhood he knew so well and he smiled at us over the piers on the waterfront, when we explained how we planned to fit them out with model ships we would build. So, thanks to Leevi, we cleared our first hurdle. And on learning that $50 worth of materials had been spent to make the model, Mike got out a checkbook and wrote a check for $50 to meet Leevi's expenses—a first contribution to the cause!

We then took up the matter of Friends of the South Street Maritime Museum. Margot Gayle, an ardent preservationist and reform Democratic District Leader in the Gramercy Park area where I'd once lived, had told me the proper dues for an infant organization was $1. She had said:

> *After all, the people you want to reach are paying you to be on your mailing list. And it's important that the member knows that he or she has an actual share in your venture—it becomes not your venture but ours. And,* she'd added, *it's important that no one be shut out for lack of funds.*

I'd followed this creative counsel in the Rutgers club, and found there was magic in it. Norma and Bob felt we should ask a little more—after all, we were going to have a newsletter to get out. But Alice, who took a friendly if (at this stage) somewhat wary interest in the project, followed Mike when he held up a single admonitory forefinger to cast his vote for the $1 dues. And so it was settled.

"Well, we'd better start up with these $1 memberships," I said. Norma, Bob and I were sitting over coffee in a drugstore to review what came next. "Let's each put in $1," I continued, "and Norma can put them in the bank tomorrow."

"Okay, that's done," said Bob. "What's next?"

"No, it isn't done," I persisted, reaching for my wallet as I spoke. "Here's my dollar," laying it on the table. "Let's see two more to open this account."

Somewhat reluctantly—what use was this penny-ante charade when there were momentous steps to be taken?—Bob and Norma put their dollars on the table and Norma picked up the three bills to put them and Seymour's check into the Chase Bank the next day. So, on the early evening of 15 November 1966, the Friends of the South Street Maritime Museum effectively entered into business as an unincorporated association, with a bank account of $53 to its credit the following day.

After our compact of 15 November our first need was people, many more people, to make our group effective. And we needed gifted people to give it wings. I thought of Dick Rath. We needed him in our project, now that it was becoming operational. From time to time Rath and I would have lunch in one of the midtown dives we frequented. We talked about Rath's handsome old schooner *March Heir*, which he'd bought from my great pal and college roommate Peter Longyear. Peter's wife, Maritza, being fond of puns, he had named the vessel for his son, born in March. The schooner had the problems that the flesh of aging wooden craft are heir to, and Rath and I talked about what it took to keep old wooden boats going, and also about Peter Longyear, who had been lost overboard in the North Sea the year before, while bringing an old cutter from Belgium to England. Since boats affect their owners and are affected by them, a new owner can never know enough about his vessel's previous relationships. We talked about Rath's idea of getting youngsters out of the mean streets of the city to go out in a schooner to catch fish in the old way, under sail. And I, of course, would fill in Rath on whatever we were up to with our explorations in the South Street venture.

I have wondered since why Rath did not get more fully involved in this earlier on. Perhaps he was sizing us up. Captain of a small freighter working out of Puerto Rico in the inter-island trade, as he was when I first met him, he came from a different world than the midtown advertising world I worked in. His growled "Rath" on the phone made you picture a worn-out reporter in a grade-B movie, wearing a green eyeshade with a cigarette dangling out of one side of his mouth as he hunted out the keys on his battered Underwood typewriter. He gloried in this image, and in upsetting people who pretended interest in things they didn't really give a damn about. He played the trombone off and on in Eddie Condon's famous jazz band, was a friend of the troubadour and great American radical Pete Seeger, and had loyal, lasting friendships all over the place. He was an outstanding sailorman, and a skilled carpenter, motor machinist and rigger. In time, we were to learn he could be a highly effective administrator. He got people to give their best by leading from the front—the only way, we both believed, to achieve real results in any field worth bothering with.

So, soon after our mid-November meeting to form the Friends of South Street, I wrote Rath inviting him to join our new group. He answered:

> *Thanks for your letter about the proposed South St. museum.*
> *Naturally you can count on my full support for such a project—*
> *including any committee work etc. where you think you might be*
> *able to use my somewhat withered talents.*

He reported that his boss, Moulton H. Farnham, had said he'd cast a favorable eye over any manuscript on the subject that we might submit. Rath went on to say:

> *I'd like very much to foregather for lunch and/or booze—almost*
> *any time that is convenient to you. Why don't you call me, since*
> *I'm one of those gray, plodding types who's always in the office?*

This was quite a letter! Getting the editor of *Popular Boating* to consider an article on the South Street project would have been enough for most people. But Rath had also made copies of our membership form and enclosed the first memberships he'd picked up, with their one-dollar dues clipped on. And he followed through on the *Boating* article, getting his boss, the skeptical Monk Farnham, to accept the piece I quickly wrote, which was to bring the first full-blooded account of the South Street project before the eyes of over 100,000 nautically-minded people.

Rath immediately zeroed in on one of the first concerns of the new Friends group. We had to know what ships we were aiming for, if we were ever to fund and install them. Ed Stackpole in Nantucket, with his friend Charlie Sayle, had awakened us to the possibilities of the coasting schooner *Alice S. Wentworth*, which they'd warned us was in pretty bad shape. And we'd learned that the former Gloucester fishing schooner *Effie M. Morrissey* was still sailing in the Brava packet trade between the Cape Verde Islands off the West Coast of Africa and the New England ports of Providence and New Bedford, under the name *Ernestina*.

We'd got a lot of background on the *Alice S. Wentworth*, a handsome schooner, now just over 100 years old. Her story brought to life an era just over time's horizon, when such craft had moved everything along the waterways as vital highways of trade. And we were agog over the discovery of the *Ernestina,* the lone example of a Gloucesterman still earning her living under sail. For this big, graceful vessel, built in 1894, had long been known as a fast and able schooner in the Gloucester fishing fleet. Her fishing days over, she served as an Arctic wildlife research vessel under the redoubtable Captain Bob Bartlett in the 1920s and '30s, thereby avoiding conversion to a motor dragger. Soon after World War II, when plans to turn her into a cruise boat fell through, Enrique Mendes bought her for the Cape Verde packet trade. Her most recent voyage had been only the previous year, 1965—the last packet ship to bring immigrants to the US under sail! Rath used his maritime connections to track down Mendes and got an idea of the old schooner's run-down condition, which was bad, indicating that the 1965 crossing would be her last. I then wrote Mendes to tell him of our interest in acquiring his schooner to be preserved for history and for training young people. That good man said he was willing to consider our interest when we were able to act on it—assuring that she would not be quietly scrapped, as seemed likely in view of her worn-out condition.

The ship search, I began to realize, would involve actively pursuing inquiries and evaluating results to form a coherent ship collection, and, of vital importance, setting up the budgets we would need. Clearly this called for a person devoted to this one project —a person with a real feeling for ships and for history, with strong connections in maritime circles. Rath was the standout choice to lead this effort, and when we met, he accepted the charge. At his lead, what we came to call the Great Ship Hunt began in earnest.

A key part of this had been launched a few months before by Norma's letter in *The Mariner's Mirror*, our first step toward realizing the great dream of getting a great square rigger on our waterfront. *Kaiulani*, the last American square rigger to carry cargo around Cape Horn under sail, was the centerpiece of the group of models Norma and I were working on to install at the South Street piers in Leevi Kiil's model. Reduced to a barge in the Philippines, her hulk had been given to the National Maritime Historical Society, destined for exhibition in Washington, DC. Norma and I were members of the society, having joined through a newspaper ad we'd seen a year earlier, and I'd written the society recently about bringing their barque to New York, but they were committed to the nation's capital. Norma's letter inquiring about surviving square riggers in *The Mariner's Mirror* had not produced any response, and we did not know where to turn next. So we chose *Kaiulani*, hoping for the best, and the model ships we whittled out in *Athena*'s cabin that autumn were dominated by *Kaiulani*, as earnest of our hopes, towering over the racehorse fishing schooners *Ernestina* and *Lady of Good Voyage*—the latter in her guise of motor dragger—and of course that sturdy Percheron of the coasting trade, the schooner *Alice S. Wentworth*.

These four, then, made up the gallant flotilla we put in the Kiil model, to give an idea of what we were looking at to revive the sailing ship waterfront. The work of funding and bringing in the ships still lay before us, but we knew what we wanted.

Meanwhile we were all conscious, intensely conscious, of the diminishing stock of the traditional American schooners which had once filled our harbor with sail like flocks of white-winged swallows coming into their nesting places along the South Street waterfront. So there was urgency in our hunt for old schooners, as there was in our plans to save the surviving buildings of the clipper-ship waterfront.

Accordingly, when we heard about a fishing schooner of 1866, now used as a yacht based in Toms River, New Jersey, Rath, Bob Ferraro, Norma and I made up a party to drive down one Saturday to visit the vessel, which bore the unromantic name *Emma C. Berry*. This was to be the style of our work for the ship committee: *Go see the ship and talk with her people.*

On a calm bright November afternoon with the clarity in the air that comes with a fine autumnal day, we walked down the wooden pier at Farragut Academy, where the old schooner lay. The vessel's master, Dayton O. Newton, welcomed us aboard and ushered us into the after cabin of his well-kept vessel, which bore gilt scrollwork on the trailboards of her clipper bow and elaborately carved paneling in the cabin. At 47 feet on deck, the *Berry* had been built as a sloop in 1886 for the coastal fisheries in southern New England, but after her first year's service she was converted to schooner rig, the more complex rig being actually more easily handled by her crew of a man and a boy. After fishing coastal waters from Cape Cod to Montauk, she migrated down east to Maine, where she continued fishing and took up carrying live lobsters to market in her fish-well, which was open to the sea. In 1924, judged to be "fished out," she was abandoned to rot away on a mudbank. An enterprising soul saw promise in her pleasing lines and rebuilt her for use as a coastal trader; coastal towns down east were better linked by the water road than by dirt roads ashore that wound their way along the deeply indented coast. In 1933 she was superseded in this service and was picked up by the well-known yachtsman F. Slade Dale, who refitted her as a yacht. She survived in that guise to end up in the Farragut Academy in the loving care of the music master, Dayton Newton.

Captain Newton was delighted to talk about the schooner, whose history he knew by heart. When we talked of having him sail a token cargo up the coast to South Street, however, he shook his head mournfully. "There are few men around today who know how to handle this old-fashioned rig," he said, "and we'd need four or five experienced hands to sail her that distance."

When I incautiously offered that it could not be all that difficult, Cap'n Newt just shook his head again. "Schooners like this were sailed by a different breed of men," he pronounced. And that was that.

We said goodbye at the rail before stepping up onto the pier. I noticed that the vessel swayed under our feet like a small boat—she was a slight thing, after all. *Athena* would hardly have stirred under our weight. Once we were out of earshot, Norma asked me: "Why does he need so many men to sail his boat? The spars and rigging seem a good deal lighter than *Athena*'s, and you and I sail her alone." "Cap'n Newt," I replied, "is a born yarn-spinner." At this, Rath quite properly gave me a reproving look, saying: "But he keeps that boat in wonderful shape." Bob Ferraro added, in a positive vein: "And she's certainly an historic boat, wouldn't you say?" On this we could all agree.

The *Emma C. Berry* never made her trip to South Street. But some years later she was picked up by Mystic Seaport, who rebuilt her in her original configuration as a sloop, and she graces the waterfront of that Valhalla for historic vessels today.

Our next trip was a weekend drive to Boston, where Norma, Bob Ferraro and I went to Anthony Athanas's Pier 4 restaurant to visit the *Alice S. Wentworth*. I had seen this graceful coasting schooner of 1863 sailing in Maine waters in my sloop *Whisper* nineteen years earlier, and we'd gotten a vivid picture of life aboard when she carried cargo from Charlie Sayle. We found the old schooner in terrible shape, with her decks kept just above water by the styrofoam stuffed into her flooded hull. We had telephoned ahead but did not get to see Mr. Athanas. When we went to the restaurant for dinner on Friday night, he did take a call from me over an internal phone, but only to make it clear that he no plans to dispose of the *Wentworth*. The next day, going on to visit USS *Constitution*, it was refreshing to see a really old ship afloat in such healthy condition. Following our quest to know more of wooden ship construction, we were awed by the weight of her massive timbers, framing different in kind from any we'd seen. From there, we had a pleasant run through ever-more countrified roads down to Woods Hole on Cape Cod, where we caught a ferry to Nantucket to see Ed Stackpole and Charlie Sayle.

They both were happy to hear how we had taken up looking seriously at vessels worth saving, and in a grand brief rendezvous we began to understand we had made two wonderful friends, both for ourselves and the South Street venture.

Two months later, we made a trip taking us deeper into the wooden world. We had learned that Rudie Schaefer, head of the Schaefer Brewing Company in Brooklyn, was having a replica of the schooner yacht *America* of 1851 built at the Goudy & Stevens yard in East Boothbay, Maine. So Norma, Bob Ferraro and I piled into our Volkswagen, agreeing to meet Rath in Maine, where he'd drive in his vintage red convertible to meet us. We'd been strongly focused on the year 1851 in South Street as the year the clipper *Flying Cloud* had astonished the maritime world by her record-breaking 89-day run to San Francisco, and 1851 was also the year the original *America*, built at Brown's 12th Street yard north of South Street, beat a fleet of Britain's fastest racing yachts to win the trophy since known as the America's Cup.

Norma and I set out early Saturday morning for Boothbay with Bob Ferraro, who cheerfully took on the task of driving our Volkswagen. Having worked late at Compton Friday night, I slept most of the way, to awake as Maine presented itself outside the car windows in farms and forest and chaste white farmhouses dusted over in snow. It was something to be there on a mission, and it was something to open the door to the great building shed at the Goudy & Stevens yard. Before us in the half light we saw the elegant shape of the *America* rising out of a bed of wood shavings in stout curved frames. The smell of fresh-hewn New England oak filled the air as Jack Dickerson, sporting his noble handlebar mustache, came forward to greet us. Wasting no time on ceremony, he took us over the details of the heavy, but precise, construction going forward. As superintendent of the work, he knew every nook and cranny in the deep, 104-foot hull taking shape. In the last century his family had sailed similar schooners in defense of the America's Cup, won by the original schooner *America*. I had met Jack when he supervised the building of a new keel for my sloop *Whisper* some years earlier, and I'd learned a great respect for his feel for the realities and possibilities of wooden boats. Jack played a prominent part in the races and cruises of the New York Yacht Club, which his brother Mahlon served as commodore. When Jack took on a job in wooden boatbuilding, however, one forgot the brass buttons and gold braid he wore on yachting occasions and watched a close-in supervisor and dedicated craftsman leading the work.

We went all over the work in progress, where thick planking was being shaped, bent, and fastened onto the massive frames by shipwrights who obviously knew their jobs and enjoyed cracking jokes with Jack. I walked up forward just to look up at the great clipper bow, framed up solid at the knightheads so that it seemed it hardly needed to be planked to keep the water out. I let my eye flow across the frames as the water would flow, seduced by the faint hollow in the bow to accept the considerable weight of the vessel following on, with the broad hindquarters that had given the original *America* her renowned ability to stand up to her canvas in a blow.

At supper that night we all agreed that a replica of this quality was worth visiting, just to see that great bow taking shape in three dimensions, pungent in its oaken reality. And we all looked forward to seeing Schaefer's *America* under sail. We felt she could play a vital role in our celebration of the South Street story—and practicality aside, the new *America* had won our hearts.

The next day, starting for home, I went with Rath in his gorgeous convertible to keep him company, while Bob Ferraro and Norma followed in our workaday Volkswagen. On the long ride, Rath tackled me on how I could justify working to establish a new museum, when the nation continued its "bomb 'em back to the Stone Age" policies in Vietnam. I was taken aback by the vehemence of his attack—or what seemed to me an attack. When our little caravan stopped off at a diner for lunch, Rath resumed his questioning of what we were doing, ripping through our explanations that we were working to achieve something valuable while we continued to protest a war we each opposed. I believe we all understood Rath's agony of mind in raising questions none of us could answer to our own satisfaction. And to my surprise, a firm response from Norma about doing what one could had a cooling effect. So after lunch, in reasonable amity, we swapped crews—Rath and Bob bound to New York City, and Norma and I home to Yorktown Heights. There we resumed the even tenor of our ways, pursuing a project we regularly characterized to ourselves and others as "something for New York."

Behind the almost magical reception we'd met at *Boating* was a circle of editors who had begun to develop their own ideas and strategies to advance the seaport cause. Rath, as associate editor, had taken the seaport idea to his boss, the editor Monk Farnham, with the resulting commitment of interest in an article on the subject, as we've seen. Along the way, he enlisted the interest of two co-workers: his fellow associate editor, Larry Kean, whose specialty was boat design and who wrote a column on the design of the month; and his immediate supervisor, managing editor Terry Walton. Terry's job was to rigorously review every piece going into the current issue, to assure factual accuracy, grammar and syntax. A well-bred young woman fascinated with the world of boats and seafaring, she took pleasure in squaring away the work that was brought to her and got on well with the formidable Monk, who was a bear about these things. This team turned out a sterling product. *Boating*'s pages were full of crisp, focused reporting on the pleasure-boating field, with bits of wit, philosophy and voyage narrative worked in.

Popular Boating, soon to be renamed simply *Boating*, was very much Monk's child. Deeply read in nautical literature, Monk made room in this practical, how-to journal for the human-interest stories that are the soul of the experience afloat, hence his readiness to run my story on Friends of South Street, an outfit made up at this point of a ragtag bobtail gathering of youthful idealists, city walkers, dock wallopers, old sailors, and a few scholars scattered around the country. Monk himself was of that same varied, difficult-to-classify stratum of society, a journalist of varied interests who had a strong bent for seafaring. Since the 1930s he'd been active in the Ship Lore & Model Club, a peripatetic organization founded the previous decade by Armitage McCann, a retired sea captain turned modelmaker. The noted marine artist Gordon Grant had been among its early members, with Captain Bob Bartlett of the *Effie M. Morrissey*, who flew the club burgee in his Arctic expeditions and held club meetings in the schooner's after cabin when she came into port in South Brooklyn, along with a varied following of souls we called ship lovers.

At *Boating*, Monk Farnham's style was to work closely with his associate editors and to encourage independent thinking, with the proviso that he would land like a ton of bricks on any writing that violated sound journalistic standards. And there had grown up a tradition of the three associates gathering in Monk's office to talk about the day's work and what came next—casual conversations enlivened, as Terry Walton has reported, with "a thimbleful of rum." In these conversations, which ranged over trade anecdotes, writers' quirks, and abstruse, almost theological debates over correct nautical usage, talk flourished about the seaport idea.

Norma and I finally finished painting and installing the model ships in Kiil's seaport model but were a little reluctant to show these crude products of our labors. But the *Boating* editors took the ships to their hearts, perhaps taken by their handhewn look and the smell of salt air they seemed to bring to the waterfront scene. They readily convinced their boss, the publisher Syd Rogers, to add the model with its little ships to the magazine's exhibit at the National Boat Show in January, where it would be seen by surging crowds of boating people.

This unanticipated breakthrough confronted us with the need to tell our story in organized form. Fortunately, I had just finished writing my article for *Boating*, so Norma and I were able to cobble together words and pictures. A professional designer and photographer, Joe Mondello, then turned up to produce these as finished placards worthy of a major ad agency. The story was simple: The first placard bore the restrained headline South Street Maritime Museum, and then the second broke out our true intention under the banner headline To Recreate in the Heart of Our City the Old Seaport of New York. These were accompanied by images ranging from a young man looking at the tall ships whose bowsprits arched across a South Street thronged with horses and wagons, to a map showing how the restored seaport would fit in the City's newly announced Lower Manhattan Plan. The plan specified a broad plaza opening on a wide vista of the East River. Fashionable planning of the day favored these vast, empty spaces that look great in aerial photographs but lifeless and barren at street level, where most city denizens live and walk and, in the Biblical phrase, have their being. The planners' vision was all very well, in our eyes, but we didn't care so much about the vista as what filled the foreground. There we looked for things that gave texture and life to the urban experience, as suggested in the seaport model and its ships.

Joe Mondello's involvement had arisen from another bit of magic that somehow came our way, independent of the vital *Boating* connection. My father had decided that Norma and I must come with him to Mystic Seaport to meet the marine artist Charles Lundgren at an art show featuring Lundgren's work. The show opened just a week before Christmas, when we were looking forward to a quiet weekend at home. But there was no stopping Al in his "Action this Day" mode, so we joined him in Mystic—and were completely captivated by a series of Lundgren paintings depicting ships from medieval times onwards, which had sailed for a Danish shipowning family named Isbrandtsen.

The show was crowded with sailing people, but Charlie, as he told us to call him, took us to a quiet corner and started right in talking with us in his quiet, thoughtful way about the South Street project. Al said nothing, but stood by with a great grin on his face while Charlie told us what his interest was.

Jakob Isbrandtsen, head of American Export-Isbrandtsen Lines, had planned a museum of shipping in Lower Manhattan, in which Charlie's paintings would be an exhibit showing the European roots of today's American merchant marine. Isbrandtsen, he added, though proud of his family heritage, was not a self-promoter and understood very well that it would take more than the Isbrandtsen collection to make a maritime museum. Moreover, as a longtime member of Mystic Seaport, Isbrandtsen had been taken with the idea of bringing actual historic ships into the South Street waterfront. When Al had called Charlie to ask a few questions about the art show, he'd told Charlie of our scheme for a restored seaport in South Street, of which not a word had yet appeared in the press.

Norma and I were stunned by Charlie's sure grasp of the seaport idea. When he asked about next steps, we told him about our model, now scheduled for the National Boat Show, for which we were working to produce illustrated placards. Charlie took down my phone number with the stub of a soft pencil, which I would learn he always carried in his jacket pocket, and said he knew a professional designer who might help out. I quickly said we had no money to pay for this, whereupon Charlie put a gentle hand on my arm and said: "We aren't talking about money here, Peter. If my pal calls, it will be to make a contribution." The following week, as Christmas loomed up before us, Joe Mondello called me at Compton Advertising to offer his services. And well before the Boat Show opened in early January, we had our finished placards to display with the first seaport model and its little ships laden with their cargoes of meaning. All done for free, from beginning to end.

It's easy in retrospect to attach too much weight to an early encounter, but in fact Norma and I were deeply stirred by our meeting with Charlie Lundgren. One saw a steadiness in his appraising eye as he sized us up, and the whole story of the Isbrandtsen interest was told in a meeting that took about ten minutes. But we left Mystic feeling that we'd known this quiet man for years.

CHAPTER 5

Tackling the Establishment, *Winter 1966–67*

Sidney Dean—City Club of New York—Membership Drive—
Frank Braynard—Need to Set Up Air Rights—
Planning Commissioner Says No to Seaport

The Great Ship Hunt was an informative pursuit, and it also brought us the interest of supporters who added new weight to our counsels. But what we urgently needed was City approval to move ahead on our plans. And to secure that approval, we'd need strong civic support. For this I turned first to the City Club of New York, a distinguished civic organization founded in 1892 in which I luckily had some standing, having been elected a trustee some years before. The City Club had led in the "good government" movement of the 1890s and had played a major role in the elections of the reform mayor Fiorello LaGuardia in the 1930s and the election of Mayor John B. Lindsay just a year before in 1965.

My election to a board mainly made up of senior judges, lawyers and leaders in city affairs was due entirely to Sidney W. Dean, Jr., whom I'd met while working in the mailroom at the giant ad agency McCann-Erickson in the 1950s.

From that casual meeting with Sid were to hang many shared adventures in civic affairs. And beyond these lay adventures in odd corners of the ocean world, from sandy beaches on New York's Long Island to North Carolina's Cape Hatteras to Mani country in the Peloponnesus in southern Greece—sites which, with the twisty streets of Greenwich Village, could be said to make up Sid's spiritual home. To these would soon be added the rumbustious, sea-haunted purlieus of South Street.

My meeting with this marvelously creative person depended on a series of unlikely events. The first was to be hired by McCann-Erickson at all, since, as I soon learned, at age 28 I was much too old for a beginner's job in the mail room. Catching the odd half-amused, half-regretful glance given me by the personnel manager, Eileen Hauck, I decided to risk all and told her that only her sympathetic manner stopped me from suing her for age discrimination (which of course there was no law against in 1955). "Oh, we can't have that," she said brightly and promptly filled out and signed a form hiring me at a weekly wage of $40. I signed with equal alacrity.

After some months in the mail room, I found myself running a training course made up of Wednesday evening lectures given by agency executives. These turned out to be mostly panegyrics to the speaker's own achievements, and, thinking that circulating notes on these sessions might encourage better lectures, I took to typing up stencils of my notes for distribution the next morning to the mail room gang with a copy for the lecturer. When Mr. Dean, McCann's vice president for marketing, signed up to give a lecture, I knew we had a big fish on the line. But I was hardly prepared for the way he launched into a rapid-fire review of recent marketing developments—a talk laced with questions like "What would you have done? Any ideas?" After trying to make notes on all this, I felt my stenciled report hardly rose to the occasion.

This feeling got worse the next day, when I got a call to see Mr. Dean right away. Quitting the mole-like mail room, I walked into his sunny upstairs office, where he asked me where I got the idea for my reports. When I explained that they were intended to improve both trainee attention and lecture performance, Sid just grinned. Next he wanted to know why I had gone for a mail room job at McCann, since, having worked in research, I could have landed a real job in his research department. I said I'd decided against research; I was interested in advertising strategy. The idea that I could learn more in the mail room than in the marketing division he presided over led him to a raised eyebrow, but persisting in his questions, he picked up a copy of my job application, which he had on his desk, and said: "I see that you spent two years in the Navy during the war and then got your BA at Harvard in three years instead four, apparently in a hurry to move on. Then why go for another two years at King's College, Cambridge?"

I fumbled a moment to find a simple, clear answer, but deciding there was none, I told the rather unusual story: Before my graduation from Harvard, John Finley, my housemaster, told me he didn't think I'd learned very much at the great university. To my astonishment he then asked if I would be interested in going on to King's College, Cambridge. The provost of King's had told him he'd take any promising student he sent along. I'd always wanted to go to England and the GI Bill was still paying college costs, so when the editor of *Yachting*, for whom I'd done some editorial work, told me that I could get a free passage across the Atlantic sailing as mate in a homeward-bound English yacht—well, the decision made itself. Sid smiled at this unlikely yarn and said he'd like to hear what came of that decision. His secretary came in at this point to remind Sid of his next appointment, and we agreed to meet over a drink next week after work. Thus began a conversation which continued for the next 41 years until Sid's death in 1997 at age 91. Our last talk, in 1996, was a multi-level discussion of seafaring's Cape Horn road, which involved archaeology, linguistics, literature, art, anthropology, history, politics, seafaring and philosophy—as Montaigne pursued them: with a laughing face. To this day I find it impossible to think of Sid without a smile on my own face, recalling his vigorous pursuit of freedom and the over-arching need to welcome varying points of view in that pursuit.

Knowing my interest in the life of the city's streets and byways, its storied waterfront and the harbor that gave it birth, Sid urged me to join the City Club. There he and I pursued some of the civic issues we were always discussing. A couple of these issues played a role in the City Club's "good government" manifesto in 1965. They also did much to shape the thinking that Sid, Norma and I, and other friends brought to the South Street venture.

The first concerned a law proposed by Governor Rockefeller to reduce the number of bars permitted in a given district. A classic good-government measure, this would have led to the closing of a number of existing neighborhood bars. But in my experience, a decent bar was a stabilizing element in the neighborhood, a workingman's club, in effect, where job information and neighborhood news could be shared, grievances aired and achievements celebrated—a center for the discourse that defines a community. Sid and I invited the trustees, who rarely frequented neighborhood bars, to join us in a South Street pub crawl, but after we'd had our say, they declared themselves satisfied and voted unanimously against the Rockefeller measure. Friends in Albany later told us that the club's dissent, which was received with some incredulity, helped sink the measure.

The second initiative stemmed from my being named chairman of the club's Education Committee. I resisted, protesting that the piled-up reports on the city's school system had all the symptoms of a problem that had been studied to death with little real progress on the ground. Ah, but just for that reason, it was explained to me, the board thought I might bring a fresh perspective to a few neighborhood problems on which the board could make specific recommendations. So I sat down with the young Harlem lawyer Basil Paterson, a new trustee on the committee, and together we decided to look at two contrasting neighborhood schools: PS 1, a successful school on Henry Street with a diverse student body (where two of my children were currently enrolled), and PS 2, a few blocks away in LaGuardia Houses, a school afflicted with rampant student alienation and outbreaks of violence. We then got Steve Stock, a public-spirited vice president at Politz Research, to design a questionnaire bringing out the differing attitudes and actions of teachers and parents that led to failure and—more important—those that led to success.

Unsurprisingly, we found that the active engagement of parents with their children's teachers made all the difference. When some teachers then complained that African-American and Hispanic parents didn't even attend parent-teacher meetings, we moved on to the action phase of the project: holding coffee klatches in these parents' kitchens in La-Guardia Houses. There we found the parents had their own complaints and their own suggestions to offer, which they simply didn't feel able to offer in the more formal atmosphere of parent-teacher meetings at the school.

We also looked into the successful Sunday afternoon trips run by young student teachers in PS 1. Paid modest stipends, these young men and women took children on trips to zoos and museums, and even ferry-boat rides across the harbor. The effect on children's vocabularies was, in a word, magical. "The kids learn more from fellow-students than from teachers," explained these aware, wide-awake student teachers, themselves eager to learn their jobs.

Thus we had two immediate, tested measures to recommend: to support the weekend educational trips, and to mandate out-of-school parent-teacher meetings in parents' homes. The City Club trustees were glad to know that we'd found effective, on-the-ground answers to seemingly intractable problems. But the educational establishment was focused on busing students out of their neighborhoods in the interests of racial integration, rather than reaching out across racial barriers to strengthen neighborhood ties. And our report on the striking success of weekend trips run by student teachers, which fostered social interchange on the neighborhood level—where that kind of integration truly counts—stirred no response.

The trustees liked what we'd discovered and asked me to draft the club's introductory statement on the problems facing the city during the run-up to the mayoral election of 1965. The club's president, I. D. Robbins, did the heavy lifting on such issues as housing and employment. The study appeared as a booklet called "A Challenge to Greatness in the Life of Our City." This set forth "cultural dispossession" as the city's central problem—a problem confronting a growing part of the population who had little sense of identity with a society whose workings they did not understand, and which did little to help them learn its ways or act on the opportunities it offered. The study concluded:

> *We therefore set as our first and overriding goal the opening of opportunity for full achievement for all who live in the city.*

To this I. D. Robbins added an appeal that went to the heart of any real effort:

> *'Hope deferred maketh the heart sick.' But action can mobilize the City's greatest resource—the aspirations of its people.*

———◆———

"The aspirations of the city's people" was my point of departure in presenting the case for the South Street venture to the City Club's board for their support. It's easy to talk about such aspirations without a strong link to street-level reality, but the City Club manifesto had made that tie. And the restored seaport would take us back to the street level to tell its story across time, offering fresh perspectives and understanding of the city's continuing story. It would invite people to find their own sense of belonging in the continuing story.

Sidney rose to point out that this sense of being part of the city's story would strengthen the city's main capital asset, its people. He added that the well-off could also benefit from a better understanding of the human story that sustained the city's wealth and act to assure people's access to its opportunities.

The board of trustees voted unanimously in favor of the South Street Seaport. Board chairman Seymour Graubard wrote:

> *I pledge my personal support. Indeed, I cannot see how anybody can do anything but approve the idea.*

So Sid's campaign for fresh, hands-on experience and the new ideas it might generate gave the seaport idea its first solid base of informed citizen support. And, not incidentally, my encounter with the educational establishment led to the growing interest in experiential education beyond the classroom, which we carried into our thinking about education of young and old aboard the ships of South Street.

Bob Ferraro had been keeping in touch with me on City Club matters, driven by his strong interest in the affairs of a city to which he, for one, felt a strong sense of belonging. Shortly before our meeting to form Friends of South Street, I'd written him a long report answering questions he had about Ed Logue's presentation to the City Club of his new housing policies for New York. To this I'd added a casual three-line note about a planned meeting with Senator Seymour. That throwaway note was about the meeting on 15 November that led to our forming Friends of South Street, after which there was little time for long exchanges on city policies. But it matters that Bob's dedication to the South Street venture sprang from those broader interests which had brought him to South Street in the first place. We were fortunate to have him with us in the shaping of the South Street experience. He has given us his own account of how his citywide interests came to a focus in South Street:

> I became involved in South Street as an outgrowth of my Peace Corps service. In Panama I'd been transformed from a 22-year-old know-nothing into "Don Roberto," a 22-year-old know-nothing with a totally unwarranted position of influence in the little farm hamlet of Guarumal. At that time just the fact of being gringo conferred status and even a smidgen of authority. So I got into the habit of thinking-up civic improvement projects. When I returned to the U.S. in 1966 I forgot I wasn't Don Roberto and was still determined to help make the world a better place. But by that time the little disturbance that was Vietnam had grown to be a full fledged disaster and the government thought I should return to serve and make that peninsula a better place.

To avoid spending another two years in the tropics, as he put it, Bob entered a teacher training program at Queens College in the summer of 1966, to begin teaching in September. There he met a fellow would-be teacher of Estonian background, Maal Kiil.

> Maal knew of my interest in the history of New York City and fondness for old architectural details. I used to take snapshots of interesting doors, stone details, rundown houses and such. And, Bob tells us, Maal said she knew of a woman who with her husband, was trying to save some old buildings in the fish market area of New York . . . The rest, as they say, is history.

Not content with making that telephone link between Bob Ferraro and Norma, Maal volunteered her architect husband, Leevi Kiil, to make a model of the South Street district to attract the members it needed to survive. As she later remembered, being newly married, she committed him casually to this major piece of work. And Lee, who never did things by halfway measures, set to work on a model which expressed the feel of the old buildings and proved a real attention-getter. Who, at the outset of our thoughts about bringing historic ships back to the Street of Ships, would have dreamt that these people, with their own lives to lead, would go to work like this to make the dream happen? When each member joined, it seemed to us a kind of miracle, which of course it was: a creative act extending beyond one's personal horizons.

And in the wide net we were casting, individuals turned up with unique contributions to make. Another member of remarkable dedication and talent was Margot Gayle, she who had urged our adoption of the $1 membership. A devoted historic preservationist, she knew the buildings of the old seaport district in intimate detail. In the gracious accents of a Southern lady, she told me she was thrilled by our project to save not just one of two of these structures, but a whole streetscape. And as always, she meant what she said, as we discovered when we began receiving dollar contributions from fashionable uptown addresses where many of her devotees lived.

Our own campaigning was tireless. We were shameless in how we picked up new members. At dinner with some advertising friends at Ed Parmelee and Claude Martinot's new Ninth Street apartment a few days after the formation of Friends, I told these old pals about the South Street venture and, before leaving, asked each of them for a dollar and their home address. There was some grumbling at this—they wanted to get on with the poker game they were just settling down to. But eventually each chipped in a dollar bill. Years later one of the party, Ian Keown, explained that they thought I was collecting taxi fare to get to Grand Central. But Ian got caught up in the venture and became a contributing member of the Friends, as did others who had joined as a favor to a pal.

And the next night, Sunday, 20 November, we invited Bob Ferraro to join us for a pot roast supper aboard *Athena*—a good spot, we thought, for talk about the floating aspect of the South Street venture. The schooner was ensconced in her winter quarters at Conroy's Marina in Westchester

Creek. There was a late-November nip in the air as evening drew on, but the schooner's cabin was cheerful by lamplight, and the coal stove cast its reassuring glow throughout the ship. It was a small but varied crew that clambered down the companionway ladder to gather round the cabin table: Bob, accompanied by his prospective brother-in-law, Victor Lawrence, who lived nearby in the Bronx; Jim Kirk, who joined us from Al Smith Houses on the Lower East Side; and Roger McCord, of the elegant magazine *Réalités*. After introductions all around, we sat down around the table, where we'd set out the model boats Norma and I had been carving to add to Leevi Kiil's South Street project model. These didn't include the big square-rigged *Kaiulani* model, which was still unfinished, but the models of the three East Coast schooners, *Lady of Good Voyage*, *Alice S. Wentworth* and *Ernestina*, gave a feeling for the traditional wooden craft which had thronged the South Street waterfront. And each of these schooners had a different story to tell. As we talked of these things in our own schooner's cabin, the curved wooden knees supporting the deck beams overhead and the massive columns of the spruce masts fore and aft suggested a wider, windswept world.

"And what about this vessel?" asked Bob. "What's she like to sail?" Irresistibly, the talk flowed to the past summer's adventures under sail: how the Tarr & Wonson Paint Manufactory in Gloucester had given a whistle salute to the schooner as she sailed into the harbor in light airs under full sail including main gaff topsail and fisherman staysail set from the mastheads; how in the open sea her heavy hull worked her way through the seas rather than skeetering across them; how a boarding sea once splashed over a huge somnolent lobster we'd bought, awakening the beast to chase us about the decks with claws extended; and how, on our homeward run, the wind gave us a riproaring beam reach, which sent *Athena* flying on her way with cresting seas breaking across the decks, while the curved oak stem of the bow plunged ahead, throwing up a bow wave with a deep-throated roar . . . and so the tales went on.

As the evening ended, everybody chipped in their dollar to become members of Friends. People were going to let Roger McCord off, since he'd brought two bottles of St. Emilion to mark the occasion, but he insisted on paying his dollar to become a member. Bob Ferraro contributed his second dollar, and has since maintained that this evening aboard *Athena* was when he first signed on. That evening aboard *Athena* gave a more solid feeling to our prospects than the few words exchanged over drugstore coffee earlier in the week when Friends was first convened.

Bob took a lively interest in the Great Ship Hunt. The following weekend saw him driving with us to Toms River, New Jersey, in our exploratory trip to visit the *Emma C. Berry*. Two weeks later he joined Norma and me on our weekend trip to visit the *Alice S. Wentworth* in Boston and on to Nantucket to foregather with Charlie Sayle, who had sailed in the *Wentworth*. Bob had indeed joined the seafaring side of our venture, to which he would contribute more.

While these developing interests enlivened our days, with my desk diary full of lunchtime and evening meetings at the Yacht Club with new recruiting officers like Margot Gayle and Dick Rath, or at Le Manoir with Roger McCord, the drumbeat of membership growth continued. A membership base was the main physical reality of the proposed South Street revival, and we needed to build up that reality right away to provide an active readership for the newsletter we planned in order to develop those readers into a corps of citizen supporters ready to do battle for the threatened South Street neighborhood. By 5 December, when we delivered the South Street model to Senator Seymour's office, now complete with ships at the piers, prior to its exhibition at the National Boat Show the following month, I counted up a total of 65 members.

I had said we must have 100 by Christmas to carry conviction and momentum into the new year, and here, halfway to Christmas, we'd gathered over half that number. But we worried about maintaining that pace, having already signed up family members and close friends, so we redoubled our efforts, and by 25 December we'd pulled in 76 more members to make a total of 141. I celebrated the occasion by getting out another 50 individual appeal letters over the three-day Christmas weekend, giving us a hefty pile to mail at the Grand Central Post Office on our way back to work on 27 December.

And at work that day I got a phone call from Frank Braynard, who said he liked a letter he'd had from me. I didn't know Frank, but I'd heard the name since he had run the successful visit of tall ships to New York in the first Operation Sail two years earlier. Running across his *Tugman's Sketchbook*, I'd noticed that he worked for Moran Towing, and I'd sent my letter to him there. I hardly expected an answer from a person so prominent in New York Harbor affairs and was startled when, instead of asking for more information or who was behind our venture (an all-too-common response), he asked me to lunch.

On 29 December, I found Frank Braynard seated in a booth with a pal, a soberly dressed man whom he introduced as Jeff Rogers of Columbus Lines. Joining the two friends in a glass of beer, I sat and listened as, after a few questions, Frank started to talk about South Street and the great shipping lines and tall windships that made South Street famous around the world as "the Street of Ships." It was evident that he had his own picture of the project.

He said: "A museum to tell the South Street story right on the street where it all happened is a must-do project. We've just got to see that this thing happens."

At this point Jeff Rogers interposed a plaintive note.

"But Frank," he said, "we've been working for years on a maritime museum in the old Custom House. What about the big story you got in the *Sunday News* earlier this month? You can't just drop that."

"This South Street thing," said Frank, "is far more important. It's a brilliant idea, simply brilliant." A broad grin accompanied this expansive statement, bolstered, I'll swear, by a wink in my direction. "You and I, Jeff, have got to do everything we can to make this thing happen. It's an idea whose time has come."

I collected one dollar from each of these new friends—Frank, catching the idea immediately, pulled out his dollar bill with a smile indicating that he knew the value of a dollar and appreciated the implications of the gift. Jeff followed suit to please his comrade-in-arms. I tramped back up into the cold winter sunlight feeling that we had gained an important ally.

Frank's unfailing enthusiasm did much to keep our spirits up in the days ahead, beginning with the second meeting I had scheduled for later that same day.

At the end of the workday, I went back downtown for an appointment at the City Planning Commission. I looked forward to a staff meeting to make the transferred development rights—or "air rights"—concept real. For this we needed someone to work out the mechanics of transferring the rights from the low-rise old buildings of the South Street project to neighboring blocks where they could be used in new high-rise development. And we needed figures to show how the sale of these rights would offset much of the cost of the land needed for the project.

This was the concept Norma and I had worked out in our early discussions of the seaport idea. Under current zoning laws, the buildings we intended to save could have been torn down and larger ones built in their place. So why not allow that surplus right to build—development rights or air rights—to be sold to the developer of a neighboring block? That way, more floors could be built on new buildings without purchasing more costly downtown real estate (a benefit for the developers), while the historic buildings would benefit from the purchase of their unused air rights, with the purchase funds used for their preservation and restoration. In effect, our low-rise buildings substituted for the developer's plaza in reaching the authorized overall density for all the land involved.

What we still had to work out was how the rights could be transferred and paid for by the developers. Such a transaction had never before been attempted in the City of New York. That was no reason to say it wouldn't work, but we really needed to get city officials working with us on this concept. I got the name of a City Planning staffer from one of my City Club friends and called for an appointment to come in and discuss the needed arrangements.

When I arrived at the City Planning Commission, however, I found that my appointment had been moved upstairs to Commissioner Harmon Goldstone's 15th-floor office—so my first talk on the mechanics of our radical proposition would be taken up, not by an aide who could help us get things spelled out, but by a high-level policy maker. In a somewhat apprehensive frame of mind, then, I walked into Commissioner Goldstone's office. It was lit only by a single desk lamp against the advancing December dusk outside the windows.

The commissioner greeted me with a weary but friendly smile—it seemed it had been a long day for him. I described our need to get the air rights transfer set up. I cited the interest of the City Club in seeing the project accomplished as a lasting asset to the life of the city. Goldstone heard me out. Then he said very gently that we were looking at some of the most sought-after real estate in the world, and the use we proposed might add an attractive amenity to city life, but it could hardly be called essential.

I pointed out that retaining our low-rise buildings would not restrict net growth, because the deficit would be made up in adjoining plots—thus enabling the city to achieve its development objectives for the area. But Goldstone shook his head, and told me how he sympathized with our project but did not see how it could possibly be worked into the city's plans.

As he walked me to the door he told me that he cherished the city's maritime heritage. He said his father had been to sea and had taken up making ship models in his retirement. It was fascinating, he said, to watch his father's big, gnarled hands at work on the delicate strands of a ship's rigging, which always came out perfect. With that, we said goodbye.

On my ride home, looking out the train window at the darkling wind-ruffled reaches of the Hudson River under the deep shadow of the Palisade bluffs, I felt numb with apprehension about our ability to get our story across. That Harmon Goldstone was clearly a noble spirit who shared our values made matters worse. It seemed that even from a sympathetic planner's point of view, and despite the support of the well-respected City Club, the whole scheme did not even merit being taken up for study. It began to look as if there would be no safe harbor for the South Street venture but what we could somehow create for ourselves.

CHAPTER 8

Headquarters In Fulton Street, *March 1967*

*The Second Reporter—The Chairman's Question—
Dinner with Joan—Headquarters and Gallery—
Expanded Budget—Others Speak Up*

On Saturday, in the chill morning air of Yorktown Heights, I reflected on the previous day's lunch. With Jakob now aboard as chairman, we had a workable board of trustees. We had $8,500 to set up an office and pay Norma's and my salary, with reasonable expenses, which should carry us through the next two months. This was a slender startup to set about changing the map of Lower Manhattan.

"We're afloat, we're on our way," I wrote in my journal, "but just barely."

Norma and I knew that the great creative force on our side was the Seaport's growing membership sustained by the *South Street Reporter*. In the turmoil of the last few weeks, the March issue was late going to press. But over the weekend Norma and I set to work to write and lay out this critical second issue from our scattered notes. We took joy in working together, juggling ideas, pictures and headlines until these fascinating disparate bits came together to make a living whole. Ideas proposed by one of us would be finished by the other, and our spirits danced as we progressed through the recreated Seaport we were building in the pages of the *Reporter*. It was heaven while the music lasted—a music of imagining things and then doing them together, a magic which still resounds through our lives together.

In this fashion the *South Street Reporter*, Vol. 1 No. 2, took shape as a four-page newsletter; we were resolved to expand and improve the journal as we went. We led off with a banner call to join "An Evening on South Street," announcing the tour and dinner at Seamen's Church Institute planned for 7 April now only a little over two weeks away, but we didn't worry about the short notice. If lots of people come, we said, of babes in the urban woods. The sidetracking of the state museum in Schermerhorn Row of course blocked any consideration of our South Street venture—which called for saving not just the historic buildings of Schermerhorn Row, but a whole city neighborhood and its waterfront.

When we did catch up with the situation early in 1967, we resolved to pursue our role of innocent amateurs. This meant pursuing our goals as if there were no opposition. And we knew that the bulldozers reshaping Lower Manhattan would leave us only memories to argue over unless we moved fast and effectively on our hopeful venture. So we set to work in good heart.

"Move to save NY's 'street of ships,'" proclaimed the headline of the *South Street Reporter*, the newsletter we'd promised our members. Beneath this headline, an engraving showed the South Street waterfront in 1818, a river crowded with sail and primitive steamers. There was a dovecote of schooners airing their sails at the lower end of the street—just the scene we'd been telling everyone that one would have seen in South Street 150 years earlier. And at center stage a providential beam of sunlight illumined the many-windowed, tall-chimneyed shape of Schermerhorn Row, anchor of our hopes for a revived seaport district. Below this appeared an account of how Friends of South Street Maritime Museum was formed "to bring into being an informed body of citizen opinion" on the venture. At the top of the page the masthead presented our officers: myself as chairman; Robert Ferraro, vice chairman; and Norma Franceschi Stanford, secretary; with Senator Seymour as honorary chairman. A sketch of *Kaiulani*'s bowsprit arched over South Street was shown with this motto:

To re-create in the heart of our city the old seaport of New York.
This was a goal reaching well beyond the role of the museum, of course—but we felt our people would understand a little stretch in a great cause.

The newsletter carried a series of news items, led by the City Club endorsement of the venture, with Sid Dean's prediction that it could "make a decisive contribution to the redevelopment of our waterfront." There was also a whitewashed version of my meeting with Commissioner

Goldstone, which noted that, despite his sympathy with the project, he "questioned some planning assumptions." And it announced a Steering Committee meeting at the Yacht Club on 26 January, ending up with a breezy: "Feel free to walk in." This was the open style of business we wanted to establish from the outset.

This *Reporter* was swiftly written by Norma and me, typed up in columned newspaper format and photocopied. All this was accomplished by 10 January. That evening, a small group gathered with Norma and me at my aunt Alice Taylor's apartment on East 38th Street to mail it out. Alice addressed envelopes in a fine Spencerian hand while urging on the work of folding, stuffing and stamping, and on the way home a jubilant crew slotted some 200 *Reporters* into the Grand Central mailbox. This left us with over half our 500 print run for future mailings as memberships came in.

We had rented a mailbox at the New York Yacht Club as a return address for Friends. But the response was more than the box could accommodate, and the club asked me to find another address. So we changed our return address to Alice Taylor's apartment. Our reserve stack of *Reporters* was quickly exhausted, and I was glad we'd said we'd get out a March issue on our promised bimonthly schedule.

The 26th of January, the day of the first regular meeting of the Steering Committee, broke fair and soft-edged on the midwinter scene, bringing unanticipated delight to the faces of people in the streets of New York. That day has lived on in my awareness, a gleaming stone on memory's beach. Heading for my midafternoon appointment at the Stock Exchange, I emerged from the Wall Street subway station rejoicing in the day, as everyone else seemed to be doing. At 2 Wall I stopped off to leave an envelope for a former schoolmate now at J. P. Morgan, and even an errand boy's job seemed fun as part of our "try all ports" approach to gathering members.

My work on the Stock Exchange account was at this time focussed on ads celebrating the Exchange's 175th anniversary. My ad featured an old print of a New York street scene and at the end of it a ship—the vehicle which led these venturesome citizens to start buying and selling shares in the commerce brought to New York in wind-driven ships. The ad was accepted as bringing some depth and color to the story of the fabled buttonwood tree under which traders met at the corner of Wall and Broad Streets—so I was earning my keep. I was able to add to my knowledge of this storied tip of Manhattan Island, whose streets had been laid out by the Dutch settlers 350 years earlier. These narrow twisting streets threaded their way through the towering buildings of the financial district, which had begun to grow toward the sky a few generations ago. Their pilastered street frontages bespoke the mannered formality of a world far removed from the midtown world of cool glass structures regimented by mathematically gridded thoroughfares. And there were still occasional clusters of brick buildings from an even earlier age, like grandparents seated at a family gathering. These generally housed small, family-owned shops and somehow seemed to offer the best bars in the district. Through the whole area one felt the presence of the harbor whose traffic had given birth to New York—a presence felt in its salt smell and the hoarse steam whistles of the tugs, freighters and ocean liners that churned the surrounding waters to a perpetual restlessness, as though the city itself were voyaging through the seaway that connected it to the world.

After an afternoon of business and some daydreaming, I made my way uptown to the Steering Committee meeting, which opened with a half dozen people seated around a table in one of the stern-cabin window embrasures in the Yacht Club's model room. The group consisted of Dick Rath, Terry Walton, Alan Frazer, Jon Feffer, Norma and me. Alan Frazer, a skilled model maker who worked for the New York Central Railroad, and Jon Feffer, a rising executive in the shipping business, had joined us through an international club of ship enthusiasts known as the World Ship Society. The Society's president, John Rodgers, had proposed that we conduct a joint walking tour and dinner in South Street in April. Arrangements had been set up, so all we had to do was say yes to launch this first public program of the South Street venture. The vote to accept this "roast lark dropping into our mouths" was unanimous.

Dick Rath's report on the Great Ship Hunt covered correspondence with vessels ranging from the schooner *Ernestina* in the Cape Verde Islands to the Cape Horn square rigger *Kaiulani* in the Philippines. And, true to form, he'd signed up a raft of new members in the boating community, led by those stars of the sailing world, Olin and Rod Stephens, who, having dominated the ocean-racing field starting in the mid-1930s, still led the pack in the changed world of the late 1960s.

My development report was dominated by a major story on our venture in the Sunday edition of New York's largest newspaper, the *New York Daily News*. I'd first heard about this Monday morning in an excited phone call from Bob Ferraro. Then a secretary had leaned into my office doorway to ask: "Is this you, Mr. Stanford?" as she passed me a copy of the paper. There was my picture at the top, and below it were two great pictures of South Street: an 1828 print of bowsprits reaching over the street toward four-story brick buildings, and a recent photograph of the buildings, battered but unbowed against the rising towers of the modern city.

The accompanying story was written by Mel Greene, a young reporter I'd talked to at a City Club luncheon the previous Friday, where I was giving a report on our venture. Mr. Greene questioned me so persistently about my talk that I had to ask him to back off—there were civic leaders and public officials in the room whose questions I really had to answer. He had thanked me, saying he felt he now had the story. As indeed, he did; it was a major story that gave wings to my report to the City Club. He established our political credentials by citing the support of two reform congressmen from Manhattan: the West Side Democrat Bill Ryan and the East Side Republican Ted Kupferman. These serendipitous bipartisan endorsements ran right up front where city bureaucrats would be sure to read on to see what their Congressional paymasters were up to. Greene then set out a clear overview of the project:

> *The museum plan*, he said, *is fourfold. It would restore the area structures built in 1811, place historic furnishings in vacant lofts, outfit clipper ships in the harbor and lease space to restaurants, marine hardware and art stores and bookshops.*

His "historic furnishings in vacant lofts" might have added "activities" to embrace our plans for restored workshops and counting-houses, with craftsmen bringing color and vitality to the scene, from sailmakers and figurehead carvers to metalworkers and printers, each producing items that aficionados seek out today. The Bowne Printing Shop, funded philanthropically by Bowne & Co., printers in New York since 1770, is a surviving example of this program in today's South Street.

In a section headed "A Sense of Belonging," he cited my remark that, for too many, life in the city was an arid experience, and that "we must offer opportunity and challenge everywhere" to get people involved in the city's story, in which they had their role to play. And winding up his account on a practical note, Greene cited an anonymous Planning Commission spokesman who conceded that a museum "could conceivably work in that area"—for which a sympathetic editor chose the inspired heading: "Museum Could Work."

People were greatly cheered by this spirited story, which presented our ideas on the future of South Street as if they were an accepted reality. I then had to report on progress in my effort to get the Planning Commission even to consider the project. But Dick Rath clapped me on the shoulder as the meeting broke up, a most un-Rathlike gesture, and invited Norma and me to join him downstairs at the bar.

"You don't seem to get it, pal," he said in his best newshawk twang as we headed downstairs. "That story isn't just a story—it's reported as positive news, in the biggest newspaper in New York. You might have written it yourself!" Noting that a Planning Commission spokesman had said a museum "could conceivably work in that area," I had seen the word "conceivably" as a dodge to avoid commitment. But Rath recognized for what it was: an admission that we might have a case, that it *could* work. This was a marked advance from the position that it couldn't work.

I belatedly realized that we had made a breakthrough. Less than three months after forming the Friends in the previous November, we had a program to back up that breakthrough into public awareness, based on our membership of some 200 and growing by leaps and bounds. Our ad-hoc Steering Committee at its first meeting had scheduled a dinner organized by an internationally renowned maritime society, set up a ship committee seeking historic ships far and wide, and got a page devoted to our project in the city's biggest newspaper.

We had outflanked the entrenched opposition to the Seaport, bypassing the opposition and going straight for our immediate goals of public and City acceptance. This gave us an opening to advance the achievement of the Seaport.

We now needed to capitalize on the lesser gains we'd made through such items as a favorable mention in New York's entertainment guide *Cue,* and a stirring salute to our efforts by Bennett Cerf in his "Tradewinds" column in *The Saturday Review of Literature.* These notices encouraged readers to see Leevi's Seaport model on exhibition at the Boat Show, which gave the columnists a peg to hang their hats on. But the *News* story caught on with no news peg; it simply told a great story and gave people a whole neighborhood to explore. Its effect went beyond a secretary's excitement over a fellow worker's picture in the paper. It led to my actually getting calls from people I had been trying to reach.

One such call came from Peter Black, a well-known member of the Yacht Club who knew his friend Melvin Conant was interested in the Seaport project but was concerned about the feasibility of our plans. So Black invited Melvin and me to lunch at the club to meet Robert F. Duncan, a management consultant known in sailing circles as the author of *A Cruising Guide to the New England Coast.* It was a convivial lunch taken up with talk of sailing in Maine waters, but as we had coffee, the conversation turned to South Street, and it became clear that Duncan was not enthusiastic about the Seaport project as I described it. For my part I had to fight off a feeling of exasperation at the questions he asked. Had we made a study of the market? No, I just knew that people stood in line to get into Sweet's Restaurant and that the newly opened Ghirardelli Square, the historic shopping complex in San Francisco, was booming.

But I also knew I should expect the same kind of questions from the new director of the Mayor's Office of Lower Manhattan Development—whom I was scheduled to meet later that very afternoon. So I walked with Duncan to Grand Central Station where he would catch his train home. We stood a moment in the vast central hall and Duncan urged me to get competent help before moving another step. This would save us a lot of heartache, particularly if the project proved to be unfeasible. But we had no way to pay a qualified person to do a study providing the kind of answers he was after. I guess Duncan saw the frustration in my face.

"Look," he said, "it isn't as difficult as you're making it out to be. For any project, there are ten basic questions you should ask yourself before proceeding. If the answers to these questions are affirmative, you've got a do-able project. If only seven or eight of the questions can be answered 'Yes,' then you've got your work cut out to change those 'Nos' to 'Yeses.' If you can't answer more than half the questions affirmatively, you haven't got a chance—you're confronting certain failure." I asked him what the ten questions were. Duncan looked a little put out; this was no way to go at the matter, standing in a station while people hurried by on the separate courses of their lives. But he briskly listed his questions, while I mentally ticked off the answers.

First came political support. Did we have the appropriate governmental authorities committed to the scheme? *No, we didn't. Our friends in Congress might be a help, but the relevant city authorities—the Planning and Landmarks Commissions—were opposed.*

Then, financing: Did we have reliable sources to fund the project? *No.*

Third: Did we have an experienced governing board, including recognized business and community leaders? *No.*

Fourth: Did we have a strong management team with a proven track record? *No.*

Fifth: Did the project have a natural constituency of people we could identify and conveniently reach? *No. We'd have to create one.*

Sixth: Was there a market for what we intended to provide, a market we could identify and cultivate? *Not really. Again, we'd just have to create one.*

Seventh: What about competition—could we offer something better than what people could get from existing sources? *Not by a long shot. Mystic offered a first-class museum experience about three hours away. We believed the two museums would complement each other, but we couldn't prove that.*

Eighth: Did we have an accurate, verifiable statement of the cost of the project? *No.*

Ninth: Could we project reliable three-year, five-year and ten-year income levels? *Not possibly.*

Tenth and finally: Did we have a plan to pull all these factors together? *No; how could we?*

"Well, there it is," said Duncan, glancing at the clock above the information booth in the center of the hall. "You've got to face these questions honestly. And I certainly wouldn't go any further until you've got answers you can count on yourself and defend to others."

"I know the answer to each one of those questions right now," I said. "In each case the answer is 'No.'"

Duncan gave me a troubled look and said goodbye. He may have felt I'd given him a flip, saucy answer. But nothing could be further from the truth. The questions were important and I was shaken by the defenseless position they had exposed. I walked the long blocks up Madison Avenue to Compton Advertising in a sombre frame of mind. Back at my office I was relieved to find a note on my desk saying my meeting with Dick Buford, director of the Office of Lower Manhattan Development, had been canceled. Something had come up to make it impossible for him to see me at five o'clock that day.

His note said to call for another appointment. I remember shrugging my shoulders as though to clear them of a burden, and, still standing by my desk, dialed a call to Buford. When he answered, I proposed we meet the following week, not at his office, but at the Yacht Club for lunch. That put me on familiar ground. To my mixed joy and trepidation, Buford accepted my invitation. But as I thought about it, trepidation won out over joy. What could I say to him to bolster the defenseless position revealed by Duncan's ten questions?

———————◆———————

Here, chance intervened. One day in the Yacht Club library I picked up Robert N. Bavier's account of how the 12-meter sloop *Constellation* had won the America's Cup three years earlier. Not wanting to buckle down to my reading on South Street, I soon became engrossed in the story. Eric Ridder, leader of the syndicate that financed the boat, had originally been at the helm, with Bavier as backup. But after test runs it became clear to Ridder that Bavier could take their graceful 12-meter—and she was a beauty—around the America's Cup course a few seconds faster than he could. So he turned over the helm to Bavier, who went on to sail *Constellation* to victory.

When I told Norma this story, I noted how Ridder had shown the spirit we were going to need to build South Street—doing the right things to make the boat go fast, sharing command decisions, using all available talent. Norma said: "Why not put him on your list?" So the next day I hammered out a letter to Eric "Ritter," as I had misremembered his name, enclosing a copy of the Sunday edition of the *Daily News* story, which we had reprinted on newspaper stock to add to its authentic feel. Ridder soon called to say he was interested in our scheme and asked me to lunch with him at India House the next day. So on Thursday, 17 February, just three days after my disheartening talk with Duncan, I showed up at India House, a splendid old brownstone mansion near the southern tip of Manhattan. There I met Eric Ridder, publisher of the *Journal of Commerce*, a lean, taut-looking man I judged to be in his early 50s. With him was an older, stoutish man with a wise, patient face like Benjamin Franklin's, who was introduced to me as Aldrick Benziger, assistant publisher of the newspaper.

We stopped off in the bar upstairs where James Farrell, son of the founder of India House, a club for people engaged in foreign commerce, presided over the scene in his chair just inside the entrance to the bar room. "Hi, Jim," said Eric, and he introduced me as the person who was trying to get a maritime museum started in South Street. Jim, white-haired, pink-faced, and dressed in the gentleman's garb of the pre-war years—a black suit with a vest and gold watch chain across his substantial middle—looked sharply at me over his square-cut rimless glasses.

"I'm a supporter of Mystic Seaport, you know," he said mildly enough. "I know that, sir," I responded. "So am I, in a modest way," which seemed a satisfactory answer. Asked what I did for a living, I said I'd written the ads for Beefeater Gin and was now working on the New York Stock Exchange account. This seemed to go down all right, as we downed two rounds of Beefeater martinis. We then proceeded up the next half flight of stairs to lunch, and over raw clams and India pale ale Eric asked me to tell him about our citizen organization. I told him we were an assorted crew from different walks of life who felt it was important for New Yorkers to learn the seaport origins of their city. He and Dick Benziger nodded agreement with this sentiment, but Dick began to look a little doubtful as I described how the old buildings, properly restored, could house commercial functions that would help support the museum, or the Seaport, as we were now beginning to call it. "That's going to cost an awful lot of money," was his comment.

Well yes, I said, but it would make money too, particularly since we believed we could get the land for practically nothing by arranging with a developer to build a big building next door, using the low density of our low-rise buildings—which did not begin to use up the building rights that came with the land they stood on. The developer could buy our land for us and then either donate it, or re-sell it to us cheap.

This was too much for Eric. "Let's skip the fancy stuff," he suggested, "and get down to cases. No matter how you slice it, this venture is going to take a lot of money." Dick nodded emphatically.

Eric continued: "We've got to find out if we can raise the kind of money we'll need in this community. It's going to come, if it comes at all, from people we already know—sailors and shipping men, bankers and insurers, people who make things go in this town."

"I wouldn't count on it till I've put it in the bank," put in Dick.

"No, we won't count on it," said Eric, "but we've got to give it our best try."

This we could all agree on.

"Now in any city," Eric continued, "there are ten or twelve people who call the shots. I'm willing to invite those people to lunch here with us. If they say 'Yes' to this project, it will almost certainly go. If they say 'No' we can forget about it."

"Wait," I said. My mind was in turmoil. I could envisage a meeting with Jim Farrell in it, concerned about the existing seaport museum at Mystic. I could see people asking costs, city approvals, all the questions for which there were no answers. And all at once it came to me that there *were* no solid answers; ours was an unprecedented venture in urban planning.

"Your gathering of movers and shakers may not agree about things. It's a complicated project. If we ask them to vote on this, we may end up with a hung jury."

The two men looked at me soberly. Evidently what I had said didn't sound crazy. And that mattered. It was, after all, their world we were proposing to move into.

"Let's get just one person," I said, "someone to be chairman."

"Have you anyone in mind?" asked Eric.

"Yes," I said, because I knew this question had to be answered. Actually I had no one in mind. But as my mind raced around I remembered Charlie Lundgren telling us of his boss Isbrandtsen's interest in a downtown maritime museum. And Isbrandtsen's name had been in the papers recently, having to do with a new container terminal.

"What about Jakob Isbrandtsen?"

"I know Pete pretty well," said Eric.

"He's a maverick," added Dick.

"Maybe that's just as well, for a project like this," Eric answered. Then he asked me: "Why did you name him?"

"The *Times* reported the other day that he's bought up the land for a new container terminal in Staten Island. That sounds like something it would take real vision and real money to do."

"Well, you may be right on both counts," said Eric. "Does he know anything about your project?"

I explained that Charlie Lundgren had told Isbrandtsen about our venture, and he'd said he wanted to be kept in touch with what we were doing. I was remembering all this as I spoke. None of these things had been in my mind when I came into India House.

"Well, gentlemen, I think we can adjourn this meeting for now," Eric said. "I'll call Pete." (I finally realized this was Isbrandtsen's nickname.) "We'll set up a luncheon meeting in the next few weeks. And, Peter, if Jakob comes in as chairman, I'll be willing to come aboard as treasurer. That's a job you'll find few takers for."

Dick Benziger rolled his eyes heavenward at this. But he gave me a broad smile as we pushed back our chairs and walked downstairs past the *Glory of the Seas* figurehead and out into the grey everyday world of New York on a winter's afternoon.

I felt new promise of change in our prospects, which no longer looked as forbidding as they had before I'd met Eric and lunched with him at India House.

CHAPTER 7

We Find the Right Chairman, *February–March 1967*

The World of India House—Buford Urges Urban Renewal—
We Incorporate—Norma Is Hired—
Jakob Isbrandtsen Takes the Chair

My lunch with Eric Ridder changed things. It opened the door to setting up a board of trustees for the new Seaport, centered on the maritime industry. And it changed my limited acquaintance with that industry, whose leaders in the 1960s still knew each other and ran across each other going about their business in streets laid down 300 years earlier. The sailing ships that carried that trade for most of those years had docked in South Street, and the bankers, insurers and shipping leaders who ran it had encamped their businesses in marble *palazzi* just inland from the working docks. This age-old pattern had begun to change in recent years as the ships, which had grown to gigantic size, had to abandon Manhattan for huge new basins dug out of the Jersey marshes. There shippers created a new seaport, Port Elizabeth, where giant cranes dominated the skyline and acres of tarmac with waiting trailer trucks received the cargoes the big ships disgorged.

But in the 1960s, top leadership in maritime affairs still carried on in Lower Manhattan. And its stamping ground was India House, the dining club Eric had summoned me to for our meeting—for reasons I began to understand. This was a world where things moved forward according to people's character and shared interests, based on experience and personal judgment. Technical studies could be hired, but purpose and such qualities as resolution, decisiveness and dedication to a cause could not.

Eric, while not one of the moguls who dominated business in Lower Manhattan, clearly played a significant role in this society as publisher of its local paper, the *Journal of Commerce*. Founded in the days when the latest news came by sailing ship, the paper covered the concerns and positions taken by the community. Eric had recently served as chairman of India House under the benevolent eye of James Farrell, whom we just met in the last chapter. I had recognized the Farrell name because the elder James Farrell's saving of the famous square rigger *Tusitala* had passed into maritime lore. Meeting his heir for a chat helped me understand the community he sprang from. It seems eminently worthwhile to step aside for a moment to take a closer look at that community, as seen through the microcosm of India House, where its leadership held forth, expressing so much of its ethos and way of viewing the world.

India House had been founded in 1914 in a period when Europe was being drawn ineluctably into World War I. The United States, resolved on a neutral stance in a world gone mad, prospered greatly by selling armaments to the Allied powers, Britain and France. The downtown crowd genuinely considered the Allies as guardians of civilization against the march of German militarism, and, since Britain's Royal Navy controlled the world's seaways, no armaments could get across the Atlantic to reach Germany in any case.

Founded, thus, in a cresting surge of maritime trade, India House reflected a new awareness of America's nascent status as a great power. A few years earlier, Germany had overtaken Britain in steel production, a key index of industrial power—but Germany's and Britain's steel production combined had been eclipsed in the same era by the unmatched output of the United States. In fact, US Steel, the leading American steel producer, alone produced more steel than all of Germany.

So it was natural that James Farrell, Sr., president of US Steel, joined with the banker and diplomat Willard Straight to found India House as a club dedicated to foreign trade. The two friends invited leaders of Chase Bank, J. P. Morgan, W. R. Grace and other moguls to a dinner, where they were informed that they would be governors of the new club, situated in the heart of the shipping and banking communities at One Hanover Square. Of course they said yes to this and, conscious of their role in the changing of the guard in world commerce, they stated in the club's charter that their mission was to "handle foreign undertakings as they had long been handled in London."

India House soon benefited from the educated tastes of its founding generation, accumulating a collection of paintings, ship models, books and papers worthy of a first-class museum. Carl Cutler, Mystic Seaport's founder, was retained to document this treasure house of marine art and artifacts in a handsome volume, *The Marine Collection at India House* (1935). James Farrell, Sr., maintained an actual sailing ship, the classic square rigger *Tusitala*, which sailed in the sugar trade from Hawaii to the US East Coast from 1924 to 1932. Born of a seafaring family himself, Farrell believed that such a ship inculcated character and seamanly values as nothing else could. In a trade that offered fair winds coming and going, *Tusitala* almost broke even financially, as Farrell insisted she must—though family records I saw show he subsidized her latter years. No one was allowed to know this at the time, and clearly this effort was not about money. Like the India House collection, it celebrated the seafaring ethos which opened the ocean world. Farrell took justifiable pride in taking visitors to see a working survivor of the age of sail at her Hoboken pier. And he maintained a prized relationship with her dauntless captain, James Barker, a veteran of Cape Horn trade under the British flag. Scrapped after World War II, the ship lives on in India House letterhead, honoring the ships that opened trade with the Pacific world and the far Indies.

By the time my meeting with Buford at the Yacht Club came round, I had met Eric, and I think I'd become imbued with some of his go-for-the-goal spirit. And, of course, I hoped the club's nautical atmosphere would help start things off with a look at the cultural asset we proposed to bring New York rather than a discussion of its feasibility.

Appointed just over a month earlier as director of the newly established Mayor's Office of Lower Manhattan Development, Buford had been hired away from Philadelphia by the Lindsay administration not just to judge different plans, but to initiate desirable projects and play an active role in bringing them about. The basic plan he was to fulfill had been published in a schematic map in the *New York Times* three months earlier. This followed the idea of "Windows on the Waterfront," the former CBS chairman Bill Paley's vision of open waterfronts embracing Manhattan—with the moldering industrial riverfront structures cleared away to establish broad plazas opening on the water and towers rising on either hand.

Our argument was that the same commercial space envisaged under Paley's towers around open plazas could be provided while retaining the old waterfront streets and structures as a public resource. By transferring the unused development rights, or air rights, above the old buildings to the new towers, it was possible to retain the historic buildings and substitute their "meaningful clutter" for the windswept open spaces that may delight the architect's eye but do little to engage the interest of the walker in city streets.

Richard Buford, when we met at the club on 23 February, turned out to be a slight, neatly dressed figure in his mid-forties, with a youthful, unlined face and occasional devil-may-care look in his eyes. And the Yacht Club turned out to be the right place to meet him. Knowing little of the boating world, he did know the fame of the America's Cup, won by the schooner yacht *America* in 1851, and was delighted to see this fabled piece of Victorian silverware, three feet high and adorned with a profusion of elaborate engravings, sitting in state amidst the sportive dolphins, swags of seaweed and magnificent ship models which enliven the lofty halls of the turn-of-the-century clubhouse. He was all attention as I walked him through the models of the English, American, and latterly Australian yachts that had raced for the cup. He had a supple mind and clearly grasped technical points in an alien field.

At lunch I outlined our Seaport scheme. To get at the root principles involved, I took him back to the argument I'd made in the Lower Eastside Neighborhoods Association over the row of well-kept houses that were torn down solely to meet zoning density requirements for a new school. I talked of the connection between architecture and culture, noting how wiping out these well-kept small buildings eradicated an oasis of visual refreshment in a neighborhood of rundown slums and fortress-like public housing, while further eroding the ethnic diversity of a neighborhood which was already losing its more successful old-immigrant groups.

Clearly not much interested in this mini-tragedy in urban planning and our hope to keep diversity and a sense of history alive in the neighborhood, Buford steered the conversation back to ships and commercial history and, above all, how we thought to present these things in our South Street museum. I told him our citizen organization, now over 400 strong, planned to bring in real working ships to the waterfront and to develop shoreside exhibits on the maritime trades in the buildings that had once housed those trades. He had seen our story in the Sunday edition of the *Daily News*, of course, so he knew of our feeling for the buildings whose windows had looked out on the sailing of packet and clipper ships.

I pressed ahead, telling him of Karl Kortum's leadership role in our work and how Ghirardelli Square (a magic name to city planners!) had been developed by one of Kortum's trustees. He was definitely interested in that, and also in the institutions represented in our Advisory Council, ranging from the Smithsonian Institution to the Museum of the City of New York.

"Well," said Buford, "I've got to go. But we want you in our plan. We'll start things rolling to make your organization the designated developer for your part of the Brooklyn Bridge Southeast Urban Renewal District." I must have been looking at him with my mouth open. Buford laughed then said: "Don't worry, you'll still have to raise your own funds to buy the land, but only you will be allowed to develop it. You'll do this according to plans you'll work out with us." I was seized with belated compunction. "Mr. Buford," I blurted out, "I don't want to be sailing under false colors. We have no money and no backing. You've got to understand that."

"Don't worry," said Buford again, pushing back his chair. "Just go out and use what I've told you to get the money and everything else you need."

"Did you mean people could call you to confirm that we were under consideration to be the designated developer?"

"Have them call me and I'll tell them what I've just told you," said Buford, "And stop calling me 'Mr. Buford,'" he added as we parted on the sidewalk outside the club. "I'm Dick, you're Peter. We'll be having a lot to do with each other, so we might as well cut through the formalities at the outset."

Returning to the office from this meeting, I was walking on air. But coming back to the Yacht Club later for the Steering Committee meeting that evening, I began to feel the weight of reality on my shoulders. Both Ridder's commitment from the private sector and Buford's from the City agency most directly concerned with our venture entailed real-world commitments we would have to scramble to meet. The committee, now ten members strong, met round a table in a private room. We agreed at the outset to hire someone at a desk to field inquiries, keep schedules, follow up assignments and pursue research on questions ranging from finding historic illustrations of the old seaport to determining present-day land costs and funding sources.

The urgency of this need was borne in by a meeting I'd had two weeks earlier with Herb Halberg, the City Commissioner of Marine & Aviation. Herb had told us he would refurbish the piers for museum use and turn them over to us gratis on a 99-year lease. This was of course a major capital gift, which depended on our getting City Planning approval. We needed that anyway, I said, to have the project happen at all. Okay, Herb had said, but you've got to move fast. Get the Rockefellers on your side, get a grip on the shoreside land. Other people with other ideas are interested in the acreage you need for your Seaport. Before our meeting had ended, Herb's able assistant, Anita, told me aside that Herb truly wanted the Seaport to happen and was worried it would not secure its land before others took it. This worried us too, I told her. But I left very encouraged by Commissioner Halberg's support of the Seaport and his active help to move it forward

By late February we had abandoned any idea of New York State's South Street Maritime Museum leading the way in saving the South

Street venture. So at this meeting, we unanimously resolved to incorporate our venture as an independent entity. Terry Walton's husband, Bob, volunteered to do this as our unpaid legal counsel. Bob Ferraro had urged us to call the new institution "South Street Seaport," a designation that included the whole neighborhood. Bob Walton, however, stoutly maintained that we needed designation as a museum; we'd then be accountable to the State Board of Regents, assuring that our educational mission would remain at the heart of our concerns. Thus we chose South Street Seaport Museum as our name.

The decision to incorporate emphasized the need to set up a staff working out of an established headquarters. I reminded our gathering that Ray Rubinow, executive director of the J. M. Kaplan Fund, who sat with me on the City Club board, had assured me that $2,500 I'd asked for would be forthcoming as soon as we got our status as a nonprofit corporation. From early on he had emphasized that we should steer an independent course and get underway as soon as we could. We'd resolved to hire a staff person—but who should it be?

We had our answer to this tough question a short while after the Steering Committee meeting. It came at a *Reporter* mailing party at Bob and Terry Walton's Greenwich Village apartment. When I raised the question, which people had had some time to think about, Terry at once raised her hand. The standout choice, she said, was Norma. She had the experience, skills and heart for the work. She knew the people and their picture of a revived South Street. All present agreed with this and we agreed to immediately telephone the rest of the Steering Committee to get their vote, which turned out to be unanimous.

Norma was stunned by this—and, to her surprise, delighted.

She knew she could do the job and felt she would enjoy it. But she also knew it was risky—the entire endeavor was risky—and she'd far rather be in the thick of the action than worrying how someone else was handling things.

I was happy that Norma had been the choice for a number of reasons, the main one, from my point of view, was that Norma's presence as manager of our enterprise would assure that there would be one of us, the volunteer founders, at the center of the evolving institution.

The Steering Committee went on next to appoint a Planning Committee to plot our course through the larger issues before us. Such a committee already existed, at the initiative of Melvin Conant, who had recruited his friend Peter Black and Robert R. Duncan (whom we've already met) as expert counsel. Their report, rendered with commendable promptness, called for me to continue my leadership role but avoid any direct involvement in the operations I would be directing. Melvin felt that if you're constantly in the front line getting out the newsletter, meeting with people to learn about prospective ships, or dreaming up future events, you will not be able to keep the whole project on course. But there were other considerations involved; such basic concerns as enlisting the creative force of human desire in our project, and forging the leadership disciplines we needed by leading from the front rather than from some remote command post.

A brief, encouraging report from Norma on membership wound up the meeting on a positive note. Membership had grown at a rate of 100 per month through January; in February it had gained 200, making a total of 450 members. We felt we were on the verge of greater things and it was time to cram on all the canvas our ship would bear! To help out, I found myself addressing envelopes in every spare moment, even riding in the subway. Such scut work helped work off the tensions Norma and I had begun to feel in the race to save the Seaport buildings. And the hand-addressed mailing pulled in responses like nets full of live fish.

It was time to bring our supporters together to let them know how the effort was progressing. So on 2 March we held a reception at the Yacht Club. We set up our Seaport model in the club, where people crowded around it, studying it, talking about it and asking questions. One troublesome question came up again and again. People who knew the East River waterfront downtown wanted to know what we planned to do about the overhead expressway. At first we'd worried about this too, for the great structure striding on giant legs the length of South Street looks from above like an enormous obstruction. We hadn't shown the expressway in the model, which we felt should reflect the street-level experience. And once in South Street, sure enough, we found that people don't see it as an obstruction.

Admiral John M. Will, a graduate of Annapolis, decorated WWII submarine commander, and postwar head of the Military Sealift Command, was a widely recognized leader in maritime affairs, who added a formal touch to the occasion, attending in dress blue uniform. Erect, decisive in manner, he played his part of sea lord to perfection, declaring that this was a project that was long overdue and that had to happen; New York had too long turned its back on the sea, and this could change all that. As chairman of American Export-Isbrandtsen Lines, Dutch Will (as he was universally known) could also carry back a good word on the project and its people to Jakob Isbrandtsen, president and principal owner of the combined lines. I believe that the report was a good one, for the next day Eric Ridder called to say that he had a date for our luncheon with Isbrandtsen—just a week later, Friday, 10 March.

We had established a direct connection with City government in Dick Buford at the Mayor's Office of Lower Manhattan Development. We'd enrolled a recognized leader of the maritime community in Eric Ridder. And we'd secured a distinguished advisory board that included leading authorities in maritime history. Moreover, we had secured widespread recognition of our goals in the press and had a lively public program scheduled for coming months.

But in the few days remaining before our meeting with Jakob Isbrandtsen, I felt we were lacking on two key points: our vital but informal relationship with the San Francisco Maritime Museum, and our own staff leadership.

On the San Francisco connection, our question answered itself when we received a response from Anita Ventura to my lengthy letter of questions.

"A go at your letter of 22 January," Anita wrote in her usual forthright style. She then tackled the opening question of whether the museum should be for scholars or a broad public:

> *Your true public should be families and children of New York*
> *and all who visit the city, as well as the historians.*

This matched our own views. The museum should be by and for New Yorkers. What will most attract visitors who come to taste the real New York is to find themselves among New Yorkers enjoying their own city. She continued:

> *If you do a good historical job, the people will be among the*
> *greatest appreciators, even though they may not understand the*
> *extent to which it is accurate history. But people can spot the*
> *exaggerated and the phony, and they lose pride in an effort that*
> *in turn debases them. It is a project of which the people of New*
> *York should feel proud and boastful, two attitudes they attain*
> *real grandeur in expressing.*

Her own interest in the Seaport stemmed, she explained, from her "enthusiasm for my old haunts in New York." Living on the third floor above a tavern, she had collected "iron stars from buildings, moldings and decoration that [she] took from demolition sites." Her home in New York was not far from the Fraunces Tavern block. But the seaport area a few blocks farther north was what resonated in her mind. Norma and I met others dismayed by the demolition of the elegant old buildings that used to line Pearl Street, but no one quite matched the poignant concern of Ms. Ventura, writing from three thousand miles away to people she had never met.

The rest of the letter was packed with helpful observations, including names and addresses of the leading developers who had made the San Francisco waterfront revival the success it was. She saw the ships, particularly the *Balclutha*, at the heart of that success; they attracted people and they brought authenticity to the scene in ways nothing else could.

She closed the letter with best wishes, saying that "if there is anything that a person in my position can further do, I would be very grateful for the chance to do it."

Neither Norma nor I ever forgot Anita's utter willingness to read herself into our situation and do everything she could to help. We were moved by the depth of her feeling for our project, expressed in her marvelously direct, but highly evocative style. Years later she made a contribution that was to prove important to the writing of this account, by gathering the papers she had on file on the connection between the San Francisco museum and our own, including memos, clippings, and, above all, Karl's and my correspondence, files which were later lost when Norma and I left South Street. Those papers proved an invaluable resource in tracing our early decision-making. And so Anita helped preserve this story of the museum as well as helping to shape it.

Anita emphasized Karl Kortum's interest in the Seaport and suggested I get in touch with Karl to talk with him directly. I promptly did so, calling from Alice Taylor's apartment for a long talk—so long it had Alice pointing at her watch to remind me of telephone charges. We reviewed the *Kaiulani* case and the importance of press support in our own cause. I told Karl of our very real admiration for his work with ships—in saving them, of course, and in so effectively telling their story in ways that awakened interest in all who saw them.

We had sent Anita a list of our advisors. Those names established credibility with anyone who knew the maritime field. To add Karl's name would give us a lift, since he was a leader of the San Francisco waterfront renaissance, a phenomenon based on his bringing in the historic ships, which brought new life and interest to the waterfront and stimulated the shoreside restoration. Karl's own interest in South Street was clearly real and he agreed to join the advisory committee on the spot. He confirmed this in two letters he sent me in the next few days.

Kortum's word pretty well set our course in historic ships, backed as it was by his sailing in the last American square rigger and his widespread reading and international correspondence in the last days of commercial sail.

But our own ship was sailing in a very loosely defined command situation. We had expected to find someone to take my place, continue the programs we had set up, and lead the Seaport into next steps according to our general plan. It was not an empty playing field, but rather one crowded with players and actions to be taken.

Melvin Conant broke into my thoughts on this with an urgent call:

Peter, the Plans Committee has decided. You've got to quit your job and go to work for the Seaport. You'll have to ask Isbrandtsen for the money to pay you when we ask him to be chairman.

Melvin went on to explain that the committee had wanted to hire a distinguished deputy curator at the Metropolitan Museum of Art. But the curator simply found the assignment unworkable; it would take a professional staff to carry it out, with museum-building piled on top of urban renewal negotiations and an unprecedented scheme for land acquisition requiring a massive fundraising effort, since we had no real money in the bank. Further inquiries with other candidates had led to the same response.

"So there's no one else to take the job," Melvin concluded.

And I then said I would do it. Norma agreed with this, though it put us both into lower-paying jobs with no security.

This meant we'd have to ask Isbrandtsen, whom we planned to invite to become chairman of the board of the new museum, to fund my salary as president in charge of operations. We reckoned that would come to $5,000 to cover two months of my $25,000 salary with something left over for expenses.

Friday arrived. I was picking up my papers to set off for the meeting with Isbrandtsen, when my account supervisor, Ralph Zeuthen, came into my office. He said we needed to have a talk: I had not taken full control of the Stock Exchange account, which in turn made it hard for him to give the attention he should to the new assignments he'd taken on. And people noticed my long lunches and of course were aware of my involvement with the new maritime museum project in Lower Manhattan.

"It's not an emergency, Peter," he said. "You do good work. It's just that your heart doesn't seem to be in it. I get the feeling that your mind is on other subjects when I walk in here. It looks to me as if you've simply got to decide on Compton Advertising and the Stock Exchange account or your marine museum."

Usually I'm at a loss when confronted with this kind of direct choice. Not this time. I simply told Ralph that I was facing that choice at lunch today, and when I came back I should have the answer, one way or the other.

Ralph raised his eyebrows. I didn't need to explain that I always made up for my long lunches with evening hours in the office, or to say that the client liked my work. He knew these things as well as I did. But the fact was that I had not shifted the center of the account into my hands; our clients at the Stock Exchange, a rather easy-going bunch compared to what I'd seen before in the advertising business, would question me about any ad I'd written, and then turn to Ralph to give their judgment and get his response. That was the root of the matter.

Ralph said simply: "Right, you'd better be on your way, then. I'll see you when you get back." With that he turned on his heel and left the room. I followed after him, to catch the downtown Lexington Avenue subway and meet Melvin in front of India House to help carry the Seaport model upstairs.

It was a sweaty, delicate business to get the model up three floors of India House to Room Four, which Eric had reserved. We placed the model on a side table and arranged our newsletter and newspaper clippings around it, while I tried to compose what I'd say to Isbrandtsen when he arrived.

Eric Ridder walked in with a smile on his face and ordered his India Pale Ale. No Beefeater martinis this time. We seated ourselves around the table and talked of this and that. We were each aware that if Isbrandtsen accepted our offer to serve as Seaport chairman, we would be in business with a functional board: Eric as treasurer, and Robert J. Tarr, a young shipping executive who'd phoned in his acceptance, as secretary, myself, a non-trustee officer of the board as president, and Melvin Conant as chair of the planning committee. There was quite a lot at stake in the little gathering. Eventually Eric said: "Well, let's have some clams, anyway," and we ordered cherrystones on the half shell. These were gobbled up. Still no Isbrandtsen. Eric said: "Gentlemen, let's have some lunch," and we all, as I remember it, ordered the classic shrimp curry, then the hallmark of the house.

While we were adding the exotic India House condiments to our curries, Isbrandtsen broke into the room, swinging the door wide open as he made his brief apologies. "I'll have what the rest of you are having. Now what are we meeting about here?" He seemed enormous, his shirt tails half out, jacket rumpled, big hands waving to underline his words.

Eric imperturbably said: "Well, Pete, Peter Stanford here would like to tell you about our idea for the South Street Seaport. Peter, why not tell him about it?"

I started talking about the Street of Ships, about Karl Kortum and the wonders he had accomplished by saving an old square rigger in San Francisco. My words were interrupted by a succession of short, brusque questions—questions about supporters, money sources, relations with Mystic Seaport, City approvals and the like. I tried to answer these briefly and factually, except when I said I could not help feeling that we were gaining the support of the people of New York. This evoked a quick grin. Isbrandtsen was on top of things and evidently following everything I said. But all at once, after just over half an hour, the questions stopped. Jakob rose to his feet, putting his hands on the tablecloth before him.

"What do you want of me?" he asked.

"We need $5,000. With what we have, that will pay Norma's and my salary for two months and cover the expenses of an office to work from in South Street," I said.

"You've got it," said Isbrandtsen. "What else?"

"We want you to be chairman," I said.

"I can't possibly do that. Too busy."

"Pete, I'm willing to be treasurer," said Eric. At almost the same moment I said: "In that case, take back your money. We need you as chairman." I've no idea what made me say that, but I meant it.

Isbrandtsen nodded to Eric. Then, with a searching look my way, he said: "Okay, I'll do it. But," pointing his finger at me, "you run it!"

With that he was out the door and gone.

There was a heap of congealed rice and curry on my plate. I had a few mouthfuls, and a cup of hot black coffee. I believe Eric said something like "We're in business," and I seem to remember Melvin saying "Well, now we go to work."

I don't really remember anything else, though we must have said goodbye as we took our departures for our separate places of business.

When I got back to Compton Advertising I went straight to Ralph Zeuthen's office. He was marking up a sheet of copy on his desk.

"Well, Ralph, it's the museum," I said. He looked at me curiously, and then incredulously. Then he got up from behind his desk and strode over to the door behind me, closing it vigorously. He was in the grip of some strong emotion and I thought that perhaps he was angry and was going to tell me that I was ruining my life or that I had let him down in some way.

Instead he rounded on me and seized my right hand.

"Well, Peter, you've done it," he said. "You've done something I've wanted to do all my life. When I came to New York I wanted to go to work as a newspaperman. I'd had some experience in Illinois, but I wanted to work in the big time. I went into advertising to pay the bills while I waited for a break. Of course it didn't happen. But you've gone ahead and made your own break.

"I wish you all the luck in the world," he finished, with a warm encouraging smile.

I couldn't say anything.

CHAPTER 8

Headquarters In Fulton Street, *March 1967*

The Second Reporter—The Chairman's Question—
Dinner with Joan—Headquarters and Gallery—
Expanded Budget—Others Speak Up

On Saturday, in the chill morning air of Yorktown Heights, I reflected on the previous day's lunch. With Jakob now aboard as chairman, we had a workable board of trustees. We had $8,500 to set up an office and pay Norma's and my salary, with reasonable expenses, which should carry us through the next two months. This was a slender startup to set about changing the map of Lower Manhattan.

"We're afloat, we're on our way," I wrote in my journal, "but just barely."

Norma and I knew that the great creative force on our side was the Seaport's growing membership sustained by the *South Street Reporter*. In the turmoil of the last few weeks, the March issue was late going to press. But over the weekend Norma and I set to work to write and lay out this critical second issue from our scattered notes. We took joy in working together, juggling ideas, pictures and headlines until these fascinating disparate bits came together to make a living whole. Ideas proposed by one of us would be finished by the other, and our spirits danced as we progressed through the re-created Seaport we were building in the pages of the *Reporter*. It was heaven while the music lasted—a music of imagining things and then doing them together, a magic which still resounds through our lives together.

In this fashion the *South Street Reporter*, Vol. 1 No. 2, took shape as a four-page newsletter; we were resolved to expand and improve the journal as we went. We led off with a banner call to join "An Evening on South Street," announcing the tour and dinner at Seamen's Church Institute planned for 7 April now only a little over two weeks away, but we didn't worry about the short notice. If lots of people come, we said, terrific; if not, we'd have a splendid private gathering. The waterfront tour gave us a reason to show the whole stretch of the waterfront from the Brooklyn Bridge to Battery Park, and we ran a photo of the street alive with shipping in 1876, taken from a tower of the uncompleted Brooklyn Bridge. Below this we showed Leevi's model of the buildings we planned to save.

We also announced the Advisors Committee, made up of nine leading citizens who had risked their good names to stand with our venture. Ed Stackpole, formerly of Mystic, had agreed to preside at the dinner. And there were three other museum leaders present: Howard Chapelle, maritime curator of the Smithsonian, Ralph Miller of the Museum of the City of New York, and Karl Kortum, founder and director of the San Francisco Maritime Museum—a strong leadership group standing together to support a new museum. The other advisors, opinion leaders in their fields, were Frank O. Braynard, past president of the Steamship Historical Society; Moulton H. Farnham, editor of *Boating* magazine; Emory Lewis, editor of *Cue;* Critchell Rimington, editor of *Yachting;* and Raymond S. Rubinow, director of the J. M. Kaplan Fund.

Serendipitously—in view of our predeliction for the schooner rig—we had fresh stories on two important schooners visited by our Ship Committee: one on the *Emma C. Berry*, celebrating her 100th year when we went aboard in 1966; and the other a replica of the great schooner-yacht *America* nearing completion in Maine for a launch this year. On the political front, in the most casual manner imaginable we announced that we were going to incorporate as South Street Seaport Museum, and that our great friend Whitney North Seymour had resigned as our honorary chairman, saying that we no longer needed his help—a generous way to put it.

Over the weekend we had summoned a meeting of the mailing team for Monday evening at Alice Taylor's apartment. There, as we folded and stuffed, we discussed the news that we had a new chairman and funds to go into business. I explained that the putative trustees wanted to delay any announcement of their appointment until they had held their first meeting and had something solid to announce. I presented the news of Buford's support as director of Lower Manhattan Development as outflanking the entrenched opposition of the Planning and Landmarks Preservation Commissions—but this left the more orderly-minded among us wondering where in the labyrinthine channels of City decision-making we actually stood.

The two radical departures from the original plan—the decision to incorporate our venture as the Seaport rather than an arm of a maritime museum in Schermerhorn Row, and Whitney North Seymour's decision to step down as honorary chairman—were accepted as steps along the path we were following. Senator Seymour had left in a friendly way, I said, and we were resolved to keep things so.

So the second *Reporter* got into the mail to our members. These now numbered 550, showing healthy growth over the 200 we'd mailed to in mid-January. As the pile of hand-addressed envelopes slithered like so many fish into the brass-lipped maw of the mailbox at Grand Central, I said to Norma: "This mailing is the most important thing we did this evening—by far." We had managed to write it, print it and mail it out— a little behind our self-imposed schedule, but in considerably expanded form. And we both felt encouraged by the positive attitude and measurable support of our crew.

Norma said: "I agree. So let's go to Costello's for a beer."

"I believe we've got things in the right order," I said over our beers. "Membership first—if we miss something important because we're concentrating too much on that, a strong citizen body will be the best thing we could have to correct the error. And if things go our way, we want a large citizen body moving ahead with us."

"But we've still got to keep pressing forward on the political front," Norma responded. "Imagine if we wake up one day to find a developer has been named for Schermerhorn Row. Then it's going to be: 'Sorry, folks, your little show is over.' It happens all the time. Remember when the City moved into East Harlem's Little Italy and forced people out of their homes? It was a neighborhood where everyone knew each other and families had lived there for generations. None of that mattered."

"And then," I said, "there's the little matter of money, which we have very little of. And the closely related question of what kind of head-quarters we set up and where. It's a crowded agenda! It's good news my boss is giving me all the time I need for Seaport business these last two weeks while I'm still on Compton's payroll."

"Of course it's just possible they're glad to get rid of you," Norma teased, "unthinkable as that may seem."

"Then they make an awfully good show of telling me they're proud of what you and I are doing," I said, perhaps a bit stiffly.

"That's nice, but I wouldn't bank on it," said Norma echoing Dick Benziger's remark at my lunch with Eric. "But," she added, "it *is* rather nice of these hard-bitten types to care," which pleased me.

"The other thing today that surprised me is that Isbrandtsen seems to be all fired up on the Seaport—he wants to see me in his office first thing Wednesday morning. And Joan Davidson called to confirm our meeting for supper at Sweet's that evening."

But Norma had begun sliding herself, not ungracefully, but rather definitely, out of her booth. "C'mon, let's get the train. We can celebrate at home."

For once, I didn't resist.

Two days later on the way to Isbrandtsen's office at 26 Broadway, I won-dered how we'd get on. Jakob was a great sailor, but many yachtsmen have no particular feel for things historical. And then—what would he expect of our gang? Here we'd asked the man to take the lead in a major real estate project, a field in which none of us had any noticeable experience and nor did he.

The first thing that met one's eyes in his office was a Baltic trading schooner of the last century encased in a glass room divider, and on the way to his room I passed a panoply of ship models, paintings, and framed documents lining the walls. Clearly ships were the heart of the Isbrandtsen story, as they were of our Seaport story.

Having come out to meet me, he expansively waved an arm at the maritime exhibits and said: "This was all intended for an Isbrandtsen museum, but the collection should be part of something bigger, the story of what Americans have achieved at sea—a story that needs telling, along with its European origins. Charlie Lundgren's got the ships right—he knows his stuff—but there are no records to go by in the early days, beyond rig and tonnage. Shipwrights knew what was wanted; why should they draw pictures? Charlie has ransacked the museums and shipping offices in Denmark for years now, and what there is, he's got. So here are the European roots of an American shipping family."

By then we had reached Jakob's desk, a massive oaken roll-top affair with docketed papers stuffed into its various pigeonholes—clearly the desk was from another world. "This was my father's," he said briefly, catching my glance.

"Now listen," he said, seating himself while he gestured me to a chair, "neither you nor I are real estate people, and here we'll be plunging right into the field, if your Seaport scheme is going to amount to anything. I hired Zeckendorf to accumulate the land for the Howland Hook container port we're doing. He had to use a Staten Island realtor, Ken Wilpon, as a blind, but Bill Zeckendorf called the shots. He's bankrupt and needs the business, and I'd like you to show him the seaport area. Are you up for that today?"

"Of course," I said, and Jakob immediately called Zeckendorf on the phone.

"Okay, Bill, Peter Stanford can do it this afternoon. What time should he show up?"

The time was set for three at Zeckendorf's midtown office; from there we'd drive to the seaport area.

"Now, look, Peter," Jakob continued, "you know what you want in the Seaport, it's his job to tell you what he can do to make it work. I want to know if he thinks it won't work at all. His won't be the last word on this, but we need to know that word. Please come right back when you're done, and tell me what happened."

After meeting Zeckendorf at this midtown office, we set off downtown in his long black chauffer-driven car. Along the way, my attempts to start a conversation on our plans for the Seaport were cut short by our distinguished host: "Let's look at the property first." We stopped off on the way at the Tweed Court House behind City Hall, where Zeckendorf had to check in daily as part of a sentence he was serving for stock fraud, as he explained. And then, to my surprise, instead of heading down Fulton Street for the Seaport neighborhood, we rolled on grandly down Broadway, turning left at its ending in Bowling Green and down Whitehall Street to drive onto the elevated FDR Drive heading north along the East River.

We had a third-story view of things as we came up to the Seaport area, and Zeckendorf asked me just what kind of commerce I hoped to attract to occupy these decrepit buildings. I pointed out the booming business Sweet's Restaurant was doing and briefly sketched out our picture of a neighborhood of bars, restaurants, marine supply houses and residential apartments, all given a special character by historic ships on the waterfront. Zeckendorf replied that stockbrokers might come on slumming trips to Sweet's, but this didn't prove anything. The building stock looked really bad, and it was unreal to think of any tenants paying more than the low-rent fish merchants, who were slated to move out under current City plans. He didn't see any way of turning things around except to clear away the aged buildings, which were nothing special to begin with, and start over.

"Not what you'd call a productive exchange," I told Jakob when I called at his office late that afternoon. He responded imperturbably: "Peter, I'm sorry he didn't get the picture. You've done well to get as many people to understand it as you have. That's the whole strength of the Seaport. Zeckendorf's eye was on the new towers near the Seaport that will be built with Seaport air rights."

I said: "So that is what the tour was about."

Jakob said: "I had to find out, and now we know what the man's about."

When Norma and I met Joan at Sweet's at six that evening, a wet heavy snow had begun to fall, hushing the traffic in the streets. The century-old buildings outside the windows of Sweet's were adorned with a fresh white trim, and in the background one felt, rather than saw, the noble form of the Brooklyn Bridge presiding over these workaday buildings of another age. This grand scene got us talking about how we had come to know this corner of New York in Sunday afternoon walks, and how we'd come to feel that the crooked streets and aged brick buildings had a great story waiting to be told. Snow always has a strange way of wiping out the passage of time for me, and this evening was no exception. Ship captains had watched Yankee packets outward bound on the rough sea road to Liverpool through these windows, and in later decades exchanged judgments on the great California clippers headed for the battle to be the first round Cape Horn to 'Frisco, where adventurers panned for gold on the banks of the Sacramento. It would not have seemed too surprising, one felt, to see one of these tall ships, like the long-lived *Young America,* emerge from the mists rising out of the East River, which the great clippers trod, dipping and nodding to the ever-present East River swell as though they knew they were making history that would be talked of wherever sailors met.

"There speaks the Peter we knew of old," said Joan. "And now you're getting a lot of interested New Yorkers to share the nautical mythos you and Norma are taken up with. Ray has kept me in touch with your doings, and it seems the Seaport is getting to be a reality. Congratulations to you both!"

Some months earlier, Ray Rubinow—who served with me on the City Club board—had told us that Joan served as an officer of the J. M. Kaplan Fund, a foundation known for backing new ventures in civic improvements in New York. And after our chance meeting on Fifth Avenue last fall, Joan had kept an eye on our South Street venture and advised Ray to make the grant we'd asked for to cover Norma's salary. So she spoke, as we now knew, as a stakeholder in our venture.

Bringing us up to date with her own affairs, Joan told us she'd moved with her family to a house in Brooklyn Heights which, we were glad to hear, looked down Pierrepont Street to the seaport district across the river. Joan had a stylish way with words, as I remembered from high school, together with a forward-leaning mind and balloon-puncturing wit. To these traits she had added a new quietude in listening. She couldn't seem to hear enough about the Seaport project and the people it had drawn into its somewhat turbulent wake.

"Anyway, Joan," I continued, to make it clear that our enthusiasm for the American clipper was no latter-day invention, "that sailing ship ethos, a set of beliefs and ways of doing things, developed over the millennia and had a real hold on people. This was much in evidence as the steam-ship began to crowd out the sailing ship, just when she was reaching her highest development. When the *Young America* was due in New York toward the end of her days, it's on record that New Yorkers flocked to see her long, sea-chasing bows and towering masts at her South Street pier. Her builder had told her first mate before she set sail: 'Take good care of her, Mister. When she's gone, there'll be no more like her.' He had named her *Young America* because he knew she stood for something important in the American spirit. And the people who came to see her knew that they were seeing something extraordinary that would be talked about long after its time."

Then Norma asked about my meeting with Jakob earlier in the day, landing us back in the present with a thump. I reported that our morning meeting had been a model of brevity, with just two topics on the table: first, an affirmation that ships, from his point of view, were the heart of the Seaport venture, as illustrated by the paintings and ship models that lined his office; and second, his recognition that neither of us knew much about New York real estate development, so he was seeking expert counsel from Bill Zeckendorf. And then, in our afternoon meeting Jakob had actually made a third point: that the Seaport idea was visibly working with New Yorkers, and this was the main strength behind the venture. He clearly recognized that public support was more important than Zeckendorf's casual dismissal of a revived seaport in historic buildings.

"Rather a waste of time, it seems to me," said Joan. "In the meantime, while you and our new chairman were settling this matter of big land dealings and high finance, what has been going on with the little matter of the New York State Maritime Museum, which we've been so concerned about?"

"Well, Joan," I responded, "I've been in regular touch with Arthur Massolo, the governor's aide, on the State Museum. And, as a matter of fact, I saw him this morning. He's sympathetic to the Seaport project, with the state museum at its center. And this morning he greeted me with something like jubilation. He said the Seaport had proved popular enough to get things moving with the state museum at last. The feeling is that Governor Nelson Rockefeller could plead the public will as his defense for breaking the agreement with David Rockefeller to hold back on the museum. And Arthur assured me that with our help, and effective behind-the-scenes work with Mike Seymour, he'd lined up a potential board for the state museum. Remember, the museum had been authorized on the condition that there would be no fundraising—that is, no museum for now. But now, says Massolo, all we need is an irreproachable president to head up the state museum board. I said we'll go to work on it"

As the snow piled up in the window embrasures, our talk turned to the kind of commerce that would work in the Seaport of the future, about our explorations of the seafaring culture, and Joan's suggestion about people we should work with for further counsels on the nexus we sought between culture and commerce—the kind of talk we needed to get a sound approach to building the revived Seaport. Norma and I came away from the evening feeling that Joan now had a keen understanding of what we needed, with a clear vision of what the Seaport could contribute to New York.

Norma had kept pointing out that putting membership first could not mean setting aside the opening of on-site headquarters. Failure to act on this would compromise both membership growth and political progress, since each depended on a working presence in the Seaport district.

I could agree with that, picturing a quiet one-room office next to a meeting room. And Bob Ferraro had found an ideal spot for this, a third-story space at the river end of Schermerhorn Row, whose windows looked out over the river—up to the Brooklyn Bridge and down the broadening waterway that led on out to sea. It was a perfect spot for peaceful deliberations with kindred spirits over the shape and nature of the new district we were planning for the city.

But Norma, supported by our architect Bill Shopsin, wanted a radically different headquarters—a space devoted to public access and participation, with doors opening onto the street with signs, exhibits and activities inviting all comers! We weren't moving into the neighborhood just to give reality to a private dream—we were moving in to be with the people of New York, to have them with us in the battle to save a vital heritage of all New Yorkers. And we would need their counsels, support, questions and even their disagreements, if we were to give life to the neighborhood and authenticity to our work together.

Of course this was the way to go! I had nothing to add to what they said. The fleeting thought did cross my mind that we had no budget for running an open public hall as part of our headquarters, but I wisely said nothing of that. If I said: "We can't afford to maintain a public hall," that was saying we couldn't afford a real public presence, thus abandoning the public strategy that had carried us so far. And with a public hall we'd have to mount an educational exhibit and run activities to attract people. As we rode the subway south from Grand Central to take a look at the ground-floor space Bill had found for us in Schermerhorn Row, I could see involvements multiply, none of which we could cover in our budget. But some wisdom made me decide to set aside the problems and go ahead with the commitment to an open public establishment.

As we emerged from the subway at Fulton Street for the ten-minute walk down Fulton to Schermerhorn Row, I reassessed our financial understanding with the board of trustees. Eric Ridder had said we would go for $1,000 corporate contributions, led by his own company, plus a more sizable startup grant from Jakob. But I had come to feel that these grants were made like sporting bets with further contributions dependent on City approvals. In fact we needed City staff to plot the mechanics of transferring air rights, a step on which our ultimate finances depended. The picture of supporters coming forward to pay the costs of developing these ultimate finances was proving illusory. Meanwhile, we were adding to expenses we could not cover.

And so the gallery began to look like a necessity rather than an interesting extra. At least we might do things there to build the income we needed to keep going beyond the two months our limited funds would cover. In that short walk, I had begun to come to grips with the financial realities that would govern our work in South Street.

Two doors down from the retail fish store at the inland corner of Schermerhorn Row we came upon the empty storefront that Bill had found for us at 16 Fulton Street. Its most recent tenant had been a clothing store, Pier 16, which had decamped to reopen in more genteel quarters uptown. There was a large street-level room with a concrete floor, which one entered through an overhead-opening garage door with a small personnel door cut into it, both inherited from the fish-stall that preceded the Pier 16 shop. A narrow wooden stairway on the left led up to a large room with a small enclosed office looking out on Fulton Street and a cramped rest room in the opposite corner. The place was dirty beyond belief and filled with heaped-up junk. Norma and I looked around and then at each other and had the same thought: "This is perfect."

That night back home in Yorktown Heights, Norma and I cleared the dining table after supper and started sketching out the display we would build around Leevi Kiil's model. As Norma later put it:

> The ideas seemed to pour out—ideas born during the months of discussing the project and working to achieve a physical presence. Now they burst onto the scene like schoolboys at the recess bell,

flowing out with an energy all their own and taking shape on the papers before us.

We covered sheet after sheet with headlines, bits of writing and sketches of display panels designed to transform our dingy hole in the wall into an inviting center for New Yorkers who shared our quest for the heritage of the tall ships that built their city. Alan Frazer volunteered to do research to fill out the story of the old seaport. Alan, a quiet, reserved employee of the New York Central Railroad, lived in nearby Seward Housing. He was also an expert ship modeler, and we were delighted when he agreed to be exhibit chairman. Kent Barwick, a young member of the Municipal Art Society who worked in advertising, had both design ideas and thoughts for the historical message we planned to present to the public. Reassuringly, others turned out as well. Bob Ferraro was constantly at hand in our weekend outings to clean up the Augean mess we had to deal with before the actual work of building the exhibition could begin.

I daily blessed my bosses at Compton for allowing me time to work on plans for the future Seaport. In these crowded two weeks at Compton between 13 and 24 March, I met with a wide variety of people who might advance the Seaport cause. In the crowded pages of my desk calendar I see that Bill Moore, of Moore-McCormack Lines, which ran splendid steamers to South America, invited me to his office in Brooklyn to discuss the Seaport—a very happy new connection for us. And Charlie Lundgren came around to offer unstinting help, making seamanlike drawings of the project on call, while Frank Braynard was a fountainhead of ideas for the exhibit and for gathering new members for the Seaport. John H. G. Pell, scion of a Revolutionary War family, who presided over the Fort Ticonderoga restoration on Lake Champlain, called to invite me to lunch with friends at the Down Town Association, a bastion of Lower Manhattan society. Pell, who had joined the Seaport after reading about it, warned me that we had a big job ahead to win over the downtown community, which, he said, thought more of heroes of the American Revolution than the hard-driving sea captains who used their new freedom to make New York America's greatest seaport.

Among those he introduced me to was James Vanderpool, another scion of Old New York and the pioneering spirit behind New York City's landmarks law. Vanderpool, telling me he was near the end of his life, said he was too feeble to be of much use, but he saluted our efforts, which he said would add a vital new dimension to the city's historic heritage. This support from these two solons of the Downtown community, who had themselves contributed greatly to its heritage, was reassuring—and challenging, especially because we'd never asked their support. We would hardly have dared to, when the Landmarks Commission, largely created by their advocacy, had voted in favor of a different project. But these two people didn't wait to be asked; they volunteered their support and were ready to put their names on the line by inviting their friends to hear our story.

When Norma asked me how things had gone at our first lunch at the Down Town Association, I said: "You know, I'd never have thought it—everyone at the table spoke up for the Seaport. Now all we've got to do is meet their expectations."

CHAPTER 9

The Seaport in the Market, *April–May 1967*

Joe Cantalupo Stops By—Wertenbaker Write-up—
"Evening in South Street"—Kortum's Call for a Diva—
"Sail and Song"

All at once it was Monday, 27 March, our first day working for the Seaport. Dressed in rough work clothes, we turned to at our new offices at 16 Fulton Street for what could hardly be called a usual office day in New York. Wanting to get the office up and running as soon as possible, a gang of us had worked over the weekend to clear the ground floor, tearing down an unwanted partition, ripping out unneeded shelves, and gathering up drifts of papers left behind by the previous tenants. Now we went to work carting the debris outside, making a messy hill of rubbish on the sidewalk. Bob Ferraro, who had taken the week off to lend a hand, set about painting the front door a pristine white, signalling to passersby that something new was afoot inside. Meanwhile, two more volunteers joined Norma and me in a thorough sweepdown of ceiling, walls and floors in preparation for scrubbing with soap and water before receiving the desk and chairs Dick Rath had secured to bring down after work. These household tasks took place under an overarching sense of far-reaching purpose, while as the place grew cleaner, we ourselves grew steadily dirtier.

It was in this confused scene of activity that Joe Cantalupo walked up to our doorstep and into our lives.

Around eleven in the morning a commanding, heavy-set figure under a broad-brimmed hat appeared in our doorway, glowering. "Who told you people you could pay my man to move that garbage outside?"

We certainly didn't want trouble with the Fish Market.

"We asked around and were told everyone uses Cantalupo," I said. "Isn't that right?"

"I am Cantalupo and you can't pay me," said the heavy man. Silence. Then a smile broke across the man's face.

"I am Joe Cantalupo. I'm a member of your museum, and Cantalupo Carting is contributing your garbage removal. So you really *can't* pay for it!"

Reaching across to shake hands with Norma and me, and with a smile now as broad as all outdoors, he continued: "I've been waiting for you guys to turn up. What took you so long?"

We explained that we had just quit our jobs to go to work to save the old buildings and cobbled streets and to bring back some of the wind-driven ships that had sailed from this waterfront. Joe smiled, held up both hands in a very New York, "enough, already" gesture—he was fluent in the argot and signage of street discourse, as we were to learn—and gently reminded us that he was a paid-up member of the Seaport Museum.

"I do read the *South Street Reporter*," he said, "every word of it." He went on to say it was chilly talking like this in the street, so we invited him in. Joe excused himself, saying "Just a minute," and left us, walking up Fulton Street with a baronial stride—a man at home in his community and counting for something in it. When he returned it was with paper cups of hot coffee for our little group of half a dozen people. He was an attentive listener as we described what we had in mind for the gallery.

While we talked he told us a little about himself. He spoke of how his father, Pasquale, had immigrated from Salerno and founded Cantalupo Carting in 1894, when fishing boats came into the market piers under sail. Encamped at first in the crowded tenement purlieus above the Brooklyn Bridge, the family had moved out to Ocean Parkway, Brooklyn, as soon as they'd saved enough money. The Brooklyn Bridge, at the north end of our district, was for them, as for many, an arched way to freedom soaring above the mean streets of the Lower East Side.

Joe, a true son of the Fish Market, became also a citizen of a wider world. He had signed up as a Seaport member in response to an item about the Seaport idea in Bennett Cerf's "Trade Winds" column in the *Saturday Review of Literature*—a journal now long gone from the scene, which in its day took pride in sharing great ideas with common people.

Joe, we were to learn, was also a long-standing member of the Municipal Art Society, the civic organization that had backed Senator Seymour's bill for a maritime museum in Schermerhorn Row. He was also a close friend of Joe Mitchell, the writer of vignettes of waterfront life for the *New Yorker* and author of *The Bottom of the Harbor* and other books on waterfront life. Joe also maintained a collection of photographs and artifacts of the Market in his small office. This was on the second floor over a garage, where his spotlessly clean garbage trucks, painted dark green with gold scrollwork, were kept. He and Joe Mitchell collaborated to save terra-cotta statuary from the cornices of the old Market building, razed a dozen years before our arrival on the scene. They even saved some columns from the neoclassical Pennsylvania Station on the West Side, whose demolition had led to the foundation of the New York City Landmarks Preservation Commission.

These things did not come up all at once, of course, but it was evident he wanted us to know his story, and from the outset it was clear that he wanted to know about us and our curious venture. He made it his practice to stop by each day to check in, usually about eleven o'clock in the morning, when cleanup in the Market was completed. He usually turned up carrying coffee for whoever was cleaning, carpentering or painting in 16 Fulton Street, always with words of encouragement and the latest Market stories. And he made an act of feigned amazement at how hard we were all going at our jobs and how dirty we got doing them.

Years later, interviewed by a Midwestern newspaper, he commented on these days of hard work and high hopes:

> *We started with 50 feet of space and $100 at 16 Fulton Street.*
> *These tough characters around here saw me in there painting*
> *with Peter and his wife and a bunch of kids. They thought I was*
> *freaked out. But we kept going.*

Work continued on the physical cleanup of our ground floor exhibition room, as well as on the dusty space upstairs. Karen Herbert, the gentle but determined wife of our lead volunteer, Robert G. Herbert, scrubbed walls, floors and glassed partitions until it all gleamed, setting a standard for the rest of us. Bob's specialty was reviewing everything we wrote for nautical accuracy. To that task he brought his experience in ships ranging from Gloucester fishing schooners to Pacific Coast freighters, and he pursued his mission with sharp-tongued relish and nearly infallible accuracy. He was also a skilled draftsman and fine modelmaker, as we came to learn.

The Herberts were a remarkable case of the skilled and dedicated volunteers who appeared out of our membership as the task of cleaning up and refurbishing our headquarters progressed. Several weeks into the project I made a curious entry in my journal on progress:

> Cold and dirty but work progresses. As of tonight it seems aston-
> ishing how it has progressed; we seem to be good at this job. But
> it also seems most likely that others will take it over, and our role,
> amid success, is threatened. Can't be helped. We may get our point
> of view across and we may, with luck, get to carry the Seaport
> further. . . . We may sell, and publish, books. Much of what we do
> can't well be torn down.

It is difficult to put a finger on what made us apprehensive about the possible takeover of the Seaport project by outside forces, but both Norma and I shared an odd feeling that this might happen. We had noticed the speculative glances Wall Street businessmen would cast at our Spartan headquarters. And the new buildings rising south of us, shimmering with slick surfaces of glass and steel, were getting ever closer, moving northward behind the sound of bulldozers and riveters.

Setting out to have a public gallery as part of our headquarters, however, opened up new possibilities. Recognition by the press and local word-of-mouth brought us new people eager to work on the gallery project. Bob Herbert and his wife Karen were forerunners of others—people with new ideas and skills whom we would never have met without having this project open to the public. George Campbell, architect of the restoration of the English tea clipper *Cutty Sark* in London, walked in our door to volunteer his services, equipping us at a stroke with a depth of background in historic ship restoration. Others volunteered their services in such vital tasks as manning the reception desk, teaching seamanship classes, researching local history, and other endless activities to build public participation in the Seaport Museum.

This influx of people and ideas brought about a major shift in the purpose of the headquarters/gallery project from a promotional outlet and meeting place to the beginnings of the Seaport Museum itself!

This shift was foreshadowed in a chance interview on our venture conducted by a young writer at the *New Yorker* who, having read about the Seaport, invited me up to his office for a chat just a week after Norma and I had quit our jobs and two days after our dinner meeting at Sweet's with Joan Davidson—a session which had us re-thinking what we would be presenting to the public in our proposed gallery. Young Bill Wertenbaker was prepared, I imagine, to write up another of the Fish Market characters Joe Mitchell had introduced to *New Yorker* readers. Instead, finding himself caught up in our scheme of a restored Seaport, he wrote what became a serious review of the whole South Street venture. The story, killed by the editors, never appeared in the magazine, but Bill saved the galley proofs, which he sent to me. The proofs made it clear that we saw the Seaport with the river as a vital part of the scene—as it had been in history. His story described the project as we then saw it with this quote:

> *The three rows of old buildings we want to save surround the Fulton Fish Market. The fourth side is the river itself. We'd have a maritime museum in the buildings and—because we want this to be a part of the city that people come to and not just an exhibit for tourists—also shops and offices associated with shipping, not excluding the ones that are already there, like Sweet's Restaurant, Sloppy Louie's and Eagle Bag & Burlap, a famous old curio shop. People should come down with their families, the poor as well as people with money in their pockets . . . .*

The restored Seaport was to be a living part of the city, one that went back to its origins.

> *A hundred years ago, South Street was all little shipping offices and stores—chandlers, sailmakers, and brokers, who functioned*

while walking up and down the street. They all vanished, and
with them their housing, except our little enclave, which the fishing
business—the most archaic business in the world—has kept intact.

But these origins were alive with the city's future—very alive, I pointed
out:

When New York was becoming a great seaport, it was at South
Street that things were happening.

The happenings ranged from New York's sending the first American
ship to China just weeks after the British evacuated the city in 1783,
to the sailing of the first regularly scheduled packet ship, *James Monroe*,
to England in 1818—and America's ensuing rise to dominance of the
North Atlantic trade.

The opening of the Erie Canal soon contributed unbelievably to
South Street; it lowered the cost of getting a ton of grain to New
York from a hundred dollars to six, and Midwest grain came on
the world market on such a major scale that soon much of Europe
would have gone hungry if deprived of it. The grain went out from
South Street, bought and sold in these little brokerages. . . . Until
the eighteen-fifties, the ships were built along here, too—built at
Corlears Hook, outfitted at Rutgers Slip, and loaded at Maiden
Lane. Great hotels were built for people with business on South
Street. One of the last of them, Meyer's, still stands. Today, it's a
seamen's home, adjacent to the buildings that we want to save. In
fact, we'd like to see it refurbished and added to the South Street
Seaport.

I went on to talk about Captain N. B. Palmer, "who kept hounding his
owners to build him a faster ship," until they built his ship *Houqua*, precursor of the China clippers, soon followed by the famous *Rainbow*, the
ship "with her bows turned inside out," generally reckoned the first of
the extreme clippers. I dwelt on the achievements of the clipper ships,
which Norma and I had discussed with Joan Davidson only a few days
earlier. Although "overmanned, expensive, and short-lived," they were
the fastest sailing ships ever built and the most beautiful, with names

that spoke for their era: "*Young America*—what a name for a ship!—and *Herald of the Morning, Flying Cloud, Neptune's Car.*"

We could not bring in a clipper from that vanished world, which, except for England's clipper *Cutty Sark,* now existed only in song and story, but we were resolved to bring in their more workaday successors, which closed out the era of working sail—the deepwater square rigger *Kaiulani* and the schooners *Effie M. Morrissey* (surviving today as *Ernestina*), *Lady of Good Voyage* and *Emma C. Berry* (now at Mystic in her original sloop rig). "Any of them," I said, "could come to New York."

Bill ended his story with news from the headquarters:

> *When we tried to reach Mr. Stanford to check the clipper-ship names and dates he'd mentioned, he called back from an office in a converted fish stall in one of Peter Schermerhorn's buildings of 1811, at 16 Fulton Street, where South Street Seaport now has its headquarters, and where the volunteers who have rallied to this project to save the last of the clipper-ship waterfronts will now repair to hold their meetings and plot the return of tall sailing ships to South Street.*

Once our phone was installed, we felt we were truly in business, in buildings that were more than a generation old when the first China clippers stood downstream outside their windows. An early call was to Karl Kortum. I waited till the seagulls that wheeled perpetually over the fish market started a prolonged screeching outside the window before making this call, and I could hear Karl's answering chuckle from the other end. He got the message—we were at last installed on the working waterfront where we had dreamed of being.

At the end of our second week, on a balmy Friday evening, 7 April, we held our first public event in South Street. This was sponsored for us by the World Ship Society, led by John Rodgers, a young maritime lawyer. Announced in our *South Street Reporter* as a walking tour and dinner on the "Street of Ships," it drew to the scene over two hundred of our own members, many of whom we'd never met, as well as a hundred-odd

World Ship Society members, for a total of 350 people. Escorted by well-informed World Ship volunteers, this sizeable group walked from Fulton Street seven blocks south to the Seamen's Church Institute on Coenties Slip—just past the bar that Norma, Jim Kirk and I stopped by to end our Sunday afternoon walks.

It was good to be following this familiar route, past the street signs for Burling Slip, Fletcher Street, Maiden Lane, Wall Street and Cuyler's Alley, names straight out of history, in streets deserted in our weekend peregrinations but now crowded with people talking, laughing and telling their own stories about the district. Our hundreds of people crowded into the great dining hall of Seamen's Church Institute, where after a simple but festive supper, Ed Stackpole regaled us with a slide show on the maritime heritage which was at the heart of our museum's purpose.

Ed had seemed to us a shy, rather quiet person, but on stage he turned out to be a savvy raconteur, who knew just what moved our people, what tickled their sense of humor, and what gave them a sense of occasion—a positive conviction that something important was taking shape, and that they all were part of it.

It was natural, he said, for islanders in Nantucket to know the world's oceans and the story of American voyages in distant waters. But it was from South Street that the great voyages leading to worldwide trade and human interchange were made—and we were here at last to tell that story, here where it happened, in the Street of Ships.

We then saw a brief NBC-TV film clip with Monk Farnham and me explaining the project, which gave a sense of immediacy to things. Chairman John Rogers, winding things up, compared the event to the sailing of the clipper *Flying Cloud* on her record-breaking maiden voyage to San Francisco in June 1851. Then Ralph Urban, chairman of the Ship Lore & Model Club, rose to his feet to lead us all in a resonant bass rendition of "Rio"—that great hymn of a sea song that begins: "The oak, the ash, the bonnie birch tree—and away, Rio!—they're all growing green in the north country." We walked out of the Institute's majestic entrance hall, guarded by a ship's figurehead of Sir Galahad in armor, with the final chorus ringing in our ears: " So fare thee well, my bonnie young girl, we are bound for the Rio Grande."

Norma and I were rather quiet on the hour-long drive home to Yorktown Heights, awed by the outpouring of support for the project we had seen. This bolstered our spirits for the actual opening of the museum, which we had resolved would take place on Monday, 22 May—National Maritime Day.

Deep groundswell forces were also moving through the South Street project, beneath the concatenation of events, laughter, confusion, woes and joys of the headquarters project. Norma and I would catch up on them at home in Yorktown Heights, or during the drive to or from work each day—times we could talk at length, undistracted by our surroundings.

Foremost among these developments was the growing presence of Karl Kortum in our work. His involvement did much to establish our credentials with people who might have raised a quizzical eyebrow at our relative youth and absolute lack of museum experience. The credentials were less important, however, than the depth and resonance that he lent to our thinking about our work.

This had begun in early 1966 when Anita Ventura responded to Norma's letter with her own advice in Kortum's absence, and had continued with that extraordinary response to my letter of a year later, as described in chapter seven. She perfectly understood Norma's and my admiration for Karl Kortum's work, noting that his operations amazed her "for their scope and the high style in which he performs this seemingly impossible feat of moving enormous hulks about the world and finding them a place to live on in the public view."

And she asserted: "Your true public should be the families and children of New York." Visitors to the city and historians were important, but the active interest of ordinary New Yorkers was critical.

Anita mentioned Mark di Suvero as a prospective supporter, the distinguished sculptor who lived in a huge attic apartment right under the lofty roof beams of Schermerhorn Row. And she knew the *New York*

Times art critic Hilton Kramer. "But these types aren't quite right, are they?" she added, knowing we needed developers and realistic city planner types. But then she added a peroration which made both Norma and me feel that Kortum was leaning over her shoulder at the typewriter:

> *I am sure, however, that the first thing you need is something real that will speak of the reality of the time you want to illustrate, and with a tangible proof of your intentions and ability to preserve the sense of the rich history of your area. Of course I mean a great ship, and that is the thing that takes doing.*

Karl's and my subsequent letters and phone conversation centered on getting a major square-rigged ship on the waterfront—the ship that Anita had called for in her letter. Karl knew of our interest in the bark *Kaiulani*, in which he'd sailed before the mast in a Cape Horn voyage twenty-six years earlier, just as America entered World War II. Built in 1899 in Sewall's yard in Bath, Maine, and now a battered, mastless hulk in the Philippines, *Kaiulani* was the last surviving example of the Down Easters, the Maine-built ships which had concluded the story of American square-rigged deepwatermen. Karl's voyage in her had gone from Port Townsend, Washington, around the Horn to Durban, South Africa, with a cargo of Oregon pine, and thence on to Sydney, Australia, with war supplies. There, *Kaiulani* was commandeered and cut down to a barge to carry supplies for MacArthur's army in its advance along the north coast of New Guinea against the Japanese invaders. At Karl's bidding the National Maritime Historical Society had been formed in 1963 to save the *Kaiulani*. The plan was to restore and re-rig the ship in the Far East and sail her home to be installed as a museum ship in Washington, DC.

In response to an ad we'd seen inviting support, Norma and I had both signed on as members of the society in 1965. Things had not worked out for the old ship, however, and I had called the society's president, Alan Hutchison, to discuss the prospects of bringing her into New York. She had put into New York for repairs in 1900 after being partially dismasted on her delivery voyage around Cape Horn to San Francisco to serve in the packet trade to Hawaii. As her captain had explained, "New York seemed the best place to go," and we cited this judgment in our case for bringing the ship to South Street.

But we couldn't come up with the guarantees Hutchison called for. Kortum then said that if the *Kaiulani* wasn't coming to New York, then we should go after some other ship—or ships. His advice on this was vintage Kortum:

> *I think that you will need at least three large, deepwater, square-rigged ships—a couple with figureheads—to complete your scene there. What originally stirred me about the Mystic project was the multiple square-rigger concept of Carl Cutler.*

And, knowing our feeling for schooners, he added:

> *Schooners are just spear carriers for square riggers, which are divas.*

Along with these Wagnerian words he sent us a sheet on the admission earnings of the ship *Balclutha* in the ten years she'd been installed on his museum's waterfront.

With this compelling picture in our minds we went back to work on the day-to-day tasks of setting up our office and building the South Street historical exhibit. More and more our thinking began to center on the presence of a great square-rigged ship on our waterfront.

Wintry blasts cut short the halcyon weather we'd had for our "Evening in South Street," and in our drafty, unheated headquarters we had to stop to warm up fingers after each bout of typing. So on Saturday, 10 April, Norma and I retreated to the National Committee for an Effective Congress headquarters in midtown to produce the May issue of the *South Street Reporter* on their fine electric typewriters. Norma had worked there for about three years before she quit to go to work for the Seaport. It was warm, bright and clean in the quiet NCEC offices. We worked all day and past midnight to get this issue right. We finally settled on a front page featuring Norma and me at the desk in Fulton Street, with the tongue-and-groove wainscoting behind us—a first step toward civilizing the barren space with its garage-door entrance. A pile of lumber with a pair of one-gallon paint cans made it clear that this was a work in progress.

Under a banner headline "Sail & Song–May 22" we announced plans for the opening of the headquarters exhibit to be followed by walking tours of the Seaport district with a party coming in by schooner to declare the South Street Seaport Museum open to the public. All this would be accompanied by traditional sea songs led by Ralph Urban of the Ship Lore & Model Club, and *Reporter* readers were grandly informed: "The public is more than welcome—they will be needed to sing the schooners in."

CHAPTER 10

Athena Opens the Museum, *May 1967*

Athena as Flagbearer—Karl and Jean Kortum Arrive—
Opening Reception—The Exhibition—
Sailing Downriver—Welcoming Crowds

The museum would be opened from the sea, so it would be known from
the outset as a place of seaborne comings and goings. And, we decided,
our message of the heritage of seafaring under sail would be delivered
by our schooner *Athena*, as a lineal descendant of the Gloucester schooners that once thronged the Fulton Fish Market. We remembered how
working people had leaned out of their factory windows to salute the old
schooner as she ghosted into Gloucester Harbor under full sail the year
before. Her role in the Seaport had been more than passive, the essential
ideas of the venture having been shaped in meetings with old salts and
young volunteers gathered around her cabin table.

And the date of this arrival by sail? Monday, 22 May, seemed made
to order, since the date had been designated National Maritime Day by
President Franklin Roosevelt in 1933, early in his administration. We'd
bring in Herb Halberg to represent the City as Commissioner of Ports
and Terminals, and Karl Kortum to represent San Francisco, a city largely
settled by tall ships sailing from South Street by way of Cape Horn. The
sea-worn ships of Karl's museum had started us on the road to opening
the new Seaport Museum, so he should be there on its opening day.
We'd found the dollars to fly Karl and his wife, Jean (an ardent urban
preservationist in her own right), to New York.

Accordingly, Friday 19 May found us battling weekend traffic to pick up
Karl and Jean at JFK Airport. When at last we met Karl face-to-face,
he turned out to be a tall man of about 50, square of countenance and
deliberate of speech; Jean was a slender, bright-eyed and quick-witted
counterpart to Karl's battleship pace and demeanor. As we drove back

into the city, Karl fired off a few ranging shots about the Seaport project and, particularly, our need for a great ship to give it the proper identity as a seaport. A ship, he was to write me later, "sends out emanations of lore, humanity, history, adventure, geography, art, literature . . ." These things, indeed, were what we felt our museum should be about.

Moreover, he now had a new ship in mind, to fill in if we couldn't get his old ship, *Kaiulani*. Discussions with Alan Hutchison of the National Maritime Historical Society had shown this might well be the case. Karl made much of the new ship, whose name and location were secret. She was a classic full-rigger of 1885, now cut down and serving as a sand barge in South America. She was British, but had traded to New York among other ports around the globe. An ad hoc luncheon with our Ship Committee had confirmed our interest in the vessel and we were eager to learn more from Karl, the discoverer of the ship, who had actually walked her decks. During his visit we came to know the ship and why she mattered. She mattered plenty. And she was to change our course for the museum and Norma's and my lives.

We left the Kortums at the Washington Square Hotel at the foot of Fifth Avenue, and they spent the weekend visiting museums and walking city streets.

Meanwhile, Norma and I had a busy weekend before us to prepare for opening day on Monday. Karl called two good friends to join us aboard *Athena* for opening day: the Cape Horn sailorman Captain Archie Horka, who'd gone on to a distinguished career in steamers in the US merchant marine, and the Australian marine artist Os Brett, who had served as a merchant mariner in World War II. We would have real seamen aboard when we sailed into South Street.

On Saturday, we readied *Athena* for the trip to Manhattan after her winter lay-up, and on Sunday Norma, Jim Kirk, David Johnston and I brought *Athena* down from the Bronx to the 23rd Street marina. We hadn't completed bending on the sails, so we did this underway. During this operation, Norma went up the mainmast in a bosun's chair to reeve off the throat halyard. But the peak halyard block on which we had hoisted her jammed and threatened to let go, leaving her stranded precariously forty-odd feet above the deck. By the time we improvised a second bosun's chair, the schooner had come into the rough water of Hell Gate, a stretch of violently swirling currents that jerked the schooner about unmercifully while Norma hung on for dear life. When we came into smoother water in the East River, we sent up a second chair on the fisherman staysail halyard (Oh, the glories of the multiple halyards on each mast in the schooner rig!), which Norma shifted to, and so was brought safely down on deck in time to help secure our mooring lines at the marina and go ashore.

From there we hurried downtown to join the volunteer crew working on the exhibit at 16 Fulton Street, due to open at noon the next day. In this preview midday reception before the public opening that evening, we saw a grand opportunity to renew ties with Senator Seymour, honoring him as author of the State Maritime Museum bill. Seymour had been president of the Municipal Art Society before being elected to the State Senate. Advised by our astute and helpful friend Margot Gayle, we invited the trustees of the Municipal Art Society to attend this reception. The work to bring all this about was performed by Kent Barwick, a young copywriter at the ad agency Batten, Barton, Durstine & Osborne (or "BBD & O," memorialized by Dorothy Parker as a name which sounds like a suitcase falling downstairs). Kent had worked as writer, carpenter and critic in the construction of our exhibit, and he now turned out to have a sure sense of protocol and connections in the right places.

"Is this the right place?" asked Ruth McAneny Loud, president of the Municipal Art Society. She stood in the doorway (where Joe Cantalupo had announced his presence two months earlier), a small but solid, tweed-clad figure who conveyed a sense of presence equal to Joe's, but in a quite different genre. Norma looked up from the pile of wood chips she was sweeping, and glanced involuntarily at her watch. This formidable guest was ten minutes early—and every minute counted in the final cleanup before guests arrived at noon.

"Yes, this is the South Street Seaport Museum," said Norma with a smile, deciding it was best to assume this was what our visitor meant by "the right place." She added: "We certainly hope we're the right place."

And this seemed to be the right thing to say. "Perfectly charming," said Mrs. Loud, and, correctly assuming that Norma had other duties than charwoman, she came in to introduce herself and said the others would be along as soon as they found a place to park. "We weren't quite sure where this was," she explained. "But it's a fascinating corner of the city, practically in the shadow of the Brooklyn Bridge. I look forward to knowing it better."

And we looked forward to knowing her better. We'd seen few people of her standing in our premises, save for Mike Seymour and Margot Gayle, but they of course had been interested in the neighborhood long before we came along. We needed to establish those uptown connections with people who supported New York City's great museums. And Mrs. Loud, for her part, did her duty, managing to meet every one of our own people, as the gallery filled up with a wonderfully variegated crowd.

Barbara Johnson, a doyenne of the Museum of American Folk Arts, had given us an imaginative gift for the reception: the services of her butler, Kirsch Masson, who, in formal attire, passed among us puffing with European formality, handing out plates of excellent cold lobster imported from Sweet's restaurant a few doors down the row.

We had thrown a tablecloth over the battered reception desk just inside the door, and I stood behind this improvised bar, popping open bottles of champagne and filling people's glasses with this and stronger stuff. Eventually, however, someone insisted on relieving me as bartender, and I steered out among the roomful of people.

I soon ran into conversation that held my attention. Karl Kortum was laying down the law to our guest of honor, Mike Seymour. Maritime museums, he stated, should be "temples of excellence," devoted to the realities of seafaring, and without historic ships a maritime museum was just a house of paper, weighted down perhaps with a few artifacts and ship models; interesting enough, but no substitute for the real thing—the ship herself. The challenge now, Karl continued, was to save the few great ocean voyagers remaining from the age of sail.

Mike listened carefully, interested to learn about the historic ships surviving in odd corners of the ocean world. The world of historic ships was new to him, but the world of museums was not. And from Karl he learned how the public interest in the historic ships on the waterfront had led William Matson Roth, a sympathetic developer who served on the board of the San Francisco Maritime Museum, to take on Ghirardelli Square, remodeling Mr. Ghirardelli's huge, sprawling chocolate factory on the North Beach into a lively complex of retail shops and restaurants overlooking San Francisco Bay—effectively launching what became known as the San Francisco Waterfront Renaissance.

Everyone knew about that, but few knew how Karl had convinced the elderly Mr. Ghirardelli to sell to Roth by promising that the name Ghirardelli, spelled out in soaring letters against the sky, would be preserved in the new center. Fewer still were aware of Jean Kortum's valiant campaign that stopped the eastward march of high-rise luxury flats just before they trampled down Ghirardelli Square, or her earlier achievement in arresting the snakelike progress of the Embarcadero Expressway before it reached the Ghirardelli waterfront.

People listened to Karl's account of these things. An incidental effect of his visit was that our guests—all of whom knew about Ghirardelli Square—learned that the *Gh* in *Ghirardelli* is pronounced with a hard G, as in *gear*, rather than the soft *G* that had sprung up in civic circles in New York.

So the festivities continued, with quite a few of our visitors stopping to read the fact-filled captions we had written for our exhibit *South Street—the Street of Ships*. Told in a flowing narrative style, we began our story with the creation of South Street from landfill after the American Revolution, following on through the establishment of packet lines, and the clipper era as the apogee of South Street as the Street of Ships; then taking on the rise of steamers on the other side of Manhattan, and ending up with the tall Down Easters of the

Cape Horn trade, the fish market and coastal schooner trades as the last of working sail.

All this was told with prints and drawings of the time and with quotations from the people who had walked the streets of the burgeoning seaport. People like a good story and this one was new to most of them.

Original watercolors by the marine artist Commander E. C. Tufnell brought the clipper era colorfully to life with hurrying ships amid foaming seas. Commissioned by our trustee Melvin Conant, these ship portraits brought lively color to our walls, celebrating that remarkable decade when American ships broke records in all oceans. Their evocative names—*Flying Cloud, Young America, Herald of the Morning*—fascinated Melvin, who later wrote a booklet on them, *Heralds of Their Age.*

And in the middle of things stood Leevi Kiil's project model, with the surviving buildings and the historic ships we planned to save shown in safe harbor at the piers along South Street.

My principal contribution to the exhibit was to insist on a photo mural to cover the entire back wall. The photo, taken by Karl aboard the *Kaiulani* on her Cape Horn passage of 1941–42, showed three men aloft, bent over the yard, working together to subdue the main upper topgallant sail in the face of an advancing squall. The immensity of the wind-lashed sea behind them stretches to the horizon, and the menace in the lowering sky is palpable. Karl's photo caught the aloneness of the hunched men working against these primordial forces—and their cohesion in the face of imminent challenge.

Our gang had objected to the huge size of this picture. It took a big chunk out of our budget and it dwarfed every other image in the place. But it showed what we were about: the ship and her people making a voyage. With its amplitude of space, and its puny figures etched against the sky, the haunting image added depth of meaning to all our other pictures.

That afternoon it was a strange crew that gathered on *Athena*'s decks at the 23rd Street marina, bound on a strange mission. This was nothing less than to reawaken a forgotten history in a forgotten stretch of the waterfront where our predecessors had built a city from the sea. There were sixteen of us aboard: Karl Kortum and Jean Kortum; their friends, the Cape Horn veteran Archie Horka and the marine artist Os Brett with his wife, Gertrude. Then there was Herb Halberg, Commissioner of Marine & Aviation, an unwavering supporter of the Seaport project, who pushed us only to get on with it before we were preempted by the bulldozers that were reshaping Lower Manhattan. With him was his fiancée, Anita, soon to become his wife. And then there were Jim Kirk; David Johnston, Bob Ferraro, Norma, my eight-year-old son Thomas, and a few others.

We still had some minor rigging work to do when we stepped aboard *Athena*, and the seamen stepped forward to help in tying off and coiling down. I noticed that Karl, Archie and Os were careful to watch how Norma, Tommy and I did things and dutifully followed our procedures. I was reminded of the sailorly adage: "Different ships, different long splices," meaning that things must be done the ship's way, to prevent confusions on a dark blowy night with half the gear under surging water.

We made sail as soon as we were clear of the marina, hoisting main, foresail, staysail and jib together, with the abundance of ready manpower we had aboard. At first I was a bit nervous about the crowd of people aboard in city clothes cumbering the decks. But with Norma at the mainmast, David at the fore, Tommy slithering out on the bowsprit to cast off the jib, and others pulling on lines as they were directed, we soon had all plain sail set. The flapping canvas was quickly sheeted home and the schooner leaned over to the damp southeasterly wind that ruffled the river water. When I switched off the engine one could hear the susurrus of broken water at the bow as *Athena* forged ahead. We were going to be able to do the passage in proper fashion—under sail! People who had been looking this way and that, unsure of how to comport themselves on this antique wooden structure moving through the heart of the towering city, smiled at each other and began commenting on the passing shoreline, dominated on the Manhattan side by the huge smokestacks of the 14th Street power station.

Ahead of us lay the Williamsburg Bridge, a rather brutal-looking structure, younger than its serene brethren, the Brooklyn and Manhattan bridges to the south. As we approached, it appeared that our slender topmast would catch and break against the steel girders overhead. This is a familiar illusion that anyone passing under bridges feels, though in our case our spar rose to less than half the height of the bridge. Years later, I learned how careless riggers had failed to lower a spar of the *Edward Sewall* that would not clear, so the spanker topmast broke and the gold ball at its head came crashing down in a manner that would have killed the young helmsman, had not the skipper ordered him to step away quickly. This was in 1916. It was the young helmsman, Adrian Raynaud of Seattle, who told me this story in 1982, sixty-six years after the incident, which, since he enjoyed being alive, he was not about to forget.

Well, each stretch of this river was full of memories like that, others and my own. Just before the Manhattan Bridge, Wallabout Channel opened up on the Brooklyn shore on our left, leading to the great docks of the Brooklyn Navy Yard, which launched a mighty fleet of warships in World War II—aircraft carriers, super battleships, cruisers and destroyers—all the while repairing battle-damaged US and Allied warships to fight again.

I had visited the Navy Yard during World War II with my father, then a lieutenant commander in the Navy stationed in New London. On one visit we went to see his sailing pal, Jack Allen, who was serving aboard a US Coast Guard cutter undergoing refit. As a high school student I had helped compile ships' data for Critchell Rimington's *Fighting Fleets* and was awed to encounter the gaunt grey ship herself, in from hard and perilous service in the Battle of the Atlantic. People seemed largely unaware of that critical struggle being fought just outside our harbor, on which the outcome of history's most terrible war depended. But I followed the harrowing losses reported in the press, and at lunch with the ship's officers, they met one teenager at least who knew, at least on paper, the unending fight against the U-boats waged on the city's doorstep.

Coming round the river's bend to the southwest after the Williamsburg Bridge, we were able to start the sheets of all the sails—that is, slack them off just a bit—as the wind now came broader on the beam. We now had a little margin to play with if the wind, always shifty in the river, came ahead. As *Athena* straightened out on her new course she picked up a little speed, and the whisper under her bows grew to a chuckling murmur. Under our lee were the clunky red brick buildings of LaGuardia Houses, where we had made some good friends in campaigning for the Rutgers Club, and ahead lay the Manhattan Bridge, an elegant complement to its noble sister, the fabled Brooklyn Bridge just beyond. We cleared these bridges with oohs and aahs from our gathered crew, who saw renewed peril as our mast tops approached each span.

To port we could see the rising hill of Brooklyn Heights, where I'd lived for my first thirteen years. The district was then still haunted by the steam whistles of shipping thronging the harbor, and for me alive with memories of things like my brother John losing control of his tricycle and hurtling down the steep sidewalk to the East River, until stopped by a hydrant at the cost of a bloody nose; and of visiting the waterfront with my father on a rainy Sunday to climb into an empty freight car and there paint our separate portraits of a South American steamer lying at a pier, whose name I wrote down as *Caribobo*. (In the 1980s, I returned to that waterfront to work in the National Maritime Historical Society headquarters in Fulton Ferry Landing, when one morning I saw the stern of a huge ship out our windows— a recent replacement for the old *Caribao*. No wonder my search for the *Caribobo* led nowhere.)

Then suddenly it was time to get canvas off the schooner and coast into the slip between the Fish Market Pier and Pier 16. The sails were doused with commendable speed and we glided into our landing gently, with the engine just turning over in neutral in case it was needed. Already in the slip and awaiting our arrival was the schooner *Volante*, a handsome vessel whose name echoed that of the immortal *Flying Cloud*.

Our arrival signaled the beginning of the song-singing, and, once we'd scrambled onto the pier, the speechmaking and general festivities began.

I first introduced Commissioner Halberg (who would be our landlord on these piers!). He delivered a first-class campaign speech, just what the occasion called for, radiating self-assurance and a businesslike outlook which gave the feeling of solid underpinnings to our somewhat ethereal vision of a center of shops, pubs, galleries and restored ships where people could enter into the experience of long-gone generations. "The museum," Herb concluded, "by bringing people down to the water's edge to celebrate the marriage of land and sea, will stress to the visitor New York's place as a world port."

Then Karl spoke with quiet conviction of the importance of historic ships, and the need to move fast to save what was left of them. My own talk was brief, dwelling on the idea that the Seaport would bring new life to South Street—and that we here assembled were the beginning of that life. It was up to us to make it happen. The rest of the evening passed in a kind of blur for me, saying hello to people I knew and many I didn't. The important thing was that the people were there!

And they were a happy crew, exalted by the project and the occasion. As a story in the Greenwich Village paper *The Villager* reported:

> Nearly 400 of what must have been the friendliest and most festive group in town were at the east end of Fulton Street Monday night to sing, cheer, walk and browse their way through the new South Street Museum.

The reporter described our gallery as "a small museum of drawings, engravings, ship models, and reprints from early publications concerning the New York seaport." The story went on to mention the volunteer guides who took groups through the neighborhood, recounting its history and pointing out such architectural features as the starfish pattern of tie rods and other maritime designs.

The writer also noted the "chilly winds" that were blowing and quoted our friend Angela Phelan, one of the guides, as saying the winds were a blessing since they enabled us to bring the *Athena* into South Street under sail. After the speeches there were sea chanteys, including "Fire Down Below" and "Leave Her Johnny," and then a hot Dixieland session by the Smith Street Jazz Band

which brought out the toe-tapping of everybody and a snappy Charleston from one couple.

Karl and Jean, ending their stay at the Washington Square Hotel, rode home with Norma and me to Yorktown Heights that evening. In our cramped Volkswagen we swept along, borne up by evening's flood tide of good will. We chattered like magpies, and Norma and I sang a chorus to one or two of the songs. It was a relief to know that all the arrangements had worked, that the people had come, and if the major newspapers had not, we had something more important going for us, which we knew would go on working for us: people. "Our kind of people," as Joe Cantalupo was wont to call them, had turned out and were clearly of a mind to turn out again.

Karl was visibly impressed; he shared in the elated feelings of the hundreds of souls who had turned out at night in a deserted industrial neighborhood. And *Athena*, clearly, had won his wholehearted approval. "That's a real schooner," he said. "A dyed-in-the-wool Down Easter." And he went on to tell us about Soule's yard, where *Athena* had been launched forty-two years before, an outfit that had been in business for the better part of a century and a half, sending tall square riggers to sea as well as coasting and fishing schooners. He said it was a privilege to sail aboard such a vessel.

At home in Yorktown Heights, as we sat with glasses of brandy in the kitchen before tramping upstairs to bed, Karl said a curious thing:

"You know, you're not going to be able to do both the schooner and the museum. It will have to be one thing or the other."

Norma and I looked at each other and then at Karl, aghast. He persisted: " You're not going to be able to keep the schooner and make this museum work."

Karl could speak bluntly on occasion, and this was such an occasion. Norma and I simultaneously decided to shrug off the remark, like water running off a duck's back. "Oh now, Karl, don't worry, we'll manage," we said. With this we said good night and made our ways to bed. What we meant was: You wait and see; we can do it.

CHAPTER 11

Kortum Finds a Ship for New York, *May–June 1967*

Kortum's World of Ships and Seamen—Fred Klebingat,
Villiers and Carr—The Great Britain *Quest—*
Discovery of Wavertree*—Karl Convinces Trustees*

The next morning, after a hearty breakfast followed by a walk around our hilly grounds, Jean, Norma, Karl and I drove into the city together. On the way we brought up Karl's strange remark that we could do the South Street project or *Athena* but not both. South Street with no *Athena*? Norma said this was a prime case for Pablo Casals's famous resolution of false dichotomies: "Why not do both?" Karl just shook his head at this. Norma teased him about it: "Don't be a bear, Karl. Why, of course we can do both. Just look at what happened yesterday! The waterfront came to life, full of happy people, with no museum, no historic ships, just the hope that it would all happen." Karl gave her an affectionate but distant look.

"It was wonderful, I'll give you that," he finally said, an Israelite prophet setting forth a stern, unwelcome judgment. "You've made a strong beginning, and that's important. My hat's off to you. But you've just embarked on a trip that will demand every waking hour, with no letup. No time for the schooner, no time for lots of things, even old friends, unless they're playing some part in making your Seaport happen. Just wait—you'll see.

"I'll do what I can to help," he added, "but it will come down again and again, and then again to just you two. You really don't know the extent of the demands, the reverses you'll come on, the upsets and backslidings—yes, they'll happen!— as well as the good moments like last night."

But to us, of course, *Athena* was part of that good moment and her very name argued the classic purposes of our venture: the dignity of man and the worth of human endeavor. Karl, curious about the schooner's name, had asked how she had come by it; and the night before, over brandies, we'd told him how we had chosen it in honor of the spirit of Periclean Athens. We had a great time with Karl and Jean, quoting Pericles' funeral oration and talking about civilization and barbarism and the American mission in the world.

As Karl, Jean, Norma and I roll through the spring countryside in our small, heavily laden Volkswagen, bound for lunch at India House with our prospective trustees Melvin Conant and Robert Tarr, it seems a good moment to get a fuller picture of the world of Karl Kortum. The saga of how he came to be the leader of a worldwide network of ship-lovers, scholars and sailors, who kept alive an awareness of historic ships, is an exciting one when you get into it, which explains why we listened so intently when he arrived among us New Yorkers.

Growing up in Petaluma, north of San Francisco Bay, Karl early began his quest for adventure in a world of wider horizons. He visited a friendly aunt across from San Francisco whose waterfront apartment looked out on the square riggers which still sailed north each spring, carrying crews for the Alaska fisheries, returning with canned salmon in the fall. This last American trade in deepwater sail died out in the early 1930s as Karl was entering his teens. Skipping college, he took to knocking about the city's harbor, doing odd waterfront jobs rather than go to work on the family chicken farm. To him the waterfront world, which then included laid-up sailing ships and their aged watchmen, opened wider horizons in space and time, an experience Karl deepened by omnivorous reading in nautical memoirs and histories and endless yarns, some true, some richly caparisoned with freshly contrived seamen's myth.

In the summer of 1941, well into these waterfront *wanderjahren*, Karl was helping the ship's watchman paint the big East Coast schooner *William H. Smith* when he spotted an incredible sight—a tall square rigger in Alameda Creek, with hands working aloft in the rigging! This turned out to be the Alaska Packers square rigger *Kaiulani* refitting for sea. Karl hastened over to the pier where she lay and persuaded Captain Hjalmar Wigsten to take him on for the old barque's voyage to South Africa by way of Cape Horn. While they were at sea, Pearl Harbor was attacked and the *Kaiulani* was re-directed to Australia. There, the

Kaiulani was commandeered by the US Army, cut down to a barge and used to support the advance in New Guinea. Karl joined the US Army Transportation Corps fleet supplying the advance and later went on to serve out the rest of the war on a hospital ship.

En route to that ending the *Kaiulani* had made history, sailed by a mixed crew of "old salts and college kids," as their skipper Wigsten described them. The young adventurers learned how to sail the 1,600-ton square rigger the hard way, picking up what they could from the old-timers who resented their eager ways and felt no compunction at not pulling their weight when there was young muscle available to do the hard work of trimming, reefing, setting and stowing the sails. This experience was of priceless value to Karl and his pal who had signed on with him, Harry Dring, who was to follow Karl into ship-keeping in the San Francisco Maritime Museum formed by Karl after World War II.

Karl's learning in the world of ships and ships' people had begun years before the *Kaiulani* voyage with his teen-age forays among the wrecks and hulks left over from the age of sail in San Francisco, and it certainly did not end now, afloat in *Kaiulani*, where he devoted his off-watch hours to hammering out the details of the experience of seagoing on a portable typewriter he had carried aboard as part of his sea kit.

When we met Karl he was deeply involved with interviewing old seamen, led by a remarkable old sea captain, Fred Klebingat, whose life luckily overlapped with ours long enough for him to contribute vital new learning to the story of square rig as we were to tell it in our exhibits and publications in South Street. After hard service in the run from Germany to San Francisco aboard the barque *Anna* in the early 1900s, Fred quit this world of battle with the screaming winds and crashing seas on the Cape Horn road to sign on with the gentler, easier-paced world of the South Seas schooners that traded among the Pacific islands. He then went on to serve as donkeyman (in charge of the small steam engine used for heavy lifting aboard the ships) and later as mate in the four-masted barque (formerly ship-rigged) *Falls of Clyde*.

He had been shipwrecked in Japan, sailed in Liberty ships in World War II and, when we met him in his eighties, was serving as relief mate in a converted Naval landing craft used as a coastal trading vessel. Karl talked with him, sailorman to sailorman, for years, taking down his words and then bringing the typed script back to Klebingat to have him add anything more he could remember. This painstaking process stimulated the old sailor's memory so that he was able to diagram obscure pieces of obsolete gear and repeat the watch bill and the orders given when the crew devised a way to tack the heavy *Falls of Clyde*, much larger than the trading schooners, without calling out the off-duty watch. This painting and overpainting gave a three-dimensional texture and resonance to Klebingat's words— making a narrative of strong evocative power.

Like most mortals, Karl was largely a product of his life experience, which was mainly of his own shaping. In 1965 Norma and I had been seized by the message of the ships he had brought into safe harbor in San Francisco; vessels that came to life in the stories of their people—owners, builders and seamen—told in Karl's words and exhibits that conveyed a sense of being in the presence of things that matter. And, as we were to learn, his deep affection for his native San Francisco made a walk with him through its sea-haunted streets an adventure in the seafaring experience.

Karl could readily grasp the stories of distant seafaring, because of the catholicity of the seafaring culture which enables a Sicilian boatman to understand the workings of a Chinese junk—cultures which flourished together, incidentally, in San Francisco Bay. Pursuing this oceanic interest in new quarters of the oceanic world—not as a stranger, but as a fellow-seaman—he built up a far-reaching circle of friends who shared his interests and worked together to save the fast-disappearing historic ships of mankind's experience at sea.

So Alan Villiers, the famous British seaman-author who had sailed in the last of the great square riggers in the oceanic trade carrying grain from Australia to England and Europe, came to know of Karl's work and visited him in San Francisco. Frank Carr, head of Britain's National Maritime Museum, who with Villiers's help saved the last China clipper ship, *Cutty Sark,* also visited Karl in his penthouse office above the museum he had established ashore—his "aerie," as we came to call it—from which he tracked down the winged ships he sought in far corners of the ocean world.

This company of ship savers came to include others besides these leading lights: the scholarly Dr. John Lyman in Chapel Hill, North Carolina; the rough-hewn (as he would always have you think) sea captain Harold Huycke in Seattle; Andy Nesdall in Waban, Massachusetts, a leading specialist in British square-rigged sailing ships; the gifted artist and photographer Robert Weinstein in Los Angeles; and of course the veteran seaman Captain Fred Klebingat in Coos Bay, Oregon. And there were also maritime labor leaders, steam-schooner veterans, and proud square riggermen from Captain P. A. McDonald of the great four-poster *Moshulu*, in Portland, Oregon, to Captain Robert Miethe of the fabled German *Potosi*, in Valparaiso, Chile—Karl got their stories, not as they would be given to a newspaper reporter, but to one of their own.

Carl Cutler, founder of Mystic Seaport in Connecticut, who had made a Cape Horn voyage as a youth, played a special role in this constellation of talents. As a young man of twenty Karl had written to Cutler in the late 1930s to ask advice on an historic ship center for San Francisco. Cutler had responded, launching a remarkable relationship between the reserved, scholarly director of what became America's leading maritime museum and the young man from Petaluma. Others were gathered up into Karl's circle, after his voyage in *Kaiulani* showed him something of the world. Among them was A. C. Daniels, the ship surveyor for Lloyds of London in the South American city of Montevideo, who kept track of the old square riggers which took up life as hulked barges in the River Plate when their sailing days were over. Daniels, like Karl, had sailed in this noble breed of vessel, which vanished from Earth's waters in his lifetime. It was through such connections that Karl became the leading authority on the surviving ships of deepwater sail.

In 1962 the directors of the new Philadelphia Maritime Museum, aware of Karl's achievements, invited him to make a trip to the East

Coast to consult with them about getting an historic ship for the young museum to exhibit in the Delaware River. Karl snapped up this invitation and urged the museum people to take on his old ship *Kaiulani* and also the *Great Britain*, a big innovative steamship of 1843 in the remote Falkland Islands. Jean came with him on this East Coast ship hunt for Philadelphia, and the couple extended their journey to New York and Connecticut. In New York they visited museums and also South Street, where Karl photographed the historic buildings of the waterfront three years before we began to think about its possibilities. At Mystic Seaport he met at last with Carl Cutler in person to exchange thoughts after their correspondence over the past quarter century.

Then, in December 1965, soon after Norma's and my October visit to San Francisco, Karl Kortum embarked on a trip that was to change the face of the historic ships movement.

Armed by William Swigert, president of the Pacific Bridge Company, with $2,000 plus his own brash confidence and unswerving dedication to historic ships, Karl left San Francisco for the Falkland Islands in the far reaches of the South Atlantic, where the hulk of Brunel's historic steamship *Great Britain* had been laid up. Stopping first at Montevideo, on the northern shore of the wide River Plate, he learned that his correspondent Daniels had died. The new Lloyd's agent, Pablo Moore, knew little of Daniels's work, but promised to look into it. Karl went on to board the little 1,793-ton steamer *Darwin* for the Falklands.

The Falkland Islands lie some 300 miles northeast of Cape Horn downwind from the Horn, so ships badly damaged in battle with the hurricane winds that lash the region could run with a following wind to the Falklands harbor of Port Stanley. In this snug port of refuge, wounded ships could replace broken spars and damaged rigging and resew torn sails. But some, like the *Great Britain*, were reckoned too old or beyond repair and never left the islands.

The 3,440-ton iron steamship *Great Britain* was built in 1843 in Bristol, England, to the revolutionary design of the visionary engineer Isambard

Kingdom Brunel. Brunel's innovations just began with building a huge iron ship, much bigger than any wooden ship ever built. Other innovations abounded, including a screw propeller instead of paddlewheels, a balance rudder, and a double bottom. Her hull was made of small iron plates (small by later standards, but the biggest the technology of the day could provide), stitched together with many thousands of rivets. The graceful overall shape Brunel achieved in these materials so impressed the American newspaperman James Gordon Bennett that when the extreme American wooden clipper *Sea Witch* appeared in South Street three years later in 1846, he could think of nothing to compare her with but Brunel's giant, three times the clipper's size.

Highly innovative vessels often fare badly on the untamed waters that enwrap our globe, which find out every weakness in a new ship. But the *Great Britain* was a success, surviving an early stranding that would have destroyed a lesser vessel. After a few years in the North Atlantic run, she went on to make a famous career in the long-haul passenger trade between Britain and Australia for a quarter century, until new, more efficient ships replaced her. Her huge, primitive engines were then removed, her big hull was reinforced with wooden sheathing to strengthen it to carry cargo, and she resumed service as a sailing ship—this time in the tough trade from England around Cape Horn to San Francisco. In 1886 she was damaged in a Cape Horn snorter and put into Port Stanley in the Falklands. There the islanders set her up as a floating warehouse for wool from the sheep they cultivated, until 1937 when, after 43 years of active sailing and 51 as a floating warehouse, her worn-out hull was finally hauled up on a remote beach and abandoned.

Karl, visiting the ship in Whalefish Bay, was stunned by the beauty of the seaworn hull. A great crack in her starboard side seemed to rule out any notion of salvage. But back in Stanley, Karl began to think of ways to close the gaping wound and float the ship home—a feat that was ultimately to be achieved with a barge, in large part because of the interest his report aroused in the British press.

Karl's great survey included other Falkland ships: the stout barque *Vicar of Bray* built in Whitehaven, England, in 1841, a survivor of the California Gold Rush of 1849; the French grain ship *Champigny* of 1902; the packet ship *Charles Cooper*, built in 1856 of Connecticut oak; the graceful iron barque *Lady Elizabeth*, English-built in 1879; the remains of the clipper ship *Snow Squall*, built in Maine in the great clipper year 1851; and the Down Easter *St. Mary*, also Maine-built, in 1890—some of which we shall encounter again in our story.

After his three-week Falklands visit Karl boarded the *Darwin* to return to Montevideo, where Pablo Moore of Lloyds' reported that none of the ships that Daniels had discussed with Karl could be found in port. But, he added, there might or might not be a few hulks remaining in Buenos Aires. And he referred Karl to John Davies of the American Bureau of Shipping in that city.

In Buenos Aires Davies led Karl to Captain Thomas Thomas of the venerable firm of Cooper Bros. Thomas, a grand old seaman, whom Norma and I later were privileged to know, had commanded square riggers at sea for seven years. And he'd noticed the *British Isles*—famous for her 1905 passage around Cape Horn in horrendously storm-beset conditions—being dragged around the river and cut down to serve as a barge. But he hadn't seen her about lately; Karl gloomily and correctly surmised she must have been scrapped, her passing unnoticed.

Karl searched the waterfront and eventually found his way to La Boca, the old harbor district at the mouth of the River Riachuelo, where it flows into the Plate. Here he found a world apart from the city of Buenos Aires with its grand parks, heroic statues, imperial buildings, and modern port with huge docks. La Boca was an unreconstructed port of the 1800s, where small craft cluster with the tugs and barges of the port at the end of the working day. Ashore one walks narrow, twisty streets alive with a coming and going of all sorts of people from numerous small shops and taverns, with here and there an art gallery or art supply store arguing the presence of a resident artists' community. Karl, in heaven in this kind of neighborhood, easily fell into conversation with three men aboard a well-kept tug of British model. Straining his phrase-book Spanish, he showed them an article by Captain Daniels which featured a picture of the *Wavertree*, formerly *Southgate*, a Liverpool ship, port painted and in her prime, with the British Red Duster flying from her spanker gaff. Daniels, ten years earlier, had uncovered nine square rigger hulks in Buenos Aires used as barges for various purposes; this one was used to carry sand dredged from the River Plate.

Did they know any like her? Karl laboriously sought to make his meaning clear. He had put together "viejos veleros" for old sailing ships, but that was about it. And his "unusual mission," as he called it, was not in the normal line of waterfront inquiries. But the men recognized a seaman in Karl, and sailors the world over will bear a hand to help one of their own kind ashore. Talking to each other in Italian, they tried to fathom just what this big, camera-toting American was about. Finally one of them gave an exclamation, pointed to a bridge farther upstream on the Riachuelo on the map Karl had shown him and gestured that he should go there. Everyone nodded at that, and with profuse thanks and farewells Karl returned to the big city to continue his inquiries in the shipping community, where he made no further progress.

On the third day of his stay Karl located a splendidly scrolled and lettered bus bound for the Avenida Vieytes and made his way to the bridge the tug men had pointed out. Looking around the dreary industrial backwater he saw nothing but an eviscerated steamer awaiting scrapping, her boilers removed and lying beside her.

Karl had become pals with an RAF pilot interested in bird study, whom he had persuaded to come on this search, hoping, as he said, to interest his new friend in a different kind of *rara avis*. But when Karl proposed walking along the industrial waterfront of the Riachuelo for the two miles now separating them from the Boca, his pal demurred. "Gerry," notes Karl, "had had enough of ship-searching in this cheerless part of the world where no bird sang."

Karl trudged on through a region of huge piles of sand and gravel, from which what he calls the "distant skyscrapers" of Buenos Aires had been built. He thought of turning back from this moonscape, but stumbling forward he rounded a sand pile and spotted across the way a craft unloading sand on the far side of the stream. It was a sailing ship! He wrote:

> *Or what had been a sailing ship—black-hulled, deep sheered, fore and mizzen lower masts still in place. Clamshell buckets were clanging in her hatches. She was in use, cared for, in a way alive. And big.*

The size was important—this was no casual trader of the coasts and rivers, but an ocean-going ship. And, as the surviving lower mizzen mast made clear, a full-rigger, square-rigged on all three masts. That meant she dated back to the 1880s, since only a few full-riggers of this size were built after that. The barque rig with fore-and-aft rigged mizzen saved the expense of the extra manpower a full-rigger demanded. All this must have gone through his head in a flash—but: *Who was she?*

An important question; to Karl, and to all who had sailed in these ships, they were individuals, each with her own reputation, and each, as the Cape Horn sailor and poet John Masefield once observed, with her own story to tell. And sailing ship stories were all different, lacking the regularity and degree of certitude that came in with the steamship. For this reason a sailing ship log of a voyage from London to Sydney, Australia, for example, was always headed: London *toward* Sydney, not *to* Sydney, for to predict arrival was to deny all the uncertainties of wind and sea.

Karl soon found a ferry to get across the "oily and Styx-like waters of the Riachuelo," and landed on the far side right under the stern of the ship. Perhaps there he'd see her name. But the brass letters that spelt out this ship's name were gone—"now only rivet holes and faint strokes of corrosion remained," as Karl reported in his journal.

> *But a pattern could be coaxed out of these . . . W . . . a V, a T, a recurring E. I played anagrams with the gaps. W-A-V-E-R-T-R-E-E.* Wavertree!

This was the deep-sheered full-rigger that Daniels had chosen to il-lustrate his article, which Karl had shown to the tug men in the Boca. She was a ship known to Karl through seamen's talk—"a well-known ship" whose name crops up in voyage narratives. Finding her was like encountering a long-lost cousin.

It was, Karl said, "As thrilling a moment as my life has known."

"Well," said Karl Kortum, popping into his mouth one of the olives from the large Beefeater Martini which had been set before him at our India House lunch, "I felt this moment deserved a celebratory drink, and after I'd boarded the ship to have a closer look and a chat with the man in charge—whose boss arrived as I was leaving the ship, just in time to let me know the ship might indeed be for sale—I found a tiny bar back across the river from the slaughterhouse the *Wavertree* was lying next to.

"Oh, I haven't told you about the slaughterhouse?" he said. "That was part of what saved the ship. Between wind and water, always the area most vulnerable to rust, she had been coated with floating lanolin from slaughtered sheep, and of course the waterline kept changing as the big sand bins they had built into the ship were loaded and unloaded. In that vulnerable region, she was well coated with the stuff.

"At any rate, I found the bar and decided a little celebration was in order. I had learned the word for beer, *cervesa*. But this was nothing to celebrate with beer, so I looked up the word for whiskey: *wisky*."

Later I learned that Karl had taken a photograph through the win-dow of that bar and, after some hounding from me, he eventually came across it, complete with the word BAR painted on the window, reading from inside the room. And beyond it is the rising bow of the *Wavertree,* partly obscured by a truck but recognizable, utterly recognizable, just from that fragmentary view. There was no other ship like her left in that Stygian river, and very few left in the world.

"Well, Karl, what's the status of the ship today?" asked Melvin Conant. Karl and I were lunching with Melvin and Bob Tarr, prospective trustees for the Seaport board. Jean and Norma were not present, lady guests not yet being admitted at lunch in businessmen's clubs in those days.

"We know the ship can be bought. Her snappily dressed owner was rubbing his thumb and forefinger together under my nose as I was leaving the ship. But we don't know for how much. I didn't want to stir up any more excitement about rich *norteamericanos* being interested in the vessel. Besides, she's really Bill Swigert's call, since he's the one who paid for the trip. You'll want to see him again when you definitely decide to buy the ship. He has some ideas about rerigging *Wavertree*, and he's president of the Pacific Bridge Company, you'll remember."

Karl went on to tell us that within days of his return to San Francisco he had gone to London with Swigert to ask the Falkland Islands Company if they would release the *Great Britain*, the initial object of his trip, to a responsible group. With the courtesy and ceremony befitting a company representing this still extant survival of the British Empire the company representatives had told their visitors that this was probably acceptable, provided there was some quid pro quo for the Falkland Islanders.

On his way back from England just a year before in 1966, Karl had stopped in New York to settle arrangements through Frank Braynard with William Van Frank, a veteran of whaling under sail who ran a one-man marine salvage business. The arrangements, successfully concluded, were to remove the topmast doubling on the foremast of the wooden barquentine *City of Beaumont*, then in use as a bulkhead in Hastings-on-Hudson. She was clearly visible from the train we rode to work from Yorktown Heights, but we had never thought of saving that heavy and complex fragment of American spars and rigging, and the topmast doubling now stands as a powerful exhibit in the San Francisco Maritime National Historical Park. Karl also stopped by to look over the site of our Seaport project, having been read into it by the heroic urbanist Anita Ventura.

Lunch ended, and as we left the dimly-lit quarters of India House to go our separate ways through the brilliant springtime streets of Lower Manhattan it was clear, I think, to all of us that we were going to bend our best efforts to secure the *Wavertree*, as the centerpiece of our bid to restore the look and ethos of the Street of Ships.

The photograph of the *Wavertree,* which had stirred the unknown tugboat hand in La Boca to steer Karl to his discovery of the great ship's hulk, had stirred some atavistic instinct in all of us, as we got into the story of her discovery. In that photo of her riding at anchor in San Francisco Bay, she seemed to us clearly a ship of destiny, ready to set sail with 3,000 tons of grain in her hold. There she was, with her sweeping sheer, her rig in perfect order with not a rope's end out of place, ready to take on her next Cape Horn passage. And Karl, in his brief visit, had made us understand what we were looking at and why it all mattered.

The next day Karl and I lunched with Eric Ridder, our prospective treasurer, who agreed with this sweeping turn in fundamental strategy with something like a gleam in his eye. Besides sailing America's Cup boats, he hunted big game in Africa and Alaska—and here was big game indeed. That night Norma and I had a farewell dinner with Karl and Jean at the Yacht Club, an occasion of considerable rejoicing, for we were now very clear what we had to do: just find the money to buy the ship, and go and get her. To Karl this was grand stuff, one of his great sea chariots to be recovered from over time's horizon.

The first resolution of the newly appointed board of trustees, held two weeks later on 8 June, was to acquire, subject to available funding and at a price to be agreed, the sailing ship *Wavertree.* Jakob Isbrandtsen as chairman ran this brief session in solid style, backed up by Eric Ridder as treasurer, with Melvin Conant and Admiral Moran as trustees. I was there as president, with Bob Walton as legal counsel to remind us of our duties, and Frank Braynard (who, it will be remembered, worked for Moran Towing) as member of the Advisory Committee. Bob Tarr, secretary, could not be with us, but I had seen him the day before and secured his ready agreement to acquiring the ship. He'd also agreed to a second resolution I felt we needed.

This resolution was simply to note that the museum was already in business as a functioning entity conducting active educational programs—with a membership now just over one thousand strong. I asked for this resolution because I wanted this recognition of the leading role of the membership to be built into the foundations of the new edifice we were erecting. Much is at stake in how one makes one's beginnings in life.

This motion of recognition, I am glad to say, was welcomed by the chairman and so was duly moved by Melvin Conant, as I remember, and warmly seconded by our treasurer—not the last time I was to be surprised by this very conservative man's openings to the left, where value questions were concerned.

CHAPTER 12

Racing the Bulldozer, *June–August 1967*

Our First Visiting Ship—Jack Kaplan Tours Seaport—Boating Magazine—Isbrandtsen and Kaplan Meet—Handel and Chanteys—A Talk With Cantalupo—Success of the $1 Membership

One of the best reasons for being alive is to see what's going to happen next. But as the Seaport's first summer opened, it began to seem that too much was happening next! The rush began on 11 June, three days after the trustees' meeting, when the sea-worn barquentine *Regina Maris* came into our river, sporting a skysail atop her square-rigged foremast. The skysail was a sail that had pretty well passed out of commercial use half a century earlier, as an extra that the hard-pressed, undermanned windships of the day could hardly afford to carry. But when the brothers John and Siegfried Wilson, Norwegian shipping people with an interest in traditional seafaring, had outfitted this wooden schooner of 1908 for a Cape Horn voyage, they had rerigged her as a barquentine to give her the driving power of square rig on the foremast—and why not a skysail while they were about it? This was the attitude that this exuberant pair carried into everything they did. They had decided to round Cape Horn on their Atlantic cruise because of the importance of this rocky outcropping in sailing-ship history. And Cape Horn had lived up to their expectations. Unexpectedly calm on the westward passage, the sea turned into a raging maelstrom on the return trip, with the stout oak ship, swept with boarding seas, staggering along under the narrow canvas strip of the fore lower topsail and two staysails set between the masts. No thought of lofty skysails in that environment. But the brothers were happy; they'd taken a skysail-yarder around the Horn!

How could we refuse this heaven-sent opportunity to have New Yorkers meet people re-enacting their forebears' voyages? We could not receive the ship at Pier 16, but the Wilsons brought her into nearby Pier 11 near the foot of Wall Street, where we sent people to visit the ship and meet her people. So this visit became part of our educational program, with the crew showing their ship to all comers and telling of their adventures. When it came time for them to set sail, we held a farewell reception at 16 Fulton Street to thank them and wish them well on their return trip across the ocean to Norway, via France and England.

As the working day ended, with the *Regina* people and guests filtering in for the reception, Norma called out to David Lutz, a teen-age volunteer who shared our vision of an active waterfront and threw himself into making it work. She asked him to stop the young woman who had just gone downstairs. Norma had been interviewing her for a staff position, and it suddenly occurred to Norma to invite her to stay for the reception. This turned out to be an inspired stroke. The young woman was Betsy Kohn. Norma had been looking for a person we urgently needed to manage public events, publicity, and volunteer affairs, so that Norma could concentrate on plans, meetings, promotional literature and funding. So Betsy, who could always turn on a dime, stayed on for the reception.

The next day Norma called to offer Betsy the job at a modest wage, and Betsy accepted. From that moment affairs in South Street began to be more orderly, rewarding and fun. Betsy, who actually flapped her hands with joy when things went right, turned out to be herself unflappable amid the swarming events that she had to handle. With what we had taken on, this help was a lifesaver.

While the days were crowded with the business and excitements of all we were doing, we also faced the riddle of how we would secure the Seaport land. This unanswered question haunted everything we did, from searching out historic ships to filling the streets with active public program. Understandably these efforts stood in the foreground of our affairs, but in the background gathered the clouds of uncertainty which we knew could sweep away all our dreams and efforts.

How to acquire the Seaport land? Walking to work each morning down Fulton Street from the subway, past honky-tonk bars, cheap jewelry shops and fast-food joints, I would recognize the low brick facades of the Water Street frontage of the Seaport as a haven at the end of the road, with the occasional traffic of ships in the river as a reminder of the ocean trades they'd been built to serve. Scrunching over the coffee beans spilt onto the sidewalk from the coffee importer's warehouse just before Water Street, I'd greet Jack Scaglione's Retail Fish Store with a mental salute, pausing before its window to admire the day's display of finny swimmers, lobsters, clams and oysters arrayed in graceful arches and arabesques worked out in seaweed, before proceeding down the frontage of Schermerhorn Row to our own headquarters gallery with its modest sign announcing the presence of the South Street Seaport Museum. What chance was there, with all our brave talk and all the faith that growing numbers of people put in our plans, that we could actually preserve this storied neighborhood? The popular interest and tentative commitments we'd secured offered no real protection against the bulldozer thrust that was reshaping Lower Manhattan.

All we knew for certain was what made us greet the days in South Street with gusto: our love affair with the old brick walls and cobbled streets that had brought us into South Street. That, and the desire to summon back a few of the vanished ships that had brought the neighborhood into being as a rich seedbed for the whole city. It was for these things that we had to secure the land.

A beginning had been made, however, when Jack Kaplan toured the Seaport site with me on 26 May. The visit was launched by a hurried phone call from Ray Rubinow asking me to drop everything and pick up Jack at a meeting he was holding with a tenants group on the Lower East Side. Ray, a great believer in the Seaport project, had been telling me for months that if Jack got seriously interested, he would find a way to acquire the Seaport land.

I found Jack Kaplan at the top floor of a five-story walkup building on Chrystie Street. He was instantly recognizable as the small, active figure in a black business suit speaking with a restive group of young African-American and Hispanic men. As I walked in the door, I caught some muttering among them, murmurs of "We don't need this," and "That's enough!" Jack broke off when he saw me in the doorway, saying "It looks like my ride is here. You gentlemen will have to resolve this." Going down the stairs to my car, I introduced myself and said that it looked like quite a meeting he was having. As we drove away, he explained the situation.

The group had come to the J. M. Kaplan Fund to seek help to buy a group of buildings owned by an exploitative landlord—a common enough situation in this rundown neighborhood. Jack had proposed they set up a cooperative tenants' organization to take over the whole block of Old Law tenements built before the building code was enacted. The Kaplan Fund was prepared to front the capital they would need, provided that all the tenants of the buildings had a share in their ownership and management. A Kaplan Fund lawyer had been made available to them to help with the legalities.

But the group had different ideas about how to handle the large sums of money involved—ideas which did not include the cooperative set-up at the heart of Jack's vision. If it was to be their money, they felt, they should use it as they saw fit. This was familiar ground to me. In the Rutgers Club I had encountered the same argument from War on Poverty workers, themselves often a heady mix of disfranchised intellectuals and would-be community leaders. The pitch was that rich white Americans were still engaged in oppressing the poor and therefore they owed a great deal of money to minority leaders who had the guts to demand it. I firmly believed that this "Stand and deliver" approach to group advancement did little but perpetuate poverty and nourish its roots in dependence, despair and futile rage.

I must have said a few words on these themes, for I remember Jack holding up his hand, smiling, to say "enough." He knew the scenes I was talking about.

Jack Kaplan clearly believed that the fortunate of the world should help the unfortunate, and not out of guilt but out of fellow-feeling. He believed that all people wanted to care for their families and to make their own way if given the opportunity to do so. So he made it his business to give disadvantaged people that opportunity in the unruly structure of the capitalist state, believing that people needed help to achieve opportunity—what President Roosevelt wisely called a helping hand, rather than a handout.

Jack's great success in business had been to get grape growers in upstate New York to unite in a cooperative to buy out the Welch's Grape Juice Company, thus taking control of manufacture and distribution of the ultimate product, grape juice. This gave Welch's a growing mass of capital to use in marketing their brand, which the firm did brilliantly, and it opened a future for farmers in which they became makers and distributors of their own product, rather than merely the suppliers of the raw materials. And here Jack was trying a stakeholding approach in an urban setting, focused on housing.

I certainly agreed with Jack's approach. But I was completely uncertain about how to express the social importance of our South Street venture to the tough-minded, highly articulate gentleman riding with me in our beat-up car. Jack may have caught a whiff of my frustrated state of mind. He turned to me and said:

"Peter, now about this project of yours. I hear a lot about it from Joan and I've talked it over with your friend Jakob, but I'm still not clear how it's going to work, and why we should want to help it. How is it really going to help the city? I understand about your feeling for old ships, but what are they going to do for New York's future?"

Seeing that I was at a loss to answer this big question, he relented and said:

"Look, suppose you just tell me how you got into this whole thing. Start at the beginning and bring me up to date. Don't try to justify anything. Just tell me how you got into it and why you're doing it yourself."

That wasn't too hard. As we filtered down through the jumbled streets of Lower Manhattan I told of our work in the Rutgers Club and the value of living history to the sense of opportunity in the mean streets of the slum—even, perhaps, the sense that the life of the city has meaning to the individual, and to struggling families. When we arrived at 16 Fulton Street, we got out of the car and walked into our exhibit.

Jack was intrigued by our model of the Seaport, with its small brick buildings facing out on our simply carved ships. And he paused reflectively before the great Kortum photograph of men aloft shortening sail in a squall, perhaps appreciating the high endeavor by sea which had built the modern city. Back outdoors, walking through the sunlit streets of the Seaport, he was full of practical questions. These were the kind of questions Zeckendorf had asked, but with this difference: Jack waited for the answer, rather than providing his own.

We were apparently reaching a broad swath of the city's population—young and old, artists and construction workers—but how would we attract wealthy people to support the commerce we needed? How would we get such people into this industrial slum that reeked of fish? I told him about the line of people waiting to get into Sweet's. And what besides food? I told him about Fulton Supply, which attracted yachtsmen from Wall Street to buy its sweaters of unscoured Norwegian wool.

And we could attract commerce that was actually educational, involving people actively in learning the rich heritage of American seafaring, just beginning with a first-class bookshop and a ship model shop. Then we'd want an art gallery and a working printing press—perhaps even a forge and . . .

Jack again held up both hands, and glanced at his watch. "Enough," he said. "You've got plenty of ideas, and Joan has been telling me about the people you're attracting. I'm interested, I'll tell you that. I'll have another talk with Jakob. We'll be in touch." He thanked me warmly for the little tour we'd taken, which I'd really begun to enjoy, and hurried off to his Wall Street luncheon, just a few blocks to the south.

I learned in time that the Kaplan Fund was concerned with the artistic, cultural, and recreational life of New York, in addition to its deep-seated concern with improving the lot of deprived citizens. Jack's idea of cooperative ownership of an entire city block eventually took root successfully in Westbeth, a West Village artists' residential project, which was personally conceived and led by his daughter Joan. His wife, Alice, who much preferred to be in the background rather than the foreground of things, was a devotee of folk art and on the board of the Museum of American Folk Art. She was later to discover for us a remarkable painting of a lift drydock in South Street, an installation which we had never heard of, though once alerted we found it in a panoramic photograph of South Street in the early 1880s. And the Folk Art Museum itself fell into a class of possible tenant in South Street, an indication of overlapping interests we were discovering with this extraordinarily creative family. Our idea in all this was to get strong, self-standing organizations working in harness together to build a genuine center of interests that contributed to the Seaport story.

And I was delighted to learn that the Kaplan family had these broader concerns beyond tackling specific social ills. My experience working in a blighted city neighborhood had led me to believe that the narrow-gauge attack on physical problems of the dispossessed of our city did only limited good without broader ventures to lift and engage the human spirit. It was exhilarating to feel this same sense in a family of such accomplishments and resources.

Still, the pressure was on to secure the Seaport land. In February, three months before we opened our doors at 16 Fulton Street, Commissioner Halberg of Ports and Terminals had told us that the City could provide the piers south of the Fish Market and might even clear away the warehouses on them and see them made good for public assembly. But, he'd warned me, nothing lasting could be done until we'd secured the Seaport land. I told Halberg that our chairman, Jakob, and Jack Kaplan were engaged in working out a scheme to buy the land, but I knew nothing of their arrangements and could not be of much help if I had. We just had to continue building support for the Seaport concept.

This day-by-day effort was helped by the article I'd written in late 1966, "Street of Ships." It appeared in the June issue of *Boating* magazine, thanks to the interest of Monk Farnham, the editor, coaxed by his managing editor, Terry Walton, and pulled along by his assistant editor, the inimitable Dick Rath. The three used to hold after-hours confabs at which nice points of syntax and word derivation were thrashed out, along with wild ideas like the Seaport. Monk, a stern taskmaster, unbent on these occasions and Rath secured his invitation for me to write the article. This was only the beginning of Monk's involvement, which was mainly on the trustee level, whereas Rath's was with the working staff and volunteers.

On 23 June, a few weeks after Jack's visit to South Street, Jack and Jakob held a meeting at the New York Yacht Club to review plans for the Seaport and consider what land should be acquired and how. Held in an upstairs room of the club under the imperious gaze of past club commodores whose portraits lined the walls, the meeting also included Joan Davidson, Jack's son Richard Kaplan, Charles Abrams, Paul Friedberg and the ever-active Ray Rubinow. I remember a certain solemnity to the occasion—these were not people who met for the sake of meeting, but to get things done. I was asked to give our picture of the restored neighborhood and the activities we expected to attract to it, based on the visitation generated by the historic ships. It was easy to cite the glowing reports of the San Francisco waterfront renaissance—an enterprise based on the presence of the ships on the waterfront. It counted for much that Karl Kortum, who had brought in those ships, had come east at our invitation to help plan our ship program.

Ray Rubinow, agreeing that ships were the heart of the story, said that we had to put that heart to work to pump life into the Seaport ashore. Joan added that we needed sophisticated guidance to make the revived Seaport work—and work to our purposes. She mentioned James Marston Fitch at the Columbia School of Architecture as a preservationist we should be in touch with.

On the question of acquiring Seaport land, we presumed the Schermerhorn Row block would at some point be acquired by the State, and it had at least the paper protection of designation for the State Maritime Museum. But the next two blocks to the north were up for grabs. Securing these threatened buildings would forestall the bulldozers chewing away at the heritage of Lower Manhattan, and would assure the future of the Seaport neighborhood.

Jack spoke enthusiastically for the Seaport as a vital addition to the life of the city and said he and Jakob were working together on the land acquisition. It wasn't clear just what commitments were shaping up to this end, but it was clear that these two men, widely different in background and life experience, were resolved to bring in these vital blocks of land. Jack also thought it important that we buy the individual building at 16 Fulton Street in Schermerhorn Row, so people would know we were there as something more than transient tenants. It would have been wise to stake this claim at this early stage, as we were to learn in the future, rather than relying on the yet-to-be-established State Maritime Museum to preserve the Schermerhorn Row block. But Jakob was focused on the larger land purchase to the north, and Jack deferred to Jakob as the principal in this matter.

Meanwhile, we were still in the dark as to what Jakob and Jack, that unlikely pair who so enjoyed each other's company, planned to do on the land acquisition front. Our part was to press forward in a continuing campaign to build up public interest in the Seaport and make an effective case to potential supporters.

To this end, Norma and I drew up a preliminary plan which we circulated in mid-July 1967. This set forth clearly what the Seaport would be and what it would do for New York—in effect, a spelling-out of my answers to Jack Kaplan's questions in his brief but memorable visit to the site. We described it as "A proposal to recreate the historic 'Street of Ships' as a major recreational and cultural resource in the heart of New York City." Drawings by our volunteer architect, Bill Shopsin, showed how the historic enclave would fit in the surrounding jungle of steel and glass, and how the ships and the activities that would grow up around them would transform the rundown waterfront. Charlie Lundgren used his artist's brush to evoke the commanding presence of the ships, whose monumental shapes carried a clear declaration of what the Street of Ships was about. And we emphasized their role in what we called "a lively center for New York City," declaring: "The ships, the commercial buildings and the excitement of South Street Seaport will all be real."

This quest of the *real thing* led to our early resolution that the ships of South Street, while serving their mission of challenging and educating the passerby at dockside, should be in all respects fit to go to sea. And we soon amended this with the principle that they should be regularly exercised at sea, if humanly possible, in order to keep the gear in working order and to keep alive the skills and sailorly culture of the ships' people. There would be nothing plastic, nothing fake or phony in the revived Street of Ships.

Plans on paper were one thing, and Norma and I delighted in develop-ing these, making sketches that were soon covered with scrawled notes as we argued out the details. But because we had opened our doors in South Street, we now had the priceless opportunity to put into action much of what we talked and wrote about.

It was not always easy to leap back and forth from long-range plans and discussions of financing ships and land to the day-to-day demands of the activities of Seaport volunteers, members and the public, who all gave the Seaport its living presence. But somehow the stretch was made, with the help of more new people now actively involved in our affairs, and our "people" programs flourished. We were signing up new members by the proverbial basketful.

The outdoor concert held in South Street at the end of June by the New Symphony Orchestra had turned out to be a magical evening, with George Frideric Handel's "Water Music" pouring out over the cobblestones and rapt faces of New Yorkers not used to this kind of splendor in their streets. Afterward, the British chanteyman Lou Killen got the crowd singing the foot-stamping "Leaving of Liverpool," which oddly enough seemed to go well following on the pure, elevated joy of Handel's work. Handel had become a British subject over 200 years earlier in quest of British freedoms guaranteed by their sea power, after all, and perhaps it is not totally illusory to think of those two quite different kinds of music as having shared ancestral strains in the glorious confusions of the English-speaking heritage.

A grant from the J. M. Kaplan Fund, through the Dynarts Foundation led by our Rutgers Club friend Irving Ruckens, paid for this classy performance—a fact that awakened us to the broad, humanist approach of the Fund to the quality of life for New Yorkers. And this particular event added a distinct new dimension to the Seaport experience—an experience we wanted to be multilayered in its celebration of the city's complex and rewarding relations with the sea.

Money remained a serious problem, however, and meeting each week's payroll had become a challenge. We were running through the startup fund, and our income from memberships and small gifts, while growing, was not yet at a point to carry the burden of operations.

Trustees were, of course, aware of our threadbare finances, but, while they were ready to tackle the major problems of acquiring land and ships, they regarded the day-to-day expenses of staying open as an operating problem that was our job to solve. If we had been running a profit-making enterprise, we could have issued stock to cover cash needs while building the business to sustain itself. But this concept, so clear to us on the scene, cut no ice with our trustees, who said we should simply stop doing anything we couldn't pay for.

That would mean closing our doors to the public. And this, we felt, was simply not an option. If we closed down operations to concentrate on plans and funding, the impetus of the operation would be lost, membership would start to dwindle away, and the bulldozer push would overrun the neighborhood we were dedicated to saving.

And it is now clear that what we were actually doing with our program of activities was beginning to re-shape the situation we faced. One by one, we were taking the existing realities and changing them through the weight and push of public opinion and the force of human desire.

We had already begun to change the answers to the ten critical questions the management consultant Bob Duncan had posed to us six months earlier. This kind of change would not be achieved in a boardroom, but in our streets—and in the expectations and desires of the people who walked them.

But the money problem would not go away. Looking at worst cases, I figured I could personally earn enough in a year or two to repay $10,000 in overdue bills if the enterprise crashed. Early in August, liabilities began to go beyond this figure. Under no conditions was I going to leave suppliers holding the bag if we went under. I had of course kept our treasurer, Eric Ridder, informed of our endangered state, and he said I might circulate the trustees to seek emergency help. So I made some unwelcome phone calls. Jakob and Admiral Moran were out of town, so, besides Eric, only Melvin Conant and Bob Tarr were available. I said that it was really a matter of finding $10,000 or closing down. Eric said his vote would be for closing down, if we could not make our way with what we had been given. Melvin said he could not help personally, but there must be some way to keep the boat afloat. Bob Tarr said he was willing to continue seeking $1,000 corporate contributions, such as his own company, Luckenbach, had made, but was in no position to do more.

I told Joe Cantalupo our problem on one of his morning visits. He took me aside and said that he knew where we could probably get $10,000 readily enough—but he recommended against our taking it. I took his meaning immediately and agreed we should not take this money. In those days organized crime still controlled the Fish Market and we wanted to stay clear of any dealings with them, as did Joe. Later in the day, Joe came by my office and suggested we take a little walk. Whatever our problems, I was always ready to talk with Joe, so we walked down Fulton Street and across South Street to look together at the river.

Finally he said: "Peter, I realize we're in a jam. I'll give you $1,000, no strings attached. I want us to succeed, you're doing a good thing here."

I said: "Joe, thank you. But it wouldn't be right to take your money. Your thousand dollars would meet this week's payroll and something more, but I can't guarantee next week's—then we'd be out of business and you'd be out your money."

"Now listen to me," said Joe. "If you were out there on a boat sinking in the river, and I didn't do whatever I could to help, I'd never forgive myself. I'd never forgive myself if I wasn't standing beside you when that boat went down. Now I want you to take this money and fight like hell to stay afloat, that's all I ask. Understand?"

I accepted Joe's gift.

And, miracle of miracles, our income, gaining a little each week, began to catch up with expenses. Our strategy of venturing everything on our public program was actually keeping us afloat financially! So we pressed on.

We believed from the outset that marine art should be at the heart of our business, so a great effort went into a marine art show we mounted at the end of August. This drew on the cadre of artists who had joined the Seaport, who in turn found ways to involve their friends. And Dick Rath invited the great folk singer Pete Seeger, writing him to say:

> Peter Stanford has asked me to: (a) prevail upon you to come down and do a few songs between 4 and 6 PM, and (b) line up a dixieland band to fill in. I can take care of (b) OK, and I hope you will agree to (a)!!

Who could say no to such an appeal? Not the great-hearted singer, who came and made the day, attracting some 3,000 people who filled our streets and made the welkin ring by joining in the choruses of Pete's songs of protest and liberation.

The welkin unkindly opened up and rained upon this occasion, but this did not stop Pete, the Dixieland band, Parks Commissioner August Heckscher or the people who turned out Saturday afternoon. Both Pete Seeger and Augie went on to become great friends of South Street, joining us cheerfully on subsequent adventures. The art show took place with artists showing their works under the much-despised expressway, which we began to view more positively as an open-air galleria. On Sunday, in fair weather, the artists were able to stand their paintings up against the friendly brick walls of Schermerhorn Row. One called us to say it was the most memorable show he'd ever taken part in, because the people came out in the rain to see art works.

People took joy in this kind of event, and the membership rolls reflected their feelings. Leon Kaplan, our volunteer membership chairman, reported that enrollment, which had reached 1,700 in July, was growing without letup. And amid the $1 memberships flooding in, there were increasing numbers of $5 contributions and an occasional $100. We specified $5 as regular membership and $1 as introductory. We expected that renewals would come in mainly at the higher level, but we could not expect them in any substantial numbers until the next year, which seemed very distant to us. But we had the good sense to welcome everyone who paid $1. As Jakob later described it, they were, in effect, paying to be put on our mailing list. Our romance with the people of New York had, in fact, sound commercial underpinnings. Had that not been true, we would soon have been out of business.

I never forgot my talk with Joe and the fact that he had bought critical days for us when we were in danger of going under. He had also changed my way of looking at our South Street venture and my stance as its leader. I knew that I could not let down this good man, nor could I let down all the people now involved in South Street.

We made it a principle to keep acting the part of a full-fledged museum, with our three-person staff and ever-active volunteers. Our leading concern was, of course, to bring in the *Wavertree*, which Jakob had said he would pay for as a gift to the museum, provided she proved sound and could be acquired for a reasonable sum. Peter Black, the importer who had recommended we get a management consultant to guide us, stayed with us although we hadn't retained a consultant or, indeed, done much that conventional wisdom recommended. He commissioned a preliminary survey of the *Wavertree* by agents in Buenos Aires, who gave us a reading that she seemed sound enough for tow with some work to secure deck openings (notably the huge empty sandbins), the replacement of a few plates in the starboard forefoot, and other details. I reported this to Jakob, who said we'd better get sonic gauging to judge the thickness of the iron plating after years of neglect.

We were also intent on fulfilling our responsibilities as a maritime museum and were working with Kent Barwick to set up preliminary arrangements with archaeologists in Washington, DC, and Holland to recover the burnt-out hulk of the Dutch ship *Tijgre*. This vessel had caught fire and been run ashore in 1613—just where crews were now about to start digging out the deep foundations for the World Trade Center. This was just one of the ship projects we tended. In this we depended enormously on informed volunteers like Rath and experts like Fred Fried, the noted collector and student of industrial archaeology, who helped shape up the local history committee we established to search out the facts and dates of our storied neighborhood.

All was not peaches and cream in these people-oriented undertakings. I wince when I re-read a harsh memo I sent to the volunteer Steering Committee when they failed to have the headquarters gallery open on a Saturday in late July—a day after the popular *Daily News* had run a prominent story saying the Seaport Museum was open Saturdays and Sundays. With Betsy now aboard, who got along famously with volunteers of every persuasion, this kind of stumble was soon cured.

However rough the journey, by late August we knew that we were under way and making significant progress in reaching and involving our public. I felt secure enough to plot our first big foray into New York Harbor.

CHAPTER 13

Aboard *Athena, Summer 1967*

Meeting Mystic's Staff—A Tale of Two Schooners—
South Street Explorer Scouts—A Rewarding Relationship—
A Gathering of Schooners—No Room for Failure

The fisherman staysail, high overhead, flapped lazily in the light breeze blowing from a halcyon sky. This sent a thin spray of water showering down onto the heads of the people sitting on the caprail of our schooner, *Athena*, so I said I'd send the sail down again. But no, said Waldo Johnston, director of Mystic Seaport, the water drops added a festive note to a wonderful occasion. So we left things as they were and continued our discursive talk, covering a multitude of shared interests. With Waldo were Ed Lynch, newly installed as curator, and one or two other members of the Mystic Seaport staff.

We had nothing to match these professionals. South Street staff consisted of just Norma and me, and neither of us had the credentials to hold a job at Mystic Seaport. But we had come to Mystic on a special mission, and with us aboard *Athena* were the distinguished merchant mariner Captain Archie Horka and marine artist Os Brett, who had been with us on our sail to open South Street Seaport two months earlier. Captain Archie's mollyhawk pennant, attesting to his having rounded Cape Horn before the mast in a working square rigger, flew at the main truck. The rest of the crew were Gertrude Brett, my children Thomas, Carol, and Tony (who were at this point in the dinghy, exploring the Mystic River harbor where the Seaport's historic ships were moored), and the ship's cat, which Carol had appropriately named Scratch.

The day before, Friday, 14 July, we had left from Port Jefferson, where we'd picked up Captain Horka and the Bretts, sailing through the night and a rather wet and blowy morning to proceed up the Mystic River and put our lines ashore in Mystic Seaport. We tied up on the pier opposite the original station house of the New York Yacht Club. This ornate structure was preserved on the Seaport waterfront along with workaday buildings housing exhibits ranging from ship models, figureheads and paintings to a working forge and cooper's workshop. But the main thing was the 330-ton whaleship *Charles W. Morgan*, which had first tasted salt water in 1841, launched from Fairhaven, Massachusetts, across the harbor from the great whaling port of New Bedford, a day's sail eastward from Mystic. Her last whaling voyage, in 1921, had been filmed as part of a movie called *Down to the Sea in Ships*, a film that had had a seminal influence on the historic ship preservation movement in the US. After that voyage she'd been preserved by Whaling Enshrined, a group of artists who painted the old New Bedford waterfront with its abandoned hulks and modern active fishing fleet—the kind of society any right-minded person would surely long to have been part of while it still flourished. But this noble effort proved unequal to preserving the aged wooden structure of the *Charles W. Morgan*. Colonel Edward Green, son of Hetty Green, "the Witch of Wall Street," who had built up a major fortune outwitting the hotshots of Wall Street in what had hitherto been a man's game, then came to the rescue. He put up the money to see the ship set up in a sand berth on the waterfront of his estate just outside the old whaling port of New Bedford. Doing right by the ship while he lived, the good Colonel, however, neglected to provide for her in his will, and after he died, the hurricane of 1938 left her shifted in her berth with her rigging disheveled and with no funds to set things right.

Carl Cutler, running the fledgling Mystic Seaport almost single-handed in the 1930s, had always planned to have an ocean-traveled square rigger at the heart of the Seaport—a port from which great wooden ships, including the Greenman Brothers' famous *David Crockett* of 1853, had been sent to sea. In an act of great grace, Cutler's trustees agreed to back him in bringing the *Charles W. Morgan* to Mystic in late 1941. The scarred old hull proved stout enough for the voyage under tow from New Bedford into Mystic, where she arrived only days before the Japanese attack on Pearl Harbor on 7 December plunged America into World War II. After that, any such venture would have been out of the question. And in Mystic, where traditional shipwrights still pursued their craft, the *Morgan* flourished. Cared for by knowing hands, the sturdy ship attracted the public—and Mystic Seaport thrived. But now more fundamental work was needed to assure the *Morgan*'s safe passage into the future.

Sitting with gin and tonics below the drying fisherman staysail, we talked of these things. With remarkable freedom, Waldo spoke of the need to concentrate on the ships at the heart of the South Street mission. He introduced his new curator, Ed Lynch, as one who had joined the staff to lead a concerted effort to make up the arrears in shipkeeping incurred in the hustle to get the shoreside establishment set up to receive crowds of visitors. Lynch's philosophy was simple and foursquare: everything to be done with original materials, keeping alive the craftsmanship that had gone into the ships in the first place, so that the ships continued as original artifacts, with materials renewed as necessary, rather than as reproductions for show.

And of course good seamanlike maintenance, such as daily saltwater washdown of the decks, would do much to slow the deterioration of the aging wooden structures. Ed asked me how old *Athena* was, and when I told him she'd been launched in 1925 he turned to Waldo and said: "The same era as our *Dunton*! This schooner is only four years younger, and look at her—just come in from a hard squall and ready to cast off her lines and put to sea again!"

He brought up the *L. A. Dunton* for a purpose, for this magnificent Grand Banks fishing schooner, brought into safe harbor at Mystic a few years earlier, was in need of serious work just to be kept afloat. She was a victim of years in which vital maintenance had been deferred. Ed Lynch regarded ships like the *Dunton* as living organisms that needed daily care, and *Athena*'s long life and robust condition gave him another example how a vessel benefitted from the day-in, day-out attention she received simply because she was in active use.

Part of our purpose sailing into Mystic Seaport with a square rigger-man in crew was to learn from Mystic's shipkeeping experience. We knew we faced a major challenge in taking care of our own historic ships after bringing them into South Street. But it was another purpose that actually set the visit in motion. In what was becoming a pattern in our ways of doing things, this was a project conceived and launched by South Street members. Led by the tireless sea diver and antiquarian Charlie Dunn, these good people had gone to work to bring a dozen youngsters from Chinatown, just north of the Brooklyn Bridge, to visit Mystic Seaport in a chartered bus. This project was well received by Mystic. Their staff was well aware that their outreach to young people was pretty much limited to the educated middle class, and they welcomed an opportunity to reach into the inner city. For our part, we were glad to be doing an active, first-class museum program before we even had a museum to do it in. So we decided to make our visit under sail on the same Saturday Charlie and his crew had chosen for their visit. With a crew of eager schoolkids arriving by bus, and our case-hardened square rig veterans by sea, our visit paid tribute in different ways to Mystic as a leader and exemplar in our business in great and narrow waters.

And then, of course, the visit to Mystic was part of our notion that we could keep *Athena* sailing while engaged in the all-consuming project of building a museum from scratch. Perhaps this, too, helped with our reception. We were voyagers come in from the sea after taking a bit of a dusting outside—as attested by the drops falling from the drying sail aloft.

Athena had indeed come through a fairly lively passage on the way to Mystic. That morning, following an overnight run from Port Jefferson, we were beating to windward against light east winds, when a hard black squall had overtaken us. Os and Archie had jumped at the chance to make a visit to Mystic Seaport under sail, and Norma and I were proud to have these veteran seamen aboard our vessel again. They both appreciated the schooner's traditional rig, in which old-fashioned block and tackles with their multiple lines were everywhere in evidence.

Soon after our usual hearty breakfast we'd run into a gathering fog, which gradually blanked out buoys, lighthouses and landmarks ashore as we approached the reef-strewn reach of Fisher's Island Sound on the way to the Mystic River. This was followed by a grey, stinging rain with mounting wind behind it. We scrambled to get in fisherman and main topsail, wrapping the thrashing canvas into wet bundles which we crammed down the forehatch. The schooner sprang forward like a startled horse, thundering across the rising sea under her working rig of jib, staysail, fore and mainsail. I called buoy sightings to Archie at the chart table below, who plotted our course to thread our way through underwater perils. The wind rapidly backed to the northwest and began to blow great guns, tearing the tops off the cresting waves. We brought *Athena* to and took in the jib and the great mainsail, shortening down to foresail and staysail, a snug rig of less than a third the sail area of the schooner's working rig. Our veterans seemed to enjoy all this sail-handling, and Archie, on deck for this, was only momentarily taken aback at Tommy's questioning one of his orders. "Why?" he said. "Because that's what's got to happen next, is why." Later he explained to Tommy that aboard ship all authority flowed from the skipper, and he was carrying out one of my orders; "passing the word," as he put it. We decided they made a good foredeck crew.

Thus under reasonable control we shot across the broad estuary of the Thames River, and on up the Sound. We sailed into rapidly easing winds under sunlit skies, with ragged black cloud formations drifting away to the northward as we came up to the rocky islands and headland of the Mystic River. As we went we reset the jib, which was Archie's and Tommy's province. Swaying up the great expanse of the mainsail under its swinging gaff took the muscle of the rest of the crew. A warm southerly breeze wafted us up the winding river until we came to the railroad bridge, where we dropped all sail, which the hands stowed with a professional-looking harbor furl as we motored through the bridge and on up to the Seaport. There we put our lines ashore around 1:30, as I see in the water-stained pages of the log, and promptly devoured the luncheon Norma had made ready on this last leg of an eventful but unexceptional trip by sea.

And there, in due course, Waldo and Ed came down to join us, as I've related. The South Street Sea Explorer Scouts from the Lower East Side were still touring the Seaport and its ships as we talked. They had already met Waldo and the senior staff, who couldn't thank us enough for bringing these young people to them. This made us feel pretty good about Mystic and the reality of their mission with all sorts and conditions of Americans. And it seemed *Athena's* end of the visit went down pretty well too.

Among our other concerns was one not on the agenda, and which was not actually discussed. We had wanted to see if we couldn't overcome some of the awkwardness that had arisen between the world-famous Mystic Seaport and our South Street Seaport project. This went beyond the fact that we had appropriated their Seaport signature. A member of Mystic's board of trustees, I'd learned, had actually telephoned a few of our South Street trustees to try to get them to pull out of South Street, complaining that our project would divert funding from Mystic. Mystic Seaport relied heavily on New York supporters generally, and had what amounted to a "special relationship" with the New York Yacht Club in particular—where we also had friends, just beginning with Jakob, Eric and myself. I, on the other hand, believed, with the customary brashness of a New York ad man, that our new museum would attract new support and also generate new interest in the great existing museum. And I believed that the word "Seaport" in our name would be recognized as acknowledging a familial tie to our great precursor. To anticipate a bit, both these things actually came to pass: Mystic's income grew as South Street's did, and South Street people have always been aware of the tie with Mystic represented in the word "Seaport" in their name.

And to anticipate still further, the Mystic trustee who'd made the phone calls to our trustees became a great pal in a year or two, who would consult with me on fundraising (of which he was a master), and who became involved in some of our own South Street plans—but that is really anticipating.

It might be far-fetched to link all these developments to *Athena's* visit to Mystic on that long-ago July weekend, but, in fact, our conference on the schooner's caprail launched a grand and rewarding relationship with Mystic Seaport.

———————◆———————

We had our own lives to lead, Norma and I, and these continued to center on *Athena*, the schooner on which we'd launched our lives together. A sizable problem in keeping *Athena* sailing was meeting the bills for her upkeep. These, by law running back, I imagine, to the days of the ancient Greeks and Phoenicians, were always more than any reasonable person would forecast. There were this year, besides the endless repairs to a balky engine, an unscheduled haul-out at Berrien's yard in Milford to recaulk some leaky seams, and a really sizable bill for a new Dacron fisherman staysail, the old canvas sail having finally ripped across in a puff of air off Port Jefferson the previous year.

Our devoted madcap volunteer Jock Bartlett, who had turned out with his brother-in-law, the artist Lenny Nodelman, for numerous painting and cleaning sessions in South Street, had fallen for the schooner and chartered her for several weekends. This helped pay the bills. Jock was a widely literate and wildly eccentric character who held a number of publishing jobs in New York. He loved left-wing causes, cooking, drinking wine and singing songs, and he was, this year, between marriages (as his sister Ellen explains it), so he could follow the advice of a grand song of this era whose protagonist wanted to go where she wanted to go and do what she wanted to do. We were fortunate that his enthusiasms embraced the schooner and the Seaport which bound us all together. Jock asked Norma and me along on an early charter of *Athena* to "show him the ropes," and I have a vivid memory of balancing a portable typewriter on my knees to hammer away at a series of South Street memos and letters while we sailed heeled over at a noticeable angle in a brisk breeze, fortunately close under the shelter of Long Island, so the motion below decks was moderate and steady. We took that typewriter everywhere we went, so I could use it in odd hours to keep up with the volume of business streaming across my desk in 16 Fulton Street.

It was crazy, this whole business of keeping up a 43-foot wooden schooner in a life situation that called for total immersion in the large and small demands of running an active museum program, while somehow bringing an urban renewal project into being. But *Athena*'s serene presence and poised look upon the water were a positive help. She drew new people into the Seaport orbit. And she inspired her crews, including Norma and me.

Indeed, *Athena* wrapped up a lot of Norma's and my dreams and feelings about our lives together, as she had from the moment we first saw her indomitable shape burdened with a snowy tarpaulin, tethered to pilings in the icy waters of Camden Harbor. Freeing this noble animal from her chill confinement and taking her to sea under her own canvas was a fundamental act of liberation in our lives as well as the old schooner's. The schooner keeps recurring in my journal. On a cool, misty day, with milky sky and quiet sea the previous October, I'd noted how she'd made her way back to her winter quarters in Conroy's Creek, "isolated, traversing the small wavelets with her own sense of where she is and where she's bound, *Athena* is a world of her own . . . a library, with moving scenery outside her portholes as you look out, and the astonishing gift of being afloat." And, of course she was filled with memories of the grand cruise to Gloucester and Nantucket and the prospect of winter evenings spent aboard with friends with the woodstove fending off the frosty nights while we plotted future voyaging.

One evening that spring, sitting with Norma over martinis as evening crept over the lawns, I noted that the old sail we'd had to retire had gone on to lead a separate, inland career in the children's endlessly reinvented world: "The fisherman staysail, ripped by a breeze warm from the sands off Port Jefferson while it stood in easy curves high off the schooner's deck, now makes a great sail for the children's boat"—their "boat" being a swing set seat on whose overhead frame the aged canvas could be hung out in full glory. And we did seize stolen weekends afloat, like one when we'd slipped out of Milford to anchor overnight in the Thimble Islands. A note written in *Athena*'s cabin records the occasion:

> *We're anchored in Thimbles, children running about decks after*
> *bucket baths from Boats, and she now aloft varnishing foremast,*
> *which David and I sanded this morning (mainly David): the*

last of the brutal job on the spars. Schooner is coming into shape
slowly—we should live more aboard her and in general, live more.
Even in this idyllic scene I added a note that the last few weeks at South
Street had been hectic, despite my best efforts. Before summer was over,
the days would become even more hectic. This stemmed from a quite
innocent remark from Norma.

"What about a gathering of schooners in New York Harbor?" said Norma.
"We've seen the interest people have in this old rig. There must be a
bond between people who sail in schooners—wouldn't they like to get
together on our waterfront, which used to be crowded with schooners?
They could meet, visit each others' boats and have a fine time telling
each other stories."

"We'd have to do something special to give the thing a sense of occasion," I said.

"The occasion is the people and the boats they come in. We could have
people get together on each others' boats for drinks, speeches, maybe
sing a song or two. We could call it a celebration of schooners. After all,
when geese get together it's a gaggle of geese—why not a celebration of
schooners?"

Ideas began to pop into our minds like fish jumping in front of a pursuing porpoise, an image that reminded me irresistibly of Lewis Carroll's
memorable line "there's a porpoise right behind us and he's treading on
my tail." Critics have translated this to mean a pursuing purpose—which
I think was probably the case with that notorious punster, and was indeed
the case with Norma and me: once again we had a purpose pushing and
nudging us forward. We could do a show on schooners in the Street of
Ships exhibit in our headquarters gallery. And we'd have a lecture by the
Sandy Hook Pilots on the pilot schooners of old.

"Yes!" said Norma. "And Al gave us that lively portrait of a pilot
schooner slipping along in the Lower Bay, so for once we wouldn't
be using copies of things, we'd have a real painting, one done at the
time. It was done at the height of clipper era, wasn't it?" It was, indeed.

The painting had been done from life sometime in the 1850s, in the era when the schooner yacht *America* astonished the world (including many Americans) by sailing to England to win the cup now famous as the America's Cup.

"And what about Rudie Schaefer's *America*?" asked Norma. Yes, what about that noble schooner yacht! After our visit to the yacht *America* taking shape among heaps of sawdust and piles of wood chips in Maine earlier in the year, we'd kept in touch with her progress—and we'd recently learned that the *America* would be coming to New York in August. All this seemed a happy conjunction of the planets for our celebration of schooners, and with this eminently satisfactory conclusion to our planning session we called dog and children in from play and adjourned for supper.

By the time Rudie Schaefer, III called us to board the *America* at City Island for her ceremonial entry into New York Harbor on 10 August, the shape of the schooner celebration had been transformed into something rich and strange. This happened without Norma and me doing more than suggesting the idea of the schooner celebration to a few of the remarkable souls we had gathered around us. With the thump of a big gaff mainsail suddenly catching a breeze, it changed into a race for schooners, rather than a gathering to talk about the old days. Though schooners had pretty well dropped out of serious racing competition, with the cups being carried off by tall marconi-rigged sloops and yawls, schooner people had by no means lost the competitive urge and the fierce desire to show the wonders of their antique rig, which drove saucy hulls that made the newer models look like stiff department-store mannequins.

It was Rath, with his instinct for the telling stroke, who said to me one day: "C'mon, let's make it a race." If we did this, he said he'd get the word out to East Coast schooners, using his *Boating* magazine connections. Larry Kean, *Boating*'s technical editor, was immediately seconded to keep track of the arcane business of rating different boats for time allowance (big boats with lots of sail had to give time to smaller vessels with less—with combinations and permutations taking in several other factors), and Monk Farnham was drafted to lead the Race Committee. This was all heady stuff, and while the fit was on me I called on F. Briggs Dalzell, fleet captain of the New York Yacht Club, to take the chair on the committee. His participation would signal that this was no fly-by-night promotion, but a serious entry in the roster of yachting events.

Briggs and his brother, Lloyd, ran the oldest tugboat company then active in New York Harbor, so clearly he would know his way around—and any authorities that had to be placated to allow slow-moving traditional craft to clutter up a busy harbor would recognize this fact. A call to the port captain in Governor's Island confirmed my belief that vessels under sail without engines running so they could get out of the way expeditiously were in fact against the rules in New York Harbor. When I told Briggs this, he said: "Don't worry. I can take care of that"—and the rule was suspended for the day.

Full of joy with all this progress, I cheerfully reported back to Norma. The scene lives starkly in my mind. She looked at me, aghast, standing beside her desk outside my office on the second floor.

"Skipper, we just can't do this," she said. "It's not that it isn't a good idea, it's a wonderful idea. We just can't do it, that's all."

She went on to explain: We were barely managing the basic tasks of keeping the museum gallery open, signing up members and developing our message and the story we were here to tell—while seeking funds and support to make the Seaport restoration happen and bring in its ships. We needed to get the existing machinery working better before we took another step. We had our work cut out to establish a reputation for steadiness and regularity. It would be awful to declare a race to which no one came. Or even worse, to mount a sloppy show, with an ill-coordinated mass of boats racing against each other where no sail had raced in half a century, and where sail was now barred.

Norma was right. The case spoke for itself. The last thing we needed was a high-risk unprecedented effort on top of what we were doing. Just staying in business, with our doors open and signing up members for a fantastic dream of saving threatened streets and buildings, and reaching out to pull historic ships back over time's horizon, this was a venture woven out of the whole cloth of risk and craziness in itself.

But I also knew there was truth in a diametrically opposed viewpoint. So I explained, and fortunately Norma listened. I said that something new was happening in this project. In the act of asking people what they thought of the idea of a race for schooners—they started to work on it! It was truly taking on a life of its own among responsible people used to doing what they said they would do. People were already calling it the Great Schooner Race.

Norma nodded. If what I reported was true, then we should set up ground rules to assure performance at every stage in this vast new endeavor: First, everyone involved must know that if people failed to do their assigned parts, the South Street Seaport would pull out. We absolutely could not bail out failure with our overstretched staff. And, very important, if we did not get a significant showing of boats, the race would be canceled.

I was delighted. In a venture of this magnitude we could not afford failure. That fact, once recognized, would stiffen everyone to the task. And of course both Norma and I saw, in this transformation from a gathering of vessels into a hotly contested revival of the schooner races that had taken place in the harbor a hundred years earlier, the breakthrough possibility of having our scrawny outfit, with its staff of just three persons, recognized as a spokesman for the heroic traditions of the New World's greatest seaport.

CHAPTER 14

The Schooner Race for the Mayor's Cup, *Autumn 1967*

America *Enters New York Harbor—De Coursey Fales's Amazing*
Niña—*The Actual Mayor's Cup—Fifteen Schooners Show Up!—A Light*
Air Start—Afternoon Sou'wester Speeds Us Home—Ed Moran's Salute

The schooner yacht *America*'s rakish varnished masts beckoned in the early morning light, as Norma and I walked down Minneford's pier in City Island to board her for her ceremonial entry into New York Harbor. Stepping aboard, we entered a world of pristine decks, glowing mahogany and polished fittings of chrome and brass, with snowy, neatly stopped sails, fore and aft, ready for hoisting. We had entered another world, a Victorian world of privilege, craftsmanship and restrained good taste— far removed from the world of working schooners of *Athena*'s lineage. But this day we were ready to luxuriate in a noble yacht from the world that financed shipping lines and railroads, owned breweries and kept the wheels of commerce turning. On this cerulean morning, with a faint breeze stirring in the rigging, who would quarrel with that?

We told Rudie Schaefer, III, who met us at the gangway, that the vessel truly fulfilled the promise of the hull framed up in oak which we had seen on our winter visit to the Goudy & Stevens yard in East Boothbay. And when young Rudie brought up the proposed visit of the *America* to South Street later in the year, the elder Rudie said he was all for it. Then, as the big schooner took in her lines and set off westward toward the city, thrumming through Hell Gate and the East River on her powerful diesel, Norma and I outlined our scheme for the Schooner Race to our hosts. Without hesitation Rudie said yes, the *America* would take part in the event. This would have to be in a ceremonial role as observation vessel, since there was no schooner yacht around of a size to race the 104-foot greyhound. That was quite all right with the elder Rudie, who really didn't need any more ornate silverware to add to the collection he had won racing his cutter, *Edlu*.

The *America* paused off the Battery, where Mayor John Lindsay came out in a police launch to join us aboard. The professional crew turned to, setting sail as we steered toward the new Verrazano Bridge in the making southerly breeze. When we bore off for Manhattan, a fireboat showed up to give us a traditional harbor welcome, the spray from the fireboat making rainbows in the bright sunlight as though the bright arcs had been planned for this occasion. The elder Rudie had invited Lindsay to take the helm and, as we came up to the Battery, the mayor put the wheel over to get a little closer to the crowd lining the waterfront.

"Rudie," he said, "she's not responding to the helm!"

Rudie then said: "Actually, Mr. Mayor, I'm steering the boat," showing him a brass lever he had his hand on at the side of the elegant round cockpit. John Lindsay understandably looked a little put out. He then had the good grace to laugh, saying:

"And they call politicians devious!"

It was a thoughtful act of Rudie to ask Norma and me to join the mayor on this trip. The Schaefer Brewery, a mile or so up the East River from the Seaport on the Brooklyn side, was a well-known business in New York. Schaefer Beer had wetted the whistles of over three generations of New Yorkers, and Rudie Schaefer was a well-known figure in New York charities and public events. When I asked John Lindsay to be honorary chairman of the schooner race, he just glanced at Rudie before saying: "Yes, Peter, I'd be honored. Just let my people know what you need."

I had met Lindsay a few weeks earlier at a luncheon he had held at Gracie Mansion for people who were doing interesting things in New York. So when he came aboard, he gave me a breezy "Hello, Peter." This surprised me and, perhaps, Rudie, and helped get us off to a good start. But it was the participation of Rudie Schaefer and the splendor of his reborn *America* that assured that our race would be known as The Schooner Race for the Mayor's Cup.

When should the race be held? This had to be settled right away, so schooner owners could include it in their plans. After Rath had done some phoning around among boating friends, we had decided to make it Saturday, 21 October. This would give the maximum notice to people, with enough time to make sure those who had come from Boston or the Chesapeake could get back home to lay up their craft for the winter before insurance coverage for active sailing ran out at the end of the month.

We knew that late October could be chilly and blowy, but we figured our tough schooner people would not be deterred by that.

Then the scramble for schooners began. There was our *Athena*, of course, the host vessel for the event, and Bill Wertenbaker's lithe *Tyehee*, a graceful flyer which we had looked at in the search which had settled on *Athena*, the heavier, more traditional craft. Rath had sold his *March Heir*, which was sadly afflicted with dry rot. But he quickly signed up his friend Teddy Charles of the Seven Seas Sailing Club, which owned the big staysail schooner *Golden Eagle*.

The staysail schooner was conceived in the late 1920s to compete with the sloops and yawls, which had begun to prevail in sailing races. Staysail schooners set a tall marconi main, and between the masts a staysail with a fisherman staysail above that. Naturally the divided rig was not so efficient as the simpler rig of sloop or yawl. The schooner's short foremast could not carry the long-luff jib that made a boat really move to windward, and it could carry only a small spinnaker. So the staysail schooner still had to get a time allowance against the single-stickers in order to compete successfully. The gaff foresail, marconi main schooner in turn has to get a time allowance against her, and the pure gaffer (like *Athena* and *Tyehee*) gets an allowance against the gaff-marconi schooner.

The most successful staysail schooner is the immortal *Niña*, a vessel built in 1928 which is still with us today. This stubby-ended, heavily canvassed 59-footer, sporting a lofty 72-foot mainmast, appears to me in a haze of glory because of her distinguished record. After winning the transAt-lantic Race of 1928, beating the much larger three-masted *Atlantic* boat for boat, and going on to win England's Fastnet Race, the fast-traveling but temperamental racer did not do well under new English owners, until DeCoursey Fales acquired her in poor shape in the mid-1930s.

DeCoursey refined her towering rig and actually added to it, giving her a longer foremast for a longer luff to the jib, and a bigger spinnaker for downwind work. He strengthened her hull (which had begun to get a hump from the wracking strains put on it by her unusual rig), and began winning races with her. This was after my old skipper Bobby Somerset had cast the unlikely vessel aside because of her over-complex rig and the problems of the leaky, strained hull. As the world changed over the next thirty years, *Niña* continued to win races against successive waves of ever-more advanced ocean-racing craft. In 1965, the official history of the New York Yacht Club notes, "the venerable ex-Commodore DeCoursey Fales was still winning races with his ancient *Niña*."

Everybody had stories to tell about this legendary pairing of the smiling yachtsman and his incredible schooner. I had witnessed *Niña's* magic under Commodore Fales racing against her in the Bermuda Race of 1952. She sailed right through *Bloodhound*, a very fast English yawl with an American rig, and she did this going to windward, outpointing us and outfooting us so that the last we saw of her that evening was her sternlight, vanishing into the night miles ahead and to windward. She had passed us close to windward on her way, and we sat marveling at the flawless fit of her overlapping sails, including a very large fisherman staysail that I wouldn't have thought could be set going to windward—but she carried it, sailing closer to the wind than we were. It was a light-air race after the start, not *Niña's* weather, and *Bloodhound* finished ahead of her, but none of us would ever forget the sight of a schooner doing what no schooner could be imagined to have done.

What accounted for DeCoursey's magic? Other acts of his offer clues to a sweeping vision combined with a mastery of fine points of detail, notably the magnificent collection of literature on the seaman-author Joseph Conrad which he left to New York University on his death, and his generosity of spirit, which I and everyone felt who knew him. When we were holding a sad-faced wake in the Yacht Club for our friend Peter Longyear, drowned at sea, DeCoursey, who was holding a reception nearby, came over to our group, asked what was going on, and ordered a round of drinks to salute our departed friend, whom he had never met—an act typical of DeCoursey.

We wanted to find a way to recognize what DeCoursey had done for the schooner rig, and the usual way would be to name a trophy for him. Talking over what the trophy might be, a story about DeCoursey came to mind. He liked things just so, as was evident in the precise fit of his sails, and though salt water might find its way below, he would have things below dried off and spread with magnificent Oriental carpets underfoot the minute the schooner was at anchor. And, getting to our point, one of his crew told me he liked to have a Beefeater martini with his cornflakes at breakfast. Whether true or not, this story was of a piece with turning a worn-out schooner into an extraordinary winner long after she had passed the wooden boat's climacteric at age 30. So it occurred to us to have a bottle of Beefeater gin and a box of cornflakes as the prize for the cook on the last boat to finish in the Schooner Race—adding a touch of glory to the traditional consolation prize.

And now, of course, it became truly vital to have *Niña* enrolled in our race. The long-lived schooner (almost as old as *Athena*) was now owned and sailed by the US Merchant Marine Academy at Kings Point, Long Island. Frank Braynard, the grand mufti of merchant marine affairs, made a call there for us, and bang, the *Niña* was in without further discussion. This news was greeted with jubilation by all hands at headquarters. Norma's grin was a mile wide. Four schooners, *Athena*, *Golden Eagle*, *Tyehee*, and now *Niña*! That made a race.

So the Schooner Race for the Mayor's Cup was now definitely on. There was then the matter of getting an actual cup for the mayor to present to the winning boat. We had no budget for this, of course, and I had no idea how to set about getting a suitable cup if we had the money. So Norma moved in on this question, thinking that if we were going to do this, it had better be done right. Right, in this case, would be something of solid traditional design, in the family of the ornate silver pitchers that accumulate in senior yacht clubs, something redolent of the most famous of all trophies, the America's Cup itself. None of the trophy suppliers had anything to offer that met Norma's ideal. So she took to exploring the junk shops, jewelry and antique stores in and around Fulton Street. She found many quaint and curious vessels but none that filled the bill.

Then one day, with time slipping away, she went into a jeweler's shop on the east side of Broadway, just south of Fulton. The window facing on the street was crammed with wonders, old and new. Once inside, she explained what she was looking for and why: "It's for the Schooner Race for the Mayor's Cup that South Street Seaport is holding. We're down at the foot of Fulton Street."

The proprietor perked up. This was interesting; a challenge. Norma then happened to look up and her eye was caught by a brown, graceful object on top of a display cabinet. It was half-hidden in shadows, so she asked the proprietor if he could bring it down for a look.

"Oh, that," he said, "I'd almost forgotten that particular piece." He fetched a step stool and brought down the pitcher, handing it to Norma.

It was an interesting shape, and beneath the encrusted dust Norma made out a small boat and a windmill, wreathed around with soul-satisfying curlicues of all descriptions.

"If only it were silver," she said.

"Oh, but it is!" said her new-found friend, fully caught up in the game. And Norma knew she had found the Mayor's Cup.

"How much is it?" Norma asked, trying to keep the quaver out of her voice. She had told the proprietor that the Seaport couldn't spend much.

"Oh, I can let you have this for $150," came the reply. "Is that all right?"

"I'll leave $15 as deposit," said Norma. "Could you clean it up and have it ready for me by the end of the week? I'll bring a check."

At the end of the day Friday Norma appeared with her check, and the proprietor handed her an elegant grey box, saying:

"Open it up." Norma took the top off, and there, lying in a bed of crushed tissue paper, was the cup, dazzling in its brightness and stunning in its boldly assertive carvings.

"It's wonderful!"

"Isn't it?" said the proprietor. "Actually it's a nickel silver water ewer from the last century, maybe a hundred years old. Worth quite a bit more than I quoted to you, but we'll stick by our word, and it's yours to take away. I hope it brings you luck in your boat race and in your museum!"

Norma felt it had brought its own luck with it, and from this moment she felt better about the Schooner Race, as did we all when we looked at the trophy, proclaiming its message of joy and robust confidence.

The evening before the race, the captains gathered for a reception to meet our gang at 16 Fulton Street. It had an element of the miraculous to see the skippers walk in from the street, greeting old friends as the crowd gathered. Was this thing really happening? The reception was followed by a captains' meeting, at which race instructions and time allowance sheets were handed out, stirring vigorous debate on how much time one boat should give another. When the meeting ended we all walked down the waterfront to Wall Street, a quiet walk on a Friday night at that time, with only the swish of an occasional car passing on the expressway overhead, and the hooting of shipping in the river to break the evening peace. It was in an exalted mood that we turned to walk out on Pier 11. There, the masts of fully fifteen schooners swayed companionably against the lights of Brooklyn across the way.

A sixteenth, the *America*, lay at the Fish Market Pier in the Seaport; she was joining us as an observation boat, not enrolled in the race. Her presence, I believe, had a lot to do with the number of schooners entering the race. She was, after all, the epitome of the classic gaff-rigged schooner, and Rudie Schaefer's presence undoubtedly reassured the doubtful that this was a worthy event.

Our crew gathered bright and early to join Norma, Tom and me aboard *Athena*. We already had aboard the devoted British crew that had done so much for the ship, David and Jane Johnston and Richard Henstock. Then Jim Kirk, Member No. 1 of South Street Seaport Museum, came down the dock to swing himself aboard by the main shrouds. He was followed by our friend, the marine artist Charles Lundgren, whom we had named mate for the passage, Norma retaining her customary title as boatswain. These were soon joined by Stanley Gerr, a new friend, who worked as a multi-lingual translator at the United Nations but had never attended college, having gained his education in coasting schooners and in the square rigger *Tusitala*. Graduating from these tough schools, with many a yarn to show for it, he devoted himself to study at the New York Public Library and so launched his career as a top-notch professional linguist. He was our best kind of member, the kind who simply walks in the door one day and asks how he can help.

The last new hand to swing himself aboard *Athena* was a short, rotund person with a grumpy expression and twinkling eyes, who introduced himself all around as Paul Loring. Paul was one of Rath's finds, an extraordinarily gifted cartoon artist from Rhode Island whose comic drawings of yachts and yachtsmen enlivened the pages of magazines like *Yachting* and *The Rudder*, infecting readers with high glee at the unfortunate situations we all strive to avoid while afloat, just beginning with groundings and capsizings. A classic work of his hangs in the New York Yacht Club to this day. It depicts an older member explaining to a neophyte that a vacant pedestal standing in a row of busts of distinguished members is reserved for the head of the person who first loses the America's Cup. Sixteen years later, the cup was finally lost to an Australian boat, after over one hundred years of successful defenses. The losing skipper kept his head and remains active in the Club, proving that Loring's cartoon was, perhaps, a bit off the wall. But no one would dream of taking it down.

Good sportsmanship was in the air as we motored downriver in light airs, making sail as we went. Bets and insults were traded back and forth between rival boats, with a freedom and nonchalance that made me feel people were actually accepting our madcap venture as a serious proposition.

The tide, which had been scheduled to start ebbing before the race start at 10:30, insistently kept flooding, so with virtually no wind, we all had to keep our engines on to keep from being swept back up the river.

When the *America* came threading her way through this tumultuous scene of swaying masts, slatting sails, and criss-crossed wakes, she seemed like an elephant stepping majestically, with due care, through a crowd of wild boars rooting for their supper in the furrowed waters of New York Harbor. A giddy, gilded note was added by a trumpeter standing in the stern of his own schooner, who played the exuberant opening bars to a commercial we had all heard on the radio:

Schaefer is the one beer to have, when you're having more than one.

I'm sure the Schaefers and their guests aboard the *America* appreciated this as much as we did, as cheers and laughter echoed across the foamy waters.

The Moran tug marking the starting line a few hundred yards off the Battery had been provided by our trustee Admiral Moran, who wasn't aboard. But the race committee and a clutch of yacht club officers were aboard, with Briggs Dalzell supervising the start, no doubt with his usual aplomb. They had to have laughed at the chaotic scene they surveyed, as schooners of all sizes ran their engines to keep somewhere near the starting line against the cheerfully flooding tide. When the preparatory signal sounded, it was mandatory to shut off engines, and the whole fleet, even the magnificent staysail schooners *Niña* and *Golden Eagle*, were carried stern-first toward the river from which they had just emerged. But after a while a vagrant southerly puff came along, and then another. A photo taken a little after the strung-out start shows the Zieglers' elegant black staysail schooner *Bounding Home* sitting on top of *Golden Eagle*—that is to windward, and a little ahead— and, surprisingly, not too far behind, *Tyehee* doing the same to our *Athena*. No one has a visible bow wave, so the boats are hardly moving through the water. Clearly the tidal current has turned at last, and is now beginning to ebb, carrying us all toward the Verrazano Bridge—and beyond to the wide waters of the Lower Bay.

Fortunately, the errant puffs of southerly air that had been teasing us began to build into a definite breeze as the morning advanced, and before noon *Athena* was rolling along close-hauled with everything set, against a steady southwest breeze. This was sheer delight, and everyone was smiling, even as *Tyehee* came up from behind to overtake us again (she'd lost her early lead when we had tacked sooner than she had to keep in the main push of the now favorable tidal thrust). As she passed us to windward with all sail set and drawing to perfection, she was the epitome of schoonerdom—and with our friend Bill Wertenbaker at the helm she looked, as indeed she proved to be, unbeatable among the gaff-rigged schooners.

Aboard *Athena* our pickup crew, nothing dismayed, worked together admirably. Norma kept a watchful eye on the set of our own sails, whose every stitch she knew—some put in with her own fingers—while Charlie Lundgren reported on wind and current shifts encountered by other boats in the panoply of sail which was now spread out in the Upper Bay like flowers strewn across the water before the Statue of Liberty. Our United Nations linguist Stanley Gerr showed us an old schooner trick by hauling down briskly on all parts of the mainsheet together to help shove the long-keeled schooner around when we were tacking in light airs after the start—this gave her a kick that brought her round in lively fashion. Up forward, Norma and Tommy between them got the jib around across the forestay at the precise moment to sheet it down hard as the breeze caught it on the new tack, while David Johnston led a gang that lowered the fisherman staysail, smothered its thrashing canvas and got it up again on the right side of the triatic stay in what seemed like seconds. When somehow the topsail sheet got jammed aloft, I quit the helm to shinny up the mainmast to clear it, an incident recorded by Paul Loring in the cartoon he presented to us after the race. But mainly it was clear sailing, with no need to touch a line or do anything but admire the russet-leaved shores of Staten Island to windward, and the sparkling waters of the Bay, which smiled back at a halcyon sky. It was all enough to make one forget the oil and garbage the harbor waters carried in those days.

There were only a few ships anchored off the land this Saturday morning, but as we came up to the Verrazano Bridge we spied the towering bulk of a great white liner coming into the harbor. She passed close to windward of *Athena* on her way in, blanketing our wind all too effectively, but we forgave even this in light of her notable beauty of form. She was the spanking new Italian liner *Raffaello*, distinguished by her fine, arched bow and perfect sheer sweeping aft to a tucked-up stern, the whole surmounted by two latticework funnels, well aft, which gave an offbeat nonchalance only a well-bred princess could get away with.

As we consumed a lunch of hot tomato soup and roast beef sandwiches, welcome against the nip in the October air, we spotted a snowy hillock of sail ahead. This turned out to be *Niña,* a low hull charging toward us under a bulging spinnaker and an airborne golliwobbler—a huge fisherman staysail tacked down at the foot of the foremast, hoisted to fore and main mastheads, and sheeted to the end of the main boom, which, when eased in a fair wind, gave a sufficiently broad sheeting base for this immense stretch of sail. To weather, ahead of the foremast, swelled the perfect hemisphere of a parachute spinnaker, drawing precariously at this angle of sailing. The fast-traveling schooner had rounded the marker buoy beyond the Verrazano Bridge and was racing flat-out for the finish line now just a few miles ahead.

We cheered the gallant *Niña* as this symphony in swelling canvas swept by, and their people returned our cheer, led by the skipper, Joe Prosser. Joe raised his cap with a flourish from his stance by the helm—while the cadet helmsman, conscious of his considerable responsibility of keeping his hurrying charger on course, took one hand off the wheel for a brief wave. The rest of the crew responded from their stations, where they were ready for instant action to keep the huge kites drawing overhead. Joe had been persuaded to quit a sail training program in Vancouver, Canada, to come East and teach the skills and attitudes of seamanship under sail to fledgling American ship's officers. This he proceeded to do in a rigorous, demanding program, with good humor and panache worthy of his predecessor, Commodore DeCoursey Fales. The aging schooner had been lucky enough to turn up with a skipper who could work her complex rig as the original maestro had done.

It was some time before we reached the buoy from which *Niña* had come galloping back, but when we did, we lowered the fisherman staysail on the run, with eager hands hauling in the canvas before it touched the water moving by to leeward, and gybed smartly around the buoy. Once around, David and his crew promptly ran the fisherman up again on the other side of the triatic stay, while Stanley and Norma set up the port backstay hard against the strong pull this sail would exert against our tall, reedlike main topmast. The good wind blew and *Athena* leaped forward, her lee scuppers gurgling as she leaned over to dip her rail in racing white water. From up forward we began to hear the growl of her advancing stem, a sound which turned into a rolling thunder as the old schooner settled down to her work. As the log entry has it, it was a "splendid roaring reach home, rail down."

Mainly, I think Norma and I felt relief—seasoned with a spice of jubilation at the grand pleasures of the day—but mainly simple relief that the schooners had come and had sailed hard with no mishaps, and everyone was enthusiastic about the day. This was the feeling we got, anyway, as we passed our lines to *Tyehee* to tie up beside her at Pier 11 at Wall Street. *Tyehee* had finished fourth, behind the three staysail schooners in the race, but first among the gaff riggers. We felt pretty good finishing right behind her, the second gaffer in the race, and actually ahead of all the marconi-headed schooners. We took the mooring lines of the other schooners as they came in, receiving thanks and congratulations from everyone. Then it was time to get dressed for the Schooner Race dinner we'd arranged at Whyte's Restaurant, a few blocks up Fulton Street.

Dress code for the schooner skippers was set as black tie and sneakers, which most captains managed to achieve, though some, perhaps at the insistence of their wives, wore black shoes instead of the white canvas sneakers everyone wore when sailing in those days. The mayor did not attend, but Briggs Dalzell, as chairman of the Race Committee, presented the Mayor's Cup with a sure sense of style, once Monk Farnham of *Boating* had read out the order of finish (taking due account of time allowances as worked out by *Boating*'s Larry Kean). It was my privilege to present the consolation prize—the cornflakes and gin—to the cook aboard the last boat to finish. The crews and guests in the crowded dining room apparently liked this tribute to Commodore Fales; all 345 of them stood to applaud the losing cook.

There were some objections to *Niña*'s racing sails and to what were felt to be unfair penalties in the time allowance system—which were a secret brew the braumeister, Larry Kean, wisely refused to divulge. As it worked out, *Niña* won in the face of heavy penalties for her slender hull and powerful rig. No one pursued these objections as formal protests, and Norma and I simply took them as evidence of the seriousness with which people took the race, born as a madcap long-shot, but now clearly on the racing map.

Seafaring Ed Moran, a seaman living at Seamen's Church Institute at 25 South Street, had sailed in coasting schooners. He had retired in a somewhat confused state of mind, and he sometimes puzzled people by his magisterial pronouncements on affairs. But everybody accepted him as seer and poet of the sailing ship heritage. He wrote us this letter about the race:

> *To the true ship lover, the region surrounding the new museum was a veritable Fiddler's Green on October 20–21. Take the new* America, *berthed at Pier 17, on the water side of the Fulton Fish Market. I admired her look of strength, stately loftiness, and grace. As to* Niña, *the winner, a finer ocean racer never wet her bobstay. Well done,* Niña! *May she float, until time is no more.*

So *Athena* brought us the two most famous schooners in America to support South Street's claim to speak for the age of sail in New York Harbor.

CHAPTER 15

The Privilege of Continuing, *November–December 1967*

Membership Grows to 3,000—Improved Finances—
Reporter *Hits its Stride*—A Walk Through South Street—
A Fish Market Christmas

Athena had gone into winter quarters soon after the Schooner Race. This followed an extraordinary summer, starting with the sail-in to open South Street Seaport Museum, on to our descent by sea on Mystic Seaport with the Cape Horn sailorman Archie Horka and the marine artist Os Brett in crew, and finally to the Schooner Race for the Mayor's Cup in October. We had our final sail of the season with Alan Frazer aboard on a weekend sail from our mooring at City Island to Cold Spring Harbor. While we were there, Mel Conant came alongside in his trim ketch *New World*, and Alan and I broke off our work over the typewritten pages of *A Walk Through South Street in the Afternoon of Sail* to review with him the photos that had come in to us from all over. Mel, always interested in visual or written evidences of the seafaring heritage, was enthralled with what he saw.

A week later, on a dank and drizzly Saturday, Norma and I motored *Athena* around from her City Island mooring to her winter home at Conroy's Marina. Norma's parents came with us for the ride, which did not exactly match anyone's picture of a yachting trip, and the family's German shepherd dog, Gina, was plainly not happy. After tying up at Conroy's, we stripped the wet sails from their spars and bundled them into our waiting car. And the following Sunday, a splendidly sunny day, we dried the great stretches of canvas out on the Franceschi lawn, making the bold image of a schooner on the grass, one composed of the actual sails that had driven us so far in fair winds and foul with, we hoped, more adventures to come. For one summer, at least, we had defied Karl's prediction that we could do South Street or *Athena*, but not both.

While we pursued our South Street work, life aboard *Athena* continued in her layup mode, a-buzz with the dreams and projects of children
and grownups alike. We visited her nearly every weekend, relying on
the faithful coal stove to warm her cabins as she slept through winter
storms and freeze-ups in the mud berth that held her fast in Westchester
Creek. Rocco's Chippewa Tavern welcomed our tumultuous crew from
time to time, but now that things were in operating order in the working
household set up within the schooner's hull, we usually had our dinners
aboard. George Campbell joined us from time to time for fascinating
talk of seafaring and ship design, often with his Scots wife, Peggy Knox
Campbell, sister of Bernard Knox, the renowned classicist. Peggy's sunlit outlook, cheerful ways, and occasional "Oh, George" helped temper
George's acerbic wit and defiant stance as a lower-deck rebel—a stance
he maintained valiantly in the face of all his own artistic and scholarly
achievements. My father, Al, and Berenice stopped by every few weeks
for dinner aboard or sometimes ashore—but then it would be at the
Sign of the Dove in Manhattan, never Rocco's, much as we might sing
its praises. Friends from South Street came aboard from time to time
on a Saturday or Sunday, led by Jim Kirk or sometimes Bob Ferraro and
his new fiancée, Paula.

We'd been assigned a new berth at the downstream end of the row of
floats—a privileged spot, clear of everyone else. It was reached, however,
by a tippy wooden walkway. Once my son Tony, bounding along in his
self-possessed way, fell off this shifty pathway into the filthy water, which
led to a thorough scrubdown by Norma and dose of whisky to kill whatever germs he had swallowed. And once Peggy Campbell, looking up
to wave to us with her beatific smile, fell off in Stygian water up to her
middle, to our horror. When we helped her back up and onto *Athena's*
deck, she wasn't actually smiling, but she gave a wry grin, and it may safely
be said she later laughed more about this than any of the rest of us ever
did.

But it was the children that set the style of things aboard *Athena* as
she lay tethered peacefully to her float. Their complete possession of the

schooner led me to write "Schooners Are Made for Children," an essay published in the year-end issue of *Boating* magazine. The story was much taken up with active sailing, relating how even small children like to haul on the clustered lines that make up a schooner's running rigging, and they delight still more in coiling down after the careless grownups have left things in a mess, and how, after getting under way, one can saunter aft to stand in an offhand manner next to whatever grownup is at the helm, to accept governance of the wheel if it is offered. And indeed, we learned that children can become fairly good helmsmen quite early in their lives.

With the success of the Schooner Race, we felt we'd won a small but noticeable foothold of New York City's awareness. The question was: What could we make of that awareness?

We couldn't do much about the ultimate challenges facing the Seaport: acquiring the blocks of land to save the buildings of the old seaport trades and bringing in the ships that carried on those trades across wide and restless seas.

The thing we *could* do was to build up our membership and create an active, supportive constituency to give a public voice to the effort, as well as a steady stream of financial support. And here the Schooner Race helped us in ways we began to feel almost immediately. The dim, practically subliminal awareness of the Seaport as a new presence in New York was enough to embolden our people to pass out Norma's brochure about the Seaport project in the offices where they worked. And in the outer boroughs of the Bronx, Queens, Brooklyn and Staten Island, where most of our volunteers lived, they could talk to friends and neighbors and pass out brochures. They found more people greeting them with a smile of recognition and a willingness to pass over a dollar bill for introductory membership or, increasingly, $5 for a regular membership. These extra dollars certainly helped, but the vital thing was to enroll the new member. Who knew what that new member might do for the Seaport!

———◆———

The lift in our affairs led to a cheery item in the year-end issue of the *South Street Reporter*, in which we reported that membership had surpassed the announced 1967 goal of 2,500—and had reached 3,000! With the growing numbers came some sizable checks, as people closed their books for the year. Income for 1967 totaled $68,000, enough to cover expenses and bring the Seaport into the coming year in reasonably good financial shape. This helped ease the tensions of our tough first year of operations. But we knew we had to keep moving ahead. So this *Reporter* carried an announcement of our plans to celebrate the 150th anniversary of the first regular transAtlantic liner service. This regular, scheduled service was launched on 5 January 1818, when the 400-ton packet *James Monroe* set sail from the Black Ball pier at the foot of Beekman Street. Os Brett designed a stamp honoring the "First Atlantic Liner, 1818–1968" for the occasion—a wonderfully lively painting showing two Black Ballers meeting in a near gale in mid-Atlantic, "carrying sail as few ships would carry it in such weather," our editorial column noted. And "Letters" carried an appeal by Mayor Lindsay calling for issuance of this commemorative stamp. The mayor cited the support of Congressman Farbstein (the old-line congressman I'd campaigned against), along with "distinguished historians and historical societies," including such luminaries as Howard Chapelle at the Smithsonian Institution; Robert G. Albion, Harvard's professor of oceanic history; and Waldo C. M. Johnston, director of Mystic Seaport, to reinforce the Seaport's case.

And, to make a good thing better, we had held public events to give an historical context to our Schooner Race. Joseph Phelan, author of a new book on the *America,* and George Campbell, the architect of the *Cutty Sark* restoration in England, together gave a remarkable seminar on the *America,* queen of schooners, aristocratic heir to the working pilot schooners that shepherded New York's arriving ships in and out of port. Their talk was backed up by Alan Frazer's new display on New York schooners, mounted on the western wall of the gallery, which we had set aside for changing exhibits. And on 2 November, George Seeth, senior member of the Sandy Hook Pilots, told stories of his experience guiding ships in and out of port. His 50-odd years' experience, no mean reach in time, was authentically extended by memories of his father's sailing days, including being at sea in the famous Blizzard of 1888. That horrendous event, which tied up the city in huge snowdrifts, took a sad toll on the pilot schooners and fishing schooners sailing out of New York and left an indelible impression on the minds of survivors—as it did on all who heard Captain Seeth tell his story.

Since our emphasis was now turning to the great square-rigged deepwatermen that had given South Street its name as the Street of Ships, we added to the *Reporter*'s crowded pages a brief biography of the *Tusitala*, last square rigger to sail under the American flag. Laid up in the post–World War I shipping slump, she was saved from the knacker's yard as a project of Christopher Morley's Three Hours for Lunch Club. And when that gallant band ran short of funds, she was kept sailing from 1925 to 1932 by James A. Farrell, father of the James Farrell I had met through Eric Ridder. Stanley Gerr, who had sailed with us in *Athena* in the Schooner Race, had sailed in *Tusitala*'s last two voyages. He contributed to our brief ship portrait a photograph of himself at the end of the bowsprit, helping to stow the ship's flying jib in a squall. The ship herself was by this time long gone, but we reached out to collect tales of her sailing as the last square rigger in commercial service under the American flag.

By this time we had hit our stride with the *Reporter*. Every page was full of brief notes that evoked whole stories, whole worlds of experience. Our mission, as we came to see it, was to send fresh lifeblood pulsing through the annals of the past and bring fresh learning, concern and dedication to the affairs of the unknowable future. The past lives on, not just in formal records, but in songs and memories, dreams, recognitions and word-of-mouth traditions, as well as in letters and diaries, sketches, poems, paintings, graffiti and the ships, buildings and the very streets where it took place. All these we regarded and acted on as within our purview—part of our story, our purpose and field of activity. And this broad-sweep voyage of exploration through time can open a person's inner vision to the fact that we are not living out our existence in our own lives only, but as part of the larger, continuing drama of humankind.

On the first page of the *Reporter*, in this final issue of the year, there appeared a small, hand-drawn advertisement for a slim book called *A Walk through South Street in the Afternoon of Sail*. This was Norma's and my effort to meet the need for something more substantial than a newsletter to draw people into the Seaport story. Our Local History Committee had been working to this end over the summer, but the interesting discussions went on with no clear picture emerging of what we wanted. The irrepressible Charlie Dunn had come out with a twenty-page account of imagined waterfront happenings on the day the *James Monroe* set sail from her South Street pier. But this didn't really fill the bill.

What were we after, then? Something that told the South Street story, the comings and goings of ships, the varied cargoes, the businesses ashore, and the people, what they were like, how they acted in the days of the Street of Ships. Robert G. Albion's magisterial *The Rise of New York Port* carried this story through to 1860, and there were other good books on the life of the port since then. We envisaged something at once smaller, livelier and more redolent of how things were done in old South Street. Back in April I'd noted in my journal: "We may sell, and publish, books," as something we could achieve to leave a mark behind, if all else failed. By August it was clear we weren't going to get a book this year, and the project was dropped.

But, then Norma and I began thinking of the great file we'd been amassing of photographs of shipping in South Street. Among these were photos strikingly expressive of the look and very heft of the big square riggers caught between their ocean passages, and of the tugs, schooners and canal boats that moved things in and out of the great entrepôt that was South Street. Karl led us to Robert Weinstein in Los Angeles, the great collector of sailing ship photos and data; to Andrew J. Nesdall in Waban, Massachusetts, who at a glance could name and date a ship from the final days of sail; and the historian John Lyman of Chapel Hill,

North Carolina, whose encyclopaedic knowledge enabled us to get small details placed in proper context in the annals of the port. These dedicated people did endless work for us, for love of the subject and because they believed America needed a museum on New York's Street of Ships. Norma and I took pleasure in odd moments poring over this growing photographic file for our own education and to build up the Seaport's records, so that people could visualize the vanished world we celebrated.

One Saturday as I went through a pile of photos at home in Yorktown Heights, I sat contemplating the stem of a fine-lined wooden Down Easter, which sprang in a compelling arch from the East River water before me. From the texture of the wood you could see the stem was new, as was the copper on her bottom, which gleamed brightly at the waterline. The hull planking, showing each seam with some ragged edges, was clearly older. She'd seen some living, and she'd just been in for some shipyard work before her next Cape Horn voyage. Her name was *Sea Witch*, a name made famous by the clipper ship of an earlier generation and the set of her bow, revealed in a gentle morning light, had the learning of the clippers in its fine strength. She was businesslike with her heavy chain bowsprit rigging and her massive anchors swung out on her catheads, ready for instant dropping if the tow failed on the way to sea. Behind her, on the other side of the pier, one caught a glimpse of other ships; the thicketed rigging of another Down Easter and the gaunt spars of a schooner. These gave a locus and sense of reality to this elegant ship, stirring a little to the wake churned up by tugs in the river—as one could tell from the wet marks from passing waves showing on her copper waterline. No wonder the photographer had stopped to catch this picture!

I called Norma over to my side of the dining room table to look at this scene. Norma was taken by the bold design of the photograph, built around that arching bow, and the soft radiance of the sunlight of a long-vanished forenoon. We talked a little about the world the ships had sailed in and what joy it would be to see such noble creatures again in South Street. And then Norma said: "Why not put this in a book?

Not just this picture, but a bunch of these photos. If we can get people to walk into these photographs, to walk through that vanished world, that would be something."

Right away I started scribbling notes on a pad. Norma brought more pictures and started going through them. The initial selection and virtually all the research had been done for us by Karl and his friends to help us get to know the old Seaport. And I had by now met enough old-time sailors to say something about the people of the ships.

One was Fred Harvey, who had told us how Captain James "Shotgun" Murphy, running across Fred on Market Street in San Francisco in 1910, hailed him across the street to invite Fred to come with him as boatswain in a passage to New York in the famous Down Easter *Shenandoah*. Sailing ship berths were getting hard to come by, so Fred said yes on the spot. The voyage went well, but as it was drawing to an end just outside New York, the cook, perhaps distracted by thoughts of the fleshpots ashore, carelessly flipped his swill bucket the wrong way when he dropped the bucket over the side to clean it out. Hanging onto the lanyard—he dared not let it go—he was dragged overboard.

The great ship was immediately hove to, the crew launched a boat, got out the oars and rowed back across a fortunately calm sea to fetch the floundering cook. "Where's the bucket?" roared Captain Murphy when the half-drowned cook was brought before him. The cook had lost it, struggling to keep afloat in the sea. Shotgun gave him living hell for losing a piece of ship's gear that had been entrusted to him. From the way Fred told the story, it was clear he thought this a proper line to take on a mistake that might have cost the cook his life. I noted, with an editor's privilege, that perhaps the cook was "a happier man than if he had been pawed over or psychoanalyzed to discover the origins of his urge to self-destruction."

Norma and I had a grand time exploring South Street in these photos of Down Easters and the streets and the surviving buildings we were coming to know so well. And the proud, self-confident stance of the people, from the seraphic-looking Captain Murphy, to riggers sending up sail to be bent on the yards aloft—or the nameless young man with opened jacket, standing at the corner of Cuyler's Alley, while across the way the bowsprits of a fleet of ships arch over South Street, all the way to the Brooklyn Bridge in the dim background. In another photo, looking out on a pier at the lower end of South Street, we pored over "a scene of forested masts and rigging towering over a jumble of unloaded cargo-boxes and barrels and heavy logs of mahogany from Honduras." We noted:

The creak of block and tackles; the shouts of stevedores and dray-men seem to echo over this remarkable scene, sounds heard here for three and a half centuries, as the ships that built the city's greatness came and went.

Thanks to the devoted and expert work of the advisors that Karl Kortum had pulled together for us, we were able to add insights on American seafaring based on factual records, which I cannot read today without being moved by the poetry of fact in the life of these ships and the men who served in them. The last photo in the book showed the handsome *A. G. Ropes* tied up in a winter scene in South Street with this valedictory note:

Topgallant masts rigged down, the famous A. G. Ropes *waits for a cargo in South Street. The learning of millennia of sail are shown in her lifting bows, burdensome hull and powerful rig. This 2,342-ton ship, built in 1884 in Bath, Maine, twice made the run to San Francisco in under 110 days, matching clipper standards. A British officer testified to her smart handling under sail: "A little bark was to leeward of us and a big Yankee ship, the* A. G. Ropes, *was passing us to windward. When the squall came up we lowered our royals and eased the topgallant halliards. The big Yankee clewed up his skysails and royals all together as if he was a frigate with a wartime crew and set them a few minutes later, all royals together and all skysails together. The little bark to leeward didn't touch anything and the squall took the maintopgallant mast out of her." In 1906 the* A. G. Ropes *was converted to a Luckenbach barge, and was lost with her crew of three on December 26, 1913.*

Beneath, there appeared this invitation:

> *The ships are gone, but they have left us proud memories, and if you come to walk down South Street today, turn in at Schermerhorn Row on Fulton Street: there you will find the offices of the South Street Seaport Museum where the story of the ships and men who sailed them is being retold.*

We were fortunate to get Mayor Lindsay to sign a brief foreword to the book, and fortunate that Edmund A. Stanley, Jr., president of Bowne & Co. printers, who had become a frequent visitor to South Street, printed it for us free of charge. So, from a standing start in late October, by December we had a small 25-page book showing harbor scenes never before gathered together, with detailed discussions of the ships in the photos, reproduced with stunning clarity and carefully critiqued by our distinguished advisors. To this day I marvel that it all happened and that we had an actual book for sale.

The Steering Committee considered this too late for Christmas sales, an attitude that reduced Norma and me to a kind of fury, so I wrote demanding that each member of the committee make three calls to sell the little book. Bennett Cerf (whom we'd never met) ran an item on it in *The Saturday Review*, and we persuaded a few bookshops to take copies. Our little ad in the *Reporter* reminded everyone to steer people to South Street to pick up a copy or two (at $2, or $1.50 for members), which also helped our membership. In this way we soon sold nearly a thousand copies, adding well over a thousand dollars to the year's income. Every dollar taken in was profit, since production was donated and Norma's and my work was done at home on volunteer hours—as was the vital authoritative work of our advisors.

As the year drew to a close, there was good feeling in the air! We were delighted when Admiral Will called to say that he had been named chairman of the New York State Maritime Museum, the office for which we'd proposed him to Arthur Massolo, our friend in the New York State

bureaucracy. We'd also proposed our treasurer, Eric Ridder, and our secretary, Bob Tarr, as trustees of the state museum, thinking this overlap
of officers an important step to pave the way for a cooperative relationship from the outset. Also named were several people put up by Mike
Seymour, including the great liner historian Walter Lord, who became
a lasting friend of South Street. We received a rather formal letter from
Eric Ridder informing us that now that he was on the State board, that
was where his main energies had to go. We had gained enough confidence
in ourselves to not be troubled by this. We wished the state museum all
the luck in the world to get the funding needed to start building the
museum in Schermerhorn Row. But it was the Seaport that had the
public program, the urban renewal designation in the making, the leads
to bring in historic ships, and, above all, the thriving, active membership
which seemed able to make all kinds of things happen. So it was with
light hearts that we held a reception for the new state museum board
and our Seaport board at 16 Fulton Street on 14 December. This turned
out to be a time of mutual congratulations and, on Norma's and my part
at least, a shared feeling of relief and thanksgiving that we had led the
South Street venture this far without crashing.

On Friday, 22 December, as we were winding up business in the office
before the long Christmas weekend, Joe Cantalupo stopped by.

"Come on, Mr. President," he said. "we've got some calls to make."

So, nothing loath, I shoved my papers into a drawer and walked out
with Joe, telling Norma on the way that we'd be back soon.

"No," said Joe, "Mrs. President is coming too."

We went first to Jack Scaglione's retail fish market in the upland end
of Schermerhorn Row. Every day Jack's establishment presented a new
window display of oysters, clams, scallops, squid, and a glorious variety
of finny denizens of deep and shallow waters in designs so appealing and
varied that we'd instinctively stop by to study the day's offerings on the
way to work each morning. This evening Jack was behind the counter and
started opening little neck clams as soon as he saw Joe in the doorway.

There were more clams for Norma and me, which we slurped up happily while Jack poured out paper cups of rye whisky, which he ordered us to down in one gulp, followed by a chaser of hot clam broth. Then it was on to our next-door neighbor, Robert Bruce, who once was quoted in the papers as saying: "I'm very fond of the fish market. It's our heritage. All of us here—we're all neighbors." More whisky there, which began to taste not so raw as we'd thought. And then upstairs to Sweet's Restaurant at the river end of the row, where Miss Leah Lake received us with appropriate gentility and brandy while her dour business manager looked on; and then on round the corner to Sloppy Louie's, where Emil Morino stood us a round of Famiglia Cribari wine, served in coffee mugs, while Mrs. Morino behind the cash register near the door held up her hands to indicate that she was not accepting any money. Joe was in his element, clearly enjoying the wisecracks that flowed with the drinks and giving as good as he got, while Norma and I smiled at each other and the world, sharing in the peace.

So it was for this Christmas, and thus it was to be for Christmases to come, while our company held together.

CHAPTER 16

Gains by Sea and Land, *January–March 1968*

The Whitehall Club—Albion Speaks at Seaport Luncheon—
"Square Riggers '68"—Albion and Chapelle on the "X Factor"—
Kaplan Grants Help Finances

The Whitehall Club opened for business in 1911 in the top floors of the grand new building at 17 Battery Place, overlooking Battery Park and the harbor, and it soon became a fixture in the maritime community of Lower Manhattan, a gathering place for bankers, shipping-line operators, dock builders and other waterfront figures. Where the more reserved and proper India House, a few blocks inland, was founded to serve owners and senior partners in shipping and foreign trade, the Whitehall Club did a rip-roaring business with the operating people who really ran things. While there was a good deal of overlap between the memberships of the two organizations, it was only in the Whitehall Club that George W. Rogers, president of Geo. W. Rogers Construction Company, could be heard (as I heard him once) declaring loudly, as Admiral John Mylan Will, Jr., USN (Ret.) stepped into the barroom: "Here comes Admiral Will, as phony as a three-dollar bill." To which "Dutch" Will responded equably: "Hello, George."

Sessions at the bar, beginning in the late morning, would not infrequently continue through the afternoon, while members threw dice for the next round of drinks. Spiro, the bartender, hired as a boy when the club opened over half a century before the time of this narrative, was a lively presence in his late sixties, when I first met him. He was to preserve into his eighties his ability to leap over the U-shaped mahogany bar to subdue any disturbances that threatened to get out of hand. He died shortly after he retired, and soon after, the club closed its doors, since much of the action that kept it going had moved to New Jersey and Connecticut, taking with it much of the gusto of the maritime culture which had for the past 350 years flourished in Lower Manhattan.

The building itself, at 17 Battery Place, was crowned with a tiara-like masonry arch, and the 31-story, yellow brick building soon became a familiar landmark for incoming ships. The club's windows, high above the treetops of the park below, were furnished with binoculars on stands, so one could look out to the shipping that thronged the Upper Bay and down through the Narrows to the open sea to the south, and over the busy shores of Jersey City to Newark Bay to the west. Tugboat dispatchers, working in the offices below, used to lean out their office windows to shout orders through megaphones to waiting tugs nested near Pier A, first in the long procession of piers that marched up Manhattan's West Side to receive the Cunarders and other liners that took over the North Atlantic traffics from the packet ships of the days of sail. The club walls were hung with a grand array of marine paintings, mostly of harbor scenes full of sailing packets, old-fashioned paddlewheel steamers and the ubiquitous tugboats of old, usually crowned with a gilded eagle until this was replaced with a more utilitarian searchlight. The club's membership and its governing board took the traditions of the maritime industry to heart, however raucous they might get in expressing that sentiment.

It was on this scene that Robert Greenhalgh Albion, professor of oceanic history at Harvard, appeared before a luncheon meeting of sixty shipping executives to launch our first James Monroe Luncheon on 5 January 1968, celebrating the 150th anniversary of the sailing of the first Black Ball packet ship, *James Monroe*. With help from Frank Braynard, his boss Admiral Edmond Moran, and the draw of Jakob Isbrandtsen's name, we had gathered the people who represented New York's shipping industry. Admiral Will cheerfully agreed to be chairman of the luncheon, which put a seal of approval on the affair. Duly assembled, the influential but irreverent guests might have expected the kind of droning lecture that you get from the retired professors who emerge from mothballs for the sake of a free lunch and captive audience on such occasions. But what they got was something else.

Bob Albion prefaced his talk by saying he was a New Englander born—as anyone could tell by his downeast twang. But, he told us, he really preferred the crowds, noise and excitement of New York, the leading center of immigration and innovation, to the quiet decorum of Boston, home of the bean and the cod. From this felicitous beginning he proceeded to bring to life the hurly-burly of seaport New York in the lusty days of the young American Republic, leading up to the sailing of the *James Monroe*, first of the big 400-ton Black Ball packets that inaugurated on-time departures, full cargo or not, in the vital North Atlantic trade. On a chilly 5 January 1818, the *Monroe* had set sail at 10AM amidst falling snow, with less than half a cargo, but exactly on schedule. In the crossing of the Western Ocean—as sailors still called the Atlantic—the Black Ball packets soon made a name for themselves for speedy, reliable, and remarkably safe passages over this turbulent sea, which Arabian sailors had named the Sea of Darkness. In the following decades the Black Ballers, together with other packet lines sailing on the same principle of on-time departures, won the cream of the oceanic carrying trade from their British rivals, hitherto rulers of the roost in the Atlantic scene as in oceans around the world.

Bob sang a chorus from that grand song "In the Black Ball Line I Served My Time," to convey something of the spirit of the time, when Yankee ships were driven as ships had never been driven before. Crossing this wide and tumultuous ocean was narrowed from a matter of months to a few weeks by their bold masters and the demanding disciplines rigorously enforced among their Anglo-American crews. To have sailed in Black Ball and achieved the rating of AB (Able-Bodied Seaman) meant that you could get a berth anywhere, in any ship, any ocean.

Having got the attention of his now-awakened audience, Albion got them to listen to a few basic facts about how New York rose to dominance in Atlantic trades. His research showed that leadership in this vital artery of trade was what made New York the New World's greatest seaport, not, as most history books had it, the opening of the Erie Canal seven years later. It was true that heavily-laden barges slipping along through the canal's smooth waters slashed the price of Midwestern wheat delivered in New York to a fraction of its prior cost when delivered by creaking ox carts struggling over rough roads. But, Albion reminded these shrewd maritime operators, the economic breakthrough had come about only because the port generated the traffic to support the huge cost of the 300-mile canal.

"Forget what you heard in school," said Bob. "The canal didn't make the seaport; the seaport made the canal. And that should tell us all something about the power of maritime trade to change the world." These unprofessorial-sounding remarks were founded on meticulous statistical research, in which Albion had been a pioneer. And his talk got some of our guests thinking about their businesses in ways they really hadn't thought before, as I later heard from some of them. Rounding things out with a few salty anecdotes about how the lifestyles of South Street took shape as the city's sea trades built America's wealth, Albion's talk was done.

Admiral Will rose to his feet to lead the room in a standing ovation. Everyone followed suit, including Will's nemesis, George Rogers; Ted Stanley of Bowne Printing; our advisory chairman Melvin Conant of Standard Oil of New Jersey; and Eric Ridder of the *Journal of Commerce* with Lloyd Dalzell of the Sandy Hook Pilots Commission, Tim Pouch of Pouch Terminals, and Johnny Caddell of Caddell Drydock, joined by the arch-rival tugboat leaders James P. McAllister and Edmond Moran.

Waldo Johnston of Mystic, Admiral George Dufek, president of the Mariners' Museum in Virginia, and Howard Chapelle of the Smithsonian Institution were also there, each plainly delighted to see the shipping industry out in force. I was awed to see these seniors in our business. Each, after all, had traveled a hundred miles or more to be there with us for this occasion, suggesting that we had not done so badly in our first eight months in our one-room museum.

Herb Halberg, representing Mayor Lindsay as Commissioner of Marine & Aviation, closed the meeting for us, conveying the mayor's consent to take part in our program of visiting square riggers in South

Street, which we had christened "Square Riggers '68." He spoke briefly and emphatically on the importance of public education in the historic role of the port, and he was listened to attentively by our guests, each of whom had business of one kind or another with him. He gave Norma and me a cheery thumbs-up before sitting down.

On the way back to our office, I remarked to Norma that I was impressed by how these nabobs of shipping and grandees of the museum world had turned out for our luncheon. A smile crept over her face and she started laughing as she grabbed my arm and gave it a squeeze.

Our one-room museum had changed for this occasion, as the new year opened. The gallery hadn't grown any bigger or more splendid, but its plain space—white-painted brick walls around a grey cement floor—now held a three-foot finely detailed model of the *James Monroe*, a gift from Ted Stanley, built for us by Bill Hitchcock of New Jersey. Our museologist visitors pronounced the model to be "of museum quality," at which we nodded gravely, secretly pleased beyond measure. And it held sailing people fascinated as they puzzled out clewlines and buntlines, topgallant brace leads and other rigging arrangements they'd never seen before. People also noticed the small galley on deck, looking like a sentry box, with a stovepipe emerging from its rounded roof. This was generally called a caboose, placed there so it could be cut away and pushed overboard in case of fire, a great danger to any ship at sea, but particularly a sailing ship with her tarry rigging and acres of flammable hemp or cotton canvas.

Along with this big, first-class model we now had a stirring portrait of the vessel setting sail as she stood downriver in a chilly north wind which whipped up sharp-crested wavelets in the East River, pathway to the world. This, the work of the artist and scholar George Campbell, was again a superbly detailed, utterly authentic presentation of a ship that changed shipping history and New York. The *James Monroe* was virtually unknown even to maritime historians—but Hitchcock's model and George's portrait gave body and life to the ship and invited you to step back into the age she sailed in.

George volunteered to stand by the model (he had helped draw its plans) to answer questions at the reception we held to introduce the Black Ball exhibit. He didn't mind innocent questions, but was not one to suffer fools gladly—and he grew a bit testy with people of less learning and wit pointing out to him that the vessel had no black ball on her foretopsail, the famous emblem of the line. So we quickly posted next to the painting a neatly lettered card stating that the Black Ball on the foretopsail was introduced well after this first voyage. This did not stop people offering their corrections to George, but George now was able to deliver his riposte by silently pointing out the sign.

We held other gatherings to discuss the contribution of the Black Ball packets to New York. These included a luncheon of our Advisory Council members before the Whitehall Club gathering. Here Bob Albion, Norma and I started a discussion launched by Norma's strong conviction that it needed something more than a big, sheltered harbor with ready access to the interior to explain the swift but enduring rise of New York to dominance in the Atlantic. We both felt that the culture we lived in, like the atmosphere we breathed, was all around us but passed unnoticed, and yet it had everything to do with how we spoke, thought and acted. Norma saw New York as a generator of new ideas which continuously bumped up against old ways of doing things, drawing on the resourcefulness and progressive ways of what she called our "mixed-up, noisy and contentious people." This was resolved by Bob's cheerful agreement that an "X factor" was indeed needed to explain the extraordinarily creative innovations which spurred New York's rise to dominance—this X factor being the questing spirit of unregenerate, unreformed New Yorkers. I believe Bob, educated in the logical positivist traditions of the age of the steam locomotive—which took you efficiently down pre-determined tracks—became quite attached to this upstart notion of an organic cultural differential as a root cause of economic progress.

Interestingly enough, the reserved Howard Chapelle heard this discussion in silence, but on the evening following the Whitehall Club luncheon he gave a learned talk on the *James Monroe,* in which he took

pleasure in offering a few thoughts on New York's achievements and
New Yorkers' brash ways. This concluding session on the Black Ball observances was at a supper we had set up at the Seamen's Church Institute
and was open to the public. It brought ordinary people into the game;
as we were learning, professionals worth their salt enjoy defending an
argument before all comers.

Norma and I had started with the strong conviction that the challenging surge of open debate was the heart of progress toward the truth
of things, and this became a core doctrine of our South Street gang. It
was a treat to see how people at the top of their profession responded
to this view of things.

With all the warmth of human interest which seemed to grow without
stopping, we had only the most tenuous hold on the territory of old
buildings and cobbled streets we aspired to save beyond the $50 monthly
rent we paid to Mr. Alliger, landlord of our building at 16 Fulton Street.
But fortunately Jack Kaplan had kept a watchful eye on our affairs since
our meeting in South Street the previous spring. A subsequent meeting
he'd held with Jakob, Tom Van Arkel and me at the Yacht Club had led to
a division of forces, with Jakob seeking banking arrangements to finance
purchase of the land, and Jack commissioning Tom's firm to develop a
feasible plan for the finances of the Seaport once established.

To us, the months seemed to crawl—for we couldn't seek the large
sums needed to restore and develop the Seaport until we had a plan and
some indication at least of initial funding for land acquisition. In the
meantime, Jack's daughter (and colleague) Joan Davidson kept pushing
for action to keep the flame we had lit in the Street of Ships burning
bright. Joan early realized the need to get leaders in the architectural
and cultural communities of New York involved in our venture, and
she spread word of our efforts far and wide. She also did everything to
encourage our maritime ventures and people-involving activities. Her
enthusiasm was infectious and brought us recruits anxious to see what
all the excitement was about.

Our own thinking about the project continued to develop. The tenor of our concerns is evident in a note in my journal in the previous August. Introducing herself as Lily Fournier, a young black woman had taken my arm and pulled me aside on the street to tell me that she and her husband, Alex, had bought 91 South Street, next to Sloppy Louie's at the river end of Schermerhorn Row. They planned to open a bar on the ground floor of the aged brick building, and were engaged in setting up living quarters on the floor above. Alex, Lily told me, was an artist, and the bar, to be named The Sketch Pad, would be a center for the artists who came to the Fish Market district to depict their impressions of a unique New York neighborhood. I noted in my journal that evening:

> Note how she and di Suvero and all the crew that live and do
> business in the capsized hulk of Schermerhorn row conflict with
> the organized idea of a big clean museum: making me wonder
> just what a museum should really be. One turns more and more
> to a broken-up series of displays salted into houses with people and
> commerce in them.

The di Suvero I mentioned was Anita Ventura's old friend Mark di Suvero, the sculptor. He lived with his wife, an Italian *contessa*, at the inland end of Schermerhorn Row. There in a cavernous attic room he had hung a group of mobile metal sculptures, including a pony made from an oil drum painted red with a mane of bright yellow rope strands, suspended from the overhead rafters. Neighborhood children were invited in to play on this pony and attendant dragons, birds and other flying machines created by Mark's genius and his skills as arc-welder of metal shapes.

These were the kind of occupants who gave life and purpose to a neighborhood. To have such native roots would encourage an organic development of the Seaport area as a living entity full of historic continuities, out of which new traditions and concerns were growing. Tom Van Arkel, who was retained to translate our citizen vision to developmental reality, closely shared our views on a living neighborhood, as did Jakob Isbrandtsen in the brief moments of attention he could give to Seaport philosophy while he was also seeking arrangements to make the whole thing happen.

On the development front, Jakob well knew how important it was to begin early to sign up tenants of the type that would set the tone we wanted. So he and I welcomed the idea of the printing shop which Ted Stanley of Bowne and Co. had proposed to open in South Street. We announced this interest in the January 1968 issue of the *South Street Reporter* in ringing terms:

> *Bowne & Co., leading New York printers since 1775, will hang their sign outside a historic printing shop in the Seaport project, according to an agreement reached between the Company and Seaport trustees.*

We hoped this announcement would assure people of the reality of our intentions and plans. With it, we ran an evocative engraving of the Bowne shop at the corner of Pearl and Wall Streets made in 1841 just prior to its 75th anniversary. We were proud to add that Bowne & Co. had made "a substantial contribution to set up the shop," and we sincerely hoped this would inspire others to follow this mixed commercial-educational endeavor. In coming years, the shop flourished as the sole survivor of this first-generation thinking in South Street.

Jakob, Tom and I also met with the eminent restaurateur and bon vivant Joe Baum, who ran the famous Four Seasons restaurant uptown and went on to establish the splendid Windows on the World at the top of World Trade Center 1—the giant tower whose cavernous cellars were at this time being dug at the other end of Fulton Street from our workaday Seaport project. Joe had a good feeling for the tenor of life in South Street. He never built the Seaport restaurant we talked of, but he remained a good friend as his works flourished, culminating in the world-renowned Windows. After we had left South Street to start over again to build up the 300-member National Maritime Historical Society, he stayed in touch and was always available for a talk about New York, a city for whose diverse roots and flowerings he had an enormous affection. We missed Joe, with his gusto and appreciative eye for the city he loved, when he died too young some fifteen years later.

The New York State Maritime Museum was very much part of the South Street Seaport scheme in this era, and soon after the Albion reception I was invited, on 18 January, to attend the first meeting of its board of trustees, headed by Admiral Will.

I felt a certain awkwardness in this and subsequent meetings. For although chartered as a state institution, the museum had no staff and no budget—nor any immediate prospects of securing either. Meanwhile, South Street Seaport Museum was charging ahead, with no government support of any kind, beyond the City's interest in its plans. For Dutch Will this situation must have chafed. Imagine a Navy man given command of a ship only to find there was no crew to man her or fuel to steam her, while the Seaport, like a rakish schooner, took the lead in going to sea with a cheering amateur crew sailing on the winds of popular support.

I felt my job was to sketch out the Seaport plan and suggest the role the state museum could fill as the academic center at its heart, indicating how vitally we depended on that learned function. Norma strongly disagreed with this. She felt that Schermerhorn Row was at the heart of the project and should be kept under our own control. To turn it over to the State of New York would create an unnecessary division in the South Street project. But I held to my vision of a glorious partnership between the two institutions. A degree of overlap and duplication of functions, it seemed to me, was a cheap price to pay for getting two quite different institutions working in partnership, in different styles, to make a new center of sea learning and experience of New York. Norma remained unconvinced but accepted the strategy of cooperation.

The state museum trustees seemed to find my ideas a bit high-flown for their deliberations and, indeed, we were never able to get them actively into planning the state museum's role in the larger Seaport project. They wanted to await the recommendations of the professionals the State would surely provide. Dutch Will always had me attend board meetings, where he was supportive of my reports, but I noticed that there was little ensuing discussion of what I reported from the Seaport front, nor of joint action to achieve our shared objectives.

One trustee at this first meeting, however, seemed to catch fire with the notion of a new public-private enterprise of shared purposes and agreed-upon roles. Introducing himself as Lloyd Dalzell, he made a date to see me a few days later, and, on 26 January, over a morning cup of coffee in my tiny office overlooking Fulton Street, he proposed we make a trip to Colonial Williamsburg together, to see how Rockefeller interests had restored that town to what it had been when it was a seedbed for the American Revolution. Lloyd, a New York State Pilot Commissioner and until recently head of Dalzell Towing, offered to pay for the trip, and on 31 January he and I caught a plane south to explore Williamsburg. The colonial gardens and sweeping lawns were dormant in winter, but colonial crafts flourished, from blacksmithing to oxen driving. There was reading out of colonial speeches and proclamations, accompanied by the lofty ceremony and catchy tunes of the day. Indoors, hearths crackled with wood fires in historic buildings brought back as closely as possible to their state when the young republic was taking shape.

We lunched with Edwin Kendrew, director of the restoration. We had been joined by Tom Van Arkel and his wife, who showed a lively interest in the whole operation. This bright young couple asked questions about philosophy and finance and kept the table alive with laughter at their wit and their obvious appreciation for all they'd seen. Lloyd was beaming throughout the proceedings, obviously happy to have brought this caring and knowledgeable group together. Kendrew, as host, asked Tom and me questions that showed that he had been following our South Street venture closely. He said he hoped we would call on him for any help he could give us in our side of the project.

Sadly, just a month later, on 27 February, we were summoned to attend Lloyd's funeral at St. James' Episcopal Church, uptown at 71st Street. We learned that he had taken his own life, afflicted by what private woes we did not know. All we knew was our sadness at losing him, and our memories of a generous, supportive and helpful soul. His intervention had helped us noticeably in our quest for joint design and good relations with the state museum, and I had been looking forward to working with him on these things and on our budding relationship with Williamsburg, which he had brought into being through the productive foray he sponsored to that grand center. I noted in the next *Reporter* how he had "worked for unity of design and high standards of execution in our project." I added: "His enthusiasm and generous vision will be remembered in South Street."

This turned out to be truer than I knew when I wrote it. My editorial note led Lloyd's younger brother, Briggs, to stop me in the front hall of the New York Yacht Club to thank me for the note I'd written in the *Reporter*. Briggs then said: "I'd be glad to step in to help out, if you like." Norma and I did like, and so we gained in F. Briggs Dalzell a new officer of the Seaport, and a friend who saw us through thick and thin for thirty-odd years to come.

Meanwhile, of course, we were still sweating out the uncertainties of the development of the Seaport land—which we always looked at as our own terrain, but of which we owned not one building, indeed not one stick or stone. A break in this situation came about on 21 February, when Jack Kaplan called a special meeting in his office. He had reviewed the Van Arkel & Moss financial study of the Seaport-to-be, which he had commissioned, and was ready to let us know his findings. His firm, recommended to us by Dick Buford, had in the early 1960s engineered the restoration of Head House Square at the heart of the revival of Philadelphia's historic downtown center. Head House Square was a general retail marketplace like the Fulton Market at the heart of our Seaport project (which later evolved into the Fulton Fish Market of our day). Along with a fine appreciation of the values we were about in South Street Seaport, Tom brought to his work a shrewd sense of marketing possibilities and the financial realities of development in a dense urban environment.

———◆———

Jack Kaplan's eyes sparkled as he welcomed us to his office on Wednesday morning, 21 February 1968. Joan and our old City Club pal Ray Rubinow, director of the J. M. Kaplan Fund, were with him, as was the Fund's expeditor Dixon Bain, Jr., who served as secretary of the meeting. Tom Van Arkel and I represented the Seaport. Dixon Bain's notes, prepared that very day, opened with an Item #1 to knock one's socks off—precisely as Jack had presented it: "The feasibility study prepared by Mr. Van Arkel is sound; it suggests that the Seaport can, in fact, be made a reality at a cost of about $11,250,000." Of this, just under half would be raised through mortgages on Seaport property leased out to suitable tenants. The remainder would have to be raised by philanthropic contributions and "conceivably, units of the state and federal governments."

Tom had estimated that the Seaport would need $70,000 to support operations over the next twelve months, and beyond this there was an agreed need for a much larger, closely detailed new model, with accompanying promotional material and more sophisticated financial analyses, costing another $30,000. Of the total $100,000, the Kaplan Fund would underwrite up to $70,000, "with the firm understanding that the Seaport staff would make every effort to raise the $100,000 as if the Kaplan Fund's pledge did not exist."

I pledged the Seaport to this kind of effort, and Jack made good his pledge, beginning immediately to pay us $5,000 a month while also covering all the Van Arkel costs for a new model, presentation materials and further financial studies. Four months later, Jack was to increase our monthly subsidy to $10,000, effectively guaranteeing our financial stability during the very active summer months. The summer program played a vital role in raising funds in the fall season, when most of our annual support would come in, as we had learned from the outpouring of support we had received in the last quarter of 1967.

After this meeting we could walk forward confidently with a longer stride, rather than stumble through a series of emergency cash infusions to keep the project going. I was also encouraged by the City's plan, announced just before the Kaplan meeting, to put housing in the western part of the district, which would accord well with the lively community we sought to bring into being in South Street. And Buford passed us word that the City would soon move to designate the Seaport as sponsor of the balance of the Brooklyn Bridge Southeast Urban Renewal District. Things were moving around us to bring the Seaport forward as a next step for New York.

Some of this new confidence may have communicated itself to people I ran into in my work. A month after this, I was walking down a city sidewalk with Ralph Miller, head of the Museum of the City of New York.

We had just come from a meeting of the State Historic Trust. At this gathering of professionals, it became clear that the State Maritime Museum was not yet in motion to forestall the bulldozers reshaping Lower Manhattan and could give no picture of their plans for Schermerhorn Row. This had left it up to me to sketch out how we envisioned the formal museum, with its library and collections, in relation to the larger Seaport project. I had presented our picture amateurishly, I imagine, but with conviction based on our experience with the ordinary New Yorkers who flocked to see our museum and join us as members.

Ralph had shown a rather frosty attitude toward our efforts, so I was startled to hear him say: "Peter, I've been thinking about the Seaport, and I've got to tell you I really like the way you're running it. You don't give a damn for what the pros tell you to do. You've got your own vision and you're making it happen. You're getting other people to see it too."

To this he added: "The Seaport needs someone like you to run it. And I'll be glad to help in any way I can."

I did not know in March 1968 that Ralph was an artist, a painter of considerable gifts and a philosopher of broad humanistic concerns. But the generous impulse behind his words appealed to me, and from then on, taking his words at face value, we were in touch on Seaport affairs.

CHAPTER 17

A Southward Foray, *May 1968*

An Intercontinental Trip—Aboard Wavertree—
Primitive Ships in Puerto Montt—Grande Luxe in Punta Arenas—
Andalucia—Wavertree's *Sheerstrake—"An Ocean Wanderer"*

"FRIDAY. May 3. Morning. Now over River Plate, I believe, on passage south to look at Southgate and Ville de Mulhouse, long trip and long shot." This airborne note marked our first step in the long journey to bring the *Wavertree* to New York. Our ship had been launched as the *Toxteth*, but entered service as *Southgate* and bore that name only for her first eighteen months in the jute trade to India. I found something onward-urging in the sound of the name *Southgate*, something perhaps which resonated with my early explorations southward in the city—always in quest of some gateway to an elder New York.

But Karl Kortum, her discoverer, called her *Wavertree*, as she was known for most of her working life. I soon yielded to Karl's call on this, particularly when he cited his aide Anita Ventura's opinion that *Wavertree* was a lovely, fresh replacement for the stolid name the ship was born with. So the ship would soon again become *Wavertree*. But to us, at this point, she was *Southgate*.

What put us aboard our continent-bridging plane was Jakob's decision that we should inspect the ship to get a clear picture of her condition and some idea of what we'd have to pay to buy her. The Lloyd's agent in Buenos Aires had provided a general notion of the vessel's condition, and it was now time for a South Street team to board the dismasted hulk and meet the people with whom we would be dealing to buy her and to make her fit for the long voyage to New York.

By this time we had written several detailed memos which summed up the qualities and conditions of a whole fleet of historic ships that Rath and others had searched out for us. Besides the National Maritime Historical Society's

American barque *Kaiulani* in the Philippines, there were other great square riggers still afloat. We planned to inspect one of these—the long-lived *Andalucia*, ex-*Ville de Mulhouse,* in the Straits of Magellan—and use her as a stalking horse to let the *Wavertree*'s owner know that there were other fish in the sea. Then there was the handsome and sturdy *Champigny* in the Falkland Islands, and the fast-traveling *Moshulu* in Finland, winner of the last Grain Race from Australia in 1939. And there were others, like the lithe colonial clipper *Antiope*, reported to us by Cape Horn sailorman Alan Villiers as beached and rusted out in East Africa with a palm tree growing through her bottom—ships of all sorts, scattered in odd corners of the ocean world, the last heirs of the deepwater sea trades under sail.

Our reports reflect the dedication of the far-flung community of people who worked to save these ships, of whom Kortum in San Francisco, Villiers in Oxford, England, and Frank G. G. Carr in London (whom we'll meet later in this story) were the recognized leaders worldwide. The reports also reveal the slowly developing criteria by which we justified our decision for the *Wavertree*. Not counting the great wooden ships already preserved—the whaling ship *Charles W. Morgan* preserved in Mystic, the clipper *Cutty Sark* in Greenwich, England, and such warships as USS *Constitution* in Boston, and Nelson's flagship HMS *Victory* in Portsmouth, England—the only remaining wooden ships were wrecks too deteriorated to save. We knew we had to go for an iron or steel ship. We looked for a full rigger, square-rigged on all three masts, which would echo the standard rig of the 1850s. Along with this traditional rig, *Wavertree*, thanks to the art of her presumed designer, Hercules Linton, had the sweeping sheer more typical of the Yankee Down Easter than her British brethren. The conservative bent of her Liverpool owners also gave us the anachronistic bonus of topmast doublings and other features carried forward from an earlier age. And she was built of iron, which rusts much more slowly than steel.

It was a glorious moment for the two of us as we stumbled out onto the airport tarmac on the morning of a brisk autumn day in Buenos Aires.

We went aboard our ship on the afternoon of our arrival, escorted by the courteous, trim-looking Moore McCormack agent Charles Crocker, to whom young Bill Moore had commended us. Charlie, who seemed genuinely keen on the project, had brought with him Captain Juan Jose P. DeValle, retired director of the naval dockyard on the Buenos Aires waterfront. Big-framed, militarily erect, and proudly moustachioed, DeValle drove us in his ancient, immaculately kept Buick to the industrial waterfront on the Riachuela, south of central Buenas Aires, where the ship lay moored alongside a stone seawall next to a dark brick slaughterhouse.

The ship, as Karl had said, was big. And though stripped to her bare iron hull and with cropped bulwarks, she was still a mass of interrelated curves wrought in old iron. This curvilinear world just began with the ship's crowned deck (all steel plate, the wooden deck long gone), the rounded edge to her poop aft, and a slight in-turning of the sides as they rose from the water, what sailors call "tumblehome," culminating in the noble upward sweep of the rusty decks toward the bow. She was a sea-defying shape so expressive she seemed to us to be aiming at far horizons beyond the industrial urban landscape she confronted. The old ship had a distinctive presence amidst the shoreside sand-heaps, soot-stained brick buildings and rusty corrugated iron shacks, making one see at a glance why local watermen called her *el gran velero*—the great sailing ship.

Charlie Crocker cautioned us not to talk to anyone about any interest in buying the ship. We were to be tourists with a special interest in historic ships. We could take a quick look at the vessel and, if still interested, Charlie would inform the owner, Señor Numeriani, of our interest in due course. Walking aft, he led us into the poop and up a passageway lined with intact cabins where the mates had lived, into the main saloon now filled with several desks with telephones and typewriters manned by one or two male secretaries, presided over by the same bulky, genial Señor Tosí whom Karl had met two years earlier. We talked about our interest in the ship's history, true to our role as *turistas* interested in maritime relics. Tosí smiled broadly, and tried us out with a few words of English.

"This ship Lor' Nelson ship in Trafalgar," he informed us. The Battle of Trafalgar of 1805 is of course well known in Spanish naval circles, as is its hero, Lord Nelson, a hero of the navies of all nations. But this claim was a stopper—how could we maintain our act, pretending to believe this preposterous statement? So I just mumbled "Verdaderamente!"

Tosí seemed pleased with this response and asked Norma if she'd like a drink. Thinking of a Coke, she nodded yes, and our host snapped his fingers in the air. A black-sweatered man sitting at one of the desks instantly rose and left the room. He returned carrying a bottle of Johnnie Walker Red Label. He filled a tumbler halfway, which he handed to Norma. Charlie and I got the same treatment, while Tosí contented himself with a glass of red wine. Cigarettes were produced from an unbroken carton of Marlboros, and Norma accepted a pack with thanks. Not knowing what to do with the full glass of Scotch whiskey, she took a sip or two, leaving it at that. Charlie and I somehow managed to finish most of our glasses, and rose from the table as soon as we courteously could to inspect the ship.

Our great discovery, besides the sheer presence of the ship with her undaunted deepwaterman's air, was the original ship's wheel. This lovely teak creation, over five feet tall, was enclosed in a boxlike iron shed at the after end of the poopdeck. Karl had missed the wheel in his brief visit to the ship and was cheered when we told him about this pristine artifact, which had been gripped by so many hands guiding the ship through fair weather and foul around the world's oceans.

The next day, a Saturday, Charlie and his wife carried us away for a sail in the River Plate in their ketch, *Sancho*. After a pleasant reach out into the broad waterway, we anchored for lunch a few miles offshore. Charlie asked us how we were faring, and we confessed to being in a bit of a daze at the strangeness of everything, but enjoying it all very much—the ornately painted buses that coursed the city streets, the grave courtesy of everyone we met, even the ceremonious way that we were served morning coffee in our hotel. And of course we were charmed by the Crockers' well-kept *Sancho*, a small, able vessel gleaming in white enamel and varnished mahogany, with cheerful hosts who enjoyed each other's company and knew how to do a luncheon afloat worthy of one of the handsome Moore-McCormack liners whose affairs Charlie handled in Buenos Aires.

That evening, we were to catch a plane to Santiago, the Chilean capital on the other side of the continent. But a partial strike by LAN Chile pilots had disrupted the flight schedule and we had to return to our hotel. This didn't bother us, for it gave us a chance to review our impressions of the *Wavertree* over an unhurried dinner and do a little planning for the next leg in our foray south. We were going to Santiago to catch a plane south to Punta Arenas on the Straits of Magellan, where we were scheduled to look at another square rigger, the *Andalucia.* This big four-masted barque, built as the French *Ville de Mulhouse* in 1899, was a possible alternative to the *Wavertree.* Alan Villiers, whom Karl and Os Brett had interested in our project, had created a sensation in our office by sending us a postcard a few months earlier from Punta Arenas, advising us of this big barque's existence. Swinging at anchor in the Strait, with her masts still in her and indeed her lower yards still crossed, she was a notable find in her own right.

After spending most of Sunday at the airport, we finally got a flight which reached Santiago at 5 PM. The trip had been an interesting one in an aircraft that weaved its way between the mountaintops of the Andes chain. We had a celebratory hotel dinner with a couple we'd met on the plane, and we were up betimes the next day to catch a plane for Punta Arenas. But the work stoppage had disrupted schedules, and there would be no flight to Punta Arenas that day, or maybe the next. But there was, we were told, a flight to Puerto Montt, a third the way down the coast, from where there were daily flights to Punta Arenas. Puerto Montt is at the head of a chain of islands reaching all the way south to the Strait of Magellan.

It was grey and blowy when we caught a plane south and arrived at the small town overlooking the sheltered inlet that made its harbor. We were curious about this town we had never expected to be in, so, after settling in at our newly-built and comfortable hotel, we made our way to the waterfront, coming upon an open-air fish market with curious spiny lobsters, fish of all shapes and sizes, tiny clams and huge snails, all laid out on beds of seaweed to keep them alive, and, in some cases, flopping. The market backed on a pebbly beach with fishing craft hauled up on it. Further north on this beach we saw a big, boxy sloop with square bilges laid ashore. Everything about the vessel was black: her hull, decks, the men's faces, hands and clothing—even her bundled mainsail had a dismal, funereal look. The men were using her gaff to swing aboard bags of coal from a donkey cart waiting alongside on the shingle. We had come upon the living act of maritime trade out of time immemorial in a new, vividly alive corner of the world of today. The locals seemed quite friendly, and with our primitive Spanish we found out that these heavy chine-bottomed craft (built heavy to withstand the strain of frequent groundings) maintained a steady trade to farms on the outlying islands which formed a protective barrier against the high winds of the Roaring Forties, surging in from across thousands of miles of the boundless Pacific Ocean.

We watched, absorbed in the activities around us, until a distinctly chilly dusk crept over the scene, dimming the clear light of the cool autumnal afternoon in this far southern latitude. Norma suggested we move on, and as we trudged up the hilly road to our hotel we turned for a last look at the harbor scene. Just outside the entrance we made out a slender fishing vessel, a different creation from the heavy trading sloops, drifting in from the skerried passage that reached for untold miles southward. As we watched, the lone figure at the helm left his post and went forward to lower his gaff mainsail. He then hauled out a long sweep which he mounted on a forked post aft, to begin sculling his way up the darkling harbor water, a silhouetted figure swaying to a timeless rhythm.

When the fisherman and his boat vanished in the thicket of tilted masts at the landing, we turned and went to our supper of clams and fresh fish, talking quietly of the day's adventures over a bottle of Chilean Riesling. We went to bed early to be ready for the morrow, when we expected to resume our way to Punta Arenas.

Clouds remained too thick the next day for our plane to take off, and we spent the day exploring the outskirts of the town. We were concerned about the continuing delays and the arrangements we had made in Punta Arenas, so the following morning we went straight to the airline office. There we were told that there would be a flight that day, but there were no openings for us.

This was too much for Norma, who had worked in the travel business in New York. She demanded to see the office supervisor and reminded him in no uncertain terms that it was an industry rule that passengers with international tickets always had priority in situations such as ours. Furthermore, the president of LAN Chile would hear about this violation of protocol unless we got seats on the plane scheduled to leave that afternoon. Courteous explanations that the airline pilots' work stoppage had inconvenienced important businessmen at a cost to the national economy and suggestions that *turistas* like ourselves should try a little *filosofia* and use the delay to enjoy our stay in Puerto Montt met with an implacable stare from Norma's usually kindly eyes. After much palaver and several phone calls from the back office, we were told we would be accommodated on that day's flight.

"Toward Cape Horn!" read my journal entry for the day. "What a long haul it is down this long bony arm of land the clippers had to fight their way round." I also noted our anxieties about getting an in-water survey of the *Wavertree* and about talking directly with her owner, since, as I noted, "we both wonder if Numeriani really means to sell." These were matters we decided to telephone Crocker about on our return to Buenos Aires after our visit to the *Andalucia*. But we didn't let the gravity of our mission interfere with our joy in pursuing it, and looking out the window at the snowy Andes through breaks in the layered clouds, we began to feel we were indeed on a grand adventure, living out a dream of high purposes and far horizons.

———————◆———————

Norma, who had gotten us airborne, renders here her account of the trip:

The bus to the airport was packed with local people carrying small bundles, and one young man carried a white hen in a net bag, which swung back and forth with every lurch of the bus, the bird remarkably unperturbed by her surroundings. When we arrived at the small and simple airport, the airplane awaiting us reminded me of the one in the final scene of "Casablanca"— small, propeller-driven, with a tiny landing wheel in the back. Peter and I had been asked to wait while the other passengers transferred from bus to plane and then we were led aboard. The stewardess (they were "stewardesses" then) led us up the sloping aisle of the passenger compartment (about the size of the bus we had just left) and past a heavy curtain, beyond which sat the pilot and copilot, who were focused on the controls. To the right was the cockpit door with a small round porthole; to the left, affixed to the port bulkhead about six feet behind the pilot, were two very small fold-out jump seats with rectangular cushions and lap belts. The young woman, looking apologetic, said this was the best they could offer.

As we lifted off for Punta Arenas, we caught glimpses of a glorious orange and crimson sunset through the cockpit windows and the porthole opposite our seats. When night fell, only a weak orange bulb illuminated our area, and as the hours passed we came into some turbulence, which thumped our backs noisily against the bulkhead on which we leaned.

Approaching the Punta Arenas airport, the aircraft descended into heavy cloud cover and we heard the pilot talking to ground control. The plane banked to the right and made a wide circle. At this point the pilot and co-pilot were each looking out the cockpit windows and exchanging comments in somewhat tense tones. With my high-school Spanish I could understand the pilot repeatedly asking the copilot if he could see anything and the response "Nada."

Still circling, we ascended above the clouds, with the pilots intently searching for any break in the clouds, any sign of lights. After about ten minutes we heard "There it is!" from the copilot. With a quick confirming glance, the pilot put us into a steep bank to the right. Peter and I—held in our jump seats only by the lap belts and centrifugal force—could see through the porthole, now below us, glimpses of lights, as we plummeted through the tiny opening in the clouds. In one motion, the plane leveled out and landed sweetly on the runway. Impressive!

Villiers's postcard suggesting our visit to the *Andalucia* had done nothing to discourage our sensations of being on a grand adventure. We had the card with us of course, with its indistinct photo of the four-master, and we pored over Alan's words, which noted the sleet rattling on the roof of his shelter while the Cape Horn gales roared by overhead—for Punta Arenas is on the north side of the Straits of Magellan, while on the south side lies Tierra del Fuego, an archipelago whose outermost island, only a little over 100 miles further south, is the dreaded Cape Horn.

The Cape Horn aura and legend dominated the region. Even the presumably primitive caravanserai from which Alan had written us bore the name Hotel Cabo de Hornos, and he, a practical-minded romantic, thoughtfully recommended we stay there. By 6:30 PM, when our plane landed after its 700-mile flight from Puerto Montt, we were at fever pitch to get out and explore this remote corner of the world. It was bitterly cold, with a smear of snow on the ground (the season was the equivalent of November in our part of the world), and Norma, who really doesn't like being cold, told me she had to clamp her jaw tight, both to stop her teeth from chattering and her mouth from uttering complaints as the unheated bus carried us through the darkness toward our destination. Once we were arrived at the Cabo de Hornos and I had thawed out my fingers, I made this entry in our log:

Arrived 7 pm at the remote fastnesses of the Straits of Magellan and found the Hotel Cabo de Hornos an enormous structure fronting

on a well kept park. The driver of the hotel bus, born here, says it is
a city of 80,000 and they expect television soon. Never mind, we
saw the Straits and across the way, like a cloud in the dim moon-
light, Tierra del Fuego. Slocum sailed through here 70 years ago.

I neglected to note the extreme formality of the hotel sheltering behind its imposing pillared and pilastered facade. As soon as we had recovered from culture shock induced by damasked walls and Persian carpetry, we made our not-so-reluctant way to the dining room, where we found three waiters attending our table, with a menu worthy of New York's Four Seasons and a wine list as long as your arm. We managed to relax and accept these amenities.

All this high living was due to the impossibly precipitous terrain along the coast. There was no railway or highway between Punta Arenas and Santiago, over a thousand miles distant to the north, and contact with civilization was only by sea. The wealthy directors of the sheep farms, which are the main business of southern Chile, had no trouble in sending their children to Europe for their education, but they quailed at making the sea passage to Santiago along this dangerous coast. Anson had lost one of his ships battling his way up the coast during his round-the-world voyage in 1737, and von Spee's powerful cruisers had been in trouble coming down the coast after sinking Cradock's gallant squadron off Coronel in 1914. A long tale of other wrecks rounds out this grim story. The end result of all this is that the prosperous sheep farmers eliminated the need to go to Santiago by creating a superb mini-metropolis of their own in Punta Arenas, which by the late 1800s had become a city of palatial residences, gracious parks and splendid restaurants amid striking natural surroundings.

This is the city we set out in early the following day, trudging through majestic streets in swirling snow flurries to meet the local authorities and secure permission and passage to board the *Andalucia* ex-*Ville de Mulhouse*. The visit was represented to us as perilous—who wanted an American tourist falling down an open hatch? The punctilious Captain Walbaum, Chilean Navy, who showed appreciation for our interest in saving the big barque, was adamant about Norma not going. I started to explain that Norma had been aboard old ships before, but Norma broke in to say she was the team's photographer (which she was), that she knew old ships, and it was her job to photograph this one. And Walbaum, surprised, had the good grace to yield the point. A motor launch took us to the ship, and we climbed the wire and wood ladder up her side accompanied by a petty officer of the Chilean Navy and two sailors. Meeting under a broken skylight in the after cabin of the "huge, desolate, windswept hulk," as I called it in my journal, we talked with the sailor already aboard, who served as watchman with his two dogs. We learned that the vessel, afloat and swinging to her anchor chain, was used as a warehouse for wool storage. Now and then parties would be held aboard, which may have explained the charred remains of a fire in the saloon's pink marble fireplace.

I climbed a little way up the main rigging to check on the condition of things aloft on the empty, cavernous vessel, but yielded quite willingly to the shouts of the petty officer and Norma's advice that I come down again right away. Still, it was something to have been even a little way aloft in the great ship's wind machinery, which, after driving her to the earth's far corners, had brought her at last to this remote port of refuge.

We learned that the vessel had actually been under sail only a quarter-century earlier, when she was pressed into service to meet the extreme shortage of shipping in World War II. She and another big barque, the *Alejandrina*, had sailed under reduced rig to deliver wool to Buenos Aires, returning with beef, grain and other foodstuffs which couldn't be raised in the harsh climate of the Straits. Both ships had had their wooden topgallant masts and yards sent down to avoid upkeep. They plodded along under reduced rig, with a tug in attendance to pull them off a lee shore if it came on to blow, and to provide steady towage through the abrupt, hurricane-force winds which howl down the canyon-like passage through the Straits.

We knew the *Wavertree* had been towed here from the Falkland Islands in the spring of 1911, following her dismasting off Cape Horn, to serve as another floating warehouse for wool until she was sold away to Buenos Aires in 1947. Asking people about her, we found a few who remembered her presence on the waterfront. One of those who definitely remembered her was a charming newsman of the old school, Osvaldo Wegmann of *La Prensa Austral*. He filled us in on much local lore and, after digging through some battered filing cases, produced a small negative of a photograph he'd made of the *Wavertree* in 1966. It was all we could do not to pick him up and waltz him around his crowded office. There was our ship, anchored in the icy waters we had just been on!

The tiny negative was difficult to read, but when we looked closely, we could see that the old ship had her mainmast still in her. The *Wavertree* had lost hers off the Horn. We didn't want to tell Osvaldo that this could not be our ship, so we didn't. This was just as well, for when we later saw a decent print, we could see that the middle spar was much thinner than the foremast or the mizzenmast. Clearly it was a replacement spar fitted with booms to swing bales of wool on and off the ship. A magnifying glass further revealed the stump of the mizzen topmast sitting in the topmast doubling, which we hadn't noticed when aboard the ship herself. We saw also that the figurehead was then still there under the aspiring bowsprit. Her figurehead hasn't yet been found. We think Pablo Neruda may have added it to his famous collection, but it did not appear in the inventory taken after his death.

Because of our delayed arrival, we had little time with much to see. Time passed like a speeded-up movie. We explored Punta Arenas and visited the small-craft breakwater, made up of the carcasses of iron ships, including one with antique quarter galleries—which were rare long before iron became common in shipbuilding in the later 1800s. (We learned later that this rusted-out hulk was that of a steamship—the *Hipparchus*, built in Newcastle in 1869.) We talked about this haunting scene over drinks with the Walbaums, who were delighted to know of our interest. But they knew nothing about the identities of the hulks. We went on exploring the stately streets to get some feeling for this remarkable city of the sea, with its leaden skies, driving snow squalls, and biting winds—and its remarkably civil population. We found not one person who had not time and interest to stop and talk and be generally helpful.

Before leaving Punta Arenas, Norma, exasperated by airline delays, went to the Lufthansa office and transferred our flight to Buenos Aires into their efficient hands. This trip included a short flight to Rio Gallegos in southern Patagonia, with a four-hour stopover before going on to B. A. So we made our departure from Punta Arenas on 10 May before dawn had lighted the snowy airfield in a gleaming British-built propjet that lifted us aloft in one swift bound. When our plane landed at the tiny airport which had no amenities to offer, we joined our fellow travellers in taking the bus into Rio Gallegos for lunch. Once there, we felt we could have been in an abandoned movie set of a Western cattle town. Its streets led out into the endless sere brown plains and disappeared into the distance with no visible living thing and no rock, hill, mound or structure to interrupt the view to the horizon. After the dense, mannered life and stately, ordered streets of Punta Arenas, this little settlement set on a bare beige billiard table of gigantic proportions made me irrationally uneasy, as America's Great Plains had unnerved pioneers on their westward trek.

We had four hours before the bus would take us to the small shelter that passed for a terminal at the airfield, so Norma and I walked the one main street looking for a haven from the overarching emptiness of the scene. The main street was intersected by smaller side streets which also provided uninterrupted views to the horizon. There was almost no traffic on the streets, and the few pedestrians seemed to be fellow flyers from the airport. Respite was offered by a modest-looking restaurant in a grey masonry building. Inside we found comfortable seating in banquettes separated by etched glass panels and attended by waiters in white coats. This was more like it! I ordered a glass of wine and *huevos flamencos*, and we settled in for a leisurely lunch to fill the hours until our bus took us all to the airfield.

———◆———

It felt like coming home to be back in our small hotel room after the exotica of Punta Arenas and the stark, harsh landscapes we had come from. We were up early the next day, Sunday, to be driven by Captain DeValle in his chromed and polished black Buick to visit the Museo Naval, in a northern suburb of the city. People on the streets were in their Sunday best, giving us a sense of occasion as we swept up quiet avenues into an older part of the city well to the north called Tigre. DeValle told us the neighborhood had been a fashionable center in the past century, but was now somewhat neglected and rundown, as people flocked to the bright lights of the central city and, for recreation, to the fashionable tennis clubs and numerous swimming beaches on the shores of the River Plate.

We came upon the museum in workmanlike brick buildings of the former navy yard, on the waterfront where the mighty Plate contracts to a marshy archipelago of wooded islands cut through by the winding waterways of the Paraná. Having glimpsed this inviting scene, we proceeded through the museum exhibits of its admirable ship models, huge battle-flags, odd swords, telescopes, gold-laced coats and other relics, and a great series of romantic paintings of the naval warfare that had first liberated Argentina from the Spanish Empire, and then made the nation a factor to be contended with in the developing continent. Outside a glorious autumn afternoon beckoned, which I duly recorded: "Golden brown water everywhere there, with slender varnished launches and pulling boats, singles and pairs, under yellowy trees on a golden afternoon."

We walked out into the celebratory scene, with couples young and old strolling about over the confetti of fallen leaves on the walkways, minding small children or pulling at oars in the shapely boats that danced through the quiet waters. DeValle seemed at first nonplussed at our blissful expressions and evident enjoyment of what was to him a quite ordinary autumn scene; he was always keen to find things these super-practical *Norteamericanos* would be interested in. But on this golden afternoon he soon relaxed his attentive posture and fell into the *paseo* mode, even yielding to a roguish smile now and then under his naval mustache as a pretty girl passed by. My journal notes on the museum visit ended with this comment: "In the Museo is a small boat like a decked canoe, varnished, with spritsail, in which someone was said to have mapped all the waterways of the estuary. Happy man."

I had expressed my concern to Crocker that we should move things forward, one way or another, with the *Wavertree*'s owner, Señor Numeriani. Charlie begged me not to push for a meeting with Numeriani now, which, he said, would be completely the wrong thing to do at this stage of the proceedings. But I pointed out that we really needed a second look at the vessel to get a better idea of the wastage in her plating and to get down into her holds to see how things looked there.

Somehow DeValle arranged this. He also arranged a luncheon with John Davies, of the American Bureau of Shipping, the day before the inspection. Davies gave us all kinds of tips on what to look for in the old ship. He said: "You've got a good thing going for you in that old English iron she's built of. That stuff lasts forever, hardly rusts at all, just gets a kind of mother on it." He volunteered to oversee the work on the ship to make her fit for the tow home and to see that she was in shape to be formally certified by ABS for insurance purposes. All this was future stuff, of course. We hadn't a dollar to our names beyond what it cost to function from day to day. But I tried not to let this feeling of walking on thin ice spoil things for us or the generous people we met. Charlie Crocker and his wife took us out to a grand farewell dinner at the end of this day, which went on with much merriment till 1:30 AM. We still had a couple of days to go, including our inspection visit to the *Wavertree*, but Charlie had a Moore-McCormack ship coming in, so this was his "bon voyage" to Norma and me.

Our second visit to the ship was set for the evening of the following day. DeValle forewarned us with a somewhat embarrassed shrug that the mysterious activities with telephones in an office aboard a sand barge with Johnnie Walker whisky and Marlboro cigarettes on demand were the operations of an outfit that dealt in the set percentage of "breakage" in imported goods to which the Buenos Aires longshoremen were entitled by contract. Operations also included betting on horse races. There were ways of arranging things with Senor Tosí and his pals, but we had to go aboard in the evening after the workmen had gone home.

So that is how we went aboard, greeting the lone night watchman conspiratorially before conducting our inspection with the flashlights DeValle provided. Everything we looked at confirmed the soundness of the old iron hull. On deck I borrowed DeValle's micrometer to measure the thickness of the metal of the sheerstrake—that important row of plates running the length of the ship at maindeck level. This, with the keel structure on the ship's bottom, forms the girder which keeps the ship from folding up like a shoebox. Having scraped away the encrusted grime until I reached shining bright metal, I applied the micrometer and read the result—25 millimeters.

"How many millimeters to the inch?" I whispered to DeValle. He came over to look at the plating with me.

"It's twenty-five to the inch," he said quietly.

"Captain, that was the specification for the sheerstrake when she was built," I said.

There had been no measurable deterioration in the 80-odd years since the ship had slid down the ways of the Oswald Mordaunt yard in Southampton. There were areas of local wastage, of course, for instance under a leaky porthole in the after cabin, where water had dripped continuously in one spot to wear away the iron in a kind of Chinese torture. But substantially, the ship was whole. DeValle shared our joy at our findings on the ship which he called the "Wovertree."

The previous day, at the end of our lunch with John Davies, we'd had an unexpected meeting which went a long way to explain our interest in the hulk and why we sought to save her. As our luncheon had ended, Davies had risen from his chair to greet an elderly gentleman of erect stature in a sober black suit, who joined us for a cup of coffee. Davies introduced the stranger as Captain Thomas Thomas, consultant to a local maritime firm, remarking that he was a distinguished veteran of square rig and might be able to help us with the restoration of the *Wavertree*.

"Did you ever run across the *Wavertree* under sail?" asked Norma, with a winsome smile. Always to the point, this girl.

"Why yes," allowed Captain Thomas, spooning a little sugar into his coffee while he turned a twinkling blue eye on Norma. "Ma'am, I ran across her more than once, here and there, I can't remember just where, but in different ports, Frisco, Newcastle in England, where I come from—there's another Newcastle in Australia, you know, much visited by sailing ships—and Tocopilla and those Chilean nitrate ports. She went where she had to, to eke out a living. I sailed in similar ships. But in truth no two of them were the same. Each had her own ways about her, her own story as it were. But they were all wanderers, picking up cargo where and when they might. The *Wavertree*, she was one of that breed—an ocean wanderer."

With these words, as you might imagine, Captain Thomas had us in thrall. I believe he knew this very well; he couldn't miss the attentive silence that greeted his words. He was clear-spoken with great, even exaggerated respect for his listeners, one of those Britons who knew his place and expected you and everyone else to respect it. After a sip of coffee he resumed:

"We took the cargos steamers were too proud to take. Of course, it wasn't pride, that's just a way of putting it. But steamers are expensive in upkeep and in making a passage—sailing ships are cheap. The wind is free, and we used every trick in the book to save money."

"What positions did you hold?" asked Norma, noting the shift to "we" in his talk.

"You commanded in sail, didn't you, skipper?" put in Davies.

"Well, yes, I did, I'm proud to say. At first of course we thought the sailing ship would go on forever. Then later, after the war [we knew which war he meant], I saw the handwriting on the wall, but I kept on in sail as long as I could. It was just a different way of life, one that made pretty stern demands. Once you get into that way of doing things other ways seem alien and, one can't help feeling, rather cheap."

"You just said the sailing ship was cheap," put in Norma, smiling.

"My dear," said Thomas (his "ma'am" forgotten), "there's cheap and there's cheap. We who served in sail were rich in our rewards, never forget that. The best way I can tell you how we were cheap is to tell you about an incident years ago, which is as fresh in my mind as the day it happened."

With that he told the story of his first trip as third mate in sail, bound from South Africa to England. Their ship lingered long in the doldrums, the area of slack or little wind one runs into after sailing across the gloriously steady northeast trades, just north of the equator. One morning he had the quarterdeck to himself in a lonely ocean as still as a millpond, as he put it. There was always work to do, and he put the watch on deck to work renewing frayed running gear aloft. This often involved cutting the worn end off a line and making a new splice around the thimble it was attached to, and similar tasks where there was a bit of old rope to be discarded. The men had canvas bags to put this discarded rope into, for eventual use in jobs like making baggywrinkle or sail stops, where strength wasn't required.

But that morning a man aloft accidentally dropped a two-foot length of old rope, which fell into the sea on the port side, alongside the motionless vessel.

Thomas knew the ship's captain was due on deck soon for the noon sight of the sun to determine his latitude. He could think of no way to recover the incriminating two feet of old rope without attracting attention—and in this no-excuses environment, he would be held responsible for that bit of rope. If he had failed to train the seaman at fault, that was his fault as the mate on watch. If he had failed to inspire the seaman with enough respect to avoid that kind of mistake, that made things even worse. Tough, acknowledged Thomas, but fair—that was how to avoid bigger mistakes than this one. And a good place to learn this is when there's no gale blowing, for example in a calm forenoon watch in the doldrums. Thomas could only wish for the wind to pick up and the ship to sail on. Well, everyone wanted that. Or perhaps the offending bit of rope would just sink out of sight; he and the offending seaman wanted that. But neither happened.

"All I could do was pray," said Captain Thomas. "And that I did. I feared the skipper would see something wrong in my face when he came up, but he didn't. I knew he would look over the rail at the water to see how the ship was moving, if at all, and this indeed he did. But I was on the port side and he glanced over the rail on the starboard side to check the ship's steerageway, so he missed the incriminating evidence floating on the port side. Finally a passing breeze caught us, and the ship sailed on."

Norma and I talked often, later, of this simple story. Captain Thomas was 80 when we met, and we never saw him again. But we remembered always that with his tight, disciplined ways, his Celtic imagination had produced the cognomen by which we decided our ship should always be known: "An Ocean Wanderer."

Lloyd's kept track of the seaports she had frequented, as they do for all ships, all oceans. And when we came to count them up we found that the *Wavertree* had called at 48 far-flung seaports in all, from Antwerp to Madras. How far she'd fared—practically a roadside beggar at the edge of the sea roads her kind had opened for mankind! She was a Gandalf dressed as mendicant, keeping open a challenging chapter of mankind's experience, which it would forget only to its ultimate impoverishment.

CHAPTER 18

Square Riggers '68, *Early Summer 1968*

Ellen & Val—Marie Lore Signs On—The Square Rigger Bar—
Urban Renewal Sponsorship—A Restoration Workshop—
The Riverboat Ball—A Week Aboard the Eagle

"Boss, I think I just hired the chairman's daughter." Norma carefully closed my office door behind her and gave me a worried look. We badly needed help to handle the fast-growing office work and errand running, and an 18-year-old girl had shown up seeking a job. Norma had heard her name as Ellen Brandon and launched right into the interview. The applicant was fresh from a year of school in Italy and admitted she had no office experience and couldn't type very well but was willing to learn. It was a wide-ranging interview and Norma liked her can-do attitude, so she hired her on the spot. But she was taken aback when she saw "Isbrandtsen" on the application sheet.

Seeing that Norma wanted to hire the girl, I said: "If you think she can handle the work, let's go ahead with it," And Norma left to usher in a tall blond girl with a direct, emphatic way of speaking. She seemed interested in the quotes we'd hung on our walls from Admiral Nelson and Pablo Casals which, I told her, we endeavored to live by. So Ellen was hired on the spot at $75 a week.

From the outset Ellen did things on the run. And she had a knack for dealing with people decisively, while making them feel that what she asked them to do was what they had meant to do on their own. She made an immediate and lasting conquest of Val Wenzel, the devoted but irascible older volunteer who worked on our local history committee and oversaw volunteer manning of the front desk. Val did original research in unexplored municipal archives. It was he who discovered that the architect of the 1880s Fulton Market, which had been torn down in the 1950s, was George W. Post, designer of the charming building which still survives on the northeast corner of Front and Beekman

Streets, across from where the old market had stood. He made other discoveries in abundance, more than most of us had time to hear. But Ellen, somehow, found time for Val. I remember once overhearing her say, on an occasion when she just couldn't stay for Val's latest news: "Mr. Wenzel, tell me later. The boss will give me hell if I don't get this done first." Val would normally reprove any female who used the word "hell" in his hearing, but as far as Val was concerned, if Ellen said "hell," then hell became respectable.

Val himself was held in respect by all of us because of his wartime service at sea, which had left him with a head injury that had required a steel plate and had affected his temper, as he explained when he signed on as a volunteer. Our respect grew when we saw the strict discipline he observed in manning the front desk—a discipline he did not hesitate to impose on others who took on that assignment. On a snowy weekend in our first winter in South Street one volunteer, who had offered to keep the place open on that particular Sunday morning, closed it up after an hour or two passed with no visitors. Val let him know firmly that when we said we were open, we must be open whether anyone came in or not. In fact, the museum was open every day of the year except two: Thanksgiving and Christmas, a schedule that could only be accomplished through the dedication of the volunteers.

Another stalwart volunteer who joined early that summer was Marie Lore, a quiet woman with white hair, smiling face and sparkling blue eyes, who worked for an insurance firm in John Street. Reading about our venture in the papers, she had walked the length of South Street to find the museum, for she had a consuming interest in ships and the sea. But she had bypassed our modest storefront on Fulton Street. When the Coast Guard sail training barque *Eagle* moved into the slip at Pier 16 on Friday, 19 June, her towering masts at the foot of Fulton Street gave Marie all the guidance she needed. The next day she was at our door with her 12-year-old son, Clinton, asking how she could help out. The two were immediately put to work tying up the balloons we were selling to celebrate the arrival of the stately square rigger at the end of the street.

Marie's yen for things maritime had survived all attempts by her parents and school teachers to have her drop this unladylike interest. She read Peter Throckmorton's books on his pioneering ventures in marine archaeology in the faraway Mediterranean—and was thrilled to meet him when Peter later became involved in our affairs. Peter knew the real thing when he met it. "Say, who is that little white-haired lady, anyway?" he said to me after they'd met. "She talks like a Midwestern schoolmarm, but she knows what she's talking about." Peter's style ran to somewhat more racy ladies, but he always sought out Marie in a crowd. I believe Marie was tickled by Peter's adventuresome ways. She'd known about him through his articles on marine archaeology in *National Geographic*, and the printed word to her was a doorway to adventure. Marie rapidly established friendships with the wide variety of people she dealt with, resulting in a circle of correspondents across the country and around the world. She wholeheartedly adopted the seamans' view of ships as having definite personalities, and took to writing lively poems about the ships of South Street, saluting their sea-challenged lives and speculating on the adventures they had met in distant seas. Marie later explained the confidence she found among our gang:

> *There was an atmosphere of "you CAN fight city hall" which seemed to be breathed in by all volunteers. We were together in enthusiasm and the conviction that the dream would be realized.*

Don and Jo Meisner were among others drawn to South Street by the *Eagle* visit. "We were looking for something to do on an idle Saturday afternoon," as Jo later recalled. They soon found plenty to do. As friends of Pete Seeger and habitués of the lively Village scene (they'd first met at a musical evening at Chumley's), they worked at promoting our get-togethers on Pier 16. They joined the Local History Committee and led in emergency archaeological recovery of such artifacts as colonial-era wooden water pipes from diggings for new conduits being installed on Water and Fulton Streets. They also became leaders in developing membership for the Seaport and in working on the ships and buildings we were to acquire, where Jo's organizational energies and Don's engineering skills were of noble service to the cause.

A new institution arrived on the scene with summer—a pub which soon became a watering-hole for staff, volunteers and visitors seeking company and refreshment in their explorations of the Seaport waterfront. The institution, the Square Rigger Bar & Grille, was the same that had stood on the north side of the old Seamen's Church Institute building on South Street at Coenties Slip. This was the bar where Norma and I had gone after our first sighting the *Lady of Good Voyage* in South Street three years before. Unhoused when Uris Bros. started to raze the entire block for their new skyscraper, the facility had moved north—that is, the battered wooden bar itself (inscribed with the initials of many forgotten sailors), the barman Joe, and a following of seamen. Joe, a small person with a black mustache, who took no nonsense, treating all comers with a cinematic tough-guy manner, was the bartender who had fussed over getting the children something hot to drink when we had come in from the wind and wet on that memorable Sunday evening. His clientele was mostly old seamen who had served in World War II, and on the wall to the right of the bar he'd hung a framed black and white photo of row after row of white crosses disappearing into the distance in a D-Day cemetery on Normandy. Set in neat type below this were the words:

Don't complain about growing old.
It's a privilege denied to many.

Joe would point to this sign when he heard too much grousing from old-timers at the bar.

We soon got to know the bar's owners, Nick and Alex Olatka, tall, quiet, sandy-haired brothers. One or the other of them would sometimes join our talk around the table. They took a polite interest in our endless stories and arguments and they advocated the Seaport cause to all comers, while Alex, through his job with International Paint, got us donated paint for the ships we brought into South Street later in this summer of "Square Riggers '68."

The arrival of the Square Rigger Bar was the first real evidence that the Seaport would attract new tenants, new commerce and activity in the streets—and, above all, people to sustain these activities.

The people thing was running strong with us, as balmy weather encouraged stockbrokers and insurance agents to throw open their coats, like any shoreside scrivener of earlier days, and amble down to the waterfront to see what might be happening on the Street of Ships. The Square Rigger became an Areopagus of museum business where everything was up to be kicked around—and generally was. Newcomers were welcome to let us have their views, and there were always volunteers on hand to invite people to sign up as museum members for $1. As the summer wore on, we experienced a surge of such renewals from the crowds of people who had flooded into South Street the year before— and who had been receiving our *Reporter* to keep them up to date with the South Street venture. The inflow of renewal fees at a rate we hadn't expected did much to stabilize our finances.

Overarching these lively scenes on the ground, basic developments were moving at last to change the Seaport's standing in the city. On Tuesday, 15 May, just before our return from Argentina, the City Planning Commission moved to designate the Seaport Museum as official sponsor of the Brooklyn Bridge Southeast Urban Renewal Area. This was swiftly approved by the Planning Commission, thanks to careful groundwork by Richard Buford of the Mayor's Office of Lower Manhattan Development. Remembering the blank unscalable wall we had encountered a year and a half earlier, this was taken by us all as a breakthrough.

A goodly crew of our volunteers were on hand to testify if needed, but only a few were called, led by our Member No. 1, Jim Kirk. On reading the next day's *New York Times* report, our gang were chagrined to find, however, that there was no mention of the citizen role in the venture, even in the air rights concept on which our acquisition of the land depended. This was distinctly a citizen initiative, though necessarily executed by City professionals.

That Friday evening a group of staff and volunteers met in the Square Rigger to express their outrage that the press had ignored their role. I said we had to let our allies in City government take what credit they could. This did not satisfy the crew, including Norma, who pointed out that those who take the credit also gain the influence for next steps. She was right of course. But for now, I said, we'd have to be satisfied that we and God knew the truth of the situation, and that truth was more important than who wangled what out of it. This was greeted with silence.

The crew's gripe was real. Without what they had done, there would be no Seaport for anyone to claim credit for. But the approval we'd won absolutely depended on the $2 million Jakob had put up to begin acquiring the Seaport land. There was a great nodding of heads when this point was made. We needed all hands pulling together, I continued, or, as Francis Drake had said before taking on Cape Horn in the *Golden Hind*, we "must have the gentleman to haul and draw with the mariner, and the mariner with the gentleman" to make the voyage.

The urban renewal designation put pressure on us to get a more detailed plan for the development of Schermerhorn Row and the two blocks to the north across Fulton Street. Jack Kaplan and Jakob Isbrandtsen played the major supportive roles in this, with Jack taking on partial underwriting of the operating expenses of the museum as well as further studies to develop the Seaport Plan. This would be followed by the large-scale project model Jack wanted to see. Tom Van Arkel, as our restoration director, assigned a young aide in the firm, George Demmy, to work with us under Tom's direction.

This quickly became a full-time job, with George joining our staff to run a restoration workshop, financed by the Kaplan Fund. George proved his mettle in research and in lively drawings for Van Arkel's reports. He also picked up other assignments, including hammer-and-nails work to open a new exhibit space in a fish stall next to ours at 18 Fulton Street. Financed by a grant from the New York State Council on the Arts arranged by Allon Schoener, this was for an exhibit, *The Destruction of*

Lower Manhattan, an epic series of photographs that recorded in close-up detail the razing of whole blocks of 19th-century buildings for the new construction that was changing lower Manhattan. It gave our visitors a dramatic depiction of the fate that would have overtaken our buildings without our intervention. In addition to his planning abilities, George proved a master craftsman and struck up a great relationship with our volunteers, who rallied round to help with any project he called them to. Norma and I found him excellent company and an innovative thinker, and we consulted with him regularly on the course ahead.

To get a sound plan we needed to get our thinking about the future of the Seaport on paper and on the table for critical review and discussion. What about a conference to pull in the best outside talent we could get? We all jumped at that idea, and Kent Barwick, who had gathered together the people and support for the opening of our 16 Fulton Street headquarters, worked with us on the outline of the panel discussions that would feed into the plan. Then he and Joan Davidson set to work to pull in the leading authorities that we needed for a useful and credible review of plans.

Norma and I had a flock of other concerns that swept us up. Our friend, the artist Charlie Lundgren, had teamed up with Howard Slotnick, an automobile dealer who was a friend of Jakob's, to organize the Riverboat Ball on 21 May aboard the paddlewheel excursion steamer *Alexander Hamilton.* This vessel, with her ornate cabins paneled with matched and contrasting woods, grand assembly rooms and threshing paddlewheels, was reminiscent of the Hudson River steamboats of a hundred years earlier. Built in 1924, she was the last of her kind. She belonged to the Circle Line, headed by Frank Barry. We had already talked with him about having her join our projected fleet in South Street when she was retired, and he cheerfully chartered the vessel to us for the night for the bare cost of fuel and crew's wages.

Using Jakob's connections and every other resource in sight, Charlie as chairman and Howard as treasurer signed up over 1,000 people at

$15 a head. Tickets included an elegant boxed supper from Le Brasserie, and dance music from bands on both the upper and lower decks. Charlie and Howard also secured a number of patrons at $100, who were each accommodated in a private cabin suggestive of Edwardian naughtiness. The Riverboat Ball gave our finances a healthy push forward and made us a multitude of new friends.

Our friends Sidney and Eugenia Dean signed up for this. Great city-lovers themselves, they had been worrying whether our grass-roots approach would ever appeal to the monied levels of society whose support we needed to meet the Seaport goals. They were in heaven; first, to be afloat in this setting, and then to know the good this would do for the cause—a cause which, it will be remembered, Sid had pushed through the City Club to give the Seaport idea its first civic endorsement in the hurried, forgetful City of New York.

As for me, I was eager to learn all I could about the paddlewheeler and, standing beside Frank Barry at an open hatch (or doorway) on the starboard side, I watched as the great liner *France* drew up to pass us on the starboard side. I asked Frank how many knots the *Alexander Hamilton* made.

"The Coast Guard limits us to nineteen miles per hour," said Frank. (I'd forgotten that river steamers used miles per hour, as people do on the neighboring riverbanks, rather than knots, which measure speed in the longer nautical miles used at sea.) "But we can do more," he added. With that, he turned to say something to the deckhand standing next to him, and a minute or two later, as the engine's beat picked up a notch, the aged paddlewheeler slid effortlessly past the *France.*

The next day was 22 May, National Maritime Day, the opening day for Square Riggers '68. Barclay Warburton had brought his smart brigantine *Black Pearl* in for the occasion, to lead a small parade of traditional craft to Battery Park at the foot of Manhattan Island. There we sailed up to fire a salute to the official party gathered to hear some speeches on bleachers erected for the occasion. The bleachers were set up to face inland, so our little demonstration upset arrangements (we were later told), as people knelt on the seats facing backward to watch the pretty sight of the brigantine, wreathed in gunsmoke as she braced her yards around to make her turn and proceed upriver within a stone's throw of the Battery seawall. The Chinese junk *Mon Lei*, steered by her redoubtable skipper, Alen York, sailed in our wake, firing bursts of Chinese firecrackers as she made her turn upriver. And that evening the Black Pearl Singers, who had come in aboard Barclay's brigantine, enlivened the occasion with song as we declared the opening of Square Riggers '68 in suitable fashion.

As the late spring dusk crept over the quiet river, we looked at the *Black Pearl*'s square yards against the sky as harbinger of things to come, when the great square riggers would return to South Street.

Somehow, in the next few weeks, we got out an enlarged issue of the *South Street Reporter*, with a front page showing the wrecked buildings of Danny Lyon's photographs, *The Destruction of Lower Manhattan*. Below this was a vignette of Jim Kirk at the City Planning Commission hearing, urging the commissioners to save the most historic surviving neighborhood of Lower Manhattan. "City Planning Commission Approves Seaport Proposal" was the banner headline, and in the editorial column inside we saluted Jakob for his $4 million fund which made this possible, and gave a listing of the 27 supporters who had given $1,000 or more to the project.

This 8-page special issue presented a selection of photos from *The Destruction of Lower Manhattan*. This presentation, like the exhibition itself, was paid for by the New York State Council on the Arts. These were important contributions, but a still more important one was buried in a back-page column, "Ports of Call." It announced that the State Council had provided funds to hire our staunch volunteer Alan Frazer as program director of the Seaport. Alan brought scholarship and careful handling of people and projects to our affairs. He continued to come down weekends and evenings from his apartment nearby to supervise volunteers as he always had.

His good relationship with this vital arm of our forces was a shining asset in our work together.

Also in this issue, Charlie Dunn appeared as chairman of Friends of South Street. Jock Bartlett had vanished up the Hudson pursuing the campaign for Pete Seeger's project to build a Hudson River sloop to be called *Clearwater*. He and his sister, Ellen, and her husband, the artist Lenny Nodelman, had hurled themselves into the effort to mount the art show and other events of the past summer, working on occasion right through the night. But now his creative energies and ebullient good will were focused on the new project.

A variety of other items crowded the *Reporter*'s pages. On one page we reported that a new Explorer Sea Scout troop had been formed by the Seaport, under the leadership of Charlie Dunn, who proposed to use the teen-age recruits in volunteer projects in South Street. On another page, an Australian correspondent told us that the coal hulk *Rona* in Melbourne had been acquired by the New South Wales National Trust to be restored to her original state as the barque *Polly Woodside*, launched in 1885 (*Wavertree*'s year). There was also an appeal for the picnic in Garrison, up the Hudson, which Jock Bartlett was working on, to promote the building of the *Clearwater*. Each of these projects went on to brilliant and enduring success. And we had our first two ads, warming my heart as an advertising man: one for the seamen's clothing shop Fulton Supply (est. 1902), and the other for Whyte's Restaurant of the same era.

In this issue we also showed an engraving of old houses in the north of the Seaport district, buildings now destroyed, including one at 11 Peck Slip, built in 1725, the oldest house in New York when it was torn down in 1946. And we ran a photograph of an anchor of the 1700s recovered from the enormous excavation being dug for the World Trade Center by Harry Druding, resident engineer in charge. We had a loving appreciation of the *Flying Cloud*, most famous of clippers, and a fine, rare lithograph by Charles Robert Patterson of the handsome three-skysail yarder *Bangalore*, lying snug under the Brooklyn Bridge.

She was a year younger than the *Wavertree,* but unlike her older sister she was lost at sea and never returned from her last Cape Horn voyage. Along with what we were doing today, we felt the *Reporter* should carry these pieces of our heritage that were "old news"—but always new to each generation.

And as for what we were doing today, we had an "All Hands on Deck" announcement in which we called for the 30–40 volunteers we'd need to handle crowds when the two tall ships, *Eagle* and *Danmark,* showed up at our pier in June and July. And our tireless volunteer Sandy Moore called for any young ladies (ages 17–20) who would serve as hostesses to entertain the cadets of the two square riggers when they stormed down the gangplanks to be received at welcome-ashore parties in 16 Fulton Street. As the busy weeks passed, crowded with preparation of all kinds, we felt the Seaport buildings themselves were awaiting the arrival of the ships whose ancestral types they had been built to serve.

While I was driving down the East River Drive to the Seaport on a Saturday morning in mid-June, an unexpected vision made me catch my breath. Before us, just beyond the grey Manhattan tower of the Brooklyn Bridge, stood the tall masts and squared yards of a great sailing ship. We had so often seen this picture in our minds' eyes, summoned from the irrecoverable past, that it hit one with a physical shock to see the long-dreamt image realized by the presence of the Coast Guard's *Eagle* at our pier.

I was still held in awe after we went aboard, and I stood aft by the wheel pointing out to Tommy the lead of braces, halyards and buntlines we had looked at only in books before this. But the solid massing of lines clustered around the masts and along the rails gradually reestablished a sense of workaday reality—albeit of a very special sort. Captain Carkeek, standing by, said: "Why don't you come out with us and try some actual sail handling?" I said something about being too busy, at which Tommy gave me an astonished look which might be translated: "Are you crazy?" But Norma spoke up to save the day.

"Captain Carkeek," she said, "you would be doing us an enormous favor if you would take my husband with you this coming week. He's been working himself to a frazzle, and he's rapidly reducing us to the same state."

Aboard the *Eagle*, I was assigned the admiral's cabin saved for visiting firemen. I found it a peaceful retreat in which to write up this note on where we stood, as the *Eagle* proceeded under power through a rainy Monday evening at sea, rolling slightly to the underlying Atlantic swell:

> *Monday, June 17. At last I would call the Seaport now a sound bet. Kaplan has picked up our expenses for this year entirely himself, and at $10K not $5K/month. This should reassure Jakob in the great step he took of putting up $2 million in funds and credits. The* Eagle *weekend seemed to work excellently. Alan Frazer has been running things himself and all the volunteers seem to have become better organized .... With so many things hanging so long and now coming in all at once (as I told Norma they would, if at all) I find myself the most shattered and dangerous person and so in most timely fashion am going to sea in the* Eagle, *ensconced now in the admiral's cabin.*

The next afternoon a light southwesterly air came in across the empty ocean around us, and the whole ship came alive with the act of setting sail. The ship slipped along under sail for the rest of the day, but at sunset the breeze died away and all sail was stowed for the night. Under the direction of the big, cheerful first mate, Hap Paulsen, I was allowed to join in sail stowing, going up the ratlines and proceeding first out along the port main yard. At the end of the yard (the yard arm) I stood on a special one-man footrope, separate from the main footrope which comes to an end at this point. Called the Flemish horse, this mini-footrope enables one to get a footing to grab the heavy lower corner of the big mainsail and fold it in neatly. But this was a cramped footing, and folding in the clew cringle presented a challenge; I had my hands full trying to accomplish it. A hearty thwack on the back from Hap, when I got back down on deck, made me feel I'd done all right for a soft-handed yachtsman.

Everything is special on these lowest sails, called the courses. The lines that draw the lower corners of square sails up to the yard above are generally called clewlines, but on the courses (the lowest sails) they are called clew garnets. The name is so old its origin is lost in the mists of time, but it was used aboard the *Eagle*—a nicety it was good to see observed in this workaday training ship. I had only a hazy general notion of the exact stations manned and orders given in sailing evolutions aboard a big square rigger, and at supper I was put through a searching exam, after which Captain Carkeek lent me his copy of Captain Felix Riesenberg's *Standard Seamanship*. Reading this in the admiral's cabin, I was charmed by the instructions for tacking a square rigger, which began: "'Hands about ship!' meant all hands, and the cook at the foresheet, a time-honored station filled by the Celestial with all the importance in the world." There was history in that: The cook was always something of an outsider, and it was only as cooks that Chinese could be signed up in US Navy crews in the Far East, a road to legal immigration to the United States.

The future of the ship we were aboard was discussed freely at the officers' mess. The captain and mates and I had all met before this, at a welcome dinner Melvin Conant had put on for us in the Commodore's Room at the New York Yacht Club. The commandant of the Coast Guard had joined us, having come up to visit his ship in New York City, and he spoke openly about the dim prospects of the ship remaining in operation for the Coast Guard. In this era, Secretary of Defense McNamara dominated governmental operations, and everything was subject to his kind of cost-benefit analysis. That was the origin, for example, of the infamous "body count" (numbers of Vietnamese slain). In this and other matters, if you couldn't pile up a measurable weight of evidence in numbers to support your case, you didn't have a case. The root values and attitudes cultivated by training aboard a sailing ship were not measurable under this system, any more than the values and attitudes of the Vietnamese people proved to be.

What was the value of training under sail? Why work people so hard to learn about clew garnets and the like, or teach them to recognize the precise moment to give the critical order "Let go and haul!" in tacking a square rigger? The techniques were of little use aboard a modern warship, at best limited to learning the effects of wind and tide with no engine power to overcome them. So, while sailors sought ways to express other values developed in the experience, they kept citing the limited values of ship-handling, rather than the limitless, imponderable values of initiative, responsibility, comradeship, loyalty, and personal leadership in a tight-knit society where these things had to be learned for the ship to make her voyage.

Everyone in the wardroom knew the importance of seafaring values and how they were instilled in cadets aboard the *Eagle*. They may have lacked the language to put their point of view across, but they did not lack the resolve. I was moved to repeat to the *Eagle*'s people afloat what I had told the commandant at Melvin's dinner ashore: "We in South Street will make the sailing of the *Eagle* one of our causes."

And—with the help of Barclay Warburton (who a few years hence would sail his little square rigger *Black Pearl* across the Atlantic with a crew of young people and return to found the American Sail Training Association), and from other kindred spirits like Dick Rath and Irving Johnson (whom we had yet to meet)—we were able to make our promise come true and to play a part in making the sail training movement the respected force it is in America today.

The actual sailing of the *Eagle* was to change dramatically as the ultimate values of sail training came to be better recognized. On our one-week trip out of New York, we shortened down to topsails at night, like the stately East Indiamen of old (as the ships of a monopoly, they had no reason to risk losing sails or spars in a midnight squall). The rule was not to have the cadets go aloft when the ship was heeled over and jumping about in the sea. We rejoiced in our light-weather cruise when we got a fresh northwest breeze, which sent the barque reeling off twelve knots across a level sea. My journal noted: "All hands merry." But we hoped the wind would get no stronger, for then the order would be given to shorten sail. And if it came on to blow, we would have to proceed with engine power under bare poles.

The *Eagle* had been taken over in Germany as a war reparation by the Coast Guard after World War II. There was no sail training doctrine in place to govern her use, so she was treated as an exhibition piece, motoring from port to port to advertise the Coast Guard's work. She made sail just enough to help give the cadets some idea of how her wind machinery worked. Fortunately, in the Coast Guard the feeling persisted that the *Eagle's* proper mission was not just to educate cadets in a bygone technology, but to teach them to pursue difficult goals in an unforgiving environment, so they could learn what they, the ship's people, could achieve together.

Hap Paulsen, Captain Carkeek's executive officer, the big, cheerful bloke who assigned me to the Flemish horse, set new standards in the following years when he took over the ship. He sailed *Eagle* hard, one of the first of her captains to make the breakthrough to treating her as what she is—a ship that comes fully to life and achieves her full purpose in being sailed hard, demanding the best the trainees have in them to give. For me, of course, sailing in the *Eagle* was the finest kind of vacation, slowing my life down to simple routines, watching others work except when I chose to join the crew hauling on a line or going aloft. I debarked at our pier in South Street, where the *Eagle* put in for a second weekend's public visitation, in a sunlit frame of mind, thoroughly unfrazzled.

The ship-rigged *Danmark* came in for a weekend a month after the *Eagle's* visit. Smaller than the *Eagle*, she surprised us all by clearing away from her berth under sail without using a tug or her own engine. Her cadets swarmed confidently into her rigging, and as she fell back out of her berth and then braced up sharp to stand downriver, the ship-handling was wonderful to watch. Her cadets were younger than the *Eagle*'s college-age cadets, and their schedule allowed them much more time at sea. The little ship had a special relationship with the US Coast Guard, for when Germany overran their country, the *Danmark* was in Florida. And when the US entered the war, her captain volunteered her as a training ship for the Coast Guard. Their wartime experience with the *Danmark* led the Coast Guard to accept the German training barque *Horst Wessel* after the war renaming her *Eagle*—an old name in the Coast Guard, to which she continues to add fresh lustre today.

Norma and I had little to do with the *Danmark* visit, however. Other events caught us up as things in South Street moved ahead at a quickening pace.

CHAPTER 19

South Street's First Ships!, *August–October 1968*

Jakob Gets Us Two Vessels—The Ambrose—
A Revolutionary Spirit—The Caviare *Sails Into South Street—
Displays for Our First Two Ships*

Of course there was a patina of grime from her years of disuse. And the mint green paint that covered the oak woodwork in the wardroom would have to come off. And oddly missing were the pipe-and-canvas bunks and the lockers for the crew's quarters—perhaps they had been needed on another ship. But, here was a working vessel, complete with all the essential equipment. Officers' quarters were intact with bunks, lockers and toilets. The enormous galley stove was functional, the wheelhouse was largely intact, and the engine room was virtually untouched and boasted two large generators, pumps, and a heating plant.

The lightship was better equipped than our drafty barren museum office at 16 Fulton Street!

These were Norma's first impressions from our inspection of Lightship #87 at the Coast Guard base in Curtis Bay, Maryland. The Coast Guard's fleet of manned lightships was being replaced by buoys and towers, and the lightships were being given away or scrapped. Lightship #87 was the first to serve on Ambrose station at the outer entrance of Ambrose Channel—the main ship channel into New York Harbor—when the channel was opened in 1908. From the beginning, we saw the stout red vessel as a gathering place for people, a center for the multifarious activities of South Street. Following our acceptance of the vessel, the Coast Guard towed her in to Pier 16 on 5 August 1968.

That no lightship had ever lain in South Street did not bother us at all. *Ambrose* was a sentinel of the sea, and her lighthouse towers had marked the entrance to New York Harbor for a quarter century, until she was replaced by a more modern vessel. It was our chairman, Jakob, who had recommended her when he learned that the Coast Guard would donate her to a suitable non-profit group. He wanted to see the Seaport afloat as well as ashore, and with her ample form and spacious decks, a new center and gathering place was added to our scene—one which swayed to the winds that had brought sailing ships up the river, and rose and fell to the wakes of passing tugs and barges today. Our waterfront scribe, Marie Lore, recorded the evening when our skilled young volunteer Chi Ling was able to get the *Ambrose*'s two powerful lights to shine again:

> We rejoiced when Ambrose *joined us. That was real solid evidence of a beginning of a fleet. One night when Chi Ling lit the lights on* Ambrose *with power from her own generators, all the volunteers, who had been below at a party, cheered. Chi pronounced: "One small step for man, one giant leap for South Street Seaport."*

This feeling was not shared by Ship Committee chairman Monk Farnham, who believed the fleet should be built up following a predetermined plan rather than an organic approach based on felt need and an instinctive feel for what would bring life and sea-learning to the waterfront. Norma and I, however, agreed with Jakob on the need for a ship that visitors could board with decks to walk on and a story to tell. We all felt a message carried by a ship swaying to the passing tides would carry more conviction than any message put up on brick walls ashore. And we foresaw her role as a mother ship for any other we might bring in; her big generators could provide quantities of electricity, and there was compressed air to work capstans and other heavy machinery. Norma noted the leading role the ship assumed in our affairs, as the vessel was "cleaned, scraped, varnished and painted. An engine room gang restocked her tool locker and got the generators running. The galley served hot coffee and chowder to work teams." And, she added:

> The public loved her. Kids swarmed aboard, attracted by her bright red hull. Most visitors had never seen a lightship in their lives and marveled at what they learned about the Lighthouse Service and the Coast Guard. Coast Guardsmen, active and retired, came by to look her over, lend advice, and delight us with anecdotes. . . .

Charlie Dunn's Explorer Scout group used her as headquarters, led by the engineering student Chi Ling, who went on to attend the Maritime College at Fort Schuyler and pursue a career at sea. The solid, distinctive lightship gave these teenagers their own clubhouse to repair to, complete with a galley stove for the preparation of shared meals, an ownership not diluted, but enriched by the fact that others, from Coast Guard veterans to volunteer work crews, also regarded the vessel as their own. It did great good also to hold trustee and Ship Committee meetings aboard. We started this as soon as Roger Campbell, eldest son of our advisor George Campbell, had restored the wardroom, leading a group of perfectionist volunteers. Using a dentist's pick to clean the mint-green paint out of the delicately fashioned carvings in the oak paneling, they had turned this room in the rounded stern of the vessel into a glowing place of milk-white paneling set off by golden varnished oak.

As a bit player in the Seaport scene, our *Athena* provided active seafaring experience to the Explorer Scouts and occasionally to staff and volunteers, as on the July Fourth weekend, when the scouts joined us for a grand rendezvous of Melvin Conant's Long Island Rum, Sailing & Chowder Society off the beach at Sheffield Island, near Westport, Connecticut. For this occasion, Norma had made a ten-foot pennant, red, white and blue with black Caslon lettering in the middle white band declaring "NOT ONE CENT FOR TRIBUTE." This flew from the main topmast in response to the Department of Ports and Terminals' demand that we insure Piers 15 and 16 against fire and liability. The liability insurance we could understand. But to require fire and damage insurance for piers the City itself had planned to demolish was plainly unreasonable.

We got in odd bits of sailing after this, but a typical log entry made late in the season reads: "Boats painted and puttied on port side, PS on office work below." We had bought an irresistible, shapely pulling boat, which gave the kids mobility even while the schooner was tied up at dockside. She was named *Owl* in honor of the bird often seen perched on the goddess Athena's shoulder, while our *Athena* carried hers lashed down on the cabin top.

Things were lively at the Seaport, with the big visiting ships of "Square Riggers '68" drawing people in numbers we hadn't seen before. To the previous year's art show we added new craft and antique shows, which pulled in their aficionados in droves, and Pete Seeger filled the streets with peaceable antiwar songs and *Clearwater* enthusiasts. Every such gathering, of course, was heavily salted with our members, drawing on a roster which by midsummer numbered 4,500. The stabilizing force of these people with an ownership stake in the venture may explain why long-haired youngsters, construction workers, naval and merchant marine veterans, Wall Street executives and yachtsmen mingled cheerfully in the streets at these diverse gatherings. Norma and I rejoiced in this evidence of South Street becoming a real neighborhood, with its own mores and expected standards of behavior.

While the summer weeks marched by, thrumming with the drumbeat of activity in South Street, Tom Van Arkel had been meeting with Jakob about ways to use the $2 million fund Jakob had put up to start the shoreside restoration. Eventually they settled on buying two buildings, one at 236 Front Street, on the southwest corner of Peck Slip, and another at 109 South Street, halfway up the row of slope-roofed fishmongers' buildings between Beekman Street and Peck Slip. Neither of these was in the three-block enclave at the heart of our project—the two blocks on the north side of Fulton Street owned by Goelet, and the Schermerhorn Row block on the south side owned by various small holders—but they did serve to establish an ownership presence in the urban renewal district.

In buying these two properties, Jakob introduced an imaginative wrinkle which resulted in saving a noble vessel for South Street. Jakob had summoned me to his office to explain this.

"Peter, I'm glad we've got the *Ambrose* lightship, but we've got to do something for the real heritage of this waterfront, which was in sailing ships. You'd been talking about that schooner *Caviare*, or whatever she's called, which Kortum got you onto. I gather this is a real Gloucester schooner, clipper bow and all. Your report says she's a generation older than Mystic's *Dunton*. You say the owner wants to sell her for $75,000, but has no takers. Offer him $50,000 cash. Then here's what I'm prepared to do."

His proposition was this: He had borrowed $130,000 to buy the 236 Front Street property, but the rundown old building actually cost about half that, leaving enough to buy the schooner *Caviare*, with money left over to get her in shape for the voyage to New York. I stared at Jakob. Imagine having the bank advance twice what was needed for the building, then turning around to bring in a survivor of the great age of fishing under sail! But his vision in this matter was unquestionably right. The battered but lovely schooner would do more for South Street as a going concern than taking on a decrepit building for which we had no ready program. And through this sleight of hand, we were actually going to bring an historic Gloucesterman into South Street!

It was Karl Kortum who'd put us on the trail of the *Caviare*, through his friend Al Swanson. Swanson had been his shipmate in the *Tuscarora*, a big troop transport for US forces in the Pacific in WWII. After Karl's voyage in the *Kaiulani* had ended in Australia, he had joined the *Tuscarora* as mate in 1942. After the war, Swanson married Shirley, a girl he had met in a USO troupe traveling aboard the *Tuscarora*. They returned to New England to raise a family of three daughters, while Al made a modest living shipping out in the boats fishing out of Gloucester. When in 1966 the *Caviare* had come into Gloucester to set up shop as a museum of the fisheries, Al told Kortum she was the real thing. He got to know the owner, Paul Henry Dunn, and helped him out by doing volunteer work on the schooner and introducing him to people in the tight fishing community. Things had not worked out for *Caviare* in Gloucester, however, and Al let Kortum know that Dunn would sell the vessel to anyone who would take proper care of her.

Kortum told us we'd better get to Gloucester and have a look.

Shortly after I had come ashore from my cruise in the *Eagle*, Norma and I squeezed in this trip as an addendum to a scheduled trip to Colonial Williamsburg. We had been invited to Williamsburg to present our thinking on South Street to a group of traditional preservationists. We enjoyed this lively exchange of ideas enormously, and, with our host paying the bills, we caught a plane to Boston. Al Swanson met us there and drove us to Gloucester to board the *Caviare*.

The aged schooner, 75 feet long, was not one of the deepwater breed of big, 120-foot schooners which fished the Grand Banks far offshore, but of the smaller class which fished the Georges Bank closer to home. But she was recognizably in the generation of Gloucestermen which appeared in the early 1890s, following bad experience with the type known as clipper schooner, a shoal-draft, fast-traveling breed which had evolved to get fish home to market fast. These vessels were prone to drive their fine bows under when running before a gale. This of course tripped them up violently, flinging them on their beam ends with no chance of recovery, due to their shallow draft. Beating to windward in heavy seas was equally hazardous. One whole fleet of these clipper schooners was lost in a winter storm that caught them with the Georges Bank to leeward.

Faced with such horrendous losses, the federal Fisheries Commission stepped in to sponsor design competitions. Yacht designers and local builders vied to produce a beautifully balanced hull and moderate rig, a boat that was rightly characterized as "fast and able." Our example of the breed showed the signs of hard usage and poor maintenance, but she radiated reality.

Paul Henry Dunn, an experienced sailor, had recognized her Gloucester hull for what it was in the motor dragger he had discovered in Pensacola, Florida. He bought her cheap, stepped disused schooner masts in her hull, took out the heavy diesel that had made her squat aft like a tug, and brought her home to Gloucester. But she had not earned her keep as an exhibition in the harbor from which she and her sisters had sailed. When I phoned Paul Henry to ask him if he would take $50,000 for the vessel, subject to survey, he said "Yes." We drove up with the check, had the vessel hauled out at Gloucester Marine Railway, and had the privilege of seeing the seductive shape of an early Gloucesterman dripping before our eyes, a Venus risen from the foam.

I had asked Jack Dickerson to survey her and to order such work as would be needed to get her insured for the trip to New York. Jack charged a token fee, $35 if memory serves. But he was tough as nails about the survey. He explained to me in words of one syllable exactly why, when he found a defective plank, the whole plank had to come out, not just the afflicted section. "The strength of the tree that the plank came from is part of the strength of the vessel," he said, as the yard hands tore out the first plank, most of it in perfect condition. "You lose that strength, or most of it, when you replace a good long plank with shorter pieces stuck in here and there."

He compromised this sterling principle to a degree when the yard manager told him he couldn't get 40-foot lengths of oak these days. And when the workmen suggested that maybe a dutchman (a wooden patch tightly fitted into an existing plank to replace a bad spot) would do, he listened and sometimes agreed. Over beers after hours, the workmen told Jack how they kept some of the old wooden hulls working with patches made out of flattened tin cans, nailed down over a bad spot on top of a brushful of hot tar. Jack listened and smiled. Knowing our tight finances, he approved a few dutchmen, but only when practically all the strength was still there in the original plank. And that was that.

These were glorious days in the first week in September. We turned to in the yard at eight, doing cleanup jobs aboard the schooner while skilled shipwrights tended to her structural problems, and we quit at five to find supper on the waterfront and retire early to bed at our member Richard Hunt's hotel, where he kindly put us up free. The smells of oak and pine shavings and Tarr & Wonson's copper bottom paint were with us all day, somewhat overlaid by the aroma of frying fish from the nearby Gorton's fish processing plant. This rather spoiled things for Norma, who was afflicted with morning sickness carrying our first child. At night we dreamed of being under sail in *Caviare*. "I have long dreamed of sailing a schooner out of Gloucester and curiously we are enacting this dream—in Gloucester," says my journal for Tuesday, 10 September 1968, "with the whistle buoy groaning outside the window in Dick Hunt's hotel...."

One fly in the ointment: Jack's strict reading of his responsibilities (for which we were grateful) had used up the money we'd allotted for work on the vessel and a bit more besides. And there was one thing that needed replacing which, while not vital to the schooner's structure, mattered a great deal to her appearance. This was the gammon knee, an oak extension of the stem arching forward under the bowsprit, which nicely completes the sweeping curve of a clipper bow. The old schooner's gammon knee had been chopped back into a stump to allow a heavy rope fender to be slung over the bow when she'd been adapted for work as a tug.

The yard manager had given me a desk and phone in his office, so I could continue to deal with the daily flow of Seaport business, while Norma worked with the yard hands on the schooner. I had only to look up to see through the window the fair shape of the schooner with her truncated bow standing outside. One morning the yard manager asked me to come down with him to look at something. As we walked toward the *Caviare* he stopped to point out a heavy, rough-sawn oak crook lying on the chip-strewn ground.

"There it is," he said, "a fine piece of seasoned oak for that knee you need under the bowsprit." I bent over to look, and saw that the grain of the wood followed the angle of the knee, an essential for strength in the piece.

"It looks ideal," I said, "but we just don't have the money for the job."

"Who said anything about money?" he retorted sharply. "I know you ran out of money, you told me. Now I'm telling you this: The yard is donating the wood, and the men are donating their work to fashion that piece and fit it into the stem. Now just give us a drawing and we'll get to work."

———◆———

"The first thing, Peter, is: Stop working the problem so hard." Howard Chapelle was gentle in his response, when I explained over the phone the problem we had with our newly acquired schooner *Caviare*. "Just have a martini with Norma when you quit work this evening, and start looking at photographs of clipper-bowed schooners of the 1890s. Learn their names and stories, that's part of the drill. Get so you can recognize the ones you really like.

"Then here's what you do. You take a nice, limber batten and tack it to the foreside of the stem. Then drag the top three feet of the batten forward until it assumes the curve you want to end up with. Secure it there and trace the curve out on a piece of plywood."

Chapelle, dean of historical naval architects and senior historian at the Smithsonian Institution, was the acknowledged authority on Gloucester schooners. He had an acerbic wit and was famous for not suffering fools gladly. However he was always kind to Norma and me, perhaps because he could see, standing outside the scene, the tremendous challenge we'd taken on in our mission to revive the historic sailing-ship waterfront of South Street. And perhaps in this instance he was moved—as we were—by the determination of the yard people that this last survivor in America of the first-generation Gloucestermen go out of their yard with the lovely curve of her clipper bow properly restored.

Norma and I did precisely as we were told and, with the ready help of two workmen, we traced the curve. We took the plywood back to the office to compare it with those old photographs. Once satisfied with the overall look, Norma drew the final lines in black marker and gave the plywood to the men to cut out. That pattern was then held up against the vessel's bow so everyone—manager, Stanfords and a crowd of workmen—could approve it. When we left on Friday, *Caviare* stood poised at the water's edge, topsides sweeping back from her arched clipper bow, gleaming in fresh black paint above the red Tarr & Wonson's copper bottom paint.

Norma and I returned the following Tuesday with our full crew for the passage to New York: George Demmy and Richard Henstock, from

Florida and Lincolnshire respectively; the indefatigable Bob Ferraro; Bill Wertenbaker of the slippery gaff schooner *Tyehee*, our nemesis in the previous year's Schooner Race for the Mayor's Cup; Al Swanson; and two retired naval officers whom Al had recruited to bolster our ranks.

Caviare was now afloat, and we were busy cleaning out her interior. Some of us started in the fo'c'sle with its common dining table wedged into the forepeak, with double bunks along each side. The companion ladder led to the forehatch just aft of the table and just forward of the stout foremast (always, on these schooners, considerably heavier than the mainmast). The great iron coal stove, surrounded by galley shelves, followed, and then the fo'c'sle ended with the wooden bulkhead that separated the deckhands' living quarters from the fishbins.

Another group tackled the fishbins that occupied the midship area, scrubbing out the gunk that had collected over the years and thoroughly washing down one bin for the ice that would cool our perishables. Another fishbin was set up to serve as a makeshift head, with a heavy piece of canvas serving as the door. Still others were cleaned to become storage areas for our other provisions and assorted gear. A third group cleaned out the after cabin, which had two bunks to starboard and two to port, under the original cabin house with its portholes and skylight for ventilation. A hatch opened aft out onto the quarterdeck, the command center of the vessel. One of the crew was surprised when we stopped him from vigorously scraping at a hard ridge of accumulated paint on the wineglass section of the cabin ceiling aft. We explained that this was irrefutable evidence of the schooner's original raised poop deck. It wasn't long before gear was stowed, bunks were made up and the schooner started to look like home.

We then set to work on deck. Two dories lying between the masts were lashed down for the voyage. The sails, which were bent to the spars for exhibition purposes, had to be overhauled and all the lashings checked. There was the great mainsail, which roughly fitted the long main boom and gaff; a foresail, which proved to be several sizes too small for the space between the masts it was meant to fill; and a staysail set from the foremast head to the stemhead in the bow. But there was no jib for the stretching length of the bowsprit. This did not bode well for any attempt to sail the vessel, which we dearly wanted to do, although, to meet insurance requirements, we had tows arranged for the whole trip. So we asked around, and a fisherman produced an old jib from his attic, which was on the small side but indisputably better than nothing to fill the gaping hole in the sail plan forward. I think we paid $15 for this vital addition to the old lady's wardrobe.

Just before we left, Dana Story, historian of the Story family, the great Gloucester schooner builders, came by to look over the vessel. Noting that she had no raised quarterdeck aft, a hallmark of the traditional Gloucestermen, he pronounced her not a Gloucesterman. But Paul Henry Dunn had produced an article from the Pensacola paper showing a Gloucester schooner undergoing a rebuild in which the raised quarterdeck was cut down to the main deck level, as shown in before-and-after photographs. And there was the hard ridge of paint in the after cabin where the old cabin sole had been, a good ten inches above the existing flooring. The new, lower floorboards had clearly been installed to maintain headroom after the raised quarterdeck above had been sawn away. I tried to interest our guest in this evidence that the vessel had once had a raised quarterdeck, but Dana just shook his head. He hadn't ever heard of such a change and couldn't see any good reason for making it. Chapelle later verified that these schooners had been so altered and their names and registries changed to get the better insurance rates available on a new vessel. (A case of bourbon whiskey customarily accompanied the application for the new registration.)

We had, however, begun to have doubts about Dunn's identification of the vessel as the *Caviare*. There was no evidence linking the original *Caviare* of 1891, wrecked off Campeche in 1916, with the rebuilt *Mystic C.* of 1923. Dunn produced a sail plan of *Caviare*, which had the notation on it, "name changed to Mystic C." The notation was made by ball-point pen, which came into use in the US a quarter century after the rebuild. The whole account began to seem weavy. And, while we had no doubts at all about her identity as a Gloucesterman of the 1890s, we resolved to keep an open mind on the schooner's identity and kept a file on this very question. And in 1970, thanks to the scrupulous research of W. J. Boughton, the schooner's identity was firmly established as the *Lettie G. Howard* of 1892, the name under which she sails today. But in 1968 and for the following two years she continued under her assigned name, *Caviare*.

Finally the last bags of provisions were brought aboard, our crew mustered on deck, and Russell Grinnell brought his tug alongside to pass us his towing line. Eyeing our Bermuda shorts and amateurish appearance a little askance, he assembled our crew to establish the disciplines of the tow before us. And I noticed that he made sure to settle the hawser around the forward bitts himself. An intense-looking person, he was all business where his profession was concerned. It was good to see that he took up the strain of the towing line very gently as we got underway—he had that respect for an aged wooden hull. So off we chugged into the gathering night on Saturday, 14 September. For dinner we had a hearty stew prepared by Norma and Richard, which we ate on deck, enjoying the cool night breeze and the sensation of being under way at last. Russ Grinnell's small tug pulled us across Cape Cod Bay at a steady rate of knots, and early the next day we came through the Cape Cod Canal, arriving at Newport, Rhode Island, in mid-afternoon. Russ shook us each by the hand and wished us Godspeed, glancing without comment at the sails that we had readied for hoisting. He had signed an undertaking with the insurance company that we were to be towed from Gloucester to Newport with no sail being set. And he'd done his part.

At Newport, our friend, Barclay Warburton, III, would take over escort duty in his brigantine *Black Pearl*. Practically from the day we opened our doors in South Street, Barclay had been an enthusiastic supporter of our efforts. He was full of ideas for the restoration and for pierside events involving the brigantine—and earlier this year had brought about such an event with the sing-along he held on our Pier 16, led by the great British chanteyman Lou Killen for Sea Day.

An athletic figure with sparkling eyes, Barclay loved adventure. And, as Norma put it, "he was a dashing figure," wearing his yachting cap at the rakish angle favored by Admiral Beatty of Jutland fame. He also loved a good song, a good story and a gathering of kindred spirits. He was devoted to history and the maritime heritage and had a strong vein of idealism which involved him in training young people for life through seafaring—an interest that would lead in a few years to his founding the American Sail Training Association. Son of Barclay Warburton, II, an Army Air Corps ace in World War I, Barclay had grown up with his mother and a stepfather whom he came to revere when his mother remarried, to William Vanderbilt, a scion of the well-known yachting family. Toward the end of his life, Barclay enjoyed recounting his days aboard the Vanderbilt steam yacht, where he berthed with the crew forward. On one occasion, when he was introduced at pre-dinner cocktails before being sent off to a child's early bedtime, he shocked the company with some fo'c'sle language. Barclay didn't exactly revolt from this background, but some time before we came to know him he had bought the 50-foot *Black Pearl*, a handsome half brig (square rigged on the foremast, fore and aft on the main; Barclay preferred the term brigantine). The vessel had been built for a round-the-world passage, which her owner-builder had had to give up due to ill health. Barclay took the *Black Pearl* to Newport, where he acquired a tavern on Bannister's Wharf. This he named the Black Pearl Tavern and, never one for halfway measures, formed the Black Pearl Singers to introduce real sea music to all who would listen. One corner of the tavern was given over to a big cage housing a green parrot, "Shipwreck," who often let loose with a salty phrase or two.

We posed Barclay a real test of his outgoing, hospitable nature when he held a party for our crew in the Tavern the night before our departure for New York. Seated together at one long table, we enjoyed a magnificent repast. Once the meal was over, our crew set about singing songs, making outrageous toasts and waging fierce arguments about the forbidden trio of topics, sex, religion and politics, raising Cain in the taproom until Norma and Barclay persuaded us out the door to board the schooner lying at the end of the wharf. There we rolled into our bunks to sleep the sleep of the carefree sea rovers we fancied ourselves to be.

A light northerly breeze greeted us as we turned to next morning to make sail. First we sweated up the giant mainsail, then the shrunken-looking foresail, and in short order the staysail and diminutive jib. We were headed into what wind there was, so all the sails were shaking softly, and I ordered lines taken in and put the helm down hard to fall off and sail away. The schooner, however, had other ends in view. With sails still shaking, she ghosted forward, toward a cluster of small craft anchored in shallow water ahead. She did not have enough way on to give her rudder enough bite to turn her, but she had enough to put us aground in short order, unless something changed right away. We backed the jib to push the schooner's head around to port and, knowing how small the jib was, backed the staysail as well—without result. We quickly hauled the foresail aback, far enough forward to effect the pivoting movement we wanted—all this to a string of wiseacre comments from our two Navy veterans. Still no result. Our own crew, who were all used to sailing schooners, did not share their amusement.

I left the useless helm and with all the remaining hands (except the two "pros") we scrambled to counter-back the main. We had a gybe preventer rigged on the main boom, which gave the hands something to haul on and, hauling with the strength of ten, we managed to get the boom right out to port against the main rigging. And the mainsail, that great stretch of old grey canvas, did the trick, kicking the schooner's stern abruptly to windward, while the headsails at last took hold and drove her bow off.

With the helm hard over, I watched the slow progress of the bowsprit under its pathetic jib (but how glad we were to have it!), as it slowly turned to port and passed close by the mast of the first of the small boats anchored ahead, then, with less room to spare, the next, and finally, by an even smaller margin, clearing the last. At that point we were still holding the main out at almost a right angle to the boat and keeping the foresail and the headsails sheeted flat to windward, with Norma and Bob Ferraro prepared to fend off any small boat we couldn't clear. We knew that the worst outcome would be a vagrant puff of the morning air filling that great mainsail and sweeping the schooner around into the wind before we'd gathered headway enough for the rudder to take effect.

But now the rudder did take effect, and the old warhorse strode nobly out toward the open sea, the water under her arching bows breaking into a lively chuckle while the bubbles streamed by her rounded flanks to join the lengthening wake astern. Running light, with less than a full load of ballast, the schooner soon out-distanced the accompanying *Black Pearl*, much to our delight. Slipping along at three knots in a light southerly breeze, she left hardly a mark on the face of the water, except for the spreading waves from under her bow. As the breeze strengthened around noon, *Black Pearl*, with her great spread of canvas, soon caught up with us, so honors were even for the day.

By mid-afternoon we were off the Mystic River in Fisher's Island Sound, where Barclay took our towline and started up the *Black Pearl*'s diesel to pull us upriver to the Mystic Seaport anchorage. Here we were guided into our berth at a wharf with the whaleship *Charles W. Morgan* across the way.

Jack Parkinson, scholarly gentleman historian of the New York Yacht Club and a great student of the schooner breed, was there to greet us. We welcomed him aboard and showed him with some embarrassment through our crude makeshift quarters below. His eyes were all for the hanging knees that bound the frames to the deck beams, and other features of traditional wooden shipbuilding. "She's a Gloucesterman, all right," he said. "And of the first generation, clearly, with that fine clipper bow. Too bad you didn't get my friend Dana Story down here in the carcass of this splendid vessel—he'd sniff out his forebears' handiwork and art—yes, actual art." I made no comment on this, for obvious reasons. Later Dana became a great friend, though we never learned if he'd accepted familial responsibility for the schooner.

Jack, whom I had known only by reputation, meant every word of what he said about the schooner. He and I left the schooner to call on John Leavitt in his office. John was a schooner veteran, having served in the coasting trade in the 1930s. When that trade died out, he went to work in the Boston office of John Alden, the yacht designer whose schooners showed the full potential of the rig, in such noble creations as our own *Athena*. Leavitt was one of the stars in the Mystic constellation of those years when preservation of historic ships was just coming of age, with its center of gravity at Mystic.

"John," said Jack Parkinson, puffing out his words, for the steep stairs had not been kind to his asthma, "you've got to see . . . what these kids have brought in. They've got . . . a vintage Gloucesterman . . . a schooner to put our *Dunton* in the shade." I remember feeling embarrassed, since it had been no great research of ours that discovered the schooner. We then hurried back to *Caviare* together. When we reached the vessel, John gave her a long look and turned to me to say: "Looks like you've got the real thing, all right."

The next morning gave us a fair wind, and Barclay suggested that we find our own way downriver. So with an anchor carried at the stern to enable us to stop if either of the two drawbridges between us and the sea had been unable to open, we proceeded in stately fashion under foresail and jib alone, since it would have been suicidal to set the main in the uncertain airs and narrow waters of the upper river. Our faithful consort *Black Pearl* followed us under power, for Barclay knew that she might be called on at short notice to give emergency service as a tug to haul our just barely manageable vessel out of trouble.

In continuing light airs, we raised the mainsail and made our way in stately fashion, up Long Island Sound toward the mecca of New York, the two ships always in company, and *Black Pearl* usually making morning coffee for both of us on their gas stove, to save our heating up our vessel with the coal stove in our galley. Eventually, on Thursday morning, we arrived at City Island. The light morning northerly sprang up into a noticeable breeze as we made our approach to Minneford's barge, where we had so often brought *Athena* in. At the helm I asked Bill Wertenbaker to call the moment when we should wipe all sail off and glide into our landing place. When Bill said "I'd do it now, Peter," I called out: "Let go everything, fore and aft," and the sails came rustling down. I put the helm down at the last minute, so George Demmy was able to step onto the barge with a spring line to bring the vessel to, and Richard Henstock leapt ashore to place a stern line. The old girl had proved marvelously responsive under sail, and sailing light, with little ballast in her, had proved able to keep up under sail with her brigantine consort, despite her unbalanced and curtailed rig. Her sweet lines made her almost too ready to start forward with the slightest push, as we'd discovered with stunned surprise, coming off the pier at Newport. And one could sit on the bowsprit for a long time, consumed in watching her sweet cutwater cleave the sea.

On Friday, 20 September, a Bronx River Towing tug showed up to pull *Caviare* out of her berth at Minneford's and on through Hell Gate into the lower reaches of the East River, where we dropped the towline and glided into our berth at Pier 16, to tie up in front of the recently-arrived *Ambrose* lightship. There the George W. Rogers Construction Company, at the instance of our friend George W. Rogers, had built a special landing stage for the schooner. There was a little misunderstanding about a permit for this stage to be used for boarding people, but when Commissioner Charles Leedham, who had succeeded our great friend Herb Halberg as commissioner of Ports and Terminals, had his photograph taken drinking water from the *Caviare*'s deck keg, these difficulties vanished and we were able to welcome the public aboard the following day, a Saturday, without let or hindrance.

Three weeks later, on 12 October, the Second Annual Mayor's Cup Race for Schooners attracted the astonishing total of thirty contestants, with the schooner *Caviare* as committee boat, and the schooner *Mystic Whaler* as observation vessel. *Niña* again swept the unrestricted class, this time in a light-weather race, and *Tyehee* again left our *Athena* in her wake, as winner of a special Alfred F. Loomis trophy which we'd set up for the gaff-rigged schooner with the best corrected time. We felt quite sure that *Tyehee* would spare us the embarrassment of winning our own trophy, and in this we were not deceived. Again, the rafters of Whyte's Restaurant on Fulton Street rang with toasts and effulgent speeches on the glory of schooners and schooner people, and the Seaport piers were crowded with a forest of swaying masts. This included the square-rigged foremast of the *Black Pearl*, which we had allowed to race as a schooner by a special dispensation of the race committee. A celebratory after-dinner mug-up in her spacious cabin confirmed the wisdom of this decision. How much we owed the generous-minded and high-spirited help and counsel of Barclay Warburton in this time! His good will even accommodated Joe Cantalupo's calling him "Washberler." When Barclay overheard this appellation one day, he pointed out to Joe that since he called him "Joe," why didn't Joe just call him "Barclay"—and so, in the usual way of things in South Street, they got on together famously, in mutual respect and admiration.

Our two new ships did everything to humanize South Street. Volunteer gatherings and work crew training sessions, historical colloquies and trustee meetings were soon held in the spacious hull of the *Ambrose*. Trustees met in her wardroom, and Eric Ridder, as treasurer, took pride in inviting people to luncheon there as part of his program of getting maritime companies to sign up with his own *Journal of Commerce* as $1,000 members of the Seaport. The luncheons were initially cold lobster salad, but were soon switched to hot bouillabaisse fresh from the kitchen of Sloppy Louie's, just across South Street. Emil Morino, the proprietor, would rush out into South Street waving his apron so that Ellen Isbrandtsen could safely cross over with the steaming pot that held this uniquely fresh and varied fish stew.

A memorable occasion came about when, with the politically conservative, by-the-numbers Eric in the chair, we became aware of a row of multi-hued young faces grinning down at us through the open skylight overhead, when one of the group said: "Look, they're eating down there." Ellen started up to go topside and close the skylight, muttering a brief apology about "those kids." Eric Ridder held up a restraining hand. "Not so fast, Ellen," he said to her. "Those kids are why we're here," and the luncheon proceeded.

The public streamed onto the pier to see for themselves these small ships that looked like nothing they'd ever seen outside picture books. From the outset we initiated sail-drying exercises on the *Caviare*, a practical necessity to keep the canvas well aired to prevent mildew and rot. This entailed an interesting drill, with people hauling on halyards to hoist the four sails, main, fore, staysail and jib, to hang loosely in the air, short of their full hoist. This gave the vessel a rather attractive disheveled look, calling to mind the Cavalier poet Robert Herrick's lines: "A sweet disorder in the dress kindles in clothes a wantonness."

But the work that produced this playful appeal was anything but casual—it was a matter of having at least two energetic haulers on both the throat and peak halyards of the mainsail, one on each of the two fore halyards, and a further two for the staysail and jib. A total of eight hands, and at that, the one hand would have to switch from the main peak halyard, which was only partly hoisted, leaving the sail in what is known as a "scandalized" state—one for you, Robert Herrick!—so that he or she could join in sweating up the last few feet of the throat halyard.

We invited morning visitors on the pier to join us in this work. And people in city clothes would cheerfully come aboard to do that, shedding their jackets to roll up their sleeves, lay hold of the bristly manila line, and *pull*, while the heavy canvas unfolded itself and lazily climbed into the morning air. In the late afternoon the sail was stowed again on its booms, faked down fisherman style, rather than in a yachtsman's furl. After these sail-handling sessions, we'd often adjourn for coffee in the fo'c'sle. These were occasions to review ship maintenance tasks on the two vessels, or even discuss future plans for the whole project with newcomers. We got new members from these unusual casual encounters. Who wouldn't give $1, or even $5, to be kept in touch with an activity like this, in which they'd played some part? And quite a few among them became volunteers, who added skilled work to supplement our slender work force in the unending tasks of active ship-keeping.

We also got a fisheries exhibit installed below decks. This was made up of photographs from my father's book, *Men, Fish & Boats,* which recorded the fisheries of the 1920s and early '30s. Al had gathered the photos from a wide range of sources, including the great photographers Albert Cook Church and Morris Rosenfeld, and a host of others, including one Doris Day (not the actress) who, Al notes, "horn-swoggled" her way into a rough fishing trip to Brown's Bank. Her studies of the men at work in dories, on deck, and ashore radiate the life and hard-learned skills of the people, and one in particular, of a lost dory signaling for pickup with an upraised oar, ineffaceably conveys the loneliness and immense cold indifference of the sea. Al himself had made a few pictures, including the frames of a new schooner rising against the sky in Story's yard in nearby Essex, birthplace of the most famous Gloucestermen, including ours. But his main contribution was to immerse himself in the stories, folkways, and speech of the fishing community.

So before we left on the ten-day trip to bring the *Caviare* to South Street, we had all the material for a ready-made exhibit. We had planned that this exhibit would be produced and the display panels brought to City Island, where we would install them before our arrival at Pier 16.

Unfortunately, the job was not done. Commissioner Leedham's reception and the opening of the ship to the public the next day had to pass with no educational display aboard. I took this as a warning that even urgent things won't get done without someone in charge with the driving purpose that moves all things before it. To nail home this point, within three working days of our return Norma had the full display printed, mounted on panels and installed below decks. Marie Lore organized volunteer tour guides to take school groups through the ships. These guides were mostly older women who had raised children of their own and could provide the discipline required both for learning and safety reasons aboard the ships. This arrangement worked wonders, and because order was maintained, children were able to develop their own thoughts about what they saw and felt in this strange setting that moved slightly in the water that embraced it.

Early on, I was thrilled to hear a boy concede that he would have been afraid to go out on the ocean in such a small vessel as the one we were aboard—particularly after seeing all the photographs of schooners sailing rail underwater and seamen dodging boarding seas on steam trawlers. But an older boy, bless him, spoke from superior knowledge: "Listen, they didn't catch the fish from this boat. They caught it from the little boats they have upstairs"—meaning the dories on deck. There, right there, was the story of long-line fishing from the Gloucester schooners!

"So what do they do when a storm comes up?"

In answer to this question Marie, or one of her recruits, was then able to tell the story of Howard Blackburn, who, blown away from his schooner, the *Grace L. Fears,* in a fierce snowstorm on the Grand Banks, rowed a hundred miles back to Newfoundland. While he rowed, his dorymate Tom Welch bailed to keep the boat afloat against the cresting seas that broke aboard, but he eventually froze to death. Blackburn, seeing that his own hands were freezing, shaped them to hold the oars, taking time out from rowing only to bail, and finally reached shore. He lost his fingers to frostbite, but went on sailing to show what a man could do if he has determination, and was given a sloop to do this in by the Cruising Club of America. Aboard the *Caviare* the youngsters could see a picture of Blackburn at the helm of his sloop, in striped pants and tie, sporting a splendid white mustache and with an unmistakable twinkle in his eye.

Joe Cantalupo was in good spirits, happy to see the *Destruction of Lower Manhattan* exhibit and genuinely delighted at the Kaplan fundings which made possible the restoration workshop and other needed measures. He was awed at the visits of the tall ships *Eagle* and *Danmark,* revenants of a distant, unknown past, and of course found himself much at home with the art, craft and antique shows, and Pete Seeger's singing, which chimed in with his own political views. And he shared the volunteers' excitement when the *Ambrose* lightship came in to stay, a visible testament to the ocean traffics that nourished South Street.

But a new chord was struck with Joe in the arrival of *Caviare*. With justifiable pride he showed us a photograph on his office wall of his father, Pasquale, on Pier 16 with a horse-drawn garbage wagon, and in the background the masts of fishing schooners. Some of the schooner masts had topmasts with topsails bundled in the crosstrees, for in 1911, when the picture was taken, engines had only begun to be installed in the fishing fleet. Schooners with engines kept their full rig of lower sails at first, using the engines only to keep going in light air, but did away with the topsails, light-weather kites, which were no longer needed. By our time, in the 1960s, our *Caviare* and the bigger *Ernestina,* ex-*Effie M. Morrissey,* were the last of these fine-lined clipper-bowed vessels from the age of sail, vessels designed to go just as fast as the wind would take them, without any kind of power assist.

Joe was stirred to make an effort to get Fish Market people interested in the museum, which they generally viewed with suspicion, since it was frequently in the papers that the market was going to be moved to the Bronx—and the market people did not want to move! But, at his behest, they gave us an ice-crushing machine of antique vintage, which had been used to fill the schooners' bins with chipped ice as they made ready for their next trip. This was exactly the kind of gear we wanted to see on our piers, things that filled in the story of these vessels and their people and brought them back to life.

CHAPTER 20

Seaport Restoration Conference, *November 1968*

Jim Diaz Leads Volunteers—New Space for Expanded Museum—
Maritime Leaders Convene on Restoration—
Moynihan Rings the Bell—Schermerhorn Row Threatened

The two ships now in South Street did wonders to establish our presence on the gritty, half-forgotten waterfront. Now people could *see* what we had been talking about, as they walked the decks of vessels that had helped build New York. And the curatorial staff we'd added gave depth to our message. These things strengthened the young museum's stance for the South Street Seaport Planning Conference we'd set up for November.

We also needed a full-time person to work with our volunteers in cleaning, painting and general maintenance of ships and buildings. Joe Cantalupo suggested a man called Jimmy Diaz, who worked as a janitor in LaGuardia Houses.

Norma interviewed Mr. Diaz in her usual relaxed and open fashion, and was drawn by his positive attitude and his interest in what we were doing in South Street. A recent transplant from Mayaguez, on Puerto Rico's western shore, he was married with two young children and wanted to secure better prospects for their lives than he could in his current job. He spoke English fluently and was a quick learner, but his first painting assignment was not up to snuff. So Norma worked with him, scraping dirt out of corners with a razor blade rather than simply painting over it, showing how to avoid "curtains" from too much paint and "holidays" from too little, along with other disciplines. He soon learned the art of doing things deliberately and getting them right the first time.

Jimmy soon showed strong initiative in his work. Within a matter of weeks he was politely correcting any volunteers with sloppy painting habits, and he suggested different ways of doing things to Norma, who regularly encouraged suggestions from people doing the work. We both came to feel that the way Jimmy went at things was a living embodiment of the ideal proposed by the shipping magnate W. R. Grace in the 1880s—in a successful company, people take "joy in the work."

Volunteer ranks were also growing apace. Jim McNamara, newly graduated from the New York State Maritime College at Fort Schuyler, was collecting steamship models for us as various downtown shipping companies went out of business or moved their headquarters out of town. Jim also used his seafaring skills to help train Chi Ling in weekend work on *Ambrose*'s machinery and *Caviare*'s rigging. His maritime connections also helped to sign up more members in the sea services, supporting Leon Kaplan's admirable work as membership chairman.

Julie Strewe and Rudy Staw served regularly as volunteer guides, especially with the school groups that began visiting, as teachers became aware of the Seaport's presence on the waterfront—thanks to news stories over the summer when our visiting ships came in, and then when our own ships arrived, and again when the schooner race filled the harbor with sail to top off the season. Charlie Dunn, stalwart of the local history committee and leader of the Sea Explorers, took over as chairman of Friends, supervising all this work. He succeeded Jock Bartlett, whose work with the Clearwater committee tied us closely to that dedicated group.

We were also expanding our foothold ashore. At Tom Van Arkel's urging, Jakob had rented the Goelet estate's vacant building at 203 Front Street, just north of Fulton Street and across from the Market Block, as a future headquarters. The four-story structure, built in 1816, had been combined with its neighbor at 204 behind a suave red-brick frontage to make a "modern" hotel in 1883. Lacking the charm of the more irregular, rosy brick of Schermerhorn Row, the smooth-faced, tall-windowed building conveyed an impression of order and respectability.

The lofty ground-floor hall, once the hotel's imposing entrance, had been used until recently as a storage room for frozen shrimp. The second floor was broken up into offices, including an interesting room at the back, running the width of the building, whose windows looked out on the alleyway behind. This potentially magnificent space was our immediate choice for our growing Seaport library, which had now reached several hundred volumes stacked up in packing cases in the upper floor of 16 Fulton. The third floor was fairly open, with a partly enclosed office space at the front, and the fourth was completely open and evidently used only for storage, once the hotel rooms had been done away with. The whole building was structurally sound, but unheated, so we could hardly occupy it in the face of the oncoming winter. But since we were almost sitting in each other's laps in 16 Fulton, we gloried in the spacious prospects before us.

This was our situation, as we prepared for the long-anticipated restoration conference. This had been largely conceived and funded by the J. M. Kaplan Fund. For our part, we wanted to have things set up so that the experts called in to review our plans would know they were dealing with a living reality rather than a dream of past glories or a fantastic vision of the future. The look and feel of the waterfront had been changed with the stout red-hulled presence of *Ambrose* and lissome black shape of *Caviare* under her rakish spars. Ashore, along with our mini-exhibit at 16 Fulton, we had the rudiments of a museum staff—though not one of them, it's interesting to note, had any prior museum experience. Also, the widespread reporting of our affairs in the papers had established another kind of presence of the Seaport: an image in people's minds.

The conference was set for Tuesday and Wednesday, 6–7 November, just three weeks after the Schooner Race. It opened with a reception aboard *Caviare* at Pier 16, at the foot of Fulton Street. The Ship Panel then adjourned for dinner at Sloppy Louie's, after which we went to their upstairs room for an evening discussion of our plans for ships in the project under the title: "Ships: the Heart of the Story." Leaders of the maritime museum community had turned out for this with typical generosity of spirit: Howard Chapelle of the Smithsonian Institution, Waldo Johnston of Mystic Seaport, Karl Kortum of the San Francisco Maritime Museum, and Harold Sniffen of the Mariners' Museum in Virginia, together with the ship historian John Lyman and the historical naval architect George Campbell—all gathered under the gavel of

Monk Farnham of *Boating* magazine, as chairman. Monk's cautionary note that we had to take care that the horse we had mounted did not run away with us was somewhat offset, if not upset, by Karl's mandate that we should think in terms of three great square-rigged ships, not just the two shown in the Seaport model now on exhibition at 16 Fulton.

How should the ships be interpreted for the public? The photographic exhibit aboard *Caviare* got good reviews, but it was agreed we needed more working gear and artifacts to flesh out the story. There was a first airing of the Ship Committee's eventual resolution that each ship should be restored "fit to go to sea," even though her mission was to be dockside for the visiting public. And there was unanimous agreement that the ships' story must permeate every aspect of the South Street restoration—as it did when the signs of packet offices, sailmakers, blockmakers, riggers, towboat operators and seamen's bars hung from the buildings of the Street of Ships.

On the land side, Joan Davidson and Kent Barwick had lined up a stellar company for the following day. In the morning session, held in the big ground floor room at 203 Front Street, a panel took up the economic and cultural aspects of "The Seaport: A Vital Place for the City," in a lively discussion led by New York City Parks Commissioner William Ginsberg. The panelists, Paul Busse of the Economic Development Council; John Hightower of the New York State Council on the Arts; and Frederick L. Rath, Jr., of the New York State Historical Association; weighed in vigorously from their diverse points of view. The idea of South Street as a place of accidental encounters, of changing events, new corners to be turned and new discoveries made, appealed to all. Commerce could play a positive role, as Fred Rath advised us, if it related to the experience the Seaport Museum presented. Colonial Williamsburg's Edwin Kendrew added the interesting fact that Williamsburg now earned more from commercial operations devoted to kindred themes than from the admission charges on which it had relied in its early years.

In our case, it was agreed that the fledgling Seaport was already attracting people who were willing customers for goods and services that complemented the experience. This was shown in the roaring success of the art and antique shows, the crowds that thronged to board visiting ships, and a very noticeable increase in business at the restaurants on or near the site. And we were only at the beginnings of building the Seaport experience!

I am not sure, however, that this simple advertising/marketing concept struck deep roots among all present. This doubt was later to grow into a real concern when top-flight professionals were eventually called in to write the Seaport financial plan. In the nature of things, they were irresistibly drawn to planning things from the top rather than from the experience that was unfolding and developing from our organic roots. For now, I just mentally logged this for future reference. And I was encouraged when everyone agreed that our efforts to attract people to the district were a success.

As to how we were going about what we were doing, Fred Rath, a traditional liberal in his views, paid us this tribute to how we were pursuing our mission in South Street: "I know of no project whose plans are more publicly discussed, or whose decisions are more openly arrived at."

On this cheery note, we got up from our chairs and tramped up the newly painted stairways in 203 Front Street to sit down to a lobster salad luncheon of no mean proportions. The feast was set out on three or four tables in the open space of the top floor, destined to be our exhibition workshop. The mood was celebratory, and as dishes were cleared away, Daniel Patrick Moynihan, then in his early forties and serving at this point in his distinguished career as director of Harvard's Joint Center for Urban Studies, rose to his feet to deliver a celebratory speech.

And what a speech it was—it echoes in my mind today. He started out, with a mock humility worthy of Mr. Finley Peter Dunne (chronicler of the great age of Irish Tammany politics), asking us to be sure, now, that we salute the noble ship captains and powerful barons of Wall Street who made America the leader among nations in providing hope and opportunity for all. This even included such humble folk as his own forebears, the Moynihans, who crossed a wide and stormy ocean to embark on new lives where the Statue of Liberty raised her light above the golden shore. Imperceptibly, then, he shifted his emphasis to the struggles of the immigrants who, despised and attacked by Know Nothings and Native Sons, had provided the sinew and impetus to dig the canals, lay the railways, man the ships and build the docks that made New York great, while fighting for the freedoms that, taken together, made New York the hope of the world.

His conclusion seemed to me the most important statement made at the conference: that these achievements were possible because of the opportunity for people to pursue their aspirations, and, equally important, that the rewards of achievement had been more widely shared than in any society on earth.

He finished by raising his glass to offer a toast to the people of South Street, the men and women of the glorious past, the challenging present, and the future which we were here to shape.

Less unanimous views emerged in "The Seaport: Past and Future Forms," a session devoted to architectural principles of the restoration. The panel was led by James Marston Fitch, presiding genius of Columbia University's School of Architecture, with the restoration architect Giorgio Cavaglieri, our friend Edwin Kendrew of Colonial Williamsburg, Loring McMillen of Historic Richmondtown in Staten Island, and the architect John Young. The panel reversed an earlier decision to remove the mansard roof added to Schermerhorn Row in 1868, when the Fulton Ferry Hotel expanded upward. Architectural consultants had called for removing the roof to maintain the original uniformity of the whole row as built in 1812–13, but that was a viewpoint which we amateurs had resisted. We had come to look on such "cultural accretions" as witnesses to a structure's passage through time, and we prized them for that reason. Loring McMillen, a leading authority on historic brick, spoke for us when he said it just didn't feel right to tear down hundred-year-old brick in the name of historic preservation.

———————◆———————

Jim Fitch enthusiastically endorsed this first finding of the panel. A leader in finding ways to be creative in preserving historic structures, he had pioneered in adaptive re-use of old structures as part of the living fabric of a modern community. He resolutely opposed the building of replica buildings in mindless idolatry of the past. His boundless good will, enormous enthusiasm for new ideas and creative work—which expressed themselves in crying "*Andiamo*" in his soft Southern accent as he led his famous explorations of the cityscape—swept all before him in such meetings as this one. Who could resist such a force of nature expressed in such courtly terms?

However, it was on this third panel, concerned with architectural treatment of buildings old and new throughout the whole Seaport neighborhood, that we came to sharp disagreements about the nature and, indeed, the very purpose of the restoration of the decaying neighborhood. These differences came to a head in Fitch's call for a new and assertively modern form for the structure that would replace the undistinguished one-story brick garage that took up the market block in the center of our area.

We—staff, trustees, volunteers, and members—had looked forward to reinstating some version of the airy, arcaded and inviting market building of 1821, which we felt embodied our purposes in reviving the historic waterfront. I believe three of the five-member panel shared our views on this, but Jim Fitch swept their ideas aside as "retrograde." He felt we must rise to the opportunity to make a bold statement for our time. We, on the other hand, felt we were here to learn from a lively and challenging era, and our structures should reflect that purpose in ways that would resonate with the existing historic structures. We had come to a division of opinion based not just on different styles, but on apparently different purposes, and we felt these differences should be resolved based on the public sense of the place, rather than on opinion handed down by professionals, however distinguished.

The company then walked down to a fine dinner at India House, where James Biddle, president of the National Trust for Historic Preservation, saluted the Seaport in terms that did indeed meet our experience of the place and our purposes, calling it

> *truly inspired effort to weave back into the fabric of New York's life some of the warmth and accessibility that has been lost over the years.* He added: *The social value of this kind of restoration in a highly urbanized setting is enormous.*

Should the door be flung wide open to the self-expression of people working in the modern idiom in the central block of the Seaport? This idea jarred upon our sense of what the neighborhood should be. We had grown accustomed to mentally walking through a reconstruction of the arcaded market of 1821 in the fine model of the project we now had on exhibition, an effort supplemented by the many detailed pictures we had gathered of the original building and the trades it housed. Its shape and varied traffics were just what we wanted to encourage the accidental encounters and exchanges of news, goods and ideas which we felt to be central to what people should find in the revived Seaport. But here we ran up against a fixed doctrine that put little stock in popular taste and the human desire for connection with the past.

As for that intangible, taste, we reminded each other that Shakespeare addressed the noblest writings in our language to the groundlings. And Virginia Woolf, in writings that soared without condescension, took pride in addressing herself to "the common reader." That was very much the way we wanted to proceed.

Because this was an issue that would not go away, it deserves a little explanation at this point. We could understand the desire not to have a new building confused with the actual historic buildings that were our patrimony in South Street. We planned to avoid that confusion by building the new market in different materials and somewhat lighter style—but reflecting an awareness of the purpose and function of the old market, whose memory we wanted to keep alive .

The following year, a contest among Jim Fitch's Columbia University architectural students for the most imaginative design for our market block was won by a neutral, featureless base with a 120-foot concrete-and-aluminum representation of a triple-decker sandwich slopped down on top. Whatever that conveyed, it was not what people came to South Street for. It was a slapstick, noisy negation of our message from an elder world.

Later, I was to show Jim sketches I had made in the Italian hill town of Modena of a new building on one side of the main square, which faced a medieval market across the square. It picked up the vaulted arcade and window heights of the old market, but used a slightly flattened arch with white marble on the inner surface of the arches, giving the arcade a lighter look. To Jim this was "the worst solution of all, a pale imitation with modern touches." But looking at the sketch, as I did to write this page, I see a vigorous new building which salutes its grandfather across the square.

The quest for novelty for its own sake is an arid one after all. The art historian and novelist Iain Pears has expressed this aridity as "a desperate search for repetitive novelty"—a phrase that captures the banality of forced innovation. Not that Pears is one for making mere copies of things. Elsewhere he cites how fakes give themselves away for what they are as time passes—for such reconstructions tend to incorporate then-current ideas of which both the copyist and his critics are alike unaware, ideas that are unspoken assumptions of the culture one breathes every day as naturally as one breathes the dense atmosphere of the planet we live on.

For our purposes, we decided to think of building consciously for our times, but in a style that remembers and celebrates what went before—a style that may be said to celebrate evolution, rather than revolution.

If the mindless quest for novelty is one obstacle to organic creativity, another is surely the deliberate celebration of meaninglessness. A modernist critic of this era actually praised the new Boston City Hall for "expressing the violence and brutality of the mid-twentieth century." Ouch! Clearly we have here a seismic shift in the idea of what art should be. This revolutionary approach was celebrated by Bostonians who improved their cityscape by tearing down the oppressive structure within a generation of its construction.

From the animal drawings made in Lascaux 17,000 years ago, until very recent times, art had been dedicated to the wonder and beauty of the world, the adventure of life, and the search for meaning—all art, that is, except art designed to impress and intimidate, which tyrants and religious fanatics used for their own oppressive purposes. And now we have come to the art of meaninglessness. It would be hard to find a view of art more radically opposed to what we felt belonged in South Street.

Not sharing the fashionable artistic outlook of our era made it all the more important to develop our own, in open discourse with all people who shared our interest in the vital roots of history and their flowering in the present day. We felt we were in a discourse started before our time which we meant to carry on into the future.

Indeed, ten years before we opened our doors in 16 Fulton Street, one John E. Nicholson wrote a letter published in the *New York Herald Tribune* in which, granted that progress in a changing city cannot and should not be stopped, he asked: "Can't one small piece of old 'maritime New York' be saved from the wreckers?" He called for saving for posterity a block front of the "old brick buildings with their long sloping roofs and their atmosphere of fast clipper ships and the Cape Horn trade." This evocation of the values we saw in old brick perfectly captures our vision of the Seaport. We had published the letter in the *Reporter* for July 1968, a few months before the conference, to avoid the temptation to think the Seaport was our idea alone. And we felt the new market building should reflect that old brick Nicholson had admired and its challenge to think across generations.

And the people of our generation clearly, and very nearly unanimously, felt the same. When the Seaport's professional plan was published in 1975, one member spoke for many when he wrote: "The new market building need not literally reproduce the old building, but it should at least evoke the ambience." Right on!

The stream of letters we published in the *Reporter* kept us in continuing discourse with the people we were there to serve—ranging from a grandson of the Sutton of Sutton's Dispatch Line at 82 South Street, which sailed the famous clipper *Young America,* along with other ships in the Cape Horn trade, to Grace Pallachino, an 8th grader from Brooklyn who wrote of her visit: "The best part I liked were the boats, almost everyone in the class said the boats were the best. And below deck was most astonishing . . . I think it's a very good idea to invite many people around the world to be astonished about New York."

"*To be astonished about New York!*" For a young New Yorker to have that sense of wonder and of discovery about what she found in South Street made grand music in our ears. That kind of response soared above the glorification of meaninglessness so fashionable in our time, from André Gide's gratuitous act to Andy Warhol's soup can. The people who wrote us were ordinary citizens without doctrinaire pretensions. They were people who could be reached by our message and who reached out to us to make themselves part of that message—this most literally, since their words were published in the *Reporter* as the official journal of the Seaport, and we were very interested in just about everything they had to tell us.

On Friday, 8 November, the day after the conference ended, we received startling news. Atlas-McGrath, one of New York's largest developers, had secretly bought up most of the Schermerhorn Row block to demolish it and build a new office building on the site. At first we took this in stride, thinking that the preliminary urban renewal designation achieved in the spring would block any such development. We met with John McGrath at Jakob's office on Broadway that Friday afternoon, the first of what became a series of meetings. At this first meeting we just agreed to disagree, and went cheerfully enough on our ways for the coming weekend.

That weekend, as it happened, included a memorable gathering of our ship people. Mel Conant had invited Karl and Jean Kortum, Norma and me to come to dinner at his East Side apartment on Saturday night.

We spent that afternoon in South Street with Os and Gertrude Brett and Dick Rath, rehashing with some joy the findings of the Ship Panel, and adding refinements to the boldly assertive memo on ship policy we had written, much of it at Karl's direction. This session concluded with a celebratory round of Guinness stout and Schaefer beer at the Square Rigger Bar, a place for which Karl had quickly developed a strong liking; it was his kind of place. Karl was never one to hurry a good drink or a good conversation, so we were late in making our departure for Mel's. That worthy soul met the bunch of us crowded at his door with a simple welcome: "Good God!"

We had neglected to tell him that there would now be seven of us instead of the four he had expected. But Mel was delighted to see Rath. He had known Rath for some years before we'd met, and he admired Rath's free-spirited ways, which contrasted with Melvin's own ordered life at Standard Oil of New Jersey—as Melvin himself once told me. He also held the Bretts in high regard and stood in positive awe of Karl, as did we all. I believe the drama of the bunch of us invading his small apartment with our talk of present ships and distant voyages appealed to his suppressed longings for the wilder shores of Bohemia. He later told Jakob that my arrival with a whole gang, where two couples had been expected, was of a piece with the way we'd steadily built up the Seaport concept from a few building frontages to become the centerpiece of an entire urban renewal district.

If the Atlas-McGrath threat was mentioned at all on this occasion, it was soon swamped in sea stories, songs, extravagant statements of all sorts, and laughter. Melvin had a gift for drawing people out, and he had his own store of tales of his family's involvement in the storied waterfront.

But the developers' threat, like the proverbial cloud on the horizon no bigger than a man's hand, was real. It grew in menace, as it became clear that the developers were steadily proceeding with their plans. We would later remember the Conant dinner as a peaceful croquet game played out on clipped lawns, while storm clouds surged into view above the swaying treetops that sheltered the game.

CHAPTER 21

South Street Besieged, *November–December 1968*

A Walk with Goldstone—Untested Landmarks Law—
Joan and Kent Write an Ad—Reaching Beyond the Mayor—
Times *Editorial—A Crucial Vote—Lunch with Emil*

Harmon Goldstone, now head of the Landmarks Preservation Commission, came hurrying down to South Street to do a walk-through review of the buildings in the Schermerhorn Row block. The commission had all the needed information on the Row itself, extending along Fulton Street, and it was in the process of designation as a City landmark. The buildings behind Schermerhorn Row on the John Street frontage were, however, of less distinction and more recent vintage. But they had housed such outfits as A. A. Low Brothers, leaders in the clipper trade to China, and were vital to the Seaport plan, which called for saving the whole block. Harmon knew they had to be included in the landmark designation, but he needed a rationale for their preservation which could stand up under the coming storm, which he clearly foresaw. Harmon paused in front of the Low building, noting its cheapjack stucco facade with some distress. Would this stand up under hostile scrutiny as a landmark building? We knew that under the stucco was an 1850 frontage of brownstone which, weathering poorly, sometimes has to be covered over for its own protection. We hastened to assure him of this fact, and, reassured, he smiled—somehow still keeping a worried look and furrowed brow.

Harmon had reason to be apprehensive. The Landmark law had been adopted just three years earlier in response to citizen outrage at the demolition of Pennsylvania Station. Its majestic columned exterior and iron-girdered interior as a cathedral of filtered light had made it a revered New York icon. The new law to stop such depredations had not yet been tested in a disputed case—and our case dealt with no marble-and-glass building serving a major public purpose, but with a huddle of down-at-the-heels brick buildings leaning against each other for mutual support, claimed by our gang, a ragtag crew who had no ownership stake in the property! And we wanted to save them for purposes that Harmon himself, in my meeting with him two years earlier, had found to be incongruous with the land-use plans of the financial district. Harmon had since come to see the Seaport's proper place in Lower Manhattan. But would others?

Jakob and his real-estate agent, Ken Wilpon, who were maintaining touch with Atlas-McGrath to seek acceptance of our plan for the block, had reported no progress. Dick Buford, as head of the Mayor's Council for Lower Manhattan Development, had assured me that the mayor stood firm and said we'd have nothing to worry about in getting the landmark designation to stick. Against these conflicting readings, Harmon Goldstone's evident concern led me to see for myself the odds we were facing in a city where political contributions by real estate interests traditionally outweighed any other interest. Also, there is something primal, indeed primeval, about private property in English-speaking countries. Private property is a bulwark against government's dictatorial action in the evolution of our freedom—and we had no ownership stake in the property we wanted to save.

"Harmon," I said as I walked with him back up Fulton Street following his visit, "you know that we've got the people with us."

Cheerful, ever modest and self-deprecating in casual discourse, on this occasion he stopped on the sidewalk and looked me squarely in the eye.

"Peter, I know you've got the people. It's a perfectly marvelous achievement. I admire all you and your friends have done to get ordinary New Yorkers involved. But now you've got to find a way to show that support in terms the Board of Estimate will understand."

There is a great tendency for people to await the outcome of events rather than set to work to change the outcome. But I realized now that we had come to a point where something had to be done to change the situation we confronted. Norma and I agreed that to do this we should mount a campaign that would field our whole strength. We met with

Joe Cantalupo and together we mapped out a campaign to get citizens writing letters on our behalf. We would not present sheets of petitions; politicians did that. We would get real letters from real people, citizens from all walks of life, and gather them up to present them personally to the mayor. This was not to convince Mayor Lindsay; with his characteristic blitheness of spirit, he was fully confident we would carry the day. Rather, we would do it to reach *others*. We'd make copies of the individual letters for other members of the Board of Estimate. Warming to the battle, Norma proposed that we make a set of copies broken down by borough to deliver to each borough president, so they would be hearing from their own constituents.

And we would go to the press with our story of the impending battle, so no one would make the mistake of thinking the Seaport could be knifed in a dark alley with no one knowing.

To add clout and reach to the campaign, I went to Joan and Kent to round up a letterhead committee. Fresh from the triumph of the restoration conference, they went to work and soon produced stunning results, initially signing up Pat Moynihan, Jim Fitch, the poet Robert Lowell, and the arch rivals Kenneth Galbraith and James Schlesinger of President Kennedy's brain trust. As the list grew, Jesse Calhoun of the Marine Engineers Beneficial Association and Joe Farr of the Brotherhood of Marine Engineers made their probably first and last appearance alongside the likes of Michael Straight of the *New Republic* and Bennett Cerf of the *Saturday Review*. The names streamed in, from the firebrand politico Paul O'Dwyer (who remained a cherished Seaport member until he departed this life years later), to the staunchly conservative R. J. Schaefer of Schaefer Brewing, Bob Albion, leading historian of the port of New York, and our great friend and mentor Pete Seeger, troubadour of radical politics and a clean Hudson River.

Just gathering the names reminded me of how much was riding on this contest and how much we owed to so many people, whom we could not let down. I began to see the campaign as an affirmation of strength and purpose, rather than a forlorn hope.

We met with Roger Starr of the Citizens' Housing and Planning Council, and with his help secured appearances on ABC and NBC-TV, both on the same day, 20 November—a month before the Board of Estimate hearing scheduled for 19 December. The following week we began the necessary political calls. Ken Wilpon arranged a meeting for Jakob and me with City Comptroller Mario Proccacino at Borough Hall on 25 November, at which his deputy, John J. Cartey, assured us of the comptroller's great interest in all cultural projects that helped New York—a washout, in short. But we had registered our interest and our respect for the office, and in days to come, Proccacino would get copies of the letters from people from all over the city, which we were now forwarding from the growing stream of letters we were receiving.

I thought Proccacino would turn first to local Democratic Party chieftains to get their take on what he should do. Here, fortunately, I knew we could count on Democratic district leader Duke Viggiano and Congressman Leonard Farbstein. For, to my surprise, we had good relations with these powerful downtown politicians, despite my active participation in the Democratic reform campaigns to unseat them both four years earlier. And our strong membership in Lower Manhattan constituted an articulate voting bloc in their districts. I felt that the media, which had always supported our efforts, would help our cause with Proccacino. He was running against Lindsay in this year's mayoral election and had taken many hits in the press for his perceived domination by special interests—such as the real estate business.

As for the mayor himself, he'd shown his interest and backed our plans, and the Seaport was part of his vision of a revived city. His shining hour had come the previous spring when he had walked the streets of Harlem and calmed the angry crowds that turned out in black communities following the assassination of Martin Luther King, Jr. That appalling deed had led to deadly riots in other big cities across America, but not in New York. Lindsay's walk among the people was an act of vision obviously based on a very real commitment to civil rights and the restoration of civility itself in the streets. His star indeed shone brightly.

However, such acts did not commend Lindsay or his views to the stalwarts of the Board of Estimate, who, with their fiefdoms to protect, did not welcome his attempts to "reform" them and their ways of doing business, and positively resented the lofty manner with which he undertook change in the city. In fact, most of them were out to get Lindsay, as it would be demonstrated in the mayoral election of the following year, 1969.

One of those who had walked the streets of Harlem with him was the charismatic African-American borough president, Percy Sutton. I knew Percy, having served as a foot soldier in civil rights campaigns, including the effort of 1963 which had culminated in King's "I have a dream" speech—which I had been there to hear. None of this, however, gave Percy or his aides any interest in the Seaport project, and I felt no fancy footwork on our part would change this.

This presented a problem. The five borough presidents each commanded two votes on the Board of Estimate, which together accounted for ten votes as against the twelve votes represented by the citywide offices of mayor, comptroller and president of the City Council, each with four votes. Understandably, the borough presidents liked to vote as a bloc, so if there were a split among the three top dogs, the borough votes would carry the day. We really needed Percy's vote to hold the others, but I felt the worst course would be to presume on past acquaintance and try to jolly him along. So instead, Alan Frazer and I met with his Community Planning Board for our district, to pay our respects and register our interest. We were well received there, because the board included several Seaport members. Oh, the glories of a large, active and open membership! But from Percy himself we still heard nothing.

The next day I went alone to meet Abe Stark, borough president of Brooklyn. Borough Hall was in easy walking distance from Orange Street in Brooklyn Heights, where I had grown up as a child. For some atavistic reason this made me confident of my ground. And meeting Mr. Stark in his book-lined office I felt instantly at home. In his solemn but cheerful manner, he bade me welcome and said he had long admired our project across the East River in Manhattan. I said well, the East River itself was the locus of our project, and with many members in Brooklyn, where I myself had been born, we wanted to have his vote to uphold the Landmark designation of Schermerhorn Row.

"I know the issue, Mr. Stanford, and I certainly sympathize with your cause," he said. "But as you must know, we borough presidents tend to vote together, and Percy Sutton will call the shot on this one, since the Seaport is in Manhattan." He smiled as he uttered this home truth. So I explained about Percy, my long-standing but remote relationship with him, and my feeling that the Seaport was not his sort of thing.

Abe Stark heard me out on this. Then he said: "You obviously know what you're doing, look what you've done with your friends and allies. But let me ask you: What do you propose doing about Mr. Sutton?"

I felt Mr. Stark was speaking as a friend and an ally himself. We had a strategy which was clear in my mind, but which I'd never put into words. So I told him:

"We'll reach Percy by mounting a campaign that he'll find taking place all around him. Our campaign will create a new situation in which new values will emerge—values we hope he can't say no to. Then he'll make his own decision based on the new situation."

"And please, Mr. Stanford, just how do you propose to create this new situation?"

"I don't know. We've just got to do it."

Mr. Stark wished me good luck as I got up to go. Not being one to prolong a good meeting, I knew that he meant what he said and would do what he could for our cause, because of his own convictions about what we were doing. I never met Abe Stark again, to my great regret, but I often think of our brief but poignant talk, and my feeling of being in the presence of a man much greater than the office he held—a rarity in politics or any human endeavor.

Sometimes I wonder how he weighed in during the borough presidents' counsels, as they checked out with each other on how to vote on

the hundreds of items that came up in the unwieldy meetings of the old
Board of Estimate of those days. It may be that he didn't have to say a
word. He conveyed much by his attitude.

My plan was to speak to each member of the Board of Estimate. This
might just transform the situation we were confronted with by making
it clear that we, with our membership of 5,500 citizens—and by extension, possibly, the people of the city—saw this issue *sub specie aeternitatis*,
as a question to be viewed in the light of eternity, rather than another
bit of business to be compromised or bargained away to gain help on a
question closer to home.

I knew that in the Bronx, Borough President Herman Badillo, an
engaging person who had spoken to support the Rutgers Reform
Democratic Club as an alternative to boss rule in the Fish Market
district, would be inclined to vote our way on principle, if practical
politics permitted. I knew that Robert T. Connor, borough president
of Staten Island, had close connections with our large and active Staten
Island membership, and that this most maritime of the city boroughs
would go our way unless, again, some *force majeure* prevented this. So I
just wrote them, and asked their friends to speak to them, and we got the
"I will if I can" responses we wanted—none, of course, in writing, which
would have broken the borough president unity rule.

That left the Borough of Queens. It was a long subway ride out to
Borough Hall, a trip I made on 6 December, with the Board of Estimate
vote due on 19 December—less than two weeks away! I walked into
the large, plain-brick building, nothing to compare with Manhattan's
wonderful Municipal Building just north of the Seaport, or Brooklyn's
classic Borough Hall presiding over the Brooklyn Heights community.
I caught an elevator up to the office of Sidney Leviss, deputy borough
president. He was busy on the phone when I walked in, and gestured to
me to take a seat. When the phone call was over, he swiveled around in
his seat to say:

"It's very good of you to make the long trip out here, Mr.—uh—
Stanford, but you're on a futile mission. Our vote is going to go with

Percy Sutton, as you should have known. He is the borough president of Manhattan and your project is in Manhattan."

"No it isn't," I was surprised to hear myself saying. "It's here in Queens."

"What! Now wait a minute," Leviss said grabbing up the letter I'd written, "I have your letter here and it shows your office in Fulton Street, Manhattan, right?"

"Mr. Leviss, it's a citywide project, even national. We have twelve hundred and fifty members right here in Queens, and they want me to ask for your vote to uphold the landmark designation of Schermerhorn Row, which is vital to the South Street Seaport project."

This got through to Leviss, who actually cracked a smile. Of course 1,250 votes in a borough of over 2,000,000 was not a major force, but it was a lot more than nothing—and it did underline the point that this was a citywide project.

We went on to chat in a friendly vein about the project and its volunteers, and suddenly Leviss said:

"Say, I seem to remember getting a handout at the subway station about a sailboat race some group was running in New York Harbor a month or two ago. Crazy thing to do. That was you guys, right?"

I told him yes, that had to be our Schooner Race for the Mayor's Cup.

"You're tight with the mayor, I take it?"

I said we knew Mayor Lindsay and had his backing. But, I added, we needed more than that to stand up to pressure from the real estate community. We needed to bring a bright spotlight to bear on the project, so that everyone understood there was nowhere to hide on this one. In fact, we needed a unanimous vote so the real estate community would accept that board members had to go with this project because it was so visibly in the public interest.

I did not add that, through transferred air rights, the Seaport would not detract significantly from commercial square footage and would add to real estate values. I had learned from experience that people just didn't get those concepts, however vital they might be.

"And where do you stand with Percy?"

"He knows us, but he seems in no hurry to give us his vote. He looks for support to help the black community, particularly on projects in Harlem. We can't help him there. But I'm hoping he'll hear from some of his fellows, like Abe Stark, who knows the project well. And he's going to receive several hundred individual letters from Manhattan residents—as you will here in Queens."

Leviss said he'd be looking forward to those letters, and that he'd do the best he could for our project. I had the feeling as I left that mentioning Abe Stark's widely respected name had not been a bad idea. But all depended, still, on Percy Sutton.

Later that same day, Jakob and I had a meeting set up with John McGrath in the New York Yacht Club. Jakob and I met in the library before McGrath's arrival, so he could tell me how things stood with Atlas-McGrath. Jakob's report was brief:

"We're nowhere. They figure they'll win the hearing hands down, and they're proceeding with their plans accordingly. Don't forget, this guy was corporation counsel for the city. He knows what he's talking about. It's not a good situation."

McGrath breezed in the door like a stage politician—white-haired, rubicund, radiating good will to all men, and smelling of eau de cologne as though he'd just come out of a barber shop. With a "Let's see if we can't wrap up this problem here and now" air, he told us he had every right to replace the decrepit buildings of Schermerhorn Row with an important new office building which would generate jobs and wealth for New Yorkers. He and his partner, Sol Atlas, understood that the Seaport was an important contribution to New York and didn't want to stand in its way. In fact, he was prepared to buy one of the New York islands as a site for us to bring in our historic ships and build our museum!

Jakob thanked McGrath for what was a very generous offer, then looked at me. I thought it right to say our charter put us in South Street, and much of our purpose lay in restoring the historic Street of Ships. We expected the City to uphold the landmarks designation of Schermerhorn

Row. With that question settled, I said, we could use the air rights over his property to build the Atlas-McGrath building on a nearby block, of which there were several available. And the City would be helpful in acquiring that alternative site, using its power to condemn the land at a fair market value, as specified in the urban renewal designation. This was not so head-in-the-clouds as it might sound. We knew McGrath had paid a generous $3 million for Schermerhorn Row; they'd had to pay the high rate of $100 per square foot in order to get all the owners to act together in selling, with no holdouts. Our solution gave them an assured sale without paying any above-market premium.

My words made no impression on McGrath. He rose from his chair with this succinct response: "All that fancy stuff is in case we lose. But let me tell you one thing: I am not accustomed to losing." He then shook a finger at Jakob for emphasis and left the room. And that was the meeting.

The following week I approved the full-page ad Kent and Joan had worked up to run in the *New York Times*. It carried Kent's challenging headline:

If there's no place in New York for South Street Seaport,
maybe there's no place here for people.

The ad used my copy for its text, sharpened by Joan and Kent, which urged people to write Mayor Lindsay, thanking him for his interest and asking his action to save Schermerhorn Row on 19 December. I was glad that my friendly editors had kept my line quoting McGrath about not being accustomed to losing. And I was grateful to him for having expressed his arrogance in better words than any I could have written about him. Kent's agency, BBD & O, gave the ad a strong layout, with the text flanked by two boldfaced columns listing the names of a hundred-member Ad Hoc Committee to Save South Street. The list began with Charles Abrams, Professor of Urban Planning at Columbia, thanks to Joan, and ended with Morton Zerdin, president of the Fishery Council, Inc., thanks to Joe Cantalupo. This appeared the next day, 13 December, six days before the hearing. It brought us a raft of new members, and I imagine it was seen by every member of the Board of Estimate.

On Tuesday the following week, 17 December, I accompanied Joan and Joe, co-chairmen of the Ad Hoc Committee, to City Hall. There, they handed the mayor a cardboard box containing one thousand individual signed letters of support. John Lindsay shook the box, which made a ticking sound as letters hit the box sides.

"Say, Mr. Cantalupo, this isn't a bomb, is it?"

"No, Mayor, it's not a bomb. But it packs a wallop. It's letters from a bunch of people who really love this city and really appreciate your support for our museum in South Street."

From there I accompanied Jim McNamara—not our new volunteer from Fort Schuyler, but our old friend from the Rutgers Club and the International Ladies' Garment Workers Union—to Percy Sutton's office in the Municipal Building. Jim and I were shown right in to meet the borough president. Percy addressed himself to Jim, his comrade-in-arms in many a fight for decent wages in the city's garment industry.

"Jim, we'll do what's right, you know that, and we'll do our best for what you want here, with our friend Peter," he said in his quick-spoken way, "but there's a lot of pressure on this one, you know, a lot of heat."

"That's when we always count on you, Mr. President," replied Jim McNamara with a winning smile. Percy had lines out everywhere; he must have picked up vibrations on this issue. But I felt that Jim convinced him that this issue was one that counted.

Frank D. O'Connor, president of the City Council, one of the triumvirate who each cast four votes on the Board of Estimate, was a more difficult problem. We knew nothing of him except that he was to retire at year-end and become a judge—the typical road to a well-paid berth in Tammany politics. I didn't find this knowledge at all reassuring. I finally called Roger Starr to once again ask his help.

"Sure, I know Frank," said Roger. "He's been laid up at home with a really bad cold. That's why you haven't been able to reach him."

I explained the situation to Roger, and asked if he knew O'Connor well enough to go see him, in bed or not. I added that since even his aides wouldn't see us, and since he was retiring to a secure lifetime appointment where no one could touch him, I was worried about whether he'd been gotten to by the real estate lobby.

Roger asked me, with just a touch of frost in his voice, what message I wanted to deliver to his old friend.

"Roger, if you can get to him today, please just tell him the we've lined up everyone but him, and at this point we need his vote. If he abstains it will be counted by all as a 'Nay' vote. His abstention, in his powerful position, will mean Procaccino may well renege on his commitment, and under that cover the borough presidents will run away. Everyone needs money, and in New York the money comes from the real estate interests."

"You're right about that," said Roger in a more friendly tone, and added that he'd do his best. He did, and later called me to say he'd delivered my message in person to Frank O'Connor.

On the morning of the 19th, I was stunned to see an editorial in the *Times* headed "Schermerhorn Row: Landmark." Reviewing what was at stake, the editorial noted:

> *Mr. McGrath, a former corporation counsel for the City of New York has excellent political connections. He says that he is not used to losing. A great many New Yorkers want to see him lose this one.*

The Old Grey Lady then startled us, as it presumably did others, by ending with the whip-crack adjuration that to fail to stop McGrath would be "an unconscionable act of cynicism by responsible public officials."

Braced by this militant support, our band of two dozen witnesses trooped into the hearing room at City Hall in good heart. They were led, as usual, by our Member No. 1, Jim Kirk, who had shown a marvelously cool conviction in previous public testimony. He was followed up by the jovial community leader Rafael Maldonado and the witty intellectual school teacher Alice Hall, both residents of public housing like Jim, and by an assorted crew of maritime, labor and business leaders, and by John Goodman, executive director of the Downtown-Lower Manhattan Association, which everyone knew spoke for David Rockefeller and the leading banking interests of New York.

First we had to hear a few items which were handled summarily with a roll-call of the board, beginning with the mayor of New York (represented by an aide) and ending with the president of the Borough of Richmond (the legal name of Staten Island). Earlier, we had been advised that our case involved too many special interests to be handled in this fashion, so it would be laid over for further consideration. Our task this day was to make a convincing show of citywide support for the unprecedented step we were asking the City to take.

Jim testified with his usual aplomb, and as he was speaking, a page hurried up to ask me to limit the number of speakers, as John McGrath planned to testify alone for the other side. I explained that our people had taken time off from their jobs to appear and would be very disappointed if they were not allowed to speak; I would pass the word to speak briefly. The page came back after whispered instructions from the bench, and at his urging I cut our list of speakers to eight.

McGrath then went to the microphone and spoke briefly. He emphasized that he owned the property and was free to develop it as he chose, that his building would bring commercial activity and jobs to the region whereas our plan wouldn't, and, finally, that since the Seaport had no ownership stake in the property, judicial review would show that we had no standing under the law. The hearings were then declared closed, and people in the audience began talking to each other.

Then, as an undertone to the noise of people talking, I began to hear familiar names being called out: "Queens . . . Manhattan . . . the Borough of Richmond." All at once I understood that the board was taking an on-the-spot roll call vote. A decision had been reached, in effect dismissing the arguments on one side as without merit! A hush came over the room. The clerk then declared in a ringing voice:

Plaintiff's suit is denied by a vote of 12 to naught. The land-
mark designation of Block 74 East is unanimously upheld.

The crowded room broke out in cheering and people started embracing each other across the backs of benches, blowing kisses at each other, waving handkerchiefs or, in many cases, using them to mop their eyes.

Others in the crowd that regularly attended these hearings were asking, "What's this all about?" And our gang was everywhere explaining what South Street Seaport was and why it mattered so much. A man in a dark suit turned to me and said: "I've never seen anything like this. And I've been attending these things for years." He spoke in such a mournful, lost-soul manner that I clapped him on the shoulder and said: "You heard our people speak. They're real people, and they've won an incredible victory for the South Street Seaport—they've just heard our main buildings will be saved from demolition. It's a great day for New York. Come down and look at our exhibit, 16 Fulton Street, you'll see what we're doing there."

He smiled and said: "I just might do that."

About a dozen of us gathered ourselves up and started down Fulton Street, headed for lunch at Sloppy Louie's. I stuck my head in the door at 16 Fulton to tell Norma the good news—she had been holding the fort in our absence. She took the news calmly, but a glow of contentment spread over her face, and no, she wouldn't join us for lunch; someone had to man the office and take the inevitable phone calls and she was happy right where she was.

"People have been calling about the *Times* editorial," she added, smiling. "Now I have something to tell them."

Emil Morino was waiting for us at the corner of Fulton and South Streets. "We won," I called ahead, and he picked up his apron and flapped it up and down like a bird's wing, executing a few steps from the tarantella all the while. It was late for lunch, no one was in the little restaurant facing on South Street, where our ships *Caviare* and *Ambrose* were visible through the front windows. Emil seated us at two of the dark wooden tables, and brought out steaming bowls of bouillabaisse for us all. This was followed by fried calamari and washed down with bottles of Famiglia Cribari wine.

"There is no charge," he said. "Don't expect us to charge for a family occasion like this." I was about to protest, but Joe Cantalupo waved a heavy forefinger to silence me, and his friend Joe Mitchell, usually reserved in expression, flashed a great grin. Mitchell, the author of incomparable harbor stories, had been one of the many supporters ready to testify at the hearing. It was a luncheon to remember.

The following night, a Friday, the volunteers staged their own impromptu celebration aboard the *Ambrose,* and the lightship's great bell rang out in rejoicing, as church bells in England rang out when the Desert Rats of the British 8th Army managed to throw Rommel's all-conquering Afrika Korps out of Africa. In their own way, on an infinitely smaller scale, our own Wharf Rats, as they sometimes called themselves, had won a similar victory against a highly professional organization whose leader was "not accustomed to losing."

CHAPTER 22

The Dreamers Get Moving, *Winter 1968–69*

Wavertree Breakthrough—Resistance on Schermerhorn Row—
Wavertree Book Completed—Return to Buenos Aires—
"Hard Work Is What It Is About"

The day after the Landmarks Preservation Commission hearing, the trustees met in the splendidly restored after cabin of the *Ambrose.* People greeted each other cheerfully, happy to meet aboard a ship of our own, with the graceful *Caviare* lying just ahead of the rubicund lightship at the pier. It was good to hear reports on the planning conference, featuring the president of the National Trust and the solid turnout of maritime museum leaders. This was followed by encouraging reports on public programs and continuing growth of the membership, now over 5,000 strong. Finances were in healthy shape, thanks to the steady support of the J. M. Kaplan Fund and the State Council on the Arts, backed up by the considerable sums now rolling in from our members in response to our year-end appeal. Joan Davidson and the dockbuilder George W. Rogers were both elected to the board, adding civic leadership and waterfront savvy to our governing body.

The outcome of the landmark vote was welcomed by the trustees, but this victory got nothing like the tumultuous reception that the unanimous roll call vote had received at the Board of Estimate the day before. Among the trustees the general feeling seemed to be: with the mayor behind us, who could be against us?

The *New York Times* editorial had stressed the gravity of the situation in racing the city's powerful real-estate lobby. After our trustees meeting, a second *Times* editorial appeared, which clearly recognized the importance of the victory in these terms: "The prompt action by the Board of Estimate raises hope that things are changing in New York."

That's what we were out to do! This second editorial went on to say:

> *Conventional cynicism, this city's traditional substitute for conventional wisdom, has long had it that the power of real estate and the pragmatism of politicians was the natural alliance that shaped this community. … Those who argued that the city existed in other terms—livability, history, function, the quality of environment and even beauty—and that the future could be foreclosed by ignoring these factors, were called bleeding hearts and dreamers.*

And it concluded simply:

> *The dreamers have turned out to be realists.*

Reality confronted us harshly, however. We still needed to buy the land to develop Schermerhorn Row as the museum's centerpiece. Only Jakob had the resources to do this, as everyone on the board understood. And Jakob decided that he and I should call on John McGrath to see what we could work out with him.

McGrath received us cordially in his office. The meeting was a brief one. All he had to tell us was that Mr. Atlas was the one who called the shots, and Mr. Atlas was determined to pursue his suit against the City and go ahead with his new building on a superblock, including the site of Schermerhorn Row. At that point, I believe Jakob decided it was best to let events take their course while he and his agent, Ken Wilpon, continued buying odd properties in the district as they came on the market. These odd lots were held in a corporation called Seaport Holdings. In time, perhaps, Atlas-McGrath, who had other dealings with the City at stake, would come to terms. Meanwhile, the Seaport's position would be strengthened by the Seaport Holdings properties, which were held for ultimate delivery to the Seaport Museum.

The campaign that won Landmark status for Schermerhorn Row had echoing consequences. It brought us new members and supporters, in a contest which established that the long-term benefits of historic preservation could win out over the immediate short-term interests of the real estate industry. The second *Times* editorial eloquently stated this case in a citywide context, which delighted all of us, for we felt South Street was a citywide resource. But much now depended on whether the Landmark designation could be made to stick. Atlas-McGrath had made clear their determination to press home the case for their new office building to be erected on the Schermerhorn Row Block and the block next inland, which would become another of the super-blocks that were changing the city's historic street plan.

If a developer decided to appeal a Landmarks designation, the Landmarks law provided a breathing space in which the champions of the historic structures had to prove their value against the developer's claims of economic benefit to the city in commerce, jobs and tax revenues for the public good. We were a long way short of being able to demonstrate the Seaport case against a well-organized attack on these lines. And we knew that just the launch of Atlas's threatened appeal would discourage new investment in our own plans to develop maritime shops and other activities vital to the Seaport development—fronts on which we had to make continued progress to demonstrate the reality of the museum's plans. And in our great *Wavertree* enterprise, it was already difficult enough to raise money for a distant hulk thousands of miles away. If any doubts were raised about there being a museum ashore to receive the big ship, an interested supporter might well hold back until that issue was settled.

So we really needed to head Atlas off at the pass before he launched his appeal against the Landmark decision. Jakob and his agent Ken Wilpon, the Staten Island realtor he'd put in charge of Seaport Holdings, proposed various schemes to get a building of the volume Atlas needed by demolishing the historic buildings on the Burling Slip side of the Schermerhorn Row block while preserving the monumental buildings of the Row itself on Fulton Street. This was a retreat from the Seaport ideal of preserving whole city blocks of the Seaport, but such a retreat might be needed to save what we could. Atlas's agents however rejected these compromise schemes.

A solution came, but it was from a totally unexpected source: the inspired generosity of a New Yorker who owned properties in the area—
including a modern ten-story office building which occupied the whole
John Street side of the inland block which Atlas planned to combine
with the Schermerhorn Row block to form the super-block for his office building. So in the thick of the Landmarks battle over Schermerhorn Row, a man we'd never met called to say that he'd read about our
effort to save the Seaport for New York—and if it would help in that
endeavor, he would be glad to sell us the John Street building for $1
million!

That figure was an incredibly low price for the building, valuable in
itself and worth much more in light of the Atlas plan. The ramshackle
buildings of the two Goelet blocks Jakob was negotiating to buy for
Seaport Holdings were priced at $5 milllion each, and these were largely
occupied by Fish Market tenants paying minimal rents. The John Street
building, on the other hand, was at the foot of John Street, where most
of New York's insurance companies made their headquarters. And Atlas
vitally needed the John Street frontage for his building—who knows
what he would have paid, if the man on the phone had been willing to
sell to him. Looking for reasons for this amazingly low price, I thought
that perhaps the owner wanted to see his building preserved as part
of the Seaport. So I felt obliged to tell him that we badly needed the
building to block the Atlas building, but it would not be saved as part
of the Seaport.

A man of few words, the caller said that all he needed to know from
me, as president of the Seaport Museum, was that this sale would benefit the Seaport. Stammering my thanks, I said that his building could
actually save the Seaport, and asked him to call Jakob Isbrandtsen as our
chairman and Ken Wilpon, director of Seaport Holdings, who would
handle the purchase. And a month later, with formalities completed on
22 January in the new year, 1969, Seaport Holdings became the building's owner. With this stopper to the Atlas building firmly in place,
the whole transaction slipped to the back of my mind. In my eagerness

to get our caller on the phone in touch with Seaport Holdings, I had neglected to note his name or phone number. Norma's and my trip to Buenos Aires to see to the *Wavertree*'s transfer of title and the need to raise the funds for the ship's tow from South America, was very much to the fore in our minds.

I did not, however, forget the man's remarkable statement that the sale at the quoted price depended on my word that the property would benefit the Seaport. But it was decades later, in the course of the many talks, debates and discoveries that accompanied the development of this account of the Seaport venture, that I realized I had to acknowledge, somehow, the great debt we and the museum owed this man of few words and great deeds. His name had passed out of Jakob's and Wilpon's memory too, I found, and it took two museum volunteers, Lee Gruzen and Michael Kramer, to ferret out the man's identity in the labyrinthian maze of City records. This proved well worth the search.

Herman Miller was our benefactor's name, a lifelong New Yorker who died in 2002 after 94 years of a life full of achievement, historical and artistic interests, and an active family life with his two children and five grandchildren. Himself the son of Lithuanian immigrants, he took an interest in immigrant, minority and other disadvantaged groups and eventually established a foundation devoted to improving their lives in a challenging city environment. His own career began with work in his father's Second Avenue paint store after finishing high school in 1925. He went on to earn a business degree from New York University while continuing in the paint business, becoming president of the New York Paint Dealers Association in the1930s. Starting in the 1940s, he and his brother took over the real estate business started by their parents in the 1920s Yorkville area, going on to manage and sell properties in the city at large.

From the beginning he maintained a strong interest in city affairs and history. In a memoir, his fellow collectors of old coins in the American Numismatic Society speak of his consuming interest in collecting objects that bring history to life, and one gets a picture of the man as a memorable story-teller of his adventures in this and other fields. He collected Greek and Roman coins and medieval illuminated manuscripts and became a devoted student of the art and culture of Etruria, the ancient country north of Rome that preceded modern Tuscany.

The treasure to be found in the quest to recover Herman Miller's identity lives on today in the Herman and Frieda L. Miller Foundation, which he co-founded with his son Myron in memory of his wife of many years, after her death in 1996. This foundation, set up in Boston where Myron runs an architectural and city planning firm, bears the hallmark of precision and creativity which characterize Herman's life and work. Rather than just throw money at the problems of deprivation and alienation, the foundation works to engage people to develop the resources to overcome problems—just the path we'd chosen in the Rutgers Club and sought to develop in the Seaport experience! The goal is "to encourage the empowerment of communities and engagement of residents." Thus it works to "support vibrant urban community life," by acting to "cultivate new and emergent leaders from the community." One has to cheer at that word "emergent," with its recognition that the task is to tap the great resource in people able, if given the chance, to act for the common good!

So I imagine Herman, rather than make a parade of his interest in the Seaport project, simply gave us a great break in the price of a property he could have sold for much more—relying on us to carry on with the job.

While we were engaged in the all-out effort to save Schermerhorn Row, centerpiece of the Seaport project, things had begun to move in our prolonged effort to secure the big square rigger we dreamed of bringing in. It sometimes happens, in long-drawn-out efforts which seem to hang endlessly in the balance, that a breakthrough develops from a completely unexpected source. Once again, that was the case in our negotiations to acquire the Cape Horn sailing ship *Wavertree* and bring her from her distant berth in Argentina to our South Street waterfront. The unlikely source for the breakthrough was one Manuel Schkulnik, ship chandler in Buenos Aires who worked as a volunteer with Juan DeValle on *Wavertree* affairs. I was surprised to get a call from him on Friday evening, 18 October 1968, asking me to come meet him that very evening in his room at the Bedford Hotel, where he was staying on one of his business trips to New York. His message was simple: "Get up here if you want to save the *Wavertree*."

I went, and Manuel told me in his hotel room how we were doing everything wrong in dealing with the owner, Señor Numeriani. He said we were trying to out-Latino the Latinos in our polite and distant way of asking Numeriani to name a price for the vessel—that's why he stuck by his original offer to exchange the battered hulk for a modern motor ship of the same tonnage.

"Look, Peter, the hulk is worth about $7,000 on the scrap market. Let me deal with Numeriani. Tell him I'm now your agent—I won't charge you anything, of course—and I'll get you the ship for $35,000, five times scrap value, maybe a little more. What I'm going to do is show some North American impatience with his wily ways, and get him worried that this fish is going to get away."

Jakob had said he was willing to go as high as $70,000 if he had to, so I told Manuel to go ahead. "Don't let our friend Mr. Crocker, or Juan DeValle speak to Numeriani," said Manuel. "They get his hopes up too much."

Manuel's business was mainly American, provisioning Moore-McCormack liners and Woods Hole Oceanographic vessels in South American waters—a blue-chip business in which the quality of the goods mattered more than the price, but, as he explained to me, he secured quality provisions at the lowest price simply by cutting out the bribes, kickbacks and miscellaneous middlemen that flourish in this line of work, particularly where rich American clients are concerned. The Woods Hole people, who had worldwide experience with ship chandlers, confirmed to me that this was so, as did our friends at Mooremack.

In November, when the Landmarks campaign was heating up, Manuel called to say the price was $37,000. I said we'd take it—and that, astonishingly, was that! Jakob pulled out $70,000 from the line of credit he'd established with the banks, to provide funds for purchase and repairs. After we wired a down payment to Argentina, the ship was acquired by the Seaport on 20 November, subject to survey in dry dock.

This action, setting things in motion in Buenos Aires, was taken on the very afternoon that Jakob and I had first met with John McGrath to fend off his plan to demolish Schermerhorn Row to build his new office building. As our campaign to avert this catastrophe proceeded, things began to move on Buenos Aires. On 30 November, *Wavertree* left her Stygian anchorage under tow, wending her way down the winding Riachuelo, out into the broad waters of the River Plate and on to the navy yard in downtown Buenos Aires to undergo the rigorous out-of-water survey we'd specified as a condition of accepting her.

There was cheering in the office when we received photographs from DeValle of the ship's anchor, caked with Riachuelo mud, at the ship's bow. It was clearly a sailing-ship anchor—part of the *Wavertree*'s original gear! And we were moved by the photo DeValle had taken from the bridge across La Boca, at the river's mouth, which showed our ocean wanderer under tow, leaving the Riachuelo behind her forever. Norma and I were confident, from what we'd seen, that she would pass her survey, though there might be bad spots of local wear calling for an iron plate to be patched or replaced. And so it proved. A survey ordered by Lloyd's found the hull remarkably intact, with over 90 percent of the thick Lomar iron she had been plated with still there. A few plates forward, dented by careless handling of her heavy anchors during her career as a barge, would need replacing, some plate edging would have to be renewed amidships at the waterline, and a scattering of loosened rivets would have to be reseated, to get the vessel certified for the long tow to New York.

It was agreed I'd go south early in the new year to sign the bill of sale and approve the plan of work to bring the vessel up to snuff. Never in the wildest dreams of childhood had I imagined signing a piece of paper to acquire a full-rigged Cape Horn sailing ship—much less being called on to approve the work to be done to get her to sea again. But these things were now agreed on in sober fact.

On the last day of the year 1968, Tom Van Arkel and I met with Jakob, much as the afterguard does in an ocean race, reviewing progress made good and the course ahead while the boat you're sailing continues to bucket her way to windward. We met at the Isbrandtsen office at 26 Broadway, a place filled with models of Isbrandtsen ships from the days of sail onward, with walls enlivened by Charlie Lundgren's paintings of these vessels at sea or entering their ports of call around the world. This was a grand spot from which to look out on the sweep of New York Harbor's Upper Bay and to appreciate these much-trafficked waters as the city's doorstep to the ocean world. It never failed to give me a lift of spirit to walk into these lofty rooms.

Jakob, despite the hard times his business was going through—in common with all American-flag shipping—rose to greet us cordially, inviting us to join him seated around a glass-topped table. It had been agreed that we should start with the land acquisition problem, and Tom led off by reviewing the situation. The City had made it clear that we really needed to secure control of the two Goelet blocks facing Schermerhorn Row, where Atlas-McGrath showed no signs of loosening their grip. Jakob nodded. He understood the situation. He told us he was seeing what could be done to set up a fund to buy the two blocks.

I then reported on the state of the museum and what we were doing to capitalize on our purchase of the *Wavertree*. We had nearly completed editorial work on a book about the ship, built around the narrative of the Australian captain, A. G. Spiers, who had sailed in her in a Cape Horn voyage, 1907–8. His journal on the voyage had been secured for us by Karl Kortum's great friend up the coast in Coos Bay, Oregon, Captain Fred Klebingat. The book, named *The Wavertree: An Ocean Wanderer*—borrowing Captain Thomas Thomas's haunting phrase—included a full account of her comings and goings from her launch on 11 December 1885 through to our recent purchase of her—an account based on Lloyd's records and the *New York Shipping Register*, fleshed out by newspaper accounts. The written record was enriched by a remarkable series of photographs of this ship and some of her sisters, procured by Karl through his network of friends. Os Brett had painted a classic picture of the ship embattled off Cape Horn, which served as a noble frontispiece. He had also made a lively set of drawings of incidents recounted in the narrative. Last, but not least, Alan Villiers had written a spirited preface for the work and, to cap this, was planning to come to New York in April and would join us for a week's campaigning for funds to restore the ship herself to her sailing glory.

Jakob reviewed my forthcoming visit to Buenos Aires with me, stressing the need to read the actual contract carefully, not relying on the copy sent us in New York, and taking the same care over the plan of work.

I was then able to report to Jakob and Tom that museum membership had reached 6,000 as of year end. The $1 membership accounted for much of the this stunning growth from the 3,000 we'd started the year with—but regular $5 members had grown even faster than the cheap memberships, belying the conventional wisdom offered us on all hands that the cheap memberships would eat up the more expensive ones. Tom and Jakob heard my report on this with smiles on their faces like two Cheshire cats. Both had early caught on that the people orientation of the place had been a telling factor in its survival and progress, and needed no urging from me to support the continued high priority I felt we should give this front.

Glancing at my watch, I took a moment to mention the growing maturity and steadiness of the volunteer corps, now well over one hundred strong. Chi Ling, our young *Ambrose* volunteer, had actually moved into Al Swanson's quarters aboard the lightship and was running ships and piers operations from there, so that Al could spend the Christmas holidays at home with his family in Danvers, Massachusetts.

On this note of good cheer we parted, Jakob for New Year's in Riverside, Connecticut, Tom to join his young family in a ski lodge in Vermont, and I to finish up office work to clear the decks for Norma's and my forthcoming trip to Buenos Aires. We were to leave in just two days' time.

I very much wanted Norma to make the Buenos Aires trip with me. The ship we were going to visit had been so much a goal in our lives together, it seemed to me she had to be there when we took charge of the ship and brought her into the South Street family. Norma, however, had another familial concern. She was expecting our first child in three months' time, and she was concerned about the twelve-hour flight to Buenos Aires and the busy schedule we would have there. But in the end she decided to come along, with the proviso that, after Buenos Aires, we add a few days in Jamaica for a much-needed rest. To me, after the strenuous days we'd been through, it was good to be getting away and, as I noted at the time, "to put one's mind on just one object, that great hull."

Having driven through the icy winter streets to JFK Airport on Thursday evening, 2 January, it was a shock the next morning to come out of the plane and walk free under the smiling sky of a Buenos Aires summer. Managing to weather the shock, we couldn't help rejoicing in the flowering trees which filled the air with the scent of their blossoms as our bus drove into the city. It was a treat to be back in Buenos Aires, surely one of the handsomest and cleanest cities in the Western Hemisphere, where trucks and buses were painted in elaborate and colorful designs and polished to gleaming brilliance. After leaving our gear at our hotel, we made the short walk to the navy yard, where the upright and dignified Captain DeValle was on hand to usher us through its imposing gates.

Once past the splendid Edwardian buildings of the yard, we saw before us the mole-colored shape of our *gran velero*, proud and bare in her dry dock, her curved iron sides gleaming dully from the vigorous washdown she'd had to facilitate inspection and necessary repairs.

———◆———

Putting on hard hats, we descended to the puddled dock floor, where "our great iron baby," as we irreverently called the vessel (but not in front of DeValle), looked huge, indeed formidable. Norma made a sketch of DeValle pointing out wasted plate edges that would need patching, as mandated by the American Bureau of Shipping. He hastened to tell me that the ABS surveyors reported that they'd seen worse decay in World War II Liberty ships just 25 years old as against the *Wavertree's* 83 years. He said senior surveyors were coming down on their lunch hours to test individual rivets with chipping hammers—any excuse to be involved with such a noble work from the long and honorable trade of shipbuilding.

The following day, a Saturday, the yard was closed and Manuel Schkulnik drove us to La Boca, the old port of Buenos Aires, a lively, bright-hued waterfront neighborhood of winding streets and jumbled buildings on the west bank of the Riachuela where it flows into the River Plate. Manuel took us through twisting, narrow lanes astir with Saturday morning's traffic of children released from school and parents from the week's routine, to arrive at a modern-looking elementary school. We entered to walk through corridors and peer into classrooms whose walls were splashed with large powerful paintings of river scenes crowded with sailing lighters, ancient steamers, tugs, barges and the occasional deepwater sailing ship.

We were joined by Manuel's friend Anibal Carrega, a ship chandler like Manuel, who explained to Norma and me that these paintings were the work of an artist who was a local hero, one Quinquela Martín. Carrega's family, he told us, had been in La Boca since 1835 in the early days of the Argentine Republic. A close friend for many years of the now 78-year-old Quinquela, he took pride in telling us the artist's story.

Quinquela had been abandoned on the doorstep of a Catholic orphanage in La Boca as an infant, wearing a tag showing his name, Benito Juan Martín. Adopted at age six by an Italian coal merchant named Chinchella, he went to work carrying gunnysacks of coal up from the barges and lighters to the merchant's coal yard. He took his adoptive father's name, changing the spelling to retain the Italian pronunciation of the hard "ch" using the Spanish "qu."

With the support of his new family he attended art classes at night, and by 1910 his work was being shown in Buenos Aires galleries. Befriended by a wealthy art patron who later became president of Argentina, he was sent in the early 1920s to spend a year as cultural attaché in the Argentine consulate in Madrid. There, his work attracted the attention of King Alfonso XIII and his court. He traveled on to Italy where the Fascist Duce, Benito Mussolini, bought several paintings from an exhibition of his work in Rome. Subsequent trips to Paris, New York and London gave his work an international reputation and made him a wealthy man. The world was his oyster and he could live as and where he wished.

"But he chose to remain in La Boca," said Carrega. "The people and the ways of the waterfront district he had grown up in, in the hardest conditions, seized not only his artist's imagination, but his deepest affections as well. He paints nothing but scenes of La Boca, and he uses his wealth to improve lives of its people. He bought the land the school is built on and challenged the city to build the school. It took years, but he got his way, and the school is run his way, celebrating the people's own history in the district where they live. He also established a museum of the art and history of La Boca, and, just recently, a new theater for the performing arts.

"He had to fight for everything he did, not for his own benefit, but to do what he believed right to do for the people. And he lives right here, on top of the school, in a penthouse apartment that includes his studio. He wouldn't be anywhere else, I tell you, and I have known him for many years now. He's upstairs as we speak, and he told me he'd be glad to see you when you came by. Only we must not stay too long and tire him out."

Quinquela turned out to be a pale, slender man with a bright, somewhat ironic gaze, who received us with easy courtesy and led us into a large, sparely furnished room, which apparently served as studio and living room. He gestured for us to sit in chairs arrayed before the big picture window that made up one wall of the room, which gave a panoramic view of the river scene, beyond the haphazard rooftops of waterfront shops and warehouses. Quinquela's aristocratic look and bearing surprised Norma and me, who had been expecting something pretty rough-hewn after hearing Carrega's story of his rugged early years.

He may have sensed this—I caught a twinkle in his eye as he said he understood that we were here to take away the last of the old square riggers that had once graced the port. We told him of our long hunt for a surviving deepwaterman of the Cape Horn trade to install on the waterfront that had been New York's Street of Ships. He commented with pleasure on our efforts to save the old waterfront buildings in a forest of skyscrapers. It had been a long time since he'd been there, he told us, but even forty years ago the towering office buildings had impressed him—there was nothing like that in Europe or, of course, in Argentina. But then, Americans did like to do things in a big way, everything new.

"Here we throw nothing away," he added, pointing out a white river excursion steamer, which, he told us, was called the *Londres*. A year and a half earlier she'd sunk where she now lay with the water washing in and out of the windows on her lower promenade deck, and no one thought to move her. The people felt sentimental about her, since many had been aboard the exotically named vessel ("London") on church picnics and other festive outings. The people of the port were wonderful, he said. "We call them *puerteños*, and I'm one of them myself, as perhaps Señor Carrega told you. I wouldn't live anywhere else, not anywhere in the world."

He reassured us that he was glad that we had come to take away the *Wavertree*, which he knew as a sand barge—while knowing, too, that the powerful hull had been built for something better than a receptacle to dry out the slurry of sand and water that was constantly being dredged from the sandbanks of the River Plate. He shook his head sadly when I asked him if he had known the great full-rigged ship *British Isles* which had ended her days here, or any of two or three others whose names I happened to remember from the list Karl had given us.

"No," he responded. "We thought they would be here forever," he went on, "first as ships, then as barges. But one day we woke up and they were gone, all except your ship up the river."

Rising, he added that he appreciated meeting the people who had got the *Wavertree* to come to life again, to raise her anchors from the river mud, unchain her from the slaughterhouse pier and come downriver bound for the open sea again and the long passage to New York.

"These ships were beautiful, even as barges," he said, outlining a boldly shaped hull with expressive hands. "And she is the last of the great sea birds that once flocked in these waters. Let me wish you all good luck with this noble ship."

Carrega insisted we stop by his house for a drink before we left, explaining that his house was a neighborhood gathering place, he would be shamed if we did not stop by on this visit. We could not let that happen, of course, so we accepted his invitation, pausing on the way to admire a raree-show going on in one of the streets we passed by. The performance was full of action and loud orations, of which we couldn't make out a word. The courteous Señor Carrega explained that the local dialect was incomprehensible to people who spoke standard Spanish—a language of which we knew just the rudiments.

Alfredo Numeriani was in formal business attire when we stopped by his office early the following week to sign the bill of sale and formally accept transfer of ownership of the barge *Don Ariano N.*, ex-*Wavertree*, ex-*Southgate,* to the South Street Seaport Museum in New York. He was seated in a swivel chair at an old-fashioned rolltop desk whose compartments, we could see, were filled with rolled-up papers. We were introduced to two young men, his sons, who were standing near him. Numeriani, a short, sturdily built man with flashing eyes, hastened to his feet when he saw that Norma was with us, snapping his fingers at one of his sons to get her a chair when he saw her condition. I don't think he was used to females in business meetings, and he addressed himself to Norma as we drew up our chairs. She acknowledged his greeting in Spanish, so he addressed her as "Señora," launching into a rapid-fire series of compliments, inquiries as to her health, and whatnot, of which we made out only the occasional word. Norma held up both hands and said her family had been Italian, so she could understand a little Spanish—but only a little.

Numeriani then explained to Manuel Schkulnik and me that he had the bill of sale—pointing out a two-inch stack of papers lying on the desk before him—and that, as a notary, he could handle all formalities on the spot. He ran through the first two pages, which stated that the Seaport hereby acquired the barge *Don Ariano N.*, No. 3973 with all her gear and equipment, which was listed in detail, for the sum of US$37,000. Having read this aloud to us in Spanish, he then turned to Norma and read it aloud to Norma in Italian, as an act of courtesy. Numeriani then signed the paper, I signed my acceptance for the museum and handed him the check which we had brought with us from New York.

Before we left I asked Numeriani what all the attached papers were for. He was puzzled by my question in pidgin Spanish, so Manuel explained to me in English that in Spanish law, the chain of ownership cannot be established simply by referring to documents on file, but has to include actual copies of each transaction relating to ownership. These attached papers proved a treasure trove of information, including the important point that the sale of the ship by her owners in Punta Arenas to Menendez Behetny in 1947 specified that she could not be used as a ship but was sold as "ferro viejo"—scrap iron! Menendez, a Chilean citizen, soon transferred ownership to an Argentine cousin, and Chilean law not being enforceable in Argentine courts meant that she could now be towed to her new destiny in Buenos Aires.

Here was another turning point in the long, intensely useful life of this stout iron hull, one of several where she had survived where her kinfolk had not. One thought, besides the many chances of seafaring under sail, of the fire that raged in her holds in Australia in 1892, which would have destroyed her had she not been in harbor where there were ready forces to save her, and of the great gale in Algoa Bay,

South Africa, ten years later. The ship rode out that crisis lying to the two great anchors she had aboard today, while boarding seas swept the ship, smashing in the after cabin doors of three-inch oak and flooding out the main saloon, while other ships in the harbor sank or were driven ashore. And there was the steamer that rammed her in Ellesmere Port, just before her last voyage, to say nothing of her dismasting off Cape Horn, ending in her staggering into the Falkland Islands with three feet of water in her hold.

Her half-life as a hulk fascinated us, it was a life that lacked the records always kept on a working ship in deepwater trade, but it was nevertheless a life, whether as a wool storage warehouse in Punta Arenas or a sand barge in the Riachuela, incidentally housing a smuggling business in her after cabin.

Numeriani was an extremely wealthy man, the owner of several blocks of downtown real estate. I think he had some feeling for the vessel in his keeping. Certainly he seemed happy that she would be preserved in a faraway museum and that his name would always appear as one of her owners.

Before we left Buenos Aires for the Jamaican half of our trip, DeValle arranged that the three of us would have lunch with Admiral Imposte in his dining room in the Navy Yard. This turned out to be a memorable occasion, marked with the ceremonial courtesy that was so pleasant a feature of Argentine life. We talked of families and children, of the great adventure of the Seaport in the heart of New York, and Imposte told us it had been decided that the *Libertad*, the Argentine Navy's great sail training ship, a full-rigged ship of lovely lines and a great reputation for speed under sail, would accept our invitation to visit our pier in the coming summer.

"You will be receiving our official response when you get back to New York," he said, "but I thought you might like to know this now, as a little surprise." Would we ever! We were delighted to have our own *Eagle* come into South Street, but to get the great Argentine ship would be something special, bringing a new and, to us, exotic culture into the heart of our project, in a ship whose lofty masts and yards would really tower over the slope-roofed buildings of Schermerhorn Row.

From the dining-room windows we could see the tall spars and tapered yards of the navy's retired training ship, *Presidente Sarmiento,* built 1897 in England—a dozen years younger than *Wavertree* but boasting many anachronisms from an earlier era, including the big single topsails which were universally replaced with double topsails before the *Wavertree*'s time, and gear to carry stuns'ls, the sails set on booms outside the regular squaresails to gain a bit more speed, which had vanished from the seas by the mid-1880s. DeValle had shown us over the ship, which had circled the globe six times in her long active career, and we'd been inspired by the high level of shipkeeping evident aboard. She was, we told Imposte, a great encouragement to us, showing what could be done to make a ship a fascinating exhibit for the veriest landsman.

Imposte told us that Captain DeValle had been the officer who persuaded the navy to make the *Libertad,* built just five years ago in Argentina, a full-rigged ship, square-rigged on all masts, whereas her older near-sisters, the Spanish *Juan Sebastián de Elcano* and the Chilean *Esmeralda,* were giant four-masted schooners, rigged with square topsails and topgallant on the foremast only.

"The ship rig makes a lot more work," observed the admiral, wagging a chiding finger at DeValle.

"Admiral, as we all know, hard work is what sail training is about," responded the retired Captain DeValle gamely, a sentiment with which Admiral Imposte had to agree, as did we all.

We were very glad to reach Jamaica, the isle of our dreams, where, we knew from Jamaican immigrants to New York, a beautiful version of English is spoken. In fact, we were glad to be anywhere at all. Here is what happened: We had to fly to Santiago, Chile, as we had the year before. From there a Chilean jet flew us to La Paz, Bolivia, where we did a crunchy, squealing landing as the pilot brought us down with a thud that shook the plane and its passengers like a James Bond martini—shaken, not stirred—and then braked hard to avoid running off the end of the landing strip and on down the Andean mountainside. "Must have been an updraft caught us wrong," I said knowledgeably. "That meant he had to drop like a stone to get us down, you know." Norma was not reassured.

"That pilot doesn't know how to fly this plane," she said flatly.

"You say that because you're worrying for two," I said. "You don't really need to do that, you know." Norma just compressed her lips, leaving it to my male imagination to guess what her response would have been had she said what she really thought.

Our next landing, at Bogota, Colombia, was even more violent. "This time I think he's broken the landing gear," said Norma. I agreed that the crunching sounds had a clattering crescendo this time, as we all went into the airport building to get a drink. There Norma informed me that she was not getting back on that plane. Before I could muster my usual "Oh, come on, now" response, I was forestalled by an announcement that, due to landing gear problems, the flight was canceled. Norma, catching sight of a Lufthansa counter, marched over to it and exchanged our tickets for the next flight to Jamaica.

From that point, everything went forward smoothly. In Jamaica, everyone we dealt with was cheerful and helpful. Riding down a mountain stream in majesty, seated side by side on a shared throne on a red velvet cushion mounted on a raft of bamboo stalks which slithered over the pebbled streambed, I remember a smiling black woman washing clothes by the wayside who paid me a flirtatious compliment, which Norma, much amused by it, has not allowed me to forget. I did no work, none, and made no notes, except to sketch a native craft pulled up in the shelter of flowering trees at Port Mourant, and to note the name of the Blue Mountain Inn, buried in the hill country, halfway across the island. There we'd had a marvelous drawn-out dinner outdoors in the murmurous night, in a pleasant glade dominated by a small waterfall making its own music running down the face of a black basalt escarpment—nothing very dramatic but just very, very peaceful. When discussing where to have dinner the following night, our last in this enchanted island, I hardly dared suggest we go back to Blue Mountain. When Norma came up with the same idea, however, I cheerfully agreed, and our second dinner there was every bit as magical as the first one.

As our plane soared through the night sky toward New York, Norma and I reflected a while on the feeling we now had for Buenos Aires as the home of a ship for whose further voyaging we and our company of South Street friends would now be responsible. I ventured the thought that our friends in Buenos Aires were also now members of this ship's company, another of her many varied crews. I believe none would ever forget the iron hulk that had now regained her historic name *Wavertree*. The ship had woven her way into their lives and they had become part of the changing crews that had driven her across oceans and round the ultimate menace of Cape Horn, where she had come so near to ending her run. The most important thing before us was to help her instill that sense of service to the ship in the very different setting that awaited us in New York. But like Jack ashore, who takes what he can get while he can get it, I think as we fell asleep we both had Jamaican smiles on our faces.

CHAPTER 23

A Home for a Distant Ship, *Winter–Spring 1969*

$10 Million Land Purchase—"This Museum Is People"—
A Ship on Ice—Local History—Starting Elissa Campaign—
Saving Eppleton Hall—Offices at 203 Front Street

The big ship was hard pressed, her great bows forced down in the cresting seas rushing at her. Black storm clouds ahead promised more and worse to come. A string of men, tiny as ants against the lowering sky, struggled aloft to stow the upper main topsail to get the ship shortened down to fighting trim. Defiantly, the ship still carried her full foresail—the big sail, its canvas spread low above the foredeck giving her the power she needed to fight her way to windward. Things would have to get a lot worse to force her to heave to and ride the seas like a bird with folded wings, the ultimate recourse. Meantime, her people were doing what had to be done to enable the tall full-rigger to make the passage she had to make around the jagged headland of Cape Horn.

This wild, darkling scene of the *Wavertree*'s battle with Cape Horn stood over our heads on the wall behind us as I stood up to introduce Jakob Isbrandtsen, chairman of the board of trustees, to open the first annual meeting of the members of the South Street Seaport Museum, on the snowy evening of Thursday, 20 February 1969, in our new headquarters in 203 Front Street. A detailed model of the ship by William Hitchcock showed her embroiled in the battle depicted in the print of Os Brett's painting which hung over our heads—emphasizing the centrality of the ship to all our purposes as a museum. A summary of operations in 1968, distributed to all hands, bore the title "Report to the Membership," to remind everyone of the second great principle of our young institution: that trustees, staff and all charged with our business were accountable to the members for all that they did.

Jakob Isbrandtsen's report as chairman began with news that rocked the membership: He had secured loans totaling $10 million from a consortium of five banks to buy the Goelet properties, the two blocks immediately north of Schermerhorn Row. These blocks constituted the center of the land designated for South Street Seaport. In his usual style, Jakob offered no details of this mighty commitment to the cause. He did say, however, that this fund assured the land needed for the Seaport plan. It would also satisfy City authorities that the Seaport project was real enough to ratify the plan and proceed with sale of the unused development rights—or air rights—over the central blocks to neighboring developers, so that they could build more densely. And Jakob spoke of the membership support that had fended off the Atlas-McGrath bid to wreck the Seaport, saying that without that victory, we might just as well fold our tents and all go home.

"A project for the public," he concluded, "requires a public to make its interest felt. In the case of South Street, the interest was there—and you can be sure it was felt."

In my report as president, I talked about Norma's and my visit to the *Wavertree* just a month earlier. I spoke of standing under that huge, shorn hull in drydock, whose lines bespoke the grace and virtue of man's deepwater adventure under sail. I told of how Lloyd's inspectors volunteered their lunch hours to tap with their hammers at her stout iron plates, marveling at how the fabric of the ship had weathered storms, fire, dismasting, neglect and abuse as a downgraded sand barge in the years and decades that had rolled by since she was launched into Southampton Water in 1885. I said to our gang that we were now the ship's company, and must do our best for her survival and continued service in a world so different from that in which she had been launched. And I reminded them that she came to us as the gift of Jakob Isbrandtsen.

This was greeted with wild cheers. Saving the Seaport land and buildings was vital to our story. But the buildings had been built, and the land they stood on had been filled in, simply to provide a base of operation for the wind-driven ships that connected us to the wider world. And people were jubilant in expressing their gratitude to the person who had acquired one of those ships to bring into their waterfront.

In Joe Cantalupo's report on behalf of Friends of South Street he talked about the great things museum members had done for us in the past year, from the high school student Chi Ling to Mayor Lindsay, with whom Joe had formed a remarkable rapport. He went on to single out Kent Barwick's contribution in running our monthly Saturday seminars which brought us direct testimony from seamen and scholars on topics of interest, and Jimmy Diaz's in leading work crews on the ships and piers. "My kind of people," he said, with a broad smile. Then he said something extraordinary—something which stuck in all our minds and was to be quoted again and again in future years.

"Other museums are for people, or about people," he declared. "This museum *is* people."

When, a year later, I was invited to talk to the American Association of Museums about our South Street venture, I gave my talk Joe's title, "This Museum *Is* People." I used as my rationale Plato's academy, a museum of discourse dedicated to the muses of the arts and sciences, where people gathered to talk together about the home truths and meanings of the human experience, walking in the shade of the trees under the fathomless depths of the Greek sky. I suggested that this was what museums should really be about, that quest for understanding of our experience of life. The artifacts museums collected were concretions of that discourse, the ideas made actual.

As to the museums' concern with artifacts, I offered the idea "a bus is an artifact," citing the exuberant celebration of life in the gold acanthus leaves garlanding the dark-green sides of the buses in Buenos Aires. We New Yorkers had once treated our trolley cars in similar fashion, as we did the workaday fishing vessels sailing from the Fulton Market, with scrollwork round their hawsepipes forward and their names picked out in gold leaf on the stern. We'd since lost something along the way—that instinct to reinvest some "joy in the work" in working vehicles and other objects. But our museum would remind people of this inspired and re-

viving concept, and it might indeed serve as a seedbed for a revival of a
more caring spirit. Modernists who deplore exploring the past for fresh
inspiration as a timid approach to the challenge of innovation and creativity would do well to consider the outpouring of new ideas and ways
of seeing things in the Italian Renaissance—sparked by a rediscovery of
the art and learning of ancient Greece and Rome.

These thoughts, it seemed to me, were implicit in Joe's saying, "This
museum *is* people." If this museum is people, then we should encourage
people to search out the sacred in the everyday and to seek meanings in
the experience of humankind across the generations.

But all this was mere theoretical vaporing unless we brought in people,
more and more people, to become part of the venture. To that end Leon
Kaplan, as Membership Committee chairman, rose to report that we had
ended the year 1968 with 6,000 members—double the 3,000 we'd had
at the end of 1967. He went on to observe that the $1 membership did
not eat up the $5 regular membership, as some had feared. Instead, the
cheap membership actually helped build the more expensive membership.

The figures Leon offered told the story. Before incorporation, just over
1 out of 10 members were regular $5 members or better. After incorpo-
ration in 1967, 1 out of 4 members were regular members, and by the
end of 1968 just over half were regular members. And these gains were
registered while membership doubled and redoubled in size! Everyone
who joined, even those at the $1 level, received our bimonthly newsletter
and other mailings, and this drew them further into the seaport story and
deeper into the affairs of the Seaport Museum. As thousands of new $1
members crowded in the door, still more joined at the regular $5 rate or
better—especially the all-important renewals, which overwhelmingly
came in at the higher rate. All this, we felt, was a remarkable tribute to
the force of human desire when harnessed to a cause that people really
wanted to see succeed.*

Monk Farnham, Ships Committee chairman, reported on the successful installation of the lightship *Ambrose* and schooner *Caviare* as our first

* For more on Leon's report, see Appendix.

museum ships. The ships immediately involved more members in museum activities and increased public visitation. The great step we had all been looking toward was of course the purchase of the *Wavertree,* and Monk reported on the first steps in her restoration begun in preparation for her long voyage home. With somewhat less enthusiasm, he reported that the *Journal of Commerce,* at Eric Ridder's bidding, had donated $5,000 to buy the hulk of the last surviving wooden packet ship—one of the flock that had changed oceanic history in their sailings from South Street.

This was a wild pigeon come home to roost at last: the 977-ton *Charles Cooper,* built of native oak in Black Rock, Connecticut, in 1856. She had put in to the Falkland Islands in 1866, leaking badly after being beaten up in battle with Cape Horn, and was put to use serving as a warehouse for the past hundred years. We bought her knowing we could not foreseeably pay the huge cost of returning the ship to New York and preserving her as an archaeological exhibit. This was distressing to Monk, who deplored commitments unbacked by resources to carry them out. But the ship did fit beautifully into Jakob's, Norma's and my ideal of saving ships to put them on ice so that they would still be available for recovery when funds became available—holding that option open for coming generations. And the icy waters of the Falklands made, indeed, a perfect icebox; witness the ship's long survival, while all her kin vanished, as if they'd never mastered the tough North Atlantic run and proved beyond peradventure of doubt that the New World had something to show the Old World in this matter of crossing deep waters under sail.

It is well, perhaps, to finish off her tale here. The museum sent off three expeditions to stabilize the ship, as the Cape Horn gales she had taken refuge from in Port Stanley sent storm surges to chew away at her planking of Connecticut oak. But finally she just collapsed into the sea and had to be junked. Before that happened, however, Norman Brouwer and Peter Throckmorton saved the great American flag carving from her stern transom. This was delivered to the Falkland Islands Museum, where it stands today, a superb testimonial to the craftsmanship and passion with which the people of her day invested the sea chariots they drove around the ocean world with such pride and such earth-shaking results. Plaster casts of the stern carving—a very well-preserved oval of the Stars and Stripes surrounded by gilded flourishes—were made with materials donated by Dow Corning, who also contributed to the cost of the expedition and sponsored a grand poetic film on the Falklands heritage in historic ships, *Ghosts of Cape Horn.*

This admirable stern carving survives in perfect replica form in South Street today, as well as in the National Maritime Historical Society's headquarters in Peekskill, New York. I am glad we have it, if only in replica, with a memorable film sequence in *Ghosts of Cape Horn* of Peter Throckmorton making the casting (the memorable line, "Pass me that stick," which occurs at a critical point in removing the casting mold from the oaken original, is repeated among the cognoscenti of this film today as a kind of password).

Other reports at the meeting were bursting with evidence of people doing things to shape the experience of their museum, beginning with a booth at the National Boat Show, manned by volunteers, while Norma and I were in Buenos Aires. Over 200 new members had been signed up, one of whom was now organizing a South Street booth at the Asbury Park Boat Show in New Jersey. And the scholarly, well-organized Fred Fried took over as chairman of the Local History Committee, bringing its labors into a more ordered state with notable acumen and good will, and supporting the work of Val Wenzel in city archives, and Jo and Don Meisner in salvage archaeology. Joe Cantalupo's agreeing to serve as chairman of Friends was a notable step forward in these efforts, for he lived the day-to-day life of the Seaport and was ideally placed to hear out the numerous complaints and occasional conflicts that characterize any body of free people working together.

We published an extensive annual report of fourteen separate committee reports for distribution at this meeting, each report written by the volunteer chairman. This thick stack of stapled typescript seemed a bit heavy for the general membership, and was definitely too much for prospective members and supporters to digest. So future annual reports were produced in a more flowing style, with pictures to show the work we were talking about—but that report of 1969 provides a good "slice of life" view of the functioning of what had become, somewhat to our surprise, an established institution strongly rooted in volunteer participation.

The solidity of an established organization was made evident to me in various small ways during this snowy midwinter. On one memorable occasion, I invited Lenny Cohen to have lunch with me at Sweet's. Lenny, district leader of a West Side reform Democratic club, worked as deputy borough president with Percy Sutton, whose offices were in the Municipal Building a few blocks away. A moderate reformer, Lenny believed in working with the old-line clubs, which predominated in black communities in New York, and I wanted Lenny's advice about what we in South Street might be doing to reach out to the black community.

There were no admission fees to our exhibits, piers or ships, and of the thousands of our visitors, a large share were from the black community, including several lead volunteers—Jim Kirk, his brother Stuart, Nat Hall, Edna Fitzpatrick and others. Our staff and volunteers had a genuinely welcoming attitude, so the museum suffered none of the black/white divisions that shook New York and other American cities at that time.

I was discussing with Lenny my notion that the mobility of our ships should enable us to take the Seaport experience to black communities— the maritime heritage was, after all, a movable feast, and there was a lot to be said about the black experience at sea besides the horrors of the slave trade. Lenny was interested and just starting to ask a question, when a high-pitched voice from the doorway behind me interrupted the quiet tenor of our discourse:

"Lenny, what are you doing in my district?"

I recognized the compelling voice as that of P. Vincent (Duke) Viggiano, whom I had run against for district leader six years earlier, so I turned in my chair and said: "Duke, it's OK, I invited him."

Duke gave a chuckle at this and came over to shake our hands, ask after our progress in South Street, and apologize that he couldn't buy us a drink—he had some people he had to meet. "Not as much fun as you two," he added.

In 1963 I had secured just over a quarter of the Democratic vote running with Nicolasa Benitez against Duke and his co-leader in the 2nd Assembly District East. One out of four does not seem like much, but it was noticeably ahead of any other reform club in a ghetto district. And more to the point, as Duke himself had told me, this showing was strong enough to justify him in retiring some what he termed "Moustache Petes," who had been captains in blocks of black and Hispanic voters. Jim Kirk became one of Duke's replacement captains when our club fell to pieces following the elections, so all was peaceable between us.

Lenny and I resumed our quiet plotting, which ultimately resulted in Percy Sutton leading a reception for our schooner, *Caviare,* when she visited Harlem's Sherman Creek some time later.

Another luncheon meeting, on 13 February, a week before our annual meeting, was at Gracie Mansion, where Mayor Lindsay had again gathered a small crowd of people doing good things for New York. The novelist Helen McInnes, a raven-haired, clear-eyed lady, sat beside me at one of the small tables scattered around the room. I said something about how I enjoyed her work; she gave me a kindly, skeptical look.

At this luncheon I also ran into George Plimpton, founder of the avant-garde magazine *Paris Review,* whom I had known as a fellow student at King's College. We had made a picaresque auto tour through England's West Country together, and his graduation party was held in my college rooms, which were about to be torn down and hence could be half-demolished in the course of the party, which indeed happened. We'd seen nothing of each other in the sixteen years since Cambridge, so I was moved when he offered to help our effort in South Street in any way he could—a promise he would keep.

———◆———

Other things moving across our desks in this time included an historic ship venture in the Mediterranean, which developed into one of the classic ship saves of our time. Joan Throckmorton, Peter's wife, flew in from Piraeus, the Greek seaport where they had taken up residence, to muster support for Peter's effort to save the motor ship *Christophoros*, which was about to be scrapped. Boarding the vessel, Peter had found a sailing ship's after cabin under the modern superstructure of a conventional powered vessel. Investigating further, he found her builder's plate. This revealed that the battered iron hull had been built in 1877 as the *Elissa*, a handsome iron barque from Alexander Hall's yard in Aberdeen, Scotland. Her clipper bow had been shorn off, and the modern superstructure and stumpy cargo masts obscured her purity of line. But Throcko, with a nose for historic ships, had sniffed her out and was seeking help to buy her.

I, of course, consulted Karl Kortum on this marvelous find and learned that Karl had already spotted this ship from his rooftop aerie in San Francisco, with helpful guidance from the Lloyd's agent in Greece. When he learned of Joan's visit, he wrote Peter, asking him to serve as agent for the San Francisco Maritime Museum to acquire this gem of the Scottish builder's art. Karl noted that they had no money for the project but were, as he put it, "resourceful." As indeed they were. In the ensuing years Karl several times found sponsors to keep the ship from being hauled ashore and cut up at the wreckers' yard where she had ended her working career. Throckmorton mortgaged his house and his archaeological research vessel *Stormie Seas* to buy the ship, and Karl found David Groos, a Canadian member of Parliament, to bail Peter out of this precarious position; but that good man Groos unexpectedly died, and his widow did not share his interest. By this time, in the late 1970s, the campaign had been waged for over a decade, with myself serving as a kind of secretary. Then a crew of South Street graduates, including Michael Creamer of the Model Shop, and Walter Rybka and David Brink of the Pioneer Marine School, found sponsors in Galveston who saved the vessel, and they ultimately restored her to sailing condition in an amazing rebirth. Karl and Peter, who made a great pair, both consummate seamen, skilled craftsmen and devoted students of the living heritage of sail, worked together over these long years. Their founding role was properly recognized when the *Elissa* set sail for the first time from Galveston in 1982. I was aboard for my small part in this amazing enterprise, which had gone through dark and troubled hours but had summoned the best energies of gifted and determined people to pull her through.

As Karl, Peter and I began work on the initial arrangements to save *Elissa*, Karl was demonstrating that "resourcefulness" he spoke of in another historic ship project, the effort to save the *Eppleton Hall*, a Tyneside paddlewheel tug of 1910. Karl had persuaded his patron Scott Newhall, managing editor of the *San Francisco Chronicle*, to take on this burnt-out hulk stranded on a riverbank in the north of England to add to the San Francisco fleet of historic ships. We were to be involved in it in unexpected ways before the year 1969 ended. The complex and somewhat shady operations that led to the acquisition of the tug were proceeding apace even as Karl set up the preliminaries of the campaign that saved the *Elissa*.

Domestic concerns progressed, as they have a way of doing, in the shade of these international undertakings. In the early months of the year Norma's father had made the unexpected decision to move to Florida and had put up the family home in Yorktown Heights for sale. Norma had found a suitable house for us in Laurelton, Queens, but we wouldn't be able to move in until May when the sellers moved out. For the interim, she found a tiny one-room furnished apartment in the pleasant purlieus of Gramercy Park, with an even tinier sleeping loft above the living room, which one reached by a ladder.

Then on 3 April, Norma's pregnancy ended at St. Luke's Hospital with the birth of our son Robert, an alert child with an amiable disposition and a resolute way of letting us know his desires with a noble roar. Our cat, Scratch, put up with these radically changed living arrangements; surely anything was better that the cesspit from which we had rescued her four years earlier.

While Norma was at St. Luke's, Betsy Kohn and Mary Davis appeared with flowers and good wishes and told Norma that they would be quitting South Street to make a trip to Mexico together in June. Norma heard this with sadness. Betsy and Mary's spirited, non-hierarchical, workmanlike ways of getting things done were a great strength to our operations. And they were friends who had been with us through tough battles. As the date of their departure neared, we were still wondering how we would ever get along without them.

With all this to deal with Norma somehow also supervised the move of the Seaport office from 16 Fulton Street into its expansive new quarters in 203 Front Street. George Demmy and Jimmy Diaz led a dedicated volunteer crew in clearing trash from the four-story structure and converting it to our various needs, building shelves, closets and partitions as needed.

The first floor served as our public display and meeting area. The models and paintings from 16 Fulton Street were shifted over, and with the extra space now available, our exhibits were enlarged and changing exhibits were added.

Offices were set up on the remaining floors, using old desks and chairs scrounged from *Boating* magazine and some, it is wonderful to report, from our good friends at the General Desk Company on the other side of the block, whose building we were soon to take over, as they well knew. They were swept up in the desire to help our efforts, as others had been.

The second floor held our most public offices. We were able to use the existing partitions at the front of the building to provide a small office for me (the size I prefer; small and crowded rather than spacious and vacuous), flanked by a larger office for Ellen Isbrandtsen as secretary, with space for a second desk for a fundraiser if we ever got one. Beyond this was the stairway with an open area for a receptionist's desk. Further on was a small office for Alan Frazer (curatorial), then another open area with room for two desks (Betsy Kohn, public relations, and volunteer librarian Gerry Boardman) and then the library/conference room at the very back of the building with its view onto the century-old brick alleyway behind it. The third floor housed the bookkeeper's office, public events coordinator and the membership department with ample room for its many file cabinets, addressing machine and table where staff and volunteers labeled, stuffed and sorted our many mailings.

And on the top floor, Norma and Steven and David Canright set up the workroom where the displays for the *Wavertree* and Pier 16 were researched, designed and created, using the heavy wooden signboards that Kortum had recommended. This place soon became redolent of pine shavings and varnish. With its electric tools, varnish room and pot belly stove for heat, it had quite a different feeling than the rest of the building.

As the most recent arrivals in a long succession of occupants, succeeding the rumbustious people of the fish market, we by this time had come to feel that we, too, belonged in this storied neighborhood. People we met in the street nodded "Hello," sometimes adding "How's the museum doing?" and the denizens of the Square Rigger Bar around the corner in Front Street certainly knew us well, from the sardonic cook John Wallace and Joe the fierce bartender to the owners Alex and Nick Olatka, who were endlessly interested and helpful to us in our work.

With these achievements we felt we were on our way to fulfilling our mission to revive the old seaport. We were reinforced in these feelings by things invisible as well as things as visible as our two ships on the waterfront. Among these unseen assets were the legal ownership of the great ship *Wavertree* in Buenos Aires—she would soon be coming *home* to New York with New York now her port of registry.

And . . . Alan Villiers, the leading chronicler of the sailing of tall ships in the Cape Horn trade, had agreed to come to see us in New York even before the *Wavertree* got here! He knew from me that we needed money, and he planned the visit to raise funds for her restoration. This was reinforcement indeed!

CHAPTER 24

Launching a Seaport Campaign, *Spring 1969*

Alan Villiers Bears a Hand—A "Twenty-one Gun Evening"—
Alliance with Atlas—Acquiring Central Seaport Blocks—
The Open Road Ahead

It was the artist Os Brett who put us in touch with Villiers and encouraged us to ask him to write an introduction for the book we planned to publish on the ship. This Villiers did, as a contribution, in an authoritative treatise on the ships and men of the last days of the Cape Horn trade in sail—in effect, an eight-page adumbration of his classic work *The War With Cape Horn*, which was to appear three years later. It set out for the first time the statistics of losses in the brutally stormy year 1905, which Villiers had recovered from old files stored in an airplane hangar in England. Full of Villiers's own experience with the ships and men he was writing about, it ran under the title "The Red-blooded Life of the Cape Horn Windjammer," and ended with this tribute to the ships and the men who served in them:

> *Their windships might kill them but while they lasted they were challenging, beautiful, noble ships in whose service there were tremendous compensations and satisfactions gone quite beyond achievement now. They exacted a price, but the men who served them took that for granted.*

At Villiers's insistence, we set up a full round of speaking engagements for him, a more concerted promotional effort than we had ever mounted before. And as the days were crossed off toward his arrival among us on 19 April, we awaited his appearance, if not with trepidation, with something like a fearful joy.

I had met Alan Villiers once before, in another lifetime it seemed, aboard his ship, the full rigger *Joseph Conrad*. The *Joseph Conrad* was in drydock in Tebo's yard off Gowanus Creek in South Brooklyn, and I have a vivid memory of Villiers in pea jacket and sea boots, poking with his foot at a crate drifting in the ship's flooded lower hold. It was early January 1935 when I was seven years of age, and the vessel, badly holed, was docked for repairs after being driven onto the Bay Ridge shore in a winter gale. The stout little square rigger, formerly the Danish sail training ship *Georg Stage*, had just finished the first leg of the round-the-world voyage Villiers planned to make in her, with young people of different nationalities in crew.

My father had driven down to see the ship in drydock, taking me with him because he knew I was crazy about square riggers as other kids were about cars and aircraft. Going aboard, I was struck by the ship's densely clustered rigging, which gave the feeling of entering a forest as we came over the rail and I stood for the first time on the decks of an ocean-going square rigger. And the decks, enclosed by bulwarks taller than I was, were indeed like a magic forest, full of legendary things I had seen only in photographs in books; the huge coils of manila rope hanging from the pinrails, the antique capstan on the foredeck, the great yards crossing the masts overhead—and what I can only call the strong, purposive look of everything in sight.

At age seven, I didn't catch much of the grownup talk, but I remember the growl in Villliers's voice as he described how the ship had been blown ashore from her anchorage in the early hours of 2 January, through a failed shackle in the anchor chain—with only an aged watchman aboard to watch helplessly as the vessel was swept away to crash on the rocky shoreline of Bay Ridge. It had been a hair-raising job to get the crippled ship off the rocks in the gale still blowing, and then to tow her at nightfall across to Staten Island, where she was put ashore until divers could patch her up for the trip to Tebo's.

Later, reading his account of the incident in the ever-memorable *Cruise of the Conrad*, I learned how he saw the gleaming lights of Lower Manhattan, signals from a distant world, while the harbor waves flooded across the decks as the ship sank lower in the icy water. The voyage almost ended on the spot, and with it, quite possibly, Villiers's life and the lives of the emergency crew embarked for this perilous passage. I am sure he said nothing of this at the time, however. We seem to have taken Villiers home for lunch, and I had a vivid mental picture of him standing in the dining-room doorway of my parents' house in Brooklyn Heights. I remember the light-grey color of the dining-room rug, because I was worried my mother might not like our visitor tracking it up with his muddy sea boots. And that was that. As it happened, we had no further meeting with Villiers during the four weeks it took to get his ship repaired, stocked with new provisions for those ruined by seawater, supplied with new gear for items that had been carried away, and at last to set sail at the end of the month.

The voyage that brought the *Joseph Conrad* to New York has since become the stuff of legend. A few years earlier, Villiers had used the money gained by his writings and lectures to buy a half-share in the great four-masted barque *Parma* to make a voyage to Australia for grain. He and his partner, Captain Ruben de Cloux, made a substantial profit on two voyages in 1931–33, and Villiers then decided to quit while he was ahead. His aim was not to get rich but to buy a ship to sail around the world with young people ready to learn the disciplines of seafaring under sail. This was to be a voyage, he said, "in defense of my poor ideals."

He regarded life under sail as deeply practical and a teacher of the truths of man's condition. Of his early years in a hard life at sea he wrote: "Here in the battered bark, all men mattered." He believed all people deserved a chance to make a decent living and that none should be excluded from life's benefits. His father had been a socialist and pacifist who advocated Australia staying out of World War I. Villiers shared his father's values, but he also admired the hard-won lessons of achievement. Making a voyage under sail called forth the best man had to give, he believed—and those disciplines were tough and demanding. He deplored a culture that valued talk above performance and had no desire to compete in the political world. He valued above all, I believe, mankind's hard-won wisdom, capacity for wonder, and appreciation of the beauty of the created world—values that shine through his memorable *Cruise of the Conrad* and all his voyage narratives.

The world in the early 1930s was not a pretty place, with Hitler arming Germany to the teeth, the capitalist system failing to provide a decent living in a worldwide economic depression that refused to go away, and Soviet communism offering only a bleak, brutal and deeply inhumane alternative. But, at sea, one could deal with honest realities and learn to make one's way by man's God-given gift to learn life's truths. So, having searched various seaports for a ship to make his voyage, when Villiers came upon a Danish sail training ship newly retired from service, it seemed like a gift from heaven. Villiers used his new-found wealth to buy her and outfit her for the world voyage he planned. He appreciated her beauty of line, and her traditional labor-intensive rig, which bespoke historic practice, delighted his eye. The ship's original name, *Georg Stage,* had been transferred to the ship that replaced her, so Villiers gave his new ship a new name, *Joseph Conrad,* for the Polish-born master mariner whose writings on seafaring and human purpose he greatly admired.

On his passage to America, the first leg of his voyage, he planned to bring along T. E. Lawrence, author of *The Seven Pillars of Wisdom*, with the New York typographer Bruce Rogers to write and print great things on a press set up in the tweendecks. That scheme collapsed when Lawrence was killed in a motorcycle accident, but Bruce Rogers came to the ship in Brooklyn and carved the figurehead of Joseph Conrad which she carried on around the world, a casting of which she carries today in Mystic Seaport.

So the voyage continued, despite every obstacle. Villiers knew that he had no new continents or islands to discover, and he made no pretense of scientific discoveries either. "But," as he later put it in *The Voyage of the Conrad*, "I could keep a form of art alive upon an earth which had grown, it thought, beyond the need of it; and I could sail for the sailing's sake, for the sake of the health and the life and the clean wind and the joy of being there."

———————◆———————

Alan, now 65, was an imposing figure when we met in the Algonquin Hotel. I correctly surmised that he would have no memory of meeting me at age seven, so I opened our talk by telling him how taken aback Norma and I had been at finding the Hotel Cabo de Hornos to be a majestic pile with uniformed waiters and a wine list a mile long—having been led to expect from Alan's postcard a crude hostel with hailstones rattling on its corrugated tin roof. Alan sat back to enjoy a good chuckle at the success of his *ruse de guerre* designed to shiver our timbers before our visit to a little-known corner of the world. Then, all business, he asked me to go over the list of his speaking engagements we had arranged. Expressing himself satisfied, he excused himself to retire early to his room.

Our schedule began the next day with Alan's talk to our membership on the evening of 21 April at the Chamber of Commerce, a noble downtown structure on Liberty Street. As I explained to Alan, our membership was our most important asset, and each individual in attendance would carry word of his message far and wide.

And what a message that was! Speaking in the Chamber's august main hall under the solemn portraits of Alexander Hamilton, DeWitt Clinton and other New York notables over the ages, Alan told the tale of the Atlantic seafaring that had brought adventurous souls to our shores. He spoke while showing slides of the sailing ships that had brought the scattered branches of mankind in touch with each other in that great oceanic adventure of the past 500 years.

Growing up in Australia in the early 1900s, Alan had been fascinated by the working sail that crowded Melbourne Harbor in that era, vessels ranging from local ketches and Tasman barques trading to New Zealand, to the big deepwatermen that still followed the long sea road back to England and European ports half a world away. He had pursued that sea road in those last survivors of the world of working sail, rounding Cape Horn sixteen times before World War II dispersed the ships and crews, with shipmates coming ashore from the last Australian grain race of 1939, sadly to become enemies in a war that ultimately engulfed all the world.

As part of his exploration of man's experience under sail, Alan was sailing in Arabian dhows when World War II broke out in 1939. He left the dhows to join the Royal Navy, and was ordered to convoy 24 LCI(L)s (Landing craft, Infantry, Large)—across the Atlantic, and later led convoys of these little ships to the invasion of Sicily and the Normandy beaches. Later, he again carried troops to the Indian Ocean for the liberation of Burma from the Japanese. By war's end, he held the rank of Commander and had been awarded the Distinguished Service Cross.

After the war, Alan returned to widening his experience in sail. He shipped out with Portuguese mariners in the schooner *Argus* to launch dories into the open sea on the Grand Banks in quest of cod. And just twelve years prior to his visit with us, he'd joined a group that built an accurate reproduction of the *Mayflower* and then sailed it across the Atlantic to her new home in Plymouth, Massachusetts. Villiers commanded the ship on that voyage, acquiring along the way new knowledge and considerable respect for the original ship and the people who had sailed her.

The tale was told with dramatic appreciation of the fury of the sea aroused and the valor of men rising to meet its challenge, and no shortage of salty language—but also with a degree of sailorly respect for the ships he'd sailed in and the people he'd sailed with. He told us we were now the ship's company for the *Wavertree*, and he wished us well in gathering the support needed to bring her to New York.

The week that followed was full of luncheon meetings with business executives and evening presentations to such outfits as the Overseas Press Club and the Larchmont Yacht Club. Alan gave his all on these occasions, ending up visibly exhausted. We learned to clear a path for him so he could quit the scene and get back to the Algonquin, where he would invariably go straight to bed.

There was a pleasant break in this hard-driven campaign when the Ship Committee met with Alan for a small private dinner at the New York Yacht Club on 24 April. George Campbell had once had,

I gathered, a somewhat acrimonious difference with Alan over the cosmetic lifts George had specified for the *Cutty Sark* restoration in England. These lifts were rigged to hold the upper topsail yard evenly spaced between the lower topsail yard below and the topgallant yard above when in the lowered position in port, thus presenting a more balanced picture than they did lowered close against the lower topsail yards, as was the practice at sea. Alan, deeply imbued with the working practices of his time at sea, had maintained in committee meetings that cosmetic lifts had never existed and were a figment of George's imagination. George came to the dinner table loaded for bear, with a large photograph of the handsome *Cutty Sark* herself, in harbor during her working career, with topsail yards evenly spaced through the use of cosmetic lifts, just as George had specified. I faced the coming showdown with some trepidation. But when George produced his photograph, Alan examined it closely and then said: "My word! Who would have thought of such a thing?" He was all smiles, and with this confrontation of the giants behind us, our small dinner became a merry one, with Alan telling story after story and George beaming like a lighthouse.

"That was a twenty-one gun evening, that was!" said master mariner Archie Horka in a letter to his friend, the marine artist Os Brett, about the Yacht Club evening. And launching into a real sailorman's tribute to another of his breed, he continued:

At long last I fell in with a man [Villiers] *whom I had been pursuing, figuratively, for most of my life as a seaman. As I mentioned to him, our paths must have crossed somewhere in the sailing-ship ports of the world. Perhaps in Sydney's Lower George Street, maybe on Stockton's "ballast bank," or in Newcastle's Hunter Street. Then again, maybe amid the horse-dust and flies in Flinders Street, Melbourne or admiring the Tassie ketches in the Little Dock. . . . He knew all these places as I did, and oft frequented them with the same dream-image in*

his eyes—the sight of a square-rigger's lofty rigging soaring
skyward above the wharf-sheds.

To catch our breaths after the week's round of engagements, I proposed that Sunday, 27 April, be a lay day—the traditional day off when
a sailor gets time to mend his clothes, write letters, or simply laze about.
Alan was put off by this, telling me plainly he had come to New York
to work for the ship, not to lie about all day. I told him what I actually
had in mind was to drive out to Mystic Seaport to visit his old ship,
Joseph Conrad, in her honored berth where she was still serving young
people, training them in the ways of the sea at dockside. Alan thought
it wasn't worth the trip, but I just said I'd be at the Algonquin at noon
to pick him up, with my son Tom, who would enjoy meeting him. He
then said if I insisted on showing up he might come along to make me
happy—just be sure it was no earlier than 12, he didn't plan to get up till
then. It was borne in on me how really exhausted he was by the relentless
schedule he'd insisted we set up for him.

Tom, now ten years old, and I met Villiers in the Algonquin lobby,
and we rolled out of the city through the quiet Sunday streets to arrive
in Mystic toward mid-afternoon. The salt air and seagoing scenery
at Mystic Seaport seemed to do wonders for Alan, who walked with
something like a spring in his step as we pursued the cobbled paths to
the wharf where the *Conrad* lay. Leading the way to board the vessel,
he turned to say: "Watch out for falling blocks, Tommy!" This is a
seaman's way of saying a ship is falling to pieces. But—there were no
falling blocks. In fact, everything about the decks and up aloft appeared in first-class order.

And Alan was delighted. He knew and admired Mystic's founder, Carl
Cutler, and must have known that Carl had stayed away from the Seaport
in his final years because of the dismal state the ships had fallen into. His
own previous visit to the *Conrad* in 1948 had been disappointing. But
luckily for us, the overhaul of the *Conrad* showed the first fruits of the
new approach to shipkeeping which Waldo Johnston had told us about

aboard *Athena* two years earlier. Alan's seaman's eye was unquestionably pleased with what he saw. Added to this, it was evident that Alan was pleased that young people were still learning the heritage of seafaring on his old ship's decks.

So it was as a merry crew that we adjourned to the bar in the Seaman's Inne, where I'd phoned ahead to have Francis E. Bowker meet us for supper. Alan had told me Biff Bowker was the one person at Mystic he wanted to see. Bowker, a captain in sail, had served in the big wooden schooners in the coastal trade which wound up the American story in working sail. At Mystic, he served as captain of the lithe and able Stephens schooner *Brilliant*, a sleek ocean racer that took Scout groups and students on cruises in local waters. Some 31 years later, toward the end of his life, Biff recalled that conversation in a valedictory letter about our talks on my visits to Mystic:

> *The time you brought Alan Villiers, against his will, was a wonderful act, and I remember he wanted to see none but me. He became a friend of Mystic and a friend of mine.*

It was indeed a friendly encounter for these old salts, who found much to talk about in their different experiences at sea. Tommy sat enraptured for a time, but after a while I thought it best to let him run around outside, as the two men got into details of sail handling in the quite different ships they'd sailed in—that, and talk of captains good and bad, were grist to Alan's mill.

For now, at 65, Alan had clearly realized his mission to record the passing of a way of life as mankind's 5,000-year sea traffics under sail were receding into the past, and he clearly didn't think there was all the time in the world to record the thoughts and memories of honest working seamen, whose experiences generally didn't make it into the books. Though the memoirs of sea captains and young people who went to sea as an adventure did often get recorded, that wasn't the case with the working stiffs who knew no other life but seafaring. Alan made a few notes, and he and Biff exchanged addresses as they parted. On the way back to the city the car got a flat tire, and Alan said to Tom: "Now, Tommy, you'll see your father doing a little real work with his hands for a change." I was delighted. You could see that he'd thoroughly enjoyed his visit.

Monday passed in a round of activities, and on Tuesday evening we had the great occasion our labors had been building toward: a presentation to the members of the New York Yacht Club in their 44th Street headquarters. The Villiers name had an electric effect on people who ventured on the sea under sail, however casually, and this was evident from the moment we walked into the clubhouse. The entryway was packed with people waiting to greet Alan, and we made a kind of state procession up the grand stairway to the Model Room—fortunately, people were polite and stood back, so we did not have to form a flying wedge to clear a path, but I worried because I feared that he'd be exhausted by dealing with so many excited people before his talk even started. I need not have worried.

Alan had refined his presentation, which never came out the same way twice, to bear down on the actualities of the experience under sail—off Cape Horn with decks awash, carrying 5,000 tons of grain in big steel ships, off Arabia in graceful wooden dhows, in Indonesian waters with handsome native schooners that maintained a network of traffic among islands that maintained a high level of civilization long before the European incursion of 400 years ago, in Australian waters where the "Tassie" (Tasmanian) ketches ply the rugged Tasman Sea, which can kick up very rough at short notice, and in the North Atlantic, where the reconstructed *Mayflower* earned her passage in bouts with violent northwesterlies that taught all hands the ways of sailors before our time. Alan's feeling for these varied craft, and his lively rendition of shipboard incidents aboard each one, shone through the photographs on the screen in a way that made you know he was not just describing the scenes before us, but reliving them. As he wound up he made a mute appeal to me to get him out of the room, and a few friends joined me to make up an escort to do just that. The next day I drove Alan to the US Lines pier to board the superliner *United States* for his return to the gentle hills and meandering streams of Oxford, where he lived with his wife, Nancie, and their three children.

So our campaign for the Seaport was launched, with leaders in the yachting community crowding the room to see Alan. However we secured only a trickle of contributions from Alan's stellar presentation; we were simply not set up to hoist in the big fish Alan had brought into our net.

What Alan's visit did accomplish, however, was to establish the legitimacy and importance of the *Wavertree* project—and, thereby, of the Seaport venture. It was a gathering no one would forget.

After the Villiers visit there was a ground-breaking ceremony at 236 Front Street, complete with gold-plated trowels and Mayor Lindsay in great form. After pointing out the benefits of the tourism the Seaport would attract, he said something that got to our educational purposes:

> *But there was something else about New York's waterfront and her link to the sea—and it is this we have lost: that sense of shared adventure New Yorkers once felt with the sea at their doorstep.*

When I, whose job it was to conduct this event with a bullhorn, said: "And here comes our beloved comptroller, Mario Proccacino," John Lindsay, knowing the highly directional pickup of the bull horn, said with mock indignation: "Peter, you liar!" Proccacino of course was running against Lindsay for the mayoralty, and the November election was less than six months away. The building itself, which was nowhere on our priorities list, collapsed a few years later, before any real work was done on it; but apparently its re-dedication achieved its purpose when, two weeks later, the City Planning Commission announced its approval of the Seaport plan. I had thought this was a foregone conclusion, but of course in city politics nothing is foregone—and of course having both the mayor and his leading challenger on the scene and both supporting the Seaport plan made good sense politically.

On that same day, Monday, 26 May, I learned that Ken Wilpon had arranged a meeting for Jakob and me with the elusive Sol G. Atlas in Babylon, Long Island. At the appointed hour on Tuesday, Jakob and Ken arrived at our offices in a long, black, chauffeur-driven limousine.

At eleven o'clock we debarked in front of a modest office building, and went up to meet Atlas in his second-floor office to find him seated behind a massive desk at the far end. Standing just behind him was an aide, who was introduced as Mr. Schuster.

"And what is the business that brings you this long way to see me?" Sol Atlas asked. A small man with a gnomish look about him, like the Wizard of Oz when he was finally unveiled, I noticed that he spoke in an extraordinarily clear and precise manner. Jakob and Ken looked at me.

In the car on the way out, both men had been talking of other concerns, but I gathered the meeting was to invite Atlas to shift his plans from Schermerhorn Row to a new 55-story building to be built on the Coffee Exchange block just inland from the Row.

So that is what I said the meeting was about. Atlas then asked me politely just what action I expected him to take. I said: "Call up Richard Buford at the Office of Lower Manhattan Development and tell him you're interested in going ahead with this proposal, in partnership with Seaport Holdings, which owns the block."

"That will never happen," said Atlas, still with studied politeness. I noticed he put his hands together in a steeple as he talked, as if to emphasize the simple truth of what he was saying. "But." he added, "I'll hear your case, since you've come such a long way."

I glanced at Jakob and Ken, who looked back at me. I then set out to explain how the new building would have the same volume as the one he'd planned, since no plaza or setbacks of upper stories would be required. He could build to twice the permitted density by taking up the air rights over Schermerhorn Row together with some from the Goelet blocks. I cited the floor area of the unused air rights over Schermerhorn Row and what was needed from the Goelet blocks, and the footage allowed in the receptor block. Mr. Schuster had his slide rule out while I was talking, and at one point he whispered, quite audibly: "The figures work out, Sol."

"Mr. Stanford, have you Mr. Buford's telephone number?" Atlas inquired with unruffled aplomb. Perhaps I imagined the faint smile I saw in his eyes as he reached for the phone I handed him, after I'd got Buford on the line. When he had set his date with Buford, I said it would be a great thing for New York if this plan went through and I thanked him for the meeting—which he waved aside with a definite smile. Jakob, seconded by Ken, reinforced my thanks, saying he hoped Mr. Atlas would find the Seaport project worthwhile as a New Yorker, and that he looked forward to working with him on the new building.

Our ride back to Manhattan was positively euphoric. Jakob and Ken told me that they hadn't expected me to explain the air rights arrangements, but simply to tell Atlas of the importance of the museum and the political clout it had built up. I remember saying that perhaps Atlas liked hearing about an innovation in his business, out of the mouth of an amateur. I didn't add that I also thought it unwise to pressure a person as careful and thoughtful as Sol Atlas had proved to be.

Atlas and Buford met the following day and reached full agreement on the new building. Jakob still hoped to bring the Goelet estate into the new building partnership, and a meeting was held to map out the economics of the new building. Atlas attended the meeting with just his aide Schuster, and Jakob brought Ken and me with him. We were confronted with half a dozen Goelet estate people. Atlas led off the meeting by citing the proposed volume of the new building, as arranged with Buford, and the costs and anticipated revenues. Here the meeting ground to a halt; a Goelet technician objected to the building costs Atlas cited as being far too low. Atlas icily responded that he had built a few office buildings in New York, and this large building, concentrated on one block, would provide considerable economies of scale. Clearly, he did not like having his figures questioned, and clearly the eager beavers running the Goelet estate interests resented Atlas's calmly assertive manner. The meeting ended with an agreement to study the problem further, but Atlas said to Jakob and me as we walked away that he saw no point in negotiating new figures. He was accustomed to building using his own figures, his own people and his own ways of getting things done, and he could not be responsible for plans based on made-up numbers.

The upshot of this was that Jakob had to give up the idea of having Goelet as a partner in the new building. So a new meeting was called to arrange that Seaport Holdings would buy the two Goelet blocks for $10 million, using the bank credits Jakob had announced in January. The Goelet team now declared that they needed an additional $1 million to cover legal and other closing costs. Jakob reluctantly accepted this, and so the deal was closed.

The rest of this saga played out sadly for the new partnership. The market for transferred air rights faded fast as the housing boom collapsed in the following year—which led to some extraordinary footwork on our part to find a way to bank the air rights—and Sol Atlas's building empire collapsed with the market, forcing the firm into bankruptcy some time later. Herman Miller, who sold us the strategic building inland from Schermerhorn Row for $1 million, went unrecognized and unthanked—though he had provided the backboard against which we were able to make Atlas an offer he couldn't really refuse, once it had been clearly presented to him. The diverse commercial empire Jakob had built up around his ownership of American Export-Isbrandtsen Lines ran into heavy weather before the year ended, as the shipping enterprises at its heart declined toward bankruptcy, as part of a general decline in American-flag shipping which saw a wipeout of virtually all such lines engaged in international trade in coming years.

But despite these harsh results for those who made it possible, the plan worked. Schermerhorn Row was definitely saved, since no one would buy the old buildings with the air rights stripped away; Seaport Holdings held the John Street building in the block inland from Schermerhorn Row, a powerful bargaining chip in ultimate land settlements; and the dearly bought central market block plus the neighboring block of historic buildings just inland of it now belonged to Seaport Holdings.

And, in coming months, we came to learn that Alan Villiers's visit had helped us more than we first realized, as we followed up with such leading supporters as Rudie Schaefer and Jack Aron and began gathering in the funds to bring in our great ship *Wavertree*.

CHAPTER 25

The Seaport Plan, *Summer 1969*

Taking Counsels—Burl Ives Makes a Record—
Libertad Celebrates Fundamentals—
A South Street School—The Unpaid Bill

It was 29 May 1969, Slash Hammock Island, Cape Hatteras: Norma and I, with our eight-week-old, Robby, were on a four-day weekend with Sid and Eugenia Dean, where we spent our days on the beach— Sid swimming in the rolling Atlantic swell, which seemed his natural habitat, and Eugenia, Norma, Robby and I splashing about in the shallows, building sand castles or just sitting and admiring the sculpted Gulf Stream clouds that blew north along the coast. Now we were back in the sturdy bungalow that Eugenia had built in a secluded spot surrounded by trees and reached by a sandy trail off the main road. It was the grownups' hour, late afternoon when the day's rhythm slows and there is time for reflection and discussion.

And, as always, the talk veered around to South Street. Sid was particularly concerned about what he felt was the lack of an agreed, coherent plan spelling out what the Seaport had to offer.

"Sid, the ship will be the tallest thing in town," I was insisting. "Well, our part of town, anyway, and that's what counts. The buildings we're saving are around 60 feet high, and when we brought in the *Eagle*, her masts towered over them at more than twice that height. The *Wavertree*'s main truck will be even higher, and her presence will give a new identity to the whole neighborhood."

"It's not just the height of the masts," Norma added, "it's the uniqueness of them—the crossed yards, the shrouds—they're like a magnet to people. And the ship will be real, with a great story to tell about how our city was built. People *can* be drawn into that story—if it's done right."

"I don't mean to be a wet blanket," said Sid, "but people watch TV for hours on end, and you're not going to change that."

"Sid, it's our job to change that," Norma said. "You should see the crowds that come down to our events—parents with kids, single young adults, grandparents, all ages, all races—they're there because they want something more than TV, something *real*. Some are interested in crafts, some come for the traditional songs, others for the art. But most just want to see a working ship up close and to know more about them. They read the displays and you can watch the parents explaining to the children what they are seeing. Now *that's* success!"

"I don't disagree with a word you've said," Sid replied. "What I'm telling you two is that you have to put your ideas in a form that marketing people and investors can recognize and respond to. And you'll need this plan as well for the philanthropists who will fund projects like the *Wavertree*. In fact, the philanthropists I run across seem very interested in knowing how the Seaport will actually work."

We had other things to talk about on this visit, notably Sid's crusade for public access in the burgeoning cable communications revolution, which promised to open myriad channels to public participation in the discourse of our time. But his call for a studied statement of what the Seaport would be and how it would work stuck in our minds.

We began to think of what should be in the plan.

Two meetings shortly before our Hatteras sojourn had helped solidify our thinking on the plan. The first was a meeting of the Restoration Committee at 203 Front Street at which we went over the principles we would follow in restoring the Seaport buildings, and it produced some welcome adjustments in previous thinking. Since Sol Atlas was now prepared to cast in his lot with our plans, it was evident to all of us that we were doing more than going through a planning exercise. What we decided would affect what happened to the buildings and streets as the Seaport district took shape in coming years.

Jim Fitch, chairman, said he liked our picture of a new market building fulfilling the variegated functions of the original Fulton Market,
which had sold all things from plowshares to local farmers' produce,
from books to ladies' fashions and china imported from abroad in the
ships that lay across South Street at the piers. And in the excited discussion of how similar functions could be fulfilled today, Jim even allowed
that a traditional design, re-embodying the arcaded experience of the old
market, might be entertained—a change from his previous mandate that
the building must rigorously express the design concepts of our own day.

The second meeting was a gathering sponsored by the Municipal
Art Society later that same day, where I received an award for my work
in South Street. The presentation was made by Waldo Johnston of
Mystic Seaport, and after the meeting Waldo presided over a dinner
at Tavern on the Green in Central Park, where speeches focussed on
how to bring fresh life to the seafaring heritage. To a degree I had not
felt before, Waldo seemed to accept South Street Seaport as a valuable
addition to the heritage scene, rather than a distraction from the great
establishment of Mystic Seaport. He asked Norma's and my opinions
on plans for a major overhaul of Mystic's flagship, the whaleship
Charles W. Morgan. The discussion bore home to me that South Street
had begun to be accepted as a respected institution in the historic ships
movement in America.

At the end of June, Norma and I moved at last into the house we'd
bought in Laurelton, near JFK Airport in Queens. This modest house
was a place where we could set up our library and other belongings, in
view of Mr. F's intended move to Florida. This move, which he seemed
determined to make, entailed sale of the Yorktown Heights establishment, where we'd been living together. So, with the help of Norma's
sturdy young cousins, Michael, Peter, and Joe Donigan, we settled into
a new house and new neighborhood with our new arrival Robby, and I
was soon busy setting up bookshelves and establishing a study to replace
the one in Yorktown Heights.

Two days after this move we received a most welcome visitor in South Street, the folk singer Burl Ives. We had invited Hamilton-Madison House to bring down some children from the public housing just north of the Brooklyn Bridge to join him in a sing-along aboard the *Caviare*. Burl performed wonders, telling the children sea stories and getting them to bawl out the chorus to songs like "Bound Away to the Westward in the *Dreadnought* We Go," and "Spanish Ladies." Later, Burl recorded these and other songs for us in a record we issued before the year ended. The album, called *Songs They Sang in South Street*, had on its cover George Campbell's noble portrait of the *James Monroe* setting sail from her Beekman Street pier on the first sailing of the Black Ball Line to Liverpool in 1818. Members were delighted to have this musical magic carpet which brought the Street of Ships into their homes—particularly one elderly member, housebound in his small apartment in the Bronx, who wrote in to say that listening to the songs made him feel truly a part of the Seaport Museum.

A visit by the US Coast Guard's *Eagle* over the weekend of 18–20 July restored a welcome square-rig presence on the waterfront. And the following week the great Argentine full rigger *Libertad* arrived on 25 July for a ten-day visit. Commissioner Charles Leedham, who had replaced Herb Halberg at the Department of Ports and Terminals and who had earlier given us some trouble over bringing the *Caviare* into Pier 16 the previous autumn, sternly ruled against *Libertad* coming into the Seaport. The ramshackle piers and grimy old buildings of South Street, he maintained, just didn't convey the right impression of New York for distinguished foreign visitors. So *Libertad* was told to go to the West Side liner piers for proper accommodations and ready access to the wonders of Times Square. But the *Libertad*'s Captain Vazquez Maiztegui had ideas of his own on this, and the office erupted in cheering when I read out a reassuring cable from him, sent from the vessel's stopover in Bermuda a few days before she arrived. It read: LIBERTAD *WILL BERTH IN NEW YORK AT SOUTH STREET SEAPORT, NO OTHER PLACE.*

———————◆———————

This was quite likely the first time in history that a visiting foreign ship had gone against the wishes of officials of the receiving port. We regarded it as a strong testament of the seamanly, stand-together spirit that defies pettifogging jacks-in-office.

At our request, *Libertad* was carrying a highly unusual cargo to the Seaport: the shattered stump of the *Wavertree*'s mizzen topmast, relic of the ship's dismasting off Cape Horn in 1910. We had noticed the wooden remnant still in place in the mizzen doubling during our visit to the vessel in drydock in Buenos Aires earlier in the year. In response to my request that he bring the relic with him, Captain Maiztegui had sent me a cable acknowledging that he had received my proposal that he take a rotten piece of a broken mast aboard the beautiful, clean Argentine Navy ship *Libertad* to carry it to New York. He further wanted me to know that he, the officers and the crew of ARA *Libertad* would consider it an honor to undertake this mission as a testimony to the brotherhood of the sea.

That he meant every word of this was plain when, once the big white-hulled ship had put her lines ashore on Pier 16, an honor guard of sailors paraded the topmast stump ashore on a black-skirted catafalque made up for the occasion. We saw nothing excessive in this, for all Seaport members knew the *Wavertree*'s story, and regarded this artifact from her last battle with Cape Horn as authentic evidence of the violence of the storm that she had come through and the valor of the men who brought her through it. And for everyone, including casual visitors to the pier, this was the only tangible evidence of the Cape Horn saga which played so stirring a role in the story of South Street, and of the Cape Horn sailing ship we planned to bring back over time's horizon to tell that story.

Jakob came hurrying over from his office on lower Broadway when he got our call announcing the *Libertad*'s arrival, and coming aft to join Captain Vazquez Maiztegui and his officers in the main saloon, he brushed past wet oilskins hanging in the passageway leading aft. Learning that the big ship had had to shorten sail in a hurry when hit by a violent summer squall in the Lower Bay, an all-hands drill which the captain described after introducing his officers, Jakob fairly beamed. When it came to sail drill and ship-handling in high winds, he was in his element. Standing amid the young officers in the mahogany-paneled ship's saloon, Jakob gave a short speech of welcome which entered into Seaport lore. Explaining that South Street had once been crowded with square riggers, he said:

> This proud ship, with her able crew, delivers a message that explains what we are about in South Street Seaport Museum. We're not just going back to the past here; we are getting back to fundamentals.

This last phrase was one that would not be forgotten and became a byword among our members and volunteers.

During the *Libertad*'s visit, on 1 August, the Hudson River Sloop *Clearwater* put in for a three-day festival celebrating her arrival in New York. The big sloop and the great square rigger gave a grand feeling of connection to a wider world tied to New York by seafaring under sail—a subject dear to our hearts! This was also encouraging to our supporters, including Mayor Lindsay, who came down from City Hall to visit the two ships, and David Rockefeller, who attended a grand dinner aboard the *Libertad*, while Pete Seeger and the English chanteyman Lou Killen made the streets echo with their singing. And Bernie Klay, now working with his newly formed Seamen's Institute group, composed of Frank Woerner, John Townley and Dan Aguiar, sang their hearts out aboard the *Caviare* in a fashion that drove the shyest dockside listeners to join in the rousing choruses.

More, perhaps, than anything that happened in that eventful summer scene in South Street, the *Libertad* and her people made a deep impression on all of us. Her people talked about their ship and how they sailed her with a gay and debonair formality; a style contrasting strongly with the New Yorker's accustomed confrontational ways. This was an aspect of the Seaport experience I felt we should encourage in our work. Here on this storied waterfront we still met people we could learn from, people from distant lands and cultures, who had made a serious voyage to get here. We felt this at the dinner we held for Captain Vazquez Maiztegui and his officers at the New York Yacht Club, where talk of Argentine history and sail training practices flowed freely round the table accompanied by circulating bottles of red wine with which we toasted our guests and they us. And Seaport staff and volunteers reported the same easy back-and-forth in exchanges with cadets and crew on the pier and in the streets—even without the fine Argentine vino rosso.

While these ship receptions were going on, we in the Seaport were sending our own young people out to encounter different cultures in a voyaging experience in our schooner *Athena*. In addition to Sea Explorer Ship No. 5, which Charlie Dunn had set up with high school boys in Chinatown (whom he irreverently called his "Red Guards") we now had Girl Mariners Troop 3-74, in which Bob and Karen Herbert organized high school girls from the neighborhood. As the *Libertad* lay in South Street in late July, Bob and Karen were on an eastward voyage in *Athena* to take part in Gloucester's "Great Schooner Race"—an event at least partly inspired by our Seaport races. With the Herberts were their son Peter and his wife, Susan, who came up from Houston, Texas, to join them in this good work, adding a wonderful new chapter to the old schooner's story.

Norma and I got in little sailing in *Athena* that summer but did break away with our British crew for a memorable trip from Stonington to Block Island for the island's race week. Ellen Isbrandtsen signed on as chief cook and bottle washer for the venture. In Block Island Jakob invited us all for drinks aboard his sleek cutter *Good News*, winner of Class B in the Bermuda Race the year before. She was a vessel much changed from the classic 1930s racing yawl we in *Bloodhound* had raced against in 1952. Jakob had replaced her heavy teak decks with light, strong plywood and fiberglass and had installed a new high-aspect ratio single-stick rig to improve her windward performance. He waxed a little nostalgic (for Jakob) when he paid a return visit to *Athena*, slapping her stout wooden mainmast as he looked aloft to trace the lead of the multi-stranded halyards, and admiring the solidity of the many-columned bulwarks that fenced in her broad decks, hung about with the heavy rope coils the schooner rig demanded. I rather expected him to ask why we were dragging so much weight around, but out of sailorly courtesy he forbore to make any such comment.

As the eventful summer progressed, Norma and I found ourselves giving concentrated attention to the Seaport plan Sid had asked us to draw up. This took shape mainly on weekends and weekday evenings at our new house in Laurelton amid a sea of papers and drawings laid out on the living room floor, arguing out our purposes and how they should be expressed in the buildings, streets and activities that would fill them. George Demmy would join us when possible, engaging in the arguments, making sketches, and adding new perspectives. Looking at the sober pages of "South Street Seaport: A Plan for a Vital New Historical Center in Lower Manhattan," I hear again the voices of the Clancy Brothers singing "We're all bound to go," or Burl Ives, singing on our own Seaport record that classic sea song "Rio." We listened to these songs as we worked and sometimes joined in the choruses. I was later to learn that Sam Morison had sung sea chanteys to his wife's accompaniment on the piano, while he wrote his classic *Maritime History of Massachusetts*. We were determined, as he had been, to get the music of seafaring, the instinct for voyaging, the story-telling, and the salt tang of the voyaging experience into the plan—which we did not envisage as a blueprint so much as an invitation to revive a vital experience in the seaport origins of New York City.

The plan opened with a brief reprise of the inter-museum conference we'd held in November the previous year. Citing the participation of "museum directors, urban planners, architects, social critics, editors, historians, economists and educators," we boldly, and I think correctly, took off on our own. The plan would be a product of citizens rediscovering their heritage. It would be an account of our working plans as evolved on the site, advised but not dictated by expert findings and tested on the pulse of the city.

We then dove right into New York's seaborne origins, noting: "Our waterfront is where the action was." To that we added: "We see this not only in retrospect; it was seen at the time. The New York papers reported all that happened and ran editorials on important new ships." Ships, indeed, were the heart of our story: "Their fortunes were followed avidly by New Yorkers. The importance of ships on our waterfront can't be understood without knowing this." And this led to our central assertion:

> *In its essential shape, as headquarters for worldwide corporations,*
> *as the world's leading marketplace for money and ideas, as a major*
> *population center and receiving port for new people, and perhaps*
> *as a cultural capital and seedbed for new social and artistic ideas,*
> *in all its leadership functions, New York is a city built from the sea.*

And then we had things to say on the heritage of seafaring under sail, a vanished way of life "abounding in terms and ways of doing things that came literally from time out of mind," in a world where seamen "sang at their work, used words and speech patterns universal to all ships but incomprehensible ashore, and showed fierce loyalties...." We further noted, of the seaman's relation to the ships he sailed in, that "sailors noticed a ship's looks like a woman's, often chose ships for their looks, defended them publicly and cursed them privately, and knew their stories and their ways by heart."

We looked at both sides of the East River as our purview, and, to us, the changing tidal waters that swept gurgling past the hulls of the ships we had brought in, was a vital texture in the experience of the seaport. So also with the changing skies which stretched above our low buildings and open piers, and the weather which seems arbitrary when winds blow or rains pour down into the city streets, but perfectly natural when you walk out into it in open space. And our interpretation of the site we said, "should be casual, ordinary, almost accidental." We did not want the citizen's encounter with the city's heritage to be sold off in pre-packaged "lessons," but rather met as a challenge to that person's own awareness and learning. So, we said:

The visitor will not be invited to step into another century .... We
believe essentially you cannot make that step and that it is better for
the 20th century citizen with his idiom and his concerns to confront
honestly the relics, records and story of men who lived before his
time, of buildings that housed different trades and ships that sailed
in the winds and sunlight of another era in the continuing story.

Accordingly, our concrete plans opened with a map of the East River centered on the Brooklyn Bridge, with recommendations on the development of the waterfront of public housing stretching north of the bridge on the Manhattan side, and the Civil War-era warehouses of Empire Stores and the foreshore of Brooklyn Heights on the Brooklyn side of the river. These plans included beer gardens and swimming barges and a marina for visiting pleasure craft on the Manhattan side—which we pointed out would provide summertime employment for young people in public housing—and a mixed-use residential and shopping waterfront community on the Brooklyn shore, providing access to the Brooklyn Heights community, then isolated from the waterfront it overlooked, linked to South Street by a revived Brooklyn ferry. South along the Brooklyn shore we optimistically looked forward to continuance of the working piers that had been there in various configurations for over three centuries.

With this scene clearly established, we took up the block-by-block development of the Seaport itself, as a congerie of "small centers gathered round special interests." This included societies like the National Maritime Historical Society, if they decided to set up shop with us, the Antique Boat & Yacht Club, and the Ship Lore & Model Club, a venerable small outfit founded in the 1920s by the deepwater veteran and modelmaker Armitage McCann, which also included such mariners as the marine artists Charles Robert Patterson and Gordon Grant, and the Arctic explorer Captain Bob Bartlett. This was a salty group. McCann, Patterson and Grant had sailed in square riggers, and Bartlett's Arctic expeditions in the Gloucester schooner *Effie M. Morrissey* were world famous. Bartlett had hosted the club's meetings aboard the *Morrissey* when she was in port in Tebo's yard in South Brooklyn.

The idea of adding an oceanographic center to this heady mix was strengthened by the visits of two important oceanographic vessels. In May the oceanographic research ship *Kellar*, operated by the Military Sea Transportation Service, had visited the Seaport, attracting a lot of interest due to the new discoveries being made by exploration of the oceanic seabed—including the verification of the theory of plate tectonics, which showed that generations of schoolchildren who had noticed that South America looked very much as if it had once been joined to Africa were correct in their naïve assumption. The later visit of the unpowered submarine *Ben Franklin* in August had fueled further interest in this new global frontier, spurred by Dr. Jacques Piccard's report on his month-long underwater drift from Florida to Nova Scotia in this highly unusual conveyance borne on the favoring currents of the Gulf Stream. These visits suggested to us the idea of an oceanographic facility in the Seaport. Perhaps, we thought, the Lamont Geological Observatory—which maintained a former sailing ship continuously at sea in their distinguished program—might sponsor such a venture in public education. And indeed, we went on to pursue our interest in oceanography as a new frontier in seafaring, by holding a seminar toward the end of the year entitled "Oceanography: Science under the Sea." Cosponsored by the Mayor's Committee on Oceanography, this demonstrated a more than passing commitment to this important potential addition to the Seaport's planned activities.

We'd also had talks with Barbara Johnson of the Museum of American Folk Art to bring their marvelous and growing collection from its midtown headquarters to the Seaport, where individual arts and crafts would be celebrated. This fitted well with our interest in an individual, ruggedly independent, non-slick view of the world, where so much one saw in the city was mass-produced, extruded in sheets, or simply poured out like cement or the asphalt that covered the city streets.

Ted Stanley's commitment as president of Bowne & Co., printers and stationers in New York since 1775, to open an historic printing shop in South Street gave us a solid beginning in a most important craft and would, we hoped, attract other historic craft activities in the reborn Street of Ships. This important installation would come to pass and was followed by other retail shops, from a major art gallery to a working forge, which we were to open in the next few years.

And we'd long been dedicated to the idea of small independent museums in the Seaport area, perhaps one devoted to the Isbrandtsen story. As we had seen in Jakob's office, Charlie Lundgren's paintings, supplemented by ship models which reached from Dutch roots in medieval times to Denmark and then to the United States, did much to bring this family saga to life. We could not cite the Isbrandtsen collection by name, any more than we could the Bowne Printing Shop, because neither installation was yet ready to announce, but these two private efforts glowed in the sky over our plans, like the loom of distant lighthouses still over the horizon one can pick up in the night-time sky at sea.

We had a clear picture of how the New York State Maritime Museum should be set up in Schermerhorn Row, as the central feature of the district. We proposed creating corridors through the row by cutting arches in the separate building walls. Visitors would pass through, picking up the thread of a chapter-by-chapter presentation, while being invited to pause in any pool of special interest. A reading room was also in the plan, where visitors might gaze out on the river running before them, and the ships moored under their eyes, where written materials on the exhibits would be provided—things for the visitor to carry away, a vital adjunct to the museum experience, as we saw things.

The piers and streets we saw filled with color and movement, "with small boats, small shops, craft activities, small restaurants, oyster stands and the like." Without this clutter of lively, individual activities, we said, these open spaces "will become empty promenades, where the story of the tall ships may echo but the sense of things happening will be gone."

And we roundly announced our intent "to hammer out a South Street school of thought." We acknowledged the help of freely given counsel from expert sources, we said: "But we must also learn from our own story.

South Street Seaport exists today as the inheritor of an old story and as an experience to be tested on the pulse."

A contrapuntal chorus of developments on the ground accompanied our work as we put the finishing touches on the Seaport Plan. The *South Street Reporter* noted our interest in Peter Throckmorton acquiring the *trehandiri* (a traditional Greek schooner) *Stormie Seas* for his marine archaeological work in the Mediterranean; and news of the dismasting of the bark *Regina Maris*, our friendly visitor of two years earlier, off the Cape Verde Islands.

Four marvelous jazz concerts were organized on the pier in August by our young volunteers Mort Dagowitz and David Lutz. One of these led to a pleasing story in the *New York Times* which noted how "jazz floated out across a breeze-swept pier on the East River" as people "sat on the wooden planking, stretched out on blankets, or strolled around examining the unusual array of ships." One might have wished the ships got a bit more attention, and the Seaport Museum which brought them in, but otherwise our reaction was one of unalloyed delight that we had got even a jazz critic to notice what we were doing! And it was critically important to our mission to reach out to people who didn't know or much care about historic ships, and get them joining the action on the pier.

The "unusual array of ships" that month included, besides the great square rigger *Libertad,* the newly launched beautiful Hudson River sloop *Clearwater* and the oceanographic submersible *Ben Franklin*—which earned its place in the September *Reporter*'s headline: "Sails, Songs, Jazz & a Yellow Submarine." We did a great business in buttons showing the Beatles' yellow submarine of song, a tubby thing looking rather like the research submersible, but with a daisy growing from her conning tower.

Bernie Klay proved a great hit with his roistering Seamen's Institute singing on the afterdeck of the *Caviare* twice during the summer, attracting folk aficionados from the far reaches of the Bronx and Queens and across the river in Hoboken and Jersey City. There was a threatening moment in the career of his new outfit when the Seamen's Church

Institute threatened legal action to get them to quit use of their name "Seamen's Institute." The venerable Seamen's Church Institute, serving sailors of all nations who arrived in the port since 1829, felt this to be too close to their own time-honored name. I called the Rev. John Mulligan about this. I knew Father John well from sessions at the bar in the Whitehall Club, where he presided with cheerful benignity. He said he had no wish to go after Bernie's group, but his directors, a rather starchy group stemming from the old established shipping aristocracy of New York, deplored the association and wanted it ended forthwith. I told him Bernie had come up with the moniker "X-Seamen's Institute," and on this Father John said he would see what he could do. I knew that meant the deal was as good as done and asked Bernie to make the change to what was, actually, a more distinctive name.

All these and a myriad other concerns were drowned out abruptly as the summer ended, when I received a cable from John Lodge, United States ambassador to the Argentine Republic. It stated simply that unless we immediately paid the $60,000 bill we owed the Argentine Navy Yard there would be an international lawsuit embarrassing to the national interest. I had been awaiting some communication about this overdue bill—but certainly nothing like this!

The fact was that we were having difficulty meeting current expenses in New York, including a $50,000 bill for needed repairs the G. W. Rogers Construction Company had made to Pier 16 in the spring. Our trustee George Rogers, head of the family firm, had agreed to accept delayed payment, but the obligation to pay for the work, done at cost, was there, it had to be met—and we were going to be strained to meet it by year-end.

And Jakob was in no position to find more funds as his maritime empire teetered on the edge of bankruptcy. He had personally paid the purchase price of the ship and all the costs of making her fit for the 6,000-mile tow home. As that was being completed, with photos which we eagerly showed him, he decided to order the extra work needed to restore the ship's bulwarks and framing for the forecastle head planking. It was bad enough bringing the *Wavertree* into New York as a dismasted hulk, he said, but we really couldn't bring her in without restoring the traditional sailing ship profile of her hull.

It was not easy to raise money for a ship so far away—there was no way, for example, to explore the cathedral spaces of the untouched forehold, or to walk the quarterdeck with its great steering wheel and surviving teak railings, and talk of the many stories that had been enacted there, as we knew from Captain Spiers's narrative. Then there was the awkward fact that people had much rather pay to see something done to the ship than to pay outstanding bills for work already done.

I could see no solution to the money problem that confronted us. So I typed out a return cable explaining that we could not pay the bill at present but were working to do so. I explained that a pledged donation had failed to come through, and that the Seaport Museum was a fledgling organization founded two years ago to save the historic South Street waterfront in Manhattan. I said we had met our other obligations and were mounting a campaign to meet this one. I added that our membership now nearing the 10,000 mark was devoted to the cause, and I invited the ambassador to join our efforts with a contribution of $10 to the South Street Seaport Museum, marked "*Wavertree*."

CHAPTER 26

Wavertree Revisited, *Autumn 1969*

An Ambassador Signs On—Galbraith's Talk— On Deck in B. A.—Change of Flag— Tigre—A New Resolve

To my surprise and considerable relief, Ambassador John Davis Lodge replied to my cable with a brief message saying he was glad to have this account of our predicament and he appreciated my personal resolve to fight our way through it to honor our obligations in full. He would convey his understanding of the situation to the Navy Yard authorities and be back in touch on further measures that we might consider.

And, he added, he was mailing me his own check for $10 to support our campaign. This rather won my heart as well as my admiration for his style in meeting what must have been, for him, an embarrassing and annoying contretemps in inter-American relations.

After further exchanges, in which Lodge continued to show a resolute style, it was decided that a formal ceremony should be held aboard the ship putting her under the American flag. This might suggest, at least, a recognized purpose to clear her debts and move her to the United States. I certainly welcomed this, having at last acquired some understanding of the formalities so highly valued in Argentine circles and some appreciation of the value of symbolic proceedings in setting the stage for actions in people's mutual interest—even if no real action could yet be taken.

Of course it was necessary that I be on the scene to publicly accept responsibility for the ship in her new career under a new flag.

So, Wednesday evening, 19 November, I boarded a plane for Buenos Aires. Settling in for the eleven-hour trip southwards, I started reviewing the bidding on what had been a pretty difficult few months following our brilliantly successful summer season. Our operating income was rising and we could handle on-the-ground operating expenses, with the notable help of the Kaplan Fund, the State Council on the Arts, and a growing roster of corporate supporters. But such capital items as the pier repair and the *Wavertree* restoration were beyond our grasp. The plain fact was that we lacked the major donors to fund the awesome responsibilities we'd taken on.

Realizing at last that fundraising was a business with its own need for special attention and support to make it work, we'd retained Hank Goldstein of Oram Associates as fundraising counsel in October. Hank was a brilliant civic activist I'd come to know through the FDR-Woodrow Wilson Club when I lived on Manhattan's Upper West Side in a grand apartment overlooking the shining reaches of the Hudson River, which my former wife and I used for receptions to support reform causes. Hank was stunned to find how weak and ill-coordinated our Seaport funding efforts were, and after he'd organized a list of prospects, he got his aide Sieglinda O'Donnell, a vivacious, take-charge person, to sit with me and get me to make needed phone calls.

And so a remarkable event had been produced to gather new supporters. Jakob got his good friend Sven Hansen to hold a lunch for two hundred guests aboard the Incres liner *Victoria* and Joan Davidson got her friend John Kenneth Galbraith, Harvard's famous liberal economist and gadfly of the state, to speak on the Seaport cause at the luncheon. And this had duly taken place on Friday, 14 November, shortly before I caught my plane to Buenos Aires the following week.

Ken Galbraith had somehow come to believe that the Seaport buildings dated from the 18th century, rather than the 1800s. We discovered this error when I picked up this very tall, very good-humored gentleman in a taxi to take him from his hotel to the *Victoria* in her berth on the Hudson River's "liner row." So as we jounced along in the taxi, into which his long body barely fitted, he hauled out the notes for his talk and started marking up the papers to transform his description of Schermerhorn Row from a princely government venture in the royal colony of New York, to a fortress of brawling American capitalism feeling its oats.

And when Ken spoke, he paid cheerful tribute to the splendid luncheon, the crowded glories of the New York waterfront, and the variety brought to it by the ships that visited here in such magnificent array. He went on to say that the Seaport was being brought into being to celebrate the heritage of the harbor that linked the city to the wider world. And he noted with approval Jimmy Biddle's statement that the Seaport would restore some of the warmth and color that had been lost in the wholesale rebuilding of the city. The glories of Rome or Paris, he then observed, depended on princely patrons. But it was up to the merchant princes of today to honor the glories of New York, a city born of the sea. I realized that he had picked up this phrase from me, during our brief, jumbled taxi ride, only because he looked over at me with a lifted eyebrow as he said it.

The crowd, including me, went wild. Everyone in the *Victoria*'s palatial dining hall knew that Ken Galbraith pooh-poohed pomposity and pricked capitalist pretensions—and they loved hearing him challenge them to do something more than pretend. I don't know when I've seen so many pillars of the financial community sway like saplings in a flow of new ideas. Ken himself seemed pleased by the reception of his remarks and, as for me, I felt he had plumbed the depths of our purposes in South Street in this one swift, deftly managed visit. He'd made the visit to please Joan, who supported liberal causes through thick and thin.

We paid a price for our inability to follow up this brilliantly successful visit, just as we had after the visit of Alan Villiers a few months earlier. Yes, a scattering of business leaders enrolled as members of the Seaport Museum, but there were no major contributions. We had no organized follow-up plan for the visit, and no time to set aside to follow such a plan if we'd had one. The truth was that I just couldn't find the hours required for the careful cultivation visits needed to build a prospect's interest till he would consider serious support—a task made much more difficult by the unresolved situation of the Seaport land.

I had discussed the problem with Hank Goldstein, explaining that I really had to concentrate on plans for the future, mixed in with the lively on-site activities which were carrying a good word throughout the city and bringing us remarkable membership growth. And then there was managing staff and volunteers to keep these vital fronts moving forward. So in fundraising, we stumbled along, badly behind the need.

Mulling the quandary as the plane leveled out at 35,000 feet, I could see no clear course of action. Perhaps the channels by which incisive thoughts find their way to the front of one's mind were clogged with my resentment at having to be the one who had to tackle fundraising on top of everything else. Trustees who might have taken on more of this burden explained their lack of progress because, they told me, no one would contribute to a museum that wouldn't own its own properties until the air rights they carried had been sold. And that, in turn, couldn't happen until the City approved all the elaborate transactions involved—which approval was taking forever to secure. It seemed that only a few visionaries like Jakob Isbrandtsen, Jack Kaplan and Allan Schoener of the New York State Council on the Arts were prepared to commit serious funds at this stage.

These frustrations enraged me to the point that, while reviewing the situation with Norma while we walked down Peck Slip a week before leaving for Buenos Aires, I had turned aside to slam my fist into the brick wall of 236 Front Street—the building the mayor had dedicated as the first restoration project of the museum. This had broken a bone, so I had to wear a plaster cast on my right hand, which forced me penitently to learn to write with my left. Fortunately I had learned to do this in readable fashion by the time I boarded the plane.

This trip would certainly be anxious time, since I would be bringing only words and good intentions to a case which called for hard cash. My job would be to express the reality of our intentions and our commitment to fulfill them. So I resolved to slow down my hurried pace and somehow enjoy this next chapter in the history of our great ship. I couldn't help wishing Norma were with me, but, I reflected, the trip would be a break for her too. For it had begun to seep through my distracted brain that I had not been particularly easy to live with in these recent frustrating ragged weeks. I resolved to write Norma a good long letter as I dropped off to sleep anticipating the renaissance of good feeling that the *Wavertree* always awakened in our spirits.

———◆———

Wavertree, back in the water and gleaming in fresh paint with grey topsides crisply set off by a checkered gunport stripe, was a bit of a shock when I went aboard her with DeValle and Schkulnik next day. She was "bare, plain, terribly clean," as I noted at the beginning of my letter to Norma—which would be written in pieces over the next two days, since I would be back from this brief visit before anything I mailed could reach her in New York. The truth was that I missed the subtle burnt umbers, greens and reds of the exposed old iron, a patina built up during decades of exposure in all weathers, which had a shimmering quality and depth to it which had lasted on even after the hull had been scrubbed down, as when we saw it last.

And then, once aboard, one saw that the decks, which earlier had been broken up by deep sandbins, were now plated over for the ocean passage to New York, making one smooth flat surface nearly the length of a football field, while the elaborate network of pipes great and small that had filled the bins with sand slurry and pumped away the excess water, had vanished as if at the wave of a magician's wand, leaving nothing behind to catch and intrigue the eye.

So I wrote that we'd have to have big photo panels on deck to summon the image of the deck spaces of a working square rigger, and we'd need to find some meaningful clutter to kill the deadly monotony of that vast steel deck.

The next morning was Friday, 21 November, a balmy day in the Argentine springtime. The ship looked much less bare and deserted, as a remarkable assortment of people crowded the broad poopdeck to observe the change-of-flag ceremony. Proceedings were opened by Admiral Imposte, commandant of the navy yard, who formally introduced first Ambassador Lodge, a tall, commanding figure who struck me as a by-the-numbers type; then our good friend Captain DeValle, technical director of the ship's restoration to date (as he had been of the *Libertad*'s rigging in Argentina); and myself representing the new owners, South Street Seaport Museum.

DeValle was called on by Imposte to give a brief account of the ship's restoration, and Lodge then took over to give a crisp account of the importance of inter-American relations, turning to me at the end to hand me the ship's new registration papers under the American flag. He then pronounced that we could hoist the ship's new colors. An impressively large United States ensign had been provided by the navy yard, and I proceeded to hoist it to the monkey gaff which had been fixed on the mizzen mast for this purpose, while DeValle paid out the downhaul, which he hung onto so that the flag would be properly spread out in the light airs stirring that morning. I had been trained in the US Navy to hoist the colors swiftly and confidently into the sky. DeValle followed a different paradigm, and for some moments there was something like a tug-of-war between us—but the flag was finally hoisted. Looking up, I found myself moved to see the Stars and Stripes flying over this vessel which had traveled so far in space and in time to reach this moment in an Argentine navy yard.

The company then adjourned below decks to the ship's main saloon, in the cabins under the poop. Here I was asked to say a few words, so I launched into a one-sentence speech: "Almirante Imposte, Señor Embajador y amigos—me agradece mucho estar a bordo de esta barco entre esta distinguida tripulación." That I was happy to be aboard this ship in this distinguished company was perhaps an OK thought; but to hail them as amigos, or pals, and as members of a tripulación, or working crew, might well have been thought below the level of the occasion. There was, indeed, a pause of a few seconds' duration, and then Admiral Imposte applauded my little offering, clapping his hands and laughing. Ambassador Lodge followed suit, his modest chuckle breaking out into an honest New England roar of laughter as he looked around the crowded room. "The cabin fairly shook," I wrote to Norma that night, "and after that, in my opinion, the party became much more bearable."

Admiral Imposte came up to me to inquire how Norma was. She had been seven months pregnant, when he had had us to lunch in January. I explained that she was well and would certainly have been here, but the arrival of our baby son, who was doing well, had kept her away from this important occasion in the life of her big iron baby. I had never before risked this formulation of Norma's relationship to the ship, which she and I used in an everyday, affectionate way, and I rather feared for our standing in the eyes of Captain DeValle, but his eyes, I saw, were on the Admiral, who seemed to find this an amusing expression of regard for the ship. A strong feeling for the ship is a common bond among seamen. Imposte, DeValle, and Captain Vazquez Maiztegui were all of them seized of the age-old formulation of man's relationship to his ships, simply expressed in English as: "The ship comes first." That was certainly our motto as well, though we did our best to live up to it in different ways.

Alfredo Numeriani was on hand and inquired solicitously as to Norma's health, expressing his admiration for her in terms suitable for a romantic novel. He was delighted to learn that she'd had a son, whom he wished long life and good health. The meticulous DeValle had made sure Numeriani was invited to join us for this occasion, and Numeriani had accepted with a letter expressing his feelings for the ship. Captain DeValle later gave me this letter, which read:

> I am moved by the honor that the South Street Seaport has accorded me, through your intervention, since the historic memory of the ship makes a deep impression, and my soul, which is susceptible of every noble passion, is touched by your magnificent efforts and by my own modest but real contribution to the noble idea of the Museum.
>
> The perfect cooperation of both has borne fruit and soon the ship of these epic times will proudly display the flag that served as a defense for the free peoples of the earth.

Manuel Schkulnik, who had played no part in the ceremonies but had done everything to make the occasion come to pass, came over to offer warm congratulations after the leading actors made their departure, and he, with DeValle and Schkulnik's brother Alberto stayed on to toast the actual crew who had worked on the ship. I recited their names for Norma:

"Montenegro (by far the most interesting man who asked after you), a wonderful old sailor called Pedro, and the watchman, also called Montenegro, who regaled us with song." At length DeValle, Schkulnik and I retired from these pleasing scenes to talk over a late lunch, after which I disengaged myself to retreat for a nap in my room at the modest hotel Romanelli on Reconquistador Avenue. This was a little closer to the harbor and notably cheaper than the Hotel Dora on Florida, where Norma and I had stayed on our previous visits.

Stretched out on the hotel bed to think things over, I reflected that the *Wavertree*'s new registry was now accomplished, and the purpose of my visit achieved. Captain Vazquez Maiztegui had invited me round to his quarters next day to a late morning reception with his officers, whom we'd met during *Libertad*'s New York visit, and Ed Pierson of Moore-McCormack had invited me to lunch after that with a wealthy lady, Señora Victoria, who might be interested in the *Wavertree* restoration. Funding for this effort remained in a crisis state, whatever reassuring face we might try to put on the situation. But I had resolved to put this out of my mind for this visit—and I held to that resolve.

Nothing else was clamoring for my attention, so I decided to walk south to the La Boca district, which we'd found so attractive on our visit to meet its resident artist, Quinquela Martìn. Here, as I made my way to the waterfront, I came upon a restaurant called "Lubek," after the famous Baltic seaport and, liking its looks, I walked in to have dinner there, and to write up my notes on the day for Norma. "The quiet, dim lit back streets of the Boca are fascinating," I wrote, "but the main drag, a few blocks away from here, is indeed a drag—huge beer and dance halls and crowds of aimless youth." I spent a quiet hour or so thinking about the neighborhood and Quinquela's powerful, creative attachment to it, before leaving to wend my way back to the Hotel Romanelli in downtown Buenos Aires.

As I walked in the hotel door at about eleven I was joined by a man who recognized me from the television broadcast that had been made of the morning's ceremony aboard the *Wavertree*. He introduced himself as González and said he was interested in our quest for the ship's figurehead. I had mentioned on TV that the figurehead was missing, and that we were anxious to hear from anyone who had heard anything about what had become of it. The poet Pablo Neruda in Chile, where the ship had lain until Numeriani had her towed to Buenos Aires in 1948, had a great collection of old ship figureheads, but his agent had told us that he knew nothing of the *Wavertree*'s figurehead.

Sr. González told me he had been the sculptor for the *Libertad*'s figurehead, which showed he knew the rather special world of sailing ship figureheads. He steered me out for a beer in a nearby restaurant which I imagine he chose for its American look, but I told him it reminded me too much of Schrafft's, a genteel place for ladies' lunches in New York, so we adjourned to the nearby Bar Bar O—which was indeed more of a walk on the wild side, as suggested by its name. There we ran into a reserved chap named Kenneth Kemble Smith, curator of an art museum in an inland town, who professed an interest in our quest. He had with him a great bear of a man, Atilio Santiago Poretti, a retired navy captain who had commanded the *Libertad* and now worked for a salvage company on the River Plate. He sailed his own boat in the Buenos Aires yacht club races and was full of local lore on old hulls in service on the Plate, including a wooden tug built as a sailing vessel in the 1820s. This seemed a stretch, admittedly. But he also knew that the *British Isles*, famous for her punishing Cape Horn voyage of 1905 under Captain James Barker, had ended her days as a hulk in the Boca, the "Bay of Dead Ships"—from which we were now liberating the *Wavertree*.

The midnight hour having passed while we exchanged views on these matters, Captain Poretti proposed a toast to the memory of President Kennedy—since it was now Saturday, 22 November, the sixth anniversary of that terrible day of the president's assassination in Dallas. This held us in mournful discourse for a time, but it was succeeded by the restorative memory of this president who patterned his inaugural address on Pericles' funeral oration of two thousand-odd years earlier, and who had the grace to be disturbed by the roar he elicited from the crowd when he declared in Germany that he was a citizen of Berlin. And who, when asked how he enjoyed being president, said he really had no complaints, the pay was reasonably good, and he could walk to work each day. We were the last to leave the Bar Bar O when it closed in the small hours.

The next morning I had to step lively to make it down to Captain Vazquez Maiztegui's quarters, which I reached at eleven o'clock to find a very festive reception in progress with the ships' officers and their ladies in attendance, all in summer dress—and to learn that I was expected for lunch! With some embarrassment I had to explain that I had an important luncheon on ship's business, which everybody seemed immediately to understand—the ship comes first, after all, and when twelve o'clock rolled around Vazquez Maiztegui walked me to the door, putting great expression into that wonderful Spanish phrase, "mi casa es su casa,"—his house was my house. He also told me that his car would drive me to my lunch, and that I must keep the car and driver for the afternoon trip I planned to make to Tigre after lunch. He seemed pleased that I would choose a place of faded glories like Tigre, rather than the fashionable *avenidas* of downtown Buenos Aires, and said I must get a boat to explore the maze of waterways which wound through that wild marsh that fed into the broad waters of the River Plate.

Señora Victoria lived in a lofty, richly furnished apartment, and lunch turned out to be an elaborate affair. There was no real opportunity to appeal for funds to aid the *Wavertree* restoration, but knowing also that I did not want to offend Ed Pierson, I played what part I could, while Ed and his wife maintained a lively discourse on our South Street project, and the heartwarming cooperation we'd had from Argentine authorities in the *Wavertree* project. I was able to contrast this with an account of our confrontation with the new Commissioner of Ports and , Terminals in New York, who had sought to keep the *Libertad* out of South Street, as the reader is aware, but which was news to Sra. Victoria, who heard the story with appropriate shocked dismay—and genuine delight at Vazquez Maiztegui's spirited riposte. On this happy note I begged my

leave, explaining that Captain Vazquez had given me a car to carry me
to Tigre for the remainder of the afternoon.

Tigre was much as I had remembered it from Norma's and my visit
the year before, but its autumnal shades had given way to the light blue
blossoms of the Tipa trees and other flowerings of every kind. Only the
waterways retained their rich, dark mahogany color. The water was alive
with launches, rowing boats, and Italianate scows carrying logs and
other cargoes for people living on its banks. I found the scene seductive enough to lure me into hiring an elegant wherry. Shoving off in
this lapstrake varnished craft, I had fun practising my rowing stroke
with long racing oars, something I hadn't done since leaving the King's
College crew seventeen years earlier. Humming the lines from the Eton
Boating Song: "Twenty years hence this weather may find us on office
stools, we'll recollect our races, though they may call us old fools . . ." I
found myself immensely entertained pulling at the oars. I might have
gone on exploring this magic place forever but realized I should get
back to shore so the driver could get to his home while light remained
in the sky, and so put back for the return trip to the central city.

That evening, back in Buenos Aires, I was slated to dine with the
oceanographer, Hector Granelli, a friend of Manuel Schkulnik, who
wanted to discuss the idea of an oceanographic center in South Street
Seaport, which he planned to visit in March. He also told me his grandfather, an Italian, came to Buenos Aires to found a piloting business in
the River Plate.

The following day, Sunday, Granelli joined Schkulnik, DeValle and
me in a thoroughgoing inspection of the *Wavertree*. DeValle reviewed
every decision that had been made: which of the sand-conveying
pipes and pumps had been removed and sold as scrap; which had been
retained; and such fine detail as replacing the starboard finial on the
half-round molding that ran along the turn of the poop whaleback
duplicating the existing port-side finial.

After Granelli left us, we held a painstaking review of our plans
to pay the outstanding bill. This was difficult ground, because it was

impossible to pledge specific monthly payments, since our income did not come in assured predictable payments. All I could really do was recite the names of supporters and how we appealed to them. I went over the development work we had done with Alan Villiers's talks on the ship's behalf, the luncheons our trustees Briggs Dalzell and Eric Ridder held with supporters aboard the lightship *Ambrose*, and the grand *Victoria* luncheon of the previous week, where Galbraith had so winningly presented our case to the downtown business community.

Neither these efforts nor our work with the fundraising firm Oram Associates was satisfactory to the good captain, and I felt helpless to do anything more. Manuel Schkulnik, who had met our trustees and seen how the struggling museum worked, was more familiar with the citizen nature of our undertaking. He explained that the museum was no longer financed by its principal supporters, but depended on our continued efforts to keep it afloat with the help of volunteers and a small cadre of supporters. DeValle simply frowned at him as if he, too, were tainted with the crookedness he seemed to find in my explanation of the situation.

When we left the ship for a late lunch ashore, Manuel did his best to lighten the conversation with stories of difficult clients he'd had to deal with, and DeValle unbent to the point of saying he knew that I personally was doing my best—but the going remained pretty heavy. After lunch, Manuel offered to take me to his home to continue our discussions, but I said I had some work that needed finishing and it would be easier to do that at the airport, where I could be sure of catching my plane on time.

DeValle again assured me of his personal regard as we said goodbye at the airport, and I repeated my pledge that we would pay the ship's bill as soon as could raise the funds.

The solitude of long-distance air travel and its isolation from day-to-day affairs appealed to me greatly at this junction, and as the plane leaped from the ground, like a great winged monster summoned from some mythic past, I felt a corresponding rise in spirits. Looking down from my window seat on the flowering avenues and crowded docks and basins of the city fronting on the silvery expanse of the River Plate, I regained my idea of Buenos Aires as a place of good times spent with good friends. Someday, I thought, we must return here, Norma and I.

That day would come only when we had paid the money we owed. And we could pay the money only if the Seaport survived. Our friend DeValle's strained sense of honor over our unpaid bill didn't help us in this vital effort, but was certainly understandable. He'd risked his name and standing in the naval circles which were his world, and it was our job to redeem his faith in us. I raised an iced glass of gin to the shimmering broad expanse of the Plate, and resolved that the grand waterway, whose radiance was now dimming with advancing dusk, would yet serve as an avenue for the *Wavertree*'s passage to New York.

CHAPTER 27

Leaning Forward, *Autumn 1969*

*Brotherhood of the Sea—*Black Pearl *in the Schooner Race—*
*A Gateway to the Wider World—*Wavertree *Report—Capital*
Charges Build Up Debts—10,000 Members . . . and Counting!

The next morning, after a dreamless sleep on the long flight from the Argentine springtime to autumn in New York, I awoke to the sudden realization that something extraordinary had happened in the past few days in Buenos Aires. The fact is, we had won a considerable victory for the ship! Or rather, our friends had. The unpaid bills which we had no way of paying, the threatened international lawsuit that confronted us, and the breaking of all relations with people whose friendship we cherished—these horrors had simply been swept away. Moreover the dire situation that bred them had been replaced by one of mutual confidence, respect, and cooperation worthy of the fellowship of the sea.

It was plain how this transformed situation had been accomplished: it was brought about by the intervention of Ambassador Lodge, who had the confidence to make a solemn ceremony of our accepting ownership of the ship under the American flag; Admiral Imposte, who did not take his office lightly, who had made a parallel commitment with nothing in hand but a promise we agreed to abide by; Señor Numeriani, who, making his smiling presence felt, had left us a letter citing our peoples' comradeship in the defense of the West; and an assortment of supporting characters ranging from the dashing Captain Vazquez Maiztegui to half-doubting Captain DeValle—people with much at stake who had made our cause their own.

This was a challenge we had to meet—but of course it was also a source of strength. The cloud of witnesses that had gathered around our cause was owed to the brotherhood of the sea. That the ship comes first is the leading tenet of that brotherhood, and it was that sense of service to the ship which had earlier this year brought us Alan Villiers, great-est of the Cape Horn sailormen, and ultimately everyone else involved. And it was my job to accept that willing service and put it to work to work to pay the *Wavertree* bills, release her from the yard that held her, and bring her to New York.

A few days before I left for Argentina, we got the sad news that Charlie Dunn, our able, good-humored and endlessly supportive volunteer, died unexpectedly in his sleep at an early age, leaving a young wife and son. Distracted with the concerns of what I had expected to be a very fraught trip, I tried to put this to the back of my mind. But coming back to my office at 203 Front Street I reached for the phone to call Charlie to seek his counsel on what I'd learned from the trip. The realization that he would be answer-ing no more phones then struck me hard and saddened me anew. That he would not be there to offer his balanced opinion or to jump into the next project left a real gap in the life of the Seaport and the lives of all who knew him. What he left us was vivid, endur-ing memories of his forward-leaning stance in life.

Another gap in our ranks was much less dire, but was still regretted by Norma and me. Al Swanson had left us as ships and piers manager, returning to his family in Danvers, Massachusetts. This was the result of maneuvering by a new friend of the Seaport, Commander Ed Ferris, to replace Al with Ed's own services. He had lobbied with our trustees to take him on as a strong managerial type who could also help out with fundraising. Ed was a member of the New York Yacht Club and a veteran of the Royal Navy in World War II, which he had joined be-fore the United States had entered the war. He was willing to work for the same picayune salary Al worked for and to live aboard the *Ambrose* in the same Spartan conditions. And he had joined the volunteers in menial jobs on the ships and cheerfully joined the crowd at the Square Rigger of an evening. Responding reluctantly to trustee pressure, I'd hired Ed on to replace Al.

This proved to be a serious mistake, as volunteer morale sagged and performance dwindled. Ed's quarterdeck manner, while friendly enough, was simply no substitute for Al's close working relationship with the crew, which bred a different sort of discipline; one founded on mutual respect. When I let Ed go, he wished us good luck and fair winds, threw me a half-salute and walked out with his customary jaunty air. Al soon settled himself in Boston Harbor, living with his family in nearby Waban. Within a few years he achieved the position of harbor historian, while doing invaluable volunteer work for the National Maritime Historical Society.

Chi Ling took up quarters in *Ambrose*, working with Jim Diaz, so life on the pier resumed its normal course heading up to the schooner race held on 4 October this year. *Tyehee* crossed the finish line rail down in a good capful of wind, to win her third straight victory over the other gaff schooners. Our friendly rivals aboard *Tyehee* had towed *Athena* down from City Island for the race, our engine having given out. But despite it being her kind of weather, *Athena* brought up the tail end of the fleet, ranking eleventh out of fourteen starters. Barclay Warburton's brigantine *Black Pearl* won the loser's prize of a box of cornflakes and bottle of Beefeater Gin, no handicap proving sufficient to make up the deficit of sailing a square rigger to windward against a bunch of fore-and-aft-rigged vessels. It was a classic demonstration of just how the schooner supplanted the brigs and brigantines of the early 1800s!

In the marvelous winds that blew, the schooner yacht *America* provided a splendid spectacle of thundering white water breaking from under her elegant bows, sailing as a Seaport patrons' observation boat in a princely gesture by Rudie Schaefer. Our friends of the *Clearwater* were on hand as well, sailing their great sloop with its huge mainsail providing a sight not seen in the harbor in this century. We were proud of their company! And we benefited directly from the presence of *Miss Circle Line*, as the official spectator boat. The money she earned for us was welcome, as was the opportunity for our members to get out on the water and see things close up.

That evening at the race supper held at Whyte's Restaurant, Barclay's crew—the Black Pearl Singers—led the schooner crews in foot-stamping ditties. The following week, staff members were still whistling "Wild Rover," as noted in the *South Street Reporter*.

No one apparently noticed that the race was smaller than expected, but if anyone had asked, the reason for this was flattering to the efforts of those who had made our first schooner race possible in 1967. For Mystic Seaport had added their own schooner race in 1968, and this year two more schooner races had been added, in Gloucester and Chesapeake Bay,

This on-deck front-page story was followed by photographs of work on the *Wavertree* to complete the bulwarks and forecastle head. These finishing touches had been ordered by Jakob in late June; he was determined that the ship should come to New York showing her classic profile rather than the shorn hulk of an odd-looking sand barge. With these photos, we ran George Demmy's presentation of the plan for the inland Goelet block to round out the picture of the full Seaport development. George's drawing included the existing marine supply shop, a house museum, and an open interior court, entered by a passageway with a coffee bar on one side—"a pleasant place where one might stop for a cup of coffee," George's description noted, "and discover the charm of sloping roofs and brick walls."

But, we did not want the *Reporter*, our lifeline to the membership, to sag off into a mere recital of our museum concerns. We saw the Seaport Museum as a doorway to the wider world of seafaring—a doorway which our journal should hold open, inviting people to further exploration. So this issue carried a rousing account of the tumultuous career of the world's last true clipper ship, *Cutty Sark* of 1869, preserved in Greenwich, England. And to keep current with new ventures, it also carried a handsome photo of the paddlewheel tug *Eppleton Hall* of 1914, which Karl Kortum's sponsor Scott Newhall was bringing in from the River Tyne in northern England, on a 10,400-mile oceanic passage to her new home in San Francisco. Karl served as mate for the passage and brought us up to date on the 20-foot seas the small river tug had encountered in the Bay of Biscay, and of their safe arrival in the Cape Verdes. We were proud to have this live connection with the voyage and hoped our members might share a little of that feeling.

"Ports of Call," a column inaugurated the previous year by the ever-active Frank Braynard, was now crammed with items from all over, as our large and active membership fed us items ranging from a plan to rebuild the Brooklyn-built pilot schooner *Thomas F. Bayard* of 1880 and return her to Brooklyn (which did not come to pass), to the building of a replica of HMS *Rose*, the British frigate that was based in occupied New York during much of the American Revolution (which *did* come to pass, the redoubtable Captain Richard Bailey making some new history in his sailing of the new frigate over the next 30-odd years). In between were sandwiched such items as the layup of the super-liner *United States*, a waterfront restoration planned for the historic Fells Point district in Baltimore, and the unhappy news that the barquentine *Regina Maris*, our first square-rigged visitor, two years earlier, had been dismasted south of the Canaries (she survived, to enter a new career under another redoubt-able skipper, George Nichols).

These matters engaged us fully. It wasn't enough to sit and wait for news, you had to be out looking for it, tweaking our network, checking facts, and, in a number of cases playing a supportive role in the varied projects coming to life in our field.

That autumn Norma's parents came to live with us in Laurelton for the winter, since health problems made them unable to cope on their own in the old farmhouse in Yorktown Heights. And we went through the business of putting *Athena* to bed for the winter. With George and Ellen Demmy in crew, we had sailed her from City Island to Milford, her new winter quarters, the weekend before my trip to Buenos Aires. The weekend following my return, we went to Milford with the Demmys and our kids—Thomas, Carol and Tony, now reinforced by Robert—to remove the nonworking engine, unlace and pack away the schooner's heavy sails, and make all secure for the winter under a crazy quilt of various tarpaulins to keep snow and ice off the decks.

On the way back, we turned off the Hutchinson River Parkway to revisit Westchester Square, where we climbed out of our heavy-laden car to walk into Rocco's Chippewa Tavern. Rocco, Schultz and the regulars all welcomed us like long-lost friends, and we sat down around the familiar long wooden table in the back room to feast on spaghetti with heavy sauces, scallops and hamburgers, which we downed like people too long exiled from Arcadia. It was late by the time we'd dropped off the children in Manhattan and wended our way out to Laurelton, but Norma agreed that it was worth the trip to be so well remembered by friends from another chapter in our lives.

As the year drew down to its ending, our trustees met to review our situation in South Street. Everyone agreed that Mayor Lindsay's re-election on 4 November was good news for us, particularly since he had won in his own right as an independent, having been defeated in the Republican primary election by the conservative State Senator John Marchi, whom we also prized as a friend. But despite Lindsay's renewed mandate, the city bureaucracy was moving at a glacial pace to approve the detailed arrangements for the sale of air rights—a sale needed to balance Seaport Holdings's books and enable them to turn over the Goelet blocks to the museum. Our close relations with City Hall did nothing to change this bureaucratic logjam, which was like some primitive animal of immense mass, impossible to spur to a livelier pace, and equally impossible to shove aside so that the way could be cleared for action by others.

Another, really worrisome obstacle to acquiring the land was the cooling-off of the boom in New York real estate that had prevailed in recent years, and in Lower Manhattan particularly. Goelet had sold out to Jakob at the precarious crest of the wave. Except for the extra development rights which Atlas was going to need for his office building, now planned to be built in partnership with Seaport Holdings, there was no longer a live market for transferred air rights.

The attitude of our trustees was that these matters were exclusively Jakob's concern, since he had put up the funds for the whole Seaport development. And Jakob clearly felt, as usual, that the best defense of his deteriorating financial situation was a spirited offense. So he regularly reported to the trustees that the city's real estate market would revive, the newly reelected mayor would push things through the creaky city machinery, and we could look forward to the museum's being in full possession of the land within a matter of months.

There were things we all wanted to see happen, but to stake everything on that immediate accomplishment was unrealistic. I knew we needed an organized, energetic effort to get money coming in to pay for both the *Wavertree* and such capital developments as pier repairs which were vital to museum operations.

But it seemed to me that it would certainly help Jakob's position, as well as the Seaport, if we could organize a real effort to get money coming in to pay the bills. The trustees, however, didn't want to discuss the problem. Let Jakob tackle the overriding problem of the Seaport land, meanwhile we should stave off any creditors as best we could—that was the message.

The rest of the financial picture, the on-the-ground, day-to-day operations, was in good order, despite the uncertain waters we were sailing. Total income for the year was headed toward $400,000, as against $301,000 the year before. This more than covered the year's operating costs. But the capital costs of over $250,000 were simply beyond our ability to pay. As a result, we were left with over $150,000 in bills still outstanding, including $54,000 owed to George W. Rogers Construction for rebuilding Pier 16, and the Argentine Navy Yard bill of $65,000 for work on the *Wavertree*. (These figures include accrued interest beyond the basic charges reported in Chapter 25.)

Presenting this general picture to the board, I found that the trustees were not interested in these small-business problems. After all, if the land deals worked out (that is to say, if the air rights could be sold and the land conveyed to the museum) these petty numbers would be swept away and thrown out with the morning trash. I did come out of the trustees' meeting with a firm determination that we would have to find some on-the-ground solutions to make it through the coming year 1970, and on to whatever the future would hold.

On the whole, we were fortunate in our trustees. Jakob was a chairman of true vision and deep-seated values vital to the Seaport cause. Eric Ridder and Briggs Dalzell shared those values, believed deeply in the cause, and did everything to encourage those working in it, staff and volunteers alike. Joan Davidson and George Rogers, from utterly different worlds, did great things for us in their fields, as, certainly, did Joe Cantalupo, who had a wonderful grasp of the dynamics, the aspirations, desires and abilities of our membership. I found myself listening with great care to Joe's words on this subject, and indeed took to writing them down to pass on to others. To add to these assets, we had planning guidance from Melvin Conant, who had the saving grace to realize that the most carefully crafted plan often did not survive an encounter with untamed wild reality, or, for that matter, creative impulses which draw strength from new understandings of that reality. And we had great potential strength in Ted Stanley's plans for a working reproduction of the historic Bowne Print Shop and his advocacy and financial support for the whole Seaport effort.

This was also true of a new trustee, Harold R. Logan, chairman of the board of Grace Line, whom Jakob had brought aboard to strengthen our ties with the shipping industry. Hal Logan showed an immediate understanding of the on-the-ground needs of our fledgling outfit and had enough confidence in its future to give us the original desk of the founder of Grace Line, W. R. Grace.

William Russell Grace, who served twice as a reform mayor of New York, emigrated as a child from Ireland to Chile in the wake of the Potato Famine of the 1840s. He launched his maritime career rowing a chandler's boat in the great Chilean seaport of Valparaiso. He then followed the sailing ships he served to New York, where he soon began chartering tall Down Easters sailing from South Street in the Cape Horn trade. His story was very much part of our story, as was his sense of public service and his conviction that people should be encouraged to take "joy in the work."

A special Seaport edition of the Grace Line newsletter set forth Hal's reasons for the Grace commitment to the Seaport in a way that went to the heart of our concerns:

> *Yes, the Seaport will bring new tourist money into the City and certainly, it will be a fitting memorial to the past. But to me that isn't the real point. The real point is that it will bring people something they need now as never before: roots and pride.*

And the Grace Line newsletter bore out this humane approach, saluting 83-year-old Cape Horn veteran Fred Harvey, who had sailed as boatswain in the famous Down Easter *Shenandoah*, and the volunteer school guide George Swede, engineer on New York tugs, who had retired in 1968, stricken with cancer, and decided to devote his final months to "doing something important." An editorial encouraged people to visit and contribute to the project, and many Grace people did make the trip up from Grace headquarters at 3 Hanover Square to 16 Fulton Street to join us in our work.

This strong affirmative commitment to our plans and to the way we were endeavoring to carry them out cheered us all. And grim as the funding prospect seemed, when I came to write the annual report for the year, this is how I described the situation:

> *Delivery of the land by Seaport Holdings to the Seaport Museum was delayed by extensive negotiations with the City over transfer and sale of disposable air rights from over the low-rise historic buildings to neighboring office buildings. These matters continued in negotiation into 1970.*

But coming into 1970 we carried forward one vital, growing asset; the membership that had carried us forward so far and would work further wonders in years to come.

On 12 January the Seaport signed up its 10,000th member, an un-precedented enrollment for any cultural institution in New York. And this was still an outfit which existed mainly in the dreams of its members.

But 10,000 members! In the January *Reporter* I reflected on this landmark achievement:

> *Confronting 10,000 members, we don't think we're a mass orga-nization; we certainly hope not. What happened on South Street in the past helped shape our city, and its story helps shape lives today—you can see it in the face of a child as he learns that men fished out of sight of land in our small schooner* Caviare . . .
>
> *We think our members come in one by one because history concerns us all, even as we lead individual lives.*

And with the brio that came with knowing we'd survived another year and achieved another significant first in our field, my *Reporter* editorial concluded with a toast:

> *Here, then, to our next 10,000 members—one by one!*

CHAPTER 28

Sea Day Ushers in a Fair Tide, *Spring 1970*

The Wavertree *Story—Stobart Paints her Portrait—*
Seafarers' Rendezvous—Ambrose Reception—
Helen Hayes—Staten Island Landing—Sea Day

We couldn't resolve the financial predicament that confronted us as 1970 opened just by studying the problems. The problems, as Winston Churchill once famously observed, could speak for themselves. What we needed to do was to change the situation by considering our assets and putting them to work to generate new funding. Accordingly, I spent New Year's Day with our fundraising counsel Hank Goldstein reviewing our strengths. Just what were our leading assets? The Seaport land wouldn't be an asset until the day we had it in our possession—a day which many believed would never come. Our great asset, besides the intangible asset of public interest and support, was the ship *Wavertree*.

Wavertree was still thousands of miles away, and no one in the New York scene could feel the mighty presence of her sea-cleaving shape—the presence which led local boatmen in Argentina's Riachuelo to hail her stripped-down hulk as *el gran velero*. The previous summer, when the tall ship *Libertad* had brought in the shattered stump of her mizzen topmast, a spar carried away in her dismasting in a Cape Horn gale in 1910, this helped establish the reality of the ship and her adventurous career, but this reached only a few. Those who got that message would have to spread the word to get others involved in funding the ship's return to New York.

And to spread the *Wavertree*'s message in some depth we of course we had our book on the ship, *Wavertree: An Ocean Wanderer*. Published in May 1969, this volume gave an on-deck picture of the ship and the world she sailed in. Led off by Villiers's resounding foreword, its contents featured a young man's scrupulously kept journal of the ship's last completed deep-sea voyage, from the American Northwest around

Cape Horn to England in 1907–08. This yarn by A. G. Spiers, a retired pilot who now lived in Australia, had appeared in print too late for the Villiers visit, but his foreword to the book enabled people to re-visit an occasion that would be remembered by everyone who attended Villiers's talks. I remembered familiar faces from these talks, R. J. Schaefer, Hal Logan of Grace Lines, the coffee importer and ship lover Jack Aron, and others who might relate directly to the ship. Their fresh interest, I felt, might do more for the ship than we found in trustees worn down through boardroom discussions in which *Wavertree* appeared as a threatening liability, rather than the priceless asset she could be.

A good many people had been involved in producing the book, a product of the Kortum network which had led to his discovery of the ship in the first place. The Spiers narrative had been discovered through this network of old sailors and ship lovers, which, activated by a call for *Wavertree* memories, led to the maritime collector A. D. Edwards in Australia reporting to Kortum's sage advisor Captain Klebingat in Oregon that Edwards's friend Captain Spiers, a retired harbor pilot, had written a lively account of his passage in the ship over half a century earlier. A whole gang of us, led by the immensely talented volunteer Ernie Blau, were then involved in producing the resulting volume in hardbound format, along with a paperback edition. The book presenting the Spiers narrative came to include seafaring photos from half a dozen countries, with illustrations by Os Brett, and plans by George Campbell, architect of the *Cutty Sark* restoration. Charlie Dunn added to this a record of all *Wavertree*'s voyages, based on reports to *Lloyd's Register of Shipping*, supplemented by newspaper reports, and accounts of different people who knew her, through to her dismasting in 1910, and subsequent career as a barge for wool storage in Punta Arenas, Chile, and a sand barge in Buenos Aires, Argentina, followed by her short tow down the Riachuelo to the navy yard two years ago to begin her refit for the long tow to New York. Charlie lived to see the work published, though he never saw the ship he'd done so much to memorialize. The subtitle of the book, *An Ocean Wanderer,* came, it will be remembered, from Captain Thomas Thomas, a veteran in square rig who, having known the ship under sail, had given us this wonderful phrase to describe her career in the closing days of sail.

After my day reviewing the story of the ship and her people, I began to think that our funding task wasn't really a matter of our need for money, but rather people's need to know what this ship and her people had to offer.

It seemed to me we should stick to fundamentals in telling our story of the ship and the heritage she represented, and it seemed best to strengthen our creative work and public programs, building on those sound foundations. We had always known that the arts were a vital aspect of the heritage we worked to give fresh life to. We carried prints of the paintings of Anton Otto Fischer and Charles Robert Patterson, in our headquarters shop at 12 Fulton Street, along with books of John Masefield's poems and the novels and essays of Joseph Conrad, and histories by Bob Albion, Sam Morison and Alan Villiers—works which we discussed and argued over aboard our ships and in our hallways and in the streets and nearby pubs. By year-end we were to have our own spacious bookshop at the corner of Fulton and Water Streets, and we were soon to be involved in active open-air theater on Pier 16 under the patronage of Helen Hayes, New York's first lady of the theater.

As for song, from our first year Pete Seeger had sung to our crowds, followed by Burl Ives. They came because they sought out authenticity and liked what they found in South Street. These troubadours of the folk music heritage were soon followed by Bernie Klay and the X-Seamen's Institute, and the Clancy Brothers who came to South Street with Barclay Warburton's Black Pearl crew and were followed by the English chanteyman Lou Killen and our own shipwright Richard Fewtrell. I remember feeling at the time that we were singing the Seaport into being. And so perhaps we were, for while our voices were raised together we felt a force that drew people into our work.

The arrival of John Stobart, the British artist who had landed on our doorstep during the landmarks battle of late 1968, served greatly to deepen our engagement in the life of ships and people where the city meets the sea. This encounter he describes in the introduction to this book as changing the course of his own life as an artist. But this change depended completely on his own keen appreciation of life and what it has to offer. Our Seaport venture had become a place where people who knew seafaring as an elemental, visceral experience gathered to celebrate the sailing ships that once coursed the world's great and narrow waters. From his earliest work as an artist, John had been attracted to these wind-driven ships that had vanished over time's horizon. After training at London's Royal Academy Schools, John earned his way painting the big steamships of major shipping lines, whose departures for far horizons he had watched as a youth. In search of new horizons in his own life, he then moved to Canada, where he spent a year working with Alan Howard, curator of the Toronto Maritime Museum, soaking in an intimate knowledge of ship models and written records of the ships of the era of sail.

In the course of this quest of a vanished age, John learned to make painted surfaces express his own feeling for the heave and yaw of a ship making her way through the sea, driven by winds one could almost feel as a physical presence in the divided habitat of sea and sky in endless play together. On his first trip to New York from Canada in 1966, John, with his aptitude for making his own luck, happened to find himself seated next to the noted art critic and editor Donald Holden. Holden first looked at John's work out of politeness but soon realized that "the paintings were extraordinary . . . and the artist was clearly a master of his subject." John's hours engaged with the ship models, records and curatorial resources of the Toronto Maritime Museum—encouraged by people willing to go out of their way to help his quest—had certainly paid off. Holden went on to note:

> *But these haunting images were more than brilliant works of*
> *documentation. They were filled with magical light and atmo-*

sphere. The sea and sky were luminous and transparent. The paintings communicated a wonderful sense of space. They conveyed the sounds and smells of ships, docks, seaside buildings, the sea air. They had poetry.

This is what John brought with him to America, where he moved after his first exhibit at New York's Kennedy Galleries sold out in 1967. He then took up residence in nearby Darien, Connecticut. There he brought the small harbor at Ring's End Landing into new prominence as the forgotten sailing ship seaport it had once been. And what he took away from his first visit to South Street, as he explains in his introduction to this book, was a new recognition of the intimate interrelationship of sea and land in seaport communities.

In his introduction he marks a tideline in his life, where, sitting with seamen in the Square Rigger bar, he went through the act of getting the *Wavertree* under way on a mad March day with the wind caroling through the rigging and the harbor seas yelping after the big ship's passage. The city she was leaving was an embracing part of the scene. Harbor craft went about their errands, while the tug assigned to tow the big square rigger scurried out of the way to avoid being run over. This effort reflecting seamen's comments and stories became John's passport to a society of working ship crews, an experience that deeply humanized the harbor scenes that from now on were his leading specialty.

Fortunately, this *Wavertree* painting was one of John's first to be reproduced as a fine art print—and that print did wonders for us in conveying a feeling for the life in the ship now lying at the Seaport pier. I remember sitting with John as he signed copies of the print to be given to the Seaport Museum for sale. How happy we all felt to have this terrific work to tell our story!

Other artists, led by John's friend Os Brett, did much to elaborate the story of the windships that bound New York to the world and the world to New York, so he, from the beginning, found good company in a growing artists' community in South Street. John's work went on to achieve a new national recognition for an art form that had languished in backwaters of public interest, but which now set sail for far horizons—a new departure perfectly expressed in this painting of the *Wavertree* outward bound.

Museum activities continued through the winter months reinforced by our resolution to stick to fundamentals. Once again we were strongly represented at the Boat Show, held in midtown in January, signing up new members with the cheerful "come along" spirit only volunteers can bring to the task. Then on 19 January two of *Caviare*'s dories, refitted by volunteers, held a race in Fulton Slip—a trial of strength between British and American merchant seamen crews which ended in victory for the Brits, after the American crew swamped their boat in the icy waters of the windy East River. Roger Campbell, a lead volunteer— son of George Campbell, the British naval architect for the *Wavertree* restoration—a thoroughly Americanized young man and Vietnam War veteran, reverted to his British allegiance to come up with the perfect victory paean:

Today the dory race, tomorrow the America's Cup!

Roger's exquisite craftsmanship, evident in his restoration work, was but one facet of an ebullient personality which flashed in coruscating wit and irreverent defiance of the rules and regs which confine most of us.

Our monthly seminars opened in January with Jerry Allen speaking about her recent book *The Sea Years of Joseph Conrad*—a fascinating account of old records and interviews with old hands in Atlantic and Pacific seaports to identify the ships and people the great novelist encountered in his seafaring career. In contrast, the following month Stanley Haas, project manager for the first commercial voyage through the fabled Northwest Passage, told how the tanker *Manhattan* had been rebuilt in Brooklyn to force a passage through the Arctic ice cap in 1969 and so make the trip around the top of North America from the Atlantic to the Pacific. For the first of these lectures (which we called seminars to encourage open discussion) we had Ms. Allen's wonderful book on Conrad as a text; for the second, we produced a special booklet, *Northwest Passage: the Manhattan on the Tides of History*, which traced the 500-year quest for a short passage to the Far East over the top of the world to replace the long passage around Africa or the long and dangerous passage round Cape Horn. In the March *South Street Reporter* I cited this publication and others we planned, remarking:

> *These little booklets should enable people to walk into the South Street story by the door that interests them, stay awhile if they will, and perhaps come back another day if the talk and the company seem good.*

Next in line was a publication we called, with what we hoped was disarming casualness, *South Street Around 1900*. This photographic exploration of the South Street scene seventy years ago was made up of 30 photographs made from wonderfully clear, detailed glass-plate negatives taken by Thomas J. Kennedy, a stroller on the Street of Ships before our time. The pictures had been recovered for us by volunteers in Bowne & Co., who found a box of the heavy glass-plate negatives about to be thrown out of a Bronx apartment closet. From these we created an exhibit in the *Ambrose* tweendecks, so a visitor to the Seaport piers could step aboard and view the scene outdoors as it appeared when sailing vessels still held their own with the steamers on the Street of Ships, and Fulton Market fishing vessels still sported lofty topmasts, just before the internal combustion engine transformed the fleet forever. With *South Street Around 1900* the visitor could walk away with a modest-priced and informative memento of what he'd seen.

The *Ambrose* was also essential to our efforts to engage supporters and bring them further into our story. On 16 February, a month before the Kennedy pictures went on display, a reception was held aboard, at which the museum was presented with Charlie Lundgren's evocative painting of the *Caviare* airing her mainsail at Pier 16 with her neighbor *Ambrose* across the pier and a George W. Rogers derrick planting new pilings at the pier end. We asked George, who knew everyone on the waterfront, to be chairman of the event, and with a bit of brass and luck we were able secure David Rockefeller as cochair.

Rockefeller, chairman of the Chase Manhattan Bank and of the Downtown-Lower Manhattan Association, had led the financial community's resistance to the South Street project, as reported in the *Times* more than three years earlier. Ultimately responsive to widespread public sentiment, Rockefeller had followed the recommendation of the Association's executive director, L. Porter Moore, to approve the project. But I felt we really needed the man's personal interest, which was another matter. Jakob saw David now and then on Seaport business, as did Eric Ridder. But this, we felt, was not enough to convey a rounded picture of the Seaport.

So, feeling he might be intrigued to hear from the person running the project that had attracted so much press coverage in his backyard, I sent him a handwritten note inviting him to join us as cochair of the *Ambrose* reception. He promptly accepted and, although some trustee feathers were ruffled at my direct approach, the reception went smoothly. At one point, when I had left David in Jakob's care in the *Ambrose's* ward room, one of the two aides who accompanied him sought me out to say Mr. Rockefeller wanted to see me right away.

When I reached the wardroom, David raised a cheerful hand to beckon me over. He told me that he was confused by the nature of the reception. He saw many people he knew, he said, but a great many who were completely unknown to him. Oh, I said, that's easy to explain. Part of the crowd were Seaport supporters and people we hoped would become supporters. The other half were volunteers who donated their services to chip paint, escort school groups and run our public programs—services which kept our ships open and made the Seaport a living, contributing presence in the community. David smiled at this answer, and nodded that he understood, as I believe he did.

Word of the event traveled, and after this we felt an improvement in the attitudes of the business people who from time to time would stop by at 16 Fulton to see what we were up to.

However, we were still hamstrung by the unsettled land arrangements and not at all helped by news of the sagging economy of the city.

When our first general membership meeting was held at 203 Front Street on 19 March, there was still no progress to report in meeting the *Wavertree*'s overdue bills. My report to the members in the May *Reporter* carried the headline "Seaport at a Critical Hour."

Facing the prospect of financial collapse due to bills we could not pay, we resolved to keep our members involved in developments in the wider world of seafaring, keeping with our philosophy that the sea is one. In our work with history and historic ships we had become in- volved early in the year in Karl Kortum's project to bring the paddle- wheel tug *Eppleton Hall* from the River Tyne in the north of England to join the fleet of historic ships Karl had been assembling in San Francisco. The launch of this unprecedented voyage had been specially noted in the past autumn's *Reporter*. The old tug Karl had reached out to pull across an ocean to add to his fleet was a survivor of the paddle- wheel tugs which had towed big ships to sea for most of the 1800s, a breed of which there were no surviving examples in the US.

Our policy of widespread reporting paid off when our West Coast members began sending us unsettling news about the impending recep- tion of the tug in San Francisco. Karl's sponsor Scott Newhall, manag- ing editor of the *San Francisco Chronicle*, had taken six months' leave of absence to bring in the tug, and the rival *San Francisco Examiner* had run a cartoon showing Scott as a wealthy playboy towing his toy tug on a string. Worse, a grand jury investigation had actually been launched to look into Karl's joining this "yachting stunt" while on the City payroll.

This news worried me enough to call Dave Nelson at the museum office. No, no, Dave assured me, don't worry, it's just the usual San Fran- cisco politics. But as I looked at successive reports in the papers, I began to think otherwise. Finally I called Jean Kortum, with apologies for bothering her about this matter.

"Don't apologize, Peter," said Jean in her forthright way. "The wolves are gathering, and there's a concerted campaign going on to get Karl out of the museum. Anything you can do would be appreciated."

That was enough for me, Norma and the rest of our gang. We set to work forthwith on a letter-writing campaign—each letter individually written to Mayor Alioto, each saluting him for his interest in the voyage. My letter opening the campaign got a printed form response, as did Dick Rath's follow-up. But by the time my aunt Alice wrote from her 38th Street apartment, she got a "Dear Miss Taylor" response signed by an aide assigned to the case. In the meantime, Mayor Alioto had also received a passionate letter from Peter Throckmorton in Greece, a solemn appeal from Howard Chapelle at the Smithsonian Institution, and supportive words from shipping magnates like Admiral Will and leaders of labor unions like the National Maritime Union. We could feel the ground shifting as we looked at clippings from the West Coast papers. Herb Caen ran an item in his column in the *Chronicle* saluting the "new Argonauts," and quoting a letter I'd sent him in which I said:

> *This is surely one of the most remarkable voyages of our time, made in a ship that was never designed to go to sea. An epic achievement, worthy of the hardy men who founded your city.*

Karl had once told me that a mention by Caen was worth more than the most favorable editorial. There must have been something to this, for on 24 March, when the *Eppleton Hall* arrived in San Francisco, Scott, Karl, and the rest of the crew were stunned at the reception they received. Fireboats and yachts turned out to escort the sea-worn tug through the Golden Gate; a crowd estimated at 11,000 filled the pier where she tied up; and the mayor with the Board of Supervisors came aboard to congratulate Scott and Karl in the tug's old-fashioned pilot house.

This considerable effort by our was made by our members for others, even while our own existence was imperilled. I felt then and feel today that the *Eppleton Hall* campaign strengthened our organization. Every member who wrote a letter could take credit for the success of the effort and for furthering the larger cause we served, the cause of American seafaring. That, in turn, strengthened our hand immeasurably for the daunting tasks ahead.

Another development in this same month that certainly helped us along was Helen Hayes, leading lady of American theater, coming down our way as part of a tour of remembered high spots and odd corners of the city she was making with her friend Anita Loos. Their discovery of the museum gallery at 16 Fulton Street, which they came across while walking through the old buildings of the Fish Market precinct, was written up by the irrepressible Ms. Loos in *Twice Over Lightly*. This lively memoir recounts the ladies meeting Val Wenzel, senior volunteer at 16 Fulton Street, who explained how in the fledgling museum, "I found something to fill my entire life." Ms. Loos notes how Val's account of his work at the Seaport thrilled Helen:

> *"Sometimes," she exclaimed, "I think our whole city is the product*
> *of these magnificent obsessions."*

In that brief statement Helen Hayes surely captured much of the magic of New York, and also the compelling strength of the dream of tall ships in South Street. The two ladies went down to the pier to board the lightship *Ambrose*, where Ms. Loos, who made satirical fun of the high life in such works as *Gentlemen Prefer Blondes*, was impressed by the near-perfect restoration our volunteers had achieved in the *Ambrose* cabins, comparing them favorably to the ocean liner accommodations with which she and Helen were familiar. Still more encouraging was Anita's reaction to the other volunteers she met aboard:

> *When Val took us up to the forecastle, we were introduced to three*
> *exceedingly handsome young men. We learned that they worked*
> *as ship custodians and guides for sightseers, even serving them*
> *with a hospitable cup of coffee. They work for the same salary that*
> *Val earns as a historian—nothing.*

"Their recompense," she adds, "is contact with the sea, for which they, too, have an obsession." The young guides whom Anita had so warmly described were indeed real, and doing their jobs. They described the museum's plans to bring in the *Wavertree* and other ships. On the strength of this meeting Val signed up both Helen and Anita as members. On parting, Anita notes that "our new, and now permanent friend Val" snagged a taxi to return the pair to their own "effete territory." Indeed, Helen went on to become cochairman, with the mayor's wife, Mary Lindsay, of Theatre Research, a group that put on regular dramatic performances beginning that same year on Pier 16 under the direction of Jean Sullivan and Michael Fischetti. And Val Wenzel comes into Anita's book again at its ending, leading the cast of characters the two decided they would stay in touch with.

On our own domestic front, Norma and I had agreed with Mr. and Mrs. F to move back to the house in Yorktown Heights together. So we made needed changes to the house, converting one bedroom into a library/study on the second floor and the lofty attic into two bedrooms for us and Robby on the third floor. Patient friends in the *Athena* crew pitched in to help this considerable move, and I kept up with South Street business by phone and unending correspondence. We had grand plans afoot for the most active summer season yet, including activities outside South Street itself, the first of which would be a real coming-together on Sea Day, our term for National Maritime Day, celebrated on 22 May as a maritime industry affair.

And Sea Day was indeed one for the books. We sailed *Athena* from Milford to the Isbrandtsens' waterfront house in Riverside, Connecticut, where we stopped for the night to join in celebrating Ellen Isbrandtsen's 21st birthday. We moored alongside Jakob's towering new sloop *Running Tide*, a long-legged beauty which went on to win Class A in the Bermuda Race the following month. The next day *Athena* motored on in calm, rainy weather, through Hell Gate and the upper East River, to reach the Seaport Pier at the end of the day. People were delighted to see her again, knowing her leading role in the Seaport story. On the following Friday, 22 May, a crew of twelve boarded the old schooner. I asked the crew to sign the log on this occasion, and besides myself, I find the following: Jakob's aide for Seaport real estate, Bob Moore, who had become a great friend; then "Seafaring" Ed Moran, who signed simply as E. F. Moran; our pal from the Rutgers Club, Jim Kirk; Val Wenzel; Val's bane, the unruly teen-age volunteer Walter Hoyeski; and our apprentice Chi F. Ling, followed by four other members of the Seaport Explorer Ship, who got their sail training aboard *Athena* and certainly deserved to be with us for the harbor parade and Staten Island landing that we planned.

It all went off like a dream. On a halcyon day with a brisk south-easterly breeze our flotilla of five sailing craft set sail, led by Barclay Warburton aboard his stately brigantine *Black Pearl*, followed by *Athena* and three other Schooner Race veterans, and accompanied by the Army Corps of Engineers cleanup vessel *Driftmaster* and three police launches. Aboard the *Pearl*, besides Barclay and the Black Pearl Singers, were Parks Commissioner Augie Heckscher and Mrs. Louis Auchincloss, a leading patron of the arts, along with our great friend and mentor, the preservationist Margot Gayle.

The main event this year was to land on the beach at the foot of Hylan Avenue on Staten Island, not far from where Villiers had put the *Conrad* ashore in sinking condition 35 years earlier. We had made no special preparations for the landing, and people had to take off shoes and socks, roll up their pants legs or lift their skirts and scramble out of the tippy dinghies carried by the brigantine and her accompanying schooners, onto the rubble-strewn, stony beach. But everyone took this in good sort. Part of our mission, we'd explained, was to get the old New York Yacht Club pier at Stapleton restored, to serve as a waterborne access to the Alice Austen House ashore. With a proper pier to receive people making future pilgrimages to the Austen House, there would be no splashing overboard and slipping and sliding on oily stones to get ashore.

Our primary mission was to preserve the Alice Austen House, originally a Dutch farmhouse built in the 1690s, later the home of the gallant Miss Austen who'd taken those haunting, evocative photographs of ships that passed her front lawn, which we'd used in our booklet *South Street in the Afternoon of Sail*. She had also pursued the ships and their people into the hurly burly of South Street, where well-bred ladies did not commonly go in the 1890s and early 1900s.

Straggling across the beach, we scrambled up a low bluff to meet a reception committee headed by Borough President Robert Connor on the Austen House lawn. I then asked Commissioner Heckscher to take the flag of the City of New York which we'd asked him to bring along, and plant it into the turf to claim the land for the people of the City of New York. When he said this might cost him his job, I told him it was worth the sacrifice.

With that, Mr. Hecksher played his part with a drama that suggested some earlier experience in amateur theater, and Bob Connor responded in similar vein. The owners of the house, a young couple who had bought it precisely to preserve it as a public resource, were delighted. So was Brad Greene, a native Staten Islander, whose tireless advocacy of the Austen House, urged on by Margot Gayle, had lain all the groundwork for the public claim we now made. And so was Bob Connor, who had willingly cast aside his prior commitment to a developer who proposed to erect a wall of high-priced, high-rise apartment buildings. This would have resulted in the demolition of the Austen House and the loss of the priceless views of the entry to the New World's greatest harbor which its sweeping lawns offer.

This little ceremony, which was followed by a joyful picnic on the grass arranged by the ship photographer and historian Frank Duffy, had no legal effect of course. But it was followed in a year or so by the City taking over the property, and a few years after that the adjoining field which included the second clubhouse of the New York Yacht Club and the foreshore where their pier had stood. Forty-odd years later the Austen House is now a National Historic Landmark and open to the public as a museum; the pier has yet to be rebuilt.

Another Sea Day mission was to encourage the clean-up of the harbor's murky waters, which was saluted by the *New York Times* in a headline referring to "the sea, the not-so-beautiful sea." We regretted the negative notion of an unlovely harbor, but we had to forgive them this miscue for the sake of the lovely photo they ran above it, which showed the beauty of the harbor on a balmy afternoon in May with our flotilla on its way back from Staten Island, passing before the rapt gaze of New Yorkers taking in the scene.

An over-arching aspect of the mission was recognized in a Connecticut paper which announced that Sea Day was proclaimed by South Street Seaport, with this grand editorial comment:

> *It seeks by this means to rescue a part of our environment which is*
> *our history, the things it takes more than one generation to learn.*

The editorialist was my father, Alfred Stanford, publisher of the *Milford Citizen*. A few weeks before the event, in a very typical fashion for us, we had all been discussing plans for Sea Day, with Dad advising me that the day should be about cleaning up the environment, a physical problem one could tackle with visible results, while I maintained that it should be about history, so that the individual has some grasp of the continuing story of mankind, and his place in that story. I had no idea that he would come out of this with the most far-reaching and reverberating statement anyone made about Sea Day. "*The things it takes more than one generation to learn.*"

The grand day on the water ended at last, and we went on to the Riverboat Ball aboard the paddlewheeler *Alexander Hamilton* (again donated by Frank Barry of Circle Line) refreshed and challenged by the day's experiences.

A week before Sea Day I had gone to an unusual luncheon, which changed the course of our long effort to rescue the ship *Wavertree* from the chains of debt that held her in Argentina.

It began with a phone call from R. J. Schaefer. The Schaefer brewery stood upriver from the Seaport on the Brooklyn shore and, looking up from his desk, Rudie could see what was happening on the Seaport piers. He had called me the previous summer to ask if I thought it wise to have Pete Seeger and the *Clearwater* in at Pier 16. This had led to a pivotal conversation: I could only explain that, yes, I thought this right, and that Pete was a good man and a good American, adding a few words on the importance of freedom of association and expression. After a short pause on the line Rudie had said: "Well, I see what you mean. Carry on." I found this a noble statement from a man who had absolutely no use for the anti-war movement in America.

But this time, the call was not about a vessel at our pier, but one that wasn't—the *Wavertree*.

"Peter, what about that ship you were going to bring in? I don't see her at your pier. Is she ever coming in?"

Pure R. J., straight and to the point. I don't remember how I answered, but I assume I had the sense to say she had to come in, but we hadn't yet got the money. Rudie didn't have much use for rationalizations or long-winded explanations, and none at all for excuses—which I appreciated. I remember very well what he said next.

"Well, I think you need a little help in that department. Why not come over for lunch one day, and I'll ask a few friends and let's see if we can't get you some money to bring in the ship."

CHAPTER 29

Our Ship Comes In, *Spring–Summer 1970*

A Schaefer Lunch—Wavertree *Redeemed*—Seaport in Curator
Magazine—*Banking Threat*—PS Elected NMHS President—
Fortnight in Italy—Wavertree *Arrives*—Lacey's Barge

Luncheon was in an oak-beamed dining room in the Schaefer Brewery.
The walls were solidly adorned with photographs of Schaefer brass bands,
featuring magnificent mustachioed and bearded men in gold-laced uniforms arrayed in Teutonically disciplined order. R. J. Schaefer, II presided
over the meeting and we talked at some length about the work of the
South Street Seaport Museum and the prospects of the New York State
Maritime Museum, of which he was a trustee. We also discussed the full
rigger *Wavertree* and her importance to both institutions.

Over coffee, R. J. asked me to explain the ship's financial plight: the
unpaid shipyard bills and the cost of the tow to New York. It was immediately agreed that any effort to redeem her must include the cost
of that vital tow. There was little point in clearing up the ship's debt
and then leaving her in Buenos Aires. No, we should go for the whole
amount to bring her in. Interest charges on the bill had brought it up
to $75,000, while the best estimate we could get on the tow to New
York came to another $75,000. So the need was for $150,000. I said
we would accept pledges and call them in only when the full amount
had been achieved, to assure that dollars received would actually bring
in the ship.

All this was satisfactory to the two Schaefers, R. J. and his son Rudie
III and to the stockbroker George F. Baker, III, but not so to Oliver Carey
of New York Dock Railway, who said he hadn't realized this was to be a
fundraising lunch and, asking to be excused, left the room. Later he was
to become a great supporter, but not this time around.

"Well, we'll do $5,000 to start things off," said R. J., whereupon George
said: "I'll do five."

"Thank you, gentlemen," I said. "That makes $15,000, a solid beginning with ten percent of what we need. With that we can make this thing work."

There was a moment's confusion about how $5,000 and $5,000 make $15,000, until I explained that I had assumed, when R. J. said "we," he had meant he and the younger Rudie each giving $5,000. R. J. gave me a stern look, suggesting that he'd meant no such thing. But he paused before speaking, then nodded his head. Everyone could see the importance of the $15,000 figure, and R. J. wanted to see that ship come in.

After lunch I called Jack Aron, who had been a generous donor of books and artifacts to the museum. I had alerted him to our $150,000 drive to bring in the *Wavertree* and now told him what the Schaefers and George Baker had done. I then asked him if the J. Aron Foundation would match the $15,000 they'd jointly pledged.

"Peter, you may know something about ships—I'll give you that," said Jack. "And you're a nice guy. But you are a terrible fundraiser. I was going to give $25,000 outright to get some serious money into the ship, but since you didn't ask for it, I won't do that. Only because I want to see that ship come in, I'll contribute the $15,000 you asked for and will give you an interest-free loan of $10,000—which I expect to see repaid after twelve months without fail."

I knew Jack meant what he said. I also knew that we now had $40,000, over a quarter of what we needed. With that solid beginning I felt we could raise the balance. And in the following weeks we received a grant of $25,000 from W. R. Grace & Co. through our trustee Hal Logan, head of Grace Lines, along with other contributions to reach a pledged total of $120,000. Hal Logan, true to form, understood the urgency of the occasion and played his part as soon as I had told him where we stood. Having reached this point, with my heart in my mouth I called in all our pledges, though we were still short of our agreed goal of $150,000. We needed the cash in hand to clear up the *Wavertree*'s bill and make a down payment on the tow to New York. Everyone understood the situation, and everyone responded. They, too, wanted to see the ship come in.

By mid-June we had paid the Navy Yard bill in Buenos Aires and we'd made a 50 percent down payment to Wijsmuller Towing for the $75,000 tow of the *Wavertree* to New York. Thanks to the Schaefer family, Jack Aron and others inspired by their gifts, we had redeemed our work with Argentine friends and saved our ship.

It seemed the days of wine and roses were upon us. The day before Sea Day, I attended a meeting of the Citizens' Union to receive the Albert S. Bard Award for civic improvements in New York. I was moved by this, because I had met Albert Bard at City Club functions and was awed by his courtly but determined demeanor and his outlook on the city as a place to be cherished and kept up as one would a private home.

And on Thursday, 2 June, I attended a conference of the American Association of Museums, where I gave a talk entitled "This Museum *Is* People."* I opened with Joe Cantalupo's declaration of this theme the previous year in the drafty ground floor hall in 203 Front Street. I went on to set forth how and why we planned "to preserve five blocks of the old waterfront as a major new cultural center devoted to museum pro-grams." I said:

> *The Seaport Museum was conceived out of a generalized affection for the old brick buildings and surviving taverns and maritime enterprises of the historic city waterfront along South Street.... Trades disappear, and the populations that serve them disperse. But one stumbles here and there upon evidences of the vanished ways of life that built the city.*

I went on to cite more current concerns, notably the principle, "a bus is an artifact," based on Norma's and my encounter with the fabulously decorated buses of Buenos Aires. Those individually named and decorated buses reflected the same care and affection that fishermen revealed in decorating working schooners with carved wreaths and gold-leaf lettering of their names. And more recently, we learned something from our Sea Day observances, held only eleven days earlier, when the newspapers, in

---

* The full text can be found in *Curator: The Museum Journal*, Vol. XIII, Issue 4 (1970).

their varying accounts, had given us a fresh vision of what Sea Day meant:

> *"We do our job well,"* I said, *"when we have the public media present our story, with insights and discoveries that only an independent reporter can dig out."*

For better or worse, we were doing what we said we'd do, learning from the experience as we developed it.

At this moment, while we basked in the prospects of the arrival in New York of our most important ship, a fresh unexpected crisis hit us like a thunderbolt. It struck out of a clear sky on a pleasant Sunday aboard *Athena* with our sailing friends Mari Ann and Barnaby Blatch.

"Peter, do you know what company I work for?" asked Barnaby in a tone of voice which wakened me from the pleasant torpor of a mid-morning sail in light weather.

We were drifting along across Long Island Sound from Port Jefferson to Milford, Connecticut, in an easterly breeze so light that the pages of the Sunday *New York Times* for 7 June 1970, which we had picked up before leaving Port Jeff, lay undisturbed all about the deck. Overhead, our lovely new fisherman staysail pulled *Athena* along, while the working sails slumbered with no pull on the lines that held them. Heaven.

"Yes, First National City Bank, I think it's called now."

"And do you know what account I work on?" he continued.

"No. Why do you ask?"

"Well, last night, after you chaps had retired, Mari Ann and I had a talk about the ethics of this situation. We decided that at this point I should tell you that at City Bank I work on the South Street Seaport account. And the bank is going to pull the plug on the whole mad venture. I'm as sorry as hell to tell you this, but that's what's about to happen."

"But Barnaby," I said, thoroughly awake now, "surely the mayor's support and the approvals by the Board of Estimate count for something. You can't just kill the project like that."

"If the City cares so much about the Seaport, the City should bear the burden of what they want done. That's what the bank will say. Bankers expect a return of capital with reasonable interest when they make a multi-million-dollar loan. We just don't see that happening here."

City Bank was one of the five banks that had formed a consortium to advance Jakob the money to buy the Seaport land. Chase was serving as the lead bank, but now, apparently, City Bank had bolted and was moving to pull out of the Seaport project.

"But you *do* finance special efforts in neighborhood development, don't you?" I protested. "I keep reading about this in the papers."

"Peter, this has been presented to us as a sure-fire money maker, not as a do-good neighborhood development project."

I could understand how Jakob had proposed the loan on a commercial basis. If the real-estate market hadn't collapsed, everyone would have come out winners, including Seaport Holdings, the company Jakob had set up to hold the Seaport land until the air rights had been sold and the blocks could be delivered to the Seaport Museum. But the collapse of the market had caught people by surprise; even the giant developer Atlas-McGrath, with the astute Sol Atlas at the helm, would soon be forced into bankruptcy after another year had passed, and with the simultaneous collapse of American flag shipping, American Export-Isbrandtsen Lines would follow down the same grim road to oblivion in another year. These things would take a little time to happen, but one could smell disaster in the air by mid-1970. No one would re-fund the land loan if City Bank dropped it, and the Seaport plan would evaporate into thin air.

"Barnaby," I said, "you've seen the people on our piers. They're not just yacht-club types. They're ordinary New Yorkers of all stripes: white collar, blue collar, from all over, including the public housing projects next door. They are there in quest of broader horizons—and a sense of belonging in the city. We are doing something more important in South Street than just fixing up a rundown neighborhood; we're helping people learn the hard work and high endeavor that built a city from the sea, and so find their own places in the city of today."

"You know that and I know that," said Barnaby. "But the bank doesn't know that. Not as things stand."

He went on to explain that there would be a meeting the next morning, where the Seaport case would be reviewed. That's why Mari Ann and he had agreed that he really had to tell us the state of affairs, even though he had no idea what we could do to save the situation.

But Norma and I knew what had to be done, and as soon as we got back to Yorktown Heights that Sunday evening, we set about doing it. We prepared a packet of plans, photos and newspaper stories showing the Seaport plan not as a commercial venture, but as an undertaking to deliver a public benefit of immense social and educational value to New York—good medicine, surely, at a time when New Yorkers were beginning to worry about the city's future and their future in the city.

Now, if ever, the free, unbought testimony of the press with its rave reviews of everything we were doing—including the three editorials in the *New York Times* over the past year and a half—would show how important it was that the venture succeed. And to any reflective mind, the public outcry that would ensue on any bank foreclosing the venture would surely begin to look like a very negative thing. Not the kind of thing a banker would like to read over his morning toast and coffee—or so we hoped.

Our presentation stuck to the high ground, with no hint of a threat in it beyond the public joy evident in the Board of Estimate victory a year and a half earlier, and big pictures in the press of the schooner races of the past three years and the Sea Day observances just over two weeks ago.

In our best "Action This Day" style, I drove to Manhattan, arriving about 3 AM to slip the papers under the door of the Blatches' apartment in Peter Cooper Village. I was relieved to find that the papers could be slipped under their door, so I did not have to awaken them at such an hour. I asked Barnaby later in the week how his meeting with his boss had come out. He said he really couldn't tell me that, but if I'd been thinking of packing up my office, I could probably hold off for a while, anyway.

So, for a while, the crisis was averted and life in the Seaport continued on its accustomed course, with everyone busy with arrangements involving the third visit of the Coast Guard's *Eagle,* and after that, the Hudson River sloop *Clearwater,* backed up by Bernie Klay's roistering X-Seamen's Institute singing on *Caviare*'s quarterdeck every week, and several performances by Jean Sullivan's Theatre Research outfit on Pier 16.

While these things were going on, another major project was taking shape in another city. On 16 June I had gone to Washington, DC, at Karl Kortum's insistence to attend a meeting of the National Maritime Historical Society. The society's finances were not in good shape, and the founding president, Alan Hutchison, was quitting Washington to take over a new real estate project in Costa Rica. At the meeting, which had originally been called to dissolve the society, I was elected president. As one of the trustees later noted, they had come to Washington expecting a funeral, and Peter Stanford jumped out of the coffin.

Norma's reaction was not quite so favorable. The next morning, driving to work together from Yorktown Heights, I told her about the meeting, what was at stake, the really dismal financial situation with something over $100,000 in debts, and my being elected president. At this, Norma, who was driving, gave me a look and said: "Tell me you didn't accept." When I said I felt obliged to accept the office, she pulled the car over onto the grassy shoulder of the Hawthorne Circle, pointed to the passenger door and calmly said: "Get out."

She had a point. We were over-extended as things were, with the land under a cloud, and a huge project on our hands when the *Wavertree* came in, and it didn't seem to make much sense to now accept responsibility for a bankrupt venture to save a half-sunken ship on the opposite side of the globe.

There were values involved in the National Maritime Historical Society of which I had only a ghostly sense, but I contented myself with saying that we owed Karl Kortum so much, that I felt I had to do what he asked. Norma thought about this. She had a high regard for Karl and felt bound, like me, to his cause in historic ships. After a while her face cleared, and she said simply: "Oh, what the hell." So we drove on round the circle and proceeded on our way to another day of the battle and the breeze in South Street.

Somehow, amid the demands of the Seaport Museum, Norma and I kept up our talks about cities, in a kind of continuing seminar. This was the interest which we'd pursued in the Rutgers Club and in the city walks that led us to South Street. Time and again Norma would cite some humanistic touch she found in the Italian towns during her college year in Rome ten years earlier—and the madcap notion of making a trip to Italy to track down these discoveries grew in our minds. As we finished paying the *Wavertree*'s bills in June, we decided we could take off two weeks for a well-earned vacation and embarked for Italy at JFK Airport on Friday, 3 July, with a complaisant 14-month-old Robert in company.

There was perhaps more than the usual flurry of urgent matters to keep us running around before departure, which included drafting a mayoral proclamation of Wavertree Day for the day of the ship's arrival, and preparing a full-page ad saluting the ship for the Seamen's Bank for Savings to run in the *New York Times*. As we loaded the car to drive to JFK, I got a call from the office about a telegram received from Juan DeValle: *Wavertree* had picked up her tow for New York that morning! So as we flew through the night over the North Atlantic, Norma and I toasted our ship then making her way north through the long reaches of the South Atlantic.

As the plane slanted down across the dusty green countryside of northern Italy the next morning, I was struck by the earthen colors of the tiled roofs of houses strung out along the winding roads we would soon be traversing in the car we'd rented for our travels. And I was much taken with the variegated look of the individual fields and vineyards. Our travels fully bore out this impression of individualism and a strong sense of place as we embarked on our land journey from Milan to Venice. There, on Sunday afternoon, we came into the Piazza San Marco just as the band struck up a trumpet voluntary which sent the resident pigeons rising in a flock, and one's spirits soaring. Robby, running toward the music on his toddler's legs, seemed completely carried away—as were we.

The next day we caught a boat to Isola San Giorgio, where the Palladian church rises from the sea in a celebration of its city. I found the structure "compelling in its clarity, vigor and vision." Then there was the city itself, full of small squares and odd corners presided over by statues of saints and heroes, with flowers bursting out of windows everywhere, giving the whole experience of the streets the feeling of an old, much lived-in family dwelling. We stopped in at a boatyard in San Trovasso Square, "a great place of chips and odd bits of planks under flowers, drying laundry and the sloped roof the people's quarters overhead," according to my journal, and we marveled at how the Rialto market foretold the layout of the Fulton Market of 1821—essentially a noble headhouse presiding over arched galleries which call irresistibly for wandering exploration. And the friendliness of the inhabitants—from the boatwrights restoring the black, lopsided gondolas in the boatyard, to the passers-by saying "Che bel bambino!" as Norma led Robby by hand through the streets—made us feel quite at home in scenes unlike anything found at home. We talked much of South Street of course, picking up hints everywhere on the special touches that made the towns we visited so alive with meaning.

Then traveling on westward we stopped at Modena, where I sketched the new market confronting a medieval market across the central square, the new one picking up the vaulted arches of the old in a lighter, airier idiom, with lovely restrained arches made possible by reinforced concrete. In the hill town of Bobbio we noted an entryway arch made up of rusticated blocks of rubble, which gave a wonderful liveliness to the doorway. And running down to the sea on the other side of the Appenines, we delighted in the noble pilasters and lively sea views painted on the sides of many of the roadside houses, as further examples of form not following function as by some *ex cathedra* ruling, but heretically following the artist's fancy, to the viewer's reward.

And always it was the people who engaged us. At Bobbio the Albergo Paolina, where we stayed, had a tiny courtyard where everyone sat together.

The teenage daughter of the hotelier volunteered to keep an eye on the sleeping Robby, so Norma and I could walk through the town and cross the Roman bridge that led to the countryside. And later, after dinner, while we sat sipping our port to the sounds of Italian songs, the young girl had Robby giggling while she danced with him amongst the tables.

Traveling on south and east, we received a warm welcome from the friendly residents of Norma's father's hometown of Vagli Sotto, where there were Franceschi names on the World War I memorial. The villagers were delighted to meet the daughter of an expatriate who'd made good and doubly delighted to know that two of his grandchildren were also along—for Norma was now visibly pregnant with our second child, due in another two months. And when we left Italy, there was the Alitalia stewardess at the airport, who put us in first class when it turned out all the coach seats were overbooked on our flight home. When a nattily dressed young buck called attention to the fact that he stood ahead of us in line, the stewardess silenced him with a glare, gesturing toward Norma and saying: "I bambini!"—that is, one in Norma's arms, and one, quite noticeably, on the way. This silenced all protest, to the approving nods of the other passengers.

Flying home in luxury, then, to pick up the daily round in South Street, Norma and I speculated about ways the humane fabric of the cities we'd seen affects the behavior of the people, as the people by their preferences shape the city. Clearly, we thought, the people and their cities interact in vital ways that affect the city's design and people's behavior—the whole process giving extra point to Joe Cantalupo's dictum about our own corner of New York: "This museum *is* people."

Not long after our return, Admiral Will called to say he wanted me to meet a man who looked like a good candidate for the formidable task of restoring the 2,000-ton ship that would be arriving at our pier in a few weeks' time. That subject had been much on my mind, and I was glad to join Dutch Will for lunch at the Whitehall Club. With him was Captain William J. Lacey, a lanky, quiet-spoken man in his late 40s, with a weather-beaten face which broke easily into a grand Irish smile. When I saw him I realized I had met him earlier in the year, at lunch with Briggs Dalzell. We had talked of Lacey's work on Dalzell tugs, but, with other concerns in hand, Lacey's name had slipped my mind. Now Dutch told me that Lacey had been the youngest captain in the merchant marine in World War II and had lost his Liberty ship to a German torpedo while carrying supplies to the embattled Russians on the perilous run to Murmansk. After the war, he had set up a floating workshop in Staten Island as a ship repair facility serving Dalzell tugs. That business ended when Dalzell was taken over by McAllister a few years before this meeting, and the odd ship-repair jobs that turned up were not enough to maintain the facility.

Then Captain Lacey read about the *Wavertree*'s impending arrival in the July issue of the *South Street Reporter*, which blazoned across its front page WAVERTREE IS COMING! This ran above an exuberant Stobart painting of the great ship making sail as she departed New York Harbor for India 75 years earlier. And the realist-romantic sea captain said to himself, as he told us over lunch: "By golly, I could do something for that ship when she comes in!"

As indeed he could, with the skilled shipwrights, mechanics and riggers in his five-man crew.

The problem, of course, was money. I explained that the museum had not yet established a solid funding base. In fact, I said, available funds barely covered routine maintenance of the ships with little left over for restoration work. We had prospects, which should begin to weigh in significantly, once the complex land arrangements had been concluded. The basic provisions had been approved by the Board of Estimate and enjoyed the personal support of Mayor Lindsay, but there had been endless delays in clearing these arrangements through the City bureaucracy. Captain Lacey then said he would like to work with us as a partner, as he had with the Dalzells. He would take his chances on payment, supplementing whatever we paid him with odd jobs working on harbor craft. He had adequate resources to carry his crew, provided that there was a future for him in the Seaport.

And that, I felt, we could assure him. Dutch Will, much involved in harbor affairs as president of American Export-Isbrandtsen Lines, strongly recommended him, as did Briggs Dalzell, and Jakob later told me we'd been lucky to get him. So, before our ship came in, Lacey's floating ship-repair facility was emplaced between Piers 15 and 16 to receive her. The barge, with its angular black-painted steel-framed superstructure housing an armory of heavy machine tools atop the bulky concrete hull, added a suitably industrial look to the Seaport scene.

As all this was being settled, we learned of a great gift that would add authenticity to the restoration of the ship's forecastle head. James P. McAllister, II, president of McAllister Towing, had made arrangements to have the forecastle-head gear of the ship *Riversdale* donated to us by Crown Zellerbach, owner of the hulk, which was part of a breakwater in Royston, British Columbia. *Riversdale*, built in 1894 as the last in the series of big square riggers acquired by Leyland Brothers, was a near-sister of *Wavertree*. These invaluable artifacts would give us not just the look, but the actuality of the capstan the forecastle gang had walked around to raise anchor at the outset of a voyage, as well as the monster windlass below the deck head and the deck leads and belaying pins for the headsail sheets—in all, 14 tons of authentic sailing-ship ironmongery, which eventually reached us, carried free of charge as deck cargo by Calmar, a shipping branch of the Bethlehem Steel Company.

This sterling example of the outreach of our New York shipping connections, and the instinct of seagoing people to "bear a hand" for the good of the ship, impressed all of us. It would have been easy, after all, for Crown Zellerbach or Calmar to have said their insurance didn't cover this risky work, or something of the kind, but they did their parts cheerfully, wishing us well in our labors from three thousand miles away. And so did Morris Green Industries, which contributed a skilled crew for the intricate work of cutting out the separate items of gear, and Pacific

Pile-Driving, which supplied the barge and crane needed to move the heavy gear to the Calmar loading dock. This was indeed "bearing a hand" in the tradition of seafaring.

A final gift, delivered to South Street on 30 June, a week before the scheduled arrival of *Wavertree*, also came to us from Canada as an impressive piece of ironmongery, again thanks to Jim McAllister's dedication to our cause. This, remarkably, was an actual operating vessel, the jaunty 72-foot steam tug *Mathilda*. Built in Sorel, Quebec, in 1899, *Mathilda* radiated the look and style of the last century, and, even better, she had the identical operating machinery of that century—the old-fashioned compound reciprocating engine she had used for some 70 years. She had steamed most of the way from Canada via the fresh-water route through Lake Champlain to the Hudson River, with connecting canals, but had to be towed from Kingston on, because, built for fresh-water work, she carried no water tanks and could not draw on the increasing degree of salt water she encountered in the Hudson without caking up her boiler tubes. New York Harbor tugs carried fresh water in tanks, which was puffed away into the air as white steam with every stroke of their revolving engines, giving a festive look to tugs at their work in old photographs. Steamers on longer runs recirculated their fresh water through condensers. But *Mathilda*, drawing her boiler water from the fresh water she had been built to work in, wasn't designed to steam in New York's salt-water harbor.

In every other respect she exactly met the need we'd felt for a working tug of the breed that would have helped *Wavertree* in and out of harbor on her visit here in 1895—for a small tug would be assigned to tow in a sailing ship, with the bigger tugs reserved for berthing cargo steamers twice her size and passenger liners bigger than that. It was with real appreciation of what the vessel meant to our work that I joined Jim McAllister aboard the little tug for the tow in from the McAllister yard in Staten Island. Captain James P. McAllister, III, was skipper of the tug that took us alongside for the tow "on the hip" to South Street Seaport. He shared his dad's delight in all things to do with harbor life and traditions, and I was proud to be in such good company on that delivery trip of the latest addition to our fleet.

And, at last, there was the ship herself. Early on Wednesday, 5 August 1970 she appeared all at once, emerging from the morning sea mist south of the Verrazano-Narrows Bridge—one moment, only damp, shifting strands of mist; the next, the ship *Wavertree* looming over the still harbor water like the revenant she was. The small Dutch tug *Titan* pulled her along like a child on a tricycle hauling a giant circus calliope, a phantasmagorical thing with a sweeping sheer line above a long line of painted gunports not seen in New York for half a century or more.

The small group of us who'd gone out to meet the vessel clambered up the rope ladder that was thrown over her towering side. A couple of hands on the McAllister tug that had taken us out wondered aloud why we'd brought this strange barge all the way from South America. They were set straight by Captain Lacey, who had brought out a few line handlers to be on hand for berthing the ship in Staten Island's Pouch Terminal. Bill knew well enough what this ship represented in the history of navigation and the story of our port, and when he reached the *Wavertree*'s deck, he stood there in silent awe. Norma wasn't with us, with our second child due in a few weeks' time. When I got back from this trip, she asked me eagerly how it felt to see the *Wavertree* in New York Harbor. She fully shared my sense that the return of this great iron ship to New York, after three quarters of a century away on her oceanic wanderings under sail, made a fundamental change in our world.

We rode the ship in silence into Pouch Terminal, whose owner, Tim Pouch, had offered us free pier space so that a work crew led by George Demmy could clean things up and install the deck exhibits we had prepared for the vessel's formal entrance to New York and her installation in South Street.

That evening, back in town, George Demmy walked with me down Pearl Street to Delmonico's, the ornate, old-fashioned restaurant at the corner of Old Slip and Beaver Street. There we met the skipper, mate, and engineer of the *Titan* to stand them to a dinner celebrating their safe delivery of our ship. They told us, in the workaday English which seamen of all nations use, that they had not understood the importance or, indeed, the use of the oddly painted vessel they had towed so far— not until a few old seamen from Sailors Snug Harbor in Staten Island had come down the road to stand speechless before the ship and gaze at her with awe. Then they understood. We then raised our glasses to the solidarity of the seafaring world and its values and traditions. Before the evening was over we had learned quite a bit about deep-sea towing, and the *Titan*'s officers got to know the story of the Cape Horn trade under sail. They had always known that the formidable headland was named for a Dutch town. Now, they said, bidding us good night to get the ferry back to their ship, they understood why old sailors shook their heads when they heard the name Cape Horn.

The next morning the *Titan* put in briefly at the Seaport pier, just long enough for the skipper to pass Jimmy Diaz a chilled bottle of Heineken. "Take this to Peter and tell him this is for him," the skipper said, "he might appreciate a cold beer from the Netherlands this morning." With that, the gallant little tug turned on her heels and chugged away to her next assignment, to pick up a Liberty ship in Norfolk, Virginia, for scrapping in Europe.

CHAPTER 30

Beautiful Necessities of Life, *August 1970*

Wavertree Arrives in South Street—Villiers's Second Visit—
Captain James Roberts Remembers a Long-Ago Trip—
Pioneer Joins the Seaport

There was a raucous hooting of sirens, foghorns and whistles as the *Wavertree* made her formal entrance to New York Harbor from her temporary berth in Staten Island. There was a clattering of helicopter blades overhead, accompanied by a brilliant plume of harbor water from an escorting New York City fireboat. The Schaefers' elegant black schooner yacht, *America,* followed at a respectful distance, accompanied by the Chinese junk *Mon Lei.* Ahead, a McAllister tug pulled our towline, while another McAllister tug snuggled up to our port side to make sure the old ship kept a steady course as she made her stately way over the six-mile distance to the Seaport Museum.

Among the crowd on the poop deck were the two veterans of the Cape Horn trade in square rig: Archie Horka and Fred Harvey, who had sailed before the mast in the big full-rigger *Fulwood* in 1906. An exact sister ship to *Wavertree, Fulwood* had gone missing with all hands in 1919 on a passage from Buenos Aires to Denmark. The seaman-artist Os Brett was aboard with his wife, Gertrude, solemnly congratulating everyone on the great ship's arrival, as was the more taciturn Bob Herbert, with his indomitable wife, Karen.

Jakob Isbrandtsen was aboard, walking his ship's decks at last. He explained how she would be rerigged to trustees who looked as if they'd never expected to see this day—for which I could hardly blame them—and to the shipping people who'd joined us, who listened with fascination to Jakob's accounts of sailing in square rig. He'd put in time in square rig as a boy, sailing a small brig in Long Island's Great South Bay, and as a youth sailing as crew in the great square-rigged yacht *Aloha.* And I was particularly glad that Captain DeValle was aboard, resolved not to miss the installation of his beloved "Wovertree" in her new domain. I saw Captain Bill Lacey interviewing him closely about the work that had been done on the ship in Buenos Aires, while Captain Ken Reynard of the *Star of India*, who'd flown in from San Diego to join us, listened attentively.

When I told Ken that we were honored to have him aboard as the *Wavertree* returned to the harbor she had left 75 years earlier, I added that I only wished Karl Kortum could have been with us. Karl had told me he just couldn't make it, he'd been held up by other matters in San Francisco. Ken then surprised me by saying that Karl should spend more time taking care of the ships in his keeping in San Francisco. I thought this over for a moment, and then contented myself with saying that if he had done that, we would none of us be here, and the *Wavertree* would have moldered her life away in the Riachuelo. This Ken acknowledged with a smile. The tension between the two men was the classic one between pioneers and settlers—the one always pushing ahead; the other laboring to make things work where he stood.

Passing ships and tugs dipped their ensigns and blew salutes on their whistles, to which our volunteer National Maritime Union signalman, Rick Miller, responded with repeated dipping of the American flag flying at the monkey gaff on which, nearly a year before, we'd first hoisted the Stars and Stripes with Ambassador Lodge presiding.

There was an electric consciousness of history in the air for every soul aboard, a consciousness that this ship, which had sailed out unnoticed 75 years earlier in a far different world, was now back and this time being hailed by her successors in the maritime trades of New York. Everyone seemed to understand that she was a last survivor of the tall ships which had built a city from the sea. "Welcome *Wavertree*!" the Seamen's Bank for Savings ad had proclaimed in that morning's newspapers, and having Archie Horka and Fred Harvey aboard gave a special fillip to the occasion for all of us.

Still, most New Yorkers might not note this arrival, so it was up to us to carry her message to the busy city.

A good beginning was made as the big ship nosed slowly into her berth on the south side of Pier 16 amid swirling water stirred up by the pushing and pulling of our two tugs. Norma and I leaned over the poop rail to watch as the first line whistled ashore, expertly hurled by Jakob Isbrandtsen from the forecastle head. We then saw the mayor's wife, Mary Lindsay, step forward to catch it. The monkey's fist, weighted with a lead pellet, brought the light messenger line snaking after it. This would be used to haul in the heavy hawser that would hold the vessel in her berth. The drill was to pick up the line after the monkey's fist had landed—not to catch the weighted fist like a baseball. But no one had told Mary this, and catch it she did.

"Wow, you guys must have mitts of steel!" she said as she came aboard once the gangplank was rigged. The word was passed to everyone to be very gentle if she offered to shake hands—and everyone was. Coffee and champagne were broken out for all hands, but few stayed long aboard. We'd made the passage; it was time to leave the ship and go about our business. So we streamed away to our varied occasions. Each of us, I imagine, took a last look at the great bow arched against the rising towers of the city of today. Henceforth, it would be our job to carry her message to the people immured in those towers, to bring them an awareness of the great sailing ships which had built their city.

Alan Villiers stopped by in October to visit the ship he had done so much to help. He was not discouraged by the lack of response to his week's intense campaigning for the *Wavertree* a year and a half earlier. On the contrary, he was full of congratulations for the feat, as he called it, of bringing her to New York. On Tuesday evening, 6 October, he gave a talk on Pier 16. This was a dramatic recalling of his experiences in the Cape Horn trade, with the *Wavertree*'s shapely stern looming over the screen on which he showed his photos of ships of her breed doing battle with the great seas that sweep around the world in the latitude of Cape Horn. This was a scene to remember—a seaman's seaman honoring his ship by telling the stories of her kind at sea, in words and images that made us feel the rushing winds and the crash of hurtling seas and giving us some sense of life as people lived it in the sailing of the great hull resting quietly at our pier.

A few days later Alan presided, in his usual bluff story-telling mode, at the opening of the Seaport bookstore. This important new resource, formerly a hash joint for fish market truckers and workers, stood at the entrance to the Seaport area at Fulton and Water Streets. Its interior had been entirely renewed by Eugenia Dean, who specialized in creating spaces that looked and felt as if they'd been there for generations. The broken tile floor was replaced with varnished wooden flooring; built-in bookshelves occupied most of the walls, with the remaining wall spaces covered in real burlap, which added a suitable tarry scent to the atmosphere; and two brass lamps hung from the stamped tin ceiling, now painted a cool sky blue. The sales area was confined to a modest wood counter supporting a gleaming antique brass cash register. This left room for two red leather banker's chairs for customers, so they could comfortably leaf through a book.

This found great favor in Alan's eyes, and he told our little group crowded in the store: "This may even wake up the burghers of Wall Street as to what happened out there on the ocean to make them all rich. A neighborhood without a bookshop is like a man without memory." No one gainsaid him on this.

After the reception Alan, Norma and I walked down to the ship and went aboard in the gathering autumnal dusk. We walked the barren decks where men had hauled away at the maze of rigging that drives a square-rigged ship, often, as we knew from Spiers's account, singing the chanteys "Haul Away Joe" and "Paddy Doyle" while at work, and "Stormalong," "Rolling Home" and other sea songs when they gathered on the fo'c'sle head in flying fish weather, running down the Trades. We walked by the after cabins to the main saloon, where Spiers tells us the skipper's uncle had done a tipsy sword dance to entertain visiting officers from the neighboring ships anchored in the dismal nitrate port of Tocopilla in 1907. Then we went up the curved stairway leading to the quarterdeck overhead. On the quarterdeck, Alan went aft to the wheel and, standing by it, gazed forward toward the ship's rising bow and beyond that to the towering city, with lights staring back at us from its glassy walls. How different this scene was from the cresting seas she'd faced off the Horn, I thought to myself—but a challenging one in its own way.

Alan must have had something of the same picture in his mind.

"It is harder to save these ships," he said, "than it was to drive them round Cape Horn."

With that, he left to catch a cab to JFK Airport and continue his journey to South America. There he would meet with Captain Miethe and other retired sea captains to write the final chapters of his masterful history, *The War with Cape Horn.* We stayed in touch with Alan, but were never to see him again.

Bill Lacey settled right into his work on the ship. We felt the first priority was to get public access to the after tweendeck under the after cabins on the main deck. This would give us a secure area where we could create a display on the life of the ship, so people would know about her even while she was being rebuilt and rerigged. Bill volunteered to lay a new steel floor to replace the rotten planking of the old deck, and to build a fireproof hatch and stairway to provide safe access for the public. To design these needed features he brought in his naval architect, Arnold de Sorio, a cheery soul with a ready supply of tales of ships and seamen, who also had a quick mind and fine hand at sketching out solutions to design problems. Anything we did on the ship would have to be approved by Ports and Terminals under Commissioner Leedham, who for some reason had a dim view of our work on his waterfront. "Leave it to Arnold," Bill would say. I am sure Bill's hospitality in receiving visitors in his well-furnished offices aboard the Lacey barge had something to do with Arnold's success in educating the people from Ports and Terminals, backed up by Arnold's designs and much learned talk between the two men of other ships they'd worked on, from tugs to the giant liners they served. And of course, the plans they proposed were perfectly sound. These were people who knew what they were doing.

There were some protests that we were going ahead too far, too fast in building this safe access to the after tweendeck, but the work was done with care not to destroy any of the ship's original fabric (except rotted-out tweendeck planking), and Jakob and I were agreed that we had to keep moving ahead to get people aboard the ship. That was how she would earn her living now.

While these first steps in the long task of restoration were being taken, an elderly gentleman showed up on the pier to add another page to the *Wavertree*'s story. Arriving on 2 November from Sailors' Snug Harbor on Staten Island in a car driven by his son, he announced himself to our pier crew as Captain James E. Roberts, adding that he'd sailed in the *Wavertree* in a voyage from England to India and back, in the years 1897–98. All kinds of people showed up with crazy stories about the ship, so when I heard about his visit, I did not take it seriously. But when he returned, two weeks later, he sent a note up to the office restating his service aboard *Wavertree*. This time we looked up the ship's articles for that voyage (one of the rare ship's articles for the *Wavertree* which we'd been able to recover from England), and we found that the signature on the note matched the 1897 signature for James E. Roberts. We were looking at records of a voyage made before the Spanish-American War, before radio, airplanes or even automobiles existed!

I hurried down to the pier, where I found a sprucely turned out gent, formal in speech and manner. I showed him the paper which he had signed three quarters of a century earlier, and he said he was glad that someone was seriously concerned with the ship's story. As his first ship, the big square rigger occupied a special place in his affections. He told how he had signed on from the training ship *Indefatigable* at age 15, with his chum George Robinson, age 16. "Poor Robinson,"

as he called him, was lost overboard when he fell from the fore upper topsail yard, stowing sail in a gale of wind in the "roaring forties"
as the ship ran her easting down after rounding the Cape of Good
Hope bound for Ceylon.

Captain Roberts, an erect, cheerful man of 88, clearly accustomed
to command, promised to be back in two weeks' time for another visit.
And he was as good as his word, coming down regularly to revisit his
old ship and tell us about his time in her. In his visits he told us how
the forecastle house where the men lived was laid out, and how the
cook, who had befriended him, burnt a hole in his only spare trousers,
drying them out as a favor on a hot oven door in the adjacent galley.
He could not give us much detail of the after cabins, because, as the
ship's boy, he was only occasionally there, hurrying down from the
poop to carry a message to Captain John Thomas or to awaken the
mate for his watch. He spoke also of the travails, risks and hardships
of life aboard a hard-case limejuicer in the days—incredibly distant
to our minds—when the bulk of the world's traffic was still carried in
deepwater sail. But the handwriting was on the wall, and a few years
before his voyage the major share of British deepwater tonnage had
already gone to steamships. Roberts himself stayed on in sail until he
shifted to steam in 1903. By 1919 he had his own command under
the American flag.

Talking with Roberts I found he had the same pride in his profession
that had been so evident in the discourse of Captain Thomas Thomas in
a Buenos Aires cafe, where he had told of his hard times under sail, but
also of the beauty of a cold dawn breaking on a wind-furrowed ocean,
the wildness of sea and sky in a gale, and, in a way, the freedom of the
life. Roberts wrote down his own words on this:

> *A sailing ship was an object of beauty and reflected life within*
> *her. A hard life and a rough one, but it was clean and free and*
> *held satisfaction.*

Again, here is that idea of freedom and reward, where a latter-day so-
ciologist might find only oppression and misery. Villiers had sounded

much the same note in the preface he wrote to our book about the *Wavertree*, speaking of service under sail in these

> *challenging, beautiful, noble ships in whose service there were tremendous*
> *compensations and rewards.*

Layer upon layer, we were learning the home truths of man's millennial experience in deepwater sail, which had ended in our lifetimes. And we learned from incorruptible sources—from men who would have scorned to tell tall tales about the sea, but who stood straighter with their eyes shining when they talked of their service under sail. We were lucky, incredibly lucky, to know such men and to have their help in learning the true story of the great iron ship that now lay on our storied waterfront.

Roberts visited with us at biweekly intervals, until shortly before his departure from this life at age 91 in 1973. He was happy, as he told us, to revisit his old ship, and to talk to our staff and our volunteers about everything he could remember of the ship under sail. But he was happiest, I believe, when the children coming down to Pier 16 gathered to ask questions of him—which, believe me, they did, when they learned that he'd sailed aboard this very ship. He always answered in straightforward fashion. There was nothing he could fabricate or invent, after all, to stand up to the hard truths and matchless rewards of his life as he'd lived it at sea under sail.

Meanwhile, another vessel launched in 1885 had come into South Street. And this vessel came in under sail!

She was the *Pioneer*, built in Marcus Hook on the Delaware River—the "American Clyde"—where shipbuilding in iron was born in America, though never quite on the massive scale of the building on Scotland's River Clyde. The *Pioneer* had been built of iron, to be a robust, buxom maid-of-all-duties to the industrial complex where she was born. Built in the early days of metal shipbuilding in America, when everything was built extra strong in this untried material, she lasted through a varied career before ending up as an oil barge in Buzzard's Bay. And then, as

Dick Rath wrote in the preface to *Pioneer Lives*, a little book we published to celebrate her history, "when patches welded over patches no longer kept the sea out," she was run up on a beach to die. Dan Clark, her owner, knew her history and sent a message to his pal Russell Grinnell, Jr., in Gloucester, to tell him that it was his turn now if this ancient, battered hulk was to be saved.

Clark, a bit of an antiquarian himself, had found the right man to save the vessel. Russ Grinnell, independently wealthy, had quit living off his investments to buy a dockbuilding company in Gloucester, which he personally managed. It was he who had provided a tug to tow the *Caviare* (later *Lettie G. Howard*) out of Gloucester for her epic trip to New York. A consummate seaman, well-read in maritime history, he took over the *Pioneer* as a hulk in 1966 and began to rebuild her in the schooner configuration she had assumed after her launch as a sloop—a typical transformation which overtook such vessels as the *Emma C. Berry*, also built as a sloop, which we had visited as a schooner in 1966, before Mystic Seaport took her over and restored her original sloop rig.

In fact, the schooner rig, albeit more complex with many more strings to pull than the sloop rig, is much more manageable with limited manpower than the sloop rig with its huge mainsail and man-killing boom. So that's how Russ re-rigged the forlorn, bent and bruised "hunk of derelict iron" at Richard Hearn's Somerset yard of Gladding-Hearn. And as a classic, saucy, broad-beamed coasting schooner, *Pioneer* was finally launched in 1968 to resume an actual working career, transporting pilings and gear from job to job on the waterfront. Except for a small auxiliary engine as an "iron jib" to aid maneuverability in tight quarters, she was still a working sailing vessel.

"It was no small project and far more expensive than I had hoped at first," Russ wrote me after the restoration was complete. "However, it would have been worse to have had to drop it."

Dick Rath had called our attention to the restoration of the *Pioneer* taking place on the Gloucester waterfront, and he had got Russ to sign up as a $1 member of South Street Seaport Museum. As Russ later explained to me, he wanted to know what damned fools thought they could recreate the old seaport of New York on the Manhattan waterfront by signing up $1 members. As a member he was kept in touch by the *South Street Reporter,* and he soon became interested in the idea of using *Pioneer* as a link between South Street and Gloucester by carrying occasional cargoes between the two ports. He was particularly interested in saving an 1850s steam hauling engine in Gloucester by taking it to New York as deck cargo, where it might become a functional centerpiece of the historic shipyard we proposed to build to the north of our piers.

We were mulling this project with Russ when on 6 April a steel beam he was hoisting in a waterfront project slipped loose and crashed on the cabin of the crane he was operating, killing him. So ended a wonderful waterfront relationship and our friendship with a tough, warm-hearted man. But our business with the Grinnell family was not yet ended, for a couple of months later two distinguished-looking young men who talked more like Bostonians than New Yorkers showed up in my small office in 203 Front Street to ask if the Seaport Museum would take on the orphaned ship. I had discussed this possibility with Rath, who told me that if we could get the vessel, he would develop a youth training program for her—fulfilling the original vision he had of helping city youngsters build a new life through the disciplines of seafaring.

So I said yes, we'd take her. I also said we could not guarantee her future, since we lived from hand to mouth financially, with no endowment or cash reserve. But we had keenly interested people led by Rath, who was well known to the Grinnells, who would sail her as a training ship. That, I said, we could promise—she would sail with city youth in crew to open new horizons in their lives.

When the decision was made to give us the *Pioneer,* there was cheering in the office—and I had one of those transcendent feelings one gets on rare occasions, that this little ship could change our whole stance in South Street by providing a vessel doing real work at sea. As Rath observed, this "could be the most useful work a coasting schooner has ever done." And true to his word, Rath leapt into action, recruiting a crew of volunteers, including Russ's nephew, George Matteson, to sail *Pioneer* in the Great Schooner Race in Gloucester in August. Our schooner, *Athena,* was already entered under the redoubtable Bob Herbert and his Girl Mariner crew, so this gave our little museum two entrants in the race. But all eyes were on *Pioneer*. Even Monk Farnham, who was understandably worried by the ship responsibilities the Seaport was assuming, cast his vote wholeheartedly to accept her as a gift from the Grinnell family.

A band of the faithful responded to Dick Rath's call to sail *Pioneer* home to New York. Bob and Terry Walton—Bob, the lawyer for the incorporation of the Seaport Museum three and a half years earlier, and Terry, the factotum of the membership drive—went with Rath and Seafarin' Ed Moran to join the *Pioneer* for the Great Schooner Race in Gloucester and then sail her to New York. The editorial circle at *Boating* magazine, with Monk as editor, Terry as managing editor, and Rath as associate editor, held firm under these demands on their time and attention. Monk, who could not join the sailing trip, was soon working with kids on the schooner's decks to teach them the rudiments of seamanship before putting to sea.

The passage from Gloucester to New York was a slow one, due to light airs from ahead, which barely moved the heavy schooner. Terry Walton, cook aboard the schooner with her crew of thirteen, remembers running out of supplies—so en route they stopped to buy fish from local fishing craft to make chowder. I told Terry this was in a time-honored tradition, relating how hungry English ships nearing home after an ocean voyage would stop to buy tunny from the Breton fishing sloops as they neared home—as indeed we did in the cutter *Iolaire* crossing from Jamaica in 1949. Ed Moran was in heaven on this passage, repeating the course with enormous formality when he relieved the helm to stand his trick at the wheel, thrilled beyond measure to be back at sea in a working schooner.

Soon after *Pioneer* tied up in South Street on 30 August, Dick Rath was in touch with Ted Gross at Mayor Lindsay's Youth Services Administration. As deputy administrator, he worked with Dick to design the cooperative measures that Gross would later run as administrator, getting teenage former addicts shaped up for hard service aboard a ship that was a real handful to sail—literally, for she had no labor-saving devices aboard except the anchor winch and auxiliary engine. Sail-handling with the heavy gear had to be done by disciplined teamwork. And in the course of the ship's sailing with the young Geo Matteson in command, there was at least one day when she simply didn't move, because the crew refused to face the indignity of hard labor to get her under way. But always, in the end, she moved. And so Mayor Lindsay, at his farewell party held in South Street in 1973, said that of all the youth programs undertaken in his administration, the Pioneer Program was the most successful.

All this was in the future and would depend on setting up a school in South Street to supplement the at-sea training—but the sea training was the indispensable ingredient of all that followed. As we launched this effort, I wrote in our book *Pioneer Lives*:

> *Those who sail in* Pioneer *today learn the loyalties, the natural order and rhythms and disciplines of life at sea. They cannot help learning, too, something of themselves, their own place in the succeeding generations....We have seen this happening now with kids who felt the world had no place for them.*

Terry Walton wrote, out of her own experience in the schooner:

> Pioneer *is in the right place. She does for her young sailors what ships and the sea have always meant to do. She is a beautiful necessity of life.*

Wavertree, the great Cape Horn sailing ship that preceded *Pioneer* into South Street, was also a "beautiful necessity." Each had her special message for the Seaport, which each delivered in a different way: the *Wavertree* for challenging voyages of the mind, *Pioneer* for the demanding realities of voyaging under sail.

CHAPTER 31

Celebrating City Waterfronts, *Autumn 1970*

Look at Our Waterfront!—*"Consider It Done"*—
*Fulton Street Scrubdown— New York's First Waterfront Festival—
Mayor Welcomes Ferry—Seaport Thrives as City Neighborhood*

Our recent ship additions had actually changed the appearance of the Lower Manhattan waterfront—and this surely was a beginning toward having the city more aware of the story we had to tell. But this was, we felt, merely a beginning. The basic idea of the storied waterfront also applied to little-known corners of the city like Staten Island's Kill van Kull, where the harbor artist John Noble was bringing to life in oil paintings and lithographs the many wrecks abandoned there. And in the Bronx's City Island the tanker captain Skip Lane, who scoured the harbor for sailing-ship relics, had set up a small museum on Fordham Street. He worked with Noble and the square rigger scholar Andy Nesdall in Massachusetts, because as youngsters the three men had explored the harbor together by rowboat, and they remained friends the rest of their lives.

We knew we needed allies to carry forward the waterfront renaissance, so we'd formed a Committee on City Waterfronts and Waterways. Cosponsored by the Municipal Art Society and the Parks Council, this outfit published a newspaper carrying progress reports and lively proposals on main water thoroughfares and quiet byways showing the whole scene as teeming with life and burgeoning possibilities. The International Longshoremen's Association (Local 1814) printed it for us—a remarkable first for a city. But something shorter and snappier was needed to get action on opening the water experience to people.

What people noticed about the existing state of city waterways and waterfronts had been demonstrated in the *New York Times* story on Sea Day earlier that year which featured the massive pollution of the water and the detritus of cast-off junk along the shoreline. Reminding people of the problem might help them become aware of the positive resources of the city waterfront. So Norma and I set to work on a collection of photographs of the wreckage strewn across our once flourishing city waterfront.

We printed the photos in a booklet called *Look at Our Waterfront! Just Look ...* In it, we pointed out the change that had led to the abandoned state of the waterfront that had for so long been a center of city life, and added this challenge:

> *The city has an economic challenge to meet in building up its share of the dollars that go to the pursuits of leisure and recreation in the modern economy.*
>
> *It has a social challenge to meet in making the urban experience more attractive, both to create a more integrated relationship among people who live and work here, and to open full cultural and recreational opportunity to all its citizens.*
>
> *The cultural and recreational development of the waterfront then becomes not a luxury but something more like a necessity.*

For action on our words, we had set up a series of public events in a waterfront festival to be held over several weeks in September, which Mayor Lindsay agreed to serve as chair.

While all this was taking shape, with Norma fully involved, on 2 September, Norma gave birth to our second child. My first day's visit with Norma at Columbia Presbyterian Hospital on the Upper West Side was taken up in domestic concerns, notably the decision to name our second son Joseph after my grandfather Joe, Al's father. Joe had led a pretty irregular life and had been treated as a reprobate by both my parents. But as a child I had adored him and, on the rare family visits my parents allowed, I delighted in talking with him. Norma readily agreed to the name, since her much-loved maternal grandfather was also named Joseph. So my second day with Norma was free to spend going over a meeting scheduled for later that afternoon with the mayor's aide, Sid Davidoff.

Davidoff had been named to take care of a list of requests for City action I had given the mayor. These were mostly for actions to facilitate the Waterfront Festival we had undertaken to run, but they would also provide improved public access to properties which belonged to the City. Norma cautioned me that to avoid having the meeting wash out in a spate of generalities, I should stick to the list of specific actions we'd asked for. I, however, reminded her of David Ogilvy's dictum that you have to sell and re-sell the reason to buy in every presentation—which in our case meant going over the reasons the festival would benefit the city, fostering public interest and citizen participation in a waterfront revival.

So I presented our case to Davidoff as "a shining opportunity" to generate new social and economic opportunity for New Yorkers. We called for two waterfront developments that would add meaningful activity and economic opportunity to life in New York: marinas on the Al Smith Houses waterfront, which would provide seasonal jobs for unemployed youth in public housing; and development of the Alice Austen House as a city park.

"And," I pointed out to Davidoff, "we urge new steps to provide for the future of today's commercial port, particularly in the growing coastal barge traffic, which can lighten the traffic burden of trucking on the highways. And we're looking forward to fast hydrofoil boats to bring commuters in from south Jersey and to take New Yorkers out to Long Island beaches, again lightening the burden on roads and bridges."

"I've seen your little book," said Davidoff, "all very nice. You told the mayor you had certain things you felt the City should be doing for you. Would you please tell me just what these things are?"

Feeling a little thrown off balance by the swift dismissal of these new perspectives we had worked out in waterfront development—these were, after all, the rationale for the Waterfront Festival—I said: "Yes, there's the matter of continuing maintenance of the City piers we lease from you, 15 and 16, at the foot of Fulton and John. I read that the City has committed $3 million to build new Upper West Side piers in the hope of winning back cargo ships to Manhattan. Meanwhile we're being stuck for expensive repairs on our piers, which are in active use by the public.

Couldn't you take over the burden of rebuilding and maintaining these existing piers, which perform a vital function for New York?"

The West Side piers had been built to appease the longshoremen's union, with no real chance of attracting any actual cargo to be dumped in Manhattan's crowded streets. Davidoff, clearly not pleased with my comment on the West Side piers, responded.

"Listen, let us worry about where and when we decide to build new piers. You stick with your old boats. And yes, we'll consider the piers you mention."

"Could we get a written agreement on that?"

"Look," said Davidoff with a sigh, "I said we'd do it. You can consider it done. Now was there anything else on your mind?"

"Yes," I said, "South Street is a trucking street, since almost all the cars use the overhead FDR Drive. The trouble is that the truck drivers know this and barrel down South Street at high speeds—and that's the street our visitors have to cross to reach our ships. And it's especially dangerous for straggling groups of school children. Could we get a traffic light installed—and if that takes more than a week to do, could we have a warning sign posted with a zebra crossing painted on the street right away? The festival begins just less than ten days from now, with a volunteer clean-up day on the 12th, less than ten days from now."

"Consider it done. Anything else?"

"Well, there's a bishop's crook street light on Peck Slip, outside Meyer's Hotel. The City is replacing these everywhere, but this one, in a landmarked district, must be preserved. Can we get this marked to be retained on City maps?"

Davidoff said I could consider it done, as he did with the next seven items, completing my list of ten. I found his crisp "consider it done" a bit overdone, and his repeated "anything else?" a bit odd, since he had the list I'd sent him on his desk and was occasionally glancing at it.

But plans for our South Street Seaport Waterfront Festival rolled on regardless. The festival involved a series of events including outdoor concerts, an art show, an antiques fair, children's puppet shows, and theater on the pier, capped by the annual Schooner Race for the Mayor's Cup, which would fill the harbor with burgeoning sail and line our piers with tall-masted vessels of traditional rig to wind up the festival on 26 September.

"Sweepers, man your brooms!" said Joe Cantalupo in a commanding voice, cheerfully borrowing the US Navy order I'd suggested. And forthwith, an ill-assorted crew of young and old, clothed in the variegated garb of Saturdays in the city, turned to, shoving the big, stiff-bristled brooms Joe had secured from the City's Sanitation Department against the accumulated papers, cigarette packs, orange peels and whatnot strewn across the cobbles of Fulton Street. Others stood waiting with shovels and garbage cans to pick up the gurry as it was gathered into piles. When this warm, sweaty work was finished, Joe opened the valve on a sidewalk hydrant, and started playing a stream of water on the sullen, dirtied stone surfaces of the swept-up street.

"Now we're going to get the last crumbs of this mess, and polish the cobblestones till they shine!"

With that, while some of the more sedately dressed retired to the banks of what became a running stream rushing down the gutters, youngsters took over the scrubbing of the cobblestones, pushing sheets of water before them. When that operation, much more fun than the dry work of stirring up clouds of dust and detritus, was finished, everyone started to smile, and a little cheering broke out.

"Not so fast, my friends," said Joe. "Our president has to inspect this street before we start congratulating ourselves on a job well done."

Accordingly, I started at the corner of Water Street, where our sweep-down had begun, and progressed toward the river, stooping over to examine the gleaming cobblestones I walked over. At length I found what I was looking for—a paper match wedged in between two cobblestones. I clawed out the sodden object and held it up so everyone could see.

"Mr. Chairman," I said (for Joe was chairman of Friends of South Street, and on this day most certainly my boss), "we can't call this street clean with this kind of obstacle clogging the way. We'll have to do this over to get this street really clean."

Joe looked around at his panting crew. "All right, ladies and gentlemen, let's tackle this job again, and this time get it right."

With that, the firehose played again across the drying stones, everybody laughing and kids playing in the gurgling gutters, and our crew of sweepers scrubbed the cobbles again until they really did shine. This time, when the sweepers reached end of the street, Joe and I strode out into the middle of it and, after a searching look up and down the gleaming way, I said: "Chairman Joe, I believe we can now pronounce this street *clean*."

I found myself moved to be part of an effort to scrub clean the streets of this run-down industrial area. The event made clear our appreciation of this neglected corner of the city—a feeling shared by all who took part in the scrubdown. And it would perhaps inspire others.

When I had first taken the idea to Joe, he had clapped his great hands together and said: "That'll show the world! When do we start?" With the date set, he had turned to and secured the City permits to close the street, provided the equipment to do the cleanup, and passed the word to volunteers to turn out for the day. He was above all the person to whom the people would listen. And when he asked them to do something, they would do it.

Some 150 people had turned out, of whom approximately half were actual workers; the spectators supplied cheers and encouragement. Among the working group was Ken Patton, Administrator of Economic Development, with his wife Helene and their young sons, Douglas and Lawrence. Lawrence, at age 6, was likely the youngest in the crew. Ken was one of Lindsay's bright young people who were out to change the city—but noticeably more feet-on-the-ground than many of these new-minted leaders. He articulated the message of the day for the *Daily News* reporter who had shown up, saying:

> *We're going to use urban renewal to save rather than to tear down. If all this city is going to get is the monotony of new growth . . . then we're going to die."*

This was an extraordinary statement coming from the prophet of re-development and growth. It had an Old Testament ring to it, echoing Solomon's pronouncement: *Where there is no vision, the people perish.*

With shadows lengthening in the street as the afternoon drew on toward evening, some of us stayed to close down and lock up before going on to the Square Rigger Bar. We all felt that the day had been more successful than we had hoped. The feeling in the street, the camaraderie created by the simple act of doing physical work together had impressed us all, even the children who saw their parents cheerfully doing what garbagemen were paid to do.

Into the Square Rigger, soon after we'd settled down, walked a sturdy, purposeful-looking man, who asked Joe the bartender: "Is there someone called Peter Stanford here?" When Joe gestured to our table, the man came over and introduced himself brusquely as William Broughton. I recognized the name: Broughton was a man from Alabama with whom I had exchanged letters. He owned a more refined sister ship of our schooner *Athena,* built to the same Alden blueprints but in a more yacht-like style. Since he was interested in old schooners and lived in the right part of the world to help with our investigation into *Caviare*'s actual name, I had asked him to look into the fishing fleet in Pensacola to see if any records survived that could prove the actual identity of the Seaport schooner—of whose alleged identity we had grown more and more doubtful with the passage of time.

"So, you've decided to hang onto that false name you've got on the fishing schooner," he said, glowering down at us. "And I thought you people were real historians."

I got to my feet.

"What on earth are you talking about?" I asked.

Broughton said he had sent us a documented report establishing the vessel's name as *Lettie G. Howard.* I said I'd seen no such report. Broughton looked at me as if I were crazy.

"No, really," I persisted, seeing that he was sincere in his indignation. "You may have sent your report—I haven't seen it.."

Then, perhaps realizing I was telling the truth, he sat down and ordered some of what we were having. Over a Guinness and beer he then explained what he had discovered. He had soon found out that people in the fleet had no idea what schooner had been rebuilt almost fifty years earlier to carry the name *Mystic C.*, the name under which Paul Henry Dunne had bought her before he renamed her *Caviare*. There were old hands willing to tell stories for a free drink, even stories about *Mystic C.*—but nothing about the schooner she had been. And E. E. Saunders, the firm that owned the vessel in 1923 when the conversion took place, had lost all its records in a fire. Undaunted, Broughton then visited the shipyard where Saunders vessels had been hauled for bottom overhaul. He tracked down the old hand, H. L. Mertyns, who had kept the hauling log in the 1920s, where plans were noted to arrange blocking of the different hulls. In Mertyns's log for 1921–34, the *Howard*'s page bore a 1923 entry: "name changed to *Mystic C.*" Eureka! An entry in a bound book, all in the same handwriting, was virtually impossible to fake. Broughton had sent us a photocopy of the log and a tape of his interview with Mertyns attesting to its authenticity. Tracking down Mertyns in his hospital bed in his final illness and securing this positive evidence, in a scene where ownership records had vanished and memories of decades-old events were blurry, was a first-class piece of scholarly research, as we all recognized on the spot, cheering Broughton and clapping him on the back.

On Monday we turned the curatorial office inside out and found Broughton's package, addressed to me, unopened in a corner. It had all the hard-won evidence in order, just as Broughton had said. The problem was that someone had messed up seriously in handling an important communication—and worse, one that we had been expecting to receive. The incident, coming after the triumphant street cleanup, bore in on me how over-stretched we were and how badly we needed the time and assistance to establish real museum disciplines.

As for the name change, further research by the historian John Lyman and by Chapelle at the Smithsonian established the pattern of removing the raised quarterdecks of old Gloucestermen and re-registering them under new names and numbers, to get better insurance rates. They accepted Broughton's solid evidence that our schooner was the *Howard*. When all the testimony was in and had been weighed by the Ship Committee and trustees, *Caviare* duly regained her rightful name, *Lettie G. Howard*, in the spring of the following year.

Mayor Lindsay cut a fine figure making his way through the crowds on Pier 16 to open the Waterfront Festival on 19 September. He came aboard *Wavertree* to make a short speech and then was treated to some rollicking songs on a sailor's life at sea and ashore, as sung by Bernie Klay, who was clad in hot oilskins on this brilliantly sunny day. He joined a luncheon of the Holland Society being held aboard and then mingled with the crowd on the pier, which extended back up Fulton Street where our antiques show was in progress, spilling out from the clean-swept sidewalk into the newly-scrubbed cobbled street. The surging, variegated, happily engaged crowd gave vivid testimony to how our ships were bringing new life to long-neglected city streets.

While the mayor was with us, he was able to watch the careful docking of the ferry *Major General William H. Hart* on the southern side of Pier 15. The *Hart* was a squat, ungainly hunk of ship, painted red with jaunty white pilot houses at each end, set off by two tall black smokestacks, side by side amidships. At 151 feet in length, she was a baby compared to the big ferries on the Staten Island and Hoboken runs, but she bulked large in our eyes and was the right size for the Fulton Ferry run to Brooklyn. She had served on other East River runs, a survivor of the breed that had churned river waters since Robert Fulton's first ferry crossed to Brooklyn in 1814.

"Who's aboard?" asked the mayor, as the ferry slid gently into her new berth, urged along by two McAllister tugs whose services had been donated to bring her in. We told him it was Benjamin Hammer, a high school senior who had initiated the negotiations that led to the vessel's donation by the US Coast Guard, who represented the Seaport on the delivery trip. John Lindsay, strong on youth and innovative arrangements as he was, looked taken aback at this, but was reassured that a Coast Guard captain had also been aboard with a handling crew to back up our teenage representative.

"She is in relatively fine shape today," wrote Benjy Hammer in the *Reporter*. "Her hull is sound, as are her engines. Brasswork abounds. Brightwork trims doors, frames, lockers, benches and bulkheads. Nearly all of her lighting fixtures are of antique style." And she soon acquired her own team of volunteers eager to clean her up, so these grand accoutrements would properly represent her days as an East River ferry.

Our headquarters crew and I were tickled to have the ferry in our fleet of ships. But Monk Farnham, chairman of our Ship Committee, was deeply offended by our haste in grabbing the vessel before she was scrapped. We had grabbed the buildings of the Seaport in order to save them—before we had any complete plans for their restoration or any funds to take care of them. Mindful of this, a majority of the Ship Committee approved the move, but this was not enough for Monk. He wanted to see spelled-out plans for the future of the ferry, money on the table to carry out those plans, and time for the committee to study the plans and reach a reasoned decision.

Time, of course, was just what we didn't have, if we were to save the ferry from scrapping. We also wanted to bring her in under the mayor's eye and in plain view of the thousands of New Yorkers we'd assembled, to make it clear that South Street Seaport was now an established part of the city scene. But Monk could not see these reasons for proceeding as we did. However, he stayed on as chairman of the Ship Committee, despite the hidden rift between us, and he continued to take pleasure in his tenure in that office, in which he performed well.

The wild ride of the Waterfront Festival ended with a very tame Schooner Race for the Mayor's Cup. This fourth race was run in light vagrant airs with a strong ebb tide, so the course was shortened to a buoy in the Narrows. This led to a pileup at the buoy, as vessels faced the ebb tide to return to the finish line. A happy result was that a small gaff-rigged schooner, the 30-foot *Mongoose*, won not only the Alfred F. Loomis Trophy for the gaff rigger finishing first, but the Mayor's Cup itself, which had hitherto been won only by the more modern, marconi-rigged schooners. Our *Pioneer*, a heavy working schooner, finished last, thereby winning the DeCoursey Fales Award: a box of cornflakes and a bottle of Beefeater Gin.

The schooner race worked well to advance the Seaport cause. Not one, but two Circle Line boats served as observation vessels, and William F. Buckley, Jr., fresh from his defeat as a mayoral candidate running against John Lindsay the year before, lent us his Bahamian schooner *Cyrano* as an observation boat for patrons of the museum. Norma and I were delighted when my mother, Dorothy, decided to sign on to watch the race from this privileged seat, since in her work for South Street she kept so rigorously out of public view, answering inquiries with handwritten letters and helping fellow volunteers as needed. And she reveled in the day on the water aboard Buckley's marvelous schooner, which sported the gloriously long bowsprit which gave rise to her name.

One schooner was notable by her absence from this race—our own *Athena*. She had done her part in the Sea Day harbor cruise which opened the Seaport's summer season in this memorable year, and in the veteran seaman Bob Herbert's June sail-training cruise with Seaport Explorer Scouts, and later with the Girl Mariners in the Great Schooner Race out of Gloucester in August. But of sixteen outings noted in the log, only five included Norma and me—for the rest, we simply could not break away to take part in the sailing.

Norma and I had not forgotten Karl Kortum's warning that we could do either the museum or the schooner, but not both. I believe from this moment, when we had neither time nor funds to get the boat's derelict engine repaired for the trip through Hell Gate to New

York, we began to believe that our great friend's fell dictum was in fact coming true. We would just have to see what the future held for our much-beloved *Athena*.

But we felt increasingly assured of the future of our South Street venture as this eventful year drew toward its close. As one passes from ebb tide to flood tide when sailing across a tide-line at sea, it takes a moment or two to realize that the tide has turned. For the Seaport Museum, whatever present troubles afflicted us or what lay ahead, the tide had turned. All of us felt this sea change. With the arrival of our great ship, *Wavertree,* and the acceptance in City Hall and, even more important, in the remote streets of the outer boroughs, the Seaport was on it way as a recognized institution in the life of the city.

CHAPTER 32

The Seaport Established, *Year-end 1970*

Membership at 15,000—Museum is Home to Six Vessels—
Civic Leaders Speak at "The Seaport in the City" conference—
Jakob Isbrandtsen on "Work and Opportunity"

"Miracle in South Street," trumpeted the headline in the November *South Street Reporter*. The editorial announced what we had all begun to recognize as a miracle, the establishment of the Seaport Museum in the heart of the city. It continued confidently:

> *It all had to happen together: major new donations to the* Wavertree; *immediate resolution of the first sale of air rights to a neighboring developer; and large increases in membership growth and publication sales.*

With the arrival of the *Wavertree*, the Seaport Museum had become keeper of an imposing collection of historic ships, backed up by a great surviving stretch of sailing-ship waterfront buildings celebrated in exhibits and publications, all supported by an active membership of 15,000 people from every walk of life. We reckoned we were doing well in our sponsorship of a major urban renewal area in the heart of the nation's leading city.

This last point was central to our vision: We saw the museum and its educational programs to be the shaping force that would determine the character of an entire seven-block neighborhood. We had already gone some way to demonstrate that its character would attract businesses linked to seafaring, whether in historic ships, sail-training ships or oceanographic vessels, working through these vital messengers from the oceanic world the transformation of a whole section of New York.

This had been achieved, and was being carried forward, on what can only be described as a shoestring budget. We had built up income from $409,000 the previous year to $730,000 in 1970. This 78-percent gain gave us $321,000 in additional funding to meet our growing obligations. By year-end we would reduce our indebtedness from $511,000 to

$401,000. Within these tight budget parameters, we survived and kept things going by a fire-brigade method of shifting our thin but highly motivated staff from one project to another, while the volunteer corps manned our public front in tasks ranging from guiding school groups to manning the ships and the desks at the exhibition hall and book shop. So we kept the Seaport Museum open 363 days a year, closed only on Thanksgiving and Christmas.

But we knew we needed to occupy and develop our waterfront in greater strength for the Seaport Museum and its neighborhood to realize their full potential.

The root problem was that we still had no clear title to the waterfront we administered! Despite Board of Estimate approval of the basic terms of the 99-year leases and the mayor's repeated assurances that the leases were being drawn up, a year and a half later, the actual signing had yet to take place.

This was a serious obstacle to the progress, and even to the survival, of the museum. Understandably, the corporations, foundations and wealthy individuals who were willing to fund our venture could not make serious investments in properties whose status was not fully established on a legal basis. We were, in essence, still squatters on the waterfront we administered.

The first sale of Seaport air rights, cited so confidently in the *Reporter*, had set a triumphant precedent in city zoning. But there was a joker in this deal. The purchase of air rights by TelCo (New York Telephone Co.) for the new office tower they planned to build in the block behind Schermerhorn Row had been arranged. But, again, the sale could not be completed until the Seaport's leases to its properties had been signed. So this vital initiative was also stalled until the signing took place.

We saw no immediate way to resolve this impasse.

But we kept working on it, and we hoped the public's high expectations reinforced by the City's reassurances would allow us to continue to increase our activities and effect gradual improvements to the Seaport buildings, ships and piers. This was all we could do, and it was what we *had* to do. The venture had come so far, after all, only because we had continuously shown it could work, and work in some excellence.

After the waterfront festival, Norma and I sat down to review our strengths. In the uncharted waters that lay before us, what did the Seaport have going for it?

First came the membership: We had 10,000 in 1969 and were on the way to reach 15,000 by the end of 1970. The yearly gains clearly signaled that membership growth, far from tapering off, was a stronger force than anyone had anticipated.

This would be a very difficult force to turn off if the land settlement began to look like failing, as it had early that summer when City Bank was moving to cancel the loan for the Seaport land. And each draft of new members brought us increased recognition and a deeper hold on the public imagination.

Second, in any reckoning of assets was the Seaport's historic fleet. Our claim to the waterfront had been made highly visible by the arrival of the *Wavertree*. The great ship now presided over a unique fleet of ships of the late sailing ship era: the tug *Mathilda* of 1899, the original *Ambrose* lightship (1907), the fishing schooner *Howard* (1893), the coastal schooner *Pioneer* (1885), and the last East River ferryboat *Hart* (1925). This grand collection was backed up by the turn-of-the-century industrial ironwork of the Lacey ship repair barge.

Captain Lacey's barge was an asset in its own right, in ways beyond what we first understood. Her presence, with her skilled crew and dedicated master, assured us of an ability to restore our ships to the highest standards. And beyond that, Bill's intimate knowledge of New York Harbor and the respect he was held in by its denizens assured us of the professional advice of working harbor operators, as well as continuous donations of materials, services and other support.

Our third asset was the quality of the Seaport's work in historical interpretation, a strength attested to by such leaders in our field as Robert G. Albion, the premier historian of New York port; Howard Chapelle, maritime curator of the Smithsonian; the seaman-author Alan Villiers, pre-eminent historian of the last days of deepwater sail; and Karl Kortum, the leading figure of the San Francisco waterfront renaissance. These people had come to us, because they knew the importance of the South Street story in both the development of worldwide seafaring and the growth of America. Once involved in Seaport affairs, they were readily caught up in the citizen dream of a restored South Street in the heart of our city. They continued with us, as we've seen in this narrative, because they wanted to see that dream achieved, and achieved in excellence worthy of the subject.

Thus, when we learned from Karl Kortum that authentic gear for the *Wavertree*'s forecastle head existed in the hulk of her younger sister *Riversdale* on the West Coast of Canada, none of us thought, oh dear, how will we ever get these relics and bring them to New York—all 14 intricate, unwieldy tons of them. Instead, the ship committee pondered this question, and when Jim McAllister told us he planned a trip to Vancouver, asking if he could do anything for us there, we told him of our need. And he set to work on it. His success in this task depended on a chain of people in responsible positions going out of their way to help in a difficult unpaid project. And they cheerfully lent a hand because they knew Jim wouldn't have asked their help if it weren't important. That trust meant every link in the chain held, despite the considerable burdens imposed on each link, each one a person whom we had never met.

The fourth and final asset was an intangible that affected everything we did and dreamed of doing: the lively style of how we went about things in South Street. This shone through the way visitors were welcomed and invited to share in our story; in the long detailed discussions held in the office, on the piers or in the street, and in off hours at the Square Rigger Bar—discussions which went to the heart of what we were doing and, most important, why. In these exchanges, our people learned to welcome raw ideas being reshaped and finished work being intensively reworked to become something better. Staff, volunteers and supporters alike were discovering that excellence was within our reach, even without the ample funding we all wished for. And they pursued that excellence with a positive joy.

So these were the strengths we could bring to bear on the scene before us: the dynamic, burgeoning membership; the ship establishment, backed up by a maritime repair facility to keep it afloat; a growing reputation for excellence in our work; and a can-do, heads-up way of going at things.
 As part of our effort to break through conventional barriers, we had embarked on two long-shot ventures.

First was the decision to undertake a program of active sail training aboard the schooner *Pioneer*. This gave wings to our work! Even before we'd developed a budget for her operations, volunteers had begun training cruises aboard, under Dick Rath's direction, and we now had the ability to take city youngsters afloat to learn the lessons of seafaring at first hand, under sail.

The second was the installation of the National Maritime Historical Society headquarters in our former office at 16 Fulton Street. The Society's founding purpose to save the *Kaiulani* was perhaps beyond achieving, but they could generate a rising tide of public interest in saving historic ships and bring fresh support to ships that had been saved, and they would sail under their own flag, with their own governing board. They might one day prove a valuable ally—who could tell?—that might actually help relieve our threatened beachhead for history in the heart of a busy metropolis.

"Well, we've certainly convinced ourselves about how right we are to charge on down the road, because the road is open and we can do it," said Norma at this point in our situation review. "But it's only going to take us so far. We've still got to get the leases signed. And we can't leave Jakob hanging out there forever, paying interest on the buildings he's bought for us."

"Boats, I would give anything to relieve Jakob's situation and see our own resolved. But the only way I can see to go is to do what we do best—drive straight ahead, enlisting New Yorkers in our cause."

"Skipper, just a minute. Let's think this through. We're counting on the support of real people, and you're asking them to believe in something that simply isn't happening. The day will come when people no longer believe in the air rights sale—they'll give up on the land ever coming to the museum. We're vulnerable while this situation lasts, and the city bureaucracy could go on stalling things forever. We've got to recognize that we don't have forever."

"No," I said, "I know we don't."

"Well, let's do something to make things happen," Norma went on. "Can't we line up some of the civic leaders and planners we've been working with—and get them to make our case? That should reach elected officials and maybe shine some light on the Atlas-McGrath back-alley work which I think is behind the City's delays. McGrath was corporation counsel for the City, wasn't he? And isn't it the corporation counsel's office that has been holding up final approval of our land arrangements?"

"Yes, and yes," I said. "And yes to getting our supporters to make our case."

This approach held a gleaming appeal to me. It meant we'd be fighting on our ground, the open field of public opinion, rather than the twisty back alleys of feudal municipal politics, out of public sight or knowledge. Perhaps I had been over-hasty in feeling sorry for John McGrath in his lonely testimony before the Board of Estimate two years before. Perhaps he had good reason not to worry too much about what elected officials decided, when he could work his interior lines of communication to wreck our citizen venture.

And it was encouraging to be doing something that would keep us moving forward. Before we went to sleep that night, Norma and I had sketched out a plan for a colloquy on what the Seaport Museum meant to the City of New York. This, we decided, should be led by Kent Barwick, who was now director of the Municipal Art Society.

With Kent's help, we readily got a panel led by Joan Davidson, and included William Kroeger, of the Lower Eastside Neighborhoods Association, with whom I had worked since the days of Rutgers Club; Allon Schoener, of the New York State Council on the Arts; Roger Starr, of the Citizens' Housing and Planning Council; and Richard Weinstein, of the Office of Lower Manhattan Development.

There would be a morning session on what these civic and government leaders believed the Seaport could contribute to New York and to New Yorkers. This would be followed by a luncheon session to review the panel's findings and to hear what some supporters of the Seaport Museum had to say about its role. Our chairman, Jakob Isbrandtsen, readily agreed to join us, along with Karl Kortum and George F. Baker, III, a supporter of the *Wavertree* project and secretary of the South Street Seaport Council, a group of supporters who had made substantial contributions to the Seaport.

I doubt that there was one of the nine people involved who did not understand the need to speed up City processes to keep pace with the needs of a great project for its people. We were a little worried about Richard Weinstein, a close friend of Dick Buford, whom he had succeeded as head of the Mayor's Office of Lower Manhattan Development. It was through his office, following up on Buford's initiative, that the first sale of any Seaport air rights had been made. But we'd received mixed messages about his feeling for the Seaport.

While Weinstein wanted the project to succeed as a cultural jewel to add to the glittering crown of Lower Manhattan development, he seemed curiously numb as to what the seafaring heritage was and not at all interested in how we celebrated it. His lack of understanding of both the Seaport's purpose and the dynamics which drove it severely hampered any real cooperative effort to move the land arrangements forward. For this reason, Norma questioned whether Weinstein should be included. But we did need his active interest, and I suggested to Norma that the session might give this bright but difficult individual a chance to learn a little about the Seaport and its ultimate objectives.

At 9:30 on the chilly morning of 3 December our old upstairs office at 16 Fulton Street rang with the sound of new voices chatting over welcome cups of steaming coffee. Kent opened the proceedings of "The Seaport in the City" by observing:

> There is probably no other cultural institution in the city that needs this conference less, and there is perhaps no other cultural institution in this city that is so anxious to have it or can do more with it.

Then he kicked off the discussion by offering this:

> One thing people notice about South Street is the great numbers and different kinds of people who support it. The old right and the new left, and hard hats and hippies, and rich men and poor men. I suppose the quintessential example of this is that both Pete Seeger and William F. Buckley, Jr., tie up their boats here.

He added:

> It cannot be that all these people see the Seaport the same way.

Joan Davidson responded with a thoughtful appreciation of human variety:

> I care about this place from two points of view: because I love the city and I think it's essential to the city, and because I care about the state of the individual in the mass society that threatens to crush us all. I think this small effort has already brought fantastic vitality to New York and will do much more.

Roger Starr of Citizens' Housing & Planning then spoke on the city's disunity. But, he said, in the Seaport New Yorkers

> can reach out through one of the senses that unified this city originally, which is that this was a seaport and remains a seaport—the fact that all of us, by ancestry at least, reached here by water from somewhere else.

Allon Schoener, who dealt with South Street among other museums, said many were in trouble with the neighborhoods they were in. He noted:

> South Street isn't in that kind of trouble—it has been built and

has conducted its affairs with effective participation by a wide variety of people.

He felt its future was assured through its investment with people, a commitment unique in his experience.

Richard Weinstein, whose viewpoint we had been awaiting with some interest, took strong exception to this. The Seaport's future, he said, was far from assured in today's economic climate. The Seaport Museum had to learn to deal with forces in the city which could either encourage or impede its growth. And he questioned whether we had developed the depth in planning to deal with the economic challenge of building and running the Seaport.

To this Allon responded that an idea so widely held would "find its way" through all obstacles. Its strength lay in the people who believed in it, who would simply make it happen by the force of people's desire to see it happen—as, in fact, it was happening today. This did not satisfy Weinstein. When asked how the Seaport had come into being, he looked puzzled for a moment and then came up with a two-word answer: "By accident."

This did not sit well with the rest of the group, who clearly felt that much more than mere accident was involved in the creation of the Seaport. But Weinstein clearly felt that we didn't understand the gravity of the problem we faced in securing the Seaport land, and—moreover—that we were not competent to deal with that challenge.

Bill Kroeger then spoke of the Seaport as "a creative factor in the development of human resources," a more assertive formulation than most of us would have ventured. He went on to explain: "The Seaport has been involved in developing an atmosphere in the Eastside." He saw the Seaport as a place where children could come after school to see what it is that the lore of seafaring and the heritage of the seaport have to offer people in our community.

As he spoke, I recalled my own encounters with neighborhood children in South Street, always guided by Julia Strew or Rudy Staw, Marie Lore, Edna Fitzpatrick or other citizen volunteers who had raised

their own children in the disciplines of the previous generation—and
who always seemed to get the youngsters to pay attention and to ask
their questions or offer their own answers in an easy but orderly way. The
"atmosphere" Bill Kroeger described was truly a product of the caring
of those volunteers and their story of what the Seaport was about. Bill
also said that he saw the Seaport Museum as a point of preservation
in our neighborhood and, at the same time, a departure point for development. Everyone liked that idea: preserving things as a point of
departure for doing the next things.

Allon Schoener then took us a little deeper into the idea of the
Seaport as a center for people and history. He first questioned whether
the Seaport should be called a museum, since most museums are
"essentially boxes . . . that you stuff things into"—and clearly the
Seaport was something more than that. Then he reflected on the era
we celebrated:

> A 19th-century lifestyle involves a direct relationship with the
> elements . . . with doing things with your hands, with your body,
> which you don't do in our society, our mechanized society.

This stirred Roger Starr to utter a gritty appreciation of what the
South Street experience should be, in words that ventured beyond his
earlier call to unity in a divided city. We should not, he suggested, make
the Seaport "a sentimental place where we preserve in pristine splendor
ships as they never were . . . un-loused up by human contact and activity." Rather, he said:

> I hope that we will maintain and recreate here a sense that people
> worked and died and were killed in accidents, and fought and
> bled, if you will, against nature and all the recalcitrant force of
> human experience to build something together here on the shore
> of this ocean.

Joan was caught up by this vision, adding:

> The kind of history that should happen here, whatever form it
> takes, should be the kind . . . that gives Americans again a kind of
> pride in who they are and where they came from . . . whether we

do it by displays, by activities, by the kind of building that happens here . . . that has to be the end of it, it has to be consummately real, never, never hokey.

As the upstairs session ended, Roger Starr made a quiet observation:

I wonder what happens to me when I come down here.

To which Allon Schoener had an answer:

South Street changes people's heads.

With that we marched off down the wooden stairway into the noontide street, joining a clump of children headed for the ships at the piers, as we walked down Fulton Street and round the corner to Sloppy Louie's. There, Emil Morino met us at the door, his customary napkin over one arm, to usher us in and tell us that our guests were waiting upstairs.

We found Jakob ensconced at one end of a long table with Karl—the two always seemed to gravitate together. With them was the young George F. Baker, III, looking from one to the other of these remarkable men, who seemed to radiate a sense of the forthright seafaring culture to which our work was dedicated.

Jakob, not always happy at being asked to speak, arose beaming at us all as he bade us welcome with a proprietary air. No wonder, since without him, none of this meeting could have occurred. And this was his formulation of what we were doing in South Street:

The city itself grew up where it did for work and opportunity, and that is why South Street Seaport Museum is here.

This formulation of "work and opportunity" was another unerring arrow shot by Jakob, getting to the heart of the occasion by getting at the fundamentals.

Karl Kortum then spoke on the vital role of ships in the story we were here to tell. He pointed out that our ships had influenced our work even before we had any ships. Their story of far voyaging had seized us—and was now driving us to tell that story in the heart of a busy city. And look how people rallied to that story! Karl pointed out that in San Francisco the success of the *Balclutha* had reshaped the surrounding neighborhood. "Success building on success in widening circles." He added:

> You will find the thing has its own inherent direction. Youth train-
> ing, publications, and all the rest grow out of this.

He then laid down this adjuration:

> You need here the strength of four big square-rigged ships—to
> match the buildings and live up to your opportunity.

This picture made us catch our breaths, the more so because Karl so evidently meant every word of what he said. The ship presence had re-shaped its surroundings, giving a potent meaning to Jakob's word "opportunity." To live up to our opportunity, in short, we had to be as expansive in our vision as the ship captains before our time had been, whose sailing built a city from the sea.

George Baker reaffirmed the central role of the *Wavertree*'s presence on our waterfront, which he had helped bring about, and said that what she meant could be seen here every day in the faces of the children who came to see her:

> Children can be shown pictures, given lectures, or confronted with
> artifacts. Here they find their way into whole systems, in context:
> the systems of work and living that built the city. . . . Such experi-
> ence changes a person. And that real change is what education is
> all about.

For me, these varied pictures of the South Street experience lit up our scene like fireworks, picking out shapes of buildings, ships and people in vivid relief. In this light, Karl's outrageous call for four big square riggers could indeed be achieved one day, if, in addition to the two big museum ships we planned on, you included a ship that might sail out of New York in sail training, and the occasional sail training ship stopping in from down the coast or abroad. Jakob's emphasis on opportunity as the theme of our work made immense sense, as did Karl's call to us to live up to our opportunity.

Both men, as it happened, were echoing Alcaeus of Mytilene's words on the city, which had resonated with me since the day I came across it:

> *Not houses finely roofed or the stones of walls well builded, nay nor canals and dockyards make the city, but men able to use their opportunity.*

As for our own prospects as keepers of the dream, I took note of Richard Weinstein's viewing our work as happening "by accident." This sent some premonitory shivers down my spine. I took heart in Joan's response, when she said the Seaport must look to its own strengths to prevail:

> *And I think those that feel it, and that care, and that want to, will help. But it has to grow out of its own being and develop from within, the way it has and the way it will continue.*

That was the essential message of the colloquy.

Toward the end of the year, laid up in bed with a cold in the snow-wrapped fields of Yorktown Heights, I thought over what I called in my journal "the amazing position we'd won" in South Street over the past three years.

I started by reflecting how our own lives had changed. Norma and I had moved our household, from the small house in Laurelton, back to Mr. and Mrs. F's farmhouse in the woods in Yorktown Heights. Mr. F had at length decided he would end his days there, as he had meant to when he bought the house in 1935. So we had settled into a multi-generational household, where we converted the third-floor attic into a roomy bedroom with a sweeping view of a big field running to a tall oak at its end, and the glint of the Croton Reservoir water showing through the woods beyond. A spare room was commandeered as our library, housing our 2,000-odd books.

Athena suffered from lack of care that year. Two-thirds of her outings under sail this year had been conducted by friends without us aboard. These included the grand trips of Girl Mariners led by Bob Herbert, and the schooner's participation in the Great Schooner Race in Gloucester. After we failed to make it to our own Schooner Race for the Mayor's Cup in September, friends sailed her back to Milford, where Al could keep an eye on the schooner as she lay at his dock in the harbor, in need of a new engine and a good deal of work on her aging wooden hull.

As for South Street, my thoughts were turned toward our work to tell the story of what mankind had learned from seafaring—a story that was the heritage of all mankind, and one that gained in value as it was more widely shared. In my year-end journal entry for 1970 I took note of a few thoughts I came across in H. G. Wells's *Outline of History* and copied out: "the only science and history of full value to men consist of what is generally and clearly known." I also noted with real delight his concern with "the ordinary men and women who are the substance of mankind."

It had been a great thing, as we all knew, to bring the *Wavertree* into South Street. Her arrival changed the look of the city waterfront and the great ship had things to say to the ordinary men and women who came by. Norma and I were resolved to do our living best to deliver her message, of man's experience coursing the world's oceans under sail.

CHAPTER 33

Gathering Strength and Purpose, *1971–1972*

Staff Changes—Pioneer's Success—*NMHS Launches*
Sea History—*Sea Museums Council*—ICOMM Conference—
Lacey's Barge—McAllister Bros. Towing—*Bicentennial Designation*

The year 1971 opened inauspiciously when, on 9 January, Piers 13 and 14, just south of our Pier 15, were swept by a five-alarm fire. Seaport members, hearing this news by radio at their breakfast tables, piled in from different parts of the city to offer help, while two McAllister tugs stood by in the river, ready to tow our ships to safety. The fires were soon put out, so no help was needed. But the response cheered us all—although the Seaport's tenure of piers and buildings might be uncertain, its hold on the loyalty of its members and tugboat captains was certain beyond doubt.

However, the same large ship establishment that made New Yorkers aware of our presence also placed heavy demands on our limited organization. There was overstretch everywhere, and these strains showed as we worked to develop the Seaport within tight budget constraints. In two of the most difficult steps we'd ever taken in South Street, early in the year we discharged George Demmy and Alan Frazer, two principal managers. Their dedication and skills were unquestioned, but critical deadlines were being missed and we felt we had no choice but to make the change. George and Alan were popular with all hands, but our decision was accepted quietly. Norma, who was then office manager, stepped in as director of ships and piers and, happily, Frank Braynard offered his services to replace Alan as program director.

Capping these unsettling developments, we had to cancel an announced run of performances of the play *Billy Budd* aboard the *Wavertree*, which had been planned and sponsored by the Amateur Comedy Club—a step forced on us by changing demands of the new Commissioner of Ports and Terminals. Although we had met US Coast Guard requirements for the *Wavertree*, and had provided more than the required access and egress,

Commissioner Leedham insisted we adhere to New York City building codes aboard the ship, including the preposterous requirement to encase all the ship's interior metal surfaces in concrete! It became obvious that these demands were about something other than public safety. Important supporters had lent their names to the performances; fortunately they stayed with us for further ventures. At the April meeting of Friends of South Street, however, I came in for criticism on my handling of the fiasco. It was also rightly noted that staff services needed strengthening.

Trustees decided to intervene on the staff question, and Jack Aron donated the services of a retired executive of the J. Aron Company to oversee ships and piers. The executive, in turn, hired as ships and piers manager a volunteer who had attracted trustee attention by strident criticism of the ships and piers staff. The new ships and piers manager then proceeded to hire a group of his pals, regardless of budget. After two months of mounting expenses, sloppy work, and raging hostilities between the new gang and the staff/volunteer crew, I let the Aron executive go, along with the newly hired pier manager and his recruits. Senior volunteers were then reinstated under Norma's direction; to our relief, they came back. The difference was felt immediately; ships and piers were soon cleaner with less than half the paid staff. And Jack Aron, to his everlasting credit, said not one word about my dismissing his former executive.

We had embarked on two special programs in late 1970 to keep the momentum of purpose needed to assure South Street's future. The first was the sailing of the schooner *Pioneer*; the second was the commitment to build up the National Maritime Historical Society as an operative entity worthy of its imposing title. Both projects were unprecedented in our field, and each was mounted with no initial resources other than the people involved, all volunteer in the first year.

The *Pioneer* program developed nicely under Rath's skilled touch. With Geo Matteson as skipper, the schooner set sail on 1 May 1971 with ten teenagers who had completed the Phoenix House program for former drug abusers—launching what the *Reporter* described as "a first-of-its-kind educational program sponsored by a maritime museum working in cooperation with an agency of city government." It was also a first for the sail training movement, which had been mostly limited to serving youngsters whose parents could pay the cost. But our bills were minimal: Our skipper, mate, cook and two hands were entirely volunteer this first year. A $10,000 grant from the Vincent Astor Foundation, supplemented by others chipping in, met out-of-pocket costs.

Some trustees said this money should go to meet our operating budget rather than to fund a new project, but Brooke Astor had already turned down a trustee approach for operating funds. A letter sent by *Boating* magazine's Terry Walton, working with Dick Rath, had secured the Astor grant for the *Pioneer* program. And *Boating* editor Monk Farnham ran on-deck training sessions for city youngsters before *Pioneer* sailed, while *Boating* publisher Syd Rogers approved these goings-on and authorized the use of the magazine's letterhead to solicit support from advertisers. All these were new resources, accessible to us only through *Pioneer*.

The summer was a triumph, with great benefit to the ninety young city-dwellers who learned to work the traditional schooner, with no injury to any of them. An unfortunate accident did occur in a race in Rhode Island waters, which *Pioneer* had entered with her crew of youngsters. In close quarters, Barclay Warburton, at the helm of his brigantine, *Black Pearl*, headed up to force *Pioneer* into the wind. This was a valid, if aggressive, tactical move. The only hitch was that the *Pearl* moved faster than the centerboard schooner could get out of the way, with the result that *Pioneer*'s main boom caught in the *Pearl*'s fore topgallant backstay. This brought the brigantine's fore topmast crashing down in a tangle of spars, cordage and flapping canvas.

With the fate of the *Pioneer* program at stake, I drove to Newport, picked up Geo from the schooner, and rowed over to the *Black Pearl* to express the regrets of the museum, Geo having already conveyed his own. We reviewed the incident, and Barclay at last understood that, despite Geo's prompt response at *Pioneer*'s helm, the old centerboard schooner simply couldn't turn quickly enough to avoid the collision. I was impressed by Geo's account of the accident from where he stood at *Pioneer*'s helm—still more by his answers to Barclay's questions about the training of the city kids aboard *Pioneer*. Geo left early to rejoin his crew, while Barclay and I went on to have a peaceful dinner talking about the British Sail Training Association and the lack of any such organization in the United States.

I continued in close touch with Barclay, while he pursued his developing interest in the sail training movement. He had told me he planned to sell *Black Pearl*, which had rot in her cabin, but that winter he had her partly rebuilt instead, and the summer of 1972 he and his son Tim (Barclay IV) sailed her to Europe for the Tall Ship Races with a crew of young trainees. When the *Pearl* came home, the American Sail Training Association was founded in her after cabin with Barclay its first president.

In the meantime, Terry Walton, Rath and I drafted a letter asking Mrs. Astor for funds to open a Pioneer Marine School to train city youth for jobs in marinas. Brooke Astor came down to talk with us about it—as we thought she might, since we had asked for a sizable grant. We met in the after cabin of *Ambrose,* where Brooke was clearly taken with the spirit of the *Pioneer* program as well as its results. As 1971 ended, we received notice of a three-year grant of $250,000. The school opened aboard the ferry *Hart* in September 1972, and the following year over 90 percent of its graduating class found jobs in the booming marina industry. Each student had two weeks of sail training at sea aboard *Pioneer* before courses in how to repair marine engines taught by personnel from the various engine manufacturers. This combination proved a heartwarming success and added a distinct dimension to the museum experience. With typical generosity, the *Pioneer* volunteers held classes for the general public on the piers, which included rowing classes held in two lifeboats donated by Moran Towing.

The National Maritime Historical Society, quite a different venture, also came through for us in 1971, starting with the publication of a small illustrated history of the historic ship movement, *The Ships that Brought Us So Far.* Norma and I produced this in odd evening hours as a first attempt to document the field of ship saving, illustrated with photos from the files of the ship museums and fleshed out with firsthand accounts of ship saves led by pioneers in the field such as Carl Cutler, Frank Carr and Karl Kortum.

We avoided blowing South Street's horn in *The Ships,* since we wanted to make it clear that the National Maritime Historical Society (NMHS) was sailing on its own, not as a dinghy towed by the South Street ship. But Peter Manigault, vice president of the National Trust, wrote a preface for the book in which he took it on himself to celebrate the South Street venture in memorable terms:

> *In the awakening and widening world of historic preservation, South Street Seaport is known both for the breadth of its planning and the practicality of its procedures.*

He went on to say that we were

> *well embarked on a plan which includes urban area redevelopment, museum building, publishing and ship preservation—in addition to a wide variety of educational and recreational programs—the latter so imaginatively conceived and exuberantly blended that it is difficult to say just where the teaching ends and the fun begins.*

In this project, as in the *Pioneer* project, we relied on volunteer leadership. But we could not have taken on either one without first-class help. In the National Maritime Historical Society we depended on the rock-solid support of our mentor Karl Kortum. And Monk Farnham's support and active intervention in the training of young people enabled us to take on both the sailing of the *Pioneer* and the establishment of the Pioneer School.

Other things happened in 1971 to assure continued progress. These ranged from Leon Kaplan's Maritime Europe Tour, leading a dozen fellow members on a three-week exploration of maritime museums and historic ships in France, Germany and Britain—signing up European members as they went!—to Norma's and my own tours covering museums and historic restoration projects as far afield as Maine and Virginia with two-year-old Robert and his younger brother, Joseph, in tow. These trips provided grist for the *Reporter*'s mill, encouraging members to make their own explorations.

Closer to home, Jim Kirk, Norma and I visited John Noble aboard his studio barge in the Kill van Kull, the crowded waterway that separates Staten Island from New Jersey, serving as the entry lane to the giant containership terminals carved out of the Jersey marshes. John was the artist of the harbor and was full of harbor lore gathered in his youthful seafaring in coastal schooners in the 1930s. We noted:

> *The stories go on, wry, sometimes bitter, sometimes funny, always scrupulous and vivid in attention to detail; they make a portrait of workaday life among people making a hard living on the waterfront.* I noted also: *Noble ran his own museum in the window front of a bar on Lower Broadway, and while the original managers lived, they refused all other offers to buy out these windows.*

That spring, Norma and I and a few friends had pulled together a small group we called the Pub Preservation Society, in collaboration with Frank Gilbert of the Landmarks Commission. This group of like-minded friends sought out interesting pubs that had the right blend of tradition and the feel of a neighborhood gathering place. These excursions led to much discussion about the possibility of a South Street pub sponsored by the museum, with regular song fests and sea music. We even chose a name for it: "We'll All Go Together," from one of Fewtrell's favorite songs "Wild Mountain Thyme." Pubs were, in fact, oases of seafaring culture. In seamen's bars like Hendrickson's Corners in Bayonne, New Jersey, the walls were crammed with John Noble's work. It also reached a wider world through seamen he'd sailed with, like Mystic's Biff Bowker, and John Stobart, who prized Noble's work and today sits on the board of the Noble Maritime Collection in Staten Island, which was established in Noble's memory. The truths of his life gleam in his work, particularly in the haunting lithographs of his later years. Norma and I made visits to Staten Island to talk with him of harbor history until his death twelve years later at age seventy.

Pursuing our explorations of other maritime museums and restoration projects, we discovered that their people were at least as interested in what we were doing as we were in what they were doing. From the crusty Admiral Dufek at The Mariners' Museum in Virginia to the affable Waldo Johnston in Connecticut's Mystic Seaport, people asked us how we had done what we did in South Street. We were invited to give talks to workshops at Colonial Williamsburg and the New York State Historical Association at Cooperstown in upstate New York, which led to quite lively discussions.

In the face of this prevailing spirit of outreach, it surprised us to find out that there was no association for the exchange of information and ideas. Noticing how our South Street members welcomed news from outside our district, we formed a committee of the museum leaders with whom we'd been in touch, this to provide a forum for inter-museum exchange. We called this group the Sea Museums Council, which embraced, besides South Street, the leading maritime museums in Pennsylvania, Maryland, Virginia, Michigan, Oregon and California, plus the Smithsonian Institution in Washington, DC—eight in all, a not inconsiderable gathering of forces. The New England museums were holdouts, led by our friends at Mystic Seaport, who I think were a bit wary of our informal ways.

Nothing daunted, in April 1972 the new Sea Museums Council tackled its first project, publishing the first issue of *Sea History*, a 34-page journal devoted to maritime heritage news, edited by Frank Braynard. Frank was helped by a few willing hands, under the direction of Robert Bruce Inverarity, director of the Philadelphia Maritime Museum, as chairman of the council. Our goal had been set forth in sweeping terms at a meeting held the previous autumn:

> *The museums of the Sea Museums Council have joined together to promote greater cooperation among maritime museums. Jointly we can share solutions, exchange technical information and unify*

the mass of maritime history, artifacts, legend and lore. Through our journal Sea History, *we disseminate our information and illuminate the activities and research being carried out in the field.*

We did not want to end up feeling we were talking to ourselves, and Bruce fortunately added a few words calling for broader communication between the keepers of history and

the public who love the waters of the earth and the vessels that ply them, from canoes and canal barges to great square riggers and steamers.

To anticipate a little, this evocative charge to involve the public in the heritage of seafaring became the mission of the magazine *Sea History*, which continued publication as the journal of the National Maritime Historical Society after the Sea Museums Council was reorganized in January 1973 as the Council of American Maritime Museums (CAMM), with Mystic's Waldo Johnston as president. The members of the old council made up most of the membership in the new CAMM, with the important addition of Mystic and three other New England museums.

After CAMM's first meeting in Mystic, the next meeting was held in June 1974, at South Street Seaport. We adjourned for lunch at India House, a short walk southward. There, our Yankee guests from the rock-bound New England coast walked softly under the stern gaze of ship captains and portraits of their vanished sailing ships—distinctly their kind of thing. Each member received a copy of the special leather-bound edition of *The Wavertree: An Ocean Wanderer*, leading Ernest Dodge of the Peabody Museum of Salem, founded in 1799, to make a suitably Bostonian comment. Plumping himself down in his chair, looking very much like President John Adams with white hair framing his ruddy face, he picked up the book and flipped through its pages.

"Good grief, Waldo," he said across the table, "I didn't know our new friends in these parts did this kind of thing." This made our day, removing the spectre of a *kulturkampf* between the brahmins of Boston and the hotshot admen of New York.

And so the National Maritime Historical Society made its way, still tied closely to South Street Seaport Museum, with its magazine *Sea History* slowly earning its way to become an accepted addition to the scene of things maritime.

Our involvement with inter-museum affairs took on a new dimension when Mystic Seaport Museum and the National Maritime Museum in Greenwich joined forces to form the International Congress of Maritime Museums. Its first meeting was held October 1972 at the National Maritime Museum, a world-famous establishment on the Thames on the outskirts of London. I attended to represent our young museum.

Walking in the portico leading up to the Queen's House, built by Inigo Jones in the early 1600s—a walk that encourages peaceable thoughts—I was startled when an earnest messenger stopped me to ask if I was Peter Stanford. When I said that I was, the equerry told me that the museum director, Basil Greenhill, wished to advise me not to make any reference in the conference to the San Francisco museum's paddlewheel tug *Eppleton Hall*. There had been a fuss, I knew, when Karl Kortum and Scott Newhall had taken the *Hall* to California, while the contemporary tug *Reliant*, meanwhile, had been partially preserved in the National Maritime Museum. With one paddlewheel lopped off, and a Cunard liner's stateroom shoved into the hull as an exhibit where the coal bunker had been, the *Reliant* was outshone by her sister tug, now steaming San Francisco Bay.

The next morning, a report on the *Reliant* presented the tug's restoration as representing long-planned advances in ship exhibitry. This was capped by Basil himself, as cochairman of the conference, stepping up to the podium to declare that Mr. Karl Kortum of San Francisco had conspired to steal the *Reliant* from the museum and would be "clapped in gaol instanter" if he dared show his face in England again! He clearly wasn't joking.

This performance did not sit well with me. So I stood up to tell the story of the authentic restoration of the *Reliant*'s sister *Eppleton Hall* and her transAtlantic voyage, recounted earlier in this narrative, and her active steaming in San Francisco Bay. I was gaveled down and ordered to be silent after two or three minutes, but I got the essential story across. At the end of the morning's proceedings, I was mobbed by a crowd of young curators from other museums, who wanted to know more about the *Eppleton Hall*. I told them that the "long-planned" restoration of the *Reliant* was in fact improvised to counter the favorable publicity earned by the *Eppleton Hall*. The museum's initial plan was to save only the *Reliant* engine. Since the *Reliant* hull was in much better shape than the burnt-out hulk of the *Eppleton Hall*, Karl and Scott had urged that the hulls be exchanged, with the *Hall* engine going to the National Maritime Museum and the *Reliant* to be restored to steaming condition. Failing to get the *Reliant*, they had embarked on a complete rebuild of the *Eppleton Hall*, which they then steamed to America in one of the great ship saves of our time. This was greeted with cheers and laughter.

As I left the lecture hall a slight, studious-looking man came up to me, introduced himself as Frank G. G. Carr, and asked me out to lunch. Carr, a friend of Karl's, had served as director of Britain's National Maritime Museum from 1948 till 1966, developing the museum from a little-known repository of naval gear and records to the world's leading maritime museum. As a child I'd read his books on sailing barges and his own pilot cutter, *Cariad*, and over lunch I found him fascinating company. Norma and I were to become Frank's partners in a number of historic ship ventures, and in future visits to England we stayed with Frank and Ruth in nearby Blackheath.

While awaiting the arrival of Norma and the boys after the conference ended, I made my first visit to London since I'd left there in 1952. When I stopped in at the Royal Ocean Racing Club headquarters in St. James's Place to say hello, I was glad to see Brian, the club bartender, still behind the bar. His response on spotting me at the door was one for the books.

"What'll it be, Mr. Stanford?" he asked cheerily, after my twenty years' absence. "The usual?" And the usual it was, "gin and it."

Norma then joined me from New York with Rob and Joe, and we went on to spend a grand week in the West Country, visiting a Devon shipyard where a replica of Drake's *Golden Hind* was taking shape, and later the City of Liverpool Museums' maritime museum. There I spoke on BBC-TV early one morning, overlooking the deserted waters of the King George docks in support of Alan Villiers's call for the museum to move to the waterfront. We made pages of notes on the wonderfully evocative seaport exhibits built by Michael Stammers, one of the young curators I'd met at the conference, which featured reconstructed waterfront alleyways echoing to street vendors' cries, the sound of horse-drawn carts, and the songs of children playing games. This look at traditional shipbuilding and fresh concepts in exhibitry was the great gain of our trip, along with meeting Frank Carr. Like Frank, Michael became an ally in our work in NMHS and *Sea History*.

With these new initiatives in sail training in the *Pioneer* and in inter-museum relations through the National Maritime Historical Society, the Seaport Museum progressed, albeit slowly, in restoring our floating empire of ships. This owed much to the efforts of Norma, Jim Diaz and the volunteer pier crew. But serious progress would have been impossible without Captain Lacey's Marine Ship Chandlery.

And in 1972 the chandlery undertook a remarkable development. Learning that Horn & Hardhardt, the big New York restaurant chain, had given up its franchise to run a snack stand at the entrance to Pier 16, Bill Lacey offered to open a stand of his own, using a shipping container on the pier. This, he said, could earn enough to keep his skilled work crew employed when work was slow. For our part, we knew we needed a place where a family could get good food at an affordable price—and we were deeply aware of the importance of keeping the Lacey crew intact. So we agreed to the Lacey proposal, supported by Jakob, Briggs and Eric. But one couldn't help wondering how Bill, a master mariner working with a crew of shipwrights, would make a go of it in fast food service, where a leading chain restaurant had failed.

I need not have wondered. From the first, the Lacey crew turned to with a will, slinging burgers and hotdogs, while they answered questions about the ships and the harbor they knew so well. The steel shipping container, christened the "Seaport Galley," became a recognized gathering place for people coming onto the pier. A large tent was soon erected with tables and chairs set out below, and as summer turned to autumn, side panels were added. By November an enormous pot-bellied stove fought off the chill air, and one often found school groups gathered about the stove's guard railing, hot cocoa in hand, enjoying their field trip to the Seaport.

This helped Bill's company, the Marine Ship Chandlery, achieve a growing income stream to offset the continuing cost of maintaining the workshop staff aboard the Lacey barge. Bill's office aboard the barge, separated by a bulkhead from the cavernous workshop with its silent machines, was visited by a stream of visitors on all kinds of business, ranging from donations of materials for the ships to new schemes for developing income on the piers. Out of this grew an informal group, known as the Wharf Rats, which held its first meeting on 30 March 1972 and monthly thereafter on Thursday evenings.

A powerful harbor presence stood behind the volunteer harbor activities that clustered around Bill Lacey's Marine Ship Chandlery barge—namely the strong interest taken in Seaport affairs by McAllister Bros. Towing. The McAllister fleet of tugs and barges, founded by James P. McAllister in 1864, is still identifiable today by the two white bands the tugs sport on their red funnels. Earlier in this narrative, we've seen how the friendly relations between James P. McAllister II and our chairman, Jakob Isbrandtsen, led Jakob to turn to Jim for help in all kinds of harbor matters. And in view of the McAllister family interest in harbor history, it was natural to appoint Jim's son James III as chairman of the Seaport's Ship Advisory Committee.

It came quite naturally for James III (as well as Jakob and myself) to stop by Bill Lacey's chandlery office for harbor news and gossip—the more so because the chandlery barge had until recently been run as a division of McAllister Bros, based in Staten Island. Bill was particularly pleased at becoming his own master, because, as he told us, McAllister paid him $3 million for two aging tugs he owned in the McAllister fleet. Having no wish to run these boats independently, he was glad to have this cash infusion from their sale as capital to run his own business—which he had now begun to do in an informal but effective partnership with the Seaport Museum by taking over the concession on Pier 16.

Harbor people have long memories, and the soundness of these intertwined relationships depended on Captain Lacey's rock-solid character, proven in his World War II service in Liberty ships, where he was decorated for saving the crew of his ship when it was torpedoed on the Murmansk run. And the long unbroken family succession in the McAllister firm proved sound enough to take to the bank when, in the next few years, refinancing was needed to build the next generation of powerful tugs to handle giant container ships

Unfortunately, what was becoming the corporate faction on our board of trustees was simply unable to understand the seamanlike values involved in Lacey's shipwrights running a food service more effectively than Horn & Hardhardt proved able to do. Nor did they see the value of keeping those highly skilled carpenters and welders available on standby for major jobs when the Seaport Museum had money to retain them. The fact that Lacey's crew proved to be able instructors in training museum volunteers in replacing their skilled services with volunteer services simply put the cap of total unbelievability on top of these unconventional arrangements.

There was no trouble, however, with the gift of towing service by McAllister Bros., which was willingly received. It was hard to say no to that kind of gift, which was worth many thousands of dollars each year, not even counting the harbor people's connections and good will that came with it.

Remarkable people continued to check in aboard the Marine Ship Chandlery barge, led by Jakob's friend, Joe Farr, a retired marine engineer labor organizer, who lent his organizing talents to sorting out volunteer assignments. We named Joe relief skipper of the *Wavertree*, and he set up his office aboard the ship in the old mate's quarters. From there, he coordinated staff and volunteer work, consulting Bill on every step, which led to comradeship and cohesive operations on the piers. Another daily visitor was Jeremiah Timothy Driscoll, who ran the harbor tanker *Sterling*, which he kept at Pier 15, supplying the museum with free fuel as rent. Every now and then Eddie Atmanchuk would make an appearance, a quiet man who ran a one-man backyard shipyard from his home on the banks of the Passaic River, off Newark Bay. And of course, there was Freddie Kosnac, who would walk up from his houseboat office moored near the foot of South Street to visit and exchange harbor news with Bill.

George Tollefsen, a tall, quiet-spoken man who ran a ship-fitting business in Brooklyn, showed up in Bill's office one day and offered to clean and repaint the *Wavertree*, sea-worn from her long tow up from Buenos Aires. When I told him we would like to see the job done but had no money to pay for it, he said: "I know that, Peter, and you know it. But we can't afford to let the world know that. She needs steam-cleaning and a lot of paint—and who said anything about money anyway? Our gang and I are proud to make the job a gift."

So it was done, and the proud full-rigger looked herself again, though still lacking her rig. George went on to help keep things shipshape in dozens of ways through his myriad harbor connections. His attitude was "these are *our* ships, and they should be kept up to snuff."

Now and then a harbor magnate would stop by with a question. One such was Francis J. Barry, president of Circle Line, which then ran harbor tours, as it does today. It held a near monopoly on the business in this era, helped by strong connections at Ports and Terminals. Bill had invited Frank Barry in to hear our plans to run a revived Fulton Ferry from the Seaport to Brooklyn. Bill wanted to be sure that we would not meet any opposition from Circle Line on this, and Frank said he would have no problems with our running the ferry. As he left, he said he had a question to ask us. He had been pilloried in Jerry Driscoll's book, *Crime Circles Manhattan*, and he wanted advice about suing Jerry, as Circle Line lawyers recommended. At this, Bill looked over to me, and I gave my view: Publicity from a lawsuit would do more damage than Jerry's accusations ever could. "That's what I thought," said Frank. He knew our friendship with Jerry, but he also knew that our advice was sincere.

While we eked things out in caring for our ships, our public program flourished under Frank Braynard. Volunteers greatly extended the outreach of limited staff, in our usual style. I met with Borough President Percy Sutton in the spring to lay the groundwork for a visit by the *Lettie G. Howard* to Harlem's Sherman Creek. This proved a great success, with over 2,000 residents boarding the schooner in a visit over the Fourth of July weekend; so we staged a repeat visit aboard our other schooner, *Pioneer*, at the end of her sailing season in the fall.

The active participation in South Street programs of New Yorkers of all ranks and backgrounds had much to do with New York City's designation of the Seaport Museum as an official site of the national bicentennial in 1976. The designation was awarded on 18 September at the Metropolitan Museum of Art, which was also receiving the designation. This recognition owed much to Frank Braynard's pioneering work on Operation Sail '76, for which we had set up an OpSail '76 Committee a year earlier. The presentation was made to South Street first, because, as the presiding official, J. Clarence Davies, pointed out, the museum was a project of so many New Yorkers of all backgrounds. Met director Tom Hoving took this in good part. Later, during a tour of the museum, he told me that a four-ton pre-Columbian statue he'd recovered from the Central American jungle was the largest artifact ever brought in one piece to New York. He was somewhat jarred when I told him that we had brought in an artifact weighing some 2,000 tons.

"What!" he exclaimed, eyebrows arched high. I explained that this was the weight of *Wavertree*'s hull. "Oh," he said, dismissively. "You mean a *ship*."

I said we regarded historic ships as artifacts, some of the most expressive that man has ever produced. After the meeting, feeling I had not made my point with Tom Hoving, I told this story to Walter Lord, an aficionado both of the Met's Mayan statuary and our ships. He expressed surprise at his friend Tom's reaction, and held forth eloquently, as we waited for the downtown Lexington Avenue subway, on the way every line in a ship's design counted in a unified vision. You couldn't make sense of a part of a ship without envisaging the whole. I was delighted to hear this simple truth so well expressed.

Bill Lacey's genius for making things work shone in a reception of a quite different nature we held for Barbara Johnson of the Museum of American Folk Art at the end of 1972. The evening meeting was held after a heavy snowfall, which only made things snugger as we gathered near the warming stove on the rugs Bill had thrown down to cover the splintery planking of the pier. Barbara was entranced with the caravanserai feel of an encampment on a trade route, and she outdid herself as she took us through her far-flung quest of the whaling heritage, handing out priceless scrimshaw carved on whale teeth to be passed around, along with other treasures, including whaling captains' journals, letters home from distant climes, and photographs of whaling men and their ships. As the company broke up to trudge homeward across the snowy pier, people were saying that they'd never attended such a meeting. It owed much to Barbara's intimate hands-on passing around of artifacts from distant waters—and much also to Bill Lacey's ability to bring people together in an unapologetically industrial setting which celebrated its seafaring origins.

A remarkable pair of people added some new dimensions to our Seaport fleet in this year 1972. Captain Ray Wallace, a West Coast artist and designer we'd come to know through Karl Kortum, had engineered the arrival of our second Cape Horn square rigger in South Street, the great barque *Moshulu*. Four years earlier, we had included a model of *Moshulu* in our Seaport exhibit, knowing well that she was still out of our reach. Her installation in South Street was financed by an adventurous entrepreneur, David Tallichet, who planned her as a restaurant ship in the Seaport fleet. Built on the Clyde in 1904, the 3,100-ton vessel, half again as big as *Wavertree*, was an early example of the big four-masters that closed out the final era of deepwater sail. Her 35-year career under sail, in fact, ended with the final grain race from Australia in 1939, which she won hands down—a stormy passage fortunately recorded in lively detail by Eric Newby in *The Last Grain Race*, a book he wrote as a member of the working crew. The vessel had a remarkably shapely hull, a fact early recognized by Norma. She had not been enthusiastic about adding another big ship to our burdens in South Street, but when she went out to greet the barque's arrival in New York, she came back a convert to her cause.

Before this installation of our second Cape Horn square rigger, Tallichet had brought in the paddlewheel steamer *Alexander Hamilton* in April, fulfilling our dream of having in our fleet this last grand paddlewheeler, famous as the "White Swan of the Hudson." Known to our members through the Riverboat Balls we'd held aboard, courtesy of Frank Barry, we realized that she was beyond our grasp, her ornate layered white wedding-cake decks presenting a maintenance problem calling for a dedicated crew assigned to her. Seeing her in the Seaport model, Tallichet had decided to take her on as a second commercial venture, believing the two very different vessels would together create a compelling destination. A bomber pilot who flew over 20 missions in World War II, Tallichet carried a strong sense of mission into his business career, including the waterfront developments Ray Wallace designed for him, and he wasn't one to go by halfway measures.

Ray Wallace, for his part, did more than design Tallichet's traditional waterfront buildings. He inspired Tallichet's interest in ships as the active agents that bring waterfronts alive. This interest had deep roots in Ray's own life. He had been saved from a tough childhood, which included brushes with the law, by going to sea in a ship surveying Pacific islands, and so became a believer in sea training for children of the city slum.

He went on to raise funds to rebuild a wooden schooner in Portugal to represent the brig *Pilgrim*, trained a crew to sail her to California, and launched a sail training program for disadvantaged youngsters—in which *Pilgrim* continues today. Ray's own career as artist and designer led to his designing ships for Disneyland, then to his being retained as designer of Tallichet's traditional seaport villages, and ultimately to bringing his ships to South Street.

So, not for the first time in our story, people of vision and ability had brought about an extraordinary development in our venture, bringing us two of the very ships we'd shown in the Seaport model. Sadly, difficulties with the City's terms for allowing the two big vessels to remain in South Street were to lead Tallichet to withdraw his plans, and the mighty *Moshulu* went to Philadelphia where she flourishes as a restaurant ship today. No lasting home could be found for the *Alexander Hamilton* and, while in Raritan Bay awaiting a promised grant, she was hit by a violent storm, smashed up beyond recovery, and eventually scrapped.

CHAPTER 34

A Place for People and for History, *Early 1973*

Lunch with Brooke and Friends—Strengthened Staff—
Banking the Air Rights—A Flood of Favorable Testimony—
Signing Seaport Lease—Progress in Exhibits and Publications

Maybe, I thought, just maybe, I had carried my total immersion approach too far. Brooke Astor, it is true, was looking perfectly at home in the deserted room we sat in, chairs stacked on tables all around us. But the tall, shy guest who had accompanied her to the meeting looked rather subdued, even a bit apprehensive—while Joe Cantalupo sat across from me with an uncharacteristic "*Now* what do we do?" expression on his face.

We had met at noon on the clear, bright Wednesday of 10 January 1973 outside 16 Fulton Street, where Brooke got out of her car, accompanied by a diffident stranger whom she introduced as Laurance Rockefeller. I was with the Danish archaeologist Ole Crumlin-Pederson, a leader in the excavation of Viking-era ships. A good-looking young man, he was one the curators who had rallied to my defense at the ICOMM conference in England a few months earlier. When he stopped by my office to say hello, I suggested he come with me to meet Mrs. Astor. After suitable protests, he joined me, to Brooke's evident pleasure, and proceeded to regale her with the story of how we'd presented the actual story of the *Eppleton Hall* at the conference, despite being warned not to do so. The story told, Ole politely bowed and left us.

We three then set out to tour the Seaport neighborhood, starting at 16 Fulton Street with the Seaport diorama and our exhibit on South Street's waterfront history, and proceeding on to the Fulton Street shops: the museum's own Seaport Books & Charts at the corner of Water Street and Fulton, where so many good things had a way of beginning; followed by Fulton Supply, a seamen's clothing shop which attracted yachtsmen and fishermen alike with its sweaters of lanolin-rich Norwegian wool and first-class foul-weather gear; and then the Fulton Retail Fish Store, where Jack Scaglione, behind his brilliant piscatorial display, after being introduced to our guests, offered us a cup of clam broth or something stronger, which Brooke declined on the grounds that we had to keep our heads about us to take in what was going on in the Seaport; and we paused to say hello to Louis Cohen, presiding in his vivid red tam-o'-shanter at Eagle Bag & Burlap, the shipping bag store which had evolved over time into a seamen's curio shop crammed with coral necklaces, exotic sea shells and a lugubrious-looking diver's outfit.

We then hastened on across South Street onto Pier 16. There we boarded the *Ambrose*, where Richard Fewtrell, manager of the *Wavertree* restoration, regaled us with stories of the men he'd met at sea who had sailed in square riggers in the Cape Horn trade, and how seafaring lore was passed down in sailing ships' fo'c'sles. Laurance, an active yachtsman, was particularly interested in the continuities of traditional ship's discipline. Richard also told how seafaring mythology lived on in the wild, haunting sea songs sung by ships' crews, which he and the volunteers sang together in the evenings. Brooke seemed fascinated to learn of this recondite form of folk art, and Richard told her he'd be glad to pipe her a stave any evening she might like to join the crew over a glass of grog. I was glad, as we left, that we'd met in the snug after saloon of the *Ambrose*, which we had chosen over meeting in the chill, echoing loneliness of the still unrestored *Wavertree*, and there was no question in my mind but that the tour had gone well. The shopkeepers had expressed a real sense of the Seaport neighborhood that was taking shape, while the charming, scholarly Ole Crumlin-Pederson and plain-spoken, salty Richard Fewtrell added a strong sense of the Seaport's connection to the wider world.

And so, ushered in by Emil Morino, we gathered for lunch in the small upstairs dining room of Sloppy Louie's. Joe Cantalupo had joined us on the pier, duly introduced as chairman of Friends of South Street, and the *Wavertree* stood just outside the window to remind us about the Seaport Museum's mission. Hoping that Brooke would get her own feel for the Seaport neighborhood, I had prepared no plan for the meeting. But something more seemed called for, so, raising a glass of Famiglia Cribari wine, I said what a pleasure it was to have Brooke with us again, and how glad we were she had brought Laurance. I then said: "Laurance, when David Rockefeller paid us a visit aboard the *Ambrose*, people would not let him alone for one minute, so I've seen how the Rockefeller name can be a real burden. But here you can stand easy, because it wasn't your name that got us seated in these exclusive surroundings, it was Joe Cantalupo's name—a name to be reckoned with in the Fulton Market."

Joe, rising to the occasion, responded: "Peter, you know that isn't so. No one listens to me in the Market. I just happen to know the Morinos as good friends, who know how to cook a bouillabaisse the Italian way."

"Fiddlesticks, Joe," said Brooke, "your name is beautifully painted in gold lettering on your trucks, which I must say are kept wonderfully clean, and Joseph Mitchell calls you the authority on Market lore in his stories about the neighborhood. Won't you tell us a little about that? How did you start out in the Market, for instance? It seems such a closed world from outside."

Joe was much taken with Brooke. So he happily launched into the story of how his father, Pasquale, had emigrated from Italy and started the carting company in 1896 to handle the garbage of the expanding Fulton Market, by that time devoted primarily to fish—which "make a lot of mess." He had grown up in the trade, resolved to have fun while maintaining the strict disciplines that gave the Cantalupos the cleanest wagons in the business. He told how he had signed a Communist Party petition in the 1930s, because he agreed with the particular issue at stake (now lost in the mists of time) and how this had very nearly led to his excommunication. And how his late cousin Angelo, who lived all his life in Little Italy on Mulberry Street, was forever telling him: "Joe, you go too far." Joe clearly looked up to Cousin Angelo, but it was apparent that he relished quoting his cousin's words in suitably doom-laden tones. Joe said visitors to the Market often asked questions about the Mafia, and one visitor from uptown had asked him if he carried a gun in dealing with these people. He had answered simply: "That would be a big mistake."

"And how about the new Seaport neighborhood?" Brooke asked, in her engagingly pertinacious way, having at one time earned her living as a reporter. Joe gave her a great smile at this question.

"For me, this is the adventure of a lifetime," he said. "With Peter and Norma and all these young people doing something about the history of this place it's like heaven. They've even got me wanting to learn more about the ships they've brought back, and I'm no sailor—I'm a land animal."

The pride Joe took in his part in the Seaport venture shone in his eyes. I told how he and Captain Lacey, who had the same ambitions for the ships Joe had for the streets and buildings, had struck up a great friendship. Dealing with maintenance problems ashore and afloat, using mainly volunteer resources to keep things up to snuff, the two talked with each other every day—and every few weeks the three of us would have a Friday lunch together, which had become part of our Seaport routine.

Over coffee we were joined by Bronson Binger, whom I introduced as our director of design and construction. I explained that he had been working for the past six months on plans for the full development of the Seaport district, an essential major step for raising the money needed to restore the ships, piers, streets and buildings in a working historic neighborhood.

Bronson then set forth the elements of the plan, as worked out with Kent Barwick, director of the Municipal Art Society, and Dick Buford, former head of the Mayor's Office of Lower Manhattan Development, both of whom held seats on our board. This was familiar ground to Brooke, who had a great interest in neighborhood revival projects, and when Bronson had finished his presentation, fielding the odd question here and there, it was Brooke who brightly asked: "And how much will it cost, Mr. Binger?"

"We can do the plan for one hundred thousand dollars," pronounced Bronson. "Any less wouldn't produce a plan that would pass muster with donors and investors."

"Well, Laurance—what do you think of that figure?" asked Brooke.

Laurance had not said much so far. Now he said: "I think your figure is wrong." Pausing while we digested this, he continued: "It's too low. From everything I've heard, you want a plan that's flexible, one that you can revise as you go, and learn from what you've done so far. Why not do a three-year plan, with regular reports on progress?"

Everyone nodded. It *was* a better way to go.

"Very well, then, I'll fund such a plan with a contribution of $200,000."

While we were stammering out our thanks, Brooke Astor rose from her chair, smiling beatifically, and said: "Come on, Laurance, we're going to be late getting uptown in this traffic."

On the way back to 16 Fulton Street, where Brooke's car awaited her, Laurance fell back to have a word with me, while Joe and Bronson went ahead with Brooke.

"I don't fully understand how you've done it, Peter, but it's clear to me that you and Mr. Cantalupo and your friends have secured the interest of the people of New York—the ordinary people, the people you're doing the Seaport for. That is a priceless asset."

"I know that," I assured him.

"Well, I believe you do. But you've got to make that clear to others: city officials, bankers and, above all, your own board. The interest of the people is an endowment that will stand as an investment against inflation and other evils that can erode money values. It's the most important asset you can have for a project like yours."

Once again, I was stunned. Here was someone who saw the real strength of our organization in the people it enrolled. And somehow he had fathomed the remoteness of our board from this scene. The board was increasingly dominated by the business executives appointed at the behest of City officialdom who maintained that they would lend credibility to our cause. Unlike earlier trustees, this new generation had not shown any prior interest in the Seaport. They seemed bored by talk of our purposes in South Street and also far removed from the concerns of philanthropy, social responsibility, or any understanding of the importance of history.

Had Brooke held her discussions with the members of the board, she might well have reached entirely different conclusions about the value of the Seaport. Fortunately, Brooke preferred to talk to people doing the work rather than those presiding from above. And Bronson had been able to show what we specifically needed to build to the vision we had established.

We had hired Bronson in May 1972, as part of a general strengthening of the staff. By living close, we'd managed to save more than half of the previous year's income of $730,767, enabling us to clear up debts and start 1972 with funds in hand. At the trustees meeting of 8 December, Ted Stanley of the Restoration Committee had called for added staff, "since restoration planning and development functions are greatly hampered by lack of staff study and follow-up." This gave me the backing I needed to hire Ellen Fletcher Rosebrock as architectural historian working with Bronson. Her assignment soon extended into exhibit development with Norma and writing studies of the Seaport neighborhood, which she pursued with a sure feeling for history, old brick, and the sense of a community evolving through time.

We also had hired Richard Fewtrell to run the *Wavertree* restoration, to which he brought a strong background in seafaring under sail, a wide range of hands-on skills, and a love of the seafaring culture. David Brink was hired as director of the new Pioneer Marine School, which he ran successfully under Dick Rath's guiding hand. And upon Karl Kortum's urgent recommendation, Norman J. Brouwer, a trained museologist with seafaring experience under his belt, was hired as historian in October 1972. Norman ventured far beyond his bookish studies and had a keen sense of the importance of volunteerism in our work. He had served as a volunteer on the *Kaiulani* project when it was headquartered in Washington, DC, before 1970. Fundraising to support this expanded staff was reinforced after Karl and I met with Marshall Streibert, who impressed us both enough to take him on as fundraising manager, a job to which he brought a clear focus and a winning style.

One of the joys of having money in the bank was to pay off the last of the Wijsmuller bill for towing *Wavertree* to New York a year and a half earlier. Arthur Wijsmuller, a solid burgher in a black suit sporting a gold watch chain, came by on 1 December to collect the outstanding balance of $5,000, which was a year and a half overdue. I handed him his check and explained that we were struggling to meet our obligations while City officials still havered over the air rights deal long ago approved by the mayor. Evidently deciding that I was telling the truth, our visitor leaned forward in his chair to say: "I can see that you and your people are doing important work." I then told him about meeting the *Titan*'s crew when they brought in our ship, and at my invitation, he told me the story of his company.

His father had died young during the shipping depression of the 1920s, whereupon his arch-rival in deep-sea towing, Smit, went to Mrs. Wijsmuller to buy up the company tugs at a very low price—and with the proviso that no Wijsmuller would work again in towing. His mother said no to this, and the banks soon foreclosed on the company. He and his brother, having lost the fleet, managed to buy one old tug. From there they had rebuilt the company to a strong position by World War II. Fascinated by this account, I asked him about the company's work in the war. Mr. Wijsmuller then told me the real names of the characters involved in Jan de Hartog's *Holland's Glory*, a tale of Dutch tugs working in exile to save ships damaged in the U-boat attack on Allied supply lines. As I started to scribble these names, our visitor raised a hand to say: "Don't bother, I have to leave now to catch my plane, but I'll send you a list of the names from Amsterdam." With that he was off, clumping down our long wooden stairway. When we did not hear from him, I called the Amsterdam office, only to learn Mr. Wijsmuller had died of a heart attack right after his return from New York. I was saddened by this, but relieved that, before he died, he had learned that we were honest people.

While our on-the-ground financial gains were making possible the strengthening of staff, a seismic change in our land dealings was taking place, in which we could practically feel the land shift under our feet. This was not a comfortable feeling at the outset, when we first learned what was afoot. We had gone to Milford in late May 1971, to spend the weekend working on *Athena*—I in the cabin at my typewriter, Norma caulking and sanding the schooner's wooden topsides while keeping an eye on Robert and Joseph. Barnaby Blatch was with us, and Saturday evening I told him that our trustees had little confidence in the air rights deal on which we based our claim to the Seaport land. Barney, from his vantage point in City Bank, told me that City Bank felt the same way. He said plainly that I'd better forget about South Street air rights, because "the Atlas-McGrath deal is fantasy."

If that were true, it meant that Atlas would not erect a new building on the block west of Schermerhorn Row in which Jakob had acquired significant holdings—so there would be no sale of air rights to that building. We both knew that Jakob's Seaport Holdings could not pay its bank debt and turn over the Seaport land to the Seaport Museum without the funding provided by the air rights sale. We were dumbfounded.

But then, when Norma and I talked about this on our drive to work on Monday, Norma insisted that the required values were still there, even though there was no immediate market for the air rights. "Why don't the banks themselves buy up the air rights?" she wanted to know. "There is real value in the air rights—any developer would love to be able to build a taller building than one zoned for his land. The banks can then hold them for future sale when the building market revives—as it surely will."

I pointed out that that was extremely unlikely, since banks are accustomed to dealing with assets that have a definite value on a definite date.

"Wait a minute, Peter, we've been here before," said Norma. "The values are there. The problem is that people don't *see* them. This is a new concept and people are always wary of new ideas. We have to change the bankers' viewpoint—get them to see that the air rights will always be useful to developers—to see them as real collateral, then wait until the market is ready to buy them."

She was right, of course. We had to give the bankers a new picture of the air rights as permanently marketable assets.

First, I needed to get Dick Buford's OK to advocate this step, which was, after all, the only solution in sight to acquiring the Seaport land. From my first meeting with Buford four years earlier, I had noticed a growing impatience whenever I raised planning questions, so Norma and I agreed that I should not argue the case with him.

"All you need is his OK for you to discuss the idea of banking the air rights with the banks."

When I presented this thinking to Dick, he said cheerfully enough: "I don't think for one moment this scheme will work. The banks will never buy it. But you're the president, so go ahead and give it a try."

So we set to work on a statement calling for banking the Seaport air rights, describing how the rights would have value for as long as New York itself had any future. Lining up support for this proposition certainly made the idea of banking the air rights seem less unreal. Kent Barwick brought the Municipal Art Society solidly into line, and Parks Commissioner August Heckscher, our hero of Sea Day 1970, called for action on "this excellent idea." And a feature editorial, "Future of South Street Seaport Is Up To Banks—Foundations," appeared July 1972 in the *Longshoreman's Voice*, journal of the International Longshoremen's Union, Local 1814. The union's endorsement added important blue-collar backing to the support of civic and cultural leaders.

In the month before the *Longshoreman's Voice* editorial, the *New York Times* had run a story featuring the Seaport as "key to Manhattan Landing"—a vast landfill project on the East River waterfront reaching to the southern tip of Manhattan. This $1.2 billion undertaking was not about to be built in the worst building recession of the postwar era, so putting our buoyant little craft alongside this giant sinking *Titanic* was not what we needed. But the article did report the City getting the New York Telephone Company to sponsor a building on the inland block where the Atlas-Isbrandtsen building was to go. Robert Graham of City Bank was named as working to have the air rights sold on an "improved real estate market." In the end, the Telephone Company deal was never ratified, and the "improved real estate market" took years to come about. Only the banks were in a position to buy and hold those rights, which, in fact, were to become a very profitable investment for them.

As we circulated reprints of the *Longshoreman's Voice* editorial, I could feel the ground begin to solidify under our feet as people saw that banking the Seaport air rights was a workable concept—and one that would save the Seaport.

As this idea gained currency, City Bank and the other banks realized that they could buy the air rights for less than half their recent market value. This would still provide enough funds to clear up almost all the debt Jakob owed the banks. (Unsurprisingly, as the market did recover, these rights were sold for more than twice what the banks paid for them!) So the banks entered their low bids, and the lawyers got busy. There was nothing routine about this transaction, and we had legal bills of just under $100,000 in 1972, even with a significant charitable discount from Hughes, Hubbard & Reed. An agreement for transfer of ownership to the museum of the land Jakob had purchased for us was finally completed, and on 8 February, 1973, soon after our meeting with Brooke and Laurance, the Board of Estimate unanimously approved the Seaport plan.

The outpouring of testimony at the Board of Estimate hearing was extraordinary, led by Karl Kortum, who pointed out in a memorable letter to Mayor Lindsay that the good news of South Street was good news for New York and for the liberal tradition. Others came from all directions of the compass, geographically and politically. We no longer had to stretch to get endorsements, we just asked and they poured in.

And the day came, on Thursday, 14 June, 1973, that the mayor's office sent down the land leases which at last authorized our occupancy of the land. We were on standby to sign them from mid-morning on, but after a few hours we went over to the Square Rigger for a sandwich lunch. And when, in due course, two impeccably dressed mayoral aides walked in, bearing the lease of some 100-odd pages, I signed cheerfully for South

Street Seaport Museum, grateful that our long march was over, and that the Seaport land was ours for the next 99 years.

And a long march it had been, particularly for Jakob. The essentials of the lease I signed had been agreed upon in 1969. As Jakob had outlined his situation to our trustees in July 1971, he had started out in 1969 with $10.7 million in loans from the banks, a debt swollen by mid-1971 to $14.3 million at 9.5% compounded interest. This cost rose relentlessly as time passed and the City's changing corporation counsels tinkered with the City lease, until by June 1973 when the lease was finally signed, Jakob's debt had grown to over $17 million. And the market for air rights had vanished. The only possible solution to bringing the air rights asset to bear had been to have the banks buy them for future sale.

The leasehold arrangements were clearly set forth in the Seaport Development Plan funded by Laurance Rockefeller. The banks' purchase of the air rights "for sale to future developers of adjacent blocks" enabled the City to acquire Schermerhorn Row and the Isbrandtsen holdings in the block just inland, "knowing that the air rights sale and prospective sale and lease agreements would reimburse the City." Further, Jakob's Seaport Holdings Company transferred the two blocks it owned north of Fulton Street to the City, along with several lots it had bought in the two neighboring blocks to the north. The New York State Maritime Museum was to purchase the Schermerhorn Row block from the City under the next year's State budget, and South Street Seaport Museum was to lease back from the City the Seaport Holding blocks "now also divested of their air rights." The turnover of Seaport Holdings properties to the City and leaseback from the City were simultaneous with the above complex transactions, effective when I signed the City lease.

Jakob was to be relieved of the $17 million bank debt which Seaport Holdings had incurred to buy the Seaport land. Of all the complex provisions of this settlement, this relief to Jakob was the only one not to be fully honored. His claim was subordinated to the banks' claim, which was fully met with a major profit, as noted earlier.

The work of drafting and securing the multi-layered approvals needed for these complex transactions was done by Kal Oravetz and his staff at Hughes, Hubbard & Reed as directed by Dick Buford and Kent Barwick, supported by Bronson Binger and his able aide, Margaret Falk. It was clear throughout how completely the whole elaborate edifice depended on the value of the transferred air rights being taken up by the banks. With the upland properties secured, a separate lease was signed with Ports and Terminals covering the four piers, 15, 16, 17 and 18, with adjacent waterfront land, thus keeping Commissioner Herb Halberg's long-ago pledge that the waterfront would be turned over to the Seaport Museum once we'd secured the land.

With the land settlement in hand, our great challenge was the ship which gave the land its Seaport character. Richard Fewtrell brought to his immense task a cool head combined with a can-do attitude. He set to work at once to replace the ship's water ballast with paving stones, and, once her stability was assured, to build, with Bill Lacey's work crew, a new mainmast to replace the one she'd lost off Cape Horn in 1910. We also continued with varied efforts to bring life to the ship's decks and involve people in her story. These ranged from an early visit to the ship by Mayor Lindsay for a reception where we served Argentine wine—the last imported to New York in a sailing ship (albeit under tow)—to a major planning conference called by the new Planning Commissioner, John Zuccotti, in May 1973, which was held in the newly restored after tweendeck—a space, Commissioner Zuccotti said, which, by its rugged and powerful curved shape designed to make its way through battering seas, should inspire City planners with a strong sense of the voyaging heritage of the city. He also had a word for the new life a revived South Street was bringing to the waterfront:

South Street, he said, *is a kind of rare place, where reality, history and romance blend in the simplest and fullest way.*

By that time Norma and I, freed up by Richard from *Wavertree*'s physical management, were working on the most ambitious museum display we had ever undertaken, an interpretation of life aboard the big Cape Horner. In this we had the staff support of the brothers Steven and David Canright, who had set up a display department workshop on the fourth floor of 203 Front Street. The *Wavertree* exhibit, as we developed it together, drew on everything Karl Kortum's compelling work had taught us, as well as the excellent exhibit techniques we'd encountered in the Liverpool Museum. After six years in the field, at last we had gained a position to take a deep breath and begin to tell our story as it should be told, in authentic materials worked into a lively display.

Major progress was made also in museum publications, which reflected the creative vitality our people were putting into their work. From the beginning we had made publishing a priority, but now publications simply leapt ahead, presenting ground-breaking work in the areas of study we were concerned with. Under Terry Walton, editor since the spring of 1973, the *Reporter* grew into a quarterly journal in magazine format, unpretentious, with no use of color—but using evocative photographs to carry the featured story, which in this first issue was "The City and the Sea," a review of New York's evolving relations with the seaways that gave it birth.

A particularly interesting story appeared in the *Reporter* as the new year 1974 opened. Called "The Black Man and the Sea," this was a six-page story in our largest-ever *Reporter* on an overlooked subject: how people of color had advanced their condition in seafaring in ways not open to them ashore. Scholars were beginning to develop this theme, and Steven Canright consulted with a group at the Brooklyn Museum to develop a wide-ranging account bringing new facts and perspectives to light. When, five years later, Michael Cohn and Michael Platzer brought out their groundbreaking book, *Black Men of the Sea*, the authors had me write a preface, knowing our early interest in the subject. But nearly a quarter century passed before W. Jeffrey Bolster's rousing *Black Jacks: African American Seamen in the Age of Sail* broke through to public consciousness in 1997, leading to publications and exhibitions which continue to open people's eyes to the achievements of a group whose story had not been told.

Geo Matteson, former *Pioneer* skipper and now director of ships and piers, in this same issue contributed a lively piece, "South Street's Working Ships," in which he urged that our ships "travel the harbor to different sites," and visitors should be called on to help sail them. Backing this up, Norman Brouwer offered an authoritative report, "Working Ships at Other Museums." And Richard Fewtrell contributed another installment of his *Wavertree* to Windward series, reporting on discoveries made as the ship was cleaned up, including original deck beams and stanchions. He was also able to report significant gifts to the ship, including the first captain's coffee pot and the ship's bell, both bearing her original name, *Southgate*, which Norman Brouwer had tracked down and obtained for the museum.

Ellen Fletcher Rosebrock, our architectural historian, gave us a history of the changing uses and remodeling of 207 Front Street, the oldest building in our office block, whose "ancient steep roof and mellow old brick" dated to 1798. Jacked up in later years to accommodate two new lower stories, as the new Fulton Market generated increased traffic in the district, and further changed with a steel lintel to provide wider ground-floor access, it presented what Ellen called "a welcome quandary" in whether to restore it to a given era or allow it to reflect the passage of time. Our vote, naturally, went resoundingly to the latter option.

Somehow Ellen, while working with a demanding Bronson Binger with one hand and with building architects and workmen in need of guidance on the other, managed to carry out her assignment as architectural historian in interpreting the streets and buildings of the Seaport in authoritative and engaging ways. Capping the individual building studies which appeared in the *Reporter*, she gave us the compendious and fascinating handbook *Walking Around in South Street* in 1974, a guide to the whole seven-block district from Burling Slip to the Brooklyn Bridge. In her introduction she wrote:

Mossy, grayed, often out of plumb, the ancient buildings in the Fulton Market neighborhood have a strong character that the passage of time has left them, dropping successive veils of heavy use, change, grime and neglect over their once-crisp brick fronts. The character is there—anyone can sense it, but to understand it specifically, to know the substance behind the illusion you must look back far into the history of the neighborhood's experience.

This interest in the character of South Street, and the strong sense of the street itself, was at the heart of our mission, an idea well summed up in the simple phrase, "the neighborhood's experience."

CHAPTER 35

Something Special for New York, *1973*

To Italy Aboard Michelangelo—Campanilismo—*Conference Aboard* Wavertree—"What Makes the City"—*Mayor Announces Seaport Plan—Trustees Refuse to Hear Staff Plan*

By 1973 the schooner *Athena*, in whose main cabin much of the talk, debate, singing of old songs, and actual written work of the Seaport Museum had been done—and whose sailing into South Street had heralded the opening of the Museum—had reached the end of the long sea road she'd traveled since her launching in 1925. She had not been sailed in 1971 or 1972, mightily as Barnaby Blatch and John Reid labored to make her fit for sea. And as she approached fifty years of age she faced the thorough rebuilding called for roughly every thirty years in the life of a wooden vessel. As early as October 1971 I had noted that we'd have to give up on "our great wooden artifact *Athena*," much as we enjoyed working together to pay seams and paint topsides, and reveled in the routines of life aboard the wooden hull that had seen so much living.

We wanted to find a new owner who would appreciate the schooner and knew we'd met the right person when Arthur Allgrove, a quiet-spoken, middle-aged building contractor, showed up and told us his plan to hire a shipwright in Maine to work on the schooner for as long as it took to rebuild her worn-out hull. We sold him *Athena* for $5,000, just what we had paid for her.

The board of trustees had continued in a state of ferment in the spring of 1973, stirred up by Jim Shepley's insistent demands for increased income and more businesslike management of our affairs. A growing membership, healthy finances, a favorable press, and the support of both the maritime community and the National Trust for Historic Preservation did nothing to satisfy Jim or his followers on the board, and discussion at board meetings withered in the face of this drumfire of criticism. As chairman, Jakob advised me to do what Shepley asked. But, since Jim had no recommendations or alternative actions to offer, I decided not to disrupt operations in a futile attempt to placate the implacable.

Our augmented staff was turning out the work of the museum in excellent form. The worst mistake, I felt, would be to compromise the good work going forward by getting embroiled with the board over impossible demands. So, Norma and I turned aside from their complaints and looked forward instead to the free weeks before us until the City leases reached us for signature.

Following the Board of Estimate approval of the Seaport plan in January, supported by the successful banking of the air rights, all was on track for the mayor's conveyance of the Seaport land. Our strengthened staff was handling these matters and a lively operational program with considerable success, and final leases were expected from the mayor's office in a month or so. We felt overstretched by the long, intense buildup to this favorable situation and longed to get away. Norma and I decided to spend part of the money from the sale of *Athena* on a different kind of voyaging.

"Aboard *Michelangelo* to Italy, by God—an incredible piece of city set loose and swaying at high speed over a cool, misty ocean." So read my journal on Saturday, 7 April. My daughter Carol, now eleven, and our sons Rob and Joe, ages four and two, were with us. The plan was to do things right and take off four weeks, traveling in an Italian superliner to roam Italy—from Norma's grandfather Petite's southern town to the Tuscan mountains where the Franceschis lived. After a farewell party, which included everyone from my aunt Alice Taylor and our old Rutgers comrade Jim Kirk, to Joe Cantalupo and Bill Lacey, hosts for the party, we set sail. As the great ship gathered way out in the stream, a South Street volunteer, Ed Squire, working as deckhand aboard Moran tugs, pursued us in the tug *Martha Moran* and wished us *bon voyage* over the tug's loud hailer.

Being new to ocean liner travel, I hugely enjoyed our dining room meals, served *con brio* by our waiter, Gino. Boasting four children of his own, he reproached me for the "Sergeant Pepper's Lonely Hearts Club Band" badge sewn onto my jacket: "That is not true what it says—you have the crowded heart!" We loved him for that, as we loved the Beatles for the soaring joy of their music. And then there was the ocean and the sky, open to us without responsibility for handling the vessel as she pursued her way like a lone planet. On the third day out, in mid-Atlantic, the weather, which had been wet and blowy, began to turn into a real gale. Looking down from the 60-foot height of the Amalfi Lounge, I noted:

> *The spectacle of the wide sea beginning to rage is something else,*
> *from this piece of city which pursues its way like some great express*
> *train. Instead of going out on a dipping bowsprit to change jibs,*
> *one hands one's wet trousers to a steward.*

The contrast with my passage as mate aboard Bobby Somerset's 43-foot cutter, *Iolaire,* in a rough crossing in the spring of 1949, bound for England, was much on my mind. Driving ahead under storm canvas most of the way, the aged vessel had been swept with boarding seas like a half-tide rock—we'd had to close the hatch smartly when going below, so half the ocean didn't follow us down. But the aroused sea—when, as the Psalmist has it, "Deep cries unto deep"—delivered its message even aboard the mighty *Michelangelo.* Just gazing down at its primordial fury cleanses one's mind wonderfully of contrived boardroom power games. The gale wore itself out, and we passed under the shelter of Cape St. Vincent, at Europe's southwest corner, on a halcyon evening.

That night we entered the Mediterranean, whose shores Dr. Johnson rated the great object of travel, and two days later our ship slid into the flamboyantly theatrical Bay of Naples. The plan was to go ashore here, travel inland to Norma's maternal grandfather's town, and visit with the scholar Tomaso Gropallo, author of a remarkable paper on the barques of nearby Sorrento. But, digging out the correspondence on the trip, I belatedly noticed that Sr. Gropallo actually lived in Genoa, not Naples. How could I have missed that! But we knew the ship was headed that way and the purser said there would be no extra charge for another day aboard his elegant ship, and Norma generously forgave my knocking the route of her long-awaited visit into a cocked hat.

At Genoa, the ship's home port, we found ourselves in a city built as an amphitheater, with its stage the harbor crammed with ships. Tomaso greeted our family like visiting royalty. Norma had offered to take the kids sightseeing while Tomaso and I had our "business lunch," but Tomaso wouldn't hear of this. So we all fitted into a big black car driven by his alert and charming daughter, Maria Angiola, whose fluent English helped communications. Driving through the stout barbican of the Casino, a maritime club housed in a medieval keep near the waterfront, we entered a lofty hall, its walls covered in silken tapestries and the huge battle flags of Genoa's long wars with Venice stirring gently beneath the clerestory windows. Genoa's ultimate defeat in the Mediterranean arena led this city of the sea to sponsor the Portuguese and Spanish voyages of Bartolemeu Dias and Cristoforo Colombo which transformed the Atlantic from "The Dark Ocean" into an international thoroughfare opening up the world—as Tomaso pointed out with justifiable pride.

It fell our lot to add a bit of history of our own to the cool, dim corridors of the Casino, when Tomaso introduced us to a gnomelike figure ensconced before an open fire on this spring day. This worthy soul, we learned, was the oldest member of the club, and, after a brief chat with Tomaso, he looked around to bid our party welcome with one quick gesture of welcome—making this the first time females and children had ever been admitted to the club. There followed a memorable luncheon in a private room with waiters lined up in attendance. To Norma's joy, the children's behavior was irreproachable—from the quiet way they stood while being looked over by the senior member, to their good manners and whispered talk at the table. The waiters, with their white gloves and military precision, certainly reinforced the formality of the occasion for them. After lunch, the Gropallos drove us on a tour of the surrounding hills, which made clear why the Genoese look to the sea, rather than the tortuous mountain roads, to connect them with the world.

The following day we rented a car and drove east through the hill country, across the north of Italy, stopping to visit friends at Cremona and proceeding on to Venice. There, our independent-minded two-year-old, Joseph, stayed on a bridge as we walked on, each of us thinking the other had him in tow. Racing back, we found Joe still on the bridge, gazing through the balustrade at the swans below, while a protective semi-circle of concerned Venetians gave us reproving glances as they expressed relief at our arrival. Then, waving goodbye, they went their different ways. One woman couldn't resist looking back to smile and shake her index finger in a reproving gesture—an expression of familial messages difficult to imagine in any but an Italian scene. As for Joe, his unruffled response was: "You were lost."

We drove on to Florence, arriving in a light, late spring snow made memorable by the city's amazing buildings resplendent in this festive dress. We soon found, however, that there was no lodging anywhere in town, not even an attic garret. No wonder—we had arrived on Good Friday, ushering in the Easter weekend! Not knowing what else to do, we sought out the apartment where Ralph Miller had been living three years earlier, finding our way there by remembering a right turn here, left there, ending up at Borgo Stella 9. In response to our ring, Ralph appeared in the doorway in his dressing gown. He paused on seeing me with the crowded car behind me, and said: "My God, it's you!" Then it was hot cocoa for the youngsters, prepared by Ralph's friend Nila, while Ralph phoned a neighbor to put them up for a few days so he could turn his apartment over to us. Nila, a very attractive and generous-minded woman, had left her family in South Africa to live an artist's life in Florence, sitting as a model for Ralph until they decided to take up life together. Ralph's entrancing portraits of her were hung throughout the apartment, and Ralph gave me a sketch of her looking out a window at the city rooftops, a piece of paper I later lost, but still hope to turn up one day. Ralph's rooms were also stacked with studies of the Tuscan landscape, which expressed the same kind of affection for its subject, with the freshness evoked by the living act of brushing color on canvas, illumined by the gleam of an unforgotten day. Ralph showed us how he ground and mixed his colors from the same earth he was depicting, which I found a moving expression of his attachment to the land he'd come to love and the life it supported. Over a late supper in a trattoria facing a square around the corner, he told us of the friends he'd made and the helpfulness of artists to one another. At Nila's urging, he later went over the paintings lined up for his one-man show, telling how each painting came about, which particularly fascinated Carol, our own budding artist.

The next day we toured Florence in a spring rain, and then, on Easter Sunday, Ralph and Nila joined us for a drive into the countryside to have a picnic lunch in a tower belonging to one of Ralph's friends—a visit enlivened by local stories related by Ralph. We had coffee together the following morning, as Ralph and Nila resumed occupancy of his apartment, both hugging us enthusiastically to send us on our way south.

Arriving in Rome, we explored Norma's student haunts of a dozen years earlier, when she was in her junior year at Marymount College, and we took in the sights of a proudly historic and seductive city, whose citizens carry themselves with an almost imperial confidence. The next day we rose early to press on southward to reach her grandfather's town of Sant' Angelo dei Lombardi, inland some miles from Naples. This proved to be an adventurous excursion through rough pastoral countryside. As we asked directions, people shook their heads at Norma's Florentine Italian, but finally, stopping before a church on whose steps three young girls were beating a huge rug, we were set right by a young woman who had overheard our query from her second-story window. This good-looking creature came down to laughingly inform us that we were already there, in Sant' Angelo dei Lombardi! We hadn't got the local accent right; "Sn·dan´·gelo," rather than the clipped "Sant' Angelo" we had been using! A soberly dressed man appeared who gave us a brief tour of the town and then led us to a modest trattoria where we had a late but delicious lunch.

We found no local Petites, but the people we met gave every sign of enjoying our stammering attempt to seek out family connections. This seemed a remarkable take on *campanilismo*, the yearning of an exile for the bell tower of one's native town—which these townspeople recognized in Norma, even when no family members remained to welcome her home. As we left the town, a passing shower gave rise to a rainbow transforming the hilltop town and its surrounding fields and groves, whose gleaming spring foliage, each leaf distinct and trembling as if just limned by Sandro Botticelli, was lit up in an atmosphere of pure joy. Such moments pass, of course, but now and then one lives on to reawaken the wonder of the created world.

Our plan was to catch the *Michelangelo* on her return voyage to New York, but a strike of the state-owned Italian Line delayed the ship's departure for a week. We took this news bravely, roaming the crooked streets of Naples where back-alley printing presses offered handbills calling for revolution against the bosses; we sang with a boatman who rowed us to the grottos of Capri, while I made sketches of local fishing craft. And we made a cliff-hanging drive along the hairpin curves of the coastal road to the isolated port of Amalfi, which had kept its ancient aspect as a medieval trading center as the centuries rolled by. This feeling was reinforced by the big rowing launches drawn up on the strand for painting in preparation for the annual contest with the maritime republics of Genoa, Pisa, Naples, and Venice. These lissome hulls gleaming in fresh colors showed us ancient custom with a lively, indeed youthful, feel.

Back aboard the *Michelangelo,* Norma and I talked of how people's life concerns were expressed in ways that shaped the character of the streets and town squares we had explored. Leafing through my journal, I came upon a sketch of a church we'd admired in Corte Morosini in Venice. It was flanked by a beer hall on one side and an art gallery on the other, so that God's creation might be celebrated in the midst of worldly concerns. The casual grace with which disparate elements of man's passage through life were piled up together here and elsewhere seemed to reflect a wonderfully abundant vision of how people living together should go about their affairs. Surely we should encourage this "mixed use" approach in South Street.

Another reason we had chosen Italy for our trip was Norma's interest in the way Italians use space in their cities and towns to a better result than we did in New York. There, every available outdoor area would have a vendor's stall, a pot of flowers, tables and chairs for an *alfresco* meal or a drink. Piazzas small and large were gathering places for leisure activities: watching the fountain, listening to an accordion playing, reading a book, chatting with a neighbor, or just relaxing and watching all the girls (or boys) go by. Our climate would limit these activities in winter, but attitudes bred in summer outdoor living could affect people's interactions year round. South Street, with its cobbled streets and low-rise buildings with their aged brick facades and a one-story central block, seemed a natural scene for similar uses.

The *Michelangelo* arrived back in New York's liner row on the Hudson on 10 May, a week late due to the vagaries of life and labor in the ever-intriguing Italian peninsula. On debarking in our own city we found the Seaport in full flower. The day after coming ashore, I attended the first meeting of the heads of the new borough planning councils, presided over by City Planning Commissioner John Zuccotti and Fred Rath, historic preservation officer of New York State. This was held aboard the *Wavertree*, as noted in the last chapter, and the context of this unprecedented conclave is worth some further note. John Zuccotti had caught my attention by declaring, "Open space should be alive" at a welcoming reception at the Century Club earlier that year. This contradicted the fashionable vision of the city, which called for sweeping views of empty space as a prime desideratum of city planning—and I felt this planner with a different view of things meant what he said.

The very concept of air rights transferred from over low-rise buildings to preserve historic neighborhoods was the philosophic rationale on which the Seaport Plan was based, and we prized this organic view of the city as a living entity making its voyage from the past into the future, showing signs of its passage through time. We also wanted to see river piers and walkways alive with activity and what we called the "meaningful clutter" people generate in pursuing their varied interests. At the *Wavertree* meeting I felt Zuccotti had fathomed the message the ship had brought to New York when he referred to South Street as "a rare place, where reality, history and romance blend in the simplest and fullest way." Who else had ever mentioned "romance" as a desideratum of city life? We treasured this, as would anyone with a real feeling for city life.

John Zucotti had also cut the Gordian knot of the Master Plan called for in the City Charter of 1936. The idea of a minutely detailed super plan on almost Sovietique lines was so rife with opportunities for corruption and machine-age notions of how to re-design the city, that over the decades no one could figure out how to sponsor or launch the monster scheme. The realities of city life and growth simply strangled the concept in knots of competing concerns.

Rather than a master plan, Zucotti believed that people working together would do a better job at planning their own futures. He mustered the organic processes of people's dreams, hopes, abilities and interests to make their own recommendations through a citywide system of borough planning councils, a system that works in growing strength and depth of experiential judgment to this day. And again, how about that word "romance" as a major factor in how people relate to the experience of the city—was this not a thing that inspired the voyaging impulse that had built New York and that lay at the heart of our business in great waters?

Romance lay thick, almost palpable, over South Street on 20 May, when hundreds of New Yorkers crowded onto Pier 16 to join Mayor Lindsay as he reopened the Fulton Ferry for its first run since the historic service was closed down in 1924. To many people, like my aunt Alice, this revived cherished memories of a waterborne run they thought had ended forever nearly a half century earlier. To others like myself it was just unmitigated joy. A light rain shower did nothing to dampen proceedings as hundreds of people crowded aboard for passage from Fulton Street in Manhattan to Fulton Street in Brooklyn. This rain-speckled but joyous event was run under the supervision of a jubilant

Bill Lacey. A retired City fireboat did duty as ferry, and her crew had a grand time taking more than 1,200 people across the river.

Alice Taylor was there, ecstatic at being in the company of her favorite mayor and fellow New Yorkers gathered to enjoy a great day together. This was the last time we were to be with her, for three weeks later she died of a stroke. She had seen the dream of a revived seaport in South Street in full flower and she was immensely proud of what New Yorkers were doing to bring this about. Alice was missed by all, particularly those who had attended the crowded meetings in her modest apartment on East 38th Street. Veterans of those festive, hard-working sessions often quoted her cheery appeal: "Come on people, we're here to get some work done."

At the end of May the Municipal Art Society gave me an award aboard the *Alexander Hamilton,* and in my acceptance speech, I called for a general shift in attitude toward the city's problems—a change based on the proposition that people are the prime resource for building the city's strengths and overcoming its problems. I quoted the wonderful statement of the Greek poet Alcaeus of Mytilene (c. 620–? BC) on the role of individual initiative:

> *Not houses finely roofed or the stones of walls well builded, nay nor canals and dockyards make the city, but men able to use their opportunity.*

"People able to use their opportunity," I said, was a phenomenon visible all around us in South Street. I pointed out the piers around us crowded with people: there was Jakob Isbrandtsen achieving his dream of a real ship museum; Joe Cantalupo finding opportunity to celebrate the heritage of a community he loved; Val Wenzel hobnobbing with the first lady of the theater, Helen Hayes; and Dick Rath achieving his great vision of taking city kids to sea aboard a traditional working schooner.

The diversity and energy of New York's people surely accounted for its rise to eminence among American cities. We took Joe Cantalupo's watchword, "This museum *is* people," as the Pole Star in our navigation.

This led to an organization involved in a constant learning process—a process, I concluded, that should never end, since it wrapped up both the purpose and the strength of our venture.

People applauded this, but it was only later that two staff members got to the heart of the matter. These were two young women hired to bolster Bronson Binger's team, as we proposed to resume responsibilities for the Seaport land. The first person hired was Ellen Fletcher Rosebrock, who soon began to enrich the pages of the *South Street Reporter* with stories of the Seaport buildings that had weathered the glory days of Western Ocean packets and China clippers sailing from our waterfront. She went on to write museum booklets on the subject—finding the funds to produce them with the help of Floyd Shumway, a professor at Columbia University who became a great friend during Norma's and my final days in South Street.

The other recruit, a remarkable young woman pursuing advanced studies at Columbia's School of Architecture, was Justine Mee, soon to become Justine Liff. She was hired to take over management of the Seaport properties we were scheduled to acquire in June 1973. Reporting to Bronson Binger, Justine showed an almost possessive grip on the Fish Market tenants, who were astounded to confront a tall, cool young lady who came round to visit them as their landlady—and who took no guff about overdue rents or remarks along the lines of "What is a nice lady like you doing in this business?"

She was all business, knowing when to yield a point but also when to insist on things. She enjoyed life hugely, showing this in her eager inquiries about other people's views, and her deep enjoyment of the natural world and of William Shakespeare's plays, in which she occasionally performed, as I was to learn.

Justine, in a closely reasoned critique of the Seaport Plan that Laurance Rockefeller had funded, gave a response going to the heart of the matter:

> *Peter, in his subjective and poetic way, is pointing to a very objective essence which is South Street. Yes, the banks and the city were there and we never would have survived without them. But that*

> *thing which makes people come to South Street and contribute to*
> *and support South Street is [the] deeply rooted social and philo-*
> *sophical belief that we can improve the quality of our lives through*
> *an understanding of South Street itself.*

Just that, the living experience of the Street itself: and that, of course,
was everything.

Amid the flowering of achievement in South Street, we found ourselves
unable to save two important ships. Richard Weinstein at the Office of
Lower Manhattan Development had mandated that Tallichet construct
new buildings ashore—under and around the overhead expressway to
hide its structure—as a requirement for City approval for the *Alexander
Hamilton* and *Moshulu* to lie at the Seaport piers. No one involved with
the Museum wanted the phony buildings, nor did any local civic
groups, but Weinstein was unyielding. So Tallichet had the *Hamilton*
towed to the Brooklyn Navy Yard to be offered for sale and towed the
Moshulu to Philadelphia, where she serves successfully as a restaurant ship
today. This was a hard blow to our plans and the loss of the two vessels
was deeply felt by all of us.

Remarkably, both these losses were made good by the vision and
energies of two Seaport members: Captain Bill Lacey brought in the
restaurant ship *Robert Fulton*; and museum trustee Jack Aron moved to
acquire the German four-masted barque *Peking*, a Cape Horn veteran
of the famous German "Flying P" line. The big barque had been serving
as a stationary training ship in England, which made her ideal for school
use; her capacious hull was filled with classrooms and even an auditorium
where she had once carried cargo.

By year-end the *Fulton* had arrived in South Street and the arrival
of the *Peking* was scheduled for 1974. Jack Aron, a sailor himself and
a painstaking manager, chose an outstanding sailorman, Hap Paulsen,
to direct the work to strengthen the *Peking* in England for her Atlantic
crossing. Hap, who had taught me the rudiments of square-rigged sailing
in the Coast Guard barque *Eagle*, gloried in the fact that he gave useful

employment to superannuated riveters, who drove hundreds of rivets for the vessel's safe passage to the New World.

As these steps were underway, we also moved to strengthen maritime preparations to celebrate the national bicentennial in 1976. So in 1974 we sent two representatives to Europe to sign up the leading vessels of the European sail training fleets. One was Frank Braynard, who became the impresario of Operation Sail '76; the other was Howard Slotnick, an active museum volunteer who became OpSail operations manager. This was to be an unparalleled visitation to American shores. Bellwether for the fleet was the Russian barque *Kruzenshtern*, formerly *Padua*, built in 1926 in Wesermünde, Germany. A near-sister of *Peking*, she was taken by the Soviet Union as a war prize after World War II. With the Cold War blocking all but a trickle of contact in the 1970s, it was a coup to get a Russian ship to New York. Frank and Howard achieved this by going aboard for the ship's voyage from England to join a tall ship rally in Germany. The $5,000 needed to fund their trip was provided in two $2,500 checks which I signed separately, avoiding trustee restrictions on checks over $2,500. From then on we continued to fund Frank's work until the OpSail corporation could pay its own way—which it more than did, giving a $320,000 surplus to the National Trust, of which $160,000 went to the *Wavertree*. The benefit to the city was a massive inflow of visitors, accompanied by an unprecedented decline in street crime, when an increase had been expected.

Pioneer, meanwhile, added some lustre to the Seaport's reputation by adding shoreside visits to her training cruises. When *Pioneer* put into the Connecticut River port of Essex as the summer of 1973 ended, my mother, Dorothy, who lived there, helped with welcoming festivities for the schooner and her student crew. Coco Lovelace at the Foot of Main Gallery put on a dazzling marine art show on the waterfront, and Essex families took home *Pioneer* students for cookouts and swimming parties—leading one mother to write a letter, published in the local paper *Deep River New Era*, regretting that her sons were away at camp and had missed seeing the good manners of these inner-city teenagers! The newspaper also published a rousing account of the Seaport Museum in New York, and Bill and Victoria Winterer, who hosted some of the youngsters, used the celebratory gathering to advance the idea of what became the future Connecticut River Museum. So *Pioneer's* sailing continued to make waves, awakening a heightened sense of the seafaring heritage, as she helped to open a brighter future in the lives of young New Yorkers.

Wavertree, still without her upper masts and rigging, continued to serve as anchor to our maritime concerns. This was illustrated in a remarkable Staten Island ceremony held on her quarterdeck to celebrate New York's Diamond Anniversary—the 75th anniversary of the unification of the five city boroughs as one city. To mark the occasion, our friend John Noble presented Borough President Robert Connor with a lithograph of the last schooner launched in New York, at the Kill Van Kull. Called "Ah, Linoleumville" in memory of the shipyard town, as John explained in a wonderful, rampageous speech, the lithograph honored the varied waterfront enclaves that bound the city together, through the schooners that brought in the pilings much of the city was built on, to the tugs that towed in the coal that kept it warm, and all the swarming life that filled its waterways.

Captain Lacey's new restaurant ship, *Robert Fulton,* was taken in hand by the Lacey crew for her new dockside mission for the Seaport Museum, the first such development in the city. The big, 180-foot, multi-decked vessel had been built in the 1930s to take low-income city families for outings around the waterways of New York. Now at the Seaport pier, this major new facility provided large, well-maintained open spaces and began to pay off immediately in late 1973, hosting gatherings, meetings and receptions, not only for the museum, but for Wall Street firms and mid-town corporations, bringing new people into the South Street sphere. The Seaport Plan funded by Laurance Rockefeller was approved aboard the *Fulton* at an October luncheon, presided over by Mayor Lindsay with Laurance and Brooke Astor as honored sponsors. Numerous catered affairs were held aboard, while Bill Lacey negotiated to secure City approval for general public assembly. That approval seemed long in coming, but Bill never wavered in his belief that it would come through. For our part, we had faith in Bill's ability, having learned that whatever he undertook to do, he did well.

Mayor Lindsay evidently shared this view, for a farewell party at the end of his second term as mayor in 1973 was held aboard the *Fulton*. This was a marvelously festive occasion involving people of all sorts—the bright young people Lindsay had brought in to transform the City bureaucracy (although with mixed results!), the seasoned Tammany pols who are always with us, silk-stocking liberals, and more people of color than any mayor had ever assembled—gathered in that hands-across-the-aisle mood too seldom found in our politics, with everyone talking to everyone like mad, while couples strolled the outside promenade decks admiring views of sailing ships and open water that had not been seen in New York in their lifetimes. Lindsay haled me to the dais to denounce me for making him sign the most complicated lease he'd had to sign in his administration to make South Street Seaport happen. I said: "Mr. Mayor, it was a pleasure."

Our first year with the South Street land secured was coming to its end, with things steadily breaking our way. The solid work done by our staff, now strengthened by the additions we'd made in 1972, made effective use of the City leases funded by Jakob Isbrandtsen's generous grant of Seaport real estate. And there was an upwelling of support from practically all sources. This resulted in doubled income: from $683,459 in 1972 to $1,370,163 in 1973. Despite declining retail sales throughout the city, museum shop sales had also doubled—encouraging evidence of people's growing interest in our venture, even in a declining city economy.

Increased expenses for the year were more than met, leaving net income of $13,422, about one percent of gross. Under the accounting system we then used, an additional $543,534 raised during the year was held aside for future use, giving the Seaport Museum a total gain of $556,956 on a gross income of nearly $2 million, which made a sound foundation to build on in 1974. Two special gifts for *Wavertree* helped build this fund. One was a check for $100,000 from the Mellon Foundation, which came with a note saying the ship did not fit foundation guidelines, but the public interest we'd aroused in historic preservation justified the grant. Another $100,000 check came from the sale of a yacht donated to us by Jakob's sailing competitor John Timken—a gift Jakob had managed to arrange while his own empire was crumbling around him.

Citing this remarkable strong beginning for the year ahead, I had asked the board to hear my report on plans for 1974 at the year-end trustees meeting on 2 December. But Jim Shepley would have none of this, saying: "We've heard enough of Peter's nonsense." Monk Farnham emphatically supported Shepley's objection, as, to my surprise, did Eric Ridder. So there was no report at all on plans for the coming year. It probably didn't help matters that I'd sent Eric a letter that summer reporting my decision to steam ahead with our successful operations without attempting to respond to trustee complaints—which I had come to feel we could never answer to their satisfaction. Norma and I had felt that our burgeoning membership growth, strong finances, and soaring public approval should have made the case for us to move ahead on the Seaport Plan with the support of Brooke Astor and Laurance Rockefeller.

At an Executive Committee meeting held a week before Christmas, all was sweetness and light, surprisingly, and a number of routine short-term actions were authorized. "Oddly everyone seemed happier at the end of the meeting," says my journal, "Buford, Farnham, the lot."

It did not occur to us that perhaps they knew something we didn't.

We went on to spend a merry Christmas. After Norma and I had been over *Wavertree* plans with Richard Fewtrell, we joined the volunteers gathered aboard the *Ambrose* for a Christmas party with much singing of carols and chanteys, and we ended up bringing Richard home with us for the holidays. There we held a serious review of plans for the shipboard *Wavertree* display we were working on under Norma's direction. Along with Norma's family, my mother, Dorothy, was with us for the weekend and sang at the piano with everyone joining in. Doffy, as the kids called her, also read from the log of my sailing in Nova Scotia in 1948, and spoke of her own memories of sailing those waters as a girl. It was Christmas as it should be observed, with songs and stories indoors while chill winds howled over the snowy grounds outside. Fewtrell added much to this with his rendition of old English songs accompanied by concertina, so we felt the sky indeed rent with angel singing, and we rested merry indeed.

CHAPTER 36

The Changing of the Guard, *January–April 1974*

Trustees' Secret Report—No Action on Funding Plan—A Trip with
Joe—Sen. Kennedy Sponsors Ship Trust—Farewell Kaiulani—*The*
Wavertree *Story Told Aboard the Ship—New Management Takes Over*

We entered the year 1974 with a troubling awareness that the trustees
were planning major changes without any discussion with those who
had brought about the successful operations of the Seaport Museum.
The founding generation of volunteers, staff and trustees had always had
a sense of guardianship of an important trust. We had a great story to
tell and we strove mightily to tell it as truly as it was in us to do. This, I
think, explains the devotion of leading maritime historians, veterans of
the sailing ship era, civic leaders, and indeed New Yorkers of all sorts to
the Seaport Museum as it then stood, with sound finances and able staff
working with skilled volunteers to head into a future bright before it.

It was difficult to imagine a good outcome arising from a total dismissal
of our way of doing things and the possible wipeout of plans that were in
mid-stride toward accomplishment. A notable case was Brooke Astor's
interest in making a $1 million grant to launch a $5 million campaign to
achieve the Stage I restoration of the Seaport in time for the National
Bicentennial two and a half years away. Granted, Brooke had called
for strengthened administration before committing this sizeable sum,
but we had agreed on that priority, in view of the large sums involved.
Clearly, cooperation between staff and trustees was essential to meet the
needs of the case, however difficult that might prove. It was time to get
a unified front, which we thought might be easier to accomplish than in
the years of struggle, in view of the solid achievements of the past year.

The trustees' actual intent, however, was quite different. This was at
last revealed to me on 22 January, at a luncheon with Jakob and Eric
Ridder at Sloppy Louie's.

It was time, said Eric, to get serious. The trustees had decided to appoint a super-manager to run things to the satisfaction of corporate leaders on the board, led by Jim Shepley as governance chair. Jim had made it clear that he was not satisfied with my administration and would resign publicly with his followers on the board unless new leadership was appointed with full executive powers. And with the public resignation of this powerful business magnate, president of the Time-Life publishing empire, any prospect of the corporate and foundation support we would need to raise the funds for the $5 million campaign would be doomed.

And I now learned that Eric had paid for a secret study calling for elimination of the present management as Shepley demanded. Stunned by what I was hearing, I tried to point out that no staff member, no volunteer, and no rank-and-file museum members had been consulted on this radical restructuring. Eric said with a smile that things are simply not done this way in the business world. Eric's eagerness to accept a corporate die-cast administration—in a museum whose dedication to individual responsibility and initiative was widely known and largely responsible for its success—left me speechless. Leaving aside the founding purposes of the museum, how on earth did he expect a solution generated by corporate fiat to work? It seemed to me that we were confronting not just difficulties, but impossibilities.

But I realized I'd better ask what else was in the trustee report beyond the appointment of a new chief executive.

"You still don't seem to understand, Peter," Eric answered. "This is confidential board material, and you can hardly expect to be consulted on all our plans. You'll be told what you need to know at the Executive Committee meeting next week."

I had worked as president but not a trustee, wanting only the power to act on the board's behalf, but not to wield a vote, so Eric was quite within his rights in a course of action I felt to be fraught with risk to the purposes and the very spirit of the Seaport Museum.

———◆———

The next day I spent in Mystic, where the reconstituted Council of American Maritime Museums was holding its first meeting, with Waldo Johnston as chairman. This meeting of CAMM, successor to the Sea Museums Council we in NMHS had pulled together, was a joyful occasion, since the New England members who had not joined the old Sea Museums Council were now part of the meeting, and there was much cheerful talk of the great things that lay ahead for the group, on which, of course, I represented South Street Seaport Museum as its president. On the way home I began to feel for the first time the burden of sustaining a hollowed-out office.

The Executive Committee meeting on 30 January was held in the South Street library. When Jim Shepley came over to say hello before the meeting—a rarity for him—I said that as president I found it strange to hear for the first time an organization plan on which I had not been consulted. Jim, patting me on the back, said I would be consulted after the meeting, where he would propose that I be elected as trustee. To this I said I hoped we would find a way of working effectively together to achieve the Seaport Plan approved late the previous year.

At the meeting we saw Jim in full campaign mode, stating at the outset that he would publicly resign if there were any attempt to modify the pending decision to appoint a new chief executive for the museum. That officer's authority would extend to all operations and public statements of policy, all financial matters, with a focus on fundraising and stringent economy to cure the excesses of the past, on which there was no need to elaborate. Peter Stanford would serve as public spokesman accountable to the CEO, who alone would shape and act on policies, accountable to the board. In recognition of Peter's past services to the museum he proposed that Peter be elected to serve on the board as trustee. He called for a unanimous vote to approve these measures, and the vote was unanimous, with everybody congratulating everyone else on this forward step in the South Street story. Not yet a trustee, I did not cast a vote.

The board offered no effective opposition to this radical turnabout in the way we had done things for the past six years. Jakob's direct stake in this was the repayment of the money he'd lent to acquire the Seaport land. He clearly felt the continued presence of the corporate leaders on our board was vital to the banks' confidence in the museum's ability to serve as urban renewal sponsor. If they reneged on the air rights sale on which the whole land deal depended, Jakob would be left high and dry. Joe Cantalupo, Dick Rath and others close to museum policies and operations were all silent, concerned that a public fight would stop development of the Seaport in its tracks and might well destroy the institution.

Not all close to the museum supported this approach, however, and some members and staff urged a public fight. They were outraged, but they were the minority and held their peace, understanding that not only the future, but the day-to-day survival of the Seaport Museum might well be at stake if there were an open battle with corporate members who controlled a solid majority on the board.

So, my own decision had made itself: I would stay on as president and try my best to make things work. Jim meant every word he said, and if he resigned, there would be no effective Stage I campaign. If I resigned, this would have meant an end to the citizen discourse and participation, which had built the museum and formed its character as an institution.

The next day Norma and I took off to spend a long weekend in Nantucket with the boys and Joe Cantalupo. Friday, 2 February, found us aboard the ferry *Islander,* bound for Nantucket with Joe Cantalupo, who had accepted our invitation to join us for a midwinter sortie to the islands. Having missed the evening ferry, we spent the night in Woods Hole, in the same rooms we had been in on the first vacation trip we'd made with Joe after we'd learned his wife, Estelle, had died. We talked a little of an article in *Sea History* on Australian historic ships, which I had first discussed with Norma and Joe on in this very room on our previous trip a year and a half earlier. We turned in early on a dark, wet and windy night, with the lights of vessels in the inner harbor moving in the swell, as restive as Norma and I felt in spirit.

Saturday morning aboard the ferry, a southwest gale sent snow flurries mixed with salt spume across the venerable steamer's decks, as we cleared the shelter of the land at Nobska Point. "God help sailors on a day like this," exclaimed Joe piously to the two boys, aged three and four. "Say," he added, arching his eyebrows in surprise, "come to think of it we're the sailors, off on a great adventure. What about that, men!" And Norma and I went on to talk to the boys of whaling voyages to distant seas launched from the sandy island we were headed for. In a lull in this conversation, while we watched the gale buffeting the steamer's windows, Joe looked up at a man in a black suit reading a newspaper at the far end of the saloon.

"Isn't that Bob Albion?" he asked, getting to his feet.

It was, and, recognizing the one and only Joe Cantalupo, Bob got up to say hello. Joe and I had been on a trip to Mystic Seaport the previous summer, and Waldo Johnston had invited us to lunch with a few others to salute Albion, who had just finished running the Munson Institute study program at Mystic. All hands had welcomed Joe as a break from the routines of academe. Then Waldo, presiding at the head of the table, chaffingly told me that I should abandon the quest to save Karl Kortum's old ship *Kaiulani* as a diversion from serious ship preservation needs. I explained that *Kaiulani* had a transcendent value to us as the property of the American people at large, for whom the National Maritime Historical Society had been designated by the president to hold in trust. Bob Albion intervened before Waldo could say another word—as guest of honor, he knew his rights: "Waldo, you lay off this young feller. He's done something beyond our dreams, bringing Cape Horn square riggers back to New York and docking them where their masts can be seen from Wall Street." At this Waldo had thrown up his hands in mock surrender while Joe beamed on the assembled company. So on this occasion aboard the *Islander*, Joe, Bob Albion, Norma and I had a grand reunion.

Our talk ranged from Sam Morison's kid-glove handling of Admiral King in his failure to provide convoy protection in the Battle of the Atlantic in the months after America entered World War II, to the theory that there was something special in the makeup of New York's diverse population that explained the city's rise to dominance in Atlantic trades—the theme we'd first discussed in Bob's New York visit of 1968, but one on which Norma and I were always ready to elaborate. When talk turned to Italian maritime city-states, where Bob had also traveled, he excused himself briefly to fetch a bottle of Spanish brandy he had in his car on the lower deck, which we enjoyed until the *Islander* pulled into her wave-lashed dock in Nantucket.

Our travels with Joe had begun a year and a half earlier, when in June 1972, having learned that Joe's wife had died, we had pressed him to join us on a summer jaunt to attend the opening of the Nantucket Lifesaving Museum. All five of us had crammed into Norma's and my car, appropriately named Sam Small, and we greatly enjoyed the trip and each other's company. This had been followed by our visit to Mystic, and then, a year later, in July 1973, we'd again joined forces with Norma and the boys for a longer expedition to Bath, Maine, stopping for a night with Barclay Warburton in Newport along the way. On this trip, which Joe insisted we make in his Mercedes Benz sedan rather than our little car, we learned of the actual existence of Joe's Cousin Angelo—a very real Angelo Beldaddi who, having lived all his life at 78 Mulberry Street, had died a week earlier at age 71. Joe told us he was a conservative person who was constantly saying: "Joe, you go too far." We took this as a tribute to Joe's championing of the poor and dispossessed—and also his role in the South Street venture.

The rest of our winter trip to Nantucket passed in what seemed like a dream, as we trudged through the snowy streets of the quiet town, attended a lecture by Ed Stackpole on discoveries made by Nantucket whalemen in the vast stretches of the Pacific, visited Charlie and Mickey Sayle to review plans to recover the schooner *Alice Wentworth*, and had a memorable luncheon at a cellar restaurant called The Brotherhood, where the dancing flames of a huge fireplace summoned up visions of the semi-legendary Compagnons de la Côte, in whose honor the restaurant was named. Travels with Joe were always full of fresh humane perspectives on the changing scene, and on this trip on our way home he talked of Things that Can Only Be Made One at a Time—a lovely concept, which he expounded at a roadside cafe in the nether reaches of Rhode Island, where the wine we had with dinner, as Joe remarked, if not quite a sipping wine, was clearly enough a *drinking* wine.

Joe's first example of something that could only be made one at a time was the shaping of a human being, not the biological creation, as he explained, but in character developed in encountering the outer world. We had seen One at a Time experiences being developed in the Apprenticeshop for building wooden boats in our trip to Maine the year before, and I stretched the concept to cover the reassuring look and sound of a cobblestone street, laid stone by stone, in contrast to an extruded sheet of asphalt. I said that Tommy had once pointed out how much livelier our passage suddenly seemed when we hit a cobbled stretch of the Lower Manhattan street we were following that day. We agreed that such One at a Time experiences had to be preserved in South Street.

We had been hard at work intensely on an overall funding plan for months now. Encouraged by the response to our year-end appeal, with its great $600,000 surge of contributions, including a surprise $100,000 check from the Mellon Foundation for the *Wavertree*, I had written Brooke Astor asking her to consider a $1 million grant to launch the $5 million campaign for the Stage I restoration of the Seaport's ships and buildings. Brooke responded that she was interested, but first she wanted to see our administration strengthened. If she had heard of the trustees' plan for a complete reorganization of Seaport operations, it was certainly understandable that she wanted to know the new setup before making any commitment.

Brooke and Laurance had publicly announced their support of the Seaport Plan the previous autumn, and the first thing to do now was to invite them to take a leadership role in the campaign. This would greatly strengthen our appeal to new supporters and would also multiply contributions from existing supporters. Both Brooke and Laurance had been interested in seeing concrete progress toward our restoration goals, so I had asked Bronson to spell out such a step-by-step restoration program and Marshall Streibert to match these steps with opportunities to give money to make each step happen. Justine Mee's outreach program to new restaurants and other prospective Seaport tenants also had to be coordinated with the philanthropically funded capital improvements, and for Fewtrell's work on the *Wavertree* we needed to line up maritime contributors in the wake of Mellon, W. R. Grace, Schaefer and J. Aron, building on support we'd already achieved. Our vital publications program, which did much to make our cause known and respected, was already being plotted with the Bicentennial and OpSail '76 in view, and for this Ellen Rosebrock and Floyd Shumway set to work to raise their own funds.

We needed to pull together these diverse but interrelated efforts in a unified campaign enlisting all our supporters and prospective supporters, and for this nothing works like public participation and positive stories in the news. We had attracted the attention of New Yorkers with public exhibitions and performances, with visiting ships, and with receptions for guest dignitaries and performers, and we had done it with much smaller resources than we now had. We saw no problem in pulling together this campaign. In fact, we all saw the road open before us.

So while trustees worked on the reorganization plan, we went ahead with staff discussions for the funding plan, culminating in a Saturday meeting with Bronson and Marshall at our house in Yorktown Heights in late March. The memos I wrote to start work on each step in the funding plan were, however, held up by trustee order, pending a final meeting of the executive committee. That meeting was held on 20 March, without any report being made to me. So if there were any organized trustee plan to raise money to fund the Seaport Plan, we were not aware of it.

———◆———

In the meantime, other things were happening. After some hesitation, Dick Buford authorized the signing of a contract with Bill Lacey to rent out to him the concession of food service aboard the newly arrived *Robert Fulton* at Pier 16—an important step for the Seaport Museum in providing both accommodation for major Seaport events and substantial income. I also signed the papers for the sale of Schermerhorn Row to New York State for $1.1 million, as previously agreed. While Norma continued to look on the State takeover as a major loss for the Seaport Museum, I believed it might be a needed base for scholarly and educational concerns, adding depth and special programs to the Seaport experience.

On National Maritime Historical Society business, I went to Washington on 1 March to meet Senator Edward M. Kennedy in response to a call from his staff. He had learned that people who had given money to NMHS to save the *Alice S. Wentworth* wanted to know what was being done for the old schooner, still a waterlogged hulk at Anthony's Pier 4 in Boston. I told him we'd bought a steel cradle on which Doug Lee, master shipwright, could haul out the shattered hull in Maine, but Captain Havileh Hawkins, whom we'd hired to tow the wreck to Maine, felt more work was needed before risking the weavy structure at sea. When the Senator asked about help from the National Trust, I told him the Trust had no program for ships. This was news to the senator, and we readily agreed on the need for a National Ship Trust. Kennedy then proposed to introduce a bill providing an initial $10 million in funding and asked us to draft a suitable bill. I had already arranged to meet with Frank Braynard, who was in Washington on OpSail business, and with our chairman Wally Schlech, who lived in nearby Annapolis, following my meeting with Senator Kennedy. They welcomed the stunning idea of a National Ship Trust, and our friend, Polly Burroughs of Martha's Vineyard, who had joined us through her interest in the *Wentworth*, got her lawyer son to set up the legal language of the bill, which he soon did to the Senator's approval.

At the same time, still on NMHS business, we bade farewell to the *Kaiulani*, stranded on a beach in Manila Bay, where the Philippine

Coast Guard had already set about scrapping her rusted-out hulk. Our last chance to save the vessel had been a plan Maritime Administrator Helen Delich Bentley worked out with us to restore *Kaiulani* to lead a Bicentennial fleet around American ports in 1976. When this was not approved, all we could do was to send Charles Witthholz, architect for the restoration, to Manila where he met with the US Ambassador and camped out on the beach to halt the scrapping. But we could not meet the Philippine Coast Guard demand that we refloat the wreck and tow it away. So scrapping resumed, with some salvaged frames set aside for shipment back to the US.

Losing *Kaiulani* was a hard blow, but with our limited resources we had done what we could for the ship that the Society was founded to save. The Ship Trust, declaring a national purpose in historic ships and providing basic funding, might become *Kaiulani*'s best memorial, assuring that other ships would be saved. As it turned out, this NMHS effort was to eventually reach to the South Street ships, though no one knew this then.

Returning to New York, I finished my work on the funding plan, reviewed and refined it with Marshall and Bronson, and we were in the initial stages of execution when I was told that trustee orders had been given to stop all fundraising work. This stunned us, since we had been working openly on plans with Brooke Astor and Laurance Rockefeller. It was a blow to our efforts and one that might well alienate those willing supporters.

Since there was nothing we could do about this, Norma and I threw ourselves into the *Wavertree* exhibit now being finished in the ship's tweendecks. Bolstered by the Mellon grant and many smaller year-end gifts, we now had funds to do something to bring the ship's story to life. So, with Dick Fewtrell capably handling the ship's restoration work, Norma took a free hand in setting up a remarkable exhibit. Working with the Canright brothers, Steven and David, they set up a proper workshop on the fourth floor of 203 Front Street, where the heavy yellow pine panels for the *Wavertree* exhibit were built, lettered, and carefully varnished in a dust-free enclosure.

In building this new exhibit, we followed the general style of Karl Kortum's work in this field, with bold-face titles followed by a lead-in sentence or two designed to draw the viewer into a longer account the visitor could linger over—as we found they frequently did. We wanted each caption to entice people to read the next one, right down to every detail of the display—calling attention to a single individual in a crowded pier scene, or pointing out an unusual vessel. There is a magic that can be created between the visual and the printed word, and that magic is what Norma and the display crew worked endlessly to achieve. To this Norma added a dimension inspired by the City of Liverpool Museums, in the exhibits we'd found so effective in our visit there in 1972. Old photos of the era were enlarged to life-size, and then set up with actual artifacts shown in the photo arranged close to it, as if they came out of the image.

Entering our new *Wavertree* exhibit in the ship's after tweendeck, one first saw a grand photograph reaching from deck to overhead, showing a ship at the end of a waterfront street, awakening people to the living past of the streets they had walked through to board our ship. The photo's title board announced "The Life of an Ocean Wanderer," and showed a deck scene of *Wavertree'* sister ship *Milverton*, followed by panels that gave an overview of the ship's career, with each voyage traced on a global map with the dates and types of cargoes carried.

The next section was "The Ship's People" where one encountered a life-size photo of a sailmaker at work with an actual sailmaker's bench in the foreground, complete with beeswax and twine and a cascade of weathered canvas draped over the bench. This canvas was from the actual foresail of *Wavertree*'s cousin *Balclutha*, given us by Karl, to tell the story of these ships with the very materials that seamen had handled aloft— "giving yell for yell to the westerly gale," in Joseph Conrad's phrase. We were fortunate in having the ship's original cast iron cook stove, which we set up with a photo of her actual cook in 1907, and nearby a notation from Spiers's voyage about how the cook allowed the young apprentices to dry their sodden clothes next to the stove.

Opposite the stove, one encountered a life-size photo of Smilin' Jack Dickerhoff—so-called because he rarely smiled—a large imposing fellow; he was the professional rigger who had rigged the *Balclutha* for Karl. Jack had come east with Karl to look over the *Wavertree*, with the intention of supervising the rigging of the ship. He had stayed with us in Yorktown Heights—a distinct privilege for us, since we were able to learn more about this exceptional and warm-hearted man. Later, when stricken with cancer and knowing he would never come back to rig the *Wavertree,* he sent us his toolbox instead. So, next to Jack's image, was a brightly lit display case, where we were able to show his rigger's tools and ditty bag with its contents laid out next to it as if ready for use, each one tagged with its name and purpose.

Right after this, one came upon a midshipman's sea chest in front of a life-size photo of three midshipmen fourteen to sixteen years of age, in their blue uniforms, with captions describing the hard training the young apprentices had to undergo. Next to it was a photo of a fourteen-year-old boy in sou'wester and oilskins, smiling with his arms wrapped over the poop deck rail with a mountainous sea in the background. With this we posted an excerpt from the teenager's journal, recounting how the rigging was slippery with ice, making it difficult to hang on. He added that the men say this is just Cape Horn, and there would be fair winds and sunlit seas ahead. Under this was a note of the boy's name, and the date he'd fallen to his death from the rigging, shortly after his last journal entry. Children and grownups alike always stopped at this gale-haunted photograph, and they talked quietly about it as they walked away. They had not known that boys that young were sent to sea for two or more years apprenticeship to do men's work and eventually earn their license as maritime officers.

In this exhibit we worked constantly to get at the drama of fact, and listened closely to how people responded to our way of presenting it. To achieve this Norma, Steven and David took turns sitting at a small table in the tweendeck display area, watching and listening to people's reaction to what they were seeing and reading. Careful attention to what people lingered over, reading down to the last small-type caption, or what they breezed by, helped us understand what attracted and engaged people. More than once we found ourselves rewriting captions or refining exhibits, based on our notes of these exchanges.

Pleased with the interest the exhibit drew from Wall Street bankers, construction workers, policemen and families out to learn the story of their city's past, I asked my former bosses at Kobrand Corp. to come to join me on a tour of the exhibit—the terms being that they give me their critical readings of the display. At first John Bush, the president, sputtered at me: "But Peter, we do not know about your ships! Wine tastings, ballet dancers by Degas, Dürer engravings, okay—but you've got us off native ground here!"

"John," I said, "with respect, it's a new field to almost everyone who comes here. I am asking you as a great favor to do something beyond the usual contribution you and Rudy send us. Give me a straight reading on this exhibit as if it were an ad for Beefeater Gin."

Silence prevailed as we walked through the tweendeck exhibits, with now and then a question from John, not a word from Rudy. Rudy, chairman of Kobrand and the prime mover of Beefeater Gin sales, always liked John to offer his views first. When we came to the life-size photo of Smilin' Jack Dickerhoff, John said: "*Mein Gott*, is that real?" to which I said: "As real as you or me, John. He stayed at our house."

I had considerable respect for these two quite different people, and I awaited their reaction. As we were leaving, John said, without even looking at Rudy—which was a first in my experience, and perhaps even in his: "That is the most convincing museum exhibit I have ever visited." He paused, and then blurted out: "Rudy and I are so happy you asked us to join you in this world of the sea." Rudy nodded his agreement with this, and I found myself quite pleased with John's judgment of the work done by Norma and the Canright brothers, which expressed our ultimate goal: to reach out to people and bring them into our story so that it is real and alive for them.

A few days later, on Monday, 8 April, the new managing director, Robert Bonham, reported aboard. I showed him to an office we'd set up down the hall from mine, just outside the entrance to the library which also served as our conference room. Bonham glanced at the office, and walked on into the library, where he plunked down his briefcase at the head of the long mahogany table in the middle of the book-lined room.

"Never mind, Peter, this will do just fine as my office," he said with a smile. All at once I understood that I was no longer in charge—and the person now in charge would have no use for my advice about keeping a small office.

Things, I understood, would be different. But—never mind! We were still young with the future before us, like the South Street venture itself, and one did not have to stamp around in charge of things to keep moving things forward. We could still dream great dreams, work to rediscover our waterfront heritage, advocate great steps recognizing the truths of our forebears' lives—and invite New Yorkers to share in a remarkable experience of their city. This resolve I endeavored to capture in the preface to the guidebook, *Walking Around in South Street*, which would appear in a few months' time. I wrote:

> *South Street is a monumental collection of ships and buildings weathering some kind of passage through the seas of time. It is a most visible argument in favor of things being (in an over-calculating and sometimes, today, despairing society), a little more natural, a little more mutually dependent, a little out of plumb.*
>
> *Hurrah for old humanity! Let us honor its cause here in South Street, where its labors are so clearly, vividly, memorably expressed in the shapes of the housing and sea chariots of an earlier age. Let us find new meanings in these old roots, so we can get on with the work of the City today with a little more grace, a little more*

dignity, a new sense of joy in the work. . . . And if you care to be part of these efforts, join the Museum! You'll find, in the words of the old sea song, "a hearty welcome waiting." Your help is needed, because our buildings, our ships, our story have no meaning and no future without you.

These words were true in the uncertain times when they were written and, across the changing decades that have passed, they still ring true today.

REVEALING HER ORIGINS as a sailing schooner in every line, the motor dragger Lady of Good Voyage *made us dream of bringing sail back to South Street. We saw her a few times at the Fish Market piers, but then she headed for southern waters and was lost in the Gulf of Mexico in the 1970s.*

AN AMERICAN FLAG and fresh white paint on the storefront at 16 Fulton Street announce a new activity for the Fish Market neighborhood in April 1967: the South Street Seaport Museum.

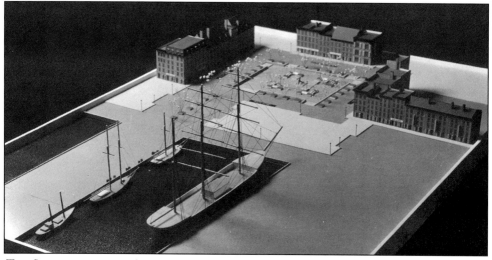

THE SEAPORT-TO-BE is shown in Leevi Kiil's model made in late 1966. Its early-1800s buildings face on the East River, grouped around an open block for outdoor activities. The square rigger Kai-ulani *is shown with (left to right) the dragger* Lady of Good Voyage, *the schooner* Ernestina, *and the coastal schooner* Alice S. Wentworth. *The simple ship models, made by the authors, showed the major role for historic ships in the Seaport plan.*

NEW YORKERS CAME TOGETHER to save the city's sailing ship waterfront. Above left, Robert Ferraro, fresh from the Peace Corps; middle, Terry Walton; and right, Richard Rath, both editors at Boating *magazine.*

JOAN K. DAVIDSON WAS THE FIRST to provide support for Norma's salary, thus opening the museum for business. She brought in the J. M. Kaplan Fund to support the programs that kept the museum's mission alive.

JAKOB ISBRANDTSEN, SHIPPING LEADER, served as founding chairman, provided funds to retain Peter and led in forming a board of trustees.

South Street Reporter

Newsletter of Friends of the South Street Maritime Museum
37 WEST 44th STREET, NEW YORK, N.Y. 10036

Honorary Chairman:
WHITNEY NORTH SEYMOUR, JR.
Chairman:
PETER STANFORD
Vice Chairman:
ROBERT FERRARO
Secretary-Treasurer:
NORMA FRANCESCHI STANFORD

VOL. I, NO. 1   • To re-create in the heart of our city the old seaport of New York •   JANUARY 1967

Move to save NY's 'street of ships'

 NEWS IN BRIEF

City Club of N Y endorsed Museum concept by unanimous vote of Trustees on Dec. 12. Chairman Seymour Graubard said: "I pledge my personal support. Indeed, I cannot see how anybody can do anything but approve the idea."

Leading citizens join Friends, including Edouard Stackpole, curator of Mystic Museum during its rise to greatness. Sidney Dean, in joining, said: "I know it can make a decisive contribution to the redevelopment of our waterfront.

Times article hails concept as "representing one of the city's last chances to retain a full block of homogeneous historical architecture of original construction." (December 17.)

Governor to appoint Trustees. Senator Seymour reports that naming of Trustees for the Museum, in accordance with State Law, is expected early this year.

Friends see planners. Comm. Harmon Goldstone, in meeting with chairman, expressed sympathy with the project but questioned some planning assumptions, asking why precise data and maps were not drawn up - though in the end, he agreed, only Planning Commission's own findings would be acceptable. Further meetings are planned.

THE HUNT FOR OLD SHIPS

A members' group visited the Alice Wentworth in Boston and an abandoned fishing vessel in New Bedford. Dick Rath at Boating is corresponding from the Cape Verde Islands to Newfoundland to gather facts on surviving historic hulls.

OPEN MEETING AT NY YACHT CLUB, JANUARY 26, 6 - 8 P.M.

Meeting at 37 W. 44 St. will consider World Ship program, reports of Ship Committee and meetings with city authorities. Steering Committee membership is informal, composed of members who are doing the work. Feel free to walk in.

City Club luncheon, January 20

Call Peter Stanford, PL 4-1100 if you wish to attend this luncheon to discuss the concept at the City Club, 6 W. 48. Luncheon is $1.50.

Organized November 15, Friends of South Street Maritime Museum works to save the only remaining part of the old N Y seaport shown in this 1818 view by Baron Klinckowstrom.

The Friends of the Museum committee exists to "bring into being an informed body of citizens opinion" on the Museum concept. Members are also studying old ships, museum operations and local history to aid Trustees. Reports are available to members on request.

A model to illustrate the idea of an open-air seaport Museum was made by Lee Kiil and is to be displayed at Seaman's Bank for Savings in April.

The World Ship Society has proposed a walking tour and dinner discussion on the South Street Museum project. The event has been tentatively agreed on for April 8.

FROM THE AUTHORS' COLLECTION.

A NEWSLETTER WAS NEEDED to keep people informed and aware of their part in an active, participating membership. By the end of the year we had 145 members—well over the 100 we felt we would need to keep the organization going into the new year.

PETER AND NORMA man the reception desk at 16 Fulton Street in April 1967. Behind them is new matchboard wainscoting, installed to give a more established look to things, while paint cans lie at hand to get on with transforming a fish stall into a museum. In this we were joined by Joe Cantalupo, in shirt sleeves below. Joe, we were to learn, cared deeply for the history of the waterfront.

JOE, WITH PIPE, and his brother Bob in the 1940s.

IN 1911, THEIR EBULLIENT FATHER Pasquale, second from right, with his crew among the schooners that bring in the fish. All this will change, as Joe, then five years old, was growing up. But he remembered it well!

PETER HOLDS FORTH to Norma and Kent Barwick about the huge photomural he plans for the back wall at 16 Fulton Street. Meanwhile Leonard Nodelman (foreground) and Jock Bartlett (on the ladder) get on with the rest of the display.

WITH THE BIG PICTURE UP, Eric Ridder (left), Ruth McAneny Loud, Barton and Walter Gubelman and the inimitable Margot Gayle line up before the photo taken aboard Kaiulani *by Karl Kortum in 1941.*

22 MAY 1967, MONDAY AFTERNOON: The schooner Athena *puts a line ashore astern of the schooner* Volante *to land Karl Kortum, Commissioner Herbert Halberg and museum friends to declare South Street Seaport Museum open to the public. Inset: Karl, Archie Horka and Os Brett, seamen all, sail* Athena *to the Seaport opening.*

Below: Peter, with Commissioner Halberg and Karl behind him, talks to the welcoming crowd, which includes a reporter (far left) with our architect Charles Evans Hughes next to him.

A MORNING TO BE ALIVE, October 1967. The crews are finishing breakfast and getting ready for the first Schooner Race for the Mayor's Cup, a considerable venture for a fledgling museum.

THE MAYOR'S CUP, an antique ewer, was discovered in a pawn shop on lower Broadway. A mahogany base carried the winners' names.

PASSING BATTERY PARK, Athena *accompanies a dozen other schooners heading for the starting line for the first sailboat race in harbor waters in half a century.*

WITH "A BONE IN HER TEETH," Athena's *mostly British crew has every sail close hauled and pulling hard, while bo'sun Norma has the helm. This photo was taken by a crew member aboard* Tyehee, *which smartly left us in her wake.*

JAMES KIRK, MUSEUM MEMBER NO. 1 and Athena's *lookout, keeps an eye to leeward.*

THE CARTOONIST PAUL LORING (below and below right) reveals an antic sense of humor with his sketch of Athena's *racing performance.*

SKIPPER PETER STANFORD

THE LAST TEN MILES IT BLEW ABOUT 30 KNOT!

FOULED TOPSAIL

THE 42 YEAR OLD ATHENA FINISHED 5TH

BARCLAY WARBURTON'S LITTLE BRIG Black Pearl *was allowed to participate as a "topsail schooner." It was a bit of a stretch, but the* Black Pearl *brought square rig back to South Street, and in the spirit of good fun, no one objected.*

OUR FIRST SEAPORT SHIPS brought people to Pier 16 in 1968. This lively watercolor by Charles Lundgren (left) shows the George Rogers construction barge and pile driver repairing the pier for our first two vessels, the lightship Ambrose *and the Gloucester fishing schooner* Caviare, *airing her mainsail.*

PHOTO: CAPT. JUAN JOSE P. DEVALLE, ARA

PHOTO: NORMA STANFORD

BOUND FOR DRYDOCK, the far-distant Wavertree *was bought by Jakob Isbrandtsen in November 1968. The ship's great seagoing hull looms over the workaday buildings of La Boca, the old seaport of Buenos Aires, as she leaves her longtime berth in the river Riachuela. There, the porteños, recognizing her deepwater lineage, called her not* ponton *(barge) but* el gran velero—*the great sailing ship.*

IN THE ARGENTINE NAVY YARD, Peter is awed by the size of the Seaport Museum's new artifact. We had already learned that over 95 percent of the ship's iron frames and plating were intact. Now professional surveyors will confirm this, to our gleeful relief. Some surveyors came on their lunch hours to tap at the old iron with their hammers, just for the experience of seeing and testing the venerable old iron, which rusts more slowly than steel.

THE TEENAGERS ON THE CAVIARE*'S MAIN GAFF helped care for the old schooner and thus had the privilege of having their photo taken during a festival on Pier 16, as Frank Woerner, with concertina, and Bernie Klay, guitar, sing songs of the sailor and fisherman for a group of youngsters.*

BURL IVES LEADS SCHOOL CHILDREN in chanteys and sea songs that tell of "diving bows under with the main skysail set." Mr. Ives went on to record an album, Songs They Sang in South Street, *which he donated to the South Street cause.*

PETE SEEGER SANG AT THE MUSEUM'S 1967 ART
SHOW and thereafter every year—to our great joy
and the museum's enduring benefit. Here, in 1969 he
arrived aboard the Hudson River sloop Clearwater
to welcome the Argentine Navy's sail training ship
Libertad to Pier 16. People filled the pier and the
streets and their voices filled the air as Pete led the
crowd in "Oh, What a Beautiful City."

HELEN HAYES ASKS HOW WE GET MEMBERS, and Peter explains that we rely on the two gents
standing behind her, Messrs. Cantalupo and Wenzel. A full account of the encounter is given in Twice
Over Lightly, a book Helen wrote with Anita Loos (standing with Joe) about rediscovering New York,
which features a rave review of the Ambrose restoration—and the volunteers who made it happen!

BEFORE OUR TIME, *people came to South Street to see the famous clipper* David Crockett *set sail toward the end of her career. Built in Mystic, Connecticut, in 1853, she rounded Cape Horn fifty times before being cut down as a barge in 1890.*

INTO THE 1930S, *the* Tusitala, *Scottish-built in 1883, kept deepwater sail alive under Capt. James Barker, who served plum duff to the crew whenever the ship overtook a steamer. She was laid up in the Depression, served as a training ship in WWII, then was scrapped.*

THE BRITISH SHIP WAVERTREE sets sail from New York bound for India in March 1895. Capt. Thomas, who knew the long-lived iron ship, called her an "Ocean Wanderer," honoring her worldwide quest for cargoes. Dismasted in a Cape Horn gale in 1910, she reeled back to the Falkland Islands and was later towed to South America. She was bought by the Seaport Museum in 1968 and came to New York in 1970. In his painting, John Stobart captures the drama of the big square rigger maneuvering in the tight quarters and tricky currents of New York harbor.

THE SCHOONER PIONEER, built of iron in Pennsylvania in 1885, sailed into South Street just after Wavertree's arrival. She served as a sail training ship for school groups, museum volunteers and visitors.

MORNING IN SOUTH STREET finds the barque Peking's masts towering over the rooftops of Schermerhorn Row. By the 1970s the Street of Ships is again alive, with Seaport Books & Charts and its quadrant sign encouraging exploration of the Seaport's heritage.

DREAMING, PERHAPS, ABOUT THE VOYAGE OF THEIR OWN LIVES, bystanders gather to watch the departure of Allerton, *sister ship of* Wavertree. *When* Wavertree *came to New York in 1895, she berthed in Brooklyn, so the artist kept faith with history by depicting an actual South Street scene.*

BOWNE & CO., STATIONERS opens in Water Street, the Seaport's face to the modern city. Restored to welcome the ships of OpSail '76, signs announce a ship chandlery and other maritime activities. Sadly, all museum shops, except Bowne, will be closed in the 1980s to make room for the mall developer, Rouse.

THE SEAPORT IS AT ITS HEIGHT, in OpSail '76. From the left: Britain's Sir
Winston Churchill *with restaurant ship* Robert Fulton *astern; the flag-dressed*
Peking *and* Wavertree *with* Ambrose *astern. At pier 15 are Norway's* Sørlandet
with Danmark *astern and the ferry* Hart *with the US Coast Guard's* Eagle.

THE STREET THAT LED AROUND THE WORLD *still offers challenge and achievement
to all comers today. The experience of that long sea road offers guidance for the future—
which, like the sea itself, is the province of uncertainty. The voyaging experience tells us
to embark with unshakable resolve and to be ever ready for what the next day brings.*

Captain Vazquez Maiztegui smiles as Peter presents our thanks for bringing the tall ship Libertad *to South Sreet in August 1969. Seated next to Norma at a dinner in his honor held at the New York Yacht Club, he and his senior officers reveled in the formal turn-of-century atmosphere of the senior club in American yachting.*

ARA Libertad, *sail-training ship of the Armada of the Republic of Argentina, makes an impressive visitor in South Street. City officials had tried to bar her coming to South Street, but Captain Vazquez announced that he was bound for South Street "and no other place."*

SEA DAY 1970, A HALCYON SPRING DAY, brings New Yorkers out to the Battery Park waterfront to watch a flotilla of visiting ships, led by our schooner Athena *and Warburton's brigantine* Black Pearl, *returning from a foray to Staten Island. Their mission was to rescue the Alice Austen House from the threat of demolition. A committee ashore, including Borough President Bob Conner and the residents of the Austen House, were on the beach to welcome our delegation, led by City Parks Commissioner August Heckscher, who planted a NYC flag on the property's lawn sweeping down to the sea, and Margot Gayle, representing the Victorian Society, to give a veneer of respectability to this raid to preserve an island treasure. Happily, the City later acted to take the property, which flourishes as a museum celebrating Ms. Austen's work as photographer of New York Harbor in the transition from sail to steam.*

THE GALLANT FULL-RIGGER DANMARK *sails into New York Harbor in 1974, headed for South Street. In 1940, when Germany invaded her homeland,* Danmark *was in Florida; the little ship helped the war effort by training US Coast Guard cadets after the United States entered the war in 1941. This encouraged the USCG to take over the barque* Eagle *after the Nazi surrender, to continue the invaluable experience of sail training to meet the fundamental demands of traditional sail.*

MAYOR JOHN V. LINDSAY, *a consistent supporter of the Seaport project, won a major victory of his administration when the Board of Estimate voted unanimously to uphold the Landmarks designation of Schermerhorn Row on 19 December 1968. This saved the Row and made possible the air rights transactions financed by Jakob Isbrandtsen's Seaport Holdings, which ultimately brought in the Seaport Land.*

Lindsay, shown here on one of his frequent visits to the Seaport, is accompanied by Peter and architectural historian Ellen Fletcher (with camera), who was an outstanding proponent for the Seaport cause.

PHOTO: MORT DAGOWITZ

AT THE MEMBERSHIP MEETING *on 20 February 1969, Peter stood with Joe Cantalupo, museum chairman Jakob Isbrandtsen and city planner Tom van Arkel to confirm that "Ships are the heart of our story." And membership chairman Joe Cantalupo described our membership philosophy by saying: "Other museums are FOR people. This museum IS people."*

Os Brett's print of Wavertree *driving through a Cape Horn gale is on the wall behind us, and a model of the ship, echoing the painting, stands on the table. Our faith in the ship and the determination of our members to bring her to New York strengthened our hand in the battles that lay ahead.*

THE FIRST RESOLUTION of the new Seaport board of trustees was to acquire a major square-rigged ship—and here she is, the full-rigger Wavertree *of 1885, in San Francisco in 1902. She is carrying 3,000 tons of grain under her hatches, with her anchor hove short to begin the 17,000-mile passage back to England. This handsome photo helped convince trustees that this was the ship they wanted.*

BOUND FOR FAR HORIZONS, Wavertree *heads into her future at the Seaport Museum, where she will serve as an educational center for people to learn the vital role of seafaring in both our national story and in the story of a city built by the sailing of such ships to the world's four corners.*

TIMELINE

These dates are based on PS notes, correspondence, personal journals and desk diaries, cross-checked with South Street Seaport Museum annual reports and the bimonthly South Street Reporter, *and with press reports of Seaport museum plans and events in this era.*

1965

Jan./Feb.	PS & NS see *Lady of Good Voyage* in Fish Market w/ Kirk, TS, CS.
Apr. 12	PS quits Ogilvy & Mather, starts work at Hicks & Greist.
Apr. 17–25	PS, NS, D. Johnston, Northup sail *Athena* from Maine to City Island, NY.
Oct. 12–18	PS & NS to West Coast for Beefeater Gin; visit LA, SF, Seattle.
Dec. 12	Al Stanford calls Ed Stackpole re our idea of East River Seaport.

1966

Jan. 20	NS letter to SF Maritime Museum re starting a maritime museum in NYC.
Jan. 26	Anita Ventura's letter to NS offering advice.
Feb.	Karl Kortum discovers *Wavertree* in Buenos Aires.
Feb. 28	PS runs into Dick Rath at office of *Popular Boating* magazine.
Aug.	NS letter in the *Mariner's Mirror*, England, re search for square rigger.
Aug. 2	Sen. Seymour's bill for SSMM signed by Gov. Rockefeller.
Aug. 4	NS & PS meet with Bob Ferraro; make list of people to call re museum.
Aug. 10	5PM: NS, PS & Ferraro meet Seymour. Agree on 5 steps. Then to South St. to survey the site w/ Maal & Leevi Kiil.
Aug. 27–Sep. 5	NS, PS, Tom on *Athena* cruise to Gloucester & Nantucket.
Aug. 30	*Athena* gets whistle salute from Tarr & Wonson's. We visit *Lady of Good Voyage* and learn of 5 other schooner hulls.
Sep. 2	*Athena* in Nantucket, meet w/ Ed Stackpole & Charlie Sayle.
Sep. 13	PS quits H & G; begins work at Compton Advertising on Oct. 15.
Nov. 15	PS, NS, Ferraro, Lee Kiil, Alice Taylor take Kiil model to Seymour. Friends of SSMM formed, w/ $50 from Seymour, $1 ea NS, PS, Ferraro.
Nov., late	Rath joins Seaport, signs up members, takes on ship search.
Nov. 25	PS, NS, Rath, Ferraro visit *Emma C. Berry* in Toms River, NJ.
Dec. 10–11	PS, NS, Ferraro to Boston to see *Alice Wentworth*, then to Nantucket to see Stackpole & Sayle.
Dec. 12	PS presents Seaport project to City Club. Board votes approval of plan.
Dec. 17	Huxtable article in *NY Times* favors Schermerhorn Row over Fraunces Tavern.
Dec. 17–18	PS & NS to Mystic w/ Al to meet Chas. Lundgren at his art exhibition.
Dec. 29	PS meets Frank Braynard & Jeff Rogers, then Harmon Goldstone.
Dec. 31	Friends of South Street ends year with 145 members. Income ca. $205.

1967

Jan. 10	First *South Street Reporter* printed and mailed out from Alice Taylor apt.

Jan. 14–20	Kiil model, with 4 model ships added, on display at NY Boat Show.
Jan. 20	PS presents Seaport plan at City Club luncheon.
Jan. 22	Mel Greene's Seaport story in *Daily News*. PS letter to Anita Ventura.
Jan. 26	First Steering Committee meeting at NYYC.
Feb. 6	Halberg says we must secure the land, before he can turn over piers.
Feb. 4–5	PS, NS, Ferraro & Rath to Boothbay, ME, to see building of *America*.
Feb. 8	Rath & PS meet w/ Melvin Conant at the Lotus Club, first time.
Feb. 14	PS lunch w/ Conant, Peter Black & Robert Duncan, who poses 10 feasibility questions.
Feb. 17	PS meets Eric Ridder for first time, w/ Aldrick Benziger & James Farrell.
Feb. 23	PS lunch w/ Buford at NYYC. Friends of South St. evening meeting decides to incorporate. Membership at 450; $600 in bank; $200 in payables.
Feb. 27	PS meets w/ Conant, Black, Duncan re Conant's $30K plan.
Mar. 2	Membership reception at NYYC. Admiral Will attending, likes Seaport idea.
Mar. 3	PS receives 5-page letter from Anita Ventura detailing Kortum ideas.
Mar. 7	Kortum accepts role as advisor & urges us to get a big square rigger.
Mar. 10	Meeting of PS, Conant, Ridder & Jakob Isbrandtsen at India House. Isbrandtsen agrees to be chairman of museum, contributes $5K.
Mar. 13	Mon. meeting Alice's; mail out March (second) *Reporter* to 550 members.
Mar. 15	PS 9AM meeting w/ J. Isbrandtsen. PS 11AM meeting w/ Arthur Massolo of Gov. Rockefeller's office, re NYS museum trustees. Afternoon: survey South St. w/ Zeckendorf. Dinner: PS, NS, Davidson meet at Sweet's in heavy snow.
Mar. 17	PS meets Wertenbaker, who writes a story for *New Yorker* (unpublished).
Mar. 20	We rent 16 Fulton for SSSM office.
Mar. 27	Mon. PS & NS start work as staff at 16 Fulton. Ferraro paints entry. Joe Cantalupo visits us for the first time.
Apr. 7	First public event in South St.: Walking tour/dinner with World Ship Soc. 350 attend.
Apr. 27	South Seaport Seaport Museum incorporated per R. Walton. PS, NS, T. Walton, William Shopsin & Jon. Feffer are founding trustees.
May 19	PS & NS welcome Karl & Jean Kortum to New York.
May 22	Museum opens w/ "Sail-in" of two schooners on National Maritime Day.
May 23	PS, Kortum lunch w/ M. Conant, R. Tarr, later Ridder, all agree on *Wavertree*.
May 26	Jack Kaplan tours South St. w/ PS, on behalf of J. M. Kaplan Fund.
June	PS article "Street of Ships" appears in *Boating*.
June 8	First meeting of SSSM Board of Trustees. PS reports 1,000+ members.
June 13	*Regina Maris* visits SSSM and Betsy Kohn is hired as factotum.
June 18	PS at Mayor Lindsay luncheon, Gracie Mansion.
June 23	PS, J. Isbrandtsen, Jack Kaplan, Davidson, Rubinow, et al. re land.
June 29	Second public event: walking tours, chanteys & New Symphony Orchestra.
July 14	PS, NS, Horka, Brett sail *Athena* to Mystic to meet w/ W. Johnston & staff.
mid July	Printed plan for Seaport is issued w/ Shopsin & Lundgren illus.

July 18	PS at second Lindsay luncheon, Gracie Mansion.
Early Aug.	Liabilities exceed $10K; PS talk with Cantalupo.
Aug. 10	Schaefer's *America* enters NY harbor w/ mayor, NS & PS aboard.
Aug. 26–27	Public event: Art Show w/ Pete Seeger & August Heckscher.
Aug. (late)	Begin work on *Tigre* remains salvage w/ Kent Barwick.
Oct. 21	First Schooner Race for the Mayor's Cup, 12 entrants, & *America* as observer.
Nov. 2	Seminar by George Seeth, Sandy Hook Pilots.
Early Dec.	SSSM book *A Walk Through South Street* published, sells out, has 2nd ed.
Dec. 31	SSSM ends year w/ 3,000 members, 3 on staff, income $68,000.

1968

Jan. 5	First James Monroe Lunch w/ Adm. Will, R. Albion & Howard Chapelle at Whitehall Club on the Black Ball Line 150th anniversary.
Jan. 6	Howard Chapelle speaks on Black Ball Line at SCI supper.
Jan.	*Reporter* announces Bowne Printing plan to open a shop in South Street.
Jan. 18	NY State Maritime Museum holds first meeting.
Jan. 31	PS, Van Arkels & Lloyd Dalzell to Williamsburg, meet w/ Kendrew, pres.
Feb. 21	Jack Kaplan OKs Seaport Plan, pledges $70,000 for financial plan.
Mar. 21	Ralph Miller of Museum of City of NY pledges support to PS in NY State Museum fracas.
May 2–16	NS & PS to South America to inspect *Wavertree* & *Ville de Mulhouse*.
May 3	In Buenos Aires NS & PS meet Crocker & DeValle, visit *Wavertree*.
May 13	NS & PS lunch w/ John Davies (ABS) and meet Capt. Thomas Thomas.
May 15	Planning Commission designates SSSM as preliminary urban renewal sponsor.
May 21	Riverboat Ball on *Alexander Hamilton*. 1,000 people at $15 ea.
May 22	National Maritime Day: "Square Riggers 68" w/ *Mon Lei, Black Pearl* et al.
Late May	George Demmy hired to run restoration workshop; Mary Brunner hired as assistant; exhibition "Destruction of Lower Manhattan" installed.
May/June	Ellen Isbrandtsen hired. Val Wenzel, Marie Lore, Jo and Don Meisner join volunteers.
June 15–16	Visit of USCGC *Eagle* to SSSM. PS joins for 5-day cruise.
June 22–23	Return visit of USCGC *Eagle* at SSSM.
June 30–July 1	Visit of *Danmark* to SSSM
July	Bernie Klay launches "Folk Arts Ring" sing-along on Pier 16.
Aug. 5	Lightship *Ambrose* arrives at pier, gift of USCG via J. Isbrandtsen.
Sep. 20	Fishing schooner *Caviare* (later *Lettie G. Howard*) arrives at South Street.
Oct. 12	Second Schooner Race, with 28 entrants and 2 observation boats.
Oct.	Jim Diaz hired. McNamara gets steamship models for SSSM. Charlie Dunn becomes chairman of Friends; J. Isbrandtsen rents 203 Front St. for SSSM.
Nov. 6–7	Restoration conference at 203 Front St. aboard Seaport ships.
Nov. 8	We learn of Atlas-McGrath hostile takeover of Schermerhorn Row block. PS starts meetings w/ Board of Estimate members.
Nov. 20	J. Isbrandtsen purchases *Wavertree* for SSSM.
Nov. 30	*Wavertree* moved from Riachuelo to Darsena Norte, Buenos Aires.

Dec. 17	PS, Davidson, Cantalupo present 1,000 letters re Schermerhorn Row to mayor.
Dec. 19	Board of Estimate upholds Landmark status for Schermerhorn Row.
Dec. 19 & 20	*NY Times* editorials support Landmark designation—and how!
Dec. 20	Davidson elected trustee of SSSM.
Dec. 31	SSSM ends year with 6,000 members; income $301,000.

1969

Jan. 2–17	PS & NS in Buenos Aires, sign *Wavertree* contract of sale.
Jan. 22	Seaport Holdings buys John St. building from Herman Miller for $1M.
Feb. 20	SSSM Annual Meeting; Cantalupo says "This museum *is* people."
Mar. 4	Kortum letter to Peter Throckmorton, who wrote PS on Feb. 1 re *Elissa*.
Apr. (mid)	Staff moves offices to 203 Front St.
Apr. 19– 30	Alan Villiers visits Seaport, many speaking dates for *Wavertree*.
May 15	Lindsay groundbreaking 236 Front St.
May 21	Riverboat Ball aboard *Alexander Hamilton* run by Slotnick & Lundgren.
May 26	City Planning Commission approves Seaport Plan dev. by staff.
May 27	AM: J. Isbrandtsen, Wilpon, PS meet w/ Atlas & Schuster. PM: PS award at Municipal Art Society; dinner w/ Waldo Johnston, et al.
May 28	*Wavertree* books are delivered.
June 30	Burl Ives sings at SSSM, records *Songs They Sang in South Street.*
July 3	Seaport Holdings buys Goelet Blocks: $10 million + 1M costs = $11M.
July 18–20	USCGC *Eagle* visits South Street.
July 24	Board of Estimate approves Seaport Plan; J. Isbrandtsen orders rebuild of *Wavertree* bulwarks & forecastle head in Buenos Aires.
July 25–Aug. 3	*Libertad* at South St., joined by P. Seeger aboard *Clearwater* on 1st visit to NYC.
July 29	Bernie Klay's X-Seamen's Institute sings at South St.
July 31	David Rockefeller dinner aboard *Libertad*.
Aug. 26	Jacques Piccard in submarine *Ben Franklin* docks at South St.
Sep.	Pier manager Al Swanson leaves, replaced by Ed Ferris.
Oct.	Staff's Seaport Plan published; price $1.50.
Oct. 4	Schooner Race, 14 entrants.
Nov. 14	J. K. Galbraith speaks at lunch aboard *Victoria* to support Seaport.
Nov. 19–23	PS to Buenos Aires for *Wavertree* change-of-flag ceremony.
Dec. 31	SSSM ends year with 10,000 members; income $408,000.

1970

Feb. 5	Jerry Allen seminar on her book *The Sea Years of Joseph Conrad.*
Feb. 16	D. Rockefeller reception aboard *Ambrose* w/ supporters & volunteers.
Feb. 21	We launch *Eppleton Hall* campaign, tug en route to San Francisco.
Mar.	Helen Hayes visits South Street, becomes chair of South St. Theater.
Mar. 26	*Eppleton Hall* makes triumphant entry to San Francisco.
May 14	Rudie Schaefer holds lunch to launch *Wavertree* Syndicate.
May 21	PS receives Albert S. Bard Award, Citizens Union.
May 22	Sea Day: 5 sail vessels & *Driftmaster* visit Alice Austen House, SI.
June 2	PS speaks at Amer. Assn. of Museums conference; published in *Curator.*

June 7–8	PS/NS develop emergency rationale for City Bank loan.
June 16	PS to Washington, DC, for NMHS meeting, is elected president.
June 25	Harbor artist John Noble visits South Street.
July	John Stobart's Wavertree *Leaves NY, 1895* in *South St. Reporter*.
July 3	*Wavertree* leaves Buenos Aires, under tow for New York.
July 3–20	PS, NS, RS to Italy by air, visit R. Miller & others.
July 17–19	Fourth USCGC *Eagle* visit to SSSM.
Aug.	Theatre Research & Four Winds Theater launch program on Pier 16.
Aug.	First air rights sale, to TelCo. bldg planned for Block 74W (later canceled).
Aug. 5	*Wavertree* arrives NYC, Pouch Terminal. Dinner for tug *Titan* crew at Delmonico's.
Aug. 11	*Wavertree* arrives at Pier 16, 11:00 AM, welcomed by Mary Lindsay.
Aug. 21–24	*Clearwater* visits South Street, 2nd of many visits.
Aug. 22	*Athena*, w/ Girl Mariners, and *Pioneer* in Great Schooner Race, Gloucester.
Aug. 30	*Pioneer* arrives in South Street as gift of Grinnell estate.
Sep. 2	PS sees Sid Davidoff w/ 10 requests for City action. No action.
Sep. 12	Over 150 volunteers conduct "South St. Cleanup Day."
Sep. 19	Mayor Lindsay visits "Waterfront for People" festival. Ferry *Hart* comes in.
Sep. 26	Schooner Race, 18 boats but no *Athena*.
Sep. 27	Theatre Research program launched on Pier 16.
Oct. 8	Alan Villiers, in second visit to SSSM, shows film on Pier 16.
Oct. 9	Villiers speaks at opening of Seaport Bookshop.
Nov. 2	James Roberts, veteran *Wavertree* hand, visits ship.
Dec. 3	"Seaport in the City" conference w/ Kortum, Schoener, Starr, Davidson.
Dec. 31	SSSM ends year with 15,000 members; income $698,000.

1971

Jan. 9	Five-alarm fire sweeps piers 13 & 14. Two McAllister tugs and volunteers ashore stand by.
Feb. 10 (ca)	Demmy leaves; NS to run *Wavertree* as manager, Ships & Piers.
Feb. 14	*Wavertree* dummy bowsprit installed.
Feb. 27	Throckmorton visits SSSM, signs on as advisor.
Mar.	Harold Lebe named vice president, Doug Burris ships & pier manager.
Mar. 19	NY Comedy Club's "Billy Budd" canceled by Dept. of Ports & Terminals.
Apr.	*Caviare* hauled at Minneford's, City Island; volunteers scrub and paint.
Apr.	Martin Rockmaker hired to manage planned ship model shop.
Apr. 12–15	NS, PS, RS, JS visit Smithsonian and Chesapeake Bay Maritime Museum at St. Michaels.
Apr. 23	PS to Cooperstown, NY, to talk to Fred Rath students.
May 1	Geo Matteson sails *Pioneer* with 10 youngsters, launching sail-training program.
May	*Caviare* renamed *Lettie G. Howard* after new evidence and review.
May 6	Pub Preservation Society formed by PS, NS and usual suspects.
May 11	Annual Meeting held aboard *Wavertree*.

May	Frank O. Braynard hired as program director, replacing Frazer.
May 25	First Astor grant to *Pioneer*: $10,000, thanks to D. Rath & T. Walton.
June 2	Trustees meeting "…peace for a while." Elect Kent Barwick & Virgil Conway trustees.
July 10	*Pioneer* in Vineyard Race.
July 15	Leon Kaplan's 21-day European maritime museum tour departs; *Wavertree* reception re *Riversdale* gear, report in *NY Times*. Trustees meeting: J. Isbrandtsen debt $10.7 million + interest $3.5M = $14.2 total. City OKs land lease held up by Board of Estimate (final OK in 8 Feb. 73; signed by mayor on 14 June '73).
July 16	PS to Newport about *Black Pearl/Pioneer* collision.
Aug. 17	NMHS book *Ships That Brought Us So Far* sent to printer.
Aug. 17	*Wavertree* agent Manuel Schkulnik visits New York with wife, Clara.
Sep. 14	J. Isbrandtsen reports "City Bank now taking the lead" in bank consortium.
Sep. 23	PS, NS & J. Kirk visit John & Susan Noble aboard his barge.
Fall	SSSM announces OpSail 1976 Committee for Bicentennial.
Oct. 4	Tallichet in NYC on plans for *Hamilton* & *Moshulu*.
Oct. 16	Schooner Race, 25 entrants.
Oct. 27	PS & Lew Roddis sign napkin agreement re Con Ed station in South St.
Dec. 1	Arthur Wijsmuller visit. We make final payment for *Wavertree* tow.
Dec. 1–6	Kortums in NYC for Dec. 2 conference at India House.
Dec. 8	Board meeting: Trustees elect Buford as trustee; decide no major fund-raising possible until land is conveyed to SSSM. Year-end appeal raises $160,000; Astor gives $250,000 to *Pioneer*.
Dec. 31	SSSM ends year with 17,000 members; income $730,767.

1972

Feb. 8	Trustees meeting ends well, due to improved financing.
Feb. 10	Dinner aboard HMS *Ark Royal* off Staten Island. PS, NS, RS, JS w/ J. & S. Noble.
Mar.	Sea Museums Council formed by NMHS. (Becomes CAMM, 8 Jan. 1973.)
Mar. 5	Schiller, Kate & Sharon leave.
Mar. 19–20	PS, NS, RS & JS to Williamsburg. Dinner w/ Kendrew, visit "Troth's Fortune."
Mar. 30	Thurs, 6PM: Inaugural meeting of Wharf Rats on Lacey Barge.
Apr.	First issue of NMHS magazine *Sea History*, including Horka journal.
Apr. 3	*Alexander Hamilton* arrives SSSM, awaiting sponsor.
Apr. 17	*NY Times* article on Seaport as "key to Manhattan Landing."
Apr. 19–24	Kortums here. To St. Michaels re proposed Restoration II Conference.
May	Bronson Binger hired on grant from Fund for the City of New York.
Summer	Richard Fewtrell hired for *Wavertree* restoration, David Brink for Pioneer School program. F. Braynard & H. Slotnick to Europe to line up ships for OpSail.
June 13	Trustees meeting, J. Kirk elected.
June 20–23	With Cantalupo to Nantucket in "Sam Small" (NS & PS auto).

July	*Longshoreman's Voice* calls for banks & foundations to buy SSSM air rights.
July 4	*Howard* visits Sherman Creek, met by Percy Sutton, 2,000 visitors.
July 14–18	PS & NS to SF to see Kortums.
Aug. 1–2	PS w/ Cantalupo to Mystic, lunch w/ W. Johnston, Albion et al.
Aug. 17	Board of Estimate OKs lease of 3 blocks & Piers 15–18 to SSSM.
Sep.	Pioneer Marine School opens aboard ferry *Hart*.
Sep. 1	Norman Brouwer starts work at SSSM.
Sep. 18 or 19	NYC Bicentennial Commission names SSSM as first NYC Bicentennial site.
Sep. 28	J. Shepley accepts US Bicentennial designation of SSSM aboard *Wavertree*.
Sep. 30	PS to London, first ICOMM meeting at National Maritime Museum.
Oct.	Joined by NS, RS, JS; to West Country, Liverpool, Cambridge; visit Carrs.
Oct. 7	Schooner Race, 13 entrants.
Oct. 12	*Moshulu* arrives at SSSM, owned by Tallichet. City disputes plan.
Nov. 27	Rath & PS meet w/ Brooke Astor in SSSM.
Dec. 31	SSSM ends year with 20,000 members, income $624,968.

1973

Jan. 8	NMHS Sea Museums Council reconsituted as CAMM in Phila.
Jan. 10	Brooke Astor, Laurance Rockefeller, Cantalupo, B. Binger & PS tour site, lunch at Sloppy Louie's; L. Rockefeller pledges $200,000 for Seaport Plan.
Jan. 18	Cantalupo, his friend Jean, Terry Williams w/ Canadian architect & PS meet re urban crisis in Bronx. NS & PS develop "General Theory of the City."
mid-Feb.	Lighter *Aqua* joins the Seaport fleet.
Mar. 18	PS & NS sell *Athena* to Arthur Allgrove.
Apr. 7–May 9	PS, NS, CS, RS, JS to Italy aboard *Michelangelo*.
May 11	Historic Preservation Conf. aboard *Wavertree*: John Zuccotti, Chair, City Planning Comm.; F. Rath, NYS Office for Historic Preservation.
May 20	Lindsay opens Fulton Ferry for one day; in 6 hours 1,200 passengers.
May 31	Municipal Art Society meeting aboard *Alexander Hamilton*.
June 14	Mayor Lindsay, then PS sign NYC lease for 3 blocks of land & Piers 15–18.
July	Board OKs Seaport Plan, funded by L. Rockefeller.
July 2	SSSM board OKs Lacey restaurant aboard barge *Robert Fulton*.
July 13–17	PS, NS, RS & JS to Bath, ME, w/ Cantalupo.
Fall	SSSM announces membership at 25,000.
Sep.	Jacques Thiry brings brig *Unicorn* to South St. for the winter.
Sep. 14–16	*Pioneer* visits Essex, CT; reception of kids by Winterers et al.
Sep. 25	John Noble's "Ah, linoleum" speech on *Wavertree*'s quarterdeck.
Oct. 13	Schooner Race, 26 entrants.
Oct. 19	Brooke Astor and L. Rockefeller approve Seaport Plan aboard *Fulton*.
Dec. 3	"Where People Come Together" conference aboard *Wavertree*, with Mayor Lindsay, et al., followed by celebratory lunch aboard *Fulton*.
Dec.	$100,000 from Mellon Foundation for *Wavertree*.
Dec.	Rick Beinecke joins NMHS as staff counsel.

Dec. 31	PS writes Brooke Astor; proposes $1 million.
Dec. 31	SSSM ends year with 25,000 members; income $1,370,163 ($1,913,697 under accounting system adopted the following year).

1974

Jan. 22	Ridder & J. Isbrandtsen tell PS of consultant's call for SSSM super-manager.
Jan. 30	Executive Committee tells PS role of new manager: total executive control.
Jan. 31–Feb. 5	Cantalupo, PS, NS, RS & JS to Nantucket; meet Albion on ferry.
Feb. 8	Buford OKs *Robert Fulton* lease.
Mar. 1	PS meets Sen. Kennedy, who agrees to sponsor National Ship Trust.
Mar. 4	Trustees meet on governance, confirm super-manager plan.
Mar. 5	SSSM bookkeeper Schiller leaves.
Mar. 8	Geo Matteson hired as Ships & Piers manager.
Mar. 9	Thiry's *Unicorn* leaves for Caribbean, w/ Jane Williams in crew.
Mar. 16	Staff meeting at Yorktown Hts. on funding plan w/ Binger & Streibert.
Mar. 20	Closed Executive Committee meeting; no report to PS.
Apr.	Gale destroys *Alice S. Wentworth* in Boston; NMHS pays $10K cleanup.
Apr. 4	Rudy Kopf & John Bush visit *Wavertree* exhibit.
Apr. 8	Robt. Bonham starts work at SSSM as CEO, cancels staff's plans.
May	*Alexander Hamilton* leaves SSSM.
June 9	Cutbacks due to funding shortfalls; NS fired, rehired June 14.
June 19	First meeting of CAMM aboard *Fulton*, lunch at India House. AIA Award to PS.
July 8	David Rockefeller hosts foreign correspondents lunch on *Fulton*.
July 8–13	PS at second Int'l Congress for Maritime History conference, UK.
Sep. 9	PS to DC, meets Hummelsine at National Trust.
Autumn	*Moshulu* leaves South Street for Philadelphia after City refuses plan.
Oct. 12	Schooner Race for Mayor's Cup, 21 entrants.
Oct. 21	NMHS Ship Trust luncheon aboard *Fulton* w/ Frank Carr, Adm. Will, et al.
Nov.	Bowne Stationers opens shop in SSSM.
Dec. 13	*Wavertree*'s new mainmast stepped, 64 years after carried away.
Dec. 31	SSSM ends year with decline to 20,000 members; income $2,629,788.

1975

Jan. 7	PS, Shepley & W. Johnston to DC in Shepley's plane; set up NTHP Maritime Committee w/ Hummelsine (chairman) & Biddle (president) of NTHP.
Jan. 8	Shepley fires Bonham at Executive Committee meeting.
Jan. 12	Buford named managing trustee, replacing Bonham as CEO.
Jan. 15	Second meeting of CAMM, at Mystic, W. Johnston, chair.
Feb. 23	Bowne Stationery dedicated by Mayor Beame on Bowne & Co.'s 200th anniv. Followed by dinner aboard *Fulton*.
Mar.	Jack Aron elected trustee.
Apr. 11	Astor $1 million challenge grant announced. SSSM must raise $3.5 million.

June 14	Executive Committee meeting: Shepley calls for "structural change."
June 28	Justine Mee & Roberta Vrona in Yorktown Heights, call on PS to take control of SSSM; PS says trustees will never agree to this.
July 17	Barwick, Cantalupo, Kirk meet at El Faro, re election of trustees.
July 22	*Peking* arrives from UK, stops in Staten Island for completion of rig.
Aug. 6	PS lunch with Ridder, who says: "Don't take outside job."
Aug. 9	Barquentine *Barba Negra* arrives for long visit.
Sep. 2	PS starts part-time at Kobrand Corp., part-time consultant at SSSM.
Sep. 20	Schooner Race, 22 entrants.
Nov. 18	NMHS withdraws Ship Trust bill at request of Nat'l Trust & CAMM.
Nov. 22	*Peking* to SSSM after 4-month refit in Staten Island.
Dec. 31	[SSSM year-end membership and financial reports not published.]

1976

Jan.	*Lady of Good Voyage* in Fulton Market for last time, en route to Honduras.
Jan.	*Mathilda* sinks at Pier 16, is later transferred to Kingston, NY, as exhibit.
Jan. 22–31	NS, PS, RS & JS rail trip to visit Kortums in SF.
Jan. 26	Alan Burrough presents *Vicar* deed to PS in San Francisco.
Feb.	NS resigns from SSSM.
Feb. 23	NS & PS attend their last Ship Advisory Committee meeting.
Feb. 25	PS & Streibert attend ICOMM meeting in Mystic.
Feb. 26	Buford and PS have showdown meeting, "complete philosophical division."
Mar. 1	PS resigns as president of SSSM at Executive Committee meeting at NYYC.
Mar. 3	PS phones Shepley to pledge NMHS support of SSSM. Meets w/ Throckmorton & Brouwer re Falklands expedition.
July 4	NMHS publishes handbill "Guide to the Ships of Operation Sail" and charters spectator boat for viewing OpSail.
Sep. 1	Buford tells *NY Times* SSSM must cut staff by 1/3, due to OpSail costs.
Dec.	Buford resigns, staying on until replaced by John Hightower in June 1977. [SSSM year-end membership and financial reports not published.]

APPENDICES

I South Street Seaport Map, 1973
Even before the Seaport Museum acquired three blocks of land on 99-year lease from the City, museum galleries and shops were opened on land bought by Seaport Holdings. By 1976 these included Seaport Books & Prints, Children's Shop, Bowne Stationers, an art gallery, a model shop, a working forge and a crafts market. While producing a healthy 15-percent profit for the museum, these varied shops also attracted visitors and added to membership growth and participation in museum programs.

II Benefits of the Low-cost Membership, Annual Report, 1968
By the museum's second year, renewals showed that the low-cost introductory membership was helping to build regular memberships, as is shown in this report by membership chairman Leon Kaplan. At its height of 25,000 members in 1973, 17,000 were regular members and 8,000 were introductory members.

III An Introduction to South Street, October 1973
This discussion of the Seaport Museum's purposes introduced in a special issue of the *South Street Reporter* summarized the professional Seaport Plan financed by Laurance Rockefeller. This added some of the humanizing ideas and measures which gave ships, streets and buildings their vitality of purpose.

IV Audited Financial Reports for 1973 and 1974
In the 1973 report, income restricted to future use was reported in a separate summary. In 1974, under new management, all income was reported under the current year, leading to an apparent surplus. In that year, the actual operating loss of $134,693 appeared only in a footnote. This led to trustee concern about the unexplained lack of available funds.

V President's Report, May 1975
This page in the Annual Report for 1974 ends in a note on the strong outreach of the museum message. The activities cited were largely discontinued in 1976, however, and following this report sent out in May 1975, annual reports were no longer sent to members.

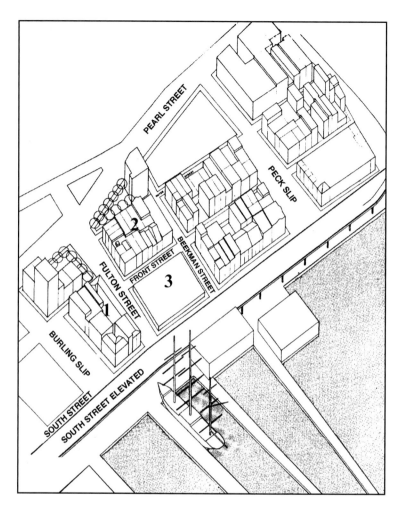

The drawing above, adapted from the official "South Street Seaport Development Plan," shows the three blocks of land conveyed to the Seaport Museum on 99-year lease in June 1973. Block **1** is Schermerhorn Row, built 1811–12, planned to house the New York State Maritime Museum. Block **2** is made up of buildings dating from 1797 to 1914, already occupied in 1973 by Seaport Museum offices and galleries. Block **3** is the Market Block, a 1950s one-story garage that will later house an arts and crafts market, including the Seaport Art Gallery and a working forge. These shops were superseded in 1982 by the Rouse Corporation's urban mall.

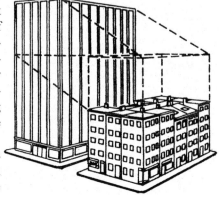

At right is a sketch of the air rights transactions which made possible Seaport Holdings acquisition of the Seaport land, which was then donated to the City of New York for leaseback to the Museum.

MEMBERSHIP COMMITTEE

Chairman: Leon Kaplan

Recruitment is carried on in a variety of ways, none more effective than word of mouth. But we extend our reach through mailings, newspaper, magazine and TV publicity, and through advertising which more than pays for itself.

Membership growth has been extraordinary, as shown in the follwing year-end totals:

$$1966 - 300$$

$$1967 - 3,000$$

$$1968 - 6,000$$

Revenue from memberships has been affected by a continuing tendency for people to join at higher membership rates.

In 1966 the ratio of members who gave $5 or more to join (since called regular members) to those who gave less that $5 (associate members) was about 1 to 10. In 1967 it was about 1 to 3. Among members who joined or renewed in 1968, the ratio of regular members to associate members was 1.2 to 1. In the first month of 1969, the ratio was 2.8 to 1.

Excerpt from the Annual Report for 1968

NOTE: In 1968 the trend was clear: Regular members ($5) made up well over half the total membership, growing faster than the introductory $1 membership. And when membership reached the unprecedented height of 25,000 five years later, this was made up of 17,000 regular members and 8,000 introductory members. Thus the cheap membership did not eat up the regular membership. Instead it acted to build up the regular and higher categories.

An Introduction to South Street

Conceived as a center for people and for history, South Street Seaport is a seven-block area of waterfront buildings in Lower Manhattan, running north from John Street to the Brooklyn Bridge on the East River. The project is unique in America, as an urban renewal project sponsored by a museum.

South Street Seaport Museum now maintains 11 ships on the historic waterfront and holds three and a half blocks of land and adjacent waterfront on 99-year lease from the City of New York. These holdings have been acquired without net charge on the city budget, by cooperative action among city, state, and banking authorities, and the generous commitment of private citizens.

The development plan calls for museum educational functions salted into a living commercial neighborhood including traditional craftsmen, theater and other museum-related functions, as well as shops, restaurants, apartments, and offices to be rented out to suitable tenants as the historic buildings are restored.

Pilot projects exist covering all these activities today. The Museum area will be visited by over one million people this year. Public participation runs strong in Museum plans and program: membership, at 25,000, is by far the largest of any historic institution in New York State or, indeed, of any sea-related museum in the world.

The South Street undertaking has been described as "the key" to the plan for development of the whole Lower Manhattan waterfront. It has been officially recognized by federal, state, and city authorities as a center of the National BiCentennial observances in 1976. Mayor Lindsay serves as the Museum's honorary program chairman, Helen Hayes as chairman of Theatre in South Street. Other distinguished New Yorkers serve in other ways.

But the bedrock on which the project is being built is the interest and participation of the ordinary New Yorker—who may not be such an ordinary person after all. People with the living interests provide the purpose of the South Street plan. They bring also, to all we undertake in South Street, an extraordinary vitality.

South Street in 1855: Most of these buildings still stand, historic ships have regathered and South Street once again is a center of city life and a vital center for people.

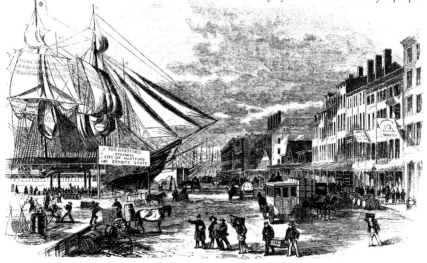

SOUTH STREET SEAPORT MUSEUM
BALANCE SHEET

DECEMBER 31

	1974	1973
ASSETS		
Cash	$ 219,539	$ 389,585
Marketable Securities	5,464	3,007
Contributions Receivable	52,127	-
Grants Receivable	240,179	49,771
Rents Receivable - Net	5,921	18,911
Notes Receivable	100,000	125,000
Merchandise Inventory	114,196	97,710
Prepaid Expenses	30,279	44,275
Leasehold, Land and Buildings, at Cost, Less Accumulated Amortization and Depreciation of $104,791 in 1974 and $42,647 in 1973	6,521,874	7,195,247
Ships, Craft and Antiquities	1,032,103	815,075
Other Assets	10,798	10,810
	$ 8,332,480	$ 8,749,391

LIABILITIES AND FUND BALANCES		
Leasehold, Land and Building Acquisition Debt	$ 6,367,076	$ 7,117,076
Notes Payable	45,252	69,813
Accounts Payable and Accrued Expenses	380,467	372,890
Grant Payable - Wildcat Service Corp.	105,001	-
Grant Payable - Other	14,000	-
Deferred Grant and Contribution Income	100,000	543,534
Fund Balance	1,320,684	646,078
	$ 8,332,480	$ 8,749,391

IV

SOUTH STREET SEAPORT MUSEUM
STATEMENT OF FUNDS INCOME AND EXPENSES

	YEAR ENDED DECEMBER 31,	
	1974	1973
	Total Funds	Total Funds
INCOME		
Membership Dues	$ 89,552	$ 93,406
Contribution Income	1,244,558	658,993
Grants	434,163	213,769
Sales - Museum Shops and Other Publications	210,237	149,240
Rental Income	271,213	186,330
Special Events	10,910	11,327
Ship Admissions	30,620	22,418
Sale of Schermerhorn Row	290,530	-
Other	48,005	34,680
	$ 2,629,788	$ 1,370,163
EXPENSES		
Salaries	$ 735,700	$ 440,197
Payroll Taxes and Employee Benefits	72,641	54,189
Stipends - Students	-	59,987
Flow Through Grant - Wildcat Service Corp.	105,001	-
Museum Acquisition, Maintenance and Repairs	191,621	146,936
Printing and Distribution	84,267	74,289
Insurance and Protection	111,590	92,855
Cost of Sales - Museum Shops and Other Publications	116,590	89,411
Special Events	4,402	61,489
Professional Fees	97,569	105,520
Rents, Utilities and Real Estate Taxes	115,257	67,657
Interest	107,294	78,472
Amortization and Depreciation of Leasehold and Buildings	71,750	42,647
Telephone	33,721	15,023
Promotion and Travel	41,511	16,828
Grants - Other	40,325	-
Other	25,943	11,241
	$ 1,955,182	$ 1,356,741

NOTE - The Museum records its income and expenses in three separate funds; Operating, Specified Purposes, and Property and Ships Operating Fund. The Operating Fund had income of $723,745 and expenses of $870,113 before net inter-fund transfer of $11,675, resulting in a deficiency of income over expenses of $134,693. A copy of the complete audit report is available upon request.

WEINTRAUB & CHASSIN

SOUTH STREET SEAPORT MUSEUM
STATEMENT OF FUNDS INCOME AND DEFERRED INCOME
FOR THE YEAR ENDED DECEMBER 31, 1973

	Deferred Income January 1, 1973	Total Fund Raising And Other Income	Total	Income Applicable To Current Year	Deferred Income December 31, 1973
GENERAL FUND					
Membership Dues	$ 8,362	$ 85,044	$ 93,406	$ 93,406	$ -
Contribution Income	207,268	375,598	582,866	341,634	241,232
Grants	12,500	60,000	72,500	52,036	20,464
Special Events	-	11,327	11,327	11,327	-
Other	-	7,142	7,142	7,142	-
	228,130	539,111	767,241	505,545	261,696
WATERFRONT FUND					
Contribution Income	16,149	324,879	341,028	103,940	237,088
Ship Admissions	-	22,418	22,418	22,418	-
Other	-	26,351	26,351	26,351	-
	16,149	373,648	389,797	152,709	237,088
PIONEER MARINE TECHNICAL SCHOOL					
Contribution Income	73,000	46,443	119,443	95,101	24,342
Grants	13,726	151,742	165,468	161,733	3,735
	86,726	198,185	284,911	256,834	28,077
PIONEER SAIL TRAINING PROGRAM					
Contribution Income	35,000	20,941	55,941	43,588	12,353
UPLANDS FUND					
Contribution Income	3,530	75,520	79,050	74,730	4,320
Rent Income	-	185,730	185,730	185,730	-
Other	-	1,787	1,787	1,787	-
	3,530	263,037	266,567	262,247	4,320
MUSEUM SHOPS PROGRAM	-	149,240	149,240	149,240	-
TOTAL	$ 369,535	$ 1,544,162	$ 1,913,697	$ 1,370,163	$ 543,534

See Notes to Financial Statements

President's Report

The Museum shops and publication sales, a vital component of Museum program and income, increased their sales from $74,000 in 1972, and $149,000 in 1973, to $210,000 in 1974.

Admissions aboard the Wavertree were only $30,000, due to delay in moving the ship to her present location on the south side of Pier 16.

The restaurant ship Robert Fulton served as a center for receptions, dances, and community events of all kinds. Technical difficulties delayed opening the ship to general public access. She is scheduled to be opened in 1975.

A Fulton Market was run in the open air in South Street under the expressway. This was successful in attracting crowds and publicity, but we erred in not opening it in the brick Market Block building as originally planned. By year-end agreement was reached to open the Market in 1975 where it was first planned.

A comprehensive review of museum program policy was held in the spring, following which Philip Yenawine joined the staff as Museum Operations Director, and Alicia Grant joined as Registrar.

Displays were significantly expanded and improved, including the Ship Model Gallery centering on the priceless Palmer collection, signs in the streets, improved gallery and shop signage, and further development of the Wavertree museum.

The Education Department expanded its program of tours, seminars, workshops and courses, and a Speakers' Bureau was established. Museum publications were enriched by a guide, "Walking Around in South Street," and booklet "Counting-house Days in South Street." The Reporter continued its flowering, as all members know.

* * *

Associate Organizations continued to add their distinctive program and purposes to South Street, which is conceived as a center of such activities. "Operation Sail — 76" continued lining up the sail training ships of the world to visit New York on July 4, 1976. The National Maritime Historical Society advanced their bill for a National Ship Trust, introduced in Congress by Senator Kennedy and Congressmen Carey and Murphy. Jean Sullivan and Michael Fischetti's South Street Theatre added to its laurels with well-received productions including "Moby Dick." Bernie Klay and the X-Seamen's Institute rampaged through an expanded program. And others, alas, too numerous to be mentioned here, did their part to make South Street's message carry — and carry truly.

Respectfully submitted:

Peter Stanford
President

INDEX

A. A. Low Brothers, 280
A. G. Ropes, sailing ship, 193
Aberdeen, Scotland, 323
Abrams, Charles, 152, 289
Ad Hoc Committee to Save South
    Street, 289–90
African-American seamen, 478–79
Aguiar, Dan, 346
air rights, 63–64, 82, 234, 289, 338–40,
    374–75, 377, 399, 435, 439–40, 473–77
Albion, Robert, ix, 188, 190, 198–200,
    202, 282, 381, 436, 502–3
Alcaeus of Mytilene, quoted, 446, 490
Alden, John, xx
Alejandrina, sailing ship, 221
Alexander Hamilton, steamboat, 236–37,
    393, 464–65, 490, 492
Alfred F. Loomis Trophy, 263, 432
Algoa Bay, 310
Alice Austen House, 391–92, 424
Alice S. Wentworth, schooner, 30–31, 42,
    45, 60–61, 503, 506
Alioto, San Francisco Mayor Joseph, 388
Allen, Jerry, 384
Allgrove, Arthur, 481
Aloha, barque yacht, 410
Amalfi, Italy, 487
Ambrose, lightship, viii 246–47, 263, 270,
    293–95, 304, 370–71, 385–86, 389, 436,
    451, 467–78, 496
America, 1851 schooner, 46, 47
America, schooner replica, 46, 47, 95, 169,
    172–73, 178, 180, 184, 410
American Association of Museums, 317,
    397
American Bureau of Shipping, 138, 225,
    306
American Eagle, fishing schooner, 28
American Export-Isbrandtsen Lines, 50,
    87, 340, 399, 406
American Sail Training Association
    (ASTA), 243, 258, 451
America's Cup, 46–47, 75, 82, 169, 177,
    179, 384

Amory, Robert, xx
Andalucia (ex-Ville de Mulhouse), sailing
    ship, 212, 215, 217, 220
Anson, Commodore George, 220
Antiope, sailing ship, 212
Antique Boat & Yacht Club, 350
Apprenticeshop, 504
Argentine Navy Yard, 354, 361, 375
Argus, codfishing schooner, 332
Aron, Jack, 340, 380, 396–7, 449, 492
artists, 157–8
Asbury Park Boat Show, 320
Astor, Brooke, 450, 451, 453–54, 466–71,
    494, 496, 498, 504–5
Athena (ex-*Heart's Desire*), schooner,
    description and history, xx
    maintenance work in Westchester
        Creek, 12–15, 19–20
    purchase, xx
    sail from Camden, Maine, xxi–xxiv
    sail to Gloucester and Nantucket,
        26–32
    sail to Mystic Seaport, 160–165
    sail to South Street for museum
        opening, 119–121, 124–127,
        129–131
    sailing in Long Island Sound, xxiv–xxvi,
        12, 20–21, 167–168, 347
    sale, 481
    Schooner Race sails, 174, 178, 181–183,
        189, 263, 371
    Sea Day participant, 390–391
    training Explorer and Mariner Scouts,
        248, 347, 432, 446
    winter layup, 59, 185–186, 373–374
    working on, xxvi–xxvii, 166, 473
Atlas, Sol, 288, 296, 297–98, 337–39,
    340, 342, 399
Atlas–McGrath, 278, 288–9, 296–8,
    338–40, 399, 473
Atmanchuk, Eddie, 461
Auchincloss, Mrs. Louis (Adéle), 391
Austen, Alice, 391–92
authenticity, 23, 28, 88, 103, 381, 401

Badillo, Herman, 286
Bailey, Capt. Richard, 373
Bain, Dixon, Jr., 209
Baker, George F. III, 395, 440, 444–45
Balclutha, sailing ship, 4–5, 17, 88, 117, 445, 508–9
Bard, Albert S., 397
Barker, Capt. James, 81, 364
Barry, Francis J., 236–37, 393, 461, 464
Bartlett, Capt. Bob, 42, 49, 350
Bartlett, Jock, 26, 166, 239
Barwick, Kent, 105, 121, 159, 236, 271, 317, 439, 469, 474, 477
Baum, Joe, 205
Bavier, Robert N., 75
Bay Ridge, 328
Beefeater gin, xxiii, xxv, 1, 22, 33, 76, 176, 510
Behetny, Menendez, 310
Ben Franklin, research submersible, 351
Bendixsen, Hans, 2
Benitez, Nicolasa, 322
Bennett, James Gordon, 137
Bentley, Helen Delich, 507
Benziger, Aldrick, 75–78, 97
Bermuda Race, 175, 347, 390
Berrien Shipyard, 166
Biddle, James, 274–75, 358
Billy Budd, play, 448
Binger, Bronson, 469–71, 477, 479, 491, 505, 507
Black, Peter, 72, 86, 158
Black Ball Line, 188, 198–99, 202–3
black community, 288, 321
Black Pearl, brigantine, 237–38, 243, 257–58, 260–61, 263, 371, 381, 391, 450–51
Black Rock, Connecticut, 319
Blackburn, Howard, 266
Blatch, Barnaby, 398–400, 473, 482
Blatch, Mari Ann, 398, 400
Blau, Ernie, 380
blizzard of 1888, 189
Block Island, 32, 347
Bloodhound, yawl, 175
Boardman, Gerry, 325
Boating magazine (formerly *Popular Boating*), 48–49, 151–52, 169, 187, 325, 420, 450

Bolster, W. Jeffrey, 478
Bonham, Robert, 511
borough presidents, New York City, 282, 284–87, 290–91, 321, 392
Boston City Hall, 276
Boughton, W. J., 257
Bounding Home, schooner, 180
Bowker, Francis E. "Biff," 335, 453
Bowne & Co., 71, 194, 205, 351, 385
Bowne Printing Shop, 71, 205, 352
Brava packet trade, 42
Braynard, Frank, 62, 95, 105, 142, 143, 176, 198, 373, 448, 454, 462, 493, 506
Brett, Gertrude, 125, 160, 279, 410
Brett, Oswald, ix, xii, 120, 125, 160, 185, 188, 279, 215, 304, 328, 333, 380, 383, 410
Brilliant, schooner, 335
Brink, David, 323, 471
Britain, 80, 137, 452, 457
British Isles, sailing ship, 138
British Sail Training Association, 451
Bronx, borough of, 12–13, 286, 385, 422
Bronx River Towing, 262
Brooklyn Bridge, xiii, xxi, 95, 100, 103, 108, 127, 239–40, 350, 479
Brooklyn Bridge Southeast Urban Renewal District, 83
Brooklyn Heights, 127, 329, 350
Brooklyn Navy Yard, 126
Brooklyn shore, 350,
Brotherhood of the Sea, 345, 369
Broughton, William, 428–30
Brouwer, Norman, 319, 471, 479
Bruce, Robert, 196
Brunel, Isambard Kingdom, 136–37
Buckley, William F., Jr., 435, 444
Buenos Aires, Argentina, 138–89, 211–13, 221, 302, 305–7, 356–7, 363, 366, 368
Buenos Aires buses, 214, 305, 397
Buford, Richard, 74, 81, 82–84, 87, 208, 210, 281, 339, 440, 469, 474, 477, 496, 506
Burroughs, Polly, 506
Bush, John, 1, 510
Busse, Paul, 271

C. A. Thayer, schooner, 2
Caddell, John, 200
Caen, Herb, 388
Cagney, James, 31
Calhoun, Jesse, 282
California, 10, 100, 465
Calmar Line, 406
Camden, Maine, xxi
Campbell, George, xi, 186, 201, 248, 270
Campbell, Roger, 248, 384
Canright, David and Steven, 326, 481, 510
Cantalupo, Joseph, xii, 107–9, 121, 156–
    8, 182, 195–6, 233, 263, 266–8, 289–90,
    317–18, 429–31, 469–73, 485, 504–7
Cantalupo, Pasquale, 108
Cape Cod Canal, 257
Cape Hatteras, 341
Cape Horn, x, 116, 119–20, 124–5,
    132–3, 135–8, 145, 219, 277–8, 303–4,
    314–15, 319, 326–7, 345, 409–10
Captains Courageous, film, 28
Carey, Oliver, 395
Cariad, pilot cutter, 457
Carkeek, Capt. Stephen, 240–42
Carr, Frank G. G., 134, 212, 452, 458
Carrega, Anibal, 306–309
Cartey, John J., 283
Casals, Pablo, quoted, viii
Cavaglieri, Giorgio, 273
Caviare, schooner, (ex-*Mystic C.*, now
    Lettie G. Howard), viii, 250–57, 259–62,
    264–67, 270, 322, 344, 346, 353, 401,
    428–30
Cerf, Bennett, 72, 282
Champigny, sailing ship, 138, 212
chanteys, 128–29, 154, 199, 346, 381, 413
Chapelle, Howard, xi, 95, 188, 197, 200,
    202, 254, 256, 270, 388, 436
Charles, Ted, 174
Charles Cooper, sailing ship, 138, 319
Charles W. Morgan, whaling ship, 161–62,
    212, 260,
children, xvii, xix, 14, 55–6, 88, 115,
    167, 186–7, 265–6, 344, 442–43, 445,
    484–85
Christmas, 15, 61–62, 195–6, 496–97
Church, Albert Cook, 265
Circle Line, 236, 432, 461–62

"The City and the Sea," 478
City Bank, 398–99, 473–75
City Club of New York, 52, 54, 56–7,
    63–4, 67, 70, 237
City Island, Bronx, xxiii, 423
city life, romance of, 489
City of Beaumont, barquentine, 142
A City Out of the Sea, novel, 7
Clancy Brothers, 348, 381
Clark, Dan, 418
Clearwater, sloop, 239, 249, 269, 346,
    371, 393, 401
clipper-ship era, 123–24
clipper ships, 70, 100–1, 112, 191
Cloux, Capt. Ruben de, 329
clubs, political, 13
Coffee Exchange block, 338
Cohen, Lenny, 321
Cohen, Louis, 467
Cohn, Michael, 478
Colonial Williamsburg, 207, 251, 271, 454
Columbia, fishing schooner, 28
Compton Advertising, 33–6, 51, 91, 93
Conant, Melvin, 72, 86, 90–3, 141, 143–
    44, 156, 248, 279, 376
concerts, 353, 428
Connecticut River Museum, 491
Connor, Robert T., 286, 392, 494
Conroy, Adrian, 14
Conroy's Creek (Westchester Creek),
    12–13, 15, 17, 19, 167
Conroy's Marina, 12–14, 59–60
Constitution, USS, sailing ship, 45
cooks, ship's, 192, 242, 416, 508
Corlears Hook, 112
Cornell, Katherine, 31
Coronel, Battle of, 220
Coulson, Jane (Johnston), xxi, xxiv–xxv,
    14
Council of American Maritime Museums
    (CAMM) (originally Sea Museums
    Council), 455, 500
Creamer, Michael, 323
Crime Circles Manhattan, book, 462
Crocker, Charles, 213–15, 225
Crown Zellerbach, 406
Cruising Club of America, 7, 266
Crumlin–Pederson, Ole, 466

Cue magazine, 72
Custom House, 62
Cutler, Carl, 81, 135–36, 161, 334
Cutty Sark, clipper ship, ix, 188, 212, 333, 372
Cuyler's Alley, 193
Cyrano, schooner, 432

Dagowitz, Mort, 353
Dale, F. Slade, 44
Dalzell, F. Briggs, 170, 180, 183, 208, 367, 376, 405–6, 458
Dalzell, Lloyd, 200, 207–8
Daniels, A. C., 135, 136, 138–39, 141
Danmark, training ship, 240, 244–45
Darien, Connecticut, 383
David Crockett, clipper ship, 161
Davidoff, Sid, 423–25
Davidson, Joan, 34–35, 100–2, 151, 152, 203, 209, 236, 271, 282, 289–90, 295, 323, 441, 443, 446
Davies, J. Clarence, 462
Davies, John, 138, 225–27
Davis, Mary, 324–25
Day, Doris, 265
Dean, Eugenia, 237, 341, 413
Dean, Sidney W., Jr., 52–54, 67, 237, 341–42
Demmy, Ellen, 373
Demmy, George, 235–36, 254, 262, 325, 348, 372, 373, 408, 448
Destruction of Lower Manhattan, exhibit, 235–36, 238
DeValle, Capt. Juan Jose P., 213, 224–26, 305–6, 311–12, 360–63, 366–68, 402
Dias, Bartolomeu, 484
Diaz, Jimmy, 268–69, 325, 371, 409, 458
Dickerhoff, Jack, 509
Dickerson, Jack, 46–47
Dodge, Ernest, 455
Down Easter, 116, 138, 191–92
Down Town Association, 105–6
Drake, Sir Francis, 235
Driftmaster, Army Corps of Engineers cleanup vessel, 391
Dring, Harry, 133
Driscoll, Jeremiah, 461
Druding, Harry, 239

Dufek, Admiral George, 200, 454
Duffy, Frank, 392
Duncan, Robert F., 72–74
Dunn, Charlie, 163, 190, 239, 269, 347, 370, 380
Dunn, Paul Henry, 250–52, 256, 429
Dynarts Foundation, 155

E. E Saunders & Co., 432
Eagle, USCGC, training ship, 240–45, 311, 341, 344, 495
Eagle Bag & Burlap, 111, 467
East River, 7–8, 285, 349–50, 430–31
Edith L. Boudreau, fishing schooner, 28
Edlu, cutter yacht, 172
Edward Sewall, sailing ship, 126
Edwards, A. D., 380
Effie M. Morrissey (see also *Ernestina*), fishing schooner, 42, 49, 113, 267, 350
Elissa, sailing ship, 323–24
Emma C. Berry, sloop, 44–45, 61, 95, 113, 418
Empire Stores, Brooklyn, 350
Eppleton Hall, steam tugboat, 324, 372, 387–88, 456–57, 466
Erie Canal, 112, 199
Ernestina (ex-*Effie M. Morrissey*), schooner, 42, 60, 70, 113, 267
Esmeralda, training ship, 312
Essex, Connecticut, 493
Evelina Goulart, fishing schooner, 28
Explorer Scouts, 164–65, 248, 432

Fales, DeCoursey, 174–76, 184
Falk, Margaret, 477
Falkland Islands, 136–38, 142, 319
Falls of Clyde, sailing ship, 133–34
Farbstein, Congressman Leonard, 283
Farnham, Moulton H. ("Monk"), 41, 48–49, 114, 151–52, 170, 183, 247, 271, 318–19, 411–12, 420, 431, 450, 452, 496
Farr, Joe, 282, 460–61
Farragut Academy, 44
Farrell, James, Jr., 75–76, 80
Farrell, James Sr, 80–81, 189
Fastnet Race, 174
Feffer, Jon, 69
Ferraro, Robert, 22, 25–26, 37, 38–39,

44–47, 57–58, 59–61, 85, 103, 105, 107, 125, 186, 260
Ferris, Commander Ed, 370–71
Fewtrell, Richard, 381, 453, 467, 471, 477, 479, 496
Fischer, Anton Otto, 381
Fischetti, Michael, 390
Fitch, James Marston, 152, 273–74, 282, 343
Fitzpatrick, Edna, 321, 442
Flying Cloud, clipper ship, 46, 113, 114, 239
Force Mulberry, book, 7
Fournier, Alex and Lily, 204
France, liner, 237
Franceschi, M. Peter, 8–9, 23, 37, 324, 446
Frazer, Alan, 69, 105, 185, 238, 284, 448
Fried, Fred, 159, 320
Friedberg, Paul, 152
Friends of South Street, 39–40, 158, 239, 264–65, 304, 317, 318, 418–9, 426–27, 449, 467,
Fulton, Robert, 430
Fulton Ferry, service reopened for one day, 461, 489–90
Fulton Ferry Hotel, 273
Fulton Fish Market, xviii–xix, 9–10, 277, 343
Fulton Supply, 150,
Fulwood, sailing ship, 410

Galbraith, John Kenneth, 282, 357–58
Galveston, Texas, 323
Gayle, Margot, 39, 59, 121, 391–2
General Desk Company, 325
Genoa, Italy, Stanford family visit, 483–84
George W. Rogers Construction, 262, 375, 385
Gerr, Stanley, 179, 181, 189
Ghirardelli Square, San Francisco, 72, 123
Ghosts of Cape Horn, film, 320
Gide, André, 278
Gilbert, Frank, 453
Ginsberg, William, 271
Girl Mariners, 347, 432
Gladding-Hearn Shipyard, 418
Glory of the Seas, clipper ship, 78

Gloucester Marine Railway, 252
Goelet property, 249, 269, 298, 303, 316, 338, 340,
Goelet estate, 339–40
Golden Eagle, schooner, 174, 180
Golden Hind, replica, 458
Goldstein, Hank, 357, 358, 379
Goldstone, Harmon, 64, 67–68, 280–82
golliwobbler, sail, 182
González, Carlos Garcia, figurehead sculptor, 363–64
Goodman, John, 291
Goudy & Stevens shipyard, 46
Grace, William Russell, 269, 376–77
Grace L. Fears, fishing schooner, 266
Grace Line, 376–77
Graham, Robert, 474
Granelli, Hector, 366
Grant, Gordon, 4, 49, 350
Graubard, Seymour, 57
Great Britain, steamship, 136–37, 142
Great Schooner Race, Gloucester, 420,
Green, Col. Edward, 161
Green, Hetty, 161
Greene, Brad, 392
Greene, Mel, 70–71
Greenhill, Basil, 456
Greenman Brothers, 161
Grinnell, Russell, 257, 418–19
Groos, David, 323
Gropallo, Tomaso, 483, 484
Gross, Ted, 420–21
Gruzen, Lee, 299

Haas, Stanley, 384
Halberg, Herbert, 84, 119, 125, 128, 151, 200–1, 477
Hall, Alice, 291
Hall, Nat, 321
Hamilton-Madison House, 344
Hammer, Benjamin, 430–31
Hansen, Sven, 357
Hartog, Jan de, 472
Harvey, Fred, 192, 377, 410
Hayes, Helen, 381, 389–90
Hearn, Richard, 418
Heckscher, August, 157, 391–92, 474
Hendrickson's Corners, bar, 453

Henstock, Richard, 30, 178, 254, 262
Herald of the Morning, clipper ship, 113, 124
Herbert, Karen, 109–10, 347, 410
Herbert, Robert G., x, 110, 347, 410, 420, 432
Herman and Frieda L. Miller Foundation, 300
Herrick, Robert, quoted, 264
Hicks & Greist, xxv, 33
Hightower, John, 271
Hipparchus, steamship, 222
Hitchcock, William, 201, 315
Holden, Donald, 382–83
Holland Society, 430
Holland's Glory, book, 472
Horka, Capt. Archie, x, 120, 125, 160, 163–64, 333–34, 410
Horst Wessel (now *Eagle*), training ship, 245
Hotel Cabo de Hornos, 219–20
Houqua, sailing ship, 112
Hoving, Thomas, 462–63
Howard, Alan, 382
Hoyeski, Walter, 391
Hughes, Hubbard & Reed, 475, 477
Hunt, Richard, 252
Hutchison, Alan, 116–17, 401
Huxtable, Ada Louise, 66
Huycke, Harold, 135

Imposte, Admiral, 311–12, 360–62, 369
Indefatigable, training ship, 415
India House, 75, 79, 80–81
International Congress of Maritime Museums, first meeting, 456–57
International Longshoremen's Association, 425, 477
Inverarity, Robert Bruce, 454
Iolaire, cutter, 420, 483
Isbrandtsen, Ellen, 230–31, 390
Isbrandtsen, Jakob, ix, 50–1, 77–78, 90–93, 97–100, 101–102, 143, 152–53, 249–50, 288–99, 296–99, 301–4, 315–16, 337–40, 345–47, 374–76, 410, 412, 440, 444, 459
Ives, Burl, 344

J. Aron Foundation, 396
J. M. Kaplan Fund, 85, 148, 150, 155, 209,
235, 270, 295, 356
James Monroe, packet ship, 112, 188, 198–99, 201–2, 344
James Monroe Luncheon, 198–201
John Street building (Herman Miller property), 298, 340
Johnson, Barbara, 122, 351, 463
Johnson, Irving, 243
Johnston, Jane (neé Coulson), 178
Johnston, David, xxi–xxiv, 120, 178
Johnston, Waldo, 160, 162, 164–65, 200, 270, 343, 455, 500, 502
Joseph Conrad, author, 381
Joseph Conrad (ex-*Georg Stage*), training ship, 327–30, 334
Journal of Commerce, 79, 263, 319
"joy in the work", 269, 317, 377
Juan Sebastián de Elcano, training ship, 312

Kaiulani, sailing ship, 43, 67, 113, 116–17, 124, 132–33, 136, 506–7
Kaplan, Jack, 147–151, 203, 208–9, 235
Kaplan, Leon, 158, 318, 452–53
Kaplan, Richard, 152
Kaplan Fund (see J. M. Kaplan Fund)
Kean, Larry, 48, 169, 184
Kellar, research vessel, 351
Kendrew, Edwin, 207, 271, 273
Kennedy, Jacqueline, 18
Kennedy, President John F., 364
Kennedy, Senator Edward, 506
Kennedy, Thomas J., 385
Kennedy Galleries, 383
Kiil, Leevi, 22, 38, 58
Kiil, Maal, 22, 58
Kill van Kull, 422, 456
Killen, Lou, 154, 258, 346, 381
Kirk, Jim, xx–xxiii, 60, 120, 125, 178, 234, 238, 291–92, 322, 343, 391, 453, 482
Kirk, Stuart, 321
Klay, Bernie, 346, 353, 381, 401, 430
Klebingat, Capt. Fred, 133–34, 135, 380
Kobrand Corporation, xxv, 1, 22–23, 510
Kohn, Betsy, 146, 324
Kopf, Rudy, 1, 22–23
Kortum, Jean, 119–20, 123, 125, 129, 131–32, 136, 143, 278, 387

Kortum, Karl, ix–x, 10
  biography, 132–136
  Buenos Aires visit, 138–43
  Falkland Islands trip, 136–38
  involvement in beginnings of SSSM,
    89, 113, 115–17
  lobbying for *Elissa*, 323–24
  New York visit (1967), 119–20, 122–25,
    128–30
  New York visit (1968), 270, 278–79
  referring *Caviare*, 250–51
  Seaport colloquy in New York (1970),
    440, 444–45, 456
  SSSM letter campaign to support
    Eppleton Hall, 387–88
Kosnac, Fred, 461
Kramer, Michael, 299
Kroeger, William, 439, 442–43
Kruzenshtern, training ship, 493
Kupferman, Ted, 70
Kyne, Peter, 3

L. A. Dunton, fishing schooner, 162
La Boca, Buenos Aires, 138–39, 306–7,
  363–64
Lacey, Capt. William J., 405–6, 408, 411,
  414, 461–62, 458–59, 460, 463, 469,
  482, 490, 492, 494–95, 498, 506
Lacey ship repair barge, 406, 436, 459–60
Lacey work crew, 458–59, 477
Lady Elizabeth, sailing ship, 138
Lady of Good Voyage, xix–xx, 21, 28–29,
  43, 113
LaGuardia Houses, 55
Lake, Leah, 196
Lamont Geological Observatory, 351
Lane, Skip, 422
Larchmont Yacht Club, 332
The Last Grain Race, book, 464
Lawrence, T. E., 330
Leavitt, John, 261
Lee, Doug, 506
Leedham, Commissioner Charles, 262,
  344, 414, 449
Lettie G. Howard, schooner (see also
  Caviare), 462
Leviss, Sidney, 286–88
Lewis, Emory, 95

Leyland Brothers, 406
Libertad, training ship, 311–12, 344–47,
  363–65
Lindsay, Mary, 390, 412
Lindsay, NYC Mayor John, 173, 188, 194,
  282–84, 289–90, 322, 337, 346, 374,
  421, 423, 430–32, 477, 489, 494–95
Ling, Chi, 247–48, 269, 304, 371
Liverpool, England, Museums of, 461, 508
Lodge, Ambassador John Davis, 354,
  356, 360–61
Logan, Harold R., 376, 396
Londres, steamer, 308
Longshoreman's Voice, 474–75
Longyear, Maritza, 40
Longyear, Peter, 40, 175
Look at Our Waterfront, booklet, 426
Loos, Anita, 389–90,
Lord, Walter, 195, 463
Lore, Clinton, 231
Lore, Marie, 231–32, 247, 265, 442–43
Loring, Paul, 179, 181
Loud, Ruth McAneny, 121–22
Lovelace, Coco, 493
Lowell, Robert, 282
Lower Eastside Neighborhoods Associa-
  tion, 18
Lower Manhattan Plan, 50
Luckenbach Steamship Company, 156
Lundgren, Charles, 50–51, 77–78, 98,
  105, 153, 179, 181, 236–37, 385
Lutz, David, 146, 353
Lyman, John, 135, 270, 430
Lynch, Ed, 160, 162
Lyon, Danny, 238

Maiden Lane, 112, 114
Major General William H. Hart, steam
  ferryboat, 430–31, 451
Maldonado, Rafael, 291
Manhattan Landing, 474
Manigault, Peter, 452
March Heir, sailing yacht, 40, 174
Marchi, NY State Senator John, 374
Marine Museum of New York, 36
Marine Ship Chandlery, 458–60
Mariner's Mirror, periodical, 17
Maritime Europe Tour, 452

Martha Moran, tugboat, 482
Martín, Quinquela, 306–9
Martinot, Claude, 30, 59
Martinot, Trevor, 30,
Masefield, John, 140, 381
Masefield's *Salt Water Ballads*, 7
Massolo, Arthur, 102
Mathilda, steam tugboat, 407
Matteson, George, 420–21, 449–51, 479
Mayflower, replica, 332
McAllister, James P. II, 406–7, 437, 459
McAllister, James P. III, 200, 407, 459–60
McAllister Towing, 410, 430, 448,
     459–60
McCann, Armitage, 49, 350
McCord, Roger, 60–61
McDonald, Capt. P. A., 135
McGrath, John, 278, 288–89, 291–92,
     296, 439
McInnes, Helen, 322
McNamara, Jim (SSSM volunteer), 269
McNamara, Jim (Rutgers Club), 290
Mee, Justine, 491–92, 505
Meisner, Don and Jo, 232–33, 320
Melbourne, Australia, 331
Mellon Foundation, 496, 504
Men, Fish & Boats, book, 7
Mendes, Enrique, 42
Mertyns, H. L., 429
Meyer's Hotel, 112
Michelangelo, liner, 482, 488
Miethe, Capt. Robert, 135, 414
Milford, Connecticut, xxiii, 7–8, 21, 373,
     446, 473
Military Sea Transportation Service, 351
Miller, Herman, 298–300, 340
Miller, Myron, 300
Miller, Ralph, 36, 95, 210, 485–86
Miller, Rick, 411
Milverton, sailing ship, 508
Minneford Shipyard, xxiii–xxiv, 172, 262
"Miracle in South Street", 437
Miss Circle Line, excursion boat, 371
Mitchell, Joseph, 109, 293–94
Modena, Italy, 276, 403
mollyhawk pennant, 160
Mon Lei, Chinese junk, 238, 410
Mondello, Joe, 49–51

Mongoose, schooner, 432
Moore, L. Porter, 386
Moore, Pablo, 136, 138
Moore, William, 105
Moore–McCormack Lines, 105
Moran, Rear Admiral Edmond, 143, 180,
     198, 200, 391
Moran, Ed, 184, 391, 420
Moran Towing, 62, 143, 451
Morino, Emil, 196, 263, 293, 444, 467
Morison, Samuel Eliot, 7, 348, 381
Morley, Christopher, 189
Morris Green Industries, 406
Moshulu, sailing ship, 212, 463, 465, 495
Moynihan, Daniel Patrick, 272–73
Mulligan, Rev. John, 354
Municipal Art Society, 109, 343, 422,
     477, 490
Murphy, Capt. James, 192
Museo Naval, Tigre, Argentina, 224
Museum of American Folk Art, 351,
     463
Museum of the City of New York, 36
Mystic Seaport Museum, 6, 45, 50–51,
     92, 160, 161–63, 165, 260, 334, 372,
     456
Mystic Whaler, schooner, 262

Nantucket Island, 29, 503
Nantucket Lifesaving Museum, 503
National Boat Show, 49, 320
National Committee for an Effective
     Congress, xxiii, 22, 117
National Maritime Day, 119, 237, 390
National Maritime Historical Society
     (NMHS), 43, 116–17, 320, 401, 438,
     449, 451–52, 455–56
National Maritime Museum, Greenwich,
     England, 456–57
National Maritime Union, 388
National Ship Trust Bill, 506
National Trust For Historic Preservation,
     493
Naverson, Harry, xxiv, 12
Nelson, Dave, 387
Nelson, Lord Horatio; quoted, x
Neptune's Car, clipper ship, 113
Neruda, Pablo, 222, 364

Nesdall, Andrew J., 135, 190, 422
New England maritime museums, 250, 454–55, 500
New Symphony Orchestra, 154
New York City
  Board of Estimate, 281–82, 284, 286, 289–90, 295, 398, 405, 442, 478
  boroughs, 286, 497
  bureaucracy, 374, 405, 442, 498
  Chamber of Commerce, 331
  City Council, New York, 284, 290
  City Planning Commission, 63–64, 234, 238, 337
  Committee on City Waterfronts and Waterways, 425–26, 450
  Department of Ports and Terminals, 119, 248, 262, 344, 365, 414, 448–49, 477
  government, 15, 87, 235, 453
  Landmarks Preservation Commission, 66, 109, 280, 295, 456
  Mayor's Committee on Oceanography, 351
  Mayor's Office of Lower Manhattan Development, 73–74, 81, 87, 234, 338, 440, 492
  officials, 63, 473, 475
  Planning Commission, 63–64, 66, 71, 234, 238, 337, 477, 488
  New York Dock Railway, 395
  New York Harbor, 168–70, 172, 180, 246, 407, 410
New York State
  Council on the Arts, 235, 271
  Historical Association, 271, 454
  Historic Trust, 210
  Maritime College, 269
  Maritime Museum, 23–24, 31, 36–37, 66–67, 102, 152–53, 194–95, 206, 352, 476
  Maritime Museum Act, 24
New York Stock Exchange, 33, 68–69, 90–91
New York Telephone Co. (TelCo), 474–75
New York Times, The, xxv, 23, 66, 82, 234, 289, 295, 353, 392, 398, 400, 402, 422, 474

New York Yacht Club,
  meetings/events at, 61, 69, 74, 82, 84, 86, 143, 152, 165, 175, 203, 242, 288, 333–34, 336, 347
  original station house, 160
  Paul Loring cartoon, 179
  pier, 391–92
New Yorker, The, xxv, 33, 109, 111,
Newby, Eric, 464
Newhall, Scott, 324, 372, 387, 456
Newport, Rhode Island, 257–58, 450
Newton, Capt. Dayton O., 44–45
Nichols, George, 373
Nicholson, John E., 277
Niña, schooner, 174–76, 182–84, 262
Noble, John, 422, 453–54, 494
Noble Maritime Collection, 453
Nodelman, Lenny, 166, 239
Numeriani, Alfredo, 213, 217, 225, 301, 309–11, 362

O'Connor, Frank D., 290–91
O'Donnell, Sieglinda, 357
O'Dwyer, Paul, 282
Ogilvy & Mather, xxv
Ogilvy, David, xv, 424
Olatka, Nick and Alex, 233, 326
Operation Sail '76, 462, 493
Oram Associates, 357
Oravetz, Kal, 477
Oswald Mordaunt Shipyard, 226
Overseas Press Club, 332

Pacific Pile–Driving Co., 406–7
Packer, Capt. Ralph, 31
Paine, Alfred W., 7
Paley, William, 82
Pallachino, Grace, 278
Palmer, Capt. Nathaniel (N. B.), 112
Parker, Dorothy, quoted, 121
Parkinson, Jack, 260–61
Parma, sailing ship, 329
Parmelee, Ed, 1, 23, 30, 59
Parmelee, Trevor, 30, 32
Paterson, Basil, 55
Patterson, Charles Robert, 239, 350, 381

Patton, Douglas and Lawrence, 427
Patton, Helene, 427
Patton, Ken, 427
Paulsen, Hap, 241–42, 244, 492–93
Peabody Museum of Salem, 455
Peace Corps, 58
Pearce, Norman, 4–5
Pears, Iain, 276
Peking, sailing ship, 492
Pell, John H. G., 105, 382–83
Pennsylvania Station, New York City,
    109, 280
Phelan, Angela, 128,
Phelan, Joseph, 188
Philadelphia Maritime Museum, 135–36,
    454
Phoenix House, 449
Piccard, Dr. Jacques, 351
Pier 16, 231–2, 258, 270, 326, 345, 354,
    375, 381, 390, 412
Pier 17, xvii
Pier A, 198
Piers 13 and 14, fire, 448
Pierson, Ed, 363, 365
Pilgrim, brig, 465
pilot schooners, 168, 188–89
Pioneer, schooner, 417–21, 432, 438, 449–
    52, 462, 493–94
Pioneer Lives, book, 418
Pioneer program, 421, 449–52
Plato's Academy, 5
Platzer, Michael, 478
Plimpton, George, 322
Polly Woodside, sailing ship, 239
Popular Boating magazine (see also *Boat-
    ing*), 17, 41, 48–49
Poretti, Capt. Atilio Santiago, 364
Port Elizabeth, New Jersey, 79
Post, George W., 230
Pouch, Tim, 200, 408
Presidente Sarmiento, training ship, 312
Price, Raymond, 15–16
Proccacino, Mario, 283, 337
Prosser, Joe, 182
Pub Preservation Society, 453
Puerto Montt, Chile, 215,
Punta Arenas, Chile, 215, 217–20, 380

Queens, Borough of, 187, 286–88,

Raffaello, liner, 182
Rainbow, clipper ship, 112
Rath, Frederick L., Jr., 271–72, 488
Rath, Richard, vi, 17, 22, 40–43, 44–45,
    46–48, 61, 69–71, 107, 152, 157, 169,
    173–74, 279, 388, 418–20, 438, 449–51,
    471, 501
Raynaud, Adrian, 126
Regina Maris, barquentine, 145, 353, 373
Reid, John, 481
Reliant, paddlewheel tugboat, 456–57
restoration workshop, 235
Retail Fish Store, 147
Reynard, Capt. Ken, 411
Riachuelo River, Buenos Aires, 138–40,
    302, 380
Ridder, Eric, 75–79, 91–93, 103, 143,
    156, 195, 200, 263–64, 319, 496,
    498–499
Riesenberg, Felix, 242
Rimington, Critchell, 95, 126
Rio Gallegos, Argentina, 223
Rise of the Port of New York, book, 190
River Plate, 135, 214, 224, 365,
Riverboat Ball,
    1968, 236–37
    1970, 393
Riversdale, sailing ship, 406, 437
Robbins, I. D., 56
Robert Fulton, restaurant barge, 492,
    494–95, 506
Roberts, Capt. James E., 415–17
Robinson, George, 415–16
Rocco's Chippewa Tavern, 13–16, 374
Rockefeller, David, 102, 291, 346, 385–
    86, 471
Rockefeller, Governor Nelson, 23, 54,
    66, 102
Rockefeller, Laurance, 466–73, 478, 497,
    507–8, 510
Rodgers, John, 69, 113–14
Rogers, Bruce, 330
Rogers, George W., 197, 200, 262, 295,
    354, 375, 385
Rogers, Jeff, 62–63
Rogers, Syd, 49, 450

Rona, sailing ship, 239
Roosevelt, Eleanor, xvii
Roosevelt, President Franklin D., 36, 119
Rose, HMS, British frigate and "HMS" *Rose*, replica ship, 373
Rosebrock, Ellen Fletcher, 471, 479, 491, 505
Rosenfeld, Morris, 265
Roth, William Matson, 123
Royal Ocean Racing Club, 460
Rubinow, Ray, 85, 95, 100–1, 147, 152, 209
Ruckens, Irving, 155
Running Tide, sloop, 390
Rutgers Reform Democratic Club, xvii, 286
Rutgers Slip, 112
Ryan, William, 70
Rybka, Walter, 323

sail, deepwater, 416–17, 440
sail training aboard USCGC *Eagle*, 243–45
Sailors' Snug Harbor, 409, 415
San Francisco, ix, 1, 5–6, 24, 87–89, 123, 324, 387–88
San Francisco Maritime Museum, 4, 9, 87–88, 134
Sancho, ketch, 214
Sandy Hook Pilots, 168, 188, 200
Santiago, Chile, 215
Sayle, Charlie, 30–32, 45–46, 50–51, 61, 503
Sayle, Mickey, 30, 503
Scaglione, Jack, 147, 195, 467
Schaefer, Rudolph II, 395–96
Schaefer, Rudolph III (Rudie), 46, 172–73, 178, 180, 340, 371, 393–94, 395–96
Schaefer Brewery, 395
Schermerhorn Row, 23–25, 273, 338, 340, 476
   Atlas-McGrath purchase, 278
   Landmark designation, 280–93, 297
Schkulnik, Manuel, 301–2, 306, 310, 360, 362–63, 367
Schlech, Rear Admiral Walter, 506
Schlesinger, James, 282
Schoener, Allon, 235, 359, 440–44

Schooner Race for the Mayor's Cup, 168–71, 172–84, 371–2, 426, 431–32
schooners
   clipper, 251
   staysail, 174
Schweitzer, Albert; quoted, viii
sea chanteys, 114–15, 128–29, 348, 413
Sea Day, 258, 390–393, 397–98, 422,
Sea Explorer Scouts, 164–65, 347
Sea History magazine, 454–56
Sea Museums Council (now Council of American Maritime Museums), 454–55, 500
Sea Witch, clipper ship, 137, 191
Sea Witch, Down Easter, 191
Seamen's Bank for Savings, 402, 411
Seamen's Church Institute, xix, 94, 114, 203, 353–54,
Seaport Books and Charts, book shop, 413, 466
Seaport buildings, 342–43, 357
Seaport Galley, 462
Seaport Holdings, 296–99, 340, 375, 377, 476
Seaport in the City colloquy, 439–446
Seaport land, the drive to acquire, 146–7, 151–53, 208, 235, 374–76, 398–400, 472–76
Seaport plan, 38, 206–7, 235–36, 280, 316, 337, 341, 343, 348–53, 399–400, 472–76, 491, 494–95, 504–5
Seaport Restoration Conference, 268–69, 271, 273, 275, 277, 279 236, 270–275
Seeger, Pete, 157, 239, 249, 282, 346, 393–94
Seeth, George, 188–89
Seven Seas Sailing Club, 174
Sewall Shipyard, 116
Seymour, Whitney North, Jr., 24–25, 38–39, 57, 61, 67, 95–96, 121–23, 195
Sheffield Island, 248
Shenandoah, sailing ship, 192, 377
Shepley, Jim, 481–82, 496, 499–501
Ship Lore & Model Club, 49, 350
Ships That Brought Us So Far, The, booklet, 452
Shopsin, William, 103, 153
Shumway, Floyd, 491, 505

Slash Hammock Island, 341
Slocum, Capt. Joshua, 220
Sloppy Louie's, 11, 196, 263, 270, 293, 444, 467, 498
Slotnick, Howard, 236, 493
Smith, Kenneth Kemble, 364
Smithsonian Institution, x, 454
Sniffen, Harold, 270
Snow Squall, clipper ship, 138
Somerset, Bobby, 175
Songs They Sang in South Street, album, 344
Sorio, Arnold de, 414–15
South Street Reporter, 67–68, 94–96, 117–118, 188–90, 205, 208, 234, 238–240, 277–78, 353, 372–73, 378, 385, 387, 405, 431, 434, 450, 478–80
South Street Seaport Museum,
   annual reports, 320–21, 377
   board of trustees, 79, 94–96, 103–4, 143–44, 155, 156, 165, 295, 374–76, 460, 470, 481, 496, 498–501
   bookstore, 413
   designation as official site of the national bicentennial, 462
   director of ships, 448, 479
   Executive Committee, 496, 500
   funding plan, 504–5, 507
   ground-breaking ceremony, 337
   headquarters at 16 Fulton Street, 13, 85, 94–95, 97, 99, 101, 103, 105, 110, 113, 118, 176, 248, 269, 298,
   headquarters at 203 Front Street, ix–x, 269–70, 325–326
   lease signing, 475–76
   library, 269–70, 325
   Local History Committee, 159, 190, 230, 232, 269, 320
   model by Leevi Kiil, 22, 38–39, 49–51, 58, 60
   planning conference, 268, 295
   Restoration Committee, 342, 471
   Saturday seminars, 317
   Ship Advisory Committee, 459
   South Street Seaport Council, 440
   Steering Committee meeting, 68–69, 84
   trustees, 141–43, 205, 263, 359, 370, 386, 410, 449–50, 470–71, 476, 481–82, 496, 498–501, 505, 507
   volunteers, ix, 109–10, 230–36, 240–41, 247–48, 267–68, 320–21, 346–67, 384–46, 389, 440–41, 452–53, 464–65, 501–2
Southgate (now *Wavertree*), sailing ship, 139, 211, 479
Spee, Admiral Maximilian von, 220
Spiers, Capt. A. G., 303–4, 380, 413, 508
Spurling, Jack, 4
Square Rigger Bar & Grille, x, 233–34, 279, 326, 383, 428, 475
Squire, Ed, 482
St. Mary, sailing ship, 138
Stackpole, Edouard, 6, 29–32, 46, 95, 114, 503
Stammers, Michael, 458
Stanford, Alfred, xviii, xxii–xxiii, 5–8, 21, 50, 126, 186, 328, 393
Stanford, Berenice, xxiii, 5, 8, 186
Stanford, Carol, xvii, xix, 14, 160, 373, 482, 486
Stanford, Dorothy, 7, 432, 493, 497
Stanford, Joseph, 423, 453, 458, 473, 482, 485
Stanford, Norma,
   "Boats" nickname, xxi
   decision to act on SSSM idea, 36–40
   job at Arts Councils of America, 22, 34
   letter to Karl Kortum, 8–10
   meeting Capt. Thomas Thomas, 227–30
   hunt for the Mayor's Cup, 176–79
   meeting John Stobart, x–xiv
   New England trips to find schooner for SSSM, 43–51
   planning the first SSSM headquarters, 100–4
   planning the Schooner Race for the Mayor's Cup, 168–73
   sailing *Athena* from Maine to New York, xxi–xxiv
   trip to Argentina, 359–63
   trip to Italy, 402–4
   trip to Jamaica, 312–14
   wedding, 1
   working on *Caviare*, 251–54,
   working on *A Walk Through South Street*, 190–94

Stanford, Peter,
  apartment in Gramercy Park, 324
  becoming president of NMHS, 401
  becoming president of SSSM, 90
  career in advertising, xxiii, xxv, xxvi,
    1–2, 22–23, 33, 52–53, 68, 90–91, 93
  City Club of New York trustee, 52,
    54–57
  education, 53–54
  house in Laurelton, Queens, 324, 343
  replaced as CEO of SSSM, 511
  house in Yorktown Heights, New York,
    36–37, 129, 324, 343, 373, 390, 446
  sailing in the USCGC *Eagle*, 241–245
  trip to Buenos Aires (1968), 211–215,
    223–229
  trip to Buenos Aires (Jan. 1969),
    305–311
  trip to Buenos Aires (Nov. 1969), 356,
    359–368
  trip to Greenwich, England, for
    ICOMM conference, 456–457, 466
  trip to Italy (1970), 402–404
  trip to Italy (1973), 482–488
  trip to Jamaica, 312–314
  trip to Punta Arenas, Chile, 212,
    215–223
  visit to fishing fleet in New York,
    xviii–xix
  visit to San Francisco, 2–5
  wedding, 1
Stanford, Robert, 324, 341, 373, 390,
  402–4, 453, 458, 482
Stanford, Thomas, xix, xxiv, 125, 138, 160,
  228–9, 373
Stanford, Tony, 160,
Stanley, Edmund A., Jr., 194, 200, 205,
  351, 376, 471
Star of India, sailing ship, 411
Stark, Abe, 284–85
Starr, Roger, 283, 290–91, 440–41, 444
Staten Island, 77, 286, 297, 328, 391–93,
  405, 407–9, 422, 453–54
Staw, Rudy, 269, 442
Stephens, Olin, 21, 70
Stephens, Rod, 70
Sterling, harbor tanker, 461
Stobart, John, vii–x, 382–83, 405, 453

Stormie Seas, Greek schooner, 323, 353
Story, Dana, 256, 260
Straight, Michael, 282
Straight, Willard, 80
Straits of Magellan, 219–20, 221
"Street of Ships," v, 25, 62, 67, 92, 113–
  14, 123, 151, 153–54, 168, 189–91
Streibert, Marshall, 471, 505
Strew, Julia, 269, 442
Sullivan, Jean, 390, 401
Sutton, Percy, 284–85, 287–88, 290, 322,
  462
Sutton's Dispatch Line, 278
Suvero, Mark di, 115, 204
Swanson, Al, 250–51, 255, 304, 370
Swede, George, 377
Sweet's Restaurant, 10, 25, 100, 111, 122,
  196, 321
Swigert, William, 136, 142
Sydney, Australia, 116

Tallichet, David, 464–65, 492
Tammany Hall, xvii, 13, 272
Tarpaulin Cove, 32
Tarr & Wonson's Paint Manufactory, 27
Tarr, Bob, 91, 132, 141, 143, 156, 195
Taylor, Alice, 38–39, 68, 89, 95, 388 482,
  489–90
teachers, 55–56, 269
Tebo Shipyard, 327, 350
TelCo (New York Telephone Co.), 435
Theatre Research, 390, 401
Thimble Islands, 167–68
"Things it takes more than a generation
  to learn," quote, 393
"This Museum is People," quote, 317,
  397, 404, 490
Thomas, Capt. John, 416
Thomas, Capt. Thomas, 138, 227–29, 303,
  380–81, 416
Thomas F. Bayard, pilot schooner, 373
Three Hours for Lunch Club, 189
Throckmorton, Joan, 322–23
Throckmorton, Peter, 232, 319–20, 323–
  24, 353, 388
Tierra del Fuego, 219
Tigre, Argentina, 224, 365–66
Tijgre, Dutch ship, 159

Tilton, Zebulon, 30–31
Timken, John, 496
Titan, seagoing tugboat, 408–9, 472
Tollefsen, George, 461
Toronto Maritime Museum, 382
Townley, John, 346
TransAtlantic Race of 1928, 174
Tufnell, E. C., 124
tugboat dispatchers, 198
tugboats, 198, 257, 324, 372–73, 387–88, 407, 408–10, 448, 456–57, 459–60, 472
Tuscarora, troopship, 250
Tusitala, sailing ship, 80, 81, 179, 189
Tyehee, schooner, 174, 176, 180–81, 183, 263, 371

United States Coast Guard, 231, 237, 240, 242, 244–45, 246–47, 344, 401, 434, 448, 492,
United States, liner, 336
Urban, Ralph, 114, 118

Vagli Sotto, Italy, 404
Valparaiso, Chile, 135
Van Arkel, Thomas, 203, 204, 207, 209, 303–05, 235, 249, 269
Van Frank, William, 142
Vanderbilt, William, 258
Vanderpool, James, 106
Vazquez Maiztegui, Capt. Fernando, 344–45, 363
Ventura, Anita, 10–11, 22, 87–89, 115–16, 211
Vicar of Bray, sailing ship, 138
Victoria, liner, 357–58
Victory, HMS, sailing ship, 212
Viggiano, P. Vincent "Duke," xx, 283, 321–22
Villager, paper, 128
Ville de Mulhouse (later *Andalucia*), sailing ship, 211, 212, 215, 220–21
Villiers, Alan, 134–35, 212, 215, 304, 326, 327–37, 340, 379–80, 381, 412–414, 416–17, 458
Vincent Astor Foundation, 450
Vision IV, sloop, 21
Volunteer Clean-up Day, 426–28

W. R. Grace & Company, 396
Walbaum, Capt., 220–21, 222
A Walk Through South Street in the Afternoon of Sail, booklet, 190–194, 391
Walking Around in South Street, book, 479–80, 511–12
Wall Street, 24, 68–69, 114, 145, 161, 178, 205, 272, 413
Wallace, Capt. Ray, 463–65
Wallace, John, 326
Walton, Robert, 85, 143, 420
Walton, Terry, 48–49, 69, 85, 152, 420–21, 450, 451, 478
Wapama, steam schooner, 3
War With Cape Horn, book, 327, 414
Warburton, Barclay II, 258
Warburton, Barclay III, 237, 243, 257–59, 263, 371, 381, 391, 450–51, 503
Warburton, Barclay IV (Tim), 451
Warhol, Andy, 278
Water Street, 11, 147, 381, 426
Waterfront Festival, 423–428, 430–32
Wavertree (ex-*Southgate*, ex-*Don Ariano N*), sailing ship,
    Alan Villiers's fundraising visit, 326, 332, 340
    arrival at SSSM, 408, 410–12
    bell, 482
    broken mast, 345
    change-of-flag ceremony, 360–61
    fittings from *Riversdale*, 406–7, 437
    decision to acquire, 143
    drydock in Argentina, 306
    discovery by Karl Kortum, 138–43
    fundraising, 395–97
    history, 221–22, 229
    history of name, 211
    negotiations and purchase, 158–59, 212–14, 225–27 300–4, 308, 309–11
    new mainmast, 477
    painting by John Stobart, 405
    painting by Oswald Brett, 315
    proposal by Karl Kortum for SSSM, 120
    onboard exhibit, 478, 510–12
    recollections of Capt. James E. Roberts, 415–17
    recollections of Capt. Thomas Thomas, 227

repairs in Argentina, 354–56

survey, 302–6

Wavertree: An Ocean Wanderer, The, book, 303–4, 379–381, 455

Wegmann, Osvaldo, 222

Weinstein, Richard, 440, 442, 446, 492

Weinstein, Robert, 135, 190

Wells, H. G., quoted, 447

Wenzel, Val, 230–31, 320, 389–91

Wertenbaker, William, 111, 174, 181

Westbeth Project, 150–51

Westchester Creek (see Conroy's Creek)

Wharf Rats, 294, 459

"White Swan of the Hudson," (*Alexander Hamilton*), 46

Whitehall Club, 197–98, 354, 404

Whyte's Restaurant, xxv, 183, 239, 263, 372

Wigsten, Capt. Hjalmar, 132–33

Wijsmuller Towing Co., 397, 472

Will, Admiral John M., Jr. "Dutch", 87, 194, 198, 200, 206, 388, 404, 406

Wilpon, Ken, 98, 281, 283, 296–98, 337

Wilson, John and Siegfried, 145

Windows on the Waterfront, 82

Windows on the World, restaurant, 205

Winterer, Bill and Victoria, 494

Witthholz, Charles, 507

Woerner, Frank, 346

World Ship Society, 69, 113–14

World Trade Center, 159, 205, 239

World War II, 7, 42, 116, 126, 244, 331–32, 370, 405

Wren, Sir Christopher; quoted, x

X–Seamen's Institute, 354, 381, 401

York, Alen, 238

Young, John, 273

Young America, clipper ship, 100–1, 113, 124, 278

Zeckendorf, Bill, 98–99, 101–2, 150

Zerdin, Morton, 289

Zuccotti, John, 477, 488–89